Archaeological Perspectives on Political Economies

Foundations of Archaeological Inquiry

James M. Skibo, series editor

Expanding Archaeology
James M. Skibo, William H. Walker, and Axel E. Nielsen

Behavioral Archaeology: First Principles
Michael Brian Schiffer

Evolutionary Archaeology: Theory and Application
Michael J. O'Brien, editor

Unit Issues in Archaeology: Measuring Time, Space, and Material
Ann F. Ramenofsky and Anastasia Steffen, editors

Pottery Ethnoarchaeology in the Central Maya Highlands
Michael Deal

Pottery and People: A Dynamic Interaction
James M. Skibo and Gary M. Feinman, editors

Material Meanings: Critical Approaches to the Interpretation of Material Culture
Elizabeth S. Chilton, editor

Social Theory in Archaeology
Michael Brian Schiffer, editor

Race and the Archaeology of Identity
Charles E. Orser Jr., editor

Style, Function, Transmission: Evolutionary Archaeological Perspectives
Michael J. O'Brien and R. Lee Lyman, editors

The Archaeology of Settlement Abandonment in Middle America
Takeshi Inomata and Ronald W. Webb, editors

Complex Systems and Archaeology: Empirical and Theoretical Applications
R. Alexander Bentley and Herbert D.G. Maschner, editors

Essential Tensions in Archaeological Method and Theory
Todd L. and Christine S. VanPool

Archaeological Perspectives on Political Economies

Edited by Gary M. Feinman and
Linda M. Nicholas

THE UNIVERSITY OF UTAH PRESS
SALT LAKE CITY

FOUNDATIONS OF ARCHAEOLOGICAL INQUIRY
James M. Skibo, editor

Printed on acid-free paper

 The Defiance House Man colophon is a registered trademark of the University of Utah
Press. It is based upon a four-foot-tall, Ancient Puebloan pictograph (late PIII) near
Glen Canyon, Utah.

2004   05   06   07   08   09
5   4   3   2   1

LIBRARY OF CONGRESS CATALOGING-IN-PUBLICATION DATA

Archaeological perspectives on political economies / edited by Gary M.
Feinman and Linda M. Nicholas.
        p. cm. — (Foundations of archaeological inquiry)
Papers originally presented at a roundtable held at the Snowbird Ski
and Summer Resort, October 20–21, 2001. Includes bibliographical references and index.
    ISBN 0-87480-776-X (hardcover : alk. paper)—ISBN 0-87480-777-8
(pbk. : alk. paper)
    1. Archaeology—Congresses. 2. Economic anthropology—Congresses.
3. Economic history—To 500—Congresses.   I. Feinman, Gary M.
II. Nicholas, Linda M., 1951–   III. Series.
    CC175.A7165 2004
    330.93—dc22   2003018795

To our parents,
for giving us the economic wherewithal
to do what we really liked

Contents

Contents

Figures

Tables

Preface

The genesis of this volume dates to a conversation between the senior editor and the series editor, James M. Skibo, at the airport cafeteria in Salt Lake City in October 1997. Both parties believed that bringing together a coterie of top scholars with research foci on the past economies of chiefdoms and states would be timely. After a series of letters and the review of a proposal submitted by the volume editors, the University of Utah Press and its director, Jeff Grathwohl, generously agreed to sponsor a roundtable at the Snowbird ski resort October 20–21, 2001.

Once the program was set, the editors were gratified by the response and interest of the outstanding group of scholars whose works are included in this collection. We also are grateful that the contributors completed their manuscripts and, for the most part, attended the roundtable despite the horror and tragedy of September 11, 2001. One member of our group was so dedicated that he drove halfway across the United States to participate in our Snowbird dialogues. Even though each participant was scarred and emotionally touched by what had happened just six weeks before, we, the editors, felt a degree of catharsis after sharing a beautiful fall weekend in a gorgeous setting with a roomful of insightful colleagues. Our discussions were provocative and stimulating, and all the authors strengthened their chapters as a direct consequence of this dialogue.

We also thank Jeff Grathwohl and the University of Utah Press for sticking with their commitment to the roundtable and the publication of the volume in the face of 9/11. We hope this volume, and the myriad ties that connect the chapters, will help solidify their rationale for giving the authors the opportunity to exchange ideas and receive constructive comments from colleagues before compiling an edited volume. We are deeply appreciative of the opportunity we had.

Finally, we thank Lauren Fishman, Ellis Murphy, and the staff at the University of Utah Press for their help in the production of this book.

Archaeology and Political Economy
Setting the Stage

GARY M. FEINMAN

From the beginnings of academic social science (including the discipline of anthropology) in North America during the latter half of the 1800s, a focal theme has been the effort to understand societal diversity and change (e.g., Boas 1932). Much of the investigation has focused on the emergence of socioeconomic inequality, leadership, classes, states, and cities, and how and why these phenomena arose in one global region or historical context versus another. From the integrative models of Herbert Spencer to the conflict frameworks of Karl Marx, economic relations generally have played a central role in the many theories, perspectives, and hypotheses that have been advanced over more than a century to account for societal change and variation (Haas 1982).

Following from these earlier writings, the more current works of Fried (1967) and Service (1962) placed key aspects of economic relations at the core of their analytical frameworks. More recently, Johnson and Earle (1987) adopted an explicitly economic focus in their synthetic treatment, *The Evolution of Human Societies*. Clearly, to understand human societal diversity and how it came to be, we must comprehend past economies and how economic relations varied and changed. Yet few of these important studies (or others, for that matter), all of which were designed to look at long-term change, were based on direct information concerning ancient (deep past) economic relations.

To a large degree, the absence of such direct economic analysis (much of which by nature would have to be discerned from the archaeological record) reflected the dearth or sketchiness, at least until recently, of such archaeological information. Beyond the broad recognition of technological transitions such as the regional shifts in tool complexes from stone to bronze to iron, archaeological information generally was not collected, processed, or organized in a manner that made the direct investigation of ancient production, distribution, and consumption readily possible. Nevertheless, given the increasing awareness afforded historical sequence, context, and contingency in contemporary anthropology, the direct use of ethnographic and documentary records and models to build narrative accounts of the deeper past (without more direct empirical perspectives) presents an array of analytical problems for deriving better understandings of societal change. Such understandings, and so more direct data on past economies, are critical not only for the construction of theory in anthropology and archaeology regarding the nature and diversity of preindustrial economies (e.g., Halperin 1988) but also for emerging dialogues in economic history (e.g., North 1994).

This volume aims to take important strides in addressing the empirical gaps that have long existed in our understanding of the economies of ancient complex hierarchical societies (chiefdoms, states, and empires, in more traditional parlance). It is important to emphasize that none of the contributors to this collection believes this to be a comprehensive treatment of this topic, nor will any general models (designed to cover all times and places or even all preindustrial contexts) be advanced. Rather, we endeavor to offer a range of current case studies that are informed by our current (and individualized) theoretical sensibilities as well as by recent findings made possible by important innovations in fieldwork and analysis strategies in archaeology. Information from a series of other relevant disciplines is incorporated as appropriate in each discussion. In a sense, this collection illustrates as much about what we do not know and still need to investigate and examine as it does about what we have learned through recent decades of field investigation, study, and analysis.

DEFINITIONS

Before reviewing the contributions to this volume as well as some of the themes that tie them together, it is worthwhile to review what is meant by economic systems, or the economy. Most of the authors follow at least in a general sense Leslie White (1959:237–260), who saw three fundamental aspects to economic systems: production, exchange, and consumption. Each of these economic facets encompasses wide realms of behaviors and is enacted at multiple scales, from the individual through the domestic unit, community, settlement, polity, region, and often macroregion (see also Blanton et al. 1997).

In this collection we focus on *political economies*, for several reasons. First, in each of the chapters the authors cover past socioeconomic contexts in which the production and circulation of goods clearly transcended domestic groups. That is, in none of the studies do we see self-sufficient households that produced exclusively for their own immediate use. In fact, in each of the chapters some production and exchange that clearly transcended the bounds of individual domestic units is evident, linking households to larger networks and institutions. Because such extrahousehold economic relations can in many situations be channeled through a diverse set of means to support integrative and/or hierarchical institutions or relationships, they more accurately constitute what many consider to be political economic relations (Johnson and Earle 1987:8–15).

To speak of political economies also is fitting, as each of the volume participants was forceful in supporting the position that all economies (preindustrial as well as industrial) are in some manner embedded in specific cultural, political, and/or social matrices. Although individual contributors certainly would not agree on the precise characterizations of all cases, all the participants expressed strongly their understanding that economic behavior and relations must be examined in (and viewed as mediated by) their broader societal contexts and could not be understood otherwise (Granovetter 1985, 1992; McCloskey 1997; Plattner 1989:14).

THEMES

As might be expected in an anthropological/archaeological discussion of political economies as opposed to a strictly or explicitly economic treatment, the focus of this collection is empirical, grounded in data (Gladwin 1989). The participants for the most part were not comfortable with constructing linear or universal models or sequences of economic relations meant to apply across time and space. Most contributors would be in basic agreement with Berdan's (1989:106) statement that "the Polanyi approach of characterizing certain economies as 'redistributive' or 'market' is therefore less fruitful than an approach that accepts the presence of a variety of exchange strategies and seeks to unravel the relationships among them." In fact, the majority of the contributions to this volume endeavor to flesh out the economies of specific past societies in a manner that Berdan (1985, 1987a) and others (Berdan et al. 1996; Hodge and Smith 1994) have shown, using both texts and archaeological findings, for the Aztecs. Of course, in many of the cases discussed here the empirical emphasis given the temporal focus is necessarily more archaeological than textual.

Although no universal models are offered here, all the volume's contributors stressed their strong commitment to comparative approaches that endeavor to dissect and understand economic differences and similarities across time and space. Some of the chapters make explicit comparisons of production and distribution patterns over time. Significantly, all the chapters are informed directly (albeit in their own distinct ways) by research questions and issues that transcend the specific regions or historical sequences under consideration. It was the general consensus of the participants that meaningful comparisons of past economic systems would be difficult in the absence of better empirical understandings of how these economies were alike and distinct.

The chapters in this book also recognize and are sensitive to the importance of analytical scale when considering both production and distribution/exchange. Across the volume, coverage and emphasis range from domestic units to macroregional networks. Many of the authors make careful efforts to distinguish and reconstruct economic processes at different scales of analysis. It is provocative that a number of the contributions emphasize the importance of domestic production largely for exchange (as opposed to immediate use); at the same time, another recurrent theme is the clear significance of long-distance or supraregional networks for understanding economic processes even in the deep past. Clearly, these patterns emphasize the importance of elucidating the highly diverse and often co-occurring modes and mechanisms through which goods were circulated and exchanged.

COMPOSITION OF THE VOLUME

The remainder of the volume comprises twelve case studies that focus on a range of themes relevant to the understanding of how past economies worked and why they changed. Each of the chapters relies to a different extent on archaeological materials in conjunction with other relevant sources. The degree of reliance on archaeology, of course, reflects the state of our knowledge as well as the topical and geographic/temporal focus of each chapter.

In Chapter 2 Charles Stanish examines the evolution of ranking, introducing an evolutionary game theory approach (Shalizi 1999) that differs in its emphasis on cooperation from those formal models more traditionally employed in anthropology. Stanish's expectations based on the model then are assessed empirically with a focus on the Middle Formative period (c. 1300–500 B.C.) in the Lake Titicaca Basin of Bolivia and Peru. Stanish argues that the emergence of ranking in the Titicaca region was part of a process that involved the establishment of new reciprocal economic relationships and included feasting and craft production.

In Chapter 3 Timothy Pauketat takes a rather different approach in endeavoring to understand pan-eastern "Mississippian political economy" circa A.D. 1000. Like Stanish, Pauketat uses a bottom-up perspective, yet his emphasis is squarely on the particular cultural practices of the people who shaped the histories of specific localities (as opposed to more general models or cross-cultural processes). Pauketat raises several significant points that weave their way through a number of subsequent chapters. He stresses the importance of not relying exclusively on one analytical scale when investigating past economic behaviors. Likewise, he reminds us not to overestimate (or focus solely on) the role of high-status or powerful people when contemplating economic practice. This chapter also illustrates how basic economic practices and relations cycle and change during long diachronic sequences.

In Chapter 4 Robert McC. Adams, whose early comparative studies (e.g., Adams 1966) served to outline and define some of the core issues that form the crux of this volume, reviews long-term economic change in southern Mesopotamia. Adams grounds his current analysis in the distinctive environmental circumstances and challenges of this plain and the response mechanisms that fostered integration and demographic concentration. He also explores the growth of cities and their implication for urban-rural relations. In Chapter 5, in an interesting contrast and complement to Adams's work, Gil Stein examines the rise of urbanism and its economic ramifications in northern Mesopotamia. Like Adams, he adopts a diachronic lens, interlaces textual with archaeological findings, and grounds his investigation in ecological factors and agrarian strategies that underpin the historical divergences between the two Southwest Asian regions. During the third millennium B.C. Stein sees northern Mesopotamian temples as being less involved in massive surplus accumulations than were temple institutions farther south. He proposes settlement discontinuity as well as relative political instability and decentralization as synergistically related consequences.

In Chapters 6 and 7 Andrew Sherratt and Glenn Storey take broad-scale views of the European and Mediterranean worlds, collectively investigating the era from the rise of the first states and cities to the growth of Rome. In a historical analysis of economic change, Sherratt considers the period between 4000 and 500 B.C., emphasizing the increasing scales of the networks of circulation that stretched across Eurasia following the rise of early cities in Mesopotamia. Storey focuses on the Roman economy, bringing an anthropologically informed view to empirically rich material generally treated by scholars of other traditions (e.g., Hopkins 1980). These chapters and others in the collection add significantly to the growing discussions regarding the nature and importance of macroregional flows of raw materials and finished goods in the past (e.g., Chase-Dunn and Hall 1991, 1997; Kardulias 1999; Peregrine and Feinman 1996).

In Chapter 8 Anne Underhill and Hui Fang endeavor to bring North China more fully into the ongoing comparative discussion of early state economies through a textual and archaeological analysis of the late Shang period (1200–1046 B.C.) and before (second

millennium B.C.). Their treatment of this topic is the most up-to-date and synthetic one available in English. Drawing on a range of empirical sources, they focus on the political economy from different scales of analysis. Mirroring arguments made by Storey and Sherratt, Underhill and Fang maintain that the nature of the connections between people living in the Shang capital of Anyang and the rest of China were different, depending on the distance from the capital. Although much research still needs to be undertaken, Underhill and Fang, like Adams, hint at important politicoeconomic changes and cycling in their focal region over time.

In Chapter 9 Patricia McAnany takes a bottom-up and diachronic look at ancient Maya political economy. Particularly for the Classic period, McAnany describes an economy based on long-distance trade connections that were expressed in hierarchical relationships of acquisition and high-status consumption. As she observes, the Classic Maya political economy, characterized by wealth (sensu D'Altroy and Earle 1985) production and exchange, palace consumption, and long-distance networks, has a significantly different dynamic than that described by Adams for southern Mesopotamia or Underhill and Fang for North China. Aspects of this diversity have been more generally characterized in the contrast drawn between the corporate and network/exclusionary modes (see Blanton et al. 1996).

In Chapter 10 Gary Feinman and Linda Nicholas turn to highland Mesoamerica (the Valley of Oaxaca) and a more synchronic study of production and exchange. The authors illustrate that most nonagricultural production in Prehispanic Mesoamerica appears to have been undertaken by household units, although much of this manufacture was for exchange. As household production would be cumbersome to control administratively, especially over large polities and without evidence for central storehouses, the significance of the market for circulation in the pre-Aztec Classic period (c. A.D. 200–800) is inferred.

In Chapter 11 Cathy Costin also relies

heavily on archaeological findings, in this case to investigate the organization of production in Andean South America. Concentrating on the Moche, Chimu, Wari, Tiwanaku, and Inka, Costin finds, like Feinman and Nicholas, that much of the identified craft production was enacted domestically although variation was present in certain contexts. No linear or progressive pattern of change was observed in the organization of production over time. By limiting her vantage principally to production, Costin explores more fully than the other contributors the relations between the contexts of manufacture and political oversight and control, and the actual characteristics of the artifacts that were made.

In the final two chapters of the volume the coverage shifts to somewhat more recent times in two areas—Southeast Asia and West Africa—that often are not given full enough consideration in comparative studies of past political economies. In Chapter 12, drawing largely from textual sources (supplemented with available archaeological findings), Laura Junker explores political economies of the first and early second millennia A.D. in Southeast Asia, which tended to be dominated by landscapes of small polities that at certain times were ultimately linked to larger distant polities (China, India). These alliance and exchange networks, which cycled in volume and direction, were maintained through strong personal connections and relations of clientage, illustrating certain parallels to the economic patterns described by McAnany for the Classic Maya (Blanton et al. 1996). Like Storey's and Sherratt's chapters, this work adds new key empirical findings to comparative analyses of macroregional economics in precapitalist times.

As she herself recognizes, Ann Stahl probably has the thinnest empirical foundation (of any of the regions considered here) on which to build for her study of West African economic systems in Chapter 13. Stahl approaches this challenge through an assessment of extant data and how it shapes and colors what we know and what others think we already understand. By clearing up old

misconceptions and evaluating the present knowledge base, Stahl, like many of the other contributors to this book, sets the foundation for defining the kinds of data that need to be collected and for indicating how a richer comprehension of past political economies will be reached.

IMPLICATIONS AND INTENTS: GOING FORWARD

In a recent thoughtful, albeit rather pessimistic, assessment of present-day cultural anthropology, D'Andrade (2000:227) bemoans that "economic anthropology is almost gone." Ensminger (2002:ix) believes that "the last decade of the twentieth century was not kind to economic anthropology." A few years earlier, in a recent important economic anthropology text, Halperin (1994:8-9) frets that economic anthropology has not been able to develop a common vocabulary and calls for the construction of a clear theoretical framework that elaborates new concepts, questions, and models. More specifically, Halperin (1994:9) asserts that "we need a revitalized economic anthropology that incorporates archaeology," a point echoed by Isaac (1996:331; see also Isaac 1993:230), who observes that "archaeologists will have to do much of the work involved in constructing a more fruitful cross-cultural/cross-temporal economic anthropology."

It is the hope of the editors and contributors that this volume will help spur a more comparative and empirically focused consideration of past political economies. As illustrated here, concerted efforts to survey large landscapes systematically for the vestiges of past occupations, to excavate broad horizontal (and statistically meaningful) household contexts, to implement a range of new compositional analytic techniques, and to interdigitate textual and archaeological findings in more systematic ways have afforded archaeologists the tools and vantage points to investigate the economies of complex societies in ways that were out of the question decades ago. Such new empirical foundations permit the more direct assessment of past economic patterns and processes in all their richness and diversity. They also offer the opportunity to assess more fully the different ways economic relations may shift over time.

As noted at the start of this essay, many of the theoretical issues addressed in this work have long been centered at the core of anthropology and anthropological archaeology. A renewed focus on these research questions (concerning economic diversity and change) using the expanded tool kit now available can serve not only to resuscitate and energize a more vital economic anthropology but to strengthen the loosening fabric that binds anthropology as a discipline at a time when centrifugal pressures threaten the integrity of the field. These are lofty goals that are perhaps well beyond the scope of any single edited volume. Yet the breadth and empirical wealth of the chapters to follow will, we hope, encourage others to rededicate themselves to reassess, advance, and eventually find answers to the core set of issues that long have been at the heart of our anthropological (and even broader social scientific and historical) endeavors.

2

The Evolution of Chiefdoms
An Economic Anthropological Model

CHARLES STANISH

This chapter reexamines one of the most perplexing questions in archaeology and anthropology: Why, after millennia of successfully living in politically egalitarian hunting-gathering bands or village societies, did some groups develop social ranking characteristic of big-man societies and simple chiefdoms? This process is a brief moment in cultural evolutionary time, but it represents the crossing of a great social threshold. The shift from a society in which each social unit of production and consumption is more or less equal to one in which a few individuals or families control or manage components of the economy constitutes a fundamental change in the way people interact with one another. The origin of state societies, in which the coercive power of one class over others becomes institutionalized, is perhaps the only other evolutionary process as significant as the development of rank.

The development of rank demands explanation for a number of theoretical reasons, not least of which is the apparent cost assumed by the bulk of the population. These individuals lose some political autonomy as rank develops and as social distances increase among members of the community. The evolution of rank creates groups of people, sometimes over generations, who are accorded or assume greater social prestige than their neighbors. Why people in egalitarian societies would give up or lose autonomy to others in their society is one of the core ques-

tions in anthropological archaeology and has intrigued scholars since classical antiquity.

The development of rank is not an event that can be explained by historical factors. Archaeology teaches us that ranked societies developed around the world. At a generational scale, ranked societies developed and collapsed at rapid rates. At a millennial scale, in contrast, ranked societies evolved around the world independently many times throughout human history. Certainly, the development of ranked societies occurred independently in both the Old World and the Americas. According to Flannery (1998:44), ranked society evolved independently in at least Central and South America, sub-Saharan Africa, Southeast Asia, Oceania, and the Pacific coast of North America. It is likely that ranked society also developed independently within these large cultural regions as well. In other words, this process occurred in a number of areas of the world among different cultures, environments, and times. From these data, we can only conclude that it is a process that can occur in any human society under the appropriate conditions.

How do ranked societies evolve out of politically and economically egalitarian societies? I argue that this process must be modeled as a voluntary phenomenon, not a coercive one, as is commonly claimed in archaeological theory. Based on the ethnographic record, commoners in nonstate societies are not forced into these relationships with their elite. Individual commoner families can withdraw from the elite-directed economic activities, and they are not obligated to participate in social activities that enhance elite prestige. In fact, in ethnographic accounts it is much more common for chiefs—both small (big man) and large—to fail than to succeed. The ethnographic record is replete with occasions when commoner families left villages or transferred their allegiance to other elite without any serious cost. In hundreds of other cases people seemingly accept the existence of rank in their communities.

In this chapter I adopt a materialist and agency approach to modeling cultural evolution (e.g., Spencer 1993, 1997; see Feinman 2000a for a review of critical issues in evolutionary anthropology). The evolution of ranked societies is a political process. I take an economic approach to the evolution of political organization, arguing that the basis of political evolution is economic surplus. I view the creation of surplus by a bounded group of people as the central factor in political evolution.

As agents, people make strategic political decisions to create, or not create, the necessary surplus that permits the emergence of an elite group. I propose that strategic decision making by individuals acting in their self-interest is an essential component of any model of the evolution of rank. This theoretical position raises the problem of free will and self-interest in cultural evolution. I support this proposition with recent theoretical work from evolutionary game theory and the evolution of cooperation. Based on this work, the best model of normative human behavior is neither a selfish rational-actor model of free will nor a utopian model of socially motivated altruistic agents. I likewise reject assumptions that people are self-interested but passive agents who respond to factors beyond their comprehension. Rather, the model of "*Homo reciprocans*," or humans as conditional cooperators, is the best assumption for normative human behavior for modeling the origins of rank. This work derives from evolutionary game theory behavior (see

Shalizi 1999 for an overview). In this model, people act in their own self-interest and are aware of the costs and benefits associated with those acts, but they act without knowledge of all information. That is, people do not make rational decisions because they lack complete information; they generally make "smart" decisions with the limited information available. In the conditional-cooperator model, cooperation actually constitutes one evolutionarily stable strategy for individuals acting in their own self-interest under the appropriate conditions. Given this new understanding of normative human behavior, the emergence of rank can be modeled as a voluntary, not coercive, phenomenon adopted by cognizant and active agents. The explanation for the origins of rank can be found in such appropriate conditions that permit the development of these more complex political and economic arrangements.

Economic theory provides the mechanism that links the emergence of cooperation as a theoretical construct embodied in conditional cooperators to this materialist model of the evolution of rank in the archaeological record. It is almost always assumed in processual archaeology that the evolution of rank entails huge economic costs to commoners. In this view the theoretical mechanisms of culture change must be coercive in some manner. They can be either directly coercive with other individuals forming classes that modify commoners' behavior to the benefit of elites, or indirectly through environmental or demographic stress that forces commoners to accept new levels of sociopolitical integration necessary to their survival but detrimental to their socioeconomic status.

I argue that this assumption is wrong. The cooperative labor organizations of ranked societies create economic efficiencies from specialized production. These organizations produce much more wealth for the same amount of labor than societies in which the household is the highest level of cooperative labor. Groups that adopt these more complex labor organizations will be substantially wealthier than egalitarian organizations. Over time, these more complex organizations will tend to dominate the cultural landscape in any one area through a variety of processes, ranging from actual conquest of smaller and poorer groups to the more common process of emulation of these organizations by less complex societies.

There is, however, a significant *social* cost to the adoption of cooperative labor organization. If there were not a cost, complex societies would have developed in the Paleolithic or Archaic periods millennia ago. This cost is the loss of control over nonsubsistence production and exchange by commoner populations. In brief, individual household production generates much lower surplus, but the laborers control all aspects of that production, including its final disposition. Cooperative labor, in contrast, produces substantially more surplus, but the control of that wealth must be managed in some way that takes decision-making autonomy about the use of that surplus out of the hands of the direct producers.

The ethnographic record is replete with examples of cooperative labor organizations in big-man and simple chiefly societies falling apart because of internal squabbles. It is difficult for elites to maintain these organizations. They must have some kind of social mechanism to ensure cooperation of all specialized laborers throughout the production process. The model presented here centers on the role of ritual in maintaining these cooperative labor organizations. The creation of a voluntary specialized labor organization implies the creation of a complex series of deferred debts that must be repaid at a later date. The establishment of rituals of production and exchange that sanctify and "schedule" the cancellation of deferred debts by the elite to the commoners can overcome this resistance to more complex labor arrangements. These rituals, embodied in material features such as platform mounds, elaborate public monuments, special buildings, valuable objects, and the like, serve as a type of "guarantee" for the redistribution of wealth that is produced. In this model of chiefdom (not state) evolution, ideology is not viewed as a mechanism to mask inequality as it is in state societies. Rather, some kinds of ideologies, given form in ritual, provide a series of benchmarks that an elite must obey that will ultimately result in a redistribution of wealth. Failure to follow those benchmarks will result in a collapse of that labor organization. Adherence to those ritual obligations provides some guarantees necessary to keep that organization together. There is, in short, an intimate link between the successful creation of ritual practices and successful specialized labor organizations.

DEFINITIONS

Definitions of ranked societies fall into two broad traditions. One is a focus on the internal political structure and hierarchy (e.g., the classic works of Fried 1967 and Service 1972). A second group of theories focuses on regional political control (Carneiro 1981, 1998; Earle 1987a, 1991, 1997:14; Johnson and Earle 2000). For the latter, a chiefdom develops when one village dominates other villages to create a regional polity. Carneiro, for instance, argues that political control over a region is the key defining characteristic of chiefdoms. Johnson and Earle (2000) define a chiefdom as a regional polity involving a number of villages under the control of a paramount.

For the first tradition, ranked society is commonly an intermediate stage between egalitarian and state societies. I follow this tradition and focus on internal political organization as the key variable. The development of a regional polity, however, is a concomitant of chiefdoms and is one of the best archaeological markers. Within the economic anthropological perspective used here, I define ranked societies as those in which a subgroup of individuals is able to command consistently greater political influence over the production and exchange of wealth.[1]

I use the term *chiefdom* very broadly to include every socioeconomic formation between egalitarian village societies and states, including all those societies that have been called simple chiefdoms, most complex chiefdoms, intermediate-level societies, big-man societies, and so forth. Chiefdoms here are understood simply as nonstate, ranked societies. With a focus on rank instead of regional political structure, a wider range of societies is brought under the concept of chiefdom. Societies such as Tikopia and the Trobriands are considered simple chiefdoms, as are the classic New Guinea big-man societies and any society in which a subgroup of people is able to direct economic activities. Redmond (1998) makes a distinction between chiefdoms and "chieftaincies." The definition used here would include the latter concept as well.

THE ECONOMIC BASIS OF RANK

The material basis of political evolution is economic surplus (e.g., Adams 1966:44–47). From the economic anthropological perspective adopted here, it is not possible to have socioeconomic rank without a surplus. The production and exchange of this surplus is the means by which rank is maintained. The most important use of the strategic redistribution of surplus is to keep allies together (e.g., Earle 1997). The evolution of ranked society out of politically and economically nonranked society is essentially an economic anthropological problem that centers on the production and allocation of wealth.

Production

I have discussed the nature of production and exchange in earlier publications (e.g., Stanish 1992) and only summarize here. Briefly, a large literature in economic anthropology recognizes that the household is the primary unit of production in virtually all societies. In politically egalitarian village societies, each household maintains a high degree of autonomy over its economic activities. Ranked societies have more complex systems of production and exchange requiring greater labor specialization between households. From an economic anthropological perspective, the development of rank requires an increase in surplus production beyond the needs of the household.

An important advance in understanding the functioning of the domestic household and labor intensification began with the observations of an early-twentieth-century Russian agricultural economist named Aleksandr Vasilevich Chayanov (1966). Chayanov analyzed data on Russian peasantry with specific reference to their economic decision-making behavior. The significance of Chayanov's observations was first extensively developed in modern anthropology by Marshall Sahlins (1972:87–92) and later elaborated by economic anthropologists and economic historians.

Succinctly stated, in the absence of pressures or inducements to the contrary, agrarian households substantially underproduce and underconsume relative to their theoretical capacity. As Sahlins describes it in his book *Stone Age Economics*, "primitive" agrarian economies "seem not to realize their own economic capacities. Labor power is underused, technological means are not fully engaged, natural resources are left untapped" (Sahlins 1972:41). Population densities are consistently below carrying capacities. He further argues that underproduction is inherent in the nature of such economies, organized by domestic groups and kinship relations. This feature of domestic economies appears to be cross-culturally valid in most historical settings, ranging from peasant households in modern nation-states, to village households peripheral to or outside state control. In other words, economies organized at the household level (i.e., by domestic groups and kinship) are characterized by a considerable "reserve" of potential labor and wealth production.

The reasons Chayanov's rule holds cross-culturally are less important for this discussion than the empirical fact that it does indeed exist. The existence of systemic underproduction is a significant factor in the evolution of more complex political economies. The difference between the potential production of the household and its actual production under these constraints acts as a reservoir of "intensifiable" wealth that can be exploited by an elite. As Adams (1966:45) noted long ago, the fact that "agricultural producers can...be induced or compelled to provide a surplus above their own subsistence needs for socially defined ends is little more than a truism." Of real theoretical concern is the means by which this surplus is procured, how it is sustained, and for what social ends it is used and distributed.

Exchange

A variety of exchange, or allocation, systems have been identified in premodern societies. The manipulation and control of these systems is the primary economic means by which rank is created and maintained. The economic historian Karl Polanyi (1957) initiated a theoretical discussion that formalized four types of allocation systems: reciprocity, redistribution, nonmarket trade, and market exchange. To these we can add competitive feasting and tribute. These six types define virtually all kinds of wealth transfers in premodern and modern economies.

Reciprocity is defined as the exchange of an equal amount of wealth, or "like value for like value." It involves a series of symmetrical obligations between individuals or groups. It may be socially mediated—a sack of potatoes to my brother-in-law for a pound of meat—or it may be an exchange between nonrelated partners, as in the famous case of the Kula as first described by Bronislaw Malinowski (1961). Reciprocity may be immediate, such as a direct exchange in a periodic fair or in commensal feasts (Dietler 1996; Hayden 1996), or it may be deferred for days, weeks, years, or even decades. Deferred reciprocity, in fact, is a fundamental feature of the Kula (Leach 1983:3) and is the most prominent feature of many ranked political economies in the ethnographic literature. Reciprocity can occur as an indirect down-the-line trade in which individuals conduct a series of reciprocal trades that link large distances through exchange partners. In virtually all types of political economies, the mechanism of reciprocity, either deferred or immediate, makes up the bulk of exchange.

Redistribution is best conceived of as "asymmetrical reciprocity." That is, there is an exchange of wealth that ideologically may be presented as equal, but the actual values exchanged are not equal. Redistribution implies the existence of some kind of social or political authority that can accumulate surplus for redistribution. Most cases of redistribution in the ethnographic record are recorded as "voluntary," with a larger group willing to give up some surplus wealth to an authority to maintain a mechanism of distribution that avoids social conflict. Likewise, most cases of redistribution involve nonsubsistence surplus (Earle 1997).

Reciprocity and redistribution are forms of barter in which values are established by custom. Exchange for profit is not a motive. In premodern political economies dominated by these mechanisms, neutral intermediaries who move goods between exchange partners are rare. Nonmarket exchange that meets these criteria is defined by Polanyi (1957:263) as "administered trade." In administered trade systems, exchange values for commodities or services are determined by a political authority and not through competitive negotiation, although as in all economies supply and demand ultimately affect exchange values. Trade is extensive in such systems, but it is not conducted in a competitive, market environment. Rather than merchants who operate for profit as in market systems, in administered trade systems middlemen act as agents for political authorities (Hodges 1988:39). Middlemen make a profit in such a system by manipulating competing political elites for rights to access to exchange partners.

Market exchange is a system in which prices are determined by negotiations between independent buyers and sellers. Media of exchange, or some kinds of money, are central to the operation of price-fixing markets. Middlemen exist and make a profit from price differences. Wealth is distributed without significant regard to political or social factors, but by largely economic ones; that is, those who bid up prices the highest receive the goods and services. In nonmarket barter economies one is socially obligated to trade with a preestablished partner, usually a kinsman. In market systems this obligation is substantially weaker.

Competitive feasting is a type of commensal feasting that, in strictly economic terms, is a form of deferred reciprocity. One person offers wealth to another with the expectation of a supposedly equal exchange in the future. However, unlike in most forms of reciprocity, the motive in competitive feasting is not the receipt of a future equal return of wealth but rather future political gain. Perhaps more so than in any other exchange mechanism, the political and the economic merge in competitive feasting. Wealth is provided strategically in order to obligate the receiver to such an extent that he or she must promise future labor or wealth. The successful host or giver may actually lose total wealth in the short term but gains political power and prestige. Most important, successful hosts increase the size of their following or faction and can command even greater numbers of non-elite laborers for future production.

Competitive feasting must be viewed as a major form of economic exchange in many premodern societies and not some kind of aberrant social behavior. It is a major mechanism of political economic evolution (Hayden 1996:127). Competitive feasting is not fully understandable as a form of redistribution, reciprocity, or trade (although cf. Polanyi 1968:13–14). It is a distinct kind of exchange that occurs under certain conditions and is central to the evolution of moderately ranked political economies.

The final mechanism of wealth transfer is tribute. This was not a mechanism for Polanyi since he was focused on the nature of internal political and economic organization. Tribute is nevertheless a mechanism of wealth exchange. It is an exploitative economic relationship in which one party materially benefits by exacting wealth from another through some kind of force. The mechanism of tribute is an integral component of archaic states and imperial political economies. Tribute takes many forms in a variety of historical and cultural contexts. The principal defining characteristic is that there is no expectation of any kind of material reciprocity.

Of these six kinds of exchange mechanisms, reciprocity, redistribution, competitive feasting, and nonmarket trade are relevant to the emergence of rank. (Market exchange and tribute are associated with more complex political economies such as complex chiefdoms and states.) These four allocation mechanisms, however, permeate all societies, and their manipulation is central to the evolution of rank.

THE PROBLEM OF INDIVIDUAL SELF-INTEREST IN PROCESSUAL THEORY

Theories that seek to explain the origin of ranked society out of egalitarian society have always confronted the problem of individual self-interest. At its most basic form, the issue is why people who live in egalitarian societies would give up some economic and political freedom, as occurs when an elite is allowed to develop. It is simply counterintuitive that people would voluntarily give up their labor time or other resources to maintain an elite. Johnson and Earle (2000:203), for instance, rhetorically ask "why food producers forgo leisure in order to generate a surplus in the first place...why are people willing to accept the burden of supporting Big Men, their expensive feasting, and public displays of wealth and status?" Why do people abandon a condition of political equality for inequality?

Sahlins (1972:82) articulates the classic economic anthropological position regarding the creation of surplus. He argues that there are only two ways to create the increased production necessary for surplus: get "people to work more or [get] more people to work." Both choices assume that people would not voluntarily give up economic and political autonomy. There are both empirical and theoretical problems with this assumption, however. The central problem is the emergence of hierarchy out of politically and economically egalitarian societies. Following traditional logic, human beings were either inherently social creatures (the Rousseauian view) who became corrupted with the advent of private property or were inherently conflict-ridden creatures (the Hobbesian view) who were willing to give up some political autonomy for survival. In this logic, complexity (hierarchy) could develop only if the bulk of individuals in any society were compelled to act against their own self-interest (economic autonomy) and accept higher levels of sociopolitical integration. Coercive theories of cultural evolution, from either internal or external factors, were the only viable ones under the theoretical constraint presented by the problems of human will and self-interest.

AN EVOLUTIONARY GAME THEORY ALTERNATIVE: CONDITIONAL COOPERATORS

Recent advances in game theory have provided what I believe to be stunning implications for archaeological theory building. This work suggests that neither the Hobbesian rational and selfish agent nor the Rousseauian social being guides human behavior. The vast majority of people in any randomly selected group are "conditional cooperators" who do not act on their immediate and optimal economic choices in all circumstances. Bowles et al. (1997:2–3) note that "important forms of cooperative behavior are commonly observed" in both controlled observations and the laboratory. The traditional rational-actor model of classical economics is insufficient. They observe that people are "irrationally" prosocial, a behavior that does not conform to economic maximization models or assumptions in classical economic theory. In fact, people tend to be both irrationally cooperative and irrationally vindictive under experimental circumstances that most approximate social life.

Although on initial appearance this conclusion seems counterintuitive, a number of experimental data support it. Nowak et al. (2000), for example, ran a series of simulations using an iterated Ultimatum Game.[2] They too discovered that there is an irrational human emphasis on fairness in games that most approximate social reality. By *irrational*, they refer to what would be expected in an economic exchange in which each actor sought to maximize resources.

The irrational behavior included the punishment of cheaters: people were ready to hurt cheaters even at a cost to themselves. When information on players' reputations (the knowledge of players' past actions) was included, cooperation emerged as an evolutionarily stable strategy. This point is critical because simulations of these behaviors indicate that so-called irrational behavior can be selected for in any population and that it is in the interest of individuals.[3]

Without information on players' reputations, Nowak et al. (2000) found that evolution always leads to the predominance of economically rational actors, that is, actors who offer little and reject nothing or offer high and accept little. With the addition of information on players, however, "fair" strategies will dominate. The ability to remember what a fellow actor will do and pass this information on to others is critical, and it is a unique property of human beings. Furthermore, whenever stochastic variation is added to the population, the "fair strategy will supersede the reasonable one in the long run." As Nowak et al. summarize their results: "When reputation is included in the Ultimatum Game, adaptation favors fairness over reason. In this most elementary game, information on the co-player fosters the emergence of strategies that are nonrational, but promote economic exchange" (2000:1774).[4]

Other work demonstrates the importance of punishment as an adaptive strategy, a seemingly irrational behavior. Bowles et al. (1997:5) note that defection (free riding) "is significantly alleviated if there is an opportunity for costly retaliation." Retaliation costs outweigh the costs of cooperation in longterm runs. Experimental evidence supports the proposition that "if costly retaliation opportunities are combined with communication opportunities almost no defection occurs and, therefore, no resources are wasted for retaliation" (Bowles et al. 1997:5–6). Bowles et al. (1997:4) argue that "a predisposition to cooperate and to undertake costly punishment are probably related phenomena," a combination they refer to as "reciprocal fairness."

Gintis (2000:169) calls this phenomenon "strong reciprocity," defining it as a predisposition "to cooperate with others and punish non-cooperators, even when this behavior cannot be justified in terms of self-interest, extended kinship, or reciprocal altruism." Gintis contrasts strong reciprocity with its weak counterpart, "reciprocal altruism." He argues that reciprocal altruism is too weak to explain the evolution of cooperative behavior because when a group is threatened, the optimal behavior for self-interested agents is defection: "precisely when a group is most in need of prosocial behavior, cooperation based on reciprocal altruism will collapse" (Gintis 2000:172). Again, in this model the role of punishment is central to the evolution of cooperation in a group of self-interested individuals.

All this work has provided us with a new assumption about the normative social behavior of humans called "*Homo reciprocans*." In this model people have a

> propensity to cooperate, they respond to the cooperation of others by maintaining or increasing their level of cooperation, and they respond to defection on the part of others by retaliating against the offenders, even at a cost to themselves, and even when they cannot reasonably expect future personal gains from such retaliation. In particular, when other forms of punishment are not available, individuals respond to defection with defection.... Homo reciprocans is thus neither the selfless altruist of utopian theory, nor the selfish hedonist of neoclassical economics. Rather, he is a conditional cooperator whose penchant for reciprocity can be elicited under the proper circumstances.
> (Bowles et al. 1997:4–5)

If indeed people are predisposed to cooperation, and if that cooperative behavior is evolutionarily stable, then we have the theoretical basis for the model for the voluntary creation of rank out of egalitarian societies.

From an economic anthropological perspective, there are two criteria that must be met for this model to be successful in historical sciences such as archaeology. First, there must be an economic mechanism that corresponds to the theoretical model in which benefits of cooperation outweigh costs for individuals. That is, the cooperative labor organization must provide greater benefits to each individual than he or she could receive by working alone, and the benefits received must be sufficiently large to compensate for the loss of autonomy in the new production process. Second, there must be a social mechanism that can maintain that labor organization: defection must be punished, and the benefits to the cooperators must be guaranteed.

ECONOMIC ANTHROPOLOGICAL MECHANISMS

Evolutionary game theory provides us with the theoretical base for an agent-based and materialist model of the evolution of rank, for we can assume that individuals act in their own self-interest and at the same time still create cooperative social organizations that are evolutionarily stable. The mechanism that parallels game theory can be found in some basic economic theory. As early as the late eighteenth century the political economist Adam Smith (1976 [1776]) outlined the now-classic argument that economic specialization (division of labor) by workers properly organized will produce far more in the same amount of time than individual laborers can produce on their own. Increasing the number of individual, nonspecialized workers will increase production arithmetically. Increasing the number of specialized workers will increase production at a much greater rate. That is, this more complex organization will result in greater productivity at the same level of labor input and without a concomitant change in technology. This phenomenon in which a specialized work organization will produce more than the sum of the individuals working alone is what Smith called "the productive powers of labor" and represents gains through efficiency of specialization.

In modern economics an economic efficiency through specialization occurs when the cost of one produced unit decreases as the capacity to produce the unit increases. In premodern economies the same general phenomenon also is evident, albeit in a much more rudimentary form. In household economies, for instance, economic efficiencies can be achieved when individuals specialize and take advantage of situations in which a marginal increase in labor cost produces a disproportionately large increase in output. This phenomenon works for any economic activity in which there are a number of distinct tasks, including the preparation of special foodstuffs, alcoholic beverages, artisan goods, and the like. In short, surplus can be increased in an economy of this nature not by getting people to work more but by getting them to work differently as specialized producers. It is significant for modeling the evolution of rank that all these specialized tasks are not qualitatively different from the non-specialized ones—there is nothing technically new to learn. What is new is the organization of the labor, not the nature or intensity of that labor.

There is a second type of specialized preindustrial economic organization that is significant for the origins of rank. This is one that allows people organized above a household level to conduct activities that are not possible for an individual household alone. Unlike the first kind of specialized organization, which exponentially increases production through the arithmetic increase in numbers and organization, the second kind is characterized by a density-dependent task that can be accomplished only with a minimum number or minimum density of people. In mathematical terms it is a nonlinear phenomenon. The number of people required is substantially larger than that available from a household organization. When that number is reached, a threshold is broken and new possibilities open up that otherwise would not be possible. Examples of such nonlinear organizations are canoe building, in which a minimum number of people are needed to lift a tree, and trading or raiding expeditions into hostile territory, for which a minimum number is necessary for protection.

The ability to get people to work differently and to maintain that new labor organization is the key to the evolution of ranked societies. Economic specialization and rudimentary economies of scale provide the economic mechanisms that link game theory with economic anthropology. To repeat, an increase in surplus can be achieved not only by getting more people to work or getting people to work more, but by getting those people *to work differently in a more efficient labor organization*. The new organization provides the material resources that increase each individual's benefits along with the wealth necessary for the emergence of an elite. There is no net labor time cost to commoners. The only cost is social: loss of their autonomy over the products of their cooperative economic activity.

The implications for the origins of ranked society are clear. When elites are able to overcome the limits of household economies, as embodied in Chayanov's rule, they are able to create more complex political economies that produce substantially more surplus than could be produced by individuals or individual households working alone. The immediate benefit is a huge increase in the number and quality of goods for the entire population, which benefits the individuals in that labor organization.

Ethnography is replete with examples of the persuasive authority of chiefs in moderately ranked societies used to maintain specialized labor organizations. In virtually all cases the material cornerstone of chiefly authority is heightened economic production through more specialized tasks that use labor in different ways. The benefits of cooperation are tangible; if a group works together in a specialized labor organization, all individuals and households benefit. People are willing to forgo these benefits if there is a perception of unfairness, however. Unfairness is perceived by individuals if they do not receive their share of the production, if they perceive that they are contributing more than others, or if they perceive that an elite is keeping too much of the product. In short, a complex labor organization can break down for a number of reasons, as seen in the ethnographic record, including (1) individuals deciding that the costs are not worth the loss of autonomy, (2) the emergence of free riders who take advantage of cooperators, (3) disputes over the share of the wealth, and (4) the desire of individuals to punish others even at a cost to themselves. The real test for an emergent elite is how to keep people working together in societies where authority is vested in kinship and economic autonomy is preserved in households.

From this perspective, the central role of elites is to keep the benefits of cooperative labor organizations consistently higher than the costs of defection from that labor. The theoretical bottom line is that if people are indeed conditional cooperators, the elite must foster and maintain those conditions that keep people working. Failure to keep benefits high will result in a collapse in the specialized labor organization to a more simple one of individual household production and exchange. An essential means of holding these specialized labor organizations together is through ritual.

RITUAL IN THE SERVICE OF SPECIALIZED LABOR ORGANIZATION

All economic activities have their magic.
—Malinowski 1961:73

Magic, in fact, in one shape or another, permeates all the economic life of the native.   —Firth 1959:245

There are many kinds of ideologies, rituals, and ceremonies documented by ethnographers and historians throughout the world's cultures in space and time. The kinds that interest us here are those that affect production and exchange. Ritual provides the guarantees to the commoner members of the labor organization that they will receive a fair share of their production. It furthermore provides sanctions against free riders and prescribes the social rewards individuals receive for cooperating over a long period of time. Ideology and its concomitant ritual is the social means by which elites guarantee the exchange of surplus wealth and thereby keep that organization alive. Among the Maori,

for instance, Firth divided all communal work into two types. One type involved people all doing the same task; the other was characterized by a specialized division of labor. He is emphatic that in the specialized division of labor "the people had to comply with a definite set of magical regulations" (Firth 1967:232). These regulations in effect constitute ritual in the service of specialized labor organization.

The most fundamental exchange mechanism, of course, is reciprocity. Reciprocity does not require intermediaries such as chiefs. Reciprocal exchange occurs in egalitarian societies, and the bulk of exchange in most societies, even very complex ones with market systems, is still reciprocal. It is significant, however, that ethnographic observations on reciprocal exchange usually include a variety of religious sanctions that ensure payment or repayment of gifts. Firth, discussing the Maori, notes the very strong cultural norm that "anything which is given must be repaid" (1959:417). The Maori maintained a principle of reciprocity called *utu*, translated as "compensation" or "obtaining an equivalent" (Firth 1967:413). Firth goes on to observe that there is serious social and supernatural sanction for failure to repay. Virtually every other ethnography in the world that discusses reciprocal exchange in ranked societies stresses the serious supernatural and earthly consequences of cheating. Marcel Mauss's celebrated essay "The Gift" (1990) describes in detail the degree to which reciprocity is socially, morally, and religiously enforced in all "archaic" societies.[5] These empirical data from around the world are quite consistent with the experimental data of evolutionary game theory that stress fairness in human transactions.

Reciprocity involves the equal exchange between individuals of similar rank. Most kinds of redistribution also maintain the fiction of equality, although the wealth reciprocated may be nonmaterial and therefore economically unequal. Given the universal importance placed on fairness in reciprocity, it is not surprising that the same kinds of religious sanctions are found with redistributive allocations as well. Malinowski's ethnography of the Trobriand Islanders is full of references to the importance of ritual and religion in organizing economic activities that lead to surpluses that are eventually redistributed under elite guidance.[6] In one example of many, he notes that "the magician inaugurates successively all the various stages [of agricultural production] which follow one another—the burning of the scrub, the clearing, the planting, the weeding and the harvesting" (Malinowski 1961:59).

According to Malinowski's own observations, the average farmer produces four times more food than he needs, the rest destined for social and political obligations to the chief and to his family. Malinowski goes on to describe how the magician uses his authority to persuade and induce people to work well beyond the needs of their household. Implicit in these observations is that this particular level of surplus production would not have been possible without the influence of the magician in invoking a community-wide ideology of work.

To keep the group working together in a specialized labor production, the elite must guarantee that the individual laborers will receive their fair share at the end of what can be a lengthy production process. Firth (1967: 306) talks about the essential role of the chief in "the apportionment of a common product among the members of a working party." It has to be fair. It has to be based on notions of reciprocity and ritually sanctioned redistribution. One of the necessary conditions for a successful economic organization in ranked societies is an ideology of reciprocity that guarantees equitable redistribution of production. In other words, these ideologies keep productive groups together and sanctify the allocation systems mediated or controlled by the elite.

Bawden (1999:140) makes a critical point about political ritual: "Essential to the persisting influence of such ritual is the mutually sustaining interaction between exact repetition of their elements and the constant meaning that they signify. Repetition in this context connotes continuity and stability, even in the face of wider social disruption." Repetition is a key here. It serves as a guarantee to the commoners working in the specialized labor organization. Ethnographic data suggest that if an organizer keeps the precise ritual order, and if economic distribution is part of that order, then the correct conduct of ritual directly ensures the "proper" distribution of those resources after the surplus is produced.

It is significant that the principal allocation mechanisms are imbued with ritual importance in at least some circumstances. Certainly, most exchange is carried out with little ritual import. But much exchange of surplus between people of different rank is carried out by socially prescribed rules. The social and religious sanctions surrounding the keeping of reciprocal debts are legion in the ethnographic literature. Redistribution used to be considered the dominant function of elites in chiefly societies. We now know that most redistribution involves nonsubsistence or prestige goods, such as exotic objects, alcohol, textiles, fancy pottery, and so forth. The offering and receipt of redistributed goods, particularly in competitive feasts, also is couched in elaborate ritual terms.

Competitive feasting, of course, is imbued with ritually prescribed behaviors: "Every feast given by one tribe to another imposed upon the recipients a stringent obligation to return this hospitality at some future time. No set term was fixed, but tribal honour required that as soon as sufficient supplies had been accumulated, a similar gathering should be convened" (Firth 1967:335). Similar observations can be found in the works of Boas (e.g., 1964), Malinowski (e.g., 1961), Oliver (e.g., 1955), and other ethnographies from around the world.

Other allocation mechanisms are wrapped in ideology as well. These three, however—reciprocity, redistribution, and competitive feasting—are the most significant ones for the origins of rank. Ritual serves to ensure the discharge of incurred obligations in the absence of legal sanctions and third parties to resolve disputes and enforce debts. Without such guarantees, complex labor organizations would not be possible.

Ritual architecture is a necessary means by which ideologies of production and exchange are expressed. Complex labor organizations are maintained through ceremonies, specifically various kinds of feasting hosted by chiefs or aspiring chiefs. As suggested above, these feasts incorporate ideologies of production and exchange. The ideologies are given expression—materialized—by a number of archaeological features. The archaeological and ethnographic examples of fancy corporate architecture—temples, ball courts, plazas, sunken courts, and the like—are the material remains of attempts by emergent elites to maintain the specialized labor organizations. Likewise, the production of elaborate art objects, the appearance of exotic materials, and the production of monuments all serve to enhance the cohesion of these organized corporate groups to prevent them from reverting to a household economic organization.

There are many ethnographic examples of this phenomenon. Public structures with religious significance are intimately associated with resource distribution. Among the Maori, Firth (1967:153) observes that the large quantities of food for feasts were heaped in ceremonial constructions called *maraes* (Firth 1967:305). This also was the case with the products of communal bird snaring. Birds were a highly valued commodity among the Maori that were collected and displayed in the *marae* after the hunt for inspection by the chief. Communal meeting houses, men's houses, and so forth also are commonly mentioned as places where ritual exchange takes place, particularly for the distribution of prestige goods.

In sum, evolutionary game theory demonstrates that one viable outcome for all individuals acting in their own self-interest, under appropriate conditions, is to create a more complex organization based on reciprocal cooperation. Economic theory shows that more complex labor organizations, in-

Figure 2.1. The Andes.

volving precisely these kinds of cooperative behaviors, increase surplus without increased labor input. There are costs for individuals in these new organizations, however, the greatest one being the loss of productive autonomy by individuals and households. Ethnographic and historical data provide the key to overcoming those costs: the ability of such surplus-producing labor organizations to provide goods and ceremonies not available to individuals or households on their own. Ritual provides the supernaturally sanctioned guarantees for individuals to participate in these organizations. We can therefore explain the origin of ranked societies out of nonranked ones with a model that assumes self-interested behavior on the part of individuals who create surplus-producing organizations and also lay out the socially prescribed rules for the redistribution of that surplus. Religious constructions such as temples represent one strategy for keeping groups together. The public buildings and the ideology behind them represent the material means of guaranteeing that the elites would

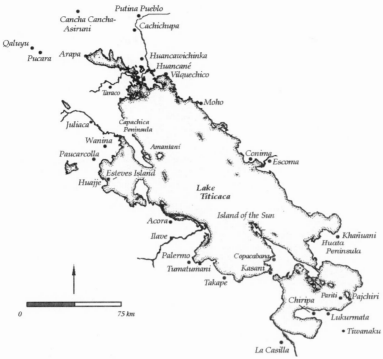

Figure 2.2. The Lake Titicaca region.

ensure the proper distribution of wealth. In the next section I outline this process with data from the Titicaca Basin of southern Peru and Bolivia.

AN ARCHAEOLOGICAL EXAMPLE OF THE EMERGENCE OF RANK: THE TITICACA BASIN OF PERU AND BOLIVIA

The Lake Titicaca region (Figures 2.1 and 2.2) is a huge geological basin that sits between two mountain ranges in southern Peru and northern Bolivia. Nestled between these two ranges, of course, is a body of water approximately 8,500 km² in size. The lowest part of the region is the surface of the lake itself, at 3,810 m above sea level. The vast bulk of the Titicaca region is above 3,800 m. This cultural and geographical area, about 50,000 km², comprises the Titicaca Basin drainage, an area about twice the size of Belize.

More than 100 years of systematic archaeological research has been conducted in the region (for a summary, see Stanish 2003). This work gives us a schematic but basic out-line of its cultural history. We know that the first occupants arrived relatively late in the Americas, sometime before 10,000 years ago. For several millennia, these hunter-gatherer-foragers lived along the rivers and other water sources. Around 4,000 years ago, some major climatic changes profoundly affected the ecology and the economic opportunities available to people of the region. The lake began to increase in size, rainfall increased, and populations grew. At this time agricultural settlements were established on the thin but very rich strip of land along the lake edge up to about 4,000 m above sea level.

Settled village life was established in at least some areas of the basin during the Early Formative period (2000–1300 B.C.). Over more than two millennia the Early Formative cultures of the circum–Titicaca Basin developed successful plant agricultural systems, maintained domesticated animal herds, consistently exploited the lake resources, and established permanent villages. Of course, there is no discrete beginning to the Early

CHRONOLOGY OF THE TITICACA BASIN

	North Titicaca	South Titicaca	Andean General
1500	Inca	Inca	Late Horizon
	Colla	Pacajes/ Lupaqa	Late Intermediate
1000		Tiwanaku V	
	Late Huaña Tiwanaku		
500			Middle Horizon
		Tiwanaku IV	
	Early Huaña	Qeya	
AD/BC	Pucara	Kalasasaya	Early Intermediate
		Late Chiripa	
500	Cusipata		Early Horizon
		Middle Chiripa	
1000		Early Chiripa	
	Qaluyu		
1500			Initial
2000	Late Archaic	Late Archaic	

Figure 2.3. Chronology of the Titicaca region.

Formative period or specific end to the Archaic. The transition to the Early Formative lifeways out of the earlier Late Archaic period was a long process, not an event. In political terms there are no indications of ranking at these Early Formative period sites. In fact, the bulk of Early Formative occupations were on multicomponent sites with early Archaic ones (Stanish et al. 1997). The Early Formative lifeway appears to be more an elaboration of the Late Archaic one, with the addition of pottery, greater sedentism, heavier reliance on domesticated plants, and so forth, than it was any kind of qualitative break in the political organization of the region.

Politically ranked societies developed for the first time in the Middle Formative period circa 1300–500 B.C. (Figure 2.3). As mentioned above, a number of anthropologists argue that the most salient characteristic of chiefdom development is the formation of intervillage polities and the loss of individual autonomy for some of these settlements. From this perspective the Middle Formative period can be understood as the development of the first political organizations in the region that transcended the village level.

Significant shifts in site location and size occurred during the Middle Formative period (Stanish 1999; Stanish et al. 1997). Unlike the Late Archaic–Early Formative transition, there were major differences between the Early Formative and Middle Formative. New sites were founded, early Formative sites were abandoned, and for the first time a recognizable site size difference developed (Stanish 1999).

There also is excavation evidence for the first substantial site architecture in the Chiripa and Qaluyu areas, to the south and north of the lake, respectively. One of the earliest corporate architectural constructions is found at the site of Chiripa, located on the Taraco Peninsula in Bolivia. During the Middle Chiripa period a depression in the middle of the mound, first reported by Wendell Bennett (1936), was most likely a sunken court. Later work by Christine Hastorf and her team (1999) supports this interpretation. Likewise, at the site of Titinhuayani on the Island of the Sun, excavations by Esteban Quelima indicated substantial remodeling of the site in late Middle Formative and Upper Formative times (500 B.C.–A.D. 400) (Bauer and Stanish 2001). The construction features included the leveling of part of the hill and the construction of what appear to be stone-walled areas, possibly sunken courts or enclosures. Similar patterns are found at Palermo and Sillumocco-Huaquina near Juli (Stanish et al. 1997). In all these cases we can see the construction of public architecture near probable elite areas. These archaeological patterns correspond to many of the village plans in ethnographic accounts.

These first corporate or public constructions represent ritual and economic areas associated with moderate chiefly ranking. By these criteria, elites were numerous in the Early Middle Formative and were found throughout the Titicaca Basin. As in the ethnographic examples described around the world, chiefly societies have many elite families. Flannery (1998:21) notes that in a chiefly village of 1,000 people, one can find as many as 15 chiefly families. Each probably had elite residences and associated ritual areas. The residences of the elites most likely represented one of several lineage heads in each larger village that had political alliances with other villages. As a result, we would expect to find numerous small courts around the region, each belonging to or associated with a lineage.

The earliest elite architectural construction in the Titicaca Basin is hypothesized to be the small, squarish, sunken court. The Llusco structure discovered by Hastorf (1999) is typical of dozens of known small sunken courts around the Titicaca Basin. Other structures similar to and roughly contemporary with the Llusco structure have been found in the region (e.g., Albarracin-Jordan 1996:105–109; Hastorf 2004; Mathews 1992:69; Portugal 1988).

The sites with sunken courts became the original primary regional centers and were the focus of efforts by the emergent elite to attract retainers or attached specialists (Figure 2.4). The Middle Formative represents the first time some people were able to organize the labor of others beyond a household level. In this sense the court complexes became the material means by which these societies began to overcome the inherent productivity limits embodied in Chayanov's rule. As Paz Soria (1999) points out for the Llusco structure at Chiripa, it likely required coordinated labor beyond a single household. The same can be said for the two other structures at the site. The question, then, is, why did the elite develop in the first place and how were they able to attract other people to their primary regional centers?

The evidence from the Titicaca Basin links

Umire

Figure 2.4. Schematic reconstruction of sunken courts in the Titicaca Basin.

the origin of rank with elite-directed feasting and ceremony at these centers during Middle Formative times. It is hypothesized that the regional centers were the settlements where elites and commoners intensified and formalized these reciprocal relationships. The sunken courts and associated architecture were the center of these political rituals. In terms of the theoretical framework outlined above, the emergent Titicaca Basin elite engaged in a number of strategies to attract followers. The northern and southern areas of the basin had the first courts. Since there were settlements throughout the basin, we hypothesize that the Chiripa and Pucara areas had favorable noncultural features that promoted elite emergence.

There is little evidence for coercion either by intentional elite behavior or by exogenous factors such as resource stress, population growth, and the like. Population densities were quite low relative to later ones. Certainly, the population levels were nowhere near the carrying capacity of the environment and levels of technological development in the Middle Formative. Furthermore, there is

little evidence of conflict in the Titicaca Basin during this period. Therefore, there is at present no evidence that populations were forced to aggregate into these centers out of fear of raiding or other dangers from neighboring groups. Finally, the regional centers show no evidence of intrasettlement conflict. Quite to the contrary, the regional centers are smaller, and individual families do not seem to have been segregated into separate areas of elite and non-elite. There is no evidence of the physical segregation of groups on these sites.

What was the nature of the reciprocal relationships between emergent elite and non-elite in the Middle Formative? In the model presented here the elite competed for the support of commoners by organizing their labor to provide goods and ceremonies not available to individuals. Elites used the organized labor of multiple households to create economies of scale, to intensify production above the levels inherent in household economies, and to create larger-scale organizations capable of activities above household-level capacities. The net effect was an economic surplus that was used by the elite to perpetuate these relationships. For instance, the elite used the labor to build and maintain the sunken courts, to maintain part-time artisans to produce the stone and ceramic objects (and probably textiles as well), and to mount trading expeditions outside the region.

The goods obtained and manufactured by this reorganized labor were redistributed to the population in competitive feasts and other ceremonies. It is hypothesized that exotic goods, particularly coca and similar substances, were obtained from the lowlands. The formation of elite alliances as evidenced in the distribution of a pan–Titicaca Basin art style known as Yaya-Mama (Chávez 1988) could have facilitated this exchange. Such alliances could include complex marriage ties and elaborate elite gift giving, strategies that created a complex set of reciprocal debt obligations among these groups (Joyce Marcus, personal communication 1999).

The existence of long-distance exchange patterns throughout the area is supported by the presence of Titicaca Basin Middle Formative period pottery styles in the eastern and western sides of the Titicaca region. It also is significant that it was during the Middle Formative that elaborate pottery styles developed around the region. How did these beautiful pottery vessels function? The first observation is that the vessels are rare and were locally produced. Second, they are shaped in such a way as to suggest a drinking or serving function. Furthermore, as in the case of the stelae, there are certain canons that were followed in manufacture, but most if not all of the assemblages were locally produced. Many vessels show signs of curation, including repair holes on used vessels. The distribution of fineware sherds near cemetery areas suggests that they were commonly buried with the dead. It is likely, therefore, that these vessels were extremely valuable until the person who "owned" them died. Then they had no value except as grave goods that were owned by an individual. In other words, these were not alienable goods but had value only in the possession of a particular person. In their owner's death, they may have had the same function as in life, being used for eating, drinking, and feasting in the afterlife.

I argue that development of these fineware pottery styles represents another persuasive strategy of elites to maintain specialized labor production. By organizing pottery production, elites were able to produce finewares not readily manufactured by individual households. The flat-bottomed bowls were used in politically ritualized feasts, where exotic or mass-produced goods were distributed by elites to their followers. The role of feasting in general, and the role of alcohol drinking in particular, is associated, I believe, with the flat-bottomed bowls. This phenomenon represents a key process of elite formation in the Middle Formative.

The political landscape of the Middle Formative was populated by numerous competing and cooperating elite families, each attempting to persuade commoners to participate in its political and economic system. There were scores of primary regional centers in the Titicaca Basin, all possessing aspiring elites competing with others to increase their factions. Archaeological evidence for the autonomy of these regional centers is strong. Pottery analysis, for instance, indicates that the vast majority of the Middle Formative period pottery was manufactured locally. The fineware pottery styles are hypothesized to be analogous to the Yaya-Mama sculpture in one regard: the canons of style were generally uniform over broad areas, but the actual objects were locally produced. The artisans at each center worked within certain regional canons, but the control of that production was local. It is no coincidence that in the few centuries in which ranked society emerged in the region, the Yaya-Mama stelae, the fancy pottery, and corporate architecture essentially coevolved.

Sites such as Khañuani, on the Huata Peninsula in the southern basin, represent successful Middle Formative elite centers but ultimately Upper Formative period failures. Khañuani appears to be a largely Middle Formative period site with some later minor occupations. The corporate architecture is modest, consisting of a probable single court and platform. Figure 2.4 is a schematic reconstruction of a Middle Formative sunken court complex. We assume, based on comparisons with similar sites excavated in the region, that there was a monolith of some sort in the court. These kinds of sites were centers of political ritual, feasting, ceremony, and faction building. In time, Khañuani and most of the other sites of similar scale and complexity were unable to successfully compete with the soon-to-be larger center in Chigani, a few kilometers to the south. Chigani most likely began as a regional center like Khañuani in the Middle Formative but emerged as a primary center in the Upper Formative, absorbing the elite alliances from the surrounding sites, including Khañuani.

In short, the model presented here is that numerous methods were employed by elites to attract commoner populations into their political sphere for the first time in the Middle Formative, particularly the hosting of feasts in and around the sunken court areas. This process represented the beginning of formal reciprocal economic relationships between elites and commoners, with the latter exchanging a part of their labor for assets provided by the elite. The organization of craft specialists to produce finewares and other goods, plus the ability of the elite to mobilize labor for heightened economic production and exchange, lie at the core of the emergence of complex society in the Titicaca region.

Notes

I gratefully acknowledge the support of Gary Feinman in the preparation of this chapter. The data presented here were obtained under grants from the National Science Foundation, the Wenner-Gren Foundation for Anthropological Research, the John H. Heinz III Foundation, the Field Museum of Natural History, and the College of Letters and Sciences at the University of California at Los Angeles. Adan Umire drew Figure 2.4. All errors of fact and interpretation are my responsibility.

1. All societies have hierarchies, of course. Even "egalitarian" societies exhibit differences among individuals and households. There is a fundamental difference between purely social hierarchies and social hierarchies that are backed with economic ones. Hierarchies that are defined by both social and economic power create their own dynamic, one that cannot be duplicated by social hierarchies alone.

2. The Ultimatum Game consists of two kinds of players: proposers and responders. The proposer has control of a sum of money. He or she can offer part or all of that amount to a responder. If the responder accepts the offer, both players can keep the divided amount. If the responder declines, neither player receives any money. In rational-actor theory the responder should accept any amount since there is no cost. However, in practice, responders are willing to give up "free" money if the offer is not deemed "fair." Cultural norms affect the amounts that people consider fair, but in all experimental studies (e.g., Nowak et al. 2000), people do not behave as rational economic agents.

3. Recent economic theory known as "behavioral economics" has accepted "irrational" behavior as a central motivation in people's choices.

4. Andreoni and Miller (1993) and Levine and Pesendorfer (2001), among many others, provide theoretical and experimental support for these conclusions.

5. Firth (1959), it should be noted, criticized Mauss's overinterpretation of the Maori data.

6. Of course, Malinowski was intent on destroying the concept of "economic man" as it was applied to non-Western peoples. He constantly pointed out that people acted on social motives, not selfish ones. Therefore, it is necessary to restrict examples to empirically described cases and not draw on the opinions that are found throughout his fine work.

3

The Economy of the Moment
Cultural Practices and Mississippian Chiefdoms

Timothy R. Pauketat

The state...is not an object...[but] an ideological project. It is first and foremost an exercise in legitimation.... It conceals real history and relations of subjection behind an a-historical mask of legitimating illusion.... The real official secret, however, is the secret of the non-existence of the state. (Abrams 1988:76–77)

It is A.D. 1000 in the middle of a continent that has not yet seen a city, has not yet witnessed the development of regional government, has not known socioeconomic classes, and arguably has not experienced the mass conversion of peoples into a people. Truncated earthen pyramids have been built for centuries, but for purposes of elevating communal rituals, not elite rulers. Modest farming villages dot the landscape of the heartland, their residents connected through the intermittent travels of wayfarers across trails and along waterways.

Now imagine that we somehow manage to excise from some remote world-historical context a founding city—say Uruk, Anyang, or Monte Albán—and plop it down in the middle of this continent. What might be the historical effects of such a transplant? Would the singular qualities of such an unusual event be determinant of the economy of the region in question, if not surrounding regions? Could we then use analogies with chiefdoms or states elsewhere in the world to understand the economy of this transplant? If not, then under what conditions are the unique historical qualities of any particular polity to be factored out of our economic comparisons?

There is a point to asking such open-ended speculative questions arising from the counterfactual exercise in imagination. The exercise, in fact, is not as outrageous as it might seem, since something akin to the transplanting of a city into a city-less continent actually happened in North America's heartland shortly after A.D. 1000. At that time the large capital center of Cahokia was founded, part of an overall transformation of the regional cultural landscape that had profound effects on the daily lives of tens of thousands of people. Thus we may use Cahokia as a case study in the investigation of the economy of a political-economic singularity, a "moment" in the cultural history of a continent.

I do not dwell here on the evidence of the Cahokia case, which I've done elsewhere (Pauketat 1994, 1997a, 1998b; Pauketat and Emerson 1997); rather, I use it and other Mississippian cultural histories to invert the usual economic model. Typically, central economies are said to have come into being through some set of processes; once emerged, these economies are thought to have constrained the activities of people. Thus economically inclined researchers generally study abstract economic systems rather than the cultural practices of people.

Contrast this with my proposal that understanding pan-eastern "Mississippian political economy" entails analyzing the cultural practices of people who shaped the histories of specific localities. I argue that economy was lived from the ground up. It was generated by the cultural practices of past people, and thus the so-called economy of a particular chiefdom or state was never a thing that existed apart from those practices. The central economy was nothing more than a conglomeration of practices. In fact, we might assert, following Abrams (1988), that the economic systems of chiefdoms and states are illusory. They existed, but only as people allowed them to exist—only to the extent that the people viewed the "invisible hand" of the economy as a force alien to their being. And if they acted accordingly, then they did in fact contribute to the making (or practicing) of the central economy (e.g., Pauketat 2000b). To understand economic processes, therefore, we must study cultural practices.

The sense that cultural practices make the economy, not vice versa, springs from the principles of what are often called practice-based and phenomenological perspectives on human history (e.g., Dietler and Herbich 1998; Dobres 2000; Meskell 1999; Pauketat 2001a, 2001b; Thomas 1996). From such perspectives, practices are the enactments, embodiments, and representations of social memories and cultural traditions. They are contingent on past practices, in fact on the whole history or genealogy of such practices. Sometimes practices are inscribed on objects, bodies, and landscapes or written in texts (Connerton 1989). Objectified in any of these ways, practices were made to seem external to the people of the past (e.g., Joyce and Hendon 2000; Pauketat and Alt 2003; Van Dyke and Alcock 2003).

This is, of course, the "official secret" of the "nonexistent" state (Abrams 1988). People can be beguiled by the "legitimating mask" of the written word and objectified practices of officialdom. In any event, we analysts also face the danger of treating practices in the aggregate as an economy that had a concrete reality apart from cultural practices. This danger is realized when we ask how the economic system emerged and then constrained the behaviors of people. It is averted when we ask how the doing and being of peoples were coordinated, thereby creating a centralized economy.

I begin with this possibly disturbing proposition: ordinary comparative analyses of central economies are insufficient to explain the relationship of economic variables to the development of chiefdoms or states. Instead, I propose that the economies of chiefdoms and states existed only as the "ideological projects" of historical moments that, in turn, constituted singularities that today we lump together as chiefdoms and states. My case material permits me to conclude that the study of economy is more properly an analysis of cultural history. Our units of comparison should be cultural histories, by which I mean genealogies of cultural practices, rather than chiefdoms or states.

Of course, to realize this sort of cultural-historical archaeology (a.k.a. "historical-processualism"), we need robust and fine-grained measures of cultural practices across space and through time (see Pauketat 2001a). For present purposes, I limit my analysis to a few observations of production and distribution practices in order to illustrate the point. These show that a bottom-up analysis of the genealogies of cultural practices refocuses our attention on the time-honored fundamentals of political economy—labor and value—even as it permits a reconceptualization of economy grounded in practice-based and phenomenological perspectives.

BACKGROUND

To some degree, my urge not to compare economies stems from what I see as a failure of eastern North American archaeology. Researchers there have sought to establish the economic attributes of pre-Mississippian and Mississippian complexes in order to interpret those societies and their role in transcontinental social evolution. Unfortunately, those interpretations have had little impact on the development of theories of change in human organizations and identities in anthropologi-

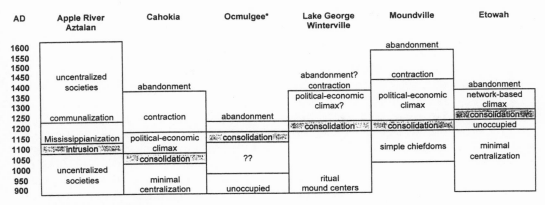

AD	Apple River Aztalan	Cahokia	Ocmulgee*	Lake George Winterville	Moundville	Etowah
1600					abandonment	
1550						
1500						
1450	uncentralized societies			abandonment? contraction	contraction	abandonment
1400		abandonment			political-economic climax	network-based climax
1350				political-economic climax?		
1300						
1250	communalization	contraction	abandonment			consolidation
1200				consolidation	consolidation	unoccupied
1150	Mississippianization	political-economic climax	consolidation			
1100	intrusion				simple chiefdoms	minimal centralization
1050		consolidation	??			
1000	uncentralized societies					
950		minimal centralization		ritual mound centers		
900			unoccupied			

*absolute dates unavailable for Ocmulgee

Figure 3.1. Mississippian political-historical trajectories compared.

cal archaeology. Perhaps this is due to a general belief that North American people fall within a realm some call noncivilized (Baines and Yoffee 1998; cf. Kehoe 1998). Perhaps it also is due to the fact that eastern North American archaeology is stuck in parochial debates over alternative explanations of particular polities or archaeological complexes.

Certainly, Cahokia has proven to be among the most controversial of the lot. Some call it a "typical" chiefdom (Milner 1998) whereas others insist it was a state (Kehoe 1998; O'Brien 1991) or a communal-utopian social experiment (Saitta 1994). Still others are content to assign either the "corporate" or "network" labels of dual-processual theory to Cahokia and to other Mississippian polities, with the implication being that one or the other kind of political strategy somehow emerged in a given region and subsequently explains the regional economy (King 2001; Trubitt 2000; contrast Feinman 2000b).

The question of what to label Cahokia or any Mississippian phenomenon is, of course, hopelessly mired in the predispositions of researchers who define chiefdom or state in a priori terms and who accordingly continue to deny American Indians both agency and history (Kehoe 1998:164). Archaeologists sympathetic to thinking about agency and history in Precolumbian North America struggle to put people back into the past and to reject labels that use measures of technology, population, or monumental architecture as correlates of some level of organization and economy (Wills 2000:25). For instance, it seems inadequate to conclude that "500 workers spending 10 days each year on moundbuilding" could have built Cahokia's earthen pyramids and thus that mound building did not require "an inordinate amount of knowledge or advance planning, certainly no more than that...undertaken by some tribal or chiefdom-scale societies elsewhere in the world" (Milner 1998:148, 150). We will remain bogged down in petty debates about what to call Cahokia, Moundville, Etowah, Ocmulgee, Lake George, Winterville, and all other Mississippian phenomena until we first seek to understand the histories of *how* labor was mobilized (Wills 2000:25).

Fortunately, as additional archaeological data become available, eastern North American archaeologists are able to make general developmental comparisons of Mississippian political histories (Figure 3.1). Ignoring obvious disparities in available data sets, we may observe that major southeastern regional polities centered at Cahokia, Moundville, Etowah, Ocmulgee, Lake George, and Winterville emerged rather abruptly either from minimally centralized village-level precursors or, in the case of Etowah and Ocmulgee, as part of a rapid infilling of virtually empty landscapes (Hally 1994; King 2001; Knight

1997; Pauketat 2000a; Williams and Brain 1983). Likewise, lesser centers seem to have "intruded" into Woodland settings to the north, at places such as Aztalan, Trempealeau, or Apple River, entailing localized reconfigurations of social arrangements and, presumably, cultural histories (e.g., Benn 1997; Emerson 1991; Goldstein and Richards 1991; Green and Rodell 1994). In both southern and northern locations impressive labor projects were organized to construct or reconstruct administrative-religious centers —earthen platforms and plazas and, in Cahokia's case, whole residential areas and farming villages.

Save appeals to dual-processual terms by some and risk-minimization terms by others, central-economic models are unpopular in the archaeology of these complexes, likely owing to an underlying bias that no native North American peoples had highly centralized economies (contrast Muller 1997 with Kehoe 1998). A few have argued that prestige-goods exchange drove the development of Mississippian polities (e.g., King 2001; Pauketat 1992; Welch 1991). But even the prestige-goods constructs have proved inadequate to explain Cahokia and Moundville, given information that exchange of finished goods across the Southeast was of a relatively low intensity (see Emerson and Hughes 2000; Muller 1995; Pauketat 1997a; Pauketat and Emerson 1997; Wilson 2001). Acquisition of exotic raw materials seemingly was for supplying local artisans with the media for manufacturing novel political-religious symbols, many of which were intended for conspicuous local purposes with values rooted in production practices rather than exchange relations (Pauketat 2002).

It seems that Cahokia and Moundville achieved apical economic positions above surrounding lesser centers apparently without much trade and, notably, also without much violence (although any level of violence has to be evaluated in relative historical terms rather than in absolute comparative ones). Etowah's regional dominance—if not the compact Lake George center—may have been imposed on or violently intruded into the lives of local people (King 2001; Little 1999). Regardless of how they emerged, though, the regional-scale polities all cast a developmental shadow across the surrounding regions, inhibiting the formation of competing centers for radii of a hundred to a few hundred kilometers (Anderson 1997; Steponaitis 1991). We could consider this an economic shadow, but given the de-emphasis on trade, it is probably better thought of as a political shadow. Later such shadows tend to coincide with cultural and linguistic boundaries (consider Drechsel 1994). Certainly the decline of all polities seems tied closely to political factors (Anderson 1994a, 1994b).

Other than these broad political-historical parallels, the histories and economic attributes of each regional Mississippian formation are potentially quite divergent, possibly scale dependent, and almost certainly historically interdigitated. If human health is used as a proxy measure of regional economy, then Moundville's complex-chiefdom economy was considerably healthier than its simple-chiefdom precursors or neighbors (Powell 1992; Welch 1990). Another neighboring polity, Summerville, is thought by John Blitz (1993) to lack the signatures of tribute mobilization and craft production that others identify at Moundville. But whereas Blitz used these data to doubt the existence of these same qualities at Moundville (and elsewhere), it is just as likely that Summerville's central economy was simply different from Moundville's. As this and other cases illustrate, all Mississippian political economies were not created equal.

The regional political histories and ultimately the physical and economic health of many mid-southern Mississippians may have been the results of historical linkages to Cahokia as North America's founding city (Kehoe 1998). By virtue of the timing and scale of its founding, Cahokia may have altered profoundly the histories of contiguous midcontinental and southern peoples in myriad ways (Pauketat 1998b). Other Mississippian centers probably played similar historical roles across the Southeast. But this assumes that Mississippiandom was defined not so much by the shared attributes of chiefly economies (contra Muller 1997; Smith 1978) as it was by the localized histories of the production of Mississippianism (consider Anderson 1997; Knight 1986, 1997). The assumption is a reasonable one from any point of view that elevates human agency and historical contingency in models of long-term change. Rather than belabor the point now, I merely note that it is important to recognize the implications of these viewpoints.

Thus, for instance, that Mississippian peoples in Arkansas and Mississippi made shell beads using Burlington chert microliths may well constitute the emulation of a Cahokian industry (even to the point of importing raw material from near Cahokia) more than it constitutes a generalizable feature of craft production in chiefdoms (Johnson 1987). Indeed, shell-bead making, microlithic technology, and craft production are attributes of any number of noncentralized eastern Woodland societies. Perhaps we should not treat shell-bead production or microlith usage merely as an economic indicator of some organization or level of complexity. Even if derived from Cahokia, the idea behind the Burlington chert and marine-shell-bead industries need not have had the same economic consequences as at Cahokia. In short, there is more to peer-polity interaction than the creation of economic peers (cf. Renfrew 1986a). To understand the economy of the outlying microlith-using, shell-bead-making Mississippians, we first need to comprehend how a Cahokian technology came to be in Arkansas and Mississippi. History first, economy second.

My point is that to explain Mississippian economies, we must appreciate Cahokia and other such formations not as examples of a "typical" kind of Mississippian political economy but as singularities not wholly comparable although possibly antecedent to other so-called Mississippian formations. As a corollary, regional economies may appear homogenized not owing to common economic processes but because of the effects of idea transmission across the Midwest and Southeast (see Drechsel 1994). In the following pages I illustrate my point primarily using Cahokian data while drawing on other Mississippian cultural histories to lesser extent.

RECENT ADVANCES IN MISSISSIPPIAN STUDIES

The last decade of theoretical change in Cahokian and mid-southern archaeology is due without a doubt to an accumulation of data reported in qualitative and quantitative detail using a 50-year chronology alongside discrete sets of even more fine-grained time-series data. The theoretical movement is, however, also a consequence of interjecting agency and history into eastern U.S. archaeology. The results? Craft production has been reappraised. Cahokia's abrupt political consolidation has been recognized as a linchpin in the history of the midcontinent and the trans-Mississippi South (Pauketat 1998b). Its scale, agricultural production, and transregional influence are again acknowledged by some to have been larger than suggested by the views of "minimalists" or "downsizers" (see Pauketat 1998b; Stoltman 1991; Yoffee et al. 1999:267). Let me provide a little background for each of these points before moving on.

In the mid-1980s Jon Muller (1984, 1987) goaded researchers to reconsider what constituted craft specialization; in the debate many realized that specialization was indeed a poor concept but that craft production was nonetheless key to explaining Mississippization less as an economic process and more as a political-cultural or "civilizing" effect (see Emerson and Hughes 2000; Pauketat 1992, 1997a, 1997b). Beads, ax heads, arrows, and other ornaments or ritual paraphernalia were made from exotic materials within the central precincts of greater Cahokia and retained, by and large, within that same greater Cahokian orbit rather than being made for exchange. Craft production was simply one dimension of a wider production of "local symbols" wherein esoteric or exotic values were incorporated into human bodies, daily routines, monuments, or whole cultural landscapes. This craft production also had a clear history, with forms and media rooted in "traditions"—albeit traditions that were doubtless already alterations of contextual and referential content. Thomas Emerson and I have since argued that most raw materials for craft production were mined from a nearby district probably held sacred in some ways owing to the meanings associated with its caves, rock outcrops, and chert-laden streams (Emerson and Hughes 2000; Pauketat and Emerson 1997). I also have argued that the "value" of raw materials was probably defined by Cahokia—things passing through there or displayed there attained value—rather than Cahokia being defined by its prestige goods (contra Peregrine 1992; Welch 1991).

Of particular interest is hypertrophic material culture—ax heads and timbers are two examples. There are buried caches of unfinished and weighty hypertrophic ax heads at administrative centers that seem to boast of the ability of somebody to mobilize the labor to acquire the raw material (from the St. François Mountain mining district) and to make them for display and disposal rather than merely for circulation and use (Pauketat 1997b). Whereas a normal ax head is 10–20 cm in length, some hypertrophic examples exceed 40 cm in length and were not finished, much less used to chop wood (Figure 3.2). Their symbolic value probably lay to an extent in the significance of wood cutting and shaping in the Cahokian realm. For instance, large timbers were cut and used as marker posts and as wall and roof members in buildings. Some of the marker posts were made from huge cypress trees, a meter in diameter, possibly hauled up the Mississippi (see J. Kelly 1997; Pauketat 1998a; Porter 1977). Where they were cut is unclear, although pine logs presumably were available only from the northernmost stand of southern pine, in the St. François Mountains some 100–200 km south and west of Cahokia. There are no native cypress swamps in the area today and

Figure 3.2. Hypertrophic *(left)* and ordinary *(right)* celts from Feature 206 at the Grossmann site.

certainly no stands of pine. Yet large quantities of uncarbonized cypress and pine bark and wood chips were found amid the presumed feasting refuse of the sub-Mound 51 pit at Cahokia, suggesting a possible ritual trimming and shaping of many logs (Pauketat et al. 2002).

Cahokian production and display of ax heads and timbers, among other things, is elsewhere argued to be part of a continuously redefined Cahokian cultural economy (e.g., Pauketat 1997a). One might say that Cahokia's economy was always one in the making. This is even more clearly seen in Cahokian monumental constructions. The abrupt and large-scale consolidation of Cahokia, occurring at a time when nothing like it existed on the continent (and, arguably, would ever exist again) may help account for the scale of this "big bang" phenomenon (the first decade or two of the Lohmann phase, cal. A.D. 1050–1100). People constructed a 19-ha plaza, two to three 9-plus-ha plazas, and the core stages of the large earthen pyramidal mounds sometime around A.D. 1050. Simultaneously, people moved into the new capital and rebuilt many downtown residences in a new thatched-roof mode sited at orthogonal angles, seemingly referencing some Precolumbian "Cahokia grid" (see Collins 1997). They raised the huge timber marker posts and intensified and localized the production of local symbols and craft items, such as the ax heads. In those years large public feasts were hosted in or near the principal plaza (Pauketat et al. 2002). The famous sacrificial pits, a falcon-warrior burial, and other suggestions of mortuary "theater" in Mound 72 date to the final years of this earliest Cahokia-Mississippian phase (Fowler et al. 2000; see also DeBoer and Kehoe 1999; Emerson and Pauketat 2002; Kehoe 1998). It is intriguing, then, that the female victims in the mass graves of Mound 72 betray isotopic signatures that stand out from the other presumed high-status individuals in this feature (Ambrose et al. 2001). The women ate more corn, suggesting culinary practices and perhaps cultural identities that differed from those of the central Cahokians (see also Bozell 1993; L. Kelly 1997; Porubcan 2000).

Given this signature of social diversity, the regional settlement pattern is even more intriguing. Contemporary with the Mound 72 burials and the monumental constructions at Cahokia, rural village farmers relocated themselves or were resettled in a series of bottomland farmsteads and in a series of more peripheral upland villages where none had existed previously (all within a 30–50-km

radius of Cahokia proper; see Alt 2001a; Pauketat 1998b, 2003). Emerson (1997) and I (Pauketat 1994; Pauketat and Lopinot 1997) have argued that the rural farmlands in the Mississippi River floodplain (the so-called American Bottom) around Cahokia were "restructured" in an at least partially top-down fashion around A.D. 1050. Villages and their kin-courtyard groups in the floodplain were dissolved or abandoned as people nucleated at Cahokia and a few administrative towns or as they moved to new single-family farmsteads in that same floodplain.

Even more significant in terms of this resettlement pattern are the discoveries of the past few years from the upland hills surrounding the floodplain. Here, in a broad prairie-forest ecotone 10–30 km south and east of Cahokia that is known for its rich agricultural soil—and known to have been largely unoccupied before A.D. 1050—we now have evidence of intrusive, displaced farmers who founded sizable villages of up to several hundred people at the same time as Cahokia's explosive Lohmann phase formation. Large-scale excavations at six of them and smaller-scale excavations at several others indicate that all these villages were probably founded in the first few years surrounding the A.D. 1050 flashpoint. These excavations also leave little doubt that the villages were then abandoned 50 to 100 years later in the early to mid-twelfth century (see Alt 2001a; Pauketat 2003).

REGIONAL ECONOMY AS VIEWED FROM THE UPLAND VILLAGES

What were the genealogies of cultural practices of these hill farmers as they relate to the central economy of Cahokia? There are six salient features of the farming villages discovered in the hills east of Cahokia. The first three are high densities of agricultural tool-resharpening debitage, low densities of meat-rich animal parts (with implications for the provisioning of Cahokia), and low densities of likely Cahokia-made or controlled objects. For instance, the upland villages have produced the highest densities (grams per cubic meter) of debitage from the resharpening of chipped-stone agricultural tool blades of any sites in the region (Alt 2002; Pauketat 1998b). The densities drop as one nears Cahokia, finally reaching a central Cahokian low (Pauketat 1998b:Figure 6), suggesting that hoe-based agriculture occupied less of a person's time at Cahokia than at a farming village. The animal-food diet of some Cahokians contrasts markedly with that of the outlying farmers, judging by quantities of various animal taxa. Notably, there are far fewer deer parts and far more small terrestrial animals in the refuse of farming villages (L. Kelly 2000). Quite plausibly, farmers supplied meat provisions to Cahokians at least periodically and perhaps for annual feasts (L. Kelly 1997, 2001).

Among the massive quantities of feasting debris in a large, former Lohmann phase borrow pit in the middle of Cahokia were significant quantities of white-tailed deer, prairie chicken, swan, and large fish bones. Conservatively extrapolating from excavated samples of single-event zones within this large (more than 56 × 19 × 3 m) pit produces MNI (minimum number of individuals) figures of 300 to more than 3,000 deer per feasting event (Pauketat et al. 2002:Table 9). Similar extrapolation of numbers of broken pots gives us figures of several hundred to several thousand containers broken per event. One might suspect that such centrifugal mobilizations of foodstuffs would leave distinct storage signatures among the contemporary settlements. Indeed, two Cahokian residential neighborhoods possess considerably more pit storage potential than the upland sites, and at least one walled elite compound at an administrative outlier of Cahokia proper enclosed a series of more than 20 storage huts (and probably considerably more outside the excavation area) that, as a set, greatly exceeded domestic storage requirements (Alt 2002; Collins 1997; J. Kelly 1997; Pauketat 1998a). The buildings at the latter (East St. Louis) site are of a type also known at various upland village sites. The East St. Louis buildings, however, had burned in a fire at about A.D.

1160, based on calibrated radiocarbon dates, with pots, shelled maize, and stored tools still inside.

A fourth salient feature of the upland sites is the presence of impoverished assemblages of likely Cahokia-made or Cahokia-distributed objects (e.g., fineware pots, pigment stones, shell beads, exotic arrowheads). For instance, marine-shell beads are abundant at Cahokia, but only one partial strand of five beads has been located among the many midden deposits at the upland villages. Likewise, fine redwares and decorated Ramey Incised jars, thought by some to have been made by a subset of potters in and around Cahokia, are found in low numbers at the upland villages (see Alt 2001a, 2001b; Pauketat and Emerson 1991). Paint stones, exotic crystals, and exotic cherts likewise exhibit a classic central-place redistributive pattern (Pauketat 1998b:Figure 6).

One building at a possible rural "administrative outpost" produced small amounts of debitage from ax-head making, along with a cache of 70 ax heads, some finished, some used, and some unfinished and unused (Alt 2001b). One has to go to Cahokia or other floodplain towns with mounds to find other caches of ax heads and significant concentrations of production debitage, and then only in some residential areas (Pauketat 1997a, 1998a). In parallel fashion, craft production appears localized among the upland farming villages (Alt 2001a, 2002). Spindle whorls best exemplify this fifth salient feature of the upland villages. These circular ceramic disks are found at most residential sites in the region, but they are invariably associated with a small fraction of the total midden deposits at any one site, suggesting some type of production localization within settlements. Moreover, some villages—and one Cahokian neighborhood—have produced high densities of the whorls whereas others have produced low densities (Alt 1999). The same pattern is known for microlithic tools used for making beads (although these data have yet to be reported in numerical form; see Alt 2001b; Department of Anthropology, University of Illinois, notes in possession of the author; John E. Kelly, personal communication 2000). Concentrations of microdrills are known from only 3 of the 250-plus houses and their middens excavated so far at 14 upland sites (Pauketat 2003).

A final salient feature of the upland villages is diversity. Pottery technological styles, architectural forms, and spatial arrangements vary within and between settlements (Alt 2001a). At three of the upland sites enough area has been excavated to identify pre-Mississippian-style single-post and semisubterranean houses around pre-Mississippian-style courtyards (with small marker posts in the central open space). The pottery-making practices represented include technological throwbacks to the preceding Woodland era mixed with newer Mississippian practices and possible nonlocal ceramic technological attributes (Alt 2001a; Pauketat 2003). On average, pots were bigger at the upland sites as well, prompting Alt (2001a, 2002) to propose a correlation with village-level corporate groups as opposed to the presumed increasingly household-based groups at and around Cahokia (see Collins 1997; Mehrer and Collins 1995; Pauketat 1998a).

In summary, the farmers living at the intrusive upland farming villages outside the Mississippi floodplain between A.D. 1050 and 1150 seem to have been an extension, and quite likely a lower-status extension, of what we could call a Cahokian economic system that was established in fairly short order during the mid-eleventh century. It is the short-order formation, though, in the context of (1) Cahokia's inclusive theatrical feasts and death rituals, (2) the intrusive appearance of the upland villagers, (3) the dietary differences between farmers and Cahokians, and (4) the cultural-practical diversity of the upland villagers that is telling us something considerably more about the cultural practices of farmers than can be captured and abstracted as an economic system.

I have recently proposed that many people living at and around Cahokia and at and around the upland villages were probably not born of local kin groups (Pauketat 2003). This argument is based on the apparent rapid rate of regional population growth leading up to the eleventh century in light of the diversity of cultural practices between the immigrant village farmers noted above. In addition, there is a well-established pattern of regional ceramic heterogeneity through the eleventh century that had been formerly thought to indicate the long-distance exchange of vessels (see J. Kelly 1980, 1991). Now, shy of chemical and petrographic evidence that the suspect pots were made in foreign locations, it is plausible that the pattern of coexisting local ceramic subtraditions indicates a degree of cultural pluralism (see also Alt 2001a; Emerson and Hargrave 2000; Pauketat 1998a). Could pluralism be an important factor in understanding a Cahokian economy?

LABOR, VALUATION, AND IDEOLOGICAL PROJECTS

If we accept that the people of and around early Cahokia included resettled families of potentially diverse social if not ethnic backgrounds, and if we look more closely at how Cahokia was constructed at and after A.D. 1050, we gain an appreciation of the possible significance of cultural practices to a Cahokian economy. An outstanding feature of Cahokia is its earthen and wooden monuments. Cahokia's largest 30-m-high earthen pyramid and the large 19-ha Grand Plaza rival the mud-brick ziggurats and adobe or rubble pyramids and adjacent plazas of other formative civilizations around the world. The central mound-and-plaza complex alone easily swallows the next largest Mississippian capital (Moundville). And this is simply the core of a sprawling "central political-administrative complex" that includes the 13-km² area of Cahokia and the several square kilometers of the adjoining 50-mound East St. Louis site and the 26-mound St. Louis center on the opposite bank of the Mississippi (Figure 3.3). In fact, in terms of numbers of earthen platforms and known or likely residential area, Cahokia, East St.

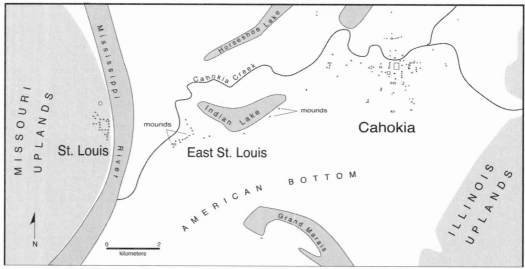

Figure 3.3. The Cahokia, East St. Louis, and St. Louis mound groups in the central political-administrative complex of the American Bottom.

Louis, and St. Louis are the first, second, and fourth largest sites in eastern North America! Proximity demands, and the knowns of the East St. Louis site affirm, that these were not sequential or autonomous political capitals. They are simply too close, all falling within several kilometers of each other in an area of less than 100 km². Instead, they were likely parts of a single unit, so that Cahokia's administrative core was easily an order of magnitude larger than any other Mississippian phenomenon.

Where evidence exists, it is clear that all plazas are more than simple empty areas; they are earthen constructions, as are the pyramids. Associated with them are huge and often rebuilt pole-and-thatch buildings and many large cypress marker posts that had been placed, pulled, and replaced numerous times (see Pauketat 1998a). All these features betray evidence of repeated construction and reconstruction. In all cases Cahokia's monuments were rebuilt with regularity. The inescapable conclusion seems to be that construction itself, as a social act, was a primary point of any Cahokia monument (see Pauketat 1993, 1996, 1997a, 1998b, 2000b).

In the same way, crafted objects were regularly produced and dispersed, some (espe-cially pots) as part of large-scale inclusive feasts. The sub-Mound 51 pit, for instance, was filled not only with high-density organic refuse but also with craft production debris, smashed well-made cooking pots, roof thatch and building parts, cypress and pine wood chips and shavings, and magico-ritual paraphernalia, possibly indicating that object manufacture, religious ceremony, and monument repair or construction were all part of one grand cultural-historical moment that generated what we see today as Cahokia (Pauketat et al. 2002). The net effect was a broadcasting of Cahokian ideology, mostly to local audiences (e.g., Pauketat and Emerson 1991). As noted earlier, even mortuary events are interpreted to have been as much about public theater as they were about honoring the dead (Emerson and Pauketat 2002:117; Kehoe 1998:169; see Porubcan 2000). The scores of female "sacrificial" victims in Mound 72 may not have been intended to accompany "someone else to the afterlife" but may have been theatrical "displays of surplus wealth" or labor (Porubcan 2000:214).

Thus we might envision Cahokia as an ongoing process, a centralized economy-in-the-making, a "cultural construction" (Pauketat

2001b), or what Abrams (1988) calls an "ideological project." In monumental construction, craft production, executions, and central feasts we are observing the ideological project itself. Surely most would agree that the rate and amplitude of the production and construction activities noted above would have entailed reliable and large-scale labor pools. If so, and if the point of monumental construction, craft production, and magicoritual object usage was the social act itself, then the labor of production and construction could reasonably be said to have created or, better, embodied Cahokian cultural meanings. It then follows that the laborers themselves were meaningful agents in the process (see also Helms 1993). Of course, how, when, and which laborers were mobilized to build, make, or enact was probably not constant. Thus the meaning of the labor and the laborers would have embodied change as well. That is, each construction cycle or production event shaped the composite economy of Cahokia. Cahokian economy, in other words, was an economy of the moment, contingent on production and construction practices and circumstances. Conceivably, change could even originate in a particular social event. Altered arrays of participants, foods, or material culture mobilized for each central gathering had implications for social relations and, literally, constituted the economy. A place or an object could gain or lose value by virtue of the addition, absence, or alteration of meaningful associations. This is nicely exemplified by historic accounts of Mississippian temples that lost their power over the lives of community members once symbolically defiled (Anderson 1994b).

The significance of process brings me to an all-important dimension of Mississippianism: value was reckoned through labor, not things. Consider the caches of ax heads or the exotic timbers that embody the labor of transport and production; consider the mobilization of produce for central feasts, the labor embodied in the regular construction of platform mounds, or the theatrical sacrifices of labor in the executions of Mound 72 people. Labor was everything. The Ca-

hokian ideological project was nothing if not a "co-optation" or a "promotion" of the labor, the cultural practices, and the very bodies of the agents of a new kind of political community (Emerson and Pauketat 2002; see also DeBoer and Kehoe 1999).

If the laborers who built and rebuilt Cahokia's landscape of earth, wood, and flesh were drawn from the diverse social groups of the recently migrated or resettled farmers, as seems necessary given the pervasive settlement-locational shifts of A.D. 1050 and Cahokia's inclusive, corporate appearance, then it becomes difficult to argue that Cahokia (and by extension a greater Cahokian economy) was merely another organically integrated Mississippian economy or the materialization of an extant Mississippian ideology. In fact, from the point of view of recent studies that elevate practice-based or phenomenological views, all things—the landscape and the laborers themselves—embody the processes of change. Production and construction, from this point of view, are not consequences of an invisible hand of economic processes. Production and construction are cultural practices, themselves the very processes of change in human relations and identities that are, in turn, contingent on the cultural history of a region's people.

Thus if one accepts this position, then we should reverse the materialization equation noted above: Mississippianism itself was the result of the creation of Cahokia and the other Mississippian formations by people with diverse interests and backgrounds. The diversity of these cultural practices that accompanied the resettlements of Cahokian centralization and the intrusions of outlying upland villages would have shaped the greater Cahokian economy in a very direct sense.

CYCLES, CLIMAXES, AND VALUATION
I have argued that early Cahokia had singular qualities that defy categorization as a typical Mississippian chiefdom and that hold implications for Mississippian political economy in general. I have posited that in order to understand Cahokia, we must begin to measure

the contingent arrays of the cultural practices of the people involved. Similar attention needs to be placed on labor, value, and cultural practices across the Mississippian Southeast. In this effort we must recognize that regional-scale summaries of political cycles, climaxes, and valuation are, at best, starting points.

For instance, in the greater Cahokia region the Stirling phase is typically said to have been the climax of Cahokia-Mississippian developments (see Pauketat 1992). The most recent excavations that might seem to bear this out have taken place at the East St. Louis site, several kilometers from Cahokia's inner core (Booth et al. 2001; J. Kelly 1997). Here are the remnants of platforms, temples, houses, storage huts, and compound walls of a twelfth-century elite precinct. Notably, that precinct has an occupation history nearly a century long, during which time buildings, walls, and earthen pyramids were rebuilt with regularity just like those of central Cahokia. Moreover, the precinct is relatively clear of concentrations of habitation debris, not counting the decorated Ramey Incised ware (here making up 50 percent of the ceramic assemblage rather than the usual 20 percent in Cahokia's residential areas). One low-lying area was intentionally filled to raise the grade at about A.D. 1100. The initial deposition into this area consisted of what seems to be a mix of high-status residential debris and ritual-feasting waste (L. Kelly 2000).

In this precinct, modest walls were built around platform mounds and the buildings on or around them. Portions of at least three walls are known around three pyramids and the surrounding space. That the walls enclosed the grounds associated with particular groups seems likely, matching the long-known pattern at Cahokia itself, where during the twelfth century the site was increasingly reserved for monumental circular and rectangular buildings (up to 400 m² in area, or nearly 20 times the size of a typical domicile). A bastioned compound is known from the same period at Cahokia proper, as is the oft-rebuilt woodhenge monument, which lies

a kilometer west of the site's central pyramid. Many of the people of the center seemed displaced at this time, presumably moving out to settlements that flank the twelfth-century capital (Pauketat and Lopinot 1997).

The increasingly apparent elite spaces of the Cahokia–East St. Louis complex may point to the emergence of distinctive and exclusive socioeconomic spheres. To some extent this development at Cahokia is comparable to what happens at other Mississippian centers. This so-called cultural climax is also the period in which an arguably elite iconography was carved into the design fields of pots that were destined for distribution to common farmers (Knight 1997; Pauketat 1992, 1994).

A pattern first recognized at Cahokia, however, and to a lesser degree now at Moundville, casts doubt on the validity of identifying the middle phases as an *economic* apex of development if we define this in terms of material goods. At Cahokia the twelfth century is characterized by less-dense accumulations of exotic waste and craft-goods production debris (chert, minerals, crystals) in residential areas than previously known during the Lohmann phase (A.D. 1050–1100). Except for continued shell-bead production, the evidence for centralized craft production is also less obvious in all residential areas. On the other hand, the iconography of Cahokia (as featured on pots), the monuments of Cahokia (buildings, posts, and mounds), and a series of carved statuettes date to this century and are rich in the symbolism of thunderbirds and fertility—more so than in the Lohmann phase (Emerson 1997; Pauketat and Emerson 1991). Food refuse too can be sorted according to elite and non-elite, with the former including the highest proportions of meaty deer waste in the history of the region (L. Kelly 1997, 2000).

For this reason, whereas the trappings of Cahokia are more readily evident in material culture and landscape, the media and symbols of Cahokian production may be said to have clearly shifted. Labor appropriation was as significant as it had been previously if not more so. Labor was devoted to centralized pottery making, limited craft production, monumental construction, and agricultural production. Symbolically speaking, however, emphasis seems to have been increasingly placed on the elite as mediators, in contrast to the inclusive "corporate" emphasis of early Cahokia (e.g., Pauketat and Emerson 1991; cf. Porubcan 2000; Trubitt 2000). This phenomenon, which I would not label a "strategy," continued into the last half-century of Cahokian hegemony, when the population of Cahokia proper had dwindled from an early high of 10,000 to 16,000 to a low of 2,000 or 3,000 (Pauketat and Lopinot 1997). By the early thirteenth century, in fact, only a token population still inhabited the East St. Louis precinct and central Cahokia. The outer hill villages had, for all intents and purposes, disappeared by A.D. 1150. The central-place redistributive pattern of earlier times is not evident. Indeed, Cahokia seems to be one of only three or four large town centers at the time, so that the three-tiered settlement hierarchy of earlier years was apparently gone (contrast Pauketat 1998b with Trubitt 2000).

The feasting debris from large-scale rituals is unknown from the thirteenth century. Monumental constructions other than earthen platforms (oversized buildings, giant posts, and woodhenges) ceased. The Cahokia-wide orientation of houses to an unseen grid disappeared by A.D. 1150, replaced by local orientation rules in which houses faced nearby platform mounds (Collins 1997; Mehrer and Collins 1995). In other ways, too, households appear to have been acting with greater autonomy, emerging by A.D. 1200 as basal socioeconomic units (earlier there was an emphasis on aggregations of houses, probably based on collective kin relations). Labor pools had shrunk even if a hypothesized "secondary climax" had been reached by these Moorehead phase Cahokians (A.D. 1200–1275).

The best data set comparable to Cahokia derives from the Moundville polity in Alabama, where a flurry of construction and production activity associated with political consolidation also appears to have given way to a prolonged decline (see Knight and Steponaitis 1998). The initial population of around 2,000 at the Moundville center dropped in later phases, even though the quantities of finished prestige goods in mortuary contexts actually appears to have increased alongside the commonplace depiction of elite themes on pots dispersed to the populace. Collapse at Moundville came slowly. The center became a point of pilgrimage and burial as political functions sloughed away by A.D. 1400 (Knight 1997).

Trubitt (2000) is thus correct in comparing early-thirteenth-century Cahokia with Moundville and Etowah in terms of the network appearances and an apparent emphasis on Southeastern Ceremonial Complex art and prestige-goods exchange. However, dual-processual models have left the reasons for such a transformation unaddressed. Notably, the most readily identifiable change in the landscape of the greater Cahokia region that separates the twelfth and thirteenth centuries now seems to have been the partitioning of centers using walls. At Cahokia this meant the construction of a more than 3-km-long, 20,000-log palisade complete with bastions (Iseminger et al. 1990). Similar walls probably went up at about the same time at the nearby Mitchell center (with its 12 mounds) and at the small mesa-top residential site of Olin (Sidney G. Denny, notes on file at the University of Illinois). Perhaps the burning of a large portion of the East St. Louis site, at about A.D. 1160, was related to the construction of walls and the transformation of Cahokia. Given the reduced population of the region (by now the upland villages have been abandoned or have been moved into unknown areas), the walls could be seen as attempts to retain political control in the face of shrinking labor pools (Pauketat 1998b: 70). As they faded into the collective memory of Mississippians, Cahokians seem in these attempts to have looked increasingly to their southern Mississippian neighbors for goods and inspiration.

Anderson (1994a) has previously noted that all Mississippian polities, large and small, coalesced and collapsed with regularity.

Earlier I stated that the shadows and demise of polities as often as not could be explained as political rather than economic in origin. Likewise, Mark Rees (2001) and I (Pauketat 1994, 1997a) have argued that "valuation"—the creation of values, interests, dispositions, and so on—can be seen as a kind of long-term process that intersects the shorter-term political cycles of the sort noted by Anderson (1994a). From a valuation perspective, the rate, scale, and overall history of a political development are in part a function of the general cultural milieu (e.g., whether or not class consciousness is a part of the culture). For instance, it could be argued that the early Cahokian regime was large, theatrical, and inclusive precisely because it happened before the formalization of a high-status stratum anywhere in the eastern United States (Pauketat 1998b).

Vernon Knight (1997) also has spoken of a long-term cultural-historical dynamic behind Mississippian history. Based on observations going back to James Griffin (1952), Knight notes that early Mississippian political economies were different from later ones. The building of huge mounds and the crafting of Southeastern Ceremonial Complex art were common in the early to middle centuries but significantly reduced after A.D. 1300. The creation of mounds and craft goods, it seems, simply did not have the same value later, at least in symbolic terms, as it had earlier. The same is true of early and late phases of any one polity.

For instance, in its earliest phase of centralization, we could say that Cahokia was a cultural dynamo, with extraordinary demographic, material-goods production, and social-diversity features. But the dynamo quickly fizzled, giving way to what I've elsewhere called "political-economic involution" and a "falling rate of political-economic expansion" (Pauketat 1994, 1998b). The inner sancta of Cahokia and, even more so, Moundville in later years became grounds for cemeteries, a use quite likely at odds with that of just a century earlier (Knight 1997; Pauketat 1997a).

Likewise, after A.D. 1200 Etowah's elites are said to have followed network strategies owing to an overall inflationary process that devalued wealth production and valued amassing finished prestige goods. And at A.D. 1400 a jumbled hoard of Mississippian artifacts from all over the Southeast could be buried at a modest site in Oklahoma—Spiro—in an apparent attempt to recapture (at this relatively insignificant site) the grandeur of early Mississippian centers. In the process, of course, what had never existed during earlier centuries was created—huge hoards of finished goods from other centers, including large amounts from Cahokia, which had by that time ceased to exist as a political entity (Brown 1996). Interestingly, here and elsewhere the symbols that had been restricted to certain central contexts in early Mississippian phases were later communalized and found in the hands of everyone (Knight 1986; Wesson 2001).

Thus, even at this coarse-grained regional scale of analysis it is clear that we are missing a great deal when we consider economy in analogous terms removed from cultural histories. How much would we learn by comparing the Moundville economy—the stereotypical precontact complex chiefdom—with the historic period Powhatan complex chiefdom (see Rountree 1989)? Labor was clearly not mobilized the same way in Powhatan as in Moundville (doubtless owing in part to different population densities). There are few public works associated with the former as opposed to the latter, and there are few to no Southeastern Ceremonial Complex symbols in the Powhatan case (see Potter 1993).

CONCLUSIONS: BEYOND CYCLES,
CLIMAXES, AND VALUATION

I contend that political explanations at a regional scale based either on cycling or valuation are insufficient without a consideration of the genealogies of cultural practices within localities. The ultimate explanations of Mississippian economies cannot be found at a regional scale of analysis, nor can they be explained through cross-cultural comparisons. Why? Allow me to return to my opening counterfactual vignette.

What if Uruk, Anyang, or Monte Albán had been excised from its world-historical context and plopped down in the middle of the Mississippi Valley at A.D. 1000? Would the result be similar to Cahokia's abrupt and large-scale beginnings? For some, the rate and scale of Cahokia's emergence, if not also the centrality of labor and resettlement in its formation, are revealing of Cahokia's singular, statelike character (consider Abrams 1988; Gailey and Patterson 1987). If nothing else, others would concede the simple point that had the mix of Cahokian sponsors, participants, and farmers been altered during Cahokia's formative years, Cahokia's economy would appear to us today differently than it does. Possibly, the history of the interdigitated Mississippian polities everywhere would have been altered to some degree.

Perhaps its singular, anomalous appearance makes Cahokia more comparable to various culture-contact situations than it is to a so-called typical Mississippian chiefdom. Indeed, given the Cahokian data at hand, culture contact models, with their emphases on cultural pluralism, syncretism, and ethnogenesis, may be better suited to Cahokia, if not also to the histories of all Mississippian centralized economies. In such culture-contact terms, explaining economic processes would entail understanding the details of how people constructed cultures and participated in ideological projects that led to historically diverse cultural practices, relations, and identities (see Pauketat 2001a).

At a regional scale some might still maintain that generalizations about political processes or valuation processes remain valid explanations. For instance, there is a worldwide pattern of corporate labor investment and goods distribution associated with the early phases of political developments, noted previously by Bruce Trigger (1990) and encoded to some degree in dual-processual models (Blanton et al. 1996). The largest and most expansive constructions of world civilizations are usually the earliest ones. Vast amounts of portable wealth may be produced at these times, and monumental constructions are commonplace. Corporate ideologies and organizations are said to predominate in those phases.

This generalization, however, is little more than a good description of the surface of a complex historical process that remains rooted in the contingent practices of many diverse people. Thus the practices of farmers, merchants, and slaves were integral parts of ideological projects and, by extension, of the constructions of regional and transregional histories. The political strategies of elites cannot be isolated in a teleological fashion to explain political histories. People need not behave in accordance with the strategies of elites. They need not follow the perceived rules of an economic system. The people themselves make history; they create the economy.

Archaeologists have tended to describe but not explain economies. How did people cooperatively labor on ideological projects and create political orders, cultural orthodoxies, or economies? To explain the projects, we must first understand them in terms of their economies of the moment. But central economies, I would argue, are always economies of the moment. Given the importance of human agents (the different mixes of peoples, their potentially divergent motivations, and the degree to which those motivations are contingent on the histories of their predecessors or their neighbors), we can appreciate that economy is inextricably caught up in a thick web of cultural history. To untangle the web, archaeologists need to measure the microhistories of settlements and their genealogies of practices in order to understand the productions, distributions, and redistributions of historical singularities. If we do not, we risk concealing the "real history and relations of subjection" behind our economic constructs as we perpetuate the official secrets of the past.

4

Reflections on the Early Southern Mesopotamian Economy

ROBERT McC. ADAMS

Unique among the world's known instances of a more-or-less autochthonous rise of early states and civilizations is southern Mesopotamia's depth and breadth of supporting written evidence. Much of this ancient written record, moreover, is directly relevant to mundane economic and administrative features of the society that are the special focus of this volume. Difficult as they may be to interpret in full context, these records are largely concerned with specific individuals, acts, and relationships, in strong contrast with the more loosely grouped aggregations of behavior patterns to which a purely archaeological record is limited. Whereas the first introduction of writing followed the advent of cities and states by several centuries and so is not a strictly contemporary record, it is at least an unequaled retrospective source of illumination of one of the great formative episodes in the human career that might otherwise remain forever mute. To be sure, the causative factors initially involved cannot be unambiguously identified with this later testimony. But before long, as I will presently argue, the exceptional range of administrative uses of cuneiform writing profoundly intensified the authoritarian character of the state itself.

There are a number of excellent, relatively recent accounts that more-or-less comprehensively summarize the major bodies of textual as well as archaeological evidence for southern Mesopotamia. It would be redundant merely to abstract them here once again. Alternatively, I seek to play a somewhat more contrarian role. While covering a 2,500-year span of time (see chronological overview in Table 4.1), I stress the importance of recent investigations of human-environmental interactions, especially for the first millennium of that span. These studies appear to lend a somewhat different emphasis to the overall interpretations that currently prevail.

Readers interested in fuller, more detailed, and more variously interpreted reviews of especially the textual evidence are referred to valuable synthetic works by J. N. Postgate (1992), Norman Yoffee (1995), Daniel C. Snell (1997), Marc Van de Mieroop (1999a) and, with greater archaeological emphasis, Gil Stein (2001a). Especially with regard to agriculture, surely the dominant economic activity, a guide to the historical trajectory that research has taken in the last century or so is provided by Benjamin R. Foster (1999). Even more detailed in this respect (if in places somewhat eclectic in coverage) is the important series *Bulletin of Sumerian Agriculture*. Finally, for the fourth millennium the recently published symposium *Uruk Mesopotamia and Its Neighbors* (Rothman, ed. 2001) includes most of the relevant information employed here.

There is a second distinctive feature of the Mesopotamian instance of the achievement of pristine early statehood—which was, after all, the earliest. It challenges the applicability

Table 4.1. Archaeological/Historical Chronology of Southern Mesopotamia

	Cassite
1500 B.C.	
	Old Babylonian
1800	
	Isin-Larsa
2000	
	Ur III
2150	
	Gutian
2250	
	Akkad
2350	
2600	Early Dynastic III
2750	Early Dynastic II
	Early Dynastic I
3000	
	Jemdet Nasr
3200	
	Late Uruk
	Middle Uruk
	Early Uruk
4000	
	Late Ubaid

of the characterization as "chiefdoms" that generally prevails in other world regions for the phase antecedent to the first appearance of cities and states. I believe it is fair to say that the substantive understanding of the concept derives entirely from ethnohistoric and ethnographic examples. That does not preclude its application to earlier settings where archaeological evidence alone is available, but it may justify taking an independent view of the question where there is an abundant—if admittedly slightly later rather than contemporary—textual record. Acknowledging that the argument cannot be conclusive at this juncture, I suggest that there is little positive evidence of any kind supporting the construct of chiefdoms antecedent to states in southern (as distinct from northern) Mesopotamia. And as Dietz Edzard has inde-

pendently concluded, reflecting his unsurpassed knowledge of the cuneiform evidence: "As far back as we can trace our historical sources, we had of course rulers' titles, but they do not connote what I would call 'chieftains.'...I would be at a loss to find a word for 'chieftain'" (in discussion, in Hudson and Levine 1996:58).

A number of features tentatively suggest the possibility of an alternative developmental path. Most important is an early and continuing architectural emphasis on ceremonial/community structures conventionally but perhaps too narrowly characterized as "temples" (Nissen 2001:154–155). These relatively large and formal buildings, although dominating the communities growing up around them, provide little to suggest an early association with individuals of authoritative, chiefly status. Organized instead around these institutions, at the time when the very earliest writing first provides us with a glimpse of their mode of operations, are somewhat abstract, functional categories of people that are not suggestive of either ascriptive kin-group membership or authoritarian, personalistic control. These features demonstrate the existence of comprehensive redistributive systems involving standardized rations, although admittedly they do little to clarify how this system originated or what decision-making powers were involved in sustaining its operations. At roughly the same time, powerful, militaristic, primarily secular figures also made their first appearance in glyptic art. But this was after the advent of true cities and was associated with a general level of scale and complexity implying the unambiguous existence of states. In summary, there are grounds for doubting that individuals of chiefly status led the way to states.

Thus it is possible that there was a different path to statehood, lacking chiefdoms as a transitional step, in at least the Mesopotamian case. Enhancements of individual status might well have been preponderantly a part of the process by which contending state organizations emerged, perhaps accompanying progressively larger and more institutionalized military activities. The seemingly rather abrupt transition to settlements of unambiguously urban size and complexity may be another factor, precipitating new forms of social organization with different, more functionally specialized internal structures than those usually associated with chiefdoms. This is certainly a plausible implication of some recent investigations, the findings of which need to be recounted at the outset.

CHANGED EVALUATION OF EARLY URBANISM'S ENVIRONMENT

The environmental context of the beginnings of southern Mesopotamian states and urbanism looks substantially different today than it did just a very few years ago. Studies of declassified satellite photographs by Jennifer

Pournelle (University of California, San Diego) shed new light on the lower plain in particular. They persuasively establish that widespread flooded areas were only gradually draining during the fourth millennium. Marshes and tidewater lagoons formed a major constituent of the landscape and played a correspondingly substantial role in human subsistence. Apart from a rich spectrum of aquatic resources, zones suitable for cereal cultivation were at first quite restricted locally so that foraging conditions were more favorable for cattle and pigs than for sheep and goats. Late 'Ubaid settlements had been sited on relatively widely separated "turtlebacks," slightly elevated islands in generally marshy surroundings. As the Flandrian marine transgression receded during the course of the fourth millennium, continuous drainage channels emerged more clearly. Adjoining levees developed, linking the earlier turtlebacks into continuous strips of slightly elevated land. As drainage continued, there were growing zones along the backslopes of the levees suitable for canal irrigation. Recent paleoclimatological research indicates that the Tigris-Euphrates hydrological cycles were more favorable to the winter cereal-growing season than they are today in the timing of the season of destructive flooding. Colder, drier winters would have inhibited the winter growing season for cereal crops that later became traditional, but on the other hand, a shift in the Indian Ocean monsoon belt made some summer precipitation likely. All this suggests an altered spectrum of subsistence techniques and choices from those extensively documented in the later Sumerian Georgica (Civil 1994) and other third-millennium textual sources.

Unclear at present is how far northward this characterization applied within the present extent of the Mesopotamian alluvium. The limits of the Flandrian transgression of the Persian Gulf itself lay some 200 km north of the present shoreline, in the vicinity of al-'Amara, but the eastern and western boundaries of this large embayment are still ill-defined and in any case graded into lagoons and marshes covering large additional areas.

Unfortunately, the northern part of the alluvium is heavily overlain with later canal levees and irrigation sediments. Hence, although there has been extensive (if erratic) wind deflation in some areas, early land surfaces tend to be progressively more deeply buried as one moves northward. It is likely that cereal cultivation and sheep and goat herding played a more prominent part there throughout the fourth millennium. But the southern part of the plain, where the Sumerian cities of the third millennium were concentrated, clearly coincides with these formerly marshy environs rather than the consistently semiarid regime found today.

Another major new finding proceeds in part from Pournelle's studies of satellite imagery but is given greater temporal precision and historical significance by a persuasive analysis of relevant economic and other textual sources by Piotr Steinkeller (2001). It has long been taken for granted that the Mesopotamian plain depended almost completely on the Euphrates. But it now seems clear that the Tigris and Euphrates were frequently if not altogether consistently linked into a naturally interconnected, anastomosing system during and after the fourth millennium as well as earlier. During much of this time the Tigris directly provided a principal source of canal transportation and irrigation water for many of the major urban centers, including Adab, Umma, and the large Lagash complex. Furthermore, a branch canal taking off the Tigris above Umma was at least a supplementary source for Uruk and continued on to reach Ur. This reconfiguration points the way to a much better understanding of barge traffic along the major rivers and canals, especially during the Ur III period at the end of the third millennium, when many cuneiform documents specify the duration of towed travel, and hence approximate distance, between cities whose location is still unknown. In prospect is a vastly improved understanding of the economic geography of the plain.

There are two striking features of the southern Mesopotamian alluvial environment during the fourth millennium that bear on its extraordinary course of development. First, it underwent a long transition away from prevailing marshy conditions and in the direction of conditions suitable for the traditional irrigation agriculture with which we today, and the texts of the third millennium (and later), associate it. But second, although the transition toward semiaridity surely presented important challenges of adjustment to which I will return, both the earlier and the later environments were potentially conducive to flourishing urban life. This is well understood for large-scale irrigation on a semiarid plain but may seem more surprising for marshes, which may have a contemporary reputation for being inhospitable. But under the different conditions then obtaining, they offered a stable multiplicity of rich subsistence and construction resources. Moreover, they made possible bulk transport by boat or barge that permitted very economical concentration of subsistence resources of every kind in large population centers. A vivid sense of the significance of both their resource and their transport potential can be found in the classic account by the early Islamic historian al-Tabarî of the Zanj rebellion in a region of the southern plain that again returned to marshlands in the later ninth century A.D. (Waines 1992).

As the uppermost centers of the settlement hierarchy moved to unprecedented levels, the diversified subsistence system responded with substantial opportunities of its own. These took two principal forms. In the first place, there were a number of distinct, complementary streams of subsistence products drawn simultaneously from a mosaic of marine, marsh, garden, field, and steppe ecosystems. Enormous as was the overall advantage that this variability provided, each individual component imposed a seasonal production cycle of its own and an accompanying set of risks that needed to be buffered and shared. Here, in other words, were major inducements to the development of specialized technologies and bodies of skill or experience. Nor was any unchanging arrangement feasible for bringing together and redistributing these resources for the common benefit, since the mosaic was in fact a continuously changing kaleidoscope as the drainage of the alluvium went forward. And superimposed on this need for continuing adaptive modification was the process of rapid population growth, urbanization involving large-scale shifts in subsistence routines and residence, and surely political centralization as well.

"THE URBAN REVOLUTION"

That these were highly favorable circumstances for a very rapid expansion of human settlement, largely by natural increase and shifts within the alluvium but probably also in part by immigration from adjoining areas in all directions, is shown by the striking increases that archaeological surveys have recorded in the numbers of sites of all size categories. Perhaps most notable was the first appearance of sites of clearly urban proportions, exceeding (and sometimes greatly exceeding) 50 ha. Uruk, in particular, already extended over 250 ha by the mid-fourth millennium. Identifiable mainly by their size, their monumental institutions (whose associated religious features and activities certainly do not exclude more encompassing socioeconomic or sociopolitical roles), and the relative wealth and diversity of their material remains, such settlements were unquestionably present before the middle of the millennium.

V. Gordon Childe's (1950) anticipatory characterization of this as an "urban revolution" decades before corroborative data to support it became available primarily from archaeological surveys (Adams 1981, 2002; Adams and Nissen 1972; Wilkinson n.d.) still accurately conveys the transformative character of the change as well as the abiding ambiguity about the respective roles of force and persuasive incentives in bringing it about. Within the limits of ceramic and radiocarbon chronologies, the evidence is increasingly convincing that this was a progressive and consistent process, although protracted over a longer period of at least several centuries rather than the truly implosive process we who were involved in the surveys originally assumed (Rothman 2001; Wright and Rupley 2001). Urban population growth could well have been encouraged by the relative advantages of politicoeconomic—as well as military—power it conferred on large concentrations of urban residents. On the other hand, cities also brought heightened problems of sanitation and disease, as well as the need to develop new logistical solutions to the challenges of longer-range subsistence procurement and storage. Nor were the reciprocal changes in the surrounding hinterlands necessarily any smoother, as Yoffee notes: "The countryside in early states, with its villages connected to cities and with its own specialized institutions of production and consumption, is utterly different than the countryside of pre-state times. The evolution of states, thus, cannot be modeled as a layer cake, with the state as the highest layer atop a stable and unchanging social base" (1995:284).

On balance, it seems fair to conclude that a concurrent emptying out of the immediately adjacent alluvial countryside was a substantial contributor to urbanization. Indeed, the surveys clearly disclose just such a process of attrition of formerly more evenly distributed small towns and villages in at least the southernmost portion of the alluvium (Pollock 2001).

The new class of urban settlements, viewed in political terms as the nuclei of emergent states, surely encouraged various economies of scale. By size alone, and by their ability to marshal unprecedented concentrations of population both as offensive military forces and as labor corvées to construct civic, defensive, and irrigation works, they could dominate their immediate neighbors. Patron deities (and their human priests, managers, skilled craftsmen, and retainers), thought of as occupying sacred households in cities, would have become the beneficiaries of growing flows of offerings in temple complexes that also were growing in monumentality. Archaeologists tend to be agnostic materialists by nature, but the symbolic aspects of urban hegemony may be no less important than the material ones.

Yet until the advent of writing late in the fourth millennium, the details of these processes remain largely obscure. Particularly at the elementary, household, or *oikos*, level where a more balanced archaeological record should in theory be most accessible, there is as yet little information available. We also are virtually ignorant of how the outlying countryside was transformed as former villagers were drawn into the orbit of the cities. Some indirect evidence of the way in which lower-status members of the community—certainly including most recent rural immigrants—would have been drawn in may be provided by the terminology employed in the early archaic tablets from Uruk for the redistribution of grain rations to dependent male and female laborers. They are listed separately according to sex and age, "herded" in exactly the same terms (although also individually named) as in parallel accounts of herds of domestic animals (Englund 1998:176).

Was agriculture carried on exclusively by herdsmen and cultivators commuting for substantial distances from urban residences, or were there new, impermanent settlements into which agriculturalists moved at times of more concentrated effort during the growing season? Might their transient, ad hoc character explain why such remains have generally resisted identification in surveys? Were there possibly, in addition, unprecedented new facilities for collecting and transporting domestic animals and harvests into the cities? The lack of answers to questions like these reflects the virtual absence heretofore of serious attention to what might be called rural archaeology once cities had come into existence. And even from much later times, much better known from the cuneiform documents, Richard Zettler has identified similar difficulties: "Were the cultivators, as has commonly been suggested or assumed, urban dwellers who moved back and forth to the countryside at certain times of the year? Or were the cultivators tribally organized persons, residing in small villages or hamlets, who had some rights to the land? These questions cannot be answered on the basis of in-formation available for the Ur III period" (1996:99).

ALTERNATIVES AND CONSTRAINTS ON INTERPRETATION

From a generalizing social science rather than philological perspective, several cautionary observations that certainly apply to southern Mesopotamia seem likely to be equally applicable to cities in other nuclear areas dealt with in this volume. To begin with, we are dealing with a *longue durée* transition of a group of institutionally similar, culturally related but at the same time individually distinct and usually contentious urban entities, irregularly undergoing a profound series of transformations. It is misleading and in most instances probably false to assume that, individually and collectively, they would have exhibited consistency or smooth, long-term continuity in economic arrangements. Textual as well as archaeological attestations of economic decisions or behavior frequently may have been representative of relatively brief periods and restricted localities and should be assumed to have had wider and lengthier application only with considerable caution.

The economy, and all the institutions, activities, and relationships we are accustomed to thinking of as composing it, was from prehistoric times onward for a millennium or more a fairly amorphous category conforming only poorly to any modern abstractions of what an economy ought to be. In other words, it was deeply intertwined with other cultural patterns whose articulations we can seldom do more than dimly surmise. This is not to deny that there also probably were domains of activity we might recognize as "economizing" and "rational" if we could adequately detect them. In general, I tend to share the recent position of Stephen Silliman in not seeing "agents acting strategically, rationally, and self-interestedly" as more than a fairly marginal presence at this time, and join him at the other end of the continuum with those "who view individuals acting meaningfully in historical and social circumstances only partly of their own making. In this scheme, individual actions are contextualized within an array of rules and resources that precede them but that give them opportunity. The dialectic is one between structure and agency. In these perspectives individuals often conduct their daily affairs in intentional and strategic *and* in routinized, nondiscursive or preconscious ways. To state the common expression, social agents are both constrained and enabled by structure" (Silliman 2001:192).

State institutions, at this early stage in their development, were surely multivalent in their routines and spheres of action and authority. Even much later in the course of Mesopotamian history, for example, when legal sanctions were proclaimed, the sources tend to be silent on their enforcement rates and procedures. Evidence of agency and motivation (not to speak of constraints on alternatives) in voluminously recorded administrative and economic activities is, in short, formalistic at best and mostly lacking. It is a step in the right direction to use instead the term *political economy* (Yoffee 1995), as a good part of our interest focuses on the emergence of states. But the articulation of state interests and institutions with those of familial, kin, community, occupational, or religious groupings, insofar as there is any evidence whatever for this at any given location or period of time, is little more than hypothetical.

Differences within the alluvium, such as in the major economic and institutional structures of individual cities (Maekawa 1973–1974:142–144) and in reportedly contrastive patterns of landholding units in northern and southern subregions (Liverani 1996; Steinkeller 1999), are receiving greater emphasis as advances are made in thematic as well as archival studies. Rates as well as trends of institutional change—not to speak of the substrate of behavioral change, which is rarely visible at all—were clearly affected by the shifting outcomes of interurban and sometimes even interpersonal rivalries. Furthermore, the inevitable accidents of discovery

mean that both the archaeological and written evidence not only is markedly discontinuous in temporal and regional distribution but also often fails to maintain consistent foci of coverage. Any assumption that we can fall back on a kind of connect-the-dots uniformity and gradualism is worse than perilous—it is almost certainly misleading.

Related to this set of issues may be a broad, ongoing shift in contemporary scholarly perspectives on the character of ancient Mesopotamian statehood—a shift, however, that is as yet prompted more by growing awareness of the limitations of the textual and archaeological evidence than by positive attestations. Discerning the same tendency, Stein has recently summarized it as replacing with more heterogeneous or non-unitary models a formerly more "integrative model of states as homeostatic systems." The result is a de-emphasis on centralized control and older interpretations from textual data that projected "vast temple and palace bureaucracies." Different groups in the same society could have radically different goals, he suggests, with conflicts between their short-term goals having quite unintended long-term consequences (Stein 2001a:214–215). I find this a very persuasive position, having independently argued for a variant of it in order better to understand the limitations of Ur III society at the end of the third millennium (see below).

The issue of unity versus heterogeneity has another, earlier manifestation, already in the fourth and earlier third millennia. It involves whether we visualize much or even all of the southern Mesopotamian plain as subordinated to the city of Uruk as a single primate center. A contending peer-polity system for much of this time range may well be a plausible alternative. It finds support in recent (illicitly excavated) finds of archaic tablets such as those from late-fourth-millennium Uruk at an uncertain site apparently farther north; in size estimates of surveyed sites that may need to be adjusted upward just as Uruk's was on more systematic, later examination; and in satellite images of major centers such as

Umma that appear to be several hundred hectares in size and are known to have early occupations but have never been scientifically excavated. No less relevant here is Pollock's observation that at least in the earlier Uruk period the Nippur-Adab area "was *not* characterized by a highly integrated economy" (italics original) like that in Uruk's immediate hinterlands farther south (2001: 208).

I am here calling into question not the virtues of the written records, which are obvious, but the substantial limitations of what ultimately gets codified into writing (cf. Civil 1980). Almost always, recorded representations of behavior are more conventionalized and slower to change than the more variable, fluid originals they purportedly reflect. In addition, whereas modern life accustoms us to think of coherent institutional structures with bounded responsibilities and designated procedures of their own, none of these features is likely to have been more than rudimentary in Mesopotamian state and religious institutions in their early antiquity. Attempts to reconstruct an overarching economic order on the basis of inductively assembled rules and norms are correspondingly perilous. Consistent application of modern analytical principles with regard to prices and markets, for example, is virtually unimaginable. What we are likely to find instead are tantalizing clues to great variability in relationships and behavior that sometimes seem to embrace what are to us contrary principles of organization.

As anthropologists, we probably should describe our objective in attempting to outline an ancient economic "system" as seeking to understand how forces of a broadly economic character affected people's lives through a lengthy, complex process. How, in other words, economic forces affected as much as is known of the full range of networks, institutions, and relationships in which the whole population was implicated. This obviously includes ownership of or access to land and other productive resources; economic and social strata and the mobility between them; regional as well as craft specialization and means of acquiring it; some reference to forces for (politico)economic integration as well as fissiparous tendencies; apparent, suitably disaggregated demographic trends as well as uncertainties; and mechanisms of circulation of goods and services, including price-fixing markets and redistributive systems as only the polar ends of a long, mostly fluid and informal continuum. Implicit in all this is a concern to discover the role of individual and group *agency*, not only the degree of diversity in people's lives but their range of preferences and motivations. Very little of this is attainable within the limits of ancient Near Eastern data, textual as well as archaeological.

Risking oversimplification in the same generalizing vein, the available archaeological as well as textual evidence is overwhelmingly suffused with an elite bias. To be sure, it is debatable how significant this limitation really is. "Consciousness," a slippery characterization even for our own times, may have had little operational significance as a basis for independent action beyond some elite segments in the periods with which we are concerned. There is little convincing evidence of elite concern for general consensus building, or for that matter for having to deal with popular opposition extending beyond the membership of the elite itself.

POWER AND COERCION

Perhaps most conspicuously missing from both the archaeological and textual evidence are indicators of the practical range and limitations, as distinct from the pretensions, of royal power and authority. In the military sphere the need for a relatively unrestrained command structure must have seemed most compelling. Enlarged representations of the "king on the battlefield" that occur in glyptic art in the late Uruk period (Pittman 2001: 436–437) and later find extensive, monumental representation tend to confirm that this was at least an aspiration. Claims in royal inscriptions of sanguinary battlefield slaughter of enemies, representations of disciplined phalanxes of identically equipped troops, and numerous attestations in economic and administrative texts of blinded, castrated, and enslaved persons who are assumed to have been war prisoners seem to point in the same direction. But the Gilgamesh epic, if behind its later, symbolic artistry is any shade of former realism, gives us a more equivocal picture of a ruler's machinations as he sought to invoke the enthusiasm of young warriors in order to overcome the opposition of the city of Uruk's assembly of elders.

Even before the onset of the Early Dynastic I period, at about the beginning of the third millennium, the process of reduction in the numbers of settlements and concurrent concentration in cities was accompanied by a significant reduction in the number of major channels of water distribution. We do not know, and may never know, how natural processes of changing river morphology associated with the reduction of the marshes intersected with human modifications of the landscape to bring this about. Nevertheless, the construction of growing irrigation systems and increasingly effective flood-control measures would have been facilitated if a greater proportion of the available flow could be consolidated in a reduced number of more stable channels. And it was clearly to the advantage of the cities, which owed their growth to their advantageous position along those channels, to concentrate the control of water in their own hands.

So it was, in any case, that a new linearity in these larger watercourses is apparent. In some cases (as around Uruk) there are suggestions of radiating patterns of smaller canals extending outward that emphasize this new pattern of more centralized control. There was, in short, "an unsettling metamorphosis in social and political life" at around the beginning of the Early Dynastic period (Yoffee 1995:287). It consisted of an ongoing transition in the direction of more coercive, hierarchically managed systems responsive to the heightened subsistence needs of the new and larger population concentrations. If Pollock's calculations for Uruk are correct, already much earlier, by early Uruk times, early in the fourth millennium, its "residents could not possibly have produced enough food to meet the needs of the city's population" (2001:195), implying a pattern of coercive extraction directed toward its neighboring dependencies that could only have intensified as Uruk continued to grow. But presently, as Hans Nissen (1976:23) has noted, it led to the Early Dynastic I introduction of new cuneiform irrigation terminology, possibly reflecting technical advances associated both with the efforts to ensure control of outlying irrigation networks and with the availability of the enlarged labor corvées that cities made possible.

We need to be mindful of the likelihood that there were many such derivative capabilities associated with urban growth that together laid the basis for quickly achieved—but also enduring—urban dominance. Among them, enhanced communications were no less important as a concomitant of urbanization than intensified attention to new irrigation requirements. Both probably played a role in the increasing linearization of the overall watercourse pattern. Towed barge traffic was facilitated by linear, well-maintained levee footpaths. The capacity for relatively inexpensive, large-scale movement of bulk as well as luxury commodities between the urban centers on the Mesopotamian plain was thenceforward surely a major factor in their collective as well as individual dominance.

Until the last few centuries of the fourth millennium we know very little directly of the mix of modes of exchange and redistribution by which resources were first concentrated in certain urban institutions and then exchanged or redistributed. Although their significance has been discounted by some, a large variety of clay tokens that were also prevalent in earlier times and that apparently functioned as counters in various contexts played a considerable part in the subsequent introduction of writing (Englund 1998:17). But in any case the existence of a well-developed system of rationing, and the hierarchically organized groupings of specialized occupations and allocations that accompanied and depended on it, is suddenly confirmed for us by the recent disclosure of the contents of the late Uruk archaic tablets (Nissen et al. 1993). Some of the system's major elements must have gradually begun to come into existence considerably earlier. Perhaps precisely because of the complex resource base and the accompanying challenge of risks or stresses that tended to focus on only one or a few elements among them at any given time, a redistribution system seems likely to have been introduced at a relatively early date under institutional auspices having a predominantly religious character.

Massive, presumably concerted, and probably centrally organized long-distance population movements (Algaze 2001a; but cf. Nissen 2001:155–167) led to replications along the Upper Euphrates and elsewhere of many features of Middle–Late Uruk urbanism in its Mesopotamian homeland. Whether this followed a deliberate decision to send out expeditionary forces over formidable distances or was a more ad hoc outgrowth of a crisis of some sort, the consequence could only facilitate the substantial and growing importation into southern Mesopotamian cities of vital classes of raw materials—timber, copper, stone, bitumen, and exotic substances from even greater distances. Surely this was not wholly unrelated to the demographic upheaval involved in the extensive depopulation of the southern Mesopotamian countryside accompanying the growth of cities, even if an altogether persuasive explanation of the connective links in the process is still lacking.

From virtually the time of their origins, cities thus constituted the most basic, enduring features on the Mesopotamian social landscape. Repeated efforts to achieve stable, larger patterns of integration multiplied scribal (and hence Assyriological) efforts and provide interrupted foci of historians' attention. But few persisted in their success for more than two or three generations at most. Piotr Michalowski has pointed out that during the span of approximately a millennium, from the beginnings of relevant records early in the third millennium to the end of the Old Babylonian period in the second, the "whole time of unity of Sumer and Akkad... consisted of 230 years, at the most" (1987:

56). Persisting through the lengthy, chaotic periods of breakdown were the cities that had resisted subordination and incorporation in larger, panregional patterns. City-states rather than ethnic-linguistic groupings or larger, territorially organized states remained the characteristic sociopolitical form until larger, durable empires emerged—in surrounding regions, not in the Mesopotamian plain itself—in the later second and first millennia B.C. (Yoffee 1995:291).

Having thus far emphasized the relatively rapid but then enduring ascendancy of cities, we also need to consider some structural consequences of how their dominance was achieved. It is simply unrealistic to view their growth as an organic, consensual process involving a shared understanding by all participants, urban elites and displaced rural immigrants alike, of the common advantages of city life. Instead, taking a long view of early Mesopotamian history as a whole, Yoffee rightly observes, "City-states were not so much directed by kings and managers as they were the primary arenas for social and economic struggle" (1995:301).

Relevant here is widespread, recently awakened archaeological interest in the role of human agency or intentionality, as distinguished from former deterministic or adaptationist approaches drawn largely from mainstream evolutionary biology. Pierre Bourdieu, whose *Outline of a Theory of Practice* was a major stimulus to this new concern, took the position that in ancient societies there was "a quasi-perfect correspondence between the objective order and the subjective principles of organization" (1977: 164). But it will not do, as Adam Smith rightly criticizes, casually to consign the practices of otherwise unexamined forerunners of modernity to the exclusive realm of *doxa*, Smith's term for unquestioned belief systems, with "lives cast as routines predicated upon the mis-recognition of social orders as natural ways of life, rather than political products.... If archaeology is to succeed in articulating the past with the present in meaningful ways, then we must actively resist the construction of rigid boundaries that set the ancient apart from the modern as an ontologically distinct entity" (2001:156–157).

Sherry Ortner hammers home Smith's point that "'agency' and 'practice' more generally must be seen as part of an essentially political problematic. A theory of practice is not an abstract metaphysical debate about the relative weight of free will versus determinism, or structure versus agency, however much it may have originated in such debates, but rather a theory of how people's actions reproduce or change a world that is never free of, and often centrally organized around, inequalities and power differentials" (2001: 272).

There were in southern Mesopotamia, I would argue, two major consequences of the operation of growing differentials in rank, status, and above all access to coercive power. The first was a persistent institutional segmentation of the elite; the second a seemingly rigid compression of the sphere of personal control of action as well as living standards of the lower economic strata of the population, urban as well as rural. The extent to which this was consciously implemented or even recognized is quite unclear, although there is virtually nothing to support the inference that something akin to "class conflict" might have been involved.

On the other hand, a different inference must be noted and highlighted. Writing and literacy, powerful technological innovations at the time, became as they improved in effectiveness the key instruments of bureaucratic control, manipulation, and propagation of the contents of the stream of political and sociocultural memory, and of rapid, accurate communication across the barriers of distance. Literacy itself, or at least authority over cadres of scribes, must have assumed a central place in the means by which these new structural features persisted for so long (Goody 1986:48–55; Larsen 1989).

FORCES OF CONTENTION AND SOCIAL RANKING

Temples (if indeed this convenient term does not overemphasize their cultic vis-à-vis other civic functions) are the earliest public buildings that archaeologists have encountered in southern Mesopotamia, with a long-continuing sequence of increasing size at Eridu, for example, originating as early as the sixth millennium. By the later Uruk period they sometimes had attained truly monumental proportions. In Uruk itself, the Eanna precinct, dominated by its formal cultic/public buildings, alone covered some 7 ha. But although an early analysis of a voluminous and important temple archive found in Early Dynastic III (mid-third millennium) Girsu led for decades to an identification of Sumerian city-states as examples of a "temple economy," that oversimplified identification tends to be used today with considerable hesitation (Foster 1981; Lipinski 1979; Nissen 1982, 1999:156–159; Snell 1997:148–149; Yoffee 1995:289; see Falkenstein 1953–1954 for a comprehensive formulation of the earlier interpretation). On the one hand, it does indeed seem that in most Mesopotamian cities temples were the largest category of landholding units. But on the other hand, they were clearly not alone in this capacity, and their articulation with—including possible subservience to—political leadership is often implied or apparent.

Emerging into the dim light of history at about the turn of the third millennium were two other substantial social blocs. The more salient, increasingly assertive on its own behalf, is the institution of kingship, which quickly was given architectural embodiment in palaces alongside temples; it then developed its own mythological rationale for hereditary succession. Kingship is clearly associated, perhaps from its very origins, with leadership in battle. It goes on to acquire the services of large numbers of retainers in a wide range of specialties and statuses. Among them, although not credited for their individual accomplishments, were skilled craftsmen producing goods to meet elite tastes that by the mid-third millennium had moved beyond mundane articles such as pottery to textiles and highly refined products of metallurgy (Stein and Blackman 1993:55). Very shortly, palace households also became great landholding institutions, acquiring vast estates at suspiciously low prices from ranked communities in which ownership or usufruct rights were hierarchically concentrated. As attested in a number of *kudurru* documents, a few leading individuals are identified as "eaters of the price" in such transactions whereas much larger numbers, listed only as witnesses, may more passively indicate some degree of assent or involvement by merely participating in a feast (Gelb et al. 1991). But how valid a view this provides of a possibly general decay of older forms of communal landholding before an aggrandizing royal power (Diakonoff 1982) is still disputed.

Here, then, we encounter a second, more heterogeneous and ill-defined but in all likelihood also very numerous group, corporate communities closely associated with the conduct of agriculture and probably of multigenerational depth. It is tempting to see in them the inhabitants of lower-level settlement hierarchies scattered around emergent cities such as Uruk who were presently swept within the walls of the cities as they grew. Their leaders might well go on to achieve various degrees of an elite status, taking their place alongside wealthy palace dependents as the nucleus of a private economic sector. Lower-ranked followers, meanwhile, must have contributed to the anonymous mass of conscripted, semifree, male and female laborers who were heavily dependent on the issuance of rations. Some such process of secular transfer, intimately associated with urbanization, also may be associated with the civic institution of assemblies. These may seem out of place next to great temple and palace estates but nevertheless persisted at least until the mid-second millennium. Falling largely outside the realm of elaborate record keeping of the "great organizations," this sector is always difficult to identify in day-to-day action. But as Gelb (1969) has repeatedly insisted, its presence alongside the palace and temple can be traced as far back as historical records take us. Although always under threat of exploitation and absorption by the dominant social strata, the assembly endured into later millennia (Van de Mieroop 1999a:107).

To confine ourselves primarily to what is better known, there is an unstable dynamic of coexistence between great temple estates and ascending royal power as the latter increasingly associated itself with administrative personnel, cadres of skilled craftsmen, and large landholdings under its direct control. This should not be taken to imply that the palace and temple were interchangeable as essentially exploitative institutions. Perhaps reflecting a much more ancient, initially largely consensual set of social arrangements, temple estates "remained important for the population as a reserve dietary fund" even while also imposing labor requirements and taxlike payments on their constituencies (Diakonoff 1982:76). In any case high officials of both temple and palace estates were compensated by relatively large grants of land that we can take for granted they played no significant part in having to cultivate. In addition, beyond these two great institutional complexes there was a substantial population that also is represented among the elite, but there is little or nothing in the existing cuneiform records to reflect any claim of some sort of "third estate" status.

How does archaeology (the original basis of my own interest and training) amplify or modify this primarily text-based account of socioeconomic status? Social differentiation, beyond an advanced division of labor, is difficult to generalize about with any confidence for essentially all the fourth millennium—that is, even for several centuries after the beginnings of writing. Archaeological exposures of house architecture for this period in southern Mesopotamia are as yet too limited to provide clear patterns of wealth or status gradation through variations in size or furnishings. Contemporary cemeteries are noteworthy mainly for their curious absence until early in the third millennium, providing little clue to what one would assume must have been slowly growing social status differentiation. In contrast with northern Mesopotamia, the impression is worth noting that personal concentrations of costly materials and objects from the alluvium were markedly less conspicuous.

Archaeological evidence on the question of royal wealth is not necessarily any better at resolving issues of discontinuous status distribution or stratified access to the primary means of production. The so-called Royal Cemetery at Ur contains wide variations in the quality and quantity of grave goods of Early Dynastic date, some but not all clearly pertaining to royal family members. But are these attestations of an individual's disposable wealth, or only of the ceremonial importance (and accompanying public offerings) attached by the community to the event of a royal or high official's death? Similarly elusive are architectural distinctions between royal palaces, identified with a secular ruler, and temples devoted to patron deities and housing personnel of a more priestly character—who might also, however, be responsible for the complex administration of vast estates. By the late third millennium, secular rulership (of course still purportedly at the service of a divine patron) and hereditary succession were firmly in the ascendancy. But the transition seems to have been subject to some brakings and reversals along the way, and it is noteworthy that there is very little evidence of hostility or even competition between prominent individuals identifying themselves with secular or priestly power.

Very large and growing gradations of wealth are evident not only in landownership as attested in the *kudurrus* but also in tomb furniture and variations in house size and furnishings. Elegantly finished stone bowls coincide with wealthier tombs in the Ur cemetery, whereas crude specimens in poorer graves may suggest some home imitations of craft products. A metalworker's shop on a public residential street in Eshnunna in late Akkadian times reveals that some craft specialists were already directing their attention to the wider public. Careful surface surveys of the site of Mashkan-shapir similarly suggest that copper or copper-alloy tools and utensils were in wide-scale, essentially universal use among residents of a third-millennium city.

By the early to mid-third millennium, increasing elements of a more recognizably politicized economy appear alongside temple estates and hierarchies, although the latter remain large and powerful economic units. With the ascendancy of political leadership came an intensification of intercity and interstate rivalry. Fairly transitory territorial states appeared in the latter part of the millennium, mostly with only a superficial influence on the city-states, which remained the fundamental units of social identification as well as economic organization and circulation. Divine assemblies are attested in the world of the myths, traceable back to the Early Dynastic period and probably reflecting human institutional forms of a considerably earlier date. Such assemblies also are mentioned in some contemporary cities. Possibly composed mainly or entirely of elders, they seem to have reached decisions by an informal process of consensus. They may have been limited to certain aspects of civic affairs and confirmation of decisions on going to war; there is nothing to suggest that they had a role in economic affairs.

The extent of authoritarian power exercised in late Early Dynastic city-states is perhaps nowhere more evident than in the scale of textile production, carried on under strict state control. Some costly garments were undoubtedly consigned to palace and temple elites or ceremonial purposes, but others constituted the chief export commodity, to be exchanged for supplies of key raw materials from distant areas. Texts from Lagash record the issuance of monthly barley rations to large numbers of female weavers and their children, many with non-Sumerian names, who had apparently been purchased as slaves (or captured, or arrested as fugitives). They were employed full-time in gangs of twenty or so that were separately accounted for under the immediate leadership of older, presumably more experienced women but with higher male supervision as well. Children accompanied them and also received rations, with girls at some age apparently being impressed into the ranks of the weavers while boys were separated and assigned to different accounting duties and units elsewhere. An overall total for the city of Lagash is not available, but these female weavers constituted as much as half the dependent population under the control of one temple (Maekawa 1980: 82).

LATER, TERRITORIALLY CONSOLIDATED STATES

The pattern of protracted rivalries between city-states was briefly interrupted just after the middle of the third millennium by a new political formation with much enlarged (if ephemeral in their realization) territorial ambitions. The Akkadian state, although withering away after three generations or so, sought seriously to incorporate urban communities on the alluvial plain and beyond within an imperial entity. Sargon, the founder, attempted to break down city-state autonomy and boundaries by appointing royal officials to serve alongside the traditional rulers, allotting the officials local lands for their support. Before long, however, these arrangements were a source of tensions and presently also successful uprisings (Foster 1993).

Toward the end of the third millennium huge archives of tablets reveal to us an astonishingly pervasive and purportedly all-encompassing bureaucratic structure that left little room for alternative modes of status gradation or resource allocation. Alongside a consolidation of military measures accompanying the formation of a standing army were the creation of a new system of provincial administration, a standardized form of taxation, a new calendar and standards of weights and measures, scribal schools, and the setting aside of a new category of crown lands (Michalowski 1987:64; Steinkeller 1987:20–21). Men who were "hired," receiving barley as their "wages," to some extent may have begun to replace those formerly impressed in corvées involving onerous labor as a major source of manpower (Englund 1991; Maekawa 1987:69). But it is the scale of state enterprises that most amazes us. To take the textile industry as the prime example, it was centered in the capital city of Ur and required

the labor of some thousands of workers to produce the small numbers of the extraordinarily labor-intensive costumes worn by the king and other elites and the great numbers of garments needed to clothe thousands of dependent laborers in the province of Ur, and to supply state controlled trade agents with large supplies destined for internal and external exchange, through which luxury goods could be secured for the ruling family and for state agencies [—a yearly production of some 630 tons of wool is accounted for, sufficient for more than 300,000 workers at then-prevailing distribution rates; this is a high figure if regarded as a sustained annual average and may indicate unrealistic elements in the accounting system]. All third millennium texts dealing with domestic production distinguish between the raw material wool and finished products. While both articles were distributed as rations according to unclear rules of disbursement, complex accounts prove that state controlled exchange mechanisms dealt primarily in wool. (Englund 1998:151)

The "wool office" in Ur appears to have been a special focus of royal interest, with elaborate credit-debit entries covering its integrated responsibilities for collecting wool and weaving as well as further processing, including fulling and perhaps bleaching the finished cloth with alkali. Calculated from the standard allotment to individuals, the number of female slaves employed must have been on the order of 19,000. As in earlier Lagash (where at this time a single text attests to the presence of more than 6,000 weavers), there were provisions for male overseers, whose residences are given in nearby villages. This seems to imply that the weaving installations were dispersed; one instance of an apparent "putting out" system involved 230 weavers who were apparently employed (and lived?) together in the same installation. Fulling and bleaching were carried on by smaller numbers of other operatives in separate establishments but under the same overall management. At least in the Lagash weaving operations at this time, male children were separated from their mothers at puberty and, judging from the terminology then applied to them, apparently castrated. Subsequently, they may have found menial employment as tow men in connection with shipping (Jacobsen 1953; Maekawa 1980).

The authoritarianism apparent here, however, may not have been as all-embracing as it first appears. To a still undetermined extent, state textual archives surely reflect an elite-focused and somewhat self-enclosed set of concerns, and something less than a uniform domain of seamless control. Of immediate interest to the palace and hence under its direct supervision was a full-time enterprise of craft production, including specialists in metalworking, goldsmiths, stonecutters, carpenters, leather workers, felters, and reed makers (Neumann 1987). But this enterprise cannot be considered a model that was slavishly followed by the society as a whole. At the other end of a continuum it seems likely that marginal and only periodically subordinated groupings and modes of organization, replenished perhaps by fugitives from the cities, would have given the region as a whole a more mixed and unstable character than was recorded, or perhaps even perceived, in the major administrative centers (Adams 2002). On the other hand, at least in the crucial agricultural sector, where gangs of unskilled men and women laborers were permanently assigned under foremen to a shifting variety of onerous tasks (with debits for failing to reach their targeted levels of performance), conditions of regulated life seem fairly appalling. If anything is reported about them at all, it is usually only the time of their termination from state employment—by flight or death (Englund 1991:259, 280). Perhaps not surprisingly, this overextended bureaucratic impulse quickly began to erode and did not survive the dynasty itself.

A proliferation of Ur III settlements, many of them only tiny hamlets, is well attested in texts of the period, especially those from uncontrolled excavations at Umma (Steinkeller 2001), and a large population for that region in particular may be reasonably inferred. But how generally the bulk of the urban population remained employed in agriculture is uncertain.

Reviewing the substantial body of somewhat disconnected, particularistic evidence, I suspect that the familiar Western models of later, plenipotentiary kings, to whom are ascribed in this case overriding rights of ownership as well as personnel control, are likely to be misleading. Functional authority may ordinarily have devolved in some never formally defined way on members of an elite with generally shared interests who were also major landholders and high officeholders. Formal title to land would be less important in this reconstruction than generally shared interests and status. Arguments over the time of origin and existence of discernibly private property, with unambiguous confirmation vainly sought in the generally equivocal evidence of buying and selling in a fluctuating market (Hudson and Levine 1996, 1999), may be of very limited relevance. During the Third Dynasty of Ur, at the end of the third millennium, some authorities report little or no evidence of the conveyance of land titles by private sale. No less forcefully, others point to indirect evidence for a contrary position (Gelb 1969). With textual evidence coming only from the "great institutions," limited or doubtful evidence would be in any case unconvincing as an argument for the absolute exercise of royal power in the assignment of usufruct and functional control of land. Members of the elite having such control would have been identified for this purpose not with reference to their largely independent interests and activities but more narrowly (and secondarily) under their titles as royal officeholders.

MARKETS, MERCHANTS, AND "PRIVATIZATION"

The emergence of local markets, probably under way well before the end of the third millennium, is still a matter of considerable dispute. Perishable goods such as fresh (not dried) fish, and cheap, mass-produced commodities such as pottery, simply do not lend themselves well to any completely centralized system of rationing or redistribution. Fortunately, the ceramic industry during the Third Dynasty of Ur is one whose production and distribution arrangements are known or can be inferred in some detail.

Operating with a considerable degree of independence, potters were responsible for making and disbursing specified types and numbers of vessels to specified individuals and institutions for only a specified number of days in a year, and for these periods received rations of barley, wool, and fat. Although the part-time affiliation was semipermanent and included provisioning of needed fuel and other raw materials and the right to recruit and release state-assigned, unskilled worker-assistants, the industry itself appears to have been carried on in home workshops without direct supervision. Moreover, committed days of labor often were devoted to other, completely unrelated corvée assignments, and there existed still another category of "potters of the countryside" without any institutional responsibilities. The implication is that much of the potters' efforts was devoted to directly fulfilling domestic demand, even though this is wholly unreported in the bureaucratic sources. Even further, Steinkeller submits that "the overwhelming majority of Ur III craftsmen worked at home, in their own workshops, and that their professional activities were to a large extent independent from the state" (1996:252).

This and other fortuitously preserved textual examples of actual behavior in some specialized occupations point to the likelihood that the seemingly all-encompassing grip of the Ur III bureaucracy may be in large part an artifact of the myopic purposes for which they were recorded. If men in these presumably somewhat higher-status occupations were only periodically employed by the state (for proportions of their annual effort that scribes took no interest in recording!), then much of their economically relevant activity lay entirely outside institutional purview and yet was clearly made available to a consuming public (Van de Mieroop 1999a:91–92).

Long-distance procurement, serving escalating needs for commodities such as metals and timber and requiring increasingly industrialized textile production to provide the pri-

mary economically transportable exchange commodity, represented an obvious priority for the state. But equally obviously, it represented an opportunity for those engaged in it to execute private commissions on their own behalf. The trade must have moved fairly quickly to somewhat standardized systems of valuation that also allowed for some variability in price. But although copper and bronze also were in common use and were accounted for as the raw materials were circulated to craftsmen, the finished articles moved outward into the population at large without intervention from central procurement offices. Additionally, a continuing need for skilled repairs and the recasting of broken implements called for craftsmen who directly supplied the community (Neumann 1992).

The existence of a market in privately held land poses similar problems of the probable inadequacy of the textual sources for addressing this question. Abrupt shifts in the relative proportions of temple and royal estates, and recorded prices for some of the lands conveyed almost a millennium earlier in the pre-Sargonic *kudurrus* for less than the value of a single year's harvest (Diakonoff 1982:68), suggest that there habitually was a large element of duress in many land transfers. Thus a lengthy coexistence of mixed, irregularly applicable systems is very likely. Unrecorded particularistic circumstances have defied some determined efforts (e.g., Farber 1978) to establish variable but intelligible exchange ratios for silver, gold, labor, and barley. Despite the arguments of some rearguard Polanyi supporters (e.g., Renger 1994, 1995), the substantial presence of many essential elements of a market seems virtually beyond dispute. As Van de Mieroop cautiously concludes, "One cannot ignore the empirical data...for the existence of some market mechanisms with the concept of profit and loss, with price fluctuations, and with situations of scarcity. But the fundamental difficulty lies in determining the relative importance of the exchange through a market within the totality of the ancient Mesopotamian economy" (1999a:117–118).

To touch only very briefly and selectively on the subsequent development of economic life and institutions, substantially different conditions can be documented in great detail for the Old Babylonian period beginning after 1800 B.C. By the earlier third of the second millennium, at any rate, the extension of literacy to permit masses of private correspondence shows that merchants had become a major, increasingly independent social force. Their entrepreneurial modes of behavior in some respects fall not far short in sophistication of those we associate with Renaissance Italian city-states. Could this behavior really have evolved so relatively suddenly, or does it again reflect an older pattern largely beyond the span of attention of the great palace- and temple-centered organizations that formally dominated in the third millennium?

There is voluminous private business correspondence involving mercantile ventures, the buying and selling of land, and provisions of credit to impoverished cultivators, leading in many cases to conditions of debt slavery. Wealthy individual creditors conducted many of their transactions with payments or receipts of silver, although measured quantities of barley continued as a recognized standard of exchange. Merchants lived in large, well-appointed, multiroom houses, nestled into the interstices among which were frequently others of poorer construction and a tenth or less the size (Elizabeth Stone, personal communication 2001; Van de Mieroop 1999b). Entrepreneurs are even seen conducting large-scale transactions with the palace and temple that involve the leasing of rights of exploitation and the selling or purchasing of large volumes of agricultural commodities (Van de Mieroop 1992:244). Of special interest is the formation of family corporate structures seeking the deity's protection for their assets through an unmarried female representative of the family (a *naditu*) permanently lodged in the temple (Harris 1964; Stone 1982). Few long-continuing private "dynasties" are in evidence, however, with wealth ordinarily dissipated over two or three generations through the capricious policies of rulers, partitive inheritance, the inevitable risks of long-distance trading ventures, and perhaps even the cyclical fortunes of ordinary economic investments in agricultural harvests.

Household slaves were present, but slavery of the kind familiar to us from classical times onward seems to have been quantitatively marginal. Much more significant are various forms of dependency, which as a general category does not correspond at all with gradations of wealth. Formal dependence on the palace or temple frequently characterized high-status individuals with official titles that could be inherited and yet with very limited duties, most of whose holdings and activities apparently were free of oversight or higher claim. Other kinds of dependents, as in earlier periods, had very inferior status. And large numbers of "free" individuals and families were by all appearances without land and survived by hired labor.

Most revealing for me has been an initiative in prosopographic history launched more than 30 years ago by A. Leo Oppenheim. It shed a fascinating light on the Old Babylonian town of Sippar by collecting all the available references to individuals in large archives there. What we seem to see at any one time is a relatively small, literate elite of perhaps a few score of individuals who combine and dispute with one another in various ventures, are appointed as judges and other civic functionaries, and serve together as officers in the town militia (at times going out into the surrounding marshes in pursuit of fleeing urban inhabitants of lower status). One gains the impression that they are self-confident in their collective standing, not particularly concerned over possible interventions by the dynastic ruler some distance away in Babylon, and irredeemably urban in their commitments and spirit (Harris 1975; Oppenheim 1965:35). On the other hand, it appears that the city was—and may always have been—a considerably less rewarding and even less-than-voluntary setting for a large proportion of their fellow inhabitants who were less economically well situated and increasingly debt-ridden (Klengel 1987; Van de Mieroop 1992:246).

Lest one is tempted by the apparent weight of documentation of multiple aspects of privatization in this period, however, it is imperative to draw attention once again to the considerable degree of our dependence on uncontrollable imbalances in our sources. If to my tastes simply too cautiously and negatively, Van de Mieroop nonetheless rightly reminds us of the need to view the entire sequence of our economic understandings of ancient Mesopotamia not necessarily as a consistent record of long-term evolutionary "progress" but as a still substantially uncertain path whose major turnings remain in some doubt:

> We are unable to draw up a balance sheet of the ancient Near East economy in any particular period, evaluating the relative importance of any particular sector, public, private or communal; hence we cannot see any evolution in their relative weight. The old idea that the Mesopotamian economy from 3000 to 1500 B.C. went through successive stages of temple, state, and private dominance is now almost universally regarded as a fantasy based on a shifting imbalance of the textual sources. But the problem is not just that we have temple archives from the Early Dynastic period, state archives from the Ur III period, and private archives from the early second millennium. Even if we had more of a variety of documents from the various sectors in different periods, we would not be able to evaluate them; a great deal of economic activity was probably never recorded at all. (Van de Mieroop 2000:42)

But to the extent that it is justified, such pessimism also can be read as an open invitation to archaeologists to devise new and innovative research strategies to help clarify the sequence of broad transitions in the society and economy that lay so discouragingly outside the purview of the subjects and writers of the texts.

CONCLUSIONS

Recent research has underlined the extraordinary environmental challenges presented by the lower Mesopotamian plain to early human settlement. Agricultural routines, long familiar by the fifth millennium in surrounding areas, could at first find little place in a prevailingly marshy landscape. With a drying land surface and progressively drier climate during the later fourth millennium, there was a changing configuration of watercourses that increased opportunities for land use intensification along a reduced number of managed, major arteries. Thus there were pressures for continuous, but surely also difficult, change for those affected, favoring some localities and subsistence regimes at the expense of others. The plain itself was characterized by a mosaic of ecosystems and consequently by different sets of subsistence resources, which also were subject to irregular change in their locations and proportions.

These stresses led simultaneously in three directions. First, they demanded a high degree of complexity in arrangements for the amassing and redistribution of different sets of specialized but potentially complementary resources. Second, they generated real pressures to form hierarchies of access to particular resources and favorable settings. And third, they induced competitive advantages for concentrations of population that presently became true cities.

Cities, in turn, drawing on larger and more specialized populations and larger resource areas, intensified the pressures for more complex and effective administrative arrangements. This was a setting in which a writing system could be expected not only to originate at a relatively simple level but to be progressively elaborated into a technology of bureaucratic control and repression. Thus it was also on the way to becoming a stratified social setting. Alongside a need for regimentation of large numbers of displaced urban immigrants was the challenge of administering an enlarged and complex hinterland on which the very survival of the city depended. As relocation of progressively more constrained water resources continued, it was, finally, a setting in which the offensive and defensive advantages of urban population concentrations became compelling.

City-states, in short, were an intelligible, "natural" outcome of an evolutionary process in a region that offered extraordinary opportunities if its challenges were met by many key advances in human organization. Contained within them were groups and structures broadly reflective of different phases or components in this irregular evolutionary process. Temple estates redistributing resources among their followers and more amorphous, quasi-kin communities probably had the deepest roots. War leaders acquiring the trappings and growing ranks of followers of kings were generally a later development, and like the other two they understandably began aggressively to pursue great landed estates of their own as a power base. Thus far, perhaps, one might have ventured, if somewhat speculatively, on the basis of archaeological evidence alone. In the context of this comparatively oriented volume, however, we should not overlook the fact that it is the absolutely unparalleled richness of the Mesopotamian textual sources, in diversity and substantive detail, that allows an account of economic life to proceed much further.

As was asserted at the outset of this chapter, all the available evidence makes it clear that there was originally a tripartite segmentation in the society that came to characterize city-states, and in the elites dominating them and imposing repressive conditions of labor service and relative impoverishment on the bulk of their fellow urbanites. But what locked this structure into place for several succeeding millennia, stoutly resisting efforts of individual, temporarily dominant city-state rulers to impose a new, territorial or proto-imperial level of control that involved the durable ascendancy of a single capital city?

Here I argue it was precisely the unparalleled effectiveness of the administrative system and the writing that enabled it, an organizational-technological linkage if you will, that we need to recognize as splendidly rising to the challenges of complexity that have been described. Cuneiform writing, in the extraordinarily versatile path of development it followed in Mesopotamia, did not merely permit effective solutions to a diverse set of administrative problems. It became the distinguishing badge and capability of a superordinate administration, a rationale for autocratic rulership and for imposing grossly differential access to collective resources, and finally, an instrument of genuinely historical consciousness. The city, as the home of a sponsoring deity with his or her supporting institution of a temple and its traditional domains and parishioners, was the all but unassailable focus of civic loyalty. This, I suggest, is what made the Mesopotamian city-state the "default" position to which the entire system reverted as successive attempts to impose higher levels of integration fell apart after a few generations. Durable territorial empires did not originate here, in spite of the economic, social, and intellectual capital that undoubtedly accumulated in city-states. Instead, they originated under a different set of conditions, on the plains of Assyria to the north.

Note

I am much indebted to Guillermo Algaze and Jennifer Pournelle for substantive as well as editorial criticisms and suggestions.

5

Structural Parameters and Sociocultural Factors in the Economic Organization of North Mesopotamian Urbanism in the Third Millennium B.C.

GIL STEIN

Urbanism as an economic system and states as political systems are often closely intertwined, and nowhere more so than in ancient Mesopotamia. The economy of ancient Mesopotamian states was almost by definition an urban economy. The emergence of this system is best known from the irrigated alluvium of southern Mesopotamia, often called the "heartland of cities" (Adams 1981). Cities first developed in southern Mesopotamia in the mid-to-late fourth millennium B.C., with the expansion of the city of Uruk/Warka to urban proportions. However, despite these precocious beginnings, the spread of city-states throughout the southern alluvium is not fully documented until the Early Dynastic period, roughly 2900–2350 B.C. (Figure 5.1). Once established, this pattern of cities and their hinterlands showed remarkable longevity, lasting as an enduring feature and basic building block of the social landscape for literally millennia through major political changes such as the emergence and collapse of empires, foreign invasions, and endemic warfare among the southern polities (Yoffee 1988a, 1988b).

However, the last three decades of research also have revealed that a second—and quite different—wave of urbanization took place across a broad region of the rain-fed agriculture zone of northern Syria, southeastern Anatolia, and northern Iraq beginning roughly in 2600–2500 B.C. (Algaze et al. 1995; Wattenmaker 1998; Weiss 1983; Weiss et al. 1993; Wilkinson 1994). Despite numerous cultural, linguistic, and economic connections between the two regions, the cities of northern Mesopotamia appear to have had a very different developmental trajectory from that of their southern counterparts. Perhaps the most notable difference lies in the comparatively ephemeral character of North Mesopotamian cities. The northern cities developed later than their southern counterparts and were mostly abandoned within a relatively short interval by the end of the third millennium. By contrast, the vast majority of South Mesopotamian cities continued to be occupied for at least another millennium.

Why did the cities of North and South Mesopotamia have such divergent developmental trajectories? In this chapter I attempt to integrate survey, excavation, and textual data from the past three decades of research to propose a descriptive model of North Mesopotamian urbanism from 2600 to 2200 B.C. I suggest that the differences between the northern and southern polities can be explained through a combination of structural parameters (mainly ecology) and historically contingent aspects of political economy. I am using the latter term in its broadest sense to encompass the relationship between political and economic organization, with the understanding that an economy must be seen as the culturally situated social organization of production, exchange, and consumption. The

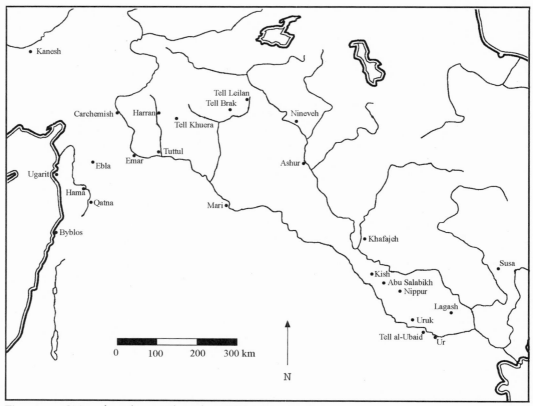

Figure 5.1. Cities of northern and southern Mesopotamia.

character and developmental history of North Mesopotamian urbanism are probably best understood as resulting from a complex mix of environmental factors, social organization, nomadic-sedentary interaction, and agropastoral technology—mainly the productivity, risk, labor requirements, and transportation costs of rain-fed agriculture.

STRUCTURAL PARAMETERS
Environment Context: Rainfall and Risk
The fundamental environmental contrast between southern and northern Mesopotamia lies in the relationship between rainfall and agriculture (Weiss 1986). Southern Mesopotamia—Sumer—is an alluvial plain that receives less than 200 mm of annual rainfall. Agriculture in the south was possible only with the aid of irrigation canals, which developed as early as the Samarran period in the sixth millennium B.C. (Oates 1969). By the Early Dynastic period in the third millennium

B.C., the focus of this chapter, each South Mesopotamian city-state had its own elaborate network of irrigation canals and river channels used to water fields, to drain runoff, and to transport goods and people cheaply and efficiently across the landscape.

By contrast, the steppe country of northern Mesopotamia (including northern Syria and southeastern Anatolia south of the Taurus Mountains) receives 200–500 mm of rainfall annually (Figure 5.2). This suffices to support a surprisingly productive system of rain-fed agriculture. However, although the *average* rainfall suffices for cereal agriculture, 30-year records of modern rainfall show an extremely high rate of interannual variability, often ranging from 30 to 35 percent (Weiss 1986:Figure 3). The relatively low average rainfall combined with the high degree of interannual variability means that "the area would have experienced a number of prolonged droughts per century which would

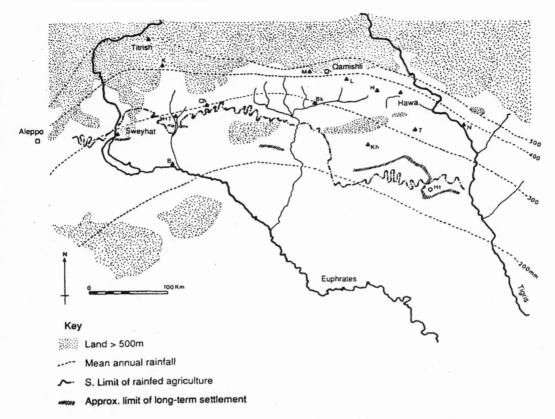

Key

Land > 500m

Mean annual rainfall

S. Limit of rainfed agriculture

Approx. limit of long-term settlement

Figure 5.2. Mean annual rainfall and main urban sites in northern Mesopotamia's dry-farming zone.

have had a significant effect on local production.... It is likely that five to ten significant droughts occurred during the millennium-long Early Bronze Age" (Wilkinson 1994: 499).

Annual rainfall decreases rapidly from north to south, so that sites in the southern edges of the dry-farming zone were in fact extremely marginal for agriculture, even during "average" rainfall years. The practical limit of rain-fed agriculture is the 200 mm annual rainfall isohyet. Agronomists working in modern Syria recognize a zone of marginal cultivation between 250 and 180 mm, where rain-fed agriculture or dry farming of drought-resistant cereals is possible but extremely risky (Wilkinson 2000b:4). In this zone sheep and goat pastoralism has major economic importance. Many of the larger North Mesopotamian urban sites of the third millennium B.C., such as Tell Bi'a, Sweyhat,

Khoshi, and Brak, are located either inside or very close to what is today the marginal zone with less than 250 mm annual rainfall (Wilkinson 2000a:5). These environmental parameters clearly played a crucial structural role in the development, functioning, and collapse of the third-millennium North Mesopotamian cities.

The Dry-Farming Urban Polities of Third-Millennium B.C. Northern Mesopotamia

The area known as northern or "Upper" Mesopotamia extends over an area approximately 700 km from east to west and about 200 km from north to south, defined by a combination of topography, water regime, and culture history. This long and narrow region of grassy steppe, grading off toward desert in the south, is bounded by the Syrian coastal mountains to the west, the eastern Taurus Mountains to the north, and the

Zagros Mountains to the east. The southern edge of this region is defined by the 200 mm annual rainfall isohyet. Northern Mesopotamia includes five subregions: southeastern Anatolia, inland Syria between the coastal mountains and the Euphrates Valley, the Euphrates Valley, the Syrian Jazira (notably the Khabur headwaters region), and the Iraqi northern Jazira.

We have three main complementary data sources for the study of mid-third-millennium North Mesopotamian urbanism. Regional surveys, both intensive and extensive, conducted in the last two decades have given us broad if patchy coverage of a wide swath across the dry-farming zone (for an overview of Mesopotamian surveys, see Wilkinson 2000a). These surveys provide a regional perspective on the growth and organization of these urban polities. Excavations (often accompanied by remote sensing/magnetometry programs) at northern urban sites such as Ebla, Chuera, Umm el Marra, Sweyhat, Banat, Kazane, Titris, Mozan, Leilan, Hamoukar, Tell Taya, and Tell el Hawa have given us an unprecedented chance to look at the spatial organization of North Mesopotamian cities.[1] Finally, a small number of northern sites such as Beydar, Brak, and Ebla have provided textual records that are invaluable as a source of information on political and economic organization. The most important of these are the royal archives of Ebla, some 15,000 cuneiform tablets recovered from the mid-late-third-millennium palace G on the citadel of Tell Mardikh/Ebla (Archi 1985; Klengel 1992; Matthiae 1980; Waetzoldt and Hauptmann 1988).

Interregional comparisons between northern and southern Mesopotamia are complicated by sampling and recovery problems (Wilkinson 2000a:229–230). Massive alluviation in southern Mesopotamia has buried most early sites and small sites while obscuring the true dimensions even of later, large mounded urban centers. Wind deflation also has been a significant factor in damaging early southern sites. In northern Mesopotamia, alluviation is much less of a problem; however, millennia of cultivation and later

occupations of sites have obscured much of the third-millennium B.C. regional settlement patterns. Overall, it is probably fair to say that in both north and south the smallest villages have been either destroyed or buried and the areal extent of the larger settlements has often been underestimated. To some extent, systematic intensive surface collections on the outer (lower) towns of at least the northern cities can make up for this problem. It also helps that many of the third-millennium urban centers of the north were abandoned and only reoccupied on a smaller scale, thereby preserving much of their surface traces reasonably intact. Thus it is still possible to compare the two parts of Mesopotamia, as long as one recognizes that (1) data on urban size may be slightly more reliable for systematically sampled cities in the north and (2) quantitative data on site size and population should always be viewed with a healthy dose of skepticism.

Urbanism

Cities emerged in the dry-farming zone of North Mesopotamia fairly rapidly sometime between 2600 and 2500 B.C. (Weiss et al. 1993:997; Wilkinson 2000a:245), at the transition from "Early Jazira" II to IIIa in the local regional sequence (Lebeau 2000:Table IX), roughly equivalent to Early Dynastic II–IIIa in southern Mesopotamia (Lebeau 2000:Table II). As noted earlier, this is almost 1,000 years later than the development of the first cities in southern Mesopotamia during the middle-to-late Uruk period, and a good four to five centuries after the spread of urbanism across the alluvium in the Jemdet Nasr and Early Dynastic I periods (Figures 5.3 and 5.4). The northern cities seem to have developed through the rapid growth of the 15–25-ha chiefly (?) centers of the early-third-millennium Ninevite 5 period in the Jazira (Schwartz 1987, 1994; Stein and Wattenmaker 1990; Wilkinson and Tucker 1995: 50–51) and the smaller centers of the Kurban V period in the Euphrates River valley to the west (Algaze 1999:555). The cities of North Mesopotamia seem to have emerged through a process of secondary state development, as

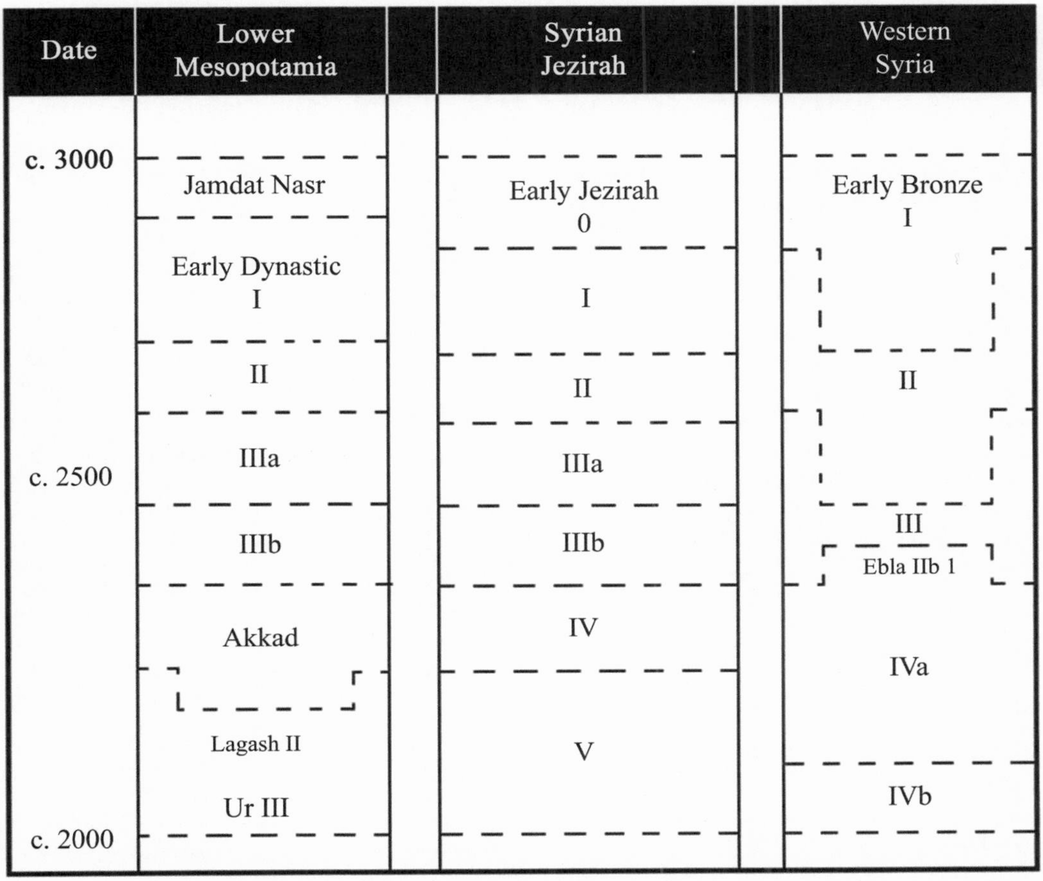

Date	Lower Mesopotamia		Syrian Jezirah		Western Syria
c. 3000	Jamdat Nasr		Early Jezirah 0		Early Bronze I
	Early Dynastic I		I		
	II		II		II
c. 2500	IIIa		IIIa		
	IIIb		IIIb		III
					Ebla IIb 1
	Akkad		IV		IVa
	Lagash II		V		
c. 2000	Ur III				IVb

Figure 5.3. Correlation of North (Jezirah) and South (Lower) Mesopotamian chronological sequences.

evidenced by the fact that urbanism emerged in this area (1) much later than in southern Mesopotamia (Lebeau 2000), (2) in the context of clear interregional interaction through exchange (Algaze et al. 2001:68) and possibly warfare (Weiss et al. 1993), and (3) with ideological models of kingship and technologies of power that clearly emulate South Mesopotamian models (Postgate 1988:113). Despite the close connections with the south, the available evidence suggests that the development of secondary states in the north took place in a context of political independence. Even taking into account a short-lived incursion by Lugalzagesi of Umma into the north (Klengel 1992:25), this region did not fall under the actual political control of South Mesopotamia until the twenty-fourth and twenty-third centuries B.C., as a result of mil-

itary conquest by the Akkadian empire under first Sargon and Naram Sin (Kuhrt 1995:49–51).

The larger unambiguously urban settlements in the Jazira fall in the size range of 50–120 ha (Table 5.1); centers seem to have been spaced about 30 km apart, suggesting an average territorial radius of about 15 km (Wilkinson 1994). Although population estimation is quite difficult (see, e.g., Postgate 1994), the general consensus is that urban population densities in the north were approximately 100–200 people/ha (Stein and Wattenmaker 1990; Weiss 1986; Wilkinson 1994:483), so that the larger cities would have had populations of 10,000 to 20,000, whereas overall population densities in the north (rural and urban combined) seem to have ranged from 29 to 60 people/km^2 in the

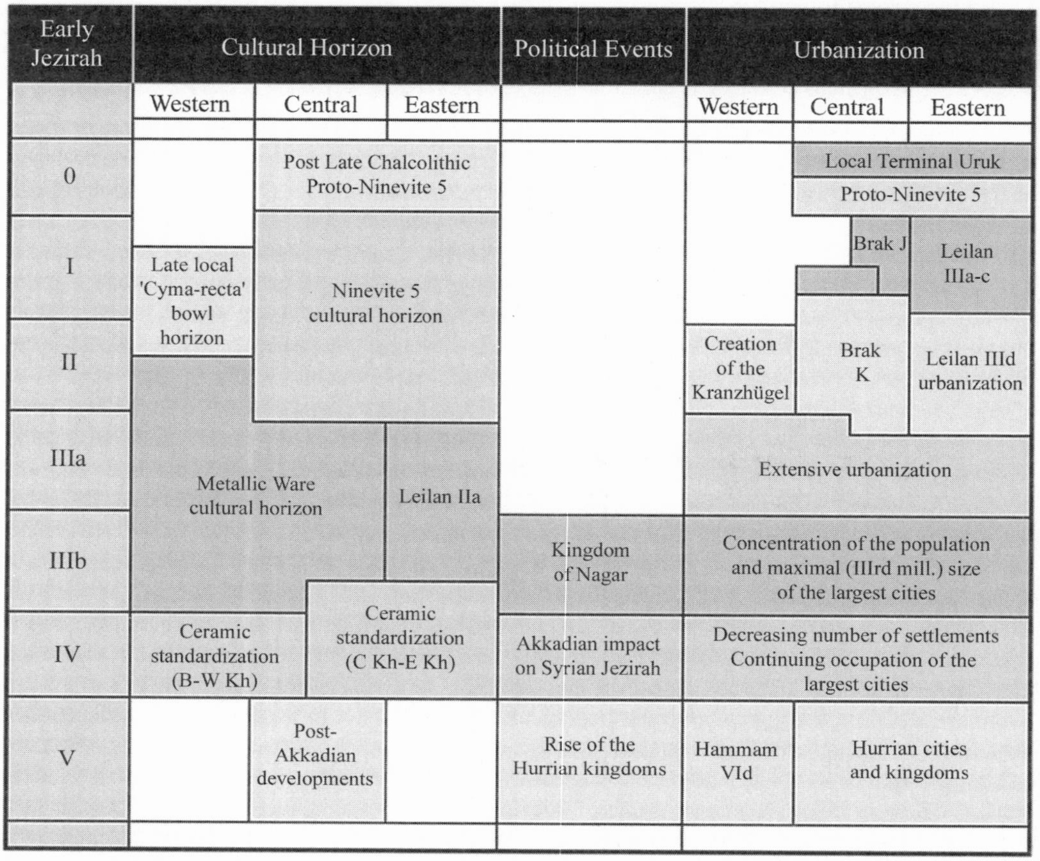

Early Jezirah	Cultural Horizon			Political Events	Urbanization		
	Western	Central	Eastern		Western	Central	Eastern
0		Post Late Chalcolithic Proto-Ninevite 5				Local Terminal Uruk	
						Proto-Ninevite 5	
I	Late local 'Cyma-recta' bowl horizon	Ninevite 5 cultural horizon				Brak J	Leilan IIIa-c
II					Creation of the Kranzhügel	Brak K	Leilan IIId urbanization
IIIa	Metallic Ware cultural horizon		Leilan IIa		Extensive urbanization		
IIIb				Kingdom of Nagar	Concentration of the population and maximal (IIIrd mill.) size of the largest cities		
IV	Ceramic standardization (B-W Kh)	Ceramic standardization (C Kh-E Kh)		Akkadian impact on Syrian Jezirah	Decreasing number of settlements Continuing occupation of the largest cities		
V		Post-Akkadian developments		Rise of the Hurrian kingdoms	Hammam VId	Hurrian cities and kingdoms	

Figure 5.4. Chronology of main social and political developments in North Mesopotamian complex societies during the third millennium B.C.

areas for which intensive survey data are available (Wilkinson 2000a:249). Wilkinson (1994) suggests that 100 ha was an effective upper limit on the size of these urban centers, given the combination of environmental uncertainty and the agricultural and transport technologies of the third millennium B.C. in the north, which necessarily relied on overland transport. More recent survey data suggest that the upper limit may be slightly higher—about 120 ha—but the basic environmental/technological limitation on site size proposed by Wilkinson remains the same.

The cities of northern and southern Mesopotamia differ markedly in their occupational histories during the late third millennium B.C. Basically, the cities of the irrigated south show continuous occupations, whereas the settlement history of the dry-farming zone shows great fluctuations and discontinuities. One of the most notable of these is the rapid abandonment of most (but not all) of the northern urban centers in the late third millennium, circa 2200 B.C. Weiss and Courty (1993; Weiss et al. 1993) have argued that this abandonment was near universal in the region and that it was due to a combination of severe drought and a major volcanic eruption. Other researchers have shown that although much of the region underwent rapid abandonment, almost certainly drought induced, the process was localized and not universal (Wilkinson 2000a:235). As a result, cities in better-watered regions such as Sweyhat on the Euphrates or Kazane in the Balikh headwaters region continued to be occupied. Although not universal, the rapid abandon-

Table 5.1. North Mesopotamian Urban Centers of the Mid to Late Third Millennium B.C.

Site	Size (ha)	Source
Chuera	65–100	Weiss 1983:Figure 11
		Jason Ur, personal communication 2002
Qatna	100	Wilkinson 1994:Table 2
Leilan	90	Weiss 1986
Mozan	120	Tony Wilkinson, personal communication 2002
		Jason Ur, personal communication 2002
Hamoukar	105	Ur 2002
Farfara	75–106	Meijer 1986:Figure 1
		Jason Ur, personal communication 2002
Kazane	100	Wattenmaker 1997
Khoshi	90	Kepinski 1990
Hadhail	90	Wilkinson 1994:Table 2
Taya	70–160	Wilkinson 1994:Table 2
Tell el Hawa	66	Wilkinson 1994:Table 2
Ebla	56	Weiss 1983:Figure 11
Hadidi	56	McClellan 1999:413
Titris	46	Algaze et al. 2001:23–24
Nineveh	45+	Wilkinson 1994:Table 2
Mohammed Diab	43	Wilkinson 1994:Table 2
Carchemish	42	McClellan 1999:413
Brak	43	Weiss 1983:Figure 11
Bia	36	McClellan 1999:413
Sweyhat	31	Wilkinson 1994:Table 2
Banat	30	McClellan 1999:413

ment of many sites in northern Mesopotamia is striking and lasted for several centuries, into the early second millennium B.C. It is important to emphasize that no such massive abandonment took place at this time in the irrigation zone of southern Mesopotamia, despite major political changes (such as the collapse of the Akkadian empire, the Gutian invasions, and the emergence and collapse of the Ur III empire).

Textual and archaeological data both suggest that the cities of northern Mesopotamia drew their sustenance from four main sectors of the economy: (1) dry farming of wheat, barley, and lentils; (2) pastoral products—mainly dairy products, wool, meat, and hides derived from sheep and goat herding; (3) production of textiles (from local wool) and metal goods (from imported copper); and (4) long-distance overland trade (Gelb 1986; Pinnock 1984, 1988; Stein and Blackman 1993; Wilkinson 2000b:6). This diversified economy probably provided an important buffer against the risk of drought-induced crop failure. There can be little doubt, however, that cereal farming and pastoral production were the most important elements in the northern economy.

Agriculture

Wheat, barley, and lentils were the main agricultural products of the northern polities

(Weiss 1983; Wilkinson 1994). The Ebla texts indicate that in the better-watered regions west of the Euphrates, olive and grapevine cultivation also was important (Matthiae 1980; Mazzoni 1988), although these crops seem to have been used more for the production of commodities such as oil and wine than as primary subsistence foods.

The area cultivated and the farming practices used in the agricultural hinterlands surrounding the northern cities can be reconstructed through site survey and offsite archaeology. These lines of evidence suggest that most third-millennium sites larger than 10 ha were surrounded by a zone of intensive cultivation, an intermediate ring of extensive cultivation and pasture, and an outer ring devoted to pasture (Wilkinson 2000b:8). Thin scatters of datable, worn potsherds are consistently found within a 3-to-5-km zone surrounding each larger settlement, dropping off to negligible amounts beyond it. Based on ethnographic analogy and historical examples, Wilkinson (1982) argues that these are the traces of ancient fertilization practices, in which night soil and ashy midden from settlements were spread on intensively cultivated fields. Clearly, transport costs would have limited this practice to the fields closest to the settlements. The hypothesized zone of intensive cultivation closely corresponds to the area of "hollow ways," or remnant roads and pathways that radiate out about 5 km in a dendritic pattern from the urban settlements (Wilkinson 1993, 1994). The hollow ways are thought to have been the paths used to transport agricultural workers to the fields and the harvest back to the city. Beyond the 5-km intensive cultivation zone, more extensive fields were located. Based on analogy with traditional farming practices in this region, it is hypothesized that these areas were farmed using a biennial fallow system (one year of "rest" between crops) to restore nitrates and retain moisture in the soil. The outer ring of cultivation also served as important pasture land for herds of sheep and goats.

Although wheat and barley were the main crops of both the northern and southern ur-

ban centers, the organization of farming differed quite markedly between the two areas. Based on modern agricultural statistics from Syria and Iraq, Weiss suggests that the yields of southern irrigation agriculture were 1.5 to 2 times larger than those of rain-fed agriculture in the north (Weiss 1986:Figures 1 and 2). At the same time, transportation costs in the south were significantly lower because of the availability of the canals and rivers for water transport. By contrast, the northern polities had to use overland transport— wheeled carts or pack animals—to bring the harvested crops from fields to consumers.

Nevertheless, by farming larger areas, the northern polities could produce *aggregate* yields comparable to those in the south (Weiss 1983). Unlike the south, where suitable land for farming was limited to those areas that could be reached by the canal system, the northern polities had available vast amounts of land for rain-fed agriculture. At the same time, labor and capital costs were lower than in the south because there were no irrigation canals to build and maintain. As a result, any northern polity that had the power to (1) control a large area of land, (2) control a large labor force, and (3) induce or compel producers to provide the surpluses to the central authorities would be able to support both a large urban population and the non-food-producing personnel of a state.

At the same time, the ecology of rain-fed agriculture would have imposed several limitations on the organization of northern urban polities in the third millennium. First, rulers would have been forced to strike a balance between their desire to farm as extensive an area as possible and the costs of overland transport. One partial solution would have been to disperse the farming population as widely as possible in the countryside (see, e.g., Archi 1990:15), so as to maximize production while minimizing the number of mouths to feed in the centers. Second, the urban centers were dependent on their hinterlands for the necessary food surpluses (Figure 5.5) (Stein 1993; Stein and Wattenmaker 1990; Wilkinson 1994) in order to survive even moderate drought years. Finally,

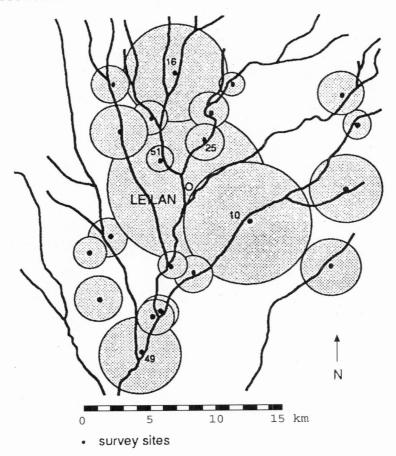

survey sites

Figure 5.5. Agricultural sustaining areas around the urban center of Tell Leilan, showing urban dependence on rural surplus production.

the dependence on rainfall agriculture meant that the centers could not depend on a reliable revenue stream, as surpluses would have varied widely from year to year, occasionally failing altogether. One would assume that the northern polities attempted to offset this unpredictability through storage, subsistence diversification, and exchange.

Herding

As would be expected in a low-rainfall steppe zone, the herding of sheep and goats played an extremely important role in the economy of the north Mesopotamian urban polities. As a mobile food resource, herds of sheep and goats can adjust to the changing seasonal and interannual availability of water and pasture. Dairy goods and meat provide reli-

able sources of protein to supplement a cereal diet. Herding is an important way to "bank" or store cereal surpluses from good years (Halstead 1993). The surplus can support the expansion of herds, which can then be either consumed or exchanged for additional cereals in years of drought (Sandford 1982). Herding and farming enjoy a symbiotic relationship in which the animals can graze on harvested stubble while fertilizing the fields with their dung. Sheep also produce wool as a valuable commodity for exchange.

Texts dealing with wool and woolen textiles are the most common form of document in the palace archives at Ebla, the most important of the northern urban polities in the mid-third millennium. As Gelb notes, "sheep raising was the mainstay of the local economy: thousands of sheep were raised, supplying the wool for the production of textiles, the main export product of Ebla. Thus wool was the mainstay of Ebla's commercial prosperity and power. Ebla, as these extraordinary tablets make clear, was an empire built on the backs of simple shepherds" (1986: 158).

Zooarchaeological data from a variety of sites in the Euphrates valley (Stein 1987; Wattenmaker 1987; Weber 1997) and the Jazira support the textual record by showing that during the mid-third millennium B.C. the sedentary pastoral economy shifted from the diversified herding of cattle, pigs, sheep, and goats to a highly specialized economy dominated by sheep and goats (Stein 1988; Wattenmaker 1987, 1998:166–167; Weber 1997; Zeder 1995:29). This intensification is consistent with the emergence of an urban-centered wool-producing economy with the attendant commodification of textiles (Kouchoukos 1998; McCorriston 1997). The herds of sheep and goats also provided an important complementary food source, mainly in the form of dairy goods such as cheese, yogurt, and milk and secondarily in the form of meat.

This pastoral economy would have been in the hands of sedentary-based herders in the urban centers and outlying villages, whereas nomadic pastoralists would have been an important economic factor both in adjacent, more arid regions and in the unoccupied interstices between sedentary settlements. Both textual (Gelb 1986) and zooarchaeological evidence (Wattenmaker 1987, 1998) suggests that the herding economy was multicentric. The state authorities clearly controlled large herds, which were often scattered in surrounding villages (Archi 1990). Secondary centers and towns provided the centers with animals and their products as a form of staple finance (Wattenmaker 1998). At the same time, it is clear that many (probably smaller) herds were in the hands of independent sedentary producers (both urban and rural), who raised them for their own subsistence needs (Stein 1987). Recent survey work has revealed a small number of third-millennium pastoral nomadic sites on the margins of the dry-farming zone (Bernbeck 1993; Wilkinson 2000b:6). Based on what we know from textual references in the very late third (Ur III period) and early second millennia from South Mesopotamia and Mari (Kupper 1957), we must assume that these campsites are the remnants of a much more extensive nomadic presence in the area. We can reasonably assume that mobile herders maintained an uneasy relationship with the sedentary states, trading pastoral products with them in good years and raiding them when drought conditions weakened the cities while stressing their normal grazing lands.

Overall, the available evidence suggests that sheep and goat herding played an extremely important role in the northern polities. This is almost certainly the case in the southern margins of the dry-farming zone (200–250 mm annual rainfall), where a series of large urban settlements (*kranzhugel*) consisting of a central mound surrounded by a lower town and a circular "ring" wall could have survived only if pastoralism played the major subsistence role, supplementing cereal farming (Wilkinson 2000a:239). Based on comparisons between mid-third-millennium textual evidence from the southern city of Girsu (capital of Lagash) and the northern city of Ebla, Gelb (1986) suggests that pastoralism played a much more important economic role relative to farming in the north than it did in the south.[2]

SOCIOCULTURAL FACTORS

It is clear that environmental parameters—specifically rainfall patterns—played a crucial structuring role in the political economy of North Mesopotamian states. However, the divergent developmental trajectories of North and South Mesopotamian urbanized polities cannot be fully explained unless one understands crucial differences in the cultural context and social organization of their inhabitants. In the following sections I examine social organization as reflected in burial practices, kingship, and the role of temples as ideological and economic institutions.

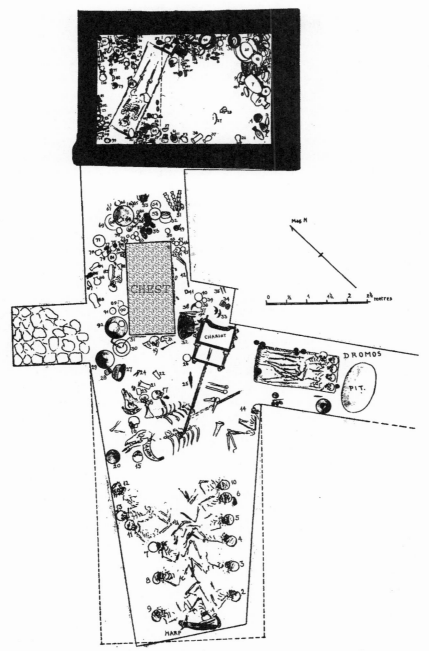

Figure 5.6. South Mesopotamian elite burials: the Royal Cemetery of Ur.

Social Organization

Although household layouts are more or less comparable in North and South Mesopotamia (Algaze et al. 1995; Henrickson 1981; Pfälzner 1996), there seems to be a higher range of variation in the south, possibly due to differences in the size of extended family households (Özbal 2002).[3] Burial practices of both elites and commoners suggest far more significant interregional differences in ideologies of kinship.

Elite burials in mid-third-millennium

southern Mesopotamia are best known from the Royal Cemetery of Ur (Pollock 1991; Woolley 1934; Zettler and Horne 1998). The sixteen burials described as "royal" were underground, richly furnished, single burials of high-status males and females, usually in masonry tombs at the bottom of pits with access ramps (Figure 5.6). Large-scale human sacrifices accompanied a number of these burials.

Recent excavations in Syria show that contemporaneous northern elites had strikingly different funerary practices. The most significant contrast is in visibility. Elites were buried in centrally located, richly furnished *aboveground* large *tumuli*, or chamber tombs. The most salient example is the White Monument at Tell Banat in the Euphrates River valley (McClellan and Porter 1999; see also Porter 1995). In its final state this *tumulus* reached a size of over 100 m in diameter and 20 m high (McClellan and Porter 1999: 107). Other aboveground elite burials have been found at Jerablus Tahtani (Peltenburg 1999), at the Tell Ahmar hypogeum (Roobaert and Bunnens 1999), and most recently at Umm el Marra (Schwartz et al. 2000). Significantly, at both Ahmar and Umm el Marra these are *multiple* elite burials with two to five adult individuals in the main chamber (the Umm el Marra tomb also includes three babies). These examples suggest that North Mesopotamian elites had fundamentally different conceptions of social identity and the relationship of rulers to the social landscape. Porter (2000) suggests that these tombs represent a form of ancestor traditions or veneration consistent with tribally organized pastoral societies.

Commoner burials show a similar contrast between North and South Mesopotamia (Creekmore 2002). Commoner burials in the southern city-states are almost always single (occasionally paired) burials. These are sometimes intramural subterranean burials, as at Khafajah (Henrickson 1981) and the Kish "Y" cemetery, or in cemeteries, as at Ur and the Kish "A" cemetery. In the north, by contrast, multiple burials are very common in both intramural and extramural cemeteries (Algaze et al. 2001; Carter and Parker 1995). As with elite funerary practices, northern intramural burials are in visible places inside residential quarters. All ages and genders are represented in these multiple intramural burials. At Titris Höyük in southeastern Turkey the intramural tombs are located in the center of blocks of residential housing in the lower town (Algaze et al. 2001). Taken together, the burial data are consistent with the idea that northern urban polities differed from the south in that the former placed a greater emphasis on corporate forms of social identity—specifically, the importance of lineage principles and tribal organization in a tribally based society.

Kingship and Political Organization

The main political units in both North and South Mesopotamia during the mid-third millennium were autonomous city-states ruled over by people called *lugal* or *en*—generally translated as "king" (Klengel 1992: 27), although *en* also has the meaning of "priest." In both regions we can see signs of increasing political consolidation as individual polities began to expand their territories through conquest and alliance. Some researchers have attempted to characterize Ebla as an "empire," but this seems unlikely on the basis of the currently available evidence. It is, however, clear that Ebla in the twenty-fourth century B.C. was an expanding state that exercised some degree of hegemony over both surrounding villages and more distant city-states (Klengel 1992:28). This process of polity growth parallels trends in southern Mesopotamia, where the city of Umma under King Lugalzagesi engaged in a major effort at military conquest at approximately the same time.

Northern kings borrowed the ideological trappings and administrative technologies of southern kingship and southern state societies—palaces, cylinder seals, writing, and royal iconography—although all these were translated into local forms and presumably into local systems of meaning as well (Post-

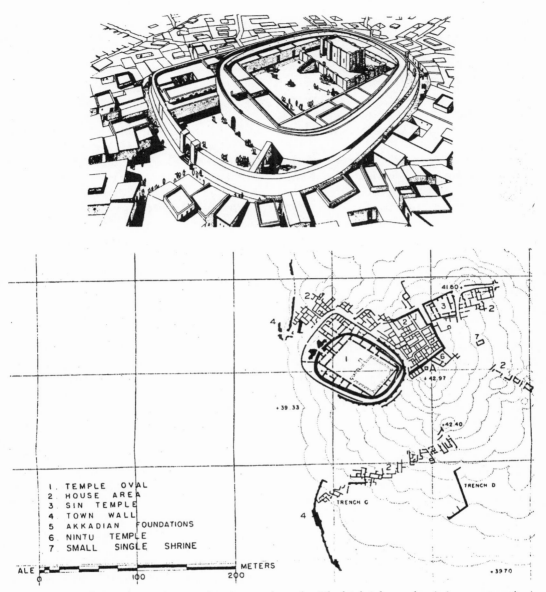

1. TEMPLE OVAL
2. HOUSE AREA
3. SIN TEMPLE
4. TOWN WALL
5. AKKADIAN FOUNDATIONS
6. NINTU TEMPLE
7. SMALL SINGLE SHRINE

Figure 5.7. South Mesopotamian temples: the temple oval at Khafajah (plan and artist's reconstruction).

gate 1988). The large complex of royal palace G, although only partially exposed, does not seem to mirror the ground plans of South Mesopotamian palaces. Northern kings even adapted the South Mesopotamian cuneiform writing system to write the local northwest Semitic language instead of simply borrowing the Sumerian language wholesale (Archi 1985; Klengel 1992:23).

We also should not assume that the concept of "king" meant the same thing in the north and south. The Ebla palace archives make it clear that North Mesopotamian kings controlled great wealth, large numbers of dependent laborers, and extensive tracts of land (Waetzoldt and Hauptmann 1988). Several lines of evidence suggest, however, that the social and ideological position of North

Mesopotamian kings may have differed from that of their southern counterparts. As noted above, elites were buried collectively rather than individually. Second, it may be significant that North Mesopotamian kings do not appear in monumental or propagandistic art. This contrasts strikingly with the depiction of South Mesopotamian kings on public monuments such as the Stele of the Vultures (Winter 1985). Finally, at Ebla, the predominant polity in mid-third-millennium North Mesopotamia, the textual evidence suggests that the power of the king may have been balanced by a council of elders, in a pattern characteristic of a "tribal type of society" (Klengel 1992:27, 28n). Whereas councils of elders existed in southern Mesopotamia as well (Jacobsen 1943), their authority appears to have been more limited (Yoffee 1995).

Temples

One of the most significant differences between the northern and southern polities can be seen in the ideological and economic role of temples. In the southern city-states of the third millennium two "great institutions" formed the central facts of urban political economy—the palace and the temple (Oppenheim 1977; Postgate 1992). Southern temples were extremely large architectural complexes. The size and central location of temples in the cities mirrored their economic and ideological importance (Van de Mieroop 1997:77) and also reflected the fact that the cities themselves had developed around earlier versions of these institutions. The shrine was laid out on a standardized tripartite ground plan of great antiquity, originating in the 'Ubaid period almost 2,000 years earlier. The building was generally decorated with niches and buttresses. They consisted of both the shrine (often raised on a platform for greater visibility) and a larger "household," or *oikos*, of the god, with residences of priests, storage facilities, and craft workshops. The temple complexes were extremely large. Thus the famous "temple oval" at Khafajah in the Diyala region of southern Mesopotamia measured 74 by 104 m (Figure 5.7) (Delougaz 1940). At the southern city of

Uruk the enormous temple complexes of Eanna and the Anu Ziggurat dominate the heart of the city (the Eanna precinct alone measures about 330 by 200 m!).

Southern temples were important economic institutions capable of generating large surpluses, providing a source of finance, and creating a subsistence buffer. Their wealth derived mainly from enormous holdings of agricultural land and irrigation works in the surrounding countryside (Powell 1990: 14). Other economic activities of the southern temples included vegetable and fruit tree cultivation; control of irrigation waters; management of large herds of sheep, goats, cattle, and equids; freshwater and saltwater fishing; manufacturing of goods from leather, wood, metal, and stone; promotion of long-distance trade; and banking (Postgate 1992: 115, 135). The southern temples controlled a large agricultural workforce of "semifree" laborers called *gurus*, in addition to attached craft specialists.

Temples were also ideologically far more important and intertwined with the idea of urbanism in the south than in the north. In the south virtually every city grew up around an earlier 'Ubaid period temple-centered town (Adams 1981). As a result, in South Mesopotamian culture it was the gods, and not humans, who were the true founders of the cities. As Van de Mieroop notes: "In the third millennium...every city of the south was closely associated with a Sumerian deity: e.g. Nippur with Enlil, Ur with Nanna, and Girsu with Ningirsu. The Mesopotamians thought that the gods had built their cities as their own dwellings.... Each [South] Mesopotamian city was the home of a god or goddess, and each prominent god or goddess was the patron deity of a city.... The connection between god and city was so close that the decline of a city was usually blamed on its abandonment by the patron deity" (1997:46–47).

The central ideological importance of the temples as households of the gods in southern cities is reflected in the tremendous temporal continuity of the physical temple complexes: "Religious sentiments dictated that temples must remain in the same location. Thus many

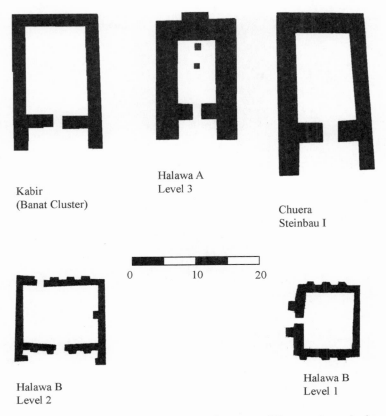

Kabir
(Banat Cluster)

Halawa A
Level 3

Chuera
Steinbau I

Halawa B
Level 2

Halawa B
Level 1

Figure 5.8. North Mesopotamian temples (note difference in scale from southern temples).

settlements were occupied continuously for several millennia starting in prehistory, and the collapse of earlier buildings provided a natural height demarcating them from their surroundings" (Van de Mieroop 1997:73).

Temples almost certainly played a different, and smaller, economic and ideological role in third-millennium B.C. North Mesopotamian cities. The architecture, location, and function of northern temples are quite distinct from those of the south. Northern temples have a single-room shrine, whose walls protrude at two sides to form a porch around the entryway (Figure 5.8). The temple structures are generally quite small[4]—often only 10 by 20 m—and are freestanding, with no associated complex of storerooms, workshops, and priestly residences. The small size, lack of ancillary facilities, and absence of writing or other record-keeping systems all suggest that temples did not play a major economic role in the northern urban polities.

Although the textual record from this area is quite limited, it is significant that among the 15,000 tablets from the royal archives at Ebla, mentions of temples as institutions are notable in their absence. Northern temples likely had a much smaller social role than their southern counterparts—they were not a "great institution"; instead, the palace appears to have been the primary social and economic sector in the polities of the dry-farming zone. The relatively small role of northern temples probably stemmed at least in part from the history of cities in this region. Unlike Sumer, North Mesopotamian urban centers do not seem to have developed from an earlier base of temple-centered towns.

Given their physical locations within the

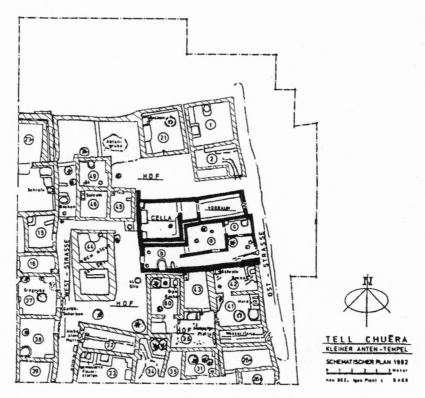

Figure 5.9. Location of northern temples in city neighborhoods: Tell Chuera Kleiner Antentempel.

northern cities, temples held a fundamentally different and smaller ideological role. In contrast with the monumentality, high visibility, and central location of the temples in the south, the small northern temples appear to have been scattered throughout the different neighborhoods of towns such as Chuera (Figure 5.9) (Orthmann 1990:Figure 5), Halawa (see McClellan 1999:Figure 3), and Taya (see, e.g., maps in Reade 1973). This pattern is more consistent with temples functioning as a focus for a lineage or other intermediate-scale, kin-based residential group in an urban setting rather than being a single ritual center for an entire community.

Thus northern temples do not seem to have had the same strong ideological association with cities as in the south. They were not "ideological attractors" to settlement, that is, they were not the initial nuclei around which the northern cities developed. They were

completely overshadowed by the palace sector in both economic and social terms. Instead, northern temples seem to have been oriented toward a much smaller level of social inclusion, that of the lineage in a tribally oriented society.

Economies of Scale and the Wealth of Cities

The clear differences in the institutional role of temples had important economic ramifications for the overall wealth and long-term stability of cities in northern and southern Mesopotamia. Southern cities were almost certainly much richer than their northern counterparts (on the sources of wealth of Sumerian cities, see Algaze 2001b). They were capable of producing and centralizing much larger agricultural surpluses, for three reasons. First, as noted above, irrigation agriculture is almost twice as productive as dry farming. Second, the lower transport costs associated with the river and canal systems of Sumer increased this profit margin still further. Finally, the organizational framework of the "great institutions"—the palace and temple sectors—made possible economies of scale in agricultural production.

Economies of scale are particularly important in irrigation agriculture, in which large amounts of land, capital, and labor make possible greater efficiencies in production. In the southern city of Girsu, for example, the Ba'u temple alone controlled more than 45 km² of prime irrigation land; other temples in the city, such as that of Ningirsu, controlled *five times* more land than the Ba'u temple (Powell 1990:8–9). This does not even take into account the palace's landholdings, which also would have been extensive. By virtue of their size and wealth, these institutions were able to make long-term agricultural investments and absorb risks in ways that individual cultivators could not (see, e.g., Rothman 1996 for a comparison of palace and private decision-making strategies in agriculture in second-millennium B.C. southern Mesopotamia). As a result, the temple and palace sectors were able to pursue strategies of economic maximization (Adams 1978) with a reasonable assurance that they had the capital and labor resources to survive environmental and localized political stresses. The vast wealth generated by these twin institutions (which was at least partially accessible to broader sectors of society through loans) endowed the southern cities with a much higher degree of economic stability than their northern counterparts.

The agricultural base of the northern cities gave lower yields to begin with, had higher transport costs, and lacked the full institutional framework to maximize production in economies of scale. As a result, northern cities could increase production only by fertilizing the fields closest to the cities, farming broader areas, and violating fallow (thereby pushing the cropping regime toward more frequent failure and greater instability). All these strategies were costly, and none yielded returns equal to those in the south.

Northern cities simply lacked the institutional framework and economic resources needed to survive periods of intense drought and the nomadic incursions that would have accompanied it.

CONCLUSIONS: STRUCTURE, HISTORY, AND COMPARATIVE URBANISM IN MESOPOTAMIA

Ecology provides a crucial structuring parameter for the nature of North Mesopotamian cities and their differences from those of the south, but only when combined with an understanding of the contingencies of culture and social organization. The southern cities were richer, more centralized, characterized by more powerful rulers, less focused on pastoralism, less "tribal" in social structure, and more grounded ideologically in the ritual system centered on large, long-lived temples. At the same time, irrigation agriculture provided a far more consistent and predictable supply of grain than did the vagaries of rain-fed agriculture in the north.

The marginal semiarid environment of the north made urbanism a risky business. Given the technology of the time, there was an upper limit of about 120 ha on urban size. The cities were dependent on their hinterlands for food but also had to maintain a dispersed rural labor force in order to produce agricultural surpluses. In times of low rainfall the cities were unable to feed themselves even with rural surpluses. The northern cities attempted to buffer against these problems by relying heavily on herding, by both sedentarists and nomads. However, the yields of sedentary pastoralism are quite low, relative to nomadic herding, because of the poor quality of grazing near permanent settlements (Martin 1982). At the same time, the herds of sedentarists are vulnerable to raiding by nomadic pastoralists. Finally, a reliance on nomadic pastoralists for dairy-based subsistence products would have been risky since pastoralists are notoriously quick to shift from trading to raiding when drought places pressure on their own grazing lands.

Northern cities thus had shaky economic foundations and were vulnerable to both the direct and indirect effects of periodic drought. However, the relatively ephemeral character of northern polities must also be understood in the context of ideology and cultural values. The historic association between temples and cities, and the central role of temples in the religious and economic life of cities, meant that cities had much more than just a political and economic function as centers of power: "In the [South] Mesopotamian concept of a city two ideas predominated: it was both a religious and a political center. Temple and palace were basic urban institutions, and they were the institutions that defined a city" (Van de Mieroop 1997: 52). Because the northern cities did not grow up around temples, and because the temples were less important as economic institutions in the north, they did not act as "ideological attractors" to bring in large populations, support them, and attract them back if a city was sacked or abandoned.

The North Mesopotamian cities seem to have developed as seats of political power in a marginal environment for agriculture. In this setting, pastoralism and a tribal form of social organization kept the option of mobility open for northern peoples. At the same time, the relative lack of wealth-generating institutions and the fact that urban places lacked the sacred character of southern cities meant that northern cities were subject to strong centrifugal forces. They were hard to maintain and easy to disperse. One might say that northern cities lacked the stability of their southern counterparts because they had only shallow roots in both the economic and the sacred landscapes.

Notes

I am grateful to Gary Feinman for inviting me to participate in the conference on the economies of ancient chiefdoms and states. Initial revisions of this chapter were presented at a colloquium in the Northwestern University Anthropology Department. I thank my colleagues there for their insightful comments and constructive criticism. This chapter has especially benefited from the comments of Robert McC. Adams, James Brown, Timothy Earle, Gary Feinman, Glenn Schwartz, Tony Wilkinson, and Jason Ur. They are not responsible for whatever errors remain.

1. I am omitting Mari from this discussion of North Mesopotamian urbanism for several reasons. First, this site is located well to the south of the 200-mm isohyet and is thus within the irrigation agriculture zone; available evidence (Margueron 1988) suggests that the site had an irrigation-based economy. Second, urbanization at Mari seems to have taken place in the Early Dynastic I period, c. 2900 B.C. (Margueron 1987), i.e., at the same time as the spread of southern Mesopotamia and some 400 years before the appearance of urbanism in the northern dry-farming zone. Third, urban structure and economy at Mari differ so markedly from those of all other northern urban sites and are so similar to those of southern Mesopotamia that the site is most accurately seen as a remote outlier of the latter area (Margueron 1996).

2. During the Ur III period, after 2200 B.C. in southern Mesopotamia, large-scale state-run herding enterprises are documented at Drehem (see, e.g., Zeder 1994), but centralized pastoralism at this scale is not documented for southern Mesopotamia in the Early Dynastic III–Akkadian periods (mid-late third millennium).

3. It should be noted, however, that we have more house-size data available from southern Mesopotamia than from the north.

4. One exception to this generalization is the "eye temple" at Tell Brak (Mallowan 1947), on the southeast edge of the dry-farming zone. This monumental temple was first constructed in the mid-late fourth millennium B.C. and underwent subsequent rebuildings in the early third millennium (Oates and Oates 1994). Unfortunately, because of the limited extent of excavations in the eye temple and the broken eroded topography of Tell Brak, it is difficult to assess how the eye temple functioned as an institution or what its relationship was to the rest of the site.

6

Material Resources, Capital, and Power
The Coevolution of Society and Culture

Andrew Sherratt

This chapter has two goals. On the one hand, it is a discussion of some later prehistoric societies in the Old World and how they were altered by contact with the first urban communities there in the period from 4000 to 500 B.C.; on the other, it is an inquiry into the relationship between social complexity and material culture. The second question arises from the first, for the effects of early urbanization on the surrounding areas originated only in part from direct mercantile or political intervention (which, though impressive, operated over limited distances); such changes also stemmed from the indirect effects of the spread of consumption habits and technologies that were pioneered in urban contexts. Much of the later part of the chapter, therefore, concerns Mesopotamia and the question of how these new modes of material consumption came about. The spread of such innovations, I would argue, had a fundamental effect on large parts of Eurasia, but for historical reasons—both the institutional separation of research activity and the recent distrust of long-distance connections that smack of "diffusionism"—the two areas are not often discussed in conjunction. The whole exercise is therefore an argument for the reintegration of specialist disciplines whose domains have become artificially separated by the growing academic division of labor, especially the distinctions between "society" and "culture" and between "history" and "prehistory" (cf. Wolf 1982). It is

also, to some extent, a reaction against the prevailing modes of interpretation (in many areas of academic discourse but notably in anthropology) of the last 30 years and an attempt to recapture some of the insights of the culture-historical mode of which they were a critique. Although it therefore resembles the kind of approach associated with writers such as Gordon Childe from the first half of the last century, it also is informed by new currents such as cultural studies and world-systems theory—themselves symptomatic of the desire to break out of these constraints in the context of contemporary society and history (Kohl 1987a). Although clearly related to twenty-first-century concerns (in a world of consumerism and globalization), these new outlooks are useful reminders of aspects that have been largely neglected in modern approaches that nonetheless have been very productive, sustaining those recent campaigns of fieldwork that have transformed our knowledge of ancient societies since the time of Childe. This essay is thus offered as an experiment in interpretation that deliberately crosses disciplinary boundaries in its search for answers.

Although this chapter principally addresses the question of how to describe changes in prehistoric Europe during the six or seven millennia between the introduction of farming and the extension of Roman power in the late first millennium B.C., it has been necessary—for two reasons—to make constant reference to the adjacent parts of western Asia discussed elsewhere in this volume (see Adams; Stein). The first is to draw contrasts between broadly contemporary societies in order to illuminate their similarities and differences. The second is because of the historical connections between them, which make it impossible to consider them in isolation. Because it would be a task beyond the scope of this chapter to offer a comprehensive review of these developments, I frequently make use of tactical comparisons in both time and space. (For a narrative overview of these periods of European prehistory, see Bogucki 1993; Price 2000; Sherratt 1994a, 1994b, 1998.) The connecting theme is the elaboration of material culture and the contrasting forms it has taken. Some periods of European prehistory are notable for their monumental constructions, such as the megalithic tombs and ceremonial centers of Neolithic northwestern Europe; others for the circulation of personal equipment, such as the metal weaponry and ornaments that were placed in hoards and burials during the Bronze Age over much of the continent. But the two forms of material display seem only rarely to coincide. This is in marked contrast to urban Mesopotamia (or Cahokia), for instance, where elaborate architecture and the manufacture of craft goods go hand in hand. Examining why this should be not only may help illuminate the relative peculiarity of prehistoric Europe in this respect but also may suggest one of the particular conjunctures of conditions that gave rise to urbanism itself.

At the root of this investigation is the question of how societies can be compared and what forms of abstraction are useful. There are broadly two answers to this question (in addition to the understandable reaction to abandon this kind of comparison altogether, which is the view of many contemporary ethnographers). The first is an evolutionary answer, which points to contrasts in scale and organizational complexity between societies at different times or in different parts of the world and arranges them on an abstract scale in order to shed light on their properties—for instance, the increasing degree of exchange-

ability between different products that accompanies the increasing scale and specialization of productive activity. Because there is an evident long-term trend in human history to move along this scale, it is tempting to proceed from an abstract scale of measurement to a temporal model and to postulate a stadial sequence of social types. The second answer is to provide a historical description of the variety of contemporary relationships between neighboring societies and the nature of their mutual influences. The categories of exposition stress cultural continuities ("genealogies") within developing local entities and the spread of particular cultural patterns. Such description can easily lead to an essentially noncomparative approach (although world-systems theory can be seen as an attempt to deal with these aspects in a comparative mode). Although discussions in this volume are closer to the spirit of the first enterprise, formulation of the problem in these terms alone leads to difficulties (well exemplified in Adams's initial querying of the universal relevance of chiefdoms in his chapter on southern Mesopotamia, for instance). Nor is the notion of an "economy" one that can be unproblematically generalized from societies with specialized systems of production and exchange to earlier forms of social organization. For these reasons, I use a series of tactical comparisons to move between periods and areas in an effort to illuminate the kinds of phenomena that have been discussed under the rubrics of "chiefdom" and "prehistoric economy."

USE AND MISUSE OF THE EVOLUTIONARY METAPHOR

The evolutionary approach has been a fundamental way of organizing ethnographic comparisons since the Renaissance; it offers a ready-made framework for describing archaeological sequences as they began to be revealed on a global scale after the mid-nineteenth century. "In the beginning," wrote John Locke in 1690, "all the world was America"; and in this lapidary phrase he summarized the usefulness of ethnographic observation in bringing to life episodes from the more remote past. Given systematic form by the "speculative historians" of the Enlightenment, this mode of argument was canonized by writers such as E. B. Tylor in the later nineteenth century as a way of integrating both the nascent discipline of anthropology and the accumulating evidence of prehistoric times. Although falling into disrepute in the early twentieth century, it was revived by L. A. White in the 1950s, was employed in popular accounts such as Peter Farb's *Man's Rise to Civilization* (1969), and is still used in textbooks such as Allen Johnson and Tim Earle's *Evolution of Human Societies* (2000). The terminology of chiefdoms and states in current use stems from this Michigan-centered movement and the early writings of Marshall Sahlins and Elman Service and has become a *koine* among anthropological archaeologists in discussing comparative sequences of change in early urban societies and their predecessors.

In the consideration of the *economies* of ancient chiefdoms and states, there is an even closer relationship with a form of evolutionary theory that began in the nineteenth century in Europe and centered on the character of the ancient Mediterranean civilizations and whether they were to be seen as part of the province of history or anthropology: the clash between "modernists" and "primitivists." This dispute was a series of debates, principally in Germany, on the nature of the ancient economy and especially whether ancient Greece was a "closed household economy" (*geschlossene Hauswirtschaft*) or a monetary economy (*Geldwirtschaft*). As with evolutionary issues in general, the debate died down in the early twentieth century but was revived by the interest of Karl Polanyi in modes of economic organization that were alternatives to capitalism. Teaching at Columbia, Polanyi (1957) gave new meaning to the primitivist interpretation, influencing both Marshall Sahlins and Moses Finley. Sahlins used these ideas in elaborating the school of economic anthropology, which he termed *substantivism* (as opposed to the formal economic models of the modernists), and Finley applied them in classics to the interpre-

tation of the ancient (Greco-Roman) economy in terms of local autarky and the relative insignificance of trade (Sherratt and Sherratt 1998).

A third stream of evolutionary thinking that particularly influenced archaeological methodologies in the 1960s was the use of central place theory in geography—which, although developed as a form of analytical description, was accommodated to the prevailing search for sequences through a largely speculative reconstruction (in textbooks of geography) that began with equally spaced villages on an isotropic plane and described the emergence of urban hierarchies serving regular hinterlands. Such models were particularly prominent at this time because of their use in urban planning. What archaeologists were less aware of was a developing critique within geography that pointed out the limited set of factors (essentially retail trips) on which these models were based and proposed an alternative set of patterns resulting from long-distance transport (wholesaling), which resulted in more linear arrangements of higher-order centers along arteries of trade (Vance 1970).

In putting together these different sorts of "origin myths," generated from different kinds of evidence in different disciplines, archaeologists initially tended to look for equations between them, or even to assume congruences—for instance, between exchange mechanisms and political organization (the much criticized idea of the "redistributive chiefdom"). It is still often assumed that terminologies arising from different fields of study (*civilization* from culture history, *urbanism* from comparative geography, *statehood* from political science) describe what are essentially different aspects of the same thing; yet in practice these labels prove increasingly difficult to apply in concrete cases. Especially where new chronologies demonstrate spans of time reckoned in millennia, it is now doubtful whether this terminology is very useful. In Mesopotamia, for instance, it might be argued that important parts of the ideological unity that we recognize as underlying "Mesopotamian civilization" were present already in Late 'Ubaid (fifth millennium), distinctively urban settlements were present in Uruk (fourth millennium), but "the state"—in the sense of recognizably secular rulership—was not present until the Early Dynastic (third millennium). I am doubtful about the procedure for recognizing statehood, for instance, from settlement patterns alone. But more generally, there seems little point in retrojecting distinctions arising from the comparative study of a handful of relatively recent societies, rather than beginning with the archaeological record itself and working out some concepts for ourselves (Yoffee and Sherratt, ed. 1993). One implication is that there should be an increasing congruence between explicitly theoretical approaches and descriptive, historical narratives—a point of view that was forcibly set out in a classic paper by Robert Adams in *Current Anthropology* in 1974.

The dominant interpretation of economic change in prehistoric Europe over the last 30 years, however, has reflected the conjunction of attitudes typical of evolutionary approaches in the various disciplines from which archaeologists have sought inspiration; these may be summarized as autonomist, subsistence oriented, and stadial in their application of ethnographic analogies. All these imported concepts have individually been very useful, and it has been part of the excitement of archaeology in the last three decades to force these ideas on the attention of largely inductive disciplines whose practitioners wanted to do little more than put pots in the right order and re-create lost civilizations by studying either their artifacts or their texts (or, in Kent Flannery's lively phrase, "would rather be buried up to their necks in fire ants than have to test an anthropological model" [1993:115]). Like nineteenth-century cultural evolutionism, half of whose argument was with creationists and degenerationists, social evolutionism has been the rhetoric of progress. But I sense that I am not alone in now wanting to go beyond this rhetorical stance and (in the words of the agenda for the roundtable from which this volume originated) "adopt a more holistic

and multiscalar view" (cf. Sherratt 1995a). Central to this exercise is the need to go beyond the regional sequences whose establishment has been one of the great achievements of this period. Even if an explicit adherence to a world-systems approach is still only a minority viewpoint, there has been a growing recognition that regional traditions have interacted with one another to the extent that it is quite artificial to describe them in isolation. Although this approach has met with some hostility from those who see it as the reintroduction of a discredited diffusionism, others have welcomed the move to an "interactionist" rather than an "autonomist" stance. This view is not without parallel in many fields of historical writing; Andre Gunder Frank has recently brought the whole phenomenon of world systems back to the Bronze Age (in effect equating it with urbanism itself; Frank and Gills 1993) and also has written a "structural" history of the last 1,000 years (Frank 1998), with China as the center of developments and Europe a latecomer, cashing in on its enlarged periphery in the New World. This is interactionism on a massive scale, both temporally and spatially, and it challenges us to explore the deeper past in a way that goes beyond a division of labor based on regional specialization. My remarks below are intended to take up that challenge. First, however, they address the two critical concepts of the present discussion: the economy and the chiefdom.

THE PROBLEM OF THE ECONOMY
The tension between "modernist" and "primitivist" (or formalist and substantivist) views as applied to European prehistory is well illustrated by the interpretation of the spread of metalworking. In his writings between 1930 and 1956 (using what is now recognized as a heavily compressed chronology, as it was based on typological comparison, before the introduction of radiocarbon dating), Childe put forward the view that metalworking had been introduced into prehistoric Europe by the Mycenaean Greeks, prospecting for new metal supplies for the Mediterranean market in the second millennium B.C.

To explain the occurrence of numerous hoards (caches) of bronze tools, weapons, and ornaments, Childe (1958) suggested that it reflected the different social context in which European metallurgy took place; instead of being bound to central institutions, metalsmiths became free craftsmen working for many patrons—and hence often had to hide their metal supplies in the form of hoards, many of which were left unrecovered in the ground. This was clearly a "modernist" scenario, owing not a little to his knowledge of the first-millennium Phoenicians and anachronistic even in the context to which he applied it. It was thus roundly criticized in the late 1960s and early 1970s by Colin Renfrew and others (e.g., Renfrew 1973), and a radiocarbon chronology showed the existence of a long European Copper Age in which metal had been used in much simpler ways. Even the techniques of alloying and bivalve-mold casting could be shown to have appeared in Europe a millennium before the Mycenaeans. At the same time, it was recognized that bronze objects—unlike the hoards of Roman coins that provided the basic analogy for this behavior—were often ritual in character and represented the deliberate deposition of wealth. The story that replaced Childe's account thus stressed a long evolutionary history of metalworking over much of Eurasia, with independent sequences of discovery of the properties of alloys and casting techniques in several different places; it used ethnographic analogies to explain the ritual destruction of wealth through competitive potlatching (e.g., Bradley 1982). There was thus a swing from modernist/formalist models to primitivist/substantivist ones.

Today a rather different picture could be put forward. Now that the chronology is clearer (and Near Eastern prehistory has been inflated by the same correction factors as that of Europe), we can see that the beginning of metalworking was a much more drawn-out process than Childe envisaged but still one in which the Near East retained overall priority (Moorey 1994). Simple copperworking, using easily smelted ores such as malachite and casting objects in simple molds, began around the margins of the Fertile Crescent before it appeared in Europe; so also—2,000 years later—did alloying and bivalve-mold casting, as well as techniques for smelting the deeper-lying sulfide ores of copper (Chernykh 1992). The Mycenaeans were indeed relatively late and irrelevant to the question of how European metalworking began, but sites such as Troy in the third millennium nevertheless appear to have been instrumental in transmitting new practices up the Danube corridor. To take one example, the use of tin appeared over a huge area, from eastern Hungary to the shores of the Persian Gulf, more or less simultaneously around the middle of that millennium (Moorey 1994; Sherratt 1993). Southeastern Europe, at any rate, was keyed in to what was happening in a much larger interaction sphere. Although Childe got the dates wrong, he correctly spotted a pattern. Moreover, although simple forms of copper metallurgy had persisted for millennia among relatively simple farming societies, the development of more complex manufacturing techniques was closely associated with the genesis of urban societies in the later fourth millennium B.C. Thus the features that European prehistorians have long recognized as marking the beginning of the "Bronze Age" can be seen in a sense as a spin-off from a social and cultural transformation taking place elsewhere.

Childe also was right in pointing to hoard deposition as a different form of behavior from that prevailing in the complex societies of the Near East and the east Mediterranean, even if his own explanation does not work. The continuing withdrawal of large quantities of craft goods and raw material for burial is in marked contrast to the relatively small quantities of metal recovered archaeologically from contemporary urban contexts farther south, where abundant finds of metalwork occur only in contexts of catastrophic destruction by fire or shipwreck (where truly impressive quantities may be recovered, such as the six tons of copper ingots in the Kaş wreck; Bass 1991). It is a contrast that was exemplified again in the Iron Age of the first millennium B.C., between the "civilized"

Mediterranean and its "barbarian" hinterland. Practically all the examples of classical Greek workmanship in precious metal come from tombs outside Greece itself, in Scythia, Thrace, Illyria, and the Celtic world (even though the shapes of metal vessels were copied by the Greeks in pottery). Textual sources record huge quantities of such objects in existence in Greek cities, so there is no doubt that they were in use there (Vickers and Gill 1994). Material wealth, even when it took the form of precisely similar objects, was used in different ways in the two areas—in one case buried, in the other retained in circulation. It would be possible to suggest an explanation along more formalist lines by saying that these different patterns of use reflect the relatively greater number of things that could be done with metal in more complex societies, and especially the fact that metals (initially bronze but later particularly precious metals) had become media of general exchange, capable of being converted into a much wider range of goods and services within complex urban societies.[1] In temperate Europe there simply wasn't the diversity of mobilized products for which metal might be exchanged, and the "ideological" (to us "irrational") uses had fewer competitors as alternative allocations of wealth.

It is tempting to summarize the situation by saying that chiefdoms (using the term to apply to groups such as the Iron Age Scythians or the Celts in the examples above) simply didn't have "economies" in the conventional meaning of the term, whereas even early examples of urban, state-based societies probably did, though they were different in many ways from recent ones. But that would be to ignore some fundamental similarities (because both groups were clearly capable of organizing regular flows of very specific products) and also to gloss over the fact that Greeks and Romans on the one hand and Scythians and Celts on the other were clearly interdependent and their societies linked by the exchange of goods. The paradox is that the same "economic system" (a network of practices concerned with the procurement

and circulation of goods) included societies sometimes using identical objects in very different ways, some of which were apparently more "economical" than others. The way out of the paradox is to suggest that in certain contexts "exchange value" came to predominate over "use value." When we describe societies as being "complex," we are pointing to precisely this fact, that there is a multiplicity of different pathways that any individual set of materials may take. It is this idea that underlies Polanyi's concept of "disembedding"—that goods, and the "economy" itself, can in some sense take on a life of their own, so goods that were once "valuables" can become "commodities" (Hart 1982). But "economic" transactions can take place between societies with different modes of economic organization, so that commodities also can become valuables in a new context when they are exported to less complex societies. This was the logic behind the concept of "prestige goods" popularized by Kajsa Ekholm and Jonathan Friedman and applied to Iron Age Europe by Susan Frankenstein and Mike Rowlands (Ekholm and Friedman 1982; Frankenstein and Rowlands 1978)—though the usefulness of this term, which originally described European manufactured goods imported into Africa in colonial times, has been diluted by archaeologists and has slipped almost unexamined into archaeological usage to describe any kind of exotic, high-value object circulating within prescribed spheres of exchange.

The degree of interdependence revealed by studies of early trade has profound implications for evolutionary models based on comparative "case studies," for it is clear that the very existence of flows of such manufactured goods (and, as I shall argue, some of the techniques of manufacturing them) served to transform surrounding societies in important ways. Iron Age "chiefdoms" such as those of the Scythians and Celts were to some extent created by their relationships with urban societies to the south. They were not (in any simple way) representatives of evolutionary stages but rather contemporary parts of a single system. Many of the later examples of chiefdoms described ethnographically were in a similar relationship with more complex neighbors. They cannot, therefore, simply be lined up in typological order to illuminate how complex societies had originally emerged, for they were themselves products of that emergence. The question of what preceded complex societies is a critical one that can be answered only by archaeology. The whole notion of differing degrees of social complexity has to be envisaged three-dimensionally, as a structure consisting of both vertical layers and horizontal zones, all of whose properties change through time. This is why the spatial component, whether approached through Childean diffusion or Wallersteinian world systems, is an essential element in understanding patterns of change. Not only ethnographic diversity but also archaeological diversity (in the sense of the multiplicity of cultural patterns identified over the last six thousand years) need to be related to processes taking place in already complex societies, whose existence altered the conditions of life of their neighbors.

Returning to the question of bronze hoards and economic analysis, it remains to be asked why objects such as bronze tools and ornaments were produced in such numbers by the indigenous communities of temperate Europe, only to be committed to the ground. A striking example is provided, for instance, by the hundreds of simple bronze neck-rings buried around the northeastern margins of the Alps in countries such as Austria and the Czech Republic around 2000 B.C. These neck-rings occur in hoards of up to a thousand or more (Harding 1983). An answer might be suggested along the following lines. Once the techniques for producing copper in quantity (e.g., by smelting sulfide ores) had arrived in the eastern Alps, there were vast and previously untouched reserves of this metal that were suddenly accessible. It was to the advantage of communities living near these sources (and already familiar with copper objects) to make use of them, and in the absence of regulation by any overarching authority, it was to the advantage of autonomous units to produce as much as possible (in a situation that economists today often describe as the "tragedy of the commons"). These objects would have circulated within immediate social networks and were then taken out of circulation, not so much to preserve their value for the common good as to prevent their falling into the hands of neighboring groups (or other members of the same societies) who could offer no comparable goods in return. There would indeed have been a local inflationary spiral—a localized precapitalist crisis of overproduction—before complementary forms of goods came to be mobilized and systems of long-distance exchange came to absorb the output. This is in fact what seems to have happened, for in a few hundred years there is evidence for central European metals reaching the Baltic, in exchange for commodities such as amber and furs. By this time the burst of localized mass deposition of bronze in central Europe was over (details in Sherratt 1993).

It is not necessary to accept this scenario in detail (and other European prehistorians might give this example a rather different emphasis; Shennan 1986, 1993a) in order to extract some general principles from it that bear on the topic of ancient economies. In the first place, this was a contact phenomenon; technologies developed in one context were transferred to another, with interesting consequences (which might well not have come about through purely internal processes). In the second place, it was not just a "spread by replication" of the kind envisaged by the simpler diffusionists; it was a translation into local terms and absorption into a new context with (presumably) new meanings and a new social significance. In the third place, it had a critical influence on the development of local exchange systems, providing a new and valuable medium of exchange with a variety of potential uses and arguably stimulating the mobilization of other goods of comparable value and their transmission over long distances. (In this case it was apparently the existence of an exchange medium that actively stimulated the diversification of production. It is perfectly possible, however, that metallurgy initially achieved this importance— way back in the Fertile Crescent—by precisely the opposite process. In a region of exceptional ecological diversity, the use of metals was a *response* to the need for a common medium of exchange in a situation in which complementary forms of local production were already taking place. The causal arrow can point in either direction.) Even if these particular interpretations are incorrect, they point to an important property of material culture, that the transmissibility of techniques can alter the conditions of local production and thus the circumstances of exchange. Therefore, practices that have their origins in a very specific set of local circumstances can eventually alter the social and economic systems of whole continents. This is an argument for basing any model of socioeconomic change on the interaction between many individual groups and areas rather than examining any one of them in isolation; it is material culture that provides the links.

THE PROBLEM OF THE CHIEFDOM

One of the characteristic features of prehistoric Europe is its long sequence of pre-state societies, between the spread of farming and the arrival of the Romans. Whereas in "nuclear" areas of the world it took something like 3,000 years to go from farming to urbanism, in Europe it took roughly twice as long. From 6000 B.C. or so to the beginning of the common era, most of the inhabitants of Europe could rather unhelpfully be described as "simple farmers," or broken down into an earlier phase of "horticulturalists" and a later one of "plow-based agriculturalists." Perhaps unsurprisingly, archaeologists have generally preferred to name them after their artifacts and call them Neolithic, Copper Age (Chalcolithic), Bronze Age, and Iron Age, or more specifically "megalith builders" or (with evident relief when ethnic labels become available from classical authors in the later Iron Age) "Celts," "Scythians," or "Thracians." None of these labels are very illuminating, despite the very interesting archaeology that lies behind them. Although there are several localized episodes of elaboration in different spheres of material culture, they lack any simple sense of overall direction and are very resistant to typological characterization. Thus unilineal sequences of social "types" are not very helpful in describing the course of change. Their analytical advantage is in providing a diversity of phenomena to examine, which in other parts of the world often occurred simultaneously. This may be helpful in distinguishing some important differences and breaking down "chiefdoms" into more elementary concepts.

One of the standing jokes among historians of English society is the phrase "the rise of the middle class." Originally introduced as an exemplar of new, social-science interpretations as opposed to old-fashioned political and dynastic descriptions (Tudors, Stuarts, Hanoverians), the middle class rose just too many times to be taken seriously. Books and articles on the sixteenth, seventeenth, eighteenth, and nineteenth centuries all attributed important developments in their periods to the rise of the middle class. Rather like "population pressure" in the founder texts of New Archaeology, it proved too generalized a concept to have much purchase on particular events. This has been the fate of the undifferentiated concept of "chiefdom" in European prehistoriography. Each millennium from the fifth to the first has produced its candidate, all looking very different and none very convincing in comparative terms until the final tenth of that time. Realizing that the term was becoming a catchall, Renfrew (1974) differentiated between "group-oriented" and "individualizing" chiefdoms, broadly corresponding to Neolithic and metal-age developments, respectively. It is this difference that is worth examining further.

There are essentially two different sets of phenomena that have attracted the "chiefdom" label: (1) the various forms of large ceremonial monuments requiring the coordinated activities of large numbers of work groups in erecting earthworks or stone structures, which occurred in the Neolithic of northern and western Europe, and (2) rich burials with concentrations of objects made of rare materials, which occurred from the Copper Age (later fifth millennium) onward, beginning in southeastern Europe and only slowly replacing the older pattern in the north and west. These concentrations of mobile wealth were not associated with ceremonial centers and until the second millennium (and then only in eastern and central Europe) were not often associated with other forms of earthmoving such as fortified settlements. The coincidence between permanent (often defended) sites and concentrations of mobile wealth only became general at the end of the second millennium and during the first. This latter pattern can be broadly related to growing relationships with the expanding urban societies of the Mediterranean. The two different phenomena that have been called chiefdoms thus differ fundamentally in character and are typical of different areas, with little continuity between them. The earlier candidates are characterized by ceremonial monumentality, the later ones by the accumulation of wealth objects in burials; only in the latest examples do the two criteria completely coincide. They point to different modes of social coordination and to the elaboration of different aspects of material culture.

Although it might be simpler in the present context just to forget about Neolithic monumentalism, it is worth spending a few moments to put it in context—in part because it occurred (perhaps rather surprisingly) on what might be accounted the outer edges of Europe, significantly distant from the continuing focus of developments in the Near Eastern nuclear area,[2] and in part because it may be illustrative of processes that are of comparative interest. The earliest farming societies in southeastern and central Europe, from 7000 B.C. onward, built villages of substantial mud or timber houses; but in northern and western Europe (and especially along the Atlantic and Baltic coasts) the farming groups that appeared after 4000 B.C. lived in less substantial domestic structures while building impressive communal tombs of stone or earth. To a large extent this contrast corresponds with areas where farming was introduced by immigrant settlers as opposed to areas where relatively dense indigenous populations selectively adopted features of farming culture and elaborated their own practices. In the former case farming spread by internal demographic increase and the proliferation of farming villages, so that the process was one of social replication; in the latter there was an element of active recruitment, as existing populations were "converted" (in both ideological and subsistence terms) to new ways of life. It is this fact that explains why the elaboration of built structures for collective burial and ceremonial purposes should occur at the outer edges rather than at the center of the continent, and why the two zones followed different paths of development (Sherratt 1994a, 1994b, 1997). While groups living in southeastern and central Europe began to use copper (and locally gold) in simple but striking ways for tools and ornaments that were sometimes deposited with individuals in graves, others—especially in the west, in Brittany and the British Isles—went on to develop large megalithic ceremonial sites with astronomical orientations and calendric significance, whose plans seem to have had their origins in those of the earlier communal tombs. These sites do not appear to have had large resident populations or to have been centers of production; they seem rather to have been fixed points in a landscape still occupied in a relatively mobile way and to have been sites of seasonal gatherings. Nevertheless, their locations point to positions in wider networks of contact, not so much as central places within territories as nodal points along the arteries by which products such as stone axes or flint were distributed from their source areas. These ceremonial monuments, although often impressive in scale, were not the starting points of a continuing process of development; they were replaced in the Bronze Age by a quite different pattern in which large monuments had no role and in which human lives were structured less by collective ceremonial and more by competition for access to material goods such as metalwork. It is as if the system had been wrenched from one path to another, ending a period of relative isolation and incorporating it in a wider world with different objectives and ideals.

Although the Neolithic societies that constructed these ceremonial monuments are not (in my view) usefully described as chiefdoms in the sense in which that term has come to be used, this episode has two points of comparative significance. This example shows how elements of centrality may emerge in areas of dense forager settlement when combined with elements of farming, as the outcome of integrating relatively mobile foragers into new social structures by a process of active recruitment and ideological conversion. It was the diversity of local ecological opportunities along the lakes, rivers, and shorelines of outer Europe that provided the circumstances for such elaboration—an ideological coordination based on metaphors drawn from striking natural phenomena (landscapes, seasons, astronomy), oriented on ancestral continuity, and set within a view of the world that could broadly be termed shamanic (including the ritual consumption of hallucinogens, in this case the henbane plant, *Hyoscyamus niger*). Had this construction of the world not been corroded by contacts with a larger set of societies structured on different principles (a historical "accident" arising from a particular set of circumstances), it is possible that such societies might have evolved further, to acquire some of the other attributes of unambiguous chiefdoms and states as they appeared in the New World (for clearly the analogies with Peru, Mesoamerica, and the Mississippi valley—and perhaps even China—are very striking). Certain patterns, therefore, seem to be potentially present on a global scale and showed a tentative manifestation in Europe before being overlain by others. Perhaps in the beginning northwestern Europe was, indeed, America.

This point is therefore not just of local but also of comparative significance, and it may be deployed to illuminate areas within the Old World that were more central to future patterns of development. Where else might similar sorts of phenomena have been manifested? Imagine a rich coastline where rivers reach the sea and unusual conditions of ecological productivity support a relatively dense foraging population, just as in Atlantic Europe. Imagine also that farming groups have spread into the adjacent interior with a pattern of villages and cereal cultivation. One might postulate a similar series of interactions between these elements, leading to similarly elaborate forms of ceremonialism growing out of the adoption of farming. Now imagine that the rivers, larger than those of northwestern Europe and occupying downfaulted basins, deposit large quantities of silt, which both precludes the construction of large stone monuments that are easy to recognize archaeologically and actively obscures the archaeological record by continuing alluvial accumulation. This area is, of course, southern Mesopotamia, but it might equally be the Nile Delta or the Indus Valley (or even the Amazon or the Orinoco). The European evidence suggests that the greatest elaboration of settlement patterns, and the emergence of ceremonial centers that then took on something of a life of their own, occurred not where farming spread by means of the straightforward proliferation of farming settlements but where more complex interactions took place with already existing foraging populations. Because we know nothing about the original, foraging inhabitants of the lower Mesopotamian plain, they have generally been given little role in discussions of the later prehistory of this area (save for speculation as to whether they spoke Sumerian). The European analogy suggests that this background may be relevant in explaining some of the distinctive features of the southern alluvium. One early aspect may well have been the presence of ceremonial centers (not necessarily initially concentrations of permanent population) arising from the diversity of food sources and the mobility of their exploitation. Such ceremonial centers would have had an important role as nodal points in the distribution of stone (and by this time also copper) resources in this largely stoneless area, just as did the ceremonial monuments of northwestern Europe.[3] These conditions could well have produced a rather different pattern of existence from that typical of areas such as northern Mesopotamia with a more "conventional" Neolithic background.[4] Although there is no direct archaeological evidence to support such a reconstruction (because there is no archaeological evidence for this period at all in southern Mesopotamia), the comparison with northwestern Europe suggests that right from the beginning—in this case the seventh millennium c. B.C.—there already could have been fundamental differences between southern and northern Mesopotamia that are historically relevant to the contrasts that increasingly emerged in the following millennia.[5] Similar considerations apply to the Nile Delta and the Indus Valley; there may be more "complexity" deeply underlying the historical patterns there than the archaeology would currently suggest.

My point in making this rather far-fetched comparison is that the conditions leading to the rapid development of social complexity are likely to be *conjunctions* of circumstances in which factors giving rise to centralization, intensification of trading relations, and technological innovation coincided and reinforced one another. Each of these features may occur in the absence of the others, without precipitating the long-term, cumulative consequences that we observe in that minority of cases in which the process "took off" into civilization, urbanism, and statehood. From the experience of prehistoric Europe, we might suggest that two sorts of power relations were present, at different times: ideological coordination of group activities leading to the construction of large ceremonial monuments (Renfrew's group-oriented chiefdoms), and control of mobile possessions including techniques of acquiring rare materials and transforming them into valuable artifacts (Renfrew's individualizing chiefdoms). In the European case these were largely dissociated and, in some sense, incompatible. In the case of Mesopotamia (and perhaps wherever pristine states emerged)

they coincided and reinforced each other synergetically. This point is likely to be lost in stadial models that are based on supposedly universal sequences of change or that privilege particular aspects as primary features. In reality, there is an element of coincidence (which is not to be confused with accident or blind chance). I shall return to the question of why these different sets of conditions may have coincided in Mesopotamia, but for the moment let us go back to prehistoric Europe.

MATERIAL CONSUMPTION AND THE TRANSFORMATION OF EUROPEAN CULTURE

Part of the problem of trying to summarize prehistoric European developments in sociological terms stems from the very abstraction that they employ: if *chiefdom* is used to describe any form of central coordination of activities, then we have constantly to be adding adjectives to specify what kinds of activities are being coordinated. It might be better to start the other way round and ask what sorts of activities were taking place before looking at what sorts of social structures they potentiate. Although this approach might seem like a return to inductive artifact description, I hope to preserve an element of comparative abstraction—or at least to balance those obvious features of the archaeological record that are canonized in period names (Stone Age, Copper Age, Bronze Age, Iron Age) with less easily recognized features that may be equally important.

I have already hinted at one innovation that separates the earlier from later phases of pre-state farming societies: plow agriculture. This was one application of a more general principle, the use of animals (initially oxen) as draft teams, and it appeared sometime around 3500 B.C. at the same time as simple wheeled vehicles. This, in turn, was part of a still larger phenomenon, the use of animals as power sources, and would include the use of horses, initially for riding or pack use (c. 3000 B.C.) and then as draft animals for specially designed light vehicles for sport and warfare (chariots, after 2000 B.C.). In addition, new breeds of sheep, with woolly fleeces, were introduced into Europe (c. 3000 B.C.), as opposed to the hairy breeds known in the Neolithic, making possible the production of woolen textiles. Animals were kept in larger numbers, and products made from milk (both from ovicaprids and cattle) probably became more important. Other features include the first use of tree crops (principally vine and olive) in the eastern Mediterranean, which are closely associated with a further element, namely, the use of fermentation processes to produce alcoholic drinks—not just from grapes but from other sugars in milk and honey. Impressed by all these new "secondary products" of domestic livestock, I suggested in 1981 that these innovations formed part of a subsistence revolution, which I called the "secondary-products revolution" (Sherratt 1981). Although it was mistaken in at least one aspect (for it has recently been demonstrated that milk products were used as early as 4000 B.C. in northwestern Europe), the rapid introduction to a large area of so many fundamental elements and the subsequent changes they made possible was indeed a radical shift, in which animal traction was the critical feature. This transition, between 3500 and 2000 B.C., also included the introduction of new ways of making metal artifacts such as bivalve-mold casting and copper alloying. Although these innovations were taken up at different rates in different areas (with tree crops confined to Mediterranean climates), most of them were widespread in Europe by 2000 B.C. and account for the much more uniform appearance of Bronze Age cultures in Europe by comparison with the diversity of Neolithic and Copper Age patterns. Whereas in southeastern Europe many of these innovations were absorbed more or less simultaneously into a new pattern, in northern and western Europe there was a more extended transition in which older patterns of monument building persisted and became more elaborate (combining, for instance, the construction of megalithic monuments with the use of animal traction for plowing). There was a period of evident tension between the older tradition of collective burial and monumental construction and the traditions that were ultimately to replace it, which stressed the individual consumption of prestige drinks (giving rise to archaeological labels such as the "bell-beaker culture") and the possession of items of weaponry such as metal daggers and archery equipment. The new features collectively transformed the primary productive systems of farming Europe and the range of products that could be made from them, as well as the sorts of social arrangements to which they gave rise.

The contrasts between earlier and later forms of pre-state societies in Europe, therefore, were intimately connected with the range of resources available to them and the modes of consumption (and monopolization of such consumption) that they allowed (cf. Dietler 1990). These features go beyond "subsistence" (in that they involved the creation of new forms of consumption) but are perhaps not yet an economy (in the sense of a generally exchangeable set of commodities). Among early farming groups there were few signs of social differentiation in the artifactual repertoire, beyond contrasts of age and gender and perhaps of role in the case of shamanic activities; after 2000 B.C. there is a clear elite consumption pattern in what was worn (woolen clothes, bronze ornaments), eaten and drunk (feasting equipment, with a heavy emphasis on drinking rituals), and used as a means of transport (horses, wheeled vehicles, boats), and especially in metal weaponry. These items of expensive personal equipment would have been available to a minority of the population, but they played a culturally prominent role. The accumulation of such items, and livestock more generally, would have been a token of success; these items were sometimes placed in graves or represented in rock art. Above all, bronze itself provided a liquid medium of exchange, as a substance that could be both accumulated and transformed into different shapes, as well as being rare and valued in itself, thus permitting a degree of local capital formation. This made possible a concentration and monopolization in individual hands, which could be translated to some degree into the ability to obtain goods or services for personal projects in a way that would have been impossible when labor was coordinated largely by ideological sanctions and arguably for communal purposes. It is this change in material opportunities that underlies Renfrew's distinction between group-oriented and individualizing elaboration. The mobility of material wealth was translated into a more fluid and overtly competitive mode of existence.

Within such arrangements there was scope for the organized long-distance flow of certain high-value materials. Although certain forms of fine stone (notably greenstone for axes and obsidian for knives and arrowheads) had achieved regional distribution in the Neolithic, in the Bronze Age there are examples of transcontinental distribution, for instance, taking amber from the Baltic to the Mediterranean. As I suggested above, the exchangeability of bronze actively encouraged the local production of other high-value exchangeables (Shennan 1999). Livestock (especially horses) may have been part of the equations, but there was no transport infrastructure capable of moving heavy bulk products, so subsistence production was inevitably localized. What did move were the materials that Wallerstein (1974) slightingly refers to as "preciosities"—substances with high value and low bulk. These materials may have included organics, and I have already mentioned furs, to which one might add honey and plant products for use as medicine. None of these underwent an elaborate manufacturing process before transportation. It was the substance, not the form, that was important, and bronze objects that moved across stylistic boundaries were usually recast into local types. Textiles, so far as one can gather from fragmentary evidence, were largely regionally produced and not items of long-distance exchange. There were no specialized transport containers, and the boats were canoes with limited tonnage. Where regular paths of trade were con-

strained by passes through mountains, they were sometimes controlled by fortified sites, though these had the character of "hillforts" rather than more substantial settlements or concentrations of population, at least until just before the arrival of the Romans. The appearance of these long-distance routes was closely related to the extension of urban communities along the Mediterranean, from east to west: (1) the "Danube corridor" was important in the late third and early second millennium B.C. (with traffic crossing the Carpathians); (2) as maritime traffic reached Italy, trans-Alpine routes became important (the classic "Amber Route"); and (3) in the first millennium B.C., as the western Mediterranean was opened up, the routes across Gaul and along the Atlantic coast became more important (Sherratt 1993).

I have presented this whistle-stop tour of temperate European prehistory in order to make the point that it is very difficult to describe this continental scale of development simply in the abstract terms of social evolutionism. The older, artifactual terminology captured something of the reality of the transformation that was taking place, which was a cumulative set of changes in material culture (and thus, in some sense, of "economy"), involving fundamental alterations in consumption patterns and thus in the sets of social arrangements that grew up to control their production and flow. It was with this in mind that I chose the phrases of my title—material resources, capital, and power: the coevolution of society and culture. It makes no sense to dichotomize these two aspects, even though there is no simple, deterministic set of relationships between one and the other. But I have had another objective in mind in cataloging all these new features, which altered the rules of the social games that could be played. For I believe that all the features I have mentioned were introduced from outside the region and that as a group they were most unlikely to have emerged endogenously from within it. Moreover most, perhaps all, of them were generated within a set of conditions that uniquely obtained within the urbanizing societies of the Near East, for reasons that have to do with the concentration of capital. Both the elements of agrarian production that I attempted to summarize as a secondary-products revolution and the advanced forms of metalworking that mark the beginning of the Bronze Age achieved their widespread application as a result of Near Eastern urbanization.[6] If I am correct in this interpretation, then Childe was absolutely right in his underlying model of European development, even though wrong in many aspects of dating and detail.

Thus stadial models are inherently misleading, or at least inadequate to capture much of what was going on. The sequence of societies cannot be described simply as a layer cake, since after the fourth millennium these groups were not so much pre-historic as para-historic, existing on the margin of literate communities whose existence critically affected their conditions of life. Instead, the situation is captured by those rather old-fashioned diagrams associated with names such as Childe, Braidwood, Willey, or Grahame Clark, which show sloping horizons with arrows going out from their V-shaped central structures. As with Andre Gunder Frank's (1978) description of the roles of Asia, Europe, and the Americas in the genesis of the Industrial Revolution, the stories of the component regions cannot be told separately. What is needed is a *structural* account of their interrelationships. For such an account, world-systems theory needs customizing for use over millennia rather than centuries.

STRUCTURAL ARTICULATION: CUSTOMIZING THE WORLD-SYSTEMS APPROACH

It was to accomplish this translation that some years ago I wrote an article titled "What Would a Bronze Age World System Look Like?" (Sherratt 1993). Like many others, I took my inspiration from Jane Schneider's brilliant 1977 review of Wallerstein's *Modern World System* (1974). Schneider accepted Wallerstein's characterization of the inner parts of the system, with its two zones, each necessary to the other: a *core* area, where manufacturing capacity (and thus the production of commoditized and added-value goods, such as textiles) was concentrated, and its *periphery*, which supplied many of the prime-value materials (e.g., metals and wool). But she also emphasized the importance of a further zone, beyond these two, for which she chose the term *margin*. This area does not participate in the bulk transfer of goods, either manufactures or raw materials, but instead is characterized by the circulation of high-value, low-bulk goods (Wallerstein's "preciosities") that were nevertheless capable of forming long-distance chains of indirect connections. The margin is thus affected by developments in the two central zones (for instance in techniques and consumption patterns) but is not incorporated so directly in complementary exchanges. This explanation has an obvious relevance to situations like that of later prehistoric Europe, in relation to the Near East, and it clarifies where Childe's descriptions were going wrong. The unsatisfactory feature of many of Childe's specific explanations stemmed from his vision, derived essentially from the first millennium B.C., of an active penetration of Europe by traders and colonists, phenomena typical of a periphery. This is indeed what was happening, from east to west along the Mediterranean, with the foundation of trading outposts from Greece and the Levant in the Bronze and early Iron Ages (A. Sherratt and S. Sherratt 1991; S. Sherratt and A. Sherratt 1993). But the processes affecting temperate Europe, of the kinds that I have described above, were very much less direct, even though they caused a profound transformation in its indigenous cultures and their social arrangements. Within a compressed chronology Childe's misperceptions are perhaps understandable (although in part he chose his chronology to suit his model), but it gives quite the wrong impression of the much more drawn-out and indirect processes that we now know were taking place.

Nevertheless, there is much to be said for Childe's basic structural analysis of what was happening; for the critical episodes of European transformation were taking place between 3500 and 2000 B.C., at a time when the rapidly urbanized societies of Mesopotamia were creating a new set of relationships with their immediate hinterlands, including the foundation of colonial settlements articulating long-distance relationships and channeling flows of raw materials from the surrounding steppe and mountain zones (Algaze 1993). This expansion had a wider impact, reflected in the creation of a large adjacent area—ultimately encompassing most of Europe and the steppe zone—to which critical innovations "escaped" and were transferred to new cultural contexts in which they were incorporated and reinterpreted, becoming integral parts of the indigenous cultures that were at the same time transformed—in terms of diet, material possessions, and modes of display—by this wave of innovations. The central area (at this stage including Mesopotamia, the Levant, and Egypt, and in the other direction the Iranian Plateau, the Indus, and the Gulf) has a recognizable, if not yet modern, economy. But in the outer, marginal zone the circulation of goods—even ones that were created by new techniques of production—were still much more embedded in local cycles of exchange and were neither produced nor traded in such quantities. Moreover, they had shorter production chains, involved fewer components, and required the coordination of fewer persons in their production; they did not show the same degree of infrastructural elaboration.

Once in existence, this whole urban and para-urban system began a process of cumulative growth, expanding both at its outer edge, through the spread of techniques, and in its inner "nucleus" (core plus periphery), through the conversion of formerly peripheral areas into secondary cores. (Such descriptions inevitably sound like cosmologists' accounts of the early phases of the universe, but that is probably inevitable when we try to talk about historical phenomena on this scale.) Within the central nucleus there were relatively rapid changes in scale and in the density of connections. This was never a smooth and continuous process and saw sudden dislocations and reorientations—the "dizzyingly abrupt shifts" of Adams's masterly description in 1974, emphasizing its historical contingencies as well as its organic pattern of proliferation.[7] Formerly peripheral areas joined a growing core region, becoming centers of manufacturing and secondary states in the later third and second millennia by the kinds of processes that economists call import substitution (well described in Jane Jacobs's classic *Economy of Cities* [1970]). These processes themselves generated a further periphery (for instance in highland Anatolia), and the inception of maritime supply routes reaching along the Mediterranean led to the emergence of successive island and peninsular centers of urban development in Crete and Greece. The core region, which began as a more or less continuous block of urbanized polities in southern Mesopotamia and Susiana, became discontinuous as further foci of development appeared (Egypt and later the Indus Valley). The growing "nuclear" structure of core and periphery extended into and incorporated adjacent areas of formerly marginal societies. The whole structure is well represented by the nested series of V-shaped horizons of culture-historical diagrams. What this description emphasizes is the organic unity underlying the whole process; urban systems were able to proliferate in the way they did because the areas into which they expanded had already been culturally transformed by the spread of consumption patterns generated when urban life itself was still locally restricted.

This nested series of expansion processes —continuing a pattern of center-edge dispersal ultimately going back to the spread of farming itself—is fundamental to understanding why urban proliferation was able to take the course that it did. This can be illustrated in a comparison between two episodes of external contact between South Mesopotamian cultures and their neighbors. The Uruk colonies on the bend of the Euphrates in Syria in the mid-fourth millennium could operate in the way they did to tap the products of surrounding regions because the societies of the adjacent areas—the upper Euphrates and the northern rim of the Fertile Crescent—were already relatively advanced. It was possible to set up a relationship in which the local mobilization of goods for exchange was to a large extent in the hands of local elites. Contrast this with another expansionist movement, from the same starting point but in the opposite direction, some two thousand years earlier, which carried 'Ubaid pottery down the Gulf to eastern Arabia, Bahrain, and Qatar but left no permanent trading stations (Oates 1977). These small exploratory missions led to no long-standing relationship because there were effectively no partners; the sparse local population lacked the infrastructure to respond to the opportunity.[8] In the first case intervention led to a lively interaction with local groups (and their further contacts arguably sparked the processes leading to the emergence of complex society in Egypt); in the second case nothing much happened at all. (Part of the answer lies in radical environmental changes involving increasing aridity in the Gulf area, but this does not affect the basic argument.) The difference lay in the relatively dense populations, with already quite sophisticated patterns of consumption, that existed in Syria and the Levant; southern Mesopotamian input was able to catalyze a more complex series of interactions in societies that already possessed considerable potential for change. In the same way the creation of a wide penumbra of "marginal" Bronze Age societies provided a set of social arrangements into which expanding urban supply networks could tap; in the right combination of circumstances they could generate new foci of urban growth. The fact that societies adjacent to the earliest urban communities had already achieved a certain degree of complexity was critical for the formation of economic complementarity and the propagation of urban networks.

This is a fundamental point in appreciating how the idea of a world system needs to be adapted in applying it to the circumstances of early urban societies. The fact that "colonial" expansion in the last few hundred years has involved the projection of power over long distances, with industrial societies taking over by force territories often occupied only by hunter-gatherers, gives a false perspective to colonial processes in the past, when "colonies" were often relatively small-scale trade missions, set up in the interstices between indigenous centers of power and owing their transformative effects to catalysis as much as conquest. This means that conceptions of world systems based on the experience of the last few centuries fail to capture the much more nuanced character of earlier encounters and the often dialectical relationships they generated. The contrast between colonizer and colonized was often slight (hence the reaction of many North Mesopotamianists in rejecting a world-systems description, because "their" sites seem in many ways no less advanced than those of the south!) and certainly did not involve conquest or even "informal empire." Instead, the transmission of lifestyles and ideologies seems to have been an important aspect of the process, reflected, for instance, in the spread of Uruk pottery assemblages (most evidently liquid containers for fermented products and bevel-rim bowls perhaps for baking leavened bread) and the food habits they imply—as much Coca-Cola-ization as colonization in its more recent sense.

Looking at regional sequences with this model in mind alters the interpretative framework for cultural change in these circumstances. The archaeological record of any particular area within this expanding system can be seen as a sequence of stages of incorporation in the larger system, from margin to periphery to core (Sherratt and Sherratt 1991). In the case of the Aegean, for instance, one could describe the area in the later fourth and earlier third millennia (with the Early Bronze Age appearance of animal traction, tree crops, textiles, and wine production) as representing a *marginal* relationship with western Asia, followed during the course of the third millennium by the production of materials for export (especially silver, extracted from lead ores by cupellation) and the adoption of western Asiatic sealing systems in a few nodal centers (such as Lerna in southern mainland Greece) in a *peripheral* relationship. This, in turn, was followed at the beginning of the second millennium by the appearance of palace-centered towns such as Knossos, linked by maritime trade (in large vessels using sails) to similarly organized societies in the eastern Mediterranean—the emergence of a secondary *core*. It is a model that, with modification, can be applied to many parts of the Mediterranean in subsequent centuries. The transitions were so gradual that if considered in isolation they might appear like phases of an autonomous, internally generated process—this was, indeed, the thesis of Colin Renfrew's *Emergence of Civilisation* (1972). But when seen in a wider setting, this sequence takes on a different light, as it fits within a pattern characterized by a consistent extension of the area of urban settlement and its surrounding supply zone. It seems more realistic to treat the whole system as a single, growing network that successively transformed the areas with which it came into contact. Nevertheless, Renfrew's insistence on the gradual and cumulative nature of the process is perfectly correct, and it did not involve mass migration or military conquest in the manner of recent episodes of incorporation in an expanding world system. It was, however, in its own small way an episode in the 5,000-year-long process of cumulative "globalization."

The notion of a world system is thus important in articulating the developmental histories of all the societies that became entangled in the nascent globalization process and the very different kinds of relationships that arose from it (Denemark et al. 2000). The mere characterization of areas as "marginal" or "peripheral" is no more sophisticated than describing societies as "chiefdoms" or "states," but it does capture the interconnectedness of the process in a way that stadial models fail to do. Moreover, it does not universally privilege the social over the material (though it is in danger of doing

the converse, if based too literally on the model of the modern world system) but leaves open the dialectical relationship between material flows and social structures, and the great diversity of specific arrangements to which they have given rise.

THE PROPERTIES OF THE CORE: COMPLEXITY, CAPITAL, AND COMMODITIZATION

All this discussion has been leading up to the critical question, how did it all start? If so much of the pattern of subsequent development can be attributed to the widening effects of early urban societies and the world system of which they were the core, how did these come about in the first place? The question is rendered more acute if we cannot use later examples of complex but nonurban (i.e., chiefdom) societies as snapshots of the historical process and models for what might have preceded urbanism itself—for, like the biological evolution of the human species, urbanization transformed its prototypes so that there are no living exemplars of the intermediate stages. It is a task for archaeology and the archaeological imagination, as that is the only body of evidence that pertains directly to the problem. The question is even more challenging if seen in a global perspective. We are fortunate in having at least two completely independent trials of the process, in the Old and New Worlds; but many of the features that have played a prominent role in our description so far—such as metallurgy and use of domestic animals for traction—are characteristic of early civilizations only in the Old World and are rare or absent (or late) in the New. We must distinguish between those aspects of the process that were historically specific and the more general set of factors that produced literate, urban societies as equifinal outcomes from very different sorts of agrarian predecessors—a tough intellectual task. Nevertheless, a consciousness of the requirements of a general model will help achieve the right degree of abstraction.

I begin with a term that I have employed loosely and descriptively here—*added value*. The defining difference between core and periphery is that the manufacturing processes are concentrated in the core, which is where the the value is added to raw materials (either imported or locally produced) by the application of labor—a point emphasized by Adams (1974) for Mesopotamia in the same year that Wallerstein's publication (1974) introduced the explicit notion of a world system. Exchanges between core and periphery involve not necessarily a complementarity of primary materials (grain versus stone and metal, in Kohl's pioneer formulation [1978]) but rather an asymmetry in the application of labor and expertise (Marfoe 1987). (Here the question of the mobilization of labor, raised above in relation to ceremonial centers, becomes relevant.) This asymmetry provides the dynamic for growth and the accumulation of capital. Exporting manufactured products (even to the areas that supplied the raw materials in the first place, and sometimes even in exchange for them) yields a profit: 1 cloth equals (say) 5 bales of raw wool (cf. Sraffa 1960). This difference is not simply a material one, however, as it is predicated on the existence of a demand for the manufactured good—it is simultaneously both material and expressive (like Calvin Klein underwear). The value is not inherent in the product; the creation of the demand for it is as critical as the production of the means to satisfy it (cf. Douglas and Isherwood 1979). The key to the problem is thus the creation of products embodying added value.

The choice of textiles in the example above is not arbitrary; the textile industry has been fundamental to economic growth down to the early stages of the Industrial Revolution in the eighteenth century. Clothing is a basic item of material culture but also one that has undergone major changes as the world has become "civilized." Indigenous peoples around the world typically wear far fewer clothes than members of urban societies, who carry around physiologically quite unnecessary quantities of woven body coverings (which encapsulate all sorts of social messages about status, role, and identity). Moreover, this is often the first element of core culture to be transferred in contact situ-

ations, as shown by photographs of "native" peoples taken around the beginning of the last century, showing women undertaking such tasks as harvesting wild seeds into baskets but now wearing long Victorian dresses (or bowler hats). Telling the natives they are naked is a traditional task of the missionaries—selling them the clothes is that of the merchants. The ideological and material aspects are complementary and indivisible, and together constitute what we inadequately describe as a change in consumption habits. This telescoped example nevertheless summarizes one of the essential attributes of urban societies and those affected by them—namely, the greatly increased volume of manufactured products they require that had not been necessary before. This elaboration of material culture is at the heart of the urbanizing process, and the lengthened chains of production and interdependence are essential to it.

Another critical area is that of diet, from which, indeed, the metaphor of consumption is literally derived. Much of the economic history of ancient Mediterranean societies can be summarized in the story of two liquid commodities. As pithily described by Pliny (*Natural History* xiv, 150), *Duo sunt liquores, humanis corporibus gratissimi: intus vini, foris olei*: There are two liquids most pleasing to human bodies—wine inside, oil outside (Sherratt 1995b). By Roman times these were bulk commodities—transported in the pottery amphorae that survive in shipwrecks or in fragmentary form on rubbish dumps around ports—that were carried in large quantities by sea around the Mediterranean. Neither is a physiological necessity, and for millennia the inhabitants of this region had existed without them. Yet they were a feature of "civilized" life there from its Bronze Age beginnings, when they were produced on a small scale in palaces and elite centers. A similar observation could be made about the civilizations of Mesopotamia that preceded those of the Mediterranean, though in this case the beverage was beer and the oil was clarified butter (ghee), produced from milk along with other lactic products (Englund 1995; Teuber 1995). The work of Hans Nissen and his colleagues (Nissen et al. 1993) on the earliest Protoliterate texts of later-fourth-millennium Mesopotamia has shown that many of these clay tablets are accounts that record the delivery of quantities of the raw materials—grain, malt, milk—and the amounts of beer, cheese, and oil that were made from them for consumption on ceremonial occasions (as the beer would not keep very long; cf. Dietler and Hayden 2001). Although these products are unlikely to have been transported very far, the implied scale of production (especially of milk, indicating the existence of specialized dairy herds of the kind that are represented on Uruk seals in association with the sign of the goddess Inanna) shows a degree of investment in both specialized production and secondary processing, which is likely to have taken place in the context of temple estates. Moreover, the occurrence of pictographic signs depicting plows and what are probably threshing sledges indicates the use of animal traction in cultivation, involving expensive draft animals (Halstead 1995; Sherratt 2002a)—forms of primary production that made sense only within economies of scale.

The manufacture of both textiles and organic consumables was thus fundamental to the processes accompanying early urbanization. The association with the earliest writing systems is not fortuitous, for many of the pictograms employed refer specifically to the commodities so far discussed and their ingredients. Moreover, the immediate antecedents of these inscribed signs were small clay models ("complex tokens," collected in a clay envelope or *bulla*, impressed with a seal), which included representations of liquid containers and, significantly, bales of raw wool. Even more interestingly, these miniature models and the pictograms that succeeded them clearly show forms of containers that are easily recognizable among contemporary pottery assemblages (such as the spouted jar) and that are characteristic of the types carried into surrounding areas by the "Uruk expansion," such as the colonial settlements on the middle Euphrates, and then reproduced in

adjacent areas (see Stein, this volume).[9] Indeed, the circulation and consumption of these liquid commodities can be related to two important technological innovations that characterize this period: the introduction of wheel-made, mass-produced pottery seems to be closely related to the need to provide containers for such liquids, whereas the manufacture of sheet-metal vessels—of silver and perhaps gold—seems to have been pioneered in connection with drinking equipment for them. The precious materials would have been appropriate for precious beverages (Sherratt and Sherratt 2001).[10] Just as historians of the Industrial Revolution point to a preceding "consumer revolution" involving especially oriental textiles, pottery, and exotic drinks (de Vries 1993), so the urban revolution in Uruk Mesopotamia involved its own consumer revolution, concerned especially with fermented food processing, animal products, and woolen textiles.[11] This entailed a degree of specialization in primary production and lengthened chains of transformation—cereal growing > malting > brewing; herding > dairying > preparation of milk products—both of which might be complicated by the addition of further herbal ingredients. Moreover, this pattern, although arising in a specific lowland environment, could be translated into other resources in the adjacent Mediterranean vegetation zone, specifically vine for the intoxicating liquor, and olive for the oil, as seems to have happened in southern Anatolia and the Levant in the later fourth millennium (Belisario et al. 1994), arguably in response to the more elaborate Uruk cuisine. The forms of elite consumption that spread along the Mediterranean in association with urban life in the subsequent millennia can be seen to have their origins in the transformation of clothing and dietary habits that accompanied the genesis of urbanism itself.

In the model being put forward here, the initial shift that created the potential for these future developments was an elaboration in lifestyle connected initially with ceremonial (and subsequently with the demonstration of social difference) in what was worn and eaten. This required the mobilization both of quantities of organic raw materials and of labor for their transformation. The materials were probably initially of local origin (in the sense that they were produced within the differentiated sectors of a single unit of production) and not initially traded far beyond the areas in which they were created (even though they quickly came to be so, once their potential was realized, as in the case of textiles). They were products of divided labor and "commodities" in the original sense of the word, namely mass-produced goods in convenient units for storage and movement, not necessarily disembedded exchangeable items moving between units of production and consumption (as with Roman wine and oil). It was the very existence of these "embedded commodities" that contained the potential for the growth of economic complexity through export and regional specialization in production. The creation of such goods was a precondition for the development of such economic rationalization. This is the missing element in portrayals of economic "takeoff" that describe the process in terms of an increasing scale of regional specialization, beginning with the emergence of economic complementarity in southern Mesopotamia and expanding to encompass surrounding areas (Algaze 2001b). Although this description is almost certainly true—and the best one so far offered—it was predicated on the emergence of these consumption patterns in the first place.[12]

The problems of describing this initial critical period are manifold because the Uruk heartland in southern Iraq is less well known than its periphery (because of alluviation, the scale of subsequent occupation, and political problems) and because of the inherent difficulty in characterizing a period of transition with all its unique features. The subsequent phases of Mesopotamian civilization in the third millennium are better understood, with a more abundant and less ambiguous textual record; but it is hard to know which features can be extrapolated back to the earlier stages. By the later third millennium employment in textile production in southern Mesopotamia had achieved a scale that dwarfs that of a comparably sized area of England on the eve of the Industrial Revolution. The figures cited by Adams (this volume) and Waetzoldt (1972) for Ur III period describe production units employing thousands of workers and, by this stage, providing extensive exports of finished cloth. To project this pattern back to the previous millennium, however, may be to miss the point that what gave this area its initial advantage was not the mass export of its commodities so much as the simultaneous export of a few durable manufactured items and of its modes of consumption, which appealed particularly to existing elites in adjacent areas. This "ideological capital" (Bourdieu 1984) was only later converted into "commodity capital," as local elites were induced to supply raw materials in exchange for their participation in a cultural as well as an economic process. An increasing scale of regional specialization in production could thus have been an emergent property of a cultural transformation, resulting from the strong positive feedback inherent in added-value production, whose outputs can be exchanged for increasing quantities of their own raw materials—the discovery of an autocatalytic cycle (cf. Kauffman 1995).

WHY DID IT HAPPEN?

A theme of this chapter has been the importance of conjuncture, the coming together of specific elements in a way that cannot be described in the language of abstract evolutionism. This coincidence (or rather co-incidence, to emphasize that the conjunction is not purely random, as our current use of *coincidence* would imply) is a necessary part of a historical account of the emergence of those properties that evolutionists have rightly emphasized. The features that came together in the genesis of urbanism were both ecological and social, in that they relate both to the resources specific to the region ("factor endowments," as economists call them) and to the social structures that motivated their exploitation in particular ways. Although their conjunction was historically contingent, the two aspects were not causally independent—social arrangements grow up in the context of particular ecologies, as my discussion of Neolithic ceremonial centers tried to show. My suggestion in this section is that the kinds of ceremonial centers that emerged in the unusual ecological conditions of southern Mesopotamia (manifested, when archaeological evidence becomes available, in the mud-brick temples of the 'Ubaid period) provided the setting for new forms of coordinated labor that explored hitherto unexploited aspects of their immediate environment. For these historical reasons, the two features that I identified in prehistoric Europe as being largely disjunct—the ideological mobilization of labor on a large scale and the negotiated flow of material goods—here came together in what proved to be an explosive combination.

Although the potential for creating added-value products had existed for many millennia, practically since the beginning of farming, these resources would come to be used on any scale only when there was some means of concentrating and coordinating the activities of different groups of workers into long chains of preparation involving delayed consumption. In disembedded economies where goods exist as commodities, this is achieved by the accumulation of capital, which in this case usually means quantities of the principal medium of exchange. Before the existence of commodities, however, such capital can take only an "ideological" form—for instance, the belief that production is "the work of the gods" (in the same way that for many farming societies it is "the work of the ancestors"; Gudeman 1986). The first element that distinguished South Mesopotamian societies was their ability to coordinate the activities of large numbers of workers both in primary production (probably male) and in manufacturing activity (probably female). There are many indications that these activities were "ideologically embedded" in a religious context and seem to have been intimately associated with temple

institutions (in the case of herding, literally "under the sign of Inanna," as shown on cylinder seals). Reaction against the oversimplified reconstruction of a monolithic *Tempelwirtschaft* in the following millennium has tended to distract attention from this fundamental aspect of Uruk organization. This degree of central (or "communal") production may have initially arisen in the context of the incorporation of indigenous foraging communities within regimes of cereal farming, but it was certainly strengthened both by the needs of irrigation and by the uncertainties associated with this unusual lowland environment, as Adams has emphasized (this volume). A degree of differentiation in productive activities, both locally and regionally, was probably present from the beginning in relation to the different potential of different areas (fishing, stock raising, and cereal growing), as Thorkild Jacobsen (1976) long ago pointed out in relation to the local deities of the emerging cities (fishing at Ur, pastoralism at Uruk, cereal farming at Nippur). The ease of movement by river would have facilitated such transfers. Irrespective of whether some degree of organized exchange took place between centers, however, it can be argued that it was the scale of their core institutions that led to the exploration of new forms of production. These depended on the nature of local resources and the degree to which they could be transformed into value-added products. Two examples of distinctive local resources may be singled out as especially important in the emergence of distinctive modes of consumption.

One of these resources was date palms, which Adams (1981) has suggested existed in considerable natural stands at the head of the Gulf and whose pits are known from 'Ubaid contexts. Dates possess the greatest natural concentration of sugar of any fruiting plant (60–70 percent in cultivated strains), and their use is likely to have led to an early familiarity with fermentation processes and to the development of forms of food and drink involving fermentation in their preparation (Sherratt 1995b, 2002b). The production of alcoholic beverages for mass consumption (probably initially in ceremonial contexts) should not be underestimated as a mechanism of social solidarity, since the mind-altering properties of earlier plant psychotropics were probably associated with the more exclusive practices of shamanism. Collective ceremonies would have been all the more powerful if they involved all the important people getting drunk periodically, and belief that production was the work of the gods all the more compelling if one of the principal tasks of the deity was the mass production of an inebriant.

A second element would have been the adornment of temples with woven fittings and exotic wood, stone, and metal. As marsh dwellers and inhabitants of riverine terrain, the populations of this area had traditionally used reed bundles and reed matting as part of their architecture, so the use of textiles was a natural feature of their design. Weaving on any scale may therefore have begun for wall hangings and coverings even before it was used extensively for clothing (as is hinted at by the schematic design of wall paintings such as those at Malatya-Arslantepe in southeastern Turkey, whose material culture was heavily influenced by Uruk practices; Frangipane 1997). Moreover, the external contacts of the lowlanders in the early fourth millennium were directed eastward to the adjacent resources of the Zagros Mountains and the Iranian Plateau, which not only supplied stone (including the semimagical lapis lazuli), metal, and exotic timber but is likely to have been the origin of a new resource for textile production in the form of wool. This important but hitherto localized secondary product of certain strains of domestic sheep imparted a new set of possibilities to large-scale textile production. The early spread of Uruk assemblages to Susiana (modern Khuzestan), which represents the first phase of Uruk expansion (Algaze 1993), may plausibly be related to obtaining supplies of wool and woolly breeds of sheep in addition to the inorganic products to which that area gave access. Use of wool provided a wider range of textile products (for instance, by its ability to take a dye) than

hitherto, and woolen textiles (and woolly sheep) became widely dispersed by subsequent Uruk expansion up the Euphrates and by their adoption in areas far beyond the Uruk periphery—as far as northwestern Europe by the middle of the third millennium B.C.

This promotion of local resources, first into basic features of the urban economy and then by selective transmission to large parts of the Old World, is what I describe as a secondary-products revolution. Just as the Neolithic revolution can be understood only in relation to the ecology of large-seeded grasses in Mediterranean environments, so the elaboration of consumption patterns at the onset of the urban revolution in the fourth millennium can be understood only in relation to the biodiversity of the Fertile Crescent and its intimate juxtaposition of contrasting ecological niches, including the specific conditions for, for example, date palms, sheep, vines, olives, and donkeys and the potential for large-scale irrigation agriculture. The ecological diversity of western Asia (a unique conjunction of the conditions of the subtropical arid zone, the Tertiary mountain belt, and the Mediterranean Tethys remnant, at the junction of the Afro-Arabian and Eurasian tectonic plates) gave it an enormously wider range of potentially tradable products than ecologically more uniform areas to either north or south. This diversity existed as a latent potential, unleashed when products were invented that could convert parts of it into socially desirable commodities. Fermentation and the use of animal fibers for textile making were two of the critical steps in realizing this potential, creating added-value products from raw materials. The advantage of southern Mesopotamia would thus lie in the existence of institutions and structures that provided a framework for coordinating labor, in circumstances where there was a variety of opportunities for elaborating production. In this respect, what I presented in 1981 as a general revolution in subsistence is better seen as a change in the nature of consumption within the unique setting of a nascent urban economy, which made possible the conversion of ideological capital into the more tangible form of stores of exchangeable commodities and productive infrastructure.

The dissemination of these modes of consumption, especially up the Euphrates (Algaze 1993),[13] took place initially within a "colonial" movement whose motivations were probably as much ideological as economic in the conventional sense. Some of the innovations that were propagated took on a life of their own as they were imitated and reinterpreted in local contexts and transformed the lives of populations far removed from direct contact with their initiators. Rather more slowly, the organizational systems pioneered by the earliest urban communities also proliferated (albeit in fits and starts) until by the middle of the third millennium there was a network of interlinked urban areas with interregional bullion flows (Marfoe 1987) that make it not unreasonable to talk of an "economy" in something like the sense in which that term is used by economists.

CONCLUSIONS

The phenomenon that Childe identified as the urban revolution seems to me to mark a more definable threshold than comparative labels such as chiefdom or state, not least because this event (in the Old World at least) not merely introduced new properties of scale but also exercised a transformative effect on the consumption habits of surrounding human populations, whether they were directly involved in its supply networks or not. So widespread were those effects that it is very hard to find ethnographically recorded societies that had not already been profoundly altered by them—save in places such as Australia and New Guinea, which were so far removed from these developments as to be irrelevant to them. I suspect, therefore, that the societies involved in the initial transformation were far less familiar to us than they appear to be through the process of ethnographic comparison. They were, in important respects, unique and therefore resistant to accommodation in typological categories. The very

process of urbanization created many features (and particularly consumption practices) that are now characteristic of a whole range of societies but were not so before.

A critical feature of this revolution that has been insufficiently theorized is thus the creation of new forms of consumption and goods that cannot be described simply as "staples" (even though the accumulation of staples and their semiproducts was an essential part of the production cycle) or "prestige goods" (in the way in which this term has come to be used, usually meaning items of prime value whose value lies in their rarity), especially in the way in which this increasingly diverse range of products broke down the previous separation between different spheres of exchange. "Wealth" was not just accumulated; its very nature was redefined. This shift cannot be reduced simply to a gain in productivity (following, for example, the development of irrigation farming), as it involved the creation of a class of meaning-laden artifacts for which earlier societies had felt no need. It seems inescapable that this set of meanings was initially impressed on material items in a religious context, which transformed ideological capital into more tangible forms. The increasing complexity of interpersonal relationships was mirrored in an increasing complexity between actors and material items. It is in this sense that it is possible (and indeed necessary) to speak of a coevolution of society and culture.

The initial step, probably taken by only very few societies in human history, was thus the creation of a set of local commodities that once in existence transformed not only the processes of production and consumption but also the processes of exchange. In particular, they initiated the conversion cycle whereby increasing quantities of raw materials could be converted into added-value goods. This cycle gave rise to two contagious processes: a diffusion of techniques and a structural incorporation of neighboring societies into an interdependent network of differentiated producers, in part made possible by the cultural transformation that had already occurred. This enlarged arena gave

scope for further diversification and specialization in production and thus for the multiplication of alternative pathways for the circulation of goods. It is this feature that gives
"the economy" an increasing autonomy from
society in general, progressively disembedding goods from their immediate social contexts as the chains of production, distribution, and ultimate consumption grow longer.
"Economic rationality" is an emergent property of this growing set of relations (Hart
1982).[14] The societies considered in this volume (ancient chiefdoms and states) had traveled only a short distance along this road, but
this phase is perhaps the most difficult to analyze, as it brings together many of the most
fundamental ideas in the social sciences, often in unexpected combinations. Nevertheless, it involves information to which only archaeologists have direct access and problems
that they are uniquely able to solve.

Notes

1. This explanation inevitably oversimplifies the
question of why wealth is deposited in tombs.
It might reasonably be pointed out that
second-millennium Egypt, no less complex
and sophisticated than classical Greece, deposited vast wealth in royal graves (although
only a small sample of the ruler's total possessions). There is clearly no mechanical correlation between burial ritual and social complexity, but it is nonetheless true that in almost
all civilizations there is a recognizable shift
through time in the character of elite graves,
from containers of wealth objects (usually below ground) to monumental constructions
(usually above ground) that do not involve the
withdrawal of precious objects from circulation. This shift has sometimes been accompanied by explicit rules forbidding the removal
of bullion. Etruscan tombs show a sequence
from rich examples with objects of precious
metal (seventh century B.C.) to ones with only
bronze and pottery equivalents (sixth and fifth
century) to ones with carved or stucco representations of these objects on the walls (fourth
century). Such changes are closely related to
growing participation in world systems in
which flows of bullion are increasingly important and the accumulation of bullion stocks
is consciously promoted ("thesaurization").
Such factors affected the Mediterranean civilizations in the later first millennium B.C. and
China in the later first millennium A.D. This
change had apparently not yet occurred in the

New World at the time of European contact;
the contrasting attitudes toward objects of
precious metal is one of the most obvious features of that collision.

2. This is why Childe (1957), following an older
tradition of diffusionism, attributed them to
the activity of "megalithic missionaries," ultimately inspired by early urban societies in the
eastern Mediterranean. But as Renfrew (1973)
pointed out, most of Europe's megalithic monuments are older than the pyramids.

3. This role does not preclude other functions for
central facilities, and the local storage of grain
supplies in landscapes liable to inundation is
likely to have been a feature of local importance.

4. Indeed, some earlier episodes of Neolithic
elaboration, such as the Çatalhöyük phenomenon, also could be related to similarly complex interactions between spreading farmers
and preexisting forager populations.

5. This idea is certainly congruent with the first
perceptible pattern, the so-called 'Ubaid o period of the early sixth millennium, revealed in
the deepest levels at Tell el-Awayli, which
shows an elaborate mud-brick building. We
do not know its antecedents (since the excavations hit the current water table at 4.5 m and
were unable to penetrate farther), but it is not
unreasonable to speculate that the Mesopotamian temple complex may have had its ultimate origins in some sort of ceremonial center generated at an early date in the encounter
between farming and foraging populations.

6. To give but one example, I believe the donkey
was first domesticated as a pack animal on
long-distance overland routes supplying the
first cities and provided a model for horse do-
mestication on the other side of the Caucasus
Mountains. Such proliferating chains of consequences and hybridization (perhaps literally,
in this case) with local elements are typical of
the process by which innovations spread and
are incorporated in new contexts (see Sherratt
2002a).

7. The largest and most dramatic example was
the collapse of the entire Indus/Gulf network
around 1800 B.C., so that the system proliferated asymmetrically (along the Mediterranean) before northern India—this time centered on the Ganges—rejoined the club in the
seventh/sixth centuries B.C.

8. Nevertheless, the southern shore of the Gulf
(and especially the metal sources in Oman)
was later to be incorporated in the growing
Mesopotamian world system, but only in the
middle of the third millennium B.C., when
the Iranian Plateau had been opened up and
the Indus Valley had undergone urbanization.
It was then possible to invest more resources in

maritime trade routes; as so often, the question turns on the process of capital formation.

9. Even the most diagnostic artifact of the Uruk expansion, the bevel-rim bowl, could find an explanation in this context, if Alan Millard (1988) is correct in interpreting these simple open containers as molds for leavened bread—another feature of the preparation of complex foods by the fermentation process, closely related to the brewing of beer (see Sherratt 2002b).

10. In the absence of tombs, actual examples from the fourth millennium are exceptionally rare and occur only outside Mesopotamia. Yet the occurrence there of vessels of lead suggests that lead ores were de-silvered by cupellation, and the cheaper by-products have survived better than the more valuable silver ones, long remelted. The occurrence of rich graves in the Early Dynastic period, such as the Royal Cemetery at Ur, gives a more representative picture, with abundant gold and silver drinking vessels (see Sherratt and Sherratt 2001).

11. What would Uruk textiles have looked like? Representations are mostly of little help, as the figures are often nude (e.g., the priests on the Warka vase, though this may be a ritual inversion of normal vestments) or, even in the third millennium, apparently wear sheepskins with the fleece out. The crucial image is the figure named—enigmatically, if provocatively—"the man in the net skirt." He, like Inanna herself, wears what might be a blanket-sized piece of (woolen?) cloth.

12. McCorriston (1997) and Joffe (1998) discuss the role of textiles and fermented drinks, respectively, in the ancient Near East. Though they both usefully amplify earlier suggestions made on these topics, they do not fully situate them in a wider economic context.

13. These two complementary expansions, to Susiana and the middle Euphrates, would have linked two existing interaction spheres (on the Persian Plateau and southern Anatolia/northern Levant, respectively), placing southern Mesopotamia in a central position to mediate between them. This nodal position within a catchment area some 4,000 km in diameter, between Egypt and eastern Afghanistan, provided a unique opportunity for arbitraging a hitherto unparalleled range of organic and inorganic materials, albeit in relatively small amounts and within a largely communitarian framework in which such treasures were still the properties of the deities and their earthly homes, the temples.

14. Commoditization is thus a cumulative process, its further stages marked by (1) the increasing liquidity provided by market mechanisms, (2) money (a commodity whose only use is as a means of exchange), (3) the use of money to make more money, and (4) the commoditization of human labor itself, in the capitalist mode of production (Hart 1982).

7

Roman Economies
A Paradigm of Their Own

Glenn R. Storey

It is high time for a new synthetic treatment of the Roman economy, and it is especially gratifying to attempt it in the context of the stimulating cross-cultural analysis of political economies of complex societies represented by this volume. In this chapter I attempt to outline a paradigm for the Roman imperial system by merging the literature of Greco-Romanist scholars with anthropological discussions of states. The tenor of the literature in both fields is converging, albeit with the usual differences in cognitive styles (Snodgrass 1986:9–12). Both disciplines should recognize that features of the Roman Empire constitute a sufficiently unique manifestation of economic behavior in a highly complex imperial society to serve as a model for cross-cultural analysis in general. The Roman economy *is* a paradigm on its own, but it illustrates a preindustrial form of state economic behavior that is perfectly understandable and expectable in an ancient complex society, eminently comparable with other imperial societies of the past, and resonant even with more recent imperial manifestations.

This new treatment also speaks of Roman econom*ies*, plural. In this I am following up previous work (Storey 1999a:230) and supporting the arguments of Archibald et al. (2001) and Cartledge et al. (2002), who have elected to call their collections *Hellenistic Economies* and *Economies of Ancient Greece*, respectively. The plural is needed to address different levels of economic behavior, as argued by Archibald (2001:3–4). For large cultural systems such as the Hellenistic world or the Roman Empire (Figure 7.1), it makes sense to distinguish economic interaction at the local, regional and/or provincial, and systemwide levels.

The other reason for the plural is that recent research on the Mediterranean ancient economy distinguishes between private and public (state) economic behavior (Archibald et al. 2001; Lo Cascio and Rathbone 2000b). Economic realms beyond those of agriculture also have recently been explored (Mattingly and Salmon 2001) and thus constitute yet another system of economic behavior, along with work identifying different economies (pastoralism versus intensive cultivation) even within the realm of agriculture (Kehoe 1990; Whittaker 1988).

Finally, as others in this volume have done, I am building from the bottom up, integrating individual economic actors, institutions, and the entire system, assessing individual and institutional economic rationality, the role and function of entrepreneurship, and the question of regional and systemwide economic integration. The key to understanding the place of Roman economies in the development of complex sociopolitical systems is the general issue of economic "rationality," the character and function of "entrepreneurship," and beginning to think of Roman

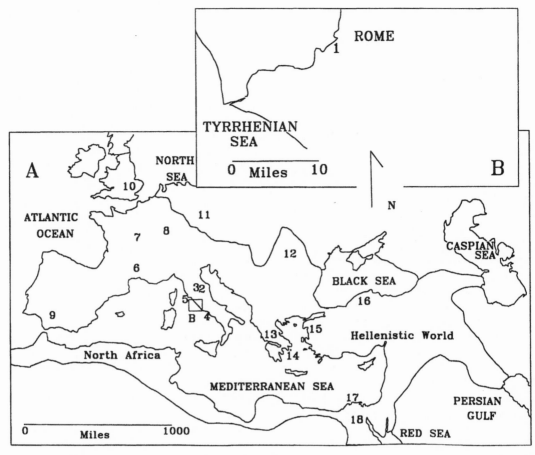

Figure 7.1. Places mentioned in the text. (1) Monte Testaccio, Rome; (2) Tifernum Tiberinum, location of Tuscan estate of Pliny the Younger; (3) Arezzo (ancient Arretium); (4) Puteoli, ancient port of Naples; (5) Cosa; (6) southern Gaul *terra sigillata* production zone; (7) central Gaul *terra sigillata* production zone; (8) eastern Gaul *terra sigillata* production zone; (9) Guadalquivir Valley, Spain; (10) Roman Britain; (11) Rhine/Danube frontier zone; (12) Dacia; (13) Roman Greece; (14) Attica (Athens); (15) Pergamon; (16) Pontus and Bithynia; (17) Roman Egypt; (18) Appianos estate, Fayûm. Because so much evidence comes from Roman North Africa and the Hellenistic world, both zones are marked.

economies as constituting an early manifestation of Wallerstein's (1974) world economy, which we should probably call an "ancient world economy."

BACKGROUND

Before setting out the Roman economies paradigm, however, it is necessary to revisit an old, related debate in both classical scholarship and economic anthropology—the primitivist versus modernist debate in the former (on the history of that debate, see Pearson 1957; for an update, see Harris 1993) and the substantivist versus formalist debate in the latter. I concur with Isaac (1993, 1996) in hoping that these dichotomies would just "go away," but they will not. We cannot make progress in the study of ancient economies without significant reliance on modeling to some degree. How we build those models and how we build a middle-range theory to make sense of archaeological data on ancient economies will confront us with features of the old dichotomies. Obviously, the more the dichotomizing traps can be avoided, the better; the issues, however, will probably always lurk in the background.

There will be those who object to my application of world-systems and world-economy hypothesizing for the Roman economies on substantivist/primitivist grounds; I would reply that criticism of legitimate attempts to "customize" world-systems theory (the term is Sherratt's, this volume), and some of the current characterizations of Roman economies, make too many formalist/modernist assumptions. The problem may be largely a discursive one, but it will arise again, as Isaac (1996) shows in recent work on the Maya. Similarly, recent research summaries on ancient Greco-Roman economies (Archibald et al. 2001; Cohen 2002; Mattingly and Salmon 2001; Parkins and Smith 1998) still deal with the classical form of the debate.

The classical form became an issue for modern scholarship with the publication of Moses Finley's *Ancient Economy* (1973). Following Polanyi (1944) and Polanyi et al. (1957), Finley defined a substantivist vision of economic life in the ancient Mediterranean world. It clearly was required as an antidote to the formalism of Rostovtzeff (1941, 1957), who thought there was very little difference between economic practice in the Roman Empire and in the modern world. The terms applied to those agreeing with Finley and those with Rostovtzeff were "primitivist" and "modernist," respectively. Since Finley, many have taken the meaning of the debate to be equivalent to the formula primitivist: substantivist = modernist:formalist. As Morris (1994:351, 354) points out, this belief is misplaced. The two dichotomies are similar but not identical (Monfort 1994:12; Storey 1999a:223–224).

Numerous commentators on the Greco-Roman world have stressed the need to abandon the primitivist/modernist dichotomy (especially Carandini 1983:202). But Andreau (1999:156) left the door open, stating, "It is time to move beyond this debate, which means understanding it first." Isaac, who tried to close the door on the formalist-substantivist debate (1993), found himself needing to reopen it: "*Future progress in understanding prehistoric economies requires us to revisit some of the basic issues of the 1960s–1970s formalist-substantivist debate in economic anthropology*" (Isaac 1996:297, emphasis in original). These comments illustrate the need to contextualize the modeling of ancient Mediterranean economies regarding the troublesome dichotomies.

The only viable position to start with is basically substantivist. As Plattner (1989:14) points out, we take for granted the substantivist truth that all economies are "embedded" (after Polanyi) and that economics are one aspect of social life rather than a separate sector. Putting it differently, without bothering with the terms *substantivism* and *formalism*, Colloredo-Mansfeld (2002:133) correctly notes that "new work by economists only reinforces what anthropologists have long argued: economy and culture are always intertwined." De Cecco (2000:270), addressing a conference on Roman markets, confirmed the new trend in economics: "In the last twenty years, there has been a complete change of direction in economics, in economic theory, towards the embedding, again, of economics into other behavioral patterns." So the dichotomizing debate was, and remains, most emphatically a non-issue.

Other commentators have emphasized that we should fully expect ancient state economies to be multidimensional (e.g., Sinopoli 1994b:224) and that the task is to unravel the interrelationships among a variety of exchange mechanisms and strategies available (Berdan 1989:106). According to Humphreys (1978:42), Polanyi himself thought the question was not "What type of economy?" but "What kind of [economic] institutions and how did they work?"

An all-encompassing, total cultural approach to economy is requisite, even to the point of identifying a cultural ethos regarding acquisition (and its rationale). Isaac (1996:329) identified the challenge of how to achieve fruitful model building as the main point of contention in the formalist-substantivist debate: "Practically speaking, this often boils down to whether we can borrow methods and models readymade from other disciplines (especially microeconomics), or *whether we have to go through the painful struggle of deriving our own anthropological methods and models*" (emphasis added).

The search for analogies and models that can appropriately be applied to the ancient context of early states is difficult, and each proposal should be evaluated on a case-by-case basis. Not every modern, modernizing, or microeconomic concept should be rejected simply because we fear anachronism. Nor should we facilely accept the assumptions behind the analysis of economic behavior that other social scientists have been constructing for years and to which we anthropologists also have turned in our need for analytical tools.

In this process, however, each new methodological or conceptual economic application will be scrutinized as to whether it smacks of primitivist or modernist assumptions, or follows more the formalist or substantivist agenda. Andreau, on Roman banking, asserted (1999:41): "The debate on the archaism [primitivism] of the ancient economy is certainly a central one; we cannot get around it." It returns like an insistent leitmotif throughout his exploration of Roman private banking. To give Andreau credit, he continued with the observation, "What is so difficult to determine is which phenomena truly are symptomatic of either modernity or archaism" (1999:41).

Cohen (1992), on Athenian banking, started with a blanket rejection of primitivism and detailed the complexity and sophistication of Athenian financial institutions. Andreau (1999) is more circumspect whereas Cohen (1992) seems at times to overstate the case for Athenian financial sophistication, as if to flog the dying horse of primitivism. Taken together, both dramatically demonstrate that previous scholarship has to a large extent misrepresented the character of Greco-Roman private financial behavior. We must now admit that banks in Mediterranean antiquity (the Greeks bequeathing the lessons of the world's first private banks to the Romans) functioned at a level and intensity of financial sophistication well beyond their standard caricature portrayal as mere pawnbrokers or money changers. The problem has simply been that "the financial life of Rome is one of the least studied parts of Roman life" (De Cecco 1985:820).

Moreover, without agreement on what constitutes a modern as opposed to a primitive feature, *primitive* and *modern* become something only in the eye of the beholder. For example, Roman bankers (like their Greek predecessors [Cohen 1992:111–114]) handled two types of deposit accounts: nonremunerated payment deposits and investment deposits. Finley (1973:141) thought the fact that the former were not remunerated made the Roman banking profession an example of primitivism. Thompson (1979:225, cited in Cohen 1992:113 n. 11) thought the similarity of the nonremunerated accounts at Athens to modern "demand deposits" (as opposed to "time deposits," which resemble the Roman investment deposits) could be considered a modern feature. But Cohen (1992:113 n. 11) noted that after 1979, transaction accounts (which are demand deposits charging interest) became popular, demonstrating that banking practices can be in constant flux and suggesting agreement with Andreau (1999: 41) that the nonremuneration deposit is not diagnostic of primitive or modern.

Rather than tender a loose judgment as to whether the ancient deposit practices were primitive or modern, it would be more useful to assess the degree of nonremunerated financial activity carried out by bankers to see if that characteristic fits within the confines of a holistic cultural economy model. A crucial aspect of such a model starts with questions of this type: in this particular case, if there was no remuneration for demand deposits, why would anyone conduct the business at all?

We thus enter the realm of agent motivations, and in the case of ancient economies, we must inquire about what motivated individuals to pursue economic activities aside from patrimonial estate management in landed wealth, which was the most culturally acceptable basis for wealth to both the Greeks and the Romans. Similarly, we must ask how landowners thought about the economic aspects of their properties, inasmuch as those properties were responsible for most of their income. These questions raise the issue of "rationality." Current analyses of Roman economic behavior have foisted largely modern (and perhaps inappropriate) assumptions onto the question of Roman rationality, a topic to which we now turn.

RATIONALITY

It is currently uncertain how necessary it is to accept rationality as a foundation for *any* analysis of the economy because we are on the threshold of a paradigm shift in the treatment of the concept in modern economics. Many economists now openly admit that rationality, defined as optimization in economic behavior, will not do as a realistic model for human economic decision making (Maital 1998; see D'Arms 1981:17 n. 58 for an early realization of this change by a classical scholar).

With regard to rationality as a foundation for economic analysis, Plattner (1989:15) maintains that if microeconomic theory was basically just searching for evidence of rational choice in economic behavior (as opposed to assuming its existence a priori), then the substantivist critique of formalism was misapplied. In a heuristic spirit of inquiry we might say, "Here is a modern microeconomic method, theory, or issue; this is how it has been analyzed and understood to function in the modern world. Does it work for the evidence from the ancient world?" An investigation starting from this premise could be perfectly legitimate.

Furthermore, what rationality means today is evolving quickly. The "new" approach to rationality comes out of the psychology, sociology, and anthropology of economic decision making (Schwartz 1998). The classic economic definition of rationality is that individuals maximize *utility* (material well-being) completely successfully because they are basing decisions on the best information

possible. Economists now doubt that rationality can be so tidily conceived of: "One of the most serious limitations of the traditional definition of rationality by economics and finance...[is] the surprisingly frequent difficulty that humans have in being consistent, even in the case of relatively simple types of problems" (Schwartz 1998:13).

Modern economics also has tended to suggest that governments (or corporations) can display this level of errorless maximizing rationality. However, recent research on invisible or alternative economies suggests that they come into being largely because of the failure of state-managed economies (Cohen 1992:190–192, especially 192 n. 10; see also Smith 1989 on informal economies). There is a particular satisfying irony in this process because Cohen's (1992) entire edifice of argument is that Athenian banking (and this is true of Roman banking also) has been ignored by modern scholarship chiefly because it was part of the Athenian invisible economy, but thereby no less important than the visible component of the economy. The irony is that the banking industry has since become respectable and part of the establishment, and now it in turn is completely bypassed in important facets of the workings of the alternative economies.

Whether for individuals or financial institutions, the problem appears to boil down to the failure of the assumption that humans can and do act on the best information. Information is always limited and of short-term application; it is culturally mediated, and the reflexive evaluation of it is constrained by considerations stemming from pragmatic, moral, aesthetic, and cosmological levels of cognitive regulation (all bounded by cultural taboos; Rocha 1996:27–30). Rationality depends on the type and form of information available, and the proper approach to this issue is not classic rationality but the analysis of choice behavior (Rocha 1996:33) or decision making (Schwartz 1998:11–12).

How does this play out for the Romans? Start with the peasant cultivator. Gallant (1991) has provided an account for ancient Greece that is equally applicable to Roman peasant cultivators: they aimed at self-sufficiency (to the extent of being "beholden to no one"); having a little of everything useful; having enough subsistence inventory in storage to tide themselves over one or two bad years; and above all, minimizing risk by crop diversification and the spatial separation of landholdings. The likelihood of this scenario is supported by consideration of the subsistence ethic (Scott 1976, cited in Colloredo-Mansfeld 1999:92) of modern peasant populations: "an obligation to utilize one's fields, help those who would help you, and be prepared to sacrifice earnings to insure the long-term economic security of the household."

It is striking that the elite landowner of the Roman Empire, as exemplified by Pliny the Younger (A.D. 61–113), also pursued the strategy of risk minimization (Kehoe 1988, 1989; Neeve 1990). Pliny discusses management of his considerable estates (especially the one at Tifernum Tiberinum in Tuscany) in his personal letters. The arrangements he made to run them suggest that although he did cash crop the rather risky product wine, he sloughed off the agricultural risks onto his tenant farmers (who had to be individuals of some means in the Roman system) and the middlemen wholesalers (*negotiatores*) who purchased the crop on the vine and were responsible for getting the product to market and recouping their costs, including the considerable cost of the seasonal labor required to harvest and process the grapes (Storey 2000:345–351; Tchernia 2001). Pliny merely wanted his approximate 6 percent yield of interest on his agricultural estates to allow him to pursue his senatorial lifestyle in Rome. It is a testament to the degree of agricultural uncertainty in the Roman world, where yields were low—on the average order of only 1:4 seed-to-harvest ratios (Spurr 1986)—that both peasants and senatorial landlords should play a risk-minimizing strategy.

Such risk avoidance may not have applied to farming on imperial estates. Kehoe (1988: 14) argues that the Roman administration of imperial properties "forced its tenants to work harder than they would have done as simple owner-cultivators." As D'Altroy (1994: 206) notes, states can be wasteful whereas private landowners cannot. So Pliny and his contemporary elite landowners could reasonably be seen as risk minimizers whereas the imperial administration ran its estates more with an eye to maximizing profit, largely because it did not need to minimize risk; it needed revenues.

Roman elites also sought reliable investments rather than high profits in their urban real estate ventures (Frier 1980:22 n. 5). Veyne (1991, cited in Andreau 1999:53) calls these attitudes a "security strategy," and Andreau (1999:24–25) refers to them as "provident management." The origin of this attitude is perhaps in the perceived responsibility to display good housekeeping—the thrust of the first economic treatise in Western literature, Xenophon's (1923) *Oikonomicos*, describing the best way to run a private estate. These trends are reflected in the Roman agricultural treatises of Cato, Varro, and Columella, which deal with the proper and efficient management of Roman agricultural estates. The notion of good housekeeping runs throughout these works, as well as an ethos recommending self-sufficiency in very much the same terms as it appears as one of the goals of the peasant subsistence farmer (to the degree possible; Macve 1985:253 n. 54).

Good housekeeping surely counts as a form of rationality. It is maximizing or optimizing what one has to work with, that is, an agrarian economic system. The background to this attitude lies in the widespread sentiment among the elite of Greco-Roman culture that the proper locus of wealth was patrimonially based inherited estates, or ones purchased as a result of money making in other realms. This elite focus on patrimony in landed estates and its maintenance via good housekeeping has not been generally admired by modern commentators and has even been treated with scorn, some sneering that the only reason for estate record keeping was to prevent fraud on the part of the staff (Mickwitz 1937; Ste. Croix 1956). Estate accounting was not undertaken to analyze productivity and guide any form of economic policy; no one used estate accounts to make improvements and increase productivity, according to these modern analysts.

Columella (1941) writes of starting up a vineyard. His motivation for this passage is thought to be his desire to persuade Roman estate owners to try viticulture instead of livestock raising or forestry, because its profitability outweighed the risks (Kehoe 1988:23–25). Columella provides a balance sheet of the expected revenues versus the costs of setting up the vineyard, but his procedure has been heavily criticized because of what he leaves out of his reckonings (Duncan-Jones 1982:33–59, 376–377; Kehoe 1988:25; Mickwitz 1937:585–586; Ste. Croix 1956:38).

Whether or not the Columellan excerpt is a good example of Roman rationality, the heavy criticism is unwarranted in light of the current discussion about what constitutes reasonable microeconomic decision making. According to Mickwitz (1937:580), rational farming did not begin until 1770, with the publication of Arthur Young's *Course of Experimental Agriculture*. The entire tenor of Mickwitz's article prompted Carandini (1983:179) to comment: "It appears that there exists a tradition from Young through Mickwitz to Finley which passes a negative judgment on the Roman economy because the Romans were not English, and did not live in the eighteenth century. Here we are still in a climate of self-deification of the modern world." Carandini has here identified the formalizing tendencies of some modern commentary on Roman economics.

By contrast, Macve (1985:241–254) concludes that Columella had not really given the issue much thought. He was trying to convince fellow estate owners that they should take up viticulture, and he just threw out some preliminary figures. What Macve emphasizes is that Columella's procedure is not about accounting practices and their effect on personal economic planning; we should "not conclude that the state of ancient accounting would have systematically misled people into making irrational decisions" (Macve 1985:247). Yet Duncan-Jones (1982:

43) finds fault mostly with Columella's figures in that they do not account for the amortization depreciation of the facilities (including the vines themselves) and personnel. It seems possible that the Romans accepted all those costs as a matter of course, as the inevitable outcome of working a farm property, and did not see the need for accounting for the percentage of loss. Carandini (1983:192–193) suggests that the ancient Roman estate was bisectorial and had a natural sector for self-support, producing for free in the eyes of the Romans, who thus conceived of a *use* value (not to be reckoned in cash terms) as opposed to an *exchange* value that was accountable in monetary terms.

Insisting on rationality in this modern sense of taking depreciation into account may be the kind of improper foisting of modern (microeconomic) thinking onto the ancient situation that Isaac (1996) so deplores. Stipulating the knowledge of depreciation may be too parochial and limiting, thus wrongly rejecting what ostensibly appears to be reasonably rational behavior ("What is the point of distorting Columella's calculations on the basis of business-school accounting criteria, rarely used in practice even today?" asks Carandini 1983:186).

One resource with relevance to this debate is ancient accounting materials, mostly from Egypt. A Hellenistic source, the Zenon archive from the estate of Apollonios (third century B.C.) in the Fayûm of Egypt shows the practices of one landowner who kept two types of accounts: *ephemerides*, or day books (balanced daily or every two to three days), for different commodities (grain, livestock, cash, etc.) and general accounts (also split up by commodity) balanced over longer periods. Although Mickwitz (1937) found little in this archive that impressed him as particularly rational, these records certainly attest to the good-housekeeping ideal, showing care for running an estate efficiently and profitably.

Rathbone (1991), in a major restudy of materials from the Heroninos archives from the estate of Appianos of A.D. 255, demonstrates that these accounts are more sophisticated than recognized in the past. Although they are monthly summaries, they are quite detailed and show integrated accounting of the various sectors of the estate. They reveal awareness of the need to account for transfers between the natural and the exchange sectors of the estate, with an explicit focus on achieving the largest profits possible from the Egyptian market system (including the probable disposing of wine surplus in the market at Alexandria). There is extensive use of credit integrated with local banking establishments that played a role in monetizing the local economy. All in all, "they give the strong impression that the management of the Appianos estate had a serious, long-term 'professional' interest in the practical aspects of maintaining and increasing productivity on the estate" (Rathbone 1991:399). These archives very much support Carandini's assertion that "the Roman [estate] thus combines the administration of domestic economy with the management of the acquisitive economy" (1983:196). Even cautious Pliny the Younger recognized that.

To Kehoe (1993, 1997), however, the Heroninos archives are impressively sophisticated but of limited scope. Kehoe rejects the claim that they demonstrate rationality because the archives were not about how Appianos managed his wealth; they did not give him a "systematic assessment of the risks and potential profits from agriculture in comparison to other types of investments" (1993: 483). So, by extension, the Romans could not really do economic planning because they had no choice but to invest their wealth in the production of crops for market, and given the constraints and risks of ancient agriculture, there was not much scope for greatly increased profits via that route (Kehoe 1997: 19). Thus the Romans (structurally) could not be "rational" because their agrarian economy did not allow it. That attitude seems restrictively and excessively formalizing, promulgating a very narrow vision of rationality. Carandini states that "the principal precondition for rational economic activity in any period is the possibility of knowing and comparing a number of productive solutions and choosing the most economical" (1983:

182). The Heroninos archives certainly are consistent with rationality according to that definition.

Finally, let us briefly consider Greco-Roman accounting practices. The standard introduction on this question remains Ste. Croix 1956, which is singularly dismissive of any hint of modernity in the ancient methods of accounting. Hunt (1987:326) sets out four characteristics of accounting advances in the thirteenth and fourteenth centuries that allegedly proved revolutionary in the growth of commerce: (1) double-entry bookkeeping, (2) customer accounts, (3) cross-references, and (4) accounts for assets and operating costs.

Customer accounts clearly existed in Roman times (Andreau 1999:40–41, 45). It is known that accounts for each client were separate; whether the transactions were simply chronological or whether separate summaries of each client's activities were maintained is unknown. The account examples we have from Roman times, especially the Heroninos archives, show the presence of accounts for assets and operating costs. The use of cross-references is ambiguous. Mickwitz (1937:582) simply states that they were unknown to the Romans. In contrast, Ste. Croix (1956:35) notes their presence in at least one Egyptian papyrus but claims that that does not indicate systematized unified accounts.

Double-entry bookkeeping is most emphatically denied by Ste. Croix (1956:35–37, 40). He does recognize, however, that one Egyptian papyrus is bilateral and comes close to the idea of double entry. The Heroninos archives also "followed a consistent bilateral format" (Rathbone 1991:397). Macve (1985: 257–260), although upholding the basic soundness of Ste. Croix's views, claims that it did not matter that the Romans did no double-entry bookkeeping. It is a myth to think that the technique was a revolution in the evolution of the modern notion of rationality and optimization through the maximization of profits. To Macve (1985:261), comparing ancient accounting with modern should consider three functions: (1) estimating profits of alternative possibilities, (2) keeping track of past transactions as a way to do number 1, and (3) double-entry book-keeping as a way to do number 2. Even in the modern world the presence of the latter two are not completely successful in guaranteeing proper estimates. Macve concludes that accounting practices had nothing to do with whether the ancients could be rational or not. Hence the ancients were capable of being as rational as need be, and their behavior in this regard is consistent with the modern shift from defining rationality as seeking "profit maximization" to defining it as seeking "a high rate of profitability" (Schwartz 1998:8).

INSTITUTIONS AND
ECONOMIC PLANNING

An examination of institutions conveniently links with individual rationality on the question of economic planning. Most of the evidence, however, is not so much about economic planning as about the degree to which the state intervened in economic affairs.

I begin with the most complex economic institution of all: the market. This is a dual concept, inasmuch as it refers to places of exchange—marketplaces—as well as the market system whereby exchange is mediated through pricing via exigencies of supply and demand. Interest in the Roman market-(place) system has grown of late (De Ligt 1993; Frayn 1993; Lo Cascio 2000; Mac-Mullen 1970; Shaw 1979). The Romans used two basic types of marketplaces—the permanent, daily, in-town facility called the *macellum* and the periodic (every eight days) shifting market called the *nundinae*. *Nundinae* market systems apparently grew up exactly as described by Blanton (1983:56–58), as a convenient exchange mechanism among primary producers in the countryside. To some, considerable state control was exerted over the market system (Frayn 1993:164), stemming more from considerations of crowd control and the Roman fear of assembly than from economic considerations.

Shaw (1979), analyzing the *nundinae* of Roman North Africa, argues that the Roman administration intervened in the *nundinae* system (changing it to a 14-day periodicity)

precisely to diffuse the social unrest that was characteristic of the pre-Roman Berber periodic market system (analogous to the modern *suq* system). De Ligt (2000) disagrees and maintains that Roman fear of assembly has been exaggerated and that Roman regulation of the *nundinae* was not motivated by it. Shaw notes that permission to set up a periodic market in North Africa was required from the emperor but that sometimes a provincial governor granted it (Shaw 1979: 101–103). That a governor or the emperor had to give permission bespeaks a great desire to control the periodic markets, but according to De Ligt (2000:240), permission was needed so that a new periodic market grant would not interfere with the existing market arrangements in nearby communities. Regional surveys all over the Roman world show dense occupation of the countryside that clearly includes marketplaces (Greene 1986:98–141). Frayn (1993:162) combines ancient and modern data to estimate that Roman Italy had about 500 towns and thus the same number of *nundinae*. State control of most of those markets would surely have been largely a local affair.

Zelener (2000), discussing Roman North African markets, focuses less on state control and more on the rationales for why such a system grew up under Roman control. He emphasizes the importance of market location at favorable ecological locales and argues that the Roman occupation led to an increase in market density (2000:226), possibly via population increase; the two may have interacted according to Hopkins's (1980) taxation intensification model to increase surplus. Some of the surplus was commandeered by Roman state mechanisms for supporting the city of Rome, but much was independently marketed, with the *nundinae* system reflecting increased surplus made available locally to the populace.

Morley (2000) adds to this picture that the *nundinae* system in Italy was purely localized for exchange among the subsistence farmers of each region. Production and exchange to support the city of Rome was carried on between elites and businessmen who dealt with the landholders on a personal and private level, which appealed to the Roman elite ethos of friendship (*amicitia*) and patronage and avoidance of open and "promiscuous" commerce in a public place. Andreau (2002) warns, however, against excessive downplaying of elite participation in the *nundinae*; the Roman elite traditional view that those markets were solely for the rustics masked their own considerable investment in them. In any event, the role of marketplaces in the empire seems prominent on any accounting.

Regarding the market supply and demand system, there is no doubt that many Roman economies functioned according to market logic, although Paterson complains that too many Roman scholars are skeptical that there even was a market economy (Paterson 1998:156–157). But the marketplace system certainly worked according to market supply and demand, and state intervention did not extend to the fixing of prices. That is clearly implied by the fact that the state did intervene to fix prices on one memorable occasion— the Edict on Maximum Prices of the Emperor Diocletian in A.D. 301. There are doubts also about the degree of independence of the market system because it is known that the Roman administration intervened in at least one major commodity—grain for the city of Rome (called the *annona*)—and also took a strong hand in supply of the military. Both are more properly examples of state redistribution.

Monfort (1994:23–25), looking at the archaeological evidence of amphorae (jars for carrying wine, olive oil, fish sauce, and exotic fruits) in Roman Britain, suggests that the fact that the amphorae are found in huge quantities at frontier forts and the point of origin for the commodities, with very few in between, strongly implies an administrative redistribution network rather than amphorae distribution according to market principles. The problem was that the long distance introduced large gaps in information that traders would need to make a true market-driven system work; without rapid information transfer they could not regulate production to demand.

With this version of the Roman amphorae trade it seems that the problem of inappropriate modern models has intervened once again. A "real" supply-and-demand market is required to have production respond perfectly to demand. Humphreys (1978:49), noting this lack of capability for prices to determine production decisions, suggests that it was perhaps *the* major distinction between modern and ancient exchange. It is not established, however, that ancient markets could not have functioned according to supply and demand because of this informational constraint. Supplying the army may have been a guarantee for demand in the eyes of amphorae commodity producers, but it also is quite possible that they could have produced those commodities "blindly" (not knowing prices and exact level of demand) because they knew that olive oil, wine, fish sauce, and fruits were preferred commodities for Mediterranean populations (including but not limited to the soldiers) living on the Roman frontier, who purchased those commodities on the open market.

Is a modern bias about information at work here? We believe ancient imperial systems had a structural problem because the administrators of the periphery had to be given too much latitude since they could not talk to their superiors in the capital city. Cowgill (1988:264) states:

> The relevance of this obvious point, especially for large, nonindustrialized states, is that sheer difficulty in communication can make it much harder for a ruler to keep physically distant subordinates accountable. It is not because of the amount of information that needs to be processed, but the time it takes for messages and responses to messages to get from one place to another. It is harder to check up on distant subordinates, and it is also necessary to give them greater legitimate powers of discretion, because they must frequently react to local events without taking time to get instructions from the political center.

The case of at least one subordinate in the Roman Empire certainly flies in the face of this obvious point—Pliny the Younger, serving as an imperial legate for the Emperor Trajan in the province of Pontus and Bithynia on the Black Sea. His case, though notable, was not unique. Millar (2000) emphasizes how the imperial government very much relied on letters exchanged between a moving emperor and moving governors. Pliny's *Epistles* Book 10 contains more than 100 letters written back and forth between Trajan and himself, asking for and receiving imperial policy decisions. One is struck by how mundane many of the included matters are, and readers are often prompted to wonder why Pliny could not have acted without Trajan's permission more often.

One modern commentator considers this correspondence "a new form of deliberative rhetoric: one embodied in correspondence internal to the organization, one that most resembles modern business memoranda" (Farnsworth 1996:35). Trajan is praised for his managerial ability, which encouraged Pliny to participate in deliberation, providing Trajan with a wider view of the situation at the top of the decision-making hierarchy while furnishing Pliny with some satisfaction for his initiatives, which gained attention and were considered seriously (Farnsworth 1996: 40–41). It is remarkable that this Roman administrative documentation should suggest to a modern rhetorician the language of business. It also is striking that the context of exchange between Pliny and Trajan is couched in the terminology of *amicitia*—the Roman institutionalized etiquette of friendship (Millar 2000:371, 374–375)—as were Pliny's own dealings with the businessmen who purchased his wine crop. As D'Arms (1981:149–171) notes, the entrepreneurial merchant class of Roman society also used the language of *amicitia* to denote business partnerships.

Pliny may have been unusually assiduous in deferring to imperial authority, but that is not likely, given how Romans reacted to authority. The bureaucrats in the Roman imperial administration simply lived with the need to consult the emperor on virtually every matter, and they did not mind having to wait to hear it: "Distances...imposed delays in time which it is genuinely hard now to comprehend, and to take into account" (Millar 2000:384). Life went on: "Come back in three months when I have an answer from the emperor" is not an unrealistic summation of the attitude. After all, "even 60 days, or two months, for the journey in each direction, by whatever route, might well seem an underestimate" (Millar 2000:383).

If the administrative system had to work within constraints that everyone knew about and lived with, there is no good reason why the economic system could not have worked in the same way. Put simply, people did more on faith in the days of very slow travel and communication. The oft-cited example of the British East India Company (which granted considerable leeway to its field officials, separated by a sea voyage of 18 to 24 months) and similar European institutions (Hunt 1987: 330–332) does not seem to be the right model for the Roman situation.

As for Monfort's construct that the amphorae trade could not work on sufficient information, given the accepted constraints of information lacunae in Roman life, there is really no reason why the trade in amphorae could not have been responding to market forces, unless one insists that a "true" interregional trade must work in a modern fashion—directly responding to marketing information. Again, a limiting formalism seems to be at work here. Besides, if the frontier distribution patterns cause some doubts, other categories of evidence counteract them. According to Zelener (2000:230), the ubiquity of African products in shipwrecks outside Africa "attests to an inter-regionally integrated system of trade." And as Paterson (1998:153) points out, "The development of Roman commercial law is another body of material, still underexploited, which provides further confirmation of trade great in scale and sophisticated in organization."

When all the evidence is taken together—the known production sites, the shipwrecks, commodity distributions on the frontier and in the interior of the empire, the local *nundinae* and the major trading relations between elite producers and private merchants selling on the open market—it strongly indicates a sophisticated level of economic integration served by equally well-developed trappings of financing.

Furthermore, Kim (2002) argues that small-denomination coinage was struck very early in the history of Greek coinage in large quantities for purely local transactions, indicating a near total suffusion throughout all levels of society from the very beginning of the use of coins in the ancient Mediterranean. Were this picture to prove generally accurate, a model of strongly developed economic integration from the micro- to the macrolevel for the Roman Empire would garner even greater support, perhaps to the extent of behaving as a Wallersteinian world economy.

Moreover, the issue of monetization continues to evolve. Previously, a vigorous debate raged between holders of the "strong" and "weak" views on the purpose of state-struck coinage (Davies 1998:239). The strong view maintains that coinage was invented to aid trade; the weak view is that coins were invented solely to facilitate state payments and that any participation in the larger economy was purely a side effect. For the Roman world, some think coins were first and foremost a means of paying the army (Crawford 1985; Wigg 1999). Howgego (1992, 1994) concludes that the Roman world was monetized, but to varying degrees, and that merely the fact that money was present in all facets of the economy is not significant. He also warns that the payment of taxes in kind in the Roman Empire has probably been underestimated.

De Cecco (1985) makes an excellent case, however, in arguing that the weak view was a product of Roman monetary historians, who were forerunners of a brand of substantivists, asserting that because Roman coinage did not work as in the modern world, it could not function in the manner envisaged by the strong view. De Cecco's critique argues implicitly what I would argue explicitly: that this kind of substantivism is in reality a species of formalism because it criticizes the Romans for not carrying out economic analysis in a modern fashion and then dubs

the Roman coinage system primitive. Coinage may thus be added to the list of cases in which this formalizing has detrimentally predominated.

In addition, Millar (1981), using Apuleius's *Golden Ass* (a Latin novel of the second century A.D.), paints a vividly evocative picture of the everyday world of Greece under the Roman Empire that eminently favors the strong view. The evidence for an all-encompassing penetration of a monetized economy deep into the rural countryside is compelling: "All the food-producing operations are specialized and the products are exchanged for cash" (Millar 1981:73). Taken with Kim's (2002) argument, this picture constitutes powerful evidence for a high level of monetization.

Whether monetization was modest or extensive, the presence at all of monetization in Roman economies confirms that we are dealing with a wealth-finance system in D'Altroy and Earle's terms (1985), but it is sometimes difficult to compare a much more heavily monetized imperial polity (Rome) on an equal footing with a nonmonetized one (Inca). Perhaps it is more helpful to illuminate Roman practice by speaking of "money finance" (as per the suggestion of Cathy Costin, at the conference on which this volume is based, 2001) as one species of wealth finance because it functions the same way, by facilitating economic transactions in a medium other than staple products. The key to defining "money finance" (suggested in De Cecco 1985:818) is that, like other forms of wealth finance in which objects can store wealth and measure value, coins serve as much more facile modes of payment and means of exchange than nonmonetary instruments in nonmonetized wealth-finance systems, such as the paradigm case of the Incas.

Despite the confidence that this neologism of money finance might engender, however, Whittaker (1985) gives pause. He argues powerfully that the bulk of the archaeological and epigraphical evidence about amphorae transport can be explained as simply the private transfer and distribution of elite-owned commodities between various private properties, resulting in the possibility that the economy of the Roman world was more a case of staple finance. The evidence of coins tends to make that option unlikely, as well as the wide distribution of many different amphora types over so many different kinds of sites (Paterson 1998:157). But it may have some element of truth. Brumfiel and Earle (1987:6) comment that the transition from staple to wealth finance was probably more feasible in a context where market demand was created by estate surpluses rather than peasant householder surpluses. That is probably the case in at least some parts of the Roman Empire. The North African *nundinae* markets discussed previously were to some degree the creatures of large-estate surplus distribution, the "domanial" model for the markets (Zelener 2000:226). It may be the case that the activity documented by Whittaker, beginning in the second century A.D., was part of this process of market demand creation. Whittaker explicitly states that the main transfer of commodities was between elite properties but that any surplus left over would have been sold on the open market. If true, Whittaker's suggestions might describe the process that helped transform the system from staple finance to the Roman form of wealth finance, which is sufficiently mediated by small-denomination coins to more accurately be termed "money finance."

Furthermore, the trade in ceramics is often cited as another example of state-administered exchange to such a degree that it can support Whittaker's staple-finance scenario, especially in terms of the production of the Roman fineware known as samian, or *terra sigillata*. Production of that fine tableware may have been directed toward the Rhine armies and thus was a form of redistribution (Middleton 1980, 1983). There may be some truth to this suggestion, in terms of the origin of the production. It should be noted, however, that this form of Roman ceramics started in Arezzo, Italy, which has no real locational advantage with regard to the Roman armies in central, western, and northern Europe. Moreover, the distribution of *terra sigillata* production loci (Tyers 1996:

106, Figure 90) suggests that even if the industry started as an army supplier, the later distribution of its production points seems to indicate something beyond that; there is no reason to believe that it was not the open market in ceramics.

Brumfiel and Earle (1987:7) distinguish two types of wealth production: universal or by attached specialists. In the universal type, items of wealth are produced everywhere, and elites merely have an advantage of means in procuring them. Attached craft specialists produce wealth items specifically for the elites or the states that employ them, in elite or state facilities. Roman wealth was clearly produced universally. D'Altroy (1994:196–197), discussing Inca ceramic production, spoke of consignment production of ceramics (supply on command). One might be tempted to suggest that the *terra sigillata* production for the Roman armies of the Rhine smacks of that kind of production, which is a form of attached craft specialization, merely on a large scale. Production loci, however, are too numerous and widely dispersed to be any form of attached specialization. And in the end, little in the Roman documentary corpus reads anything like the kinds of attached specialization that figure in the evidence from Mesoamerica.

If it is true that the Roman state did not intervene extensively in the production of either agricultural staples (aside from acting to ensure adequate supply to the city of Rome itself) or ceramics for the Rhine armies, it may still be true that the Roman state intervened in other ways to influence the economy. Andreau (1999:100–126) comments on the Roman administration's attitude toward intervention, especially regarding coinage: "In my opinion, the Romans were conscious of a system of financial relations that functioned in an autonomous fashion, mechanically, and knew that it was important to get it going again when it broke down. But they did not theorize this idea.... And the financial policy of the public authorities was far more in evidence when the system broke down. When times were 'normal,' they tended not to intervene" (109).

Whatever the effect of the intervention of the Roman authorities in the supply of money, the issue of state intervention in the economy comes up frequently (in general, see Brumfiel and Earle 1987:4; Sinopoli 1994a: 166; for the Greco-Roman world, see Archibald et al. 2001; Lo Cascio and Rathbone, eds. 2000; for Vijayanagara, see Sinopoli 1994b:236–237; for the Inca, see D'Altroy 1994:170; for the Aztec, see Berdan 1983: 84–85). According to the record of states and their economies, however, the issue of state intervention in the economy is also a non-issue because *all* state administrations intervene in the economy. The only difference from one state to another is the degree to which a government might interfere and to what purpose.

Love (1991) goes so far as to suggest that capitalism was the prevalent economic mode in the ancient world, but it was administered by the state, leading him to coin the phrase *political capitalism*. This is in essence a formalizing approach to characterizing the anthropologically recognized command economy (Carrasco 1983), perhaps overly interpreting ancient behavior as capitalist when it need not be so described. Similarly, Monfort (1994:361–374) characterizes state interventionism with the new terms *market interventionism* and *parasitic trade*. These, too, seem unnecessary elaborations attempting to capture state institutional behavior that is known to occur cross-culturally. Lo Cascio and Rathbone (2000:1–2), perhaps more fruitfully, are especially interested in determining how much states of the ancient Mediterranean world intervened explicitly to stimulate production, inasmuch as that factor strongly suggests that someone in the government was engaging in economic planning, without necessarily requiring it to look like modern economic planning.

Beyond the role of coinage, then, there is the question of to what degree people in the past, in their role as servants of the state, engaged in economic planning—a hallmark of modern economic behavior. Kemp (1997: 129) refers to Egyptian temple and pharaonic accounting: "Within the confines of a single foundation, an instinctive feeling for good housekeeping, manifested in careful record keeping, would have urged that expenditures did not exceed income. Economic man was at work here.... A fascinating and ultimately unanswerable question is whether the most senior of the officials, overseeing these huge accounting exercises, gained, even if intuitively, an overall sense of how the country's economy was performing, and what shape the accounts were in, when they considered imperial activity."

Rationality returns here in the notion of good housekeeping and *Homo economicus*, with the added issue of what to advise the monarch to do. Smith (1997:304) discusses a pharaoh's options to pursue either building activities or military expeditions: "He had to have enough grain and supplies to feed both army and artisans. The only way that this could be ensured was through careful accounting and some degree of economic forecasting, including a consideration of cost and benefit."

These comments about Egypt apply equally to the Roman Empire. It will be difficult, however, to establish whether Roman imperial officials did economic planning. Lo Cascio (1981) is quite certain that Roman administrators did so in respect to coinage, but Andreau's comment on state intervention quoted above shows a less sanguine view. One wonders if ancient monarchs really did do even the basic accounting that Smith alleges. When Trajan decided to invade Dacia in A.D. 101, he probably did not call in the accountants to ask if it was feasible. The Roman honor of arms demanded it. It is likely that Domitian's fiscal care had amassed enough surplus for Trajan to invade (Storey 2000:344). The evidence for that is weak, however, and in the end, Dacia's gold ensured that the enterprise about broke even. However, Trajan *may* have known that when a Roman army moved, its costs increased threefold (MacMullen 1984:576–577 n. 21), but he might not have taken much note, and even then the knowledge might not have deterred him from invading.

To us, governments obviously have to do

some economic planning, however rudimentary. That may be, however, just another modern idea that does not apply to the ancient world because ancient elites took so many things for granted. Day-to-day costs were matters for their subordinates. When contemplating large transactions for which they may not have had the full sum, they simply turned to one another for (reciprocal) short-term loans. Their goal was maintenance of the patrimony of the state that they tended (as it was for their own personal patrimonies), and territorial expansion was the engine of that process, so they did not question its necessity. In both private and public sectors the notion that the costs would somehow take care of themselves may have prevailed far more than (modernly) thought prudent.

So great was their faith that public debt was unheard of in Greco-Roman antiquity (Andreau 1999:121–124), providing a possible explanation of why major financing of businesses and a healthier credit system never developed. Instead, the Greco-Roman world depended on *euergetism*, the generosity of elites in providing monetary assistance to the administration of cities and regions. In a way, this practice was akin to one rich person going to another rich person to borrow money, as Andreau (2002:128) describes for Cicero: "At the very high consular level on which Cicero operated within the Senate the chief transactions undertaken were less to do with the patrimony's productive side than with the expenses that political and social life entailed, and the occasional complementary gains that arose directly or indirectly therefrom."

There were even cases in which private finance was aimed at big profits only to have them potlatched away in a grand gesture of liberally generous *euergetism* (Andreau 1999: 145). Although the Roman elite remained committed to an ethos that disparaged gain from commerce, D'Arms (1981:18) concludes that "the attitude of disparagement was largely that of nostalgia for a bygone era and had lost its power to influence conduct significantly," for the Roman elite did become heavily involved in commerce. D'Arms (1980) summarizes the considerable archaeological evidence for the business dealings of the Sestii, a senatorial family with three generations practicing large-scale wine production and export based in Cosa.

This public patrimonialism, balanced by private (nearly hidden) commercialism, was the milieu in which the Romans functioned economically. Regarding their attitudes to economic behavior, Shaw (2001:430 n. 50) argues that individual rationality was not as important as the character of the social system, whether it allowed "'individual rational calculators'...to have a more dominant place in the economy which in turn transforms the economy itself." To address that question and tie together the strands of rationality, both private and public, I now turn to a consideration of the "spirit of entrepreneurship."

ENTREPRENEURSHIP

Entrepreneurs seem to play an important role in the development of inequality, hierarchy, and the state itself, if they are considered equivalent to aggrandizers (Diehl 2000; Price and Feinman 1995). Somewhere along the way in the ontology of complex society, aggrandizers are transformed into entrepreneurs and become progressively incorporated into the social and political power structures of the society. The degree and character of this incorporation is crucial to defining the normative economic behavior in a particular culture.

Given that *aggrandizer* connotes bad acquisitiveness whereas *entrepreneur* connotes good acquisitiveness, the original aggrandizing role is recalled in the frequent social sanctions that seem to be applied cross-culturally to entrepreneurs. For example, the notion of the "just price," which is a societal sanction in reaction to allowing traders a totally free hand in the market, aims to prevent the buyer from being exploited by the trader (Humphreys 1978:52). D'Arms (1981:2–3 n. 5) reviewed evidence of negative perceptions of commerce from Roman and medieval Europe, comparing those with similar evidence even from Han China on attitudes toward merchants. In the ancient world, aggrandizers were sanctioned but maintained low status, even as their role evolved toward the entrepreneurial dimension.

There were three types of entrepreneurs in the Roman world (Andreau 1999:3–4). First, there were the bankers, who were mostly ex-slaves, with not a single member of the municipal decurial (town council) aristocracy or the imperial aristocracy of knights and senators being counted in their number. Second, there were elite entrepreneurs, such as Crassus (of the First Triumvirate) and Quintus Axius, both senators, and Atticus, Cicero's friend and correspondent, and his uncle Quintus Caecilius, both knights; all these individuals were active in the first century B.C. (Andreau 2002:122–128). These elites lent money to their peers, but their activity was confined to other members of their class. Third, there was a very limited number of entrepreneurs who hovered on the margin of the elites and were the most "modern" of the three because they invested large sums of money in the hopes of making large profits (especially in risky maritime commerce). The line between the first and second types was clear, but the distinction between the second and third types could be vague because a member of the elite could be an entrepreneur of this third type.

What is not at issue is that the bankers, those really pursuing banking as a profession, were of uniformly low status and made little significant impact on the socioeconomic structure of Roman culture. That was to some extent due to the fact that there were no bills of exchange, credit was limited (although clearly known and used), and "coins constituted the only organized system of monetary instrument," which is "one very important difference between Greco-Roman antiquity and modern Europe" (Andreau 1999:1).

Regarding the elite financiers, one role was, as with all elites, to set an example and to serve their communities through the aforementioned euergetism, a route to status and enhanced honor. There is a fascinating similarity between euergetism in the Greco-Roman world and the Maya cargo (Cancian 1965, 1989; Storey 2000:362). In both cases the rationale of such an institution may be related to the problem of diffusing popular anger at the elites, by attempting to homogenize all social levels according to Eric Wolf's "enforced philanthropy"—the societal pressure to participate in community rituals and level wealth via the expenditure on these rituals (quoted in Cancian 1989:133; see also Colloredo-Mansfeld 1999).

The cargo system, however, does not necessarily work that way. In the Zinacantan cargo system the richest individuals undertook the most expensive cargoes both early and late in their careers, without affecting their wealth, but the poor families that undertook cargoes remained poor (Cancian 1989:147; Hayden and Gargett 1990). There is the same break among elites in the case of euergetism in the Roman Empire. The imperial elites (the senators and knights) were wealthy enough to pay for community benefits all through their careers (equivalent to rich cargo holders); the municipal elites, the decurial class of the cities of the empire, struggled more to pay for the necessary benefits (equal to the poor cargo holders). The decurial class was continually impoverished throughout the first four centuries A.D. (Storey 2000:351–353 with references). Paradoxically, members of this class acted in accordance with the prevailing patrimonial ethos, stifling the entrepreneurial spirit that would have furnished them the wherewithal to keep up and continue to play the euergetism game on the same level as the imperial elites.

There did exist a class of true entrepreneurs among the Romans, however, in the merchant financiers, probably some of whom had elite status or were very wealthy freedmen, but their role was limited because of the small size of their numbers. The best example of one is fictional, the ex-slave Trimalchio in Petronius's *Satyricon*. Petronius was clearly making fun of a real type and seems well informed on the true situation of Rome's merchant entrepreneurial class; D'Arms (1981:

97–120) builds a plausible case for considering Trimalchio to be very like a member of the merchant class of Puteoli, the port of Naples, and thus a reasonable exemplar.

Trimalchio made his fortune in maritime commerce. Its dangers are highlighted by the fact that a storm bankrupted him once, but he repeated his business ventures, recouping and increasing his wealth many times over. His story is strikingly similar to that of a modern indigenous entrepreneur from Otavalo in the Andes, Galo Ajala, described by Colloredo-Mansfeld (1999:125–129). Galo traded in indigenous handicrafts and made and lost fortunes punctuated by four misfortunes: two robberies of his inventory, a fire in a storeroom, and the confiscation of his inventory by customs agents.

That such series of disasters can occur and that the individual can recover from them is demonstrated in real life by Galo Ajala, adding plausibility to Trimalchio's fictional history. Both this real-life entrepreneur and Trimalchio are perhaps unusually persistent because of their low social status, which may have served as an engine for them to overcome their adversities and fulfill their ambitions. Trimalchio is truly entrepreneurial in that he totally stepped out of the logic of patrimony and pursued the maximum profits that he could by the means at his disposal; he started by using his master's money—confirming how much elite entrepreneurial activity was accomplished through slave agents.

What Trimalchio and many other real-life Roman entrepreneurs did with their wealth amounted to the reassertion of the logic of patrimony, however. Once fortunes had been made, the entrepreneurs bought land and tried to enter the ranks of the elites. It was largely impossible for them but not for their children. The stigma of the entrepreneur/ aggrandizer equation remained institutionalized because although commerce could bring wealth, the descendant of a trader, on entering the ranks of the elites, ceased to be a trader (Andreau 1999:61).

Such entrepreneurial histories highlight the need to distinguish types of entrepreneurial behavior and analyze how a cultural system integrates entrepreneurial/aggrandizing behavior. Here I am introducing new terminology, although some of the terms have been used before in ways distinct from their use in this context.

When entrepreneurs are a dominant faction in the actual governing power structure, we might call this *directorial entrepreneurship*. I originally thought to use the term *structural entrepreneurship* but rejected it because Brumfiel (1994:3–4) distinguishes "instrumentalist" economies (state personnel as servants of the capitalist class) and "structuralist" economies (incomplete dominance by the capitalists). Brumfiel's use of *structuralist* is almost the opposite of what I mean, and her *instrumentalist* is close to what I mean by *directorial*. Medieval Venice and Genoa are good examples of this type (Hunt 1987:326–328). Although it often seems as though modern governments are unduly deferential to entrepreneurial capitalists, frequent government regulation of multinational corporations (Hunt 1987:346–354) suggests that, unlike in medieval Venice and Genoa, the government is not run by them directly for their interests.

Modern capitalistic entrepreneurship can be called *independently institutionalized, connected, commercial entrepreneurship*. Entrepreneurs are independent of the state but institutionalized through corporations (which are recent phenomena; see Hunt's 1987 analysis), sharing transnational relations and connections, seeking survival and aggrandizement through commerce (whether manufacturing or trading).

The Roman form of entrepreneurship might best be called *adventitious, symbiotic entrepreneurship*. Roman entrepreneurs were independent of the state, but the state needed them. Even in highly administered trade such as the grain trade, emperors granted traders favorable concessions to ensure supply (evidence cited in Paterson 1998:157)—hence the term *symbiotic* (suggested by Hunt 1987: 347). They were adventitious because much of their success came from piggybacking onto the state's need to transfer certain commodities. That several ancient states cultivated this adventitious symbiotic entrepreneurship seems clear. The oft-cited *pochteca* of the Aztec empire fit this definition well, being both servants of the state and private entrepreneurs (Berdan 1983:85, 1989:89).

The market niche success of Roman entrepreneurs may have come directly from exploiting transport routes opened up by the Roman administration. The great Spanish olive oil trade with Rome might be an example. Olive oil was transshipped from the Guadalquivir River valley in southwest Spain (in what are called Dressel 20 amphorae) at such a scale that the emptied vessels broken on arrival in Rome formed a small mountain, the Monte Testaccio in the Aventine commercial district of Rome. This trade grew as a result of being attached to the transport of metals to Rome for coins, which was the whole reason the Romans conquered Spain in the first place. Roman North Africa's grain fed Rome, and then the ceramic trade that followed the grain, the African Red Slip Ware—the most ubiquitous pottery from the classical world—took over the world market (both cases in Mattingly 1988). The Roman *terra sigillata* produced in Gaul also probably was attached to the metals transport routes (Middleton 1980).

In any event, none of the three types of entrepreneurs in the Roman Empire were part of the power structure to the extent that entrepreneurial interests could be directly advanced. Nor were Roman entrepreneurs remotely like modern entrepreneurial capitalists. Roman entrepreneurs were truly marginal; they did not constitute a group or a bourgeoisie, not even an emergent one (Andreau 1999:154). They were unconcentrated and unconnected, the opposite of the modern corporation. Their associations were horizontal networks, not vertical institutionalized hierarchies; that is, entrepreneurs could associate and cooperate but mostly as equals. Hence they used the same language of *amicitia* as the elite administration. There were no wholly owned subsidiaries, as Fülle (1997) demonstrates in discussing the evolution of the Arezzo ware into the *terra sigillata* industry. Entrepreneurs in the Roman world were

individual aggrandizers, not an institution of them, as is a multinational corporation (Hunt 1987).

One possible resonance between Roman entrepreneurship and the modern version, however, is the notion of the winner-take-all economy (Frank and Cook 1995), in which there are many participants but very few who really strike it rich. This case seems especially true of the third class of Roman entrepreneurs we have examined. In essence, one may have to risk much to win big, and only the true entrepreneurs (people willing to invest in risky but profitable maritime commerce) were playing in the context in which the few can succeed markedly. But as with the Maya cargo, where the richest continue to be winners who take all, the top elite of the Roman Empire also continued to be winners who took all. One has to be placed advantageously to get close to being the winner who takes all; senators were best situated to take economic advantage of their governing roles, and they frequently did, even under the stricter regime of the Principate.

The winner-take-all result seems true of other contexts. It is notable how Roman *terra sigillata* ceramics moved from production centered in Italy, to southern Gaul, to central Gaul, to eastern Gaul, each industry superseding the previous one and coming to dominate production (Tyers 1996:111–114). Similarly, Italian wine may have given way to provincial wine (Purcell 1985; however, Purcell thinks Italian wine changed its focus from the high-quality market to high-quantity production), and Italian olive oil gave way to Spanish oil, which gave way to North African oil, the biggest winner (Mattingly 1997). Just as today, competition among commodities yielded clear winners and losers, but the exact implications of these patterns are still not completely clear.

Another modern parallel is with the native crafts artisans from Otavalo in Ecuador (Colloredo-Mansfeld 1999, 2002), who have moved into an international market thanks to a very spirited entrepreneurial sense. The manufacturers and marketers for Roman *terra sigillata* similarly moved into an international market. Both industries began in small, remote places with highly concentrated production. They both exploited new markets quickly and moved into new market niches opportunistically. How Roman products may have been marketed is a neglected topic and should be taken up; for a start, Dyson (1985) recommends considering the marketing of Roman *terra sigillata* in the light of historical parallels such as the practices of Josiah Wedgwood.

DUAL PROCESSUALITY

The final elements required for the groundwork of the paradigm concern dual processuality. Elsewhere I have discussed the change from the Roman republican to the Roman imperial system as a transition from a corporate to a network political economy (Storey 1999b). The Roman republican system was an excellent example of a corporate state. There were two equally powerful executive magistrates—the consuls—who served for only one year. They were presidents of the body of elite officeholders—the Senate—numbering either 300 or 600 men, depending on the period. The same families dominated the consulship, the holding of which ennobled a family forever. Yet occasional "new men" such as Gaius Marius and Marcus Tullius Cicero achieved the office, which was never an ascribed one. The repeat of family names over generations appearing as the eponymous list of consuls for record keeping illustrates that under the republic the Roman concept of time was cyclical; thus the glories of the state were repeated (Walters 1996).

In contrast, the system founded by Augustus, technically called the Principate but usually referred to as the imperial system, was clearly a network state. The emperor came to hold *imperium maius* (greater power) that put him above all other magistrates. The Senate ceased to function as the legislative and executive body through the consuls. Although the imperial system allowed other Romans besides the emperors to hold the consulship, the office became largely ceremonial. Timekeeping became linear, with the years counted for each emperor's "tribuni-

cian power," the sacral inviolability of person that under the republic had been the prerogative of a minor magistrate, the tribune of the people. The network Principate clearly paraded its corporate republican pedigree. The genius of Augustus's solution was to fashion a system that made one-man rule acceptable in a context of a consensual oligarchy consisting of the landed elite. Also, the office of emperor never really became hereditary and ascriptive.

Thus the tradition of consensual dispositions in the Roman administration, with multiple officeholders, many with predominantly accounting duties, such as Pliny the Younger (who served as a financial officer for most of his career), mitigated against the development of a very powerful state or command economy, even though the Principate was a network polity and might have been expected to display greater tendency toward that kind of state interventionism. The tradition of a senatorial class, economically independent, looking after its own patrimonies, was too well established to bypass.

TAXES AND TRADE

Hopkins's (1980) taxation-intensification model holds that the Roman administration's increased demand for taxation, paid in coin, had the effect of stimulating production in the empire. Paterson (2001) supports Hopkins's model on the grounds that all the evidence points to growth (both demographic and economic) in the Roman Empire. Zelener (2000) questions it, however, noting that taxation would have had to affect different regions at different times, as those regions were progressively incorporated into the empire, and because, for example, Roman North Africa's economic development started long after the takeover by Rome. One wonders, also, if what is being seen is more a natural growth of populations living at the bounds of subsistence (as modeled cross-culturally by Wood 1998). Hopkins (2000) has recently modified the model, arguing that taxes and rents to elite landlords competed for the limited surplus produced by the high-risk Roman agricultural regime, contributing at least in part to some of the structural weakness in the empire that ultimately led to its collapse.

For the Aztec empire, Berdan (1983:92) acknowledges that taxation proved a political device for controlling economic production, as in Hopkins's model. But Sinopoli (1994a: 166), in her review of imperial systems, suggests that although imperial incorporation could have had the effect of intensifying production, it was by no means inevitable. Notably, Sinopoli's counterexample is Greece under the Roman Empire, as thoroughly analyzed by Alcock (1993), which experienced economic decline under Roman rule compared with other parts of the empire.

WORLD SYSTEMS AND
WORLD ECONOMIES

An obvious model for the Roman Empire is world-systems analysis (Wallerstein 1974). There has been early and continuing criticism of world-systems analysis (Kohl 1987b; Schneider 1977). Dietler (1998) and Stein (1998a) both argue powerfully that the world-systems model is not applicable to Old World polities of early periods, leaving the question open about whether the model is acceptable for later polities (see Sherratt, this volume, for the Bronze Age). World-systems analysis has remained popular, though, even being extended to times and contexts strikingly dissimilar to Wallerstein's original formation context (Blanton and Feinman 1984; Blanton et al. 1992; Chase-Dunn 1992; Collins 1992; Hall and Chase-Dunn 1993; Peregrine and Feinman 1996). Recently, Small (2001) has urged that we not become overly focused on matching data with models and acknowledge the basically heuristic nature of this kind of analogical reasoning. I agree in principle, but I also wish to explore how closely the Roman Empire resembles Wallerstein's well-documented construct.

Reviewing some of Wallerstein's most formulaic statements on what constitutes a world economy, especially regarding various kinds of workers and the division of labor (1974:86), we find that (1) slaves are found on sugar plantations and in mines; (2) serfs tend large domains of grain production and

wood extraction; (3) tenant farmers produce cash crops, including grain; (4) some proportion of free laborers are found in agricultural production; (5) there is a new class of "yeoman" farmers (well-off non-elite landholders, the instigators and benefiters of the "enclosures"); (6) a small layer of intermediate personnel supervises the laborers; (7) there are a few independent and skilled artisans; and (8) at the top is a thin layer of a ruling class. With some minor adjustments it is not too difficult to find strong parallels in the Roman Empire for each of these requirements. Similarly, in Wallerstein's discussion of what is found in the urban colonialism of the nascent European world economy (Wallerstein 1974:120), it is notable that the Roman Empire also had (1) overall market expansion, (2) growth of towns, (3) multiplication of urban markets, (4) increased penetration of the money economy into the rural sector, (5) growth of hired labor, (6) leasing of private properties for money rent, and (7) large profits from foreign trade.

The Roman Empire features are not a perfect fit, and the most crucial missing element is that a capitalist world economy requires multiple political systems so that economic loss can be absorbed by political entities and profits fall into "private" hands (Wallerstein 1974:348–349). The feature of multiple political entities is lacking in the Roman Empire—it is a unified world empire. It is worth considering, however, whether the differently disposed provinces of the Roman Empire could serve as proxies for the required nation-states in order to constitute a Roman world economy. That question deserves further consideration in future work.

Monfort (1994:33) considers whether the Roman Empire was the first "economy of scale," given that the different provinces were economically integrated with complementing production regimes and highly developed interprovincial trade, even of bulk production destined for long-distance export. He thoroughly analyzes the amphorae of Roman Britain to dispel this possibility (Monfort 1994:356–379). As we noted, however, his criteria for defining an economy of scale require perhaps overly stringent integration of production based on information from consumption in a context of inadequate information transfer.

Jongman (2000) likewise rejects the idea that most Roman industries produced at the levels required of an economy of scale, on the grounds that economies of scale require concentration of production, which was manifestly not the case in the Roman world, especially regarding his topic, textile production. This is somewhat odd, because he states that "this dispersed manufacture of textiles is, perhaps surprisingly, a sign of the greater integration and larger scale of the Roman economy, compared to medieval Europe" (2000: 189).

Thus Jongman takes widely distributed manufacture as a characteristic that could be modern, even if the production was for local markets chiefly: "The Roman Empire was not only one huge market for goods (even though most goods were produced for local consumers), but also for skills and technology" (Jongman 2000:196). He concludes that the Industrial Revolution was a major break that makes the modern world completely different (economically) from the medieval or ancient, but his formalizing stance cannot dispel the impression his own analysis has given in attributing a greater complexity to Roman economies than has hitherto been appreciated.

Given reasonable questions about these two rejections of Roman economies of scale, why is it then impossible for a loosely integrated system such as the Roman Empire's to constitute a regionally integrated market sufficient to count as an ancient world economy? Paterson (1998:164) characterizes the Roman Empire as a network of microregional economies: "These micro-economies have their own natural rhythms and structures designed to meet local needs.... But at certain periods some of these economies become more closely linked with the wider world and find a wider market for their goods." That seems to summarize the situation aptly. The Roman Empire as a whole still appears qualitatively distant from Europe of the emerging modern world system. However, little by little, it is becoming plausible to countenance the Roman Empire as a proto- or emergent world economy, so I am tentatively suggesting this construct as a dimension for characterizing Roman economies. As Woolf (1990:53) notes, a systematic archaeological demonstration of a Roman world economy has yet to be attempted. This should be a focus of future research.

"PRECESSION" OF WORLD SYSTEMS

In the meantime, to tie together the strands of thought on world systems here and in Sherratt's chapter (this volume), I suggest that world systems may behave in a way that can be described as a process of "precession" (as in the astronomical expression *precession of the equinoxes*—that wobbling of the earth's axis that shifts the earth's orientation to the stars and thus shifts the region of the sky by which equinoxes and solstices are marked). Sherratt here paints a world-systems scene with a wide brush on a large canvas, and the evidence of history supports him to the degree that there were shifting bases of power. Neolithic Mesopotamia (perhaps not quite a world system) yielded to Bronze Age Anatolian and eastern Mediterranean empires (which may have been), which in turn yielded to the Iron Age Aegean, to classical Greece, to the Hellenistic world, on to the Roman Empire (clearly a world empire), then to the Ottoman Empire, and so on.

These shifts occurred because the areas that were margins to the cores of these systems became incorporated peripheries that in time became the cores of new systems themselves. Thus Roman Italy was a margin to the eastern Mediterranean world system and transformed from a margin into a periphery and then a core. The sequence of world systems seen in this scenario resembles a "wobbling" in a westward direction (and also to the east, as Sherratt suggested, from the Iranian Plateau to the Indus and beyond) that created the phenomena of classical, Hellenistic, and Roman complex polities. One aspect of this hypothesized process is that it accounts for the cultural similarities that are so obvious in the series of cultures from the Near East to Rome, without invoking the tired old hyperdiffusionism that was so belittling to the cultures that could not lay claim to pristine development of the institutions or technological complexities of state-level societies.

And yet this model will explain a common cultural *koinonia*—a community of shared human experience in populated landscapes and institutional elaboration that is so well captured by the ancient expression *oikoumene*, the "inhabited world" of the Roman Empire, surviving in the modern expression *ecumenical*. This wobbling of cultural systems is responsible for the similarity of landscapes—both figurative and literal—in the succession of complex polities that fanned out from the original "heartland of cities" in this region (Adams 1981), the oldest manifestation of complex societies in the world, which we call civilizations.

And so it is possible to push the Roman world-economy view by noting that the characterization here is the beginning of an attempt to "customize" (Sherratt's term) a model for the highly but imperfectly (in modern terms) integrated economic system of Rome. It is the ancient equivalent of a modern world economy, and with it we have a reasonable example of an ancient world economy.

MODELING ROMAN ECONOMIES

I now attempt to set out a general model for Roman economies. Humphreys (1978:137) describes what a model of ancient Greco-Roman economies should address: "We still have to face today the task of finding an interpretation of ancient economic history which accommodates not only primitive technology, small-scale organization, and a general contempt for economic enterprise, but also wide-spread trade, the beginnings of banking and economic analysis, and attitudes characterized by contemporary sources as individualistic and mercenary. Neither modernists nor primitivists gave a successful account of this combination."

My model is as follows. The Roman economy was a wealth-finance system, with a largely monetized economy (money finance) and universal wealth production (i.e., not through attached specialization) functioning in a patrimonialist (versus capitalist) ethos, with mostly non-elite-based limited banking and credit facilities, characterized by adventitious, symbiotic entrepreneurship with winner-take-all consequences, exercised in horizontal associations of networks rather than commercial companies, and with mostly individual aggrandizement strategies. The preponderant financial strategies were inspired by the ideal of good housekeeping (running an efficient household, or *oikos*) and were focused on risk minimization, security, and provident management rather than strictly optimizing profit and utility maximization. Economic rationality, though, was present and could be described as consistent with the modern redefinition of rationality as seeking a "high rate of profitability." Government intervention in the economy was deliberate, although probably more or less comparable with the level in other state societies, including those of today. The degree of economic planning was minimal and purely a reaction to disorder in monetary flow. The Roman Empire was a network political economy (arising out of a corporate one)—possibly an example of a Hopkins taxes-and-trade intensification economy—that also could be considered an ancient example of a Wallerstein world economy.

I hope this model—an attempt to integrate general anthropological archaeological economic factors into a discussion of Roman economies—is at least a small step forward. The most controversial aspect is the world-systems framework. Many classicists have expressed hostility to the world-systems or world-economy model (discussed by Woolf [1990], who is somewhat more sympathetic; for other criticism, see Davies 2001:41–42; Shipley 1993). I would argue, however, that customizing world systems to the ancient world by admitting that modern features do not apply in all elaborations and trying to find proper analogues, where appropriate, is a better approach than, for example, Love's (1991) attempt to push capitalism back into the ancient world. That seems to me too formalizing a model to apply convincingly to the ancient situation.

Regarding the world-economy model for the Hellenistic world, Shipley characterizes the Hellenistic world as too multicentered, with too much of a plurality of economic spheres to count as a world economy of the Wallerstein type (1993:280–283), despite the recognition that there was some interlinking of these plural economic systems. Davies, more dismissive yet, criticizes world systems on the grounds that "high-generality analogies can mislead horribly" and that "one person's centre is another person's periphery" (Davies 2001:42).

In answer to Shipley, the key here is fungibility of different monetary instruments (De Cecco 1985:819); both the Hellenistic world and the Roman Empire had different monetary instruments that sometimes did not exchange easily. For the Hellenistic world, Foraboschi (2000:38) notes that several standard currencies—the Attica drachma, the Pergamene *cistophorus*, and the Egyptian drachma—were not commonly interchangeable. But it is significant that individuals could conceive of them being exchanged, as was the case with similarly impermeable Roman instruments, even if it was not commonly done. To De Cecco (1985:819–820), "market imperfection" and "segmentation" determine that even in the modern world it has not always been easy to use some instruments. Twenty-dollar bills were hard to use for groceries in the 1960s, and it is still true that one's personal check may not be accepted far from home. Yet these imperfections and segmentations, found even in developed countries today, are held against the ancient world and said to be sufficient grounds for attributing labels such as "imperfect monetization" or "incomplete interregional economic integration."

In answer to Davies, careful customizing of models should not be rejected simply because previous ones have misled. Davies's second comment should be taken as a possible strength for the kind of precession of world systems posited here, conceived by Sherratt. It just seems that the concept of world systems is rejected by classicists precisely because it is not a perfect fit; this appears to be a somewhat formalistic stance, as if to argue that aspects of the Hellenistic world (Foraboschi 2000), aspects of Roman banking practices (Duncan-Jones 1990, 1994), the accounting of the Heroninos estate (Kehoe 1993, 1997), the distribution of Roman amphorae (Monfort 1994), Columella's account keeping (Duncan-Jones 1982), or the entire issue of Roman monetization itself (De Cecco 1985) *do not count as economic institutions comparable to modern manifestations unless they* are *completely isomorphic with their modern counterparts.* We are back to Carandini's complaint that Anglo-Saxon scholarship seems to hold it against the Romans that they did not study economics. But they did not have a word for it. De Cecco (1985:822) aptly comments: "Economics, as…eminent [modern] historians use this word, is a discipline invented by [John Maynard] Keynes. But if knowing economics means to be aware of the results attendant upon some actions in the economic spheres, then a careful study of Roman literary and legal evidence [we may add archaeological] will convince anybody that the Romans knew a lot of it [and]…they had never found it necessary to study it formally to talk about it."

In closing, a final reason for pursuing a world-systems perspective for the Roman Empire is the tenor of current work on Roman economies. Until September 11, 2001, this was an age of such economic confidence in the Western world that it seems to have tinged how many scholars of the ancient economy wrote. Many favored the Hopkins model and its implied approval of minimally restrained capitalism, with consequent beneficial trickle-down effects. And yet the same investigators rejected wholesale the Wallerstein worldview because it is too reductionist or center-centric, while either downplaying or ignoring its analysis of systematic exploitation.

What is compelling about the world-systems view is the refusal to back away from the likely (if not outright obvious) asymmetry between economic life in the core and the peripheries, and the inequalities of and among different groups in the core itself. And the ancient world can never escape the taint of slavery, immortalized in Ste. Croix's (1981) stunning indictment. That is what empires do, after all. A little dose of reminder about the inequality inherent in the system would be a welcome antidote to the unrelenting optimism of some recent analysis of ancient economic life. If Plattner (1989:17) is correct that Marxism is the historical study of "how the patterns of inequalities in control over productive assets are reproduced over time," then inequality (especially economic inequal-ity) is an inevitable dimension of what we must study about complex societies, whether we like it or not.

Note

I would like to thank Gary Feinman for inviting me to participate in this roundtable and volume and for giving me so much encouragement and so many valuable suggestions. I also would like to thank all the volume's participants, who taught me in two days at the conference as much as I had ever learned about political economies. I am grateful to my sister, Rebecca Storey, for reading and commenting on a draft of this chapter, and to Rudi Colloredo-Mansfeld for valuable discussions on economic anthropology. Katharine Dale and Gwendolyn Gruber were tireless and outstanding research assistants. Thanks also to my patient wife, Andrea Lucia Piermarini Storey.

8

Early State Economic Systems in China

ANNE P. UNDERHILL AND HUI FANG

A fundamental issue in anthropological archaeology is the development and nature of economic systems in early state societies. During the past decade, research in several areas has accentuated the need to investigate variation in systems of production, distribution, and consumption. Recent studies emphasize the importance of considering patterns that characterize specific historical contexts and investigating change in economic systems over time (Brumfiel 1994; Feinman and Marcus 1998; Stein 2001b). Political and domestic economies in early states are not static entities but dynamic ones that change in response to shifting strategies of elite and non-elite households. There is increasing recognition that early states were composed of diverse social groups with competing economic interests.

A key research question is how early state officials attempted to increase economic power through control over production of prestige goods, acquisition of tribute, control of agricultural production, or other means (Brumfiel 1994; Brumfiel and Earle 1987; Haas 1982; Stein 2001b; Wright 2000). Investigating these kinds of issues requires analyzing interactions between communities at different social scales (Feinman 1998:101). The degree of control over systems of production and distribution has important implications for understanding the nature and extent of regional economic integration in early states. Research in several world areas

indicates that elite control of the economy was limited and fluctuating (Marcus and Feinman 1998; Stein 2001b).

Ancient China has not been considered adequately in these discussions. A major problem is lack of accessibility to relevant publications, including important studies in English that are out of print (e.g., Chang 1980). One valuable study in Chinese by Liu and Chen (2000) considers control of copper, lead, and salt over peripheral areas by regional centers during the Erlitou and Shang periods, especially in west-central Henan and southern Shanxi. In this chapter we employ both textual and archaeological data to discuss the nature of the political economy during the late Shang period (c. 1200–1046 B.C.; Qiu and Cai 2001). We discuss control over farmers and utilitarian craft specialists near the capital of Anyang, control of skilled labor to produce prestige goods at Anyang, exchange of prestige goods and wealth items among elites, acquisition of tribute by state officials, and acquisition of important raw materials (salt, jade, ores). Laborers were essential for farming, production of basic craft goods for elites in the capitals, production of prestige goods, and large-scale construction projects. At the same time, ruling elites expended considerable effort to establish alliances with peoples beyond the Shang core area and to extract valuable raw materials and finished objects. This process had an impact on the size and integration of the Shang

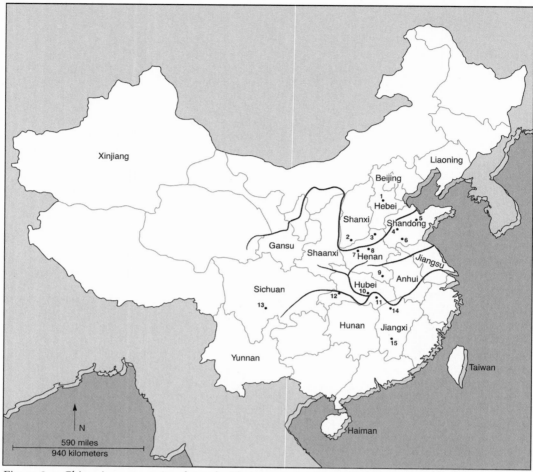

Figure 8.1. China: important sites from the Shang period. (1) Taixi; (2) Yuanqu; (3) Anyang; (4) Daxinzhuang; (5) Sufutun; (6) Qianzhangda; (7) Erlitou and Yanshi; (8) Zhengzhou; (9) Tianhu; (10) Panlongcheng; (11) Tonglushan; (12) Zhongbaodao; (13) Sanxingdui; (14) Tongling; (15) Xingan. (Illustration by Jill Seagard)

state. We conclude that relations of economic and political control were fragile and fluctuated throughout the Shang period.

EARLY STATES IN NORTHERN CHINA
There is a consensus that complex societies emerged in more than one area of the Yellow River valley after about 2500 B.C. (Chang 1983a, 1986; Su 1994). There is great debate, however, about the periods during which the earliest states developed. Until recently, the prevailing view has been that the Erlitou period (c. 1900–1500 B.C.) represents the emergence of states. Research has fo-

cused on identifying the origins of the Xia dynasty, mentioned in later historical texts. This task has been made more difficult by the fact that no written records from the Xia dynasty have been discovered. The remains from the Erlitou site (Figure 8.1) and Erlitou period, including population centers, palaces, bronze items, and other prestige goods such as jade and turquoise, are qualitatively different from those found at earlier sites in the area (see Barnes 1993:127; Chang 1986; Institute of Archaeology 1999; Liu and Chen 2001; Thorp 1991). Some recent publications argue instead that states developed during the preceding Longshan period (c. 2600–1900 B.C.) in the Yellow River valley (Dematte 1999; Wiesheu 1997:100–101; Zhang 1997). These debates cannot be resolved until more data on social, political, and economic organization in individual regions are collected.

Regardless of when states first emerged, there is compelling evidence that the degree of political centralization in the Shang state increased during occupation of the late Shang period capital at Anyang. Several discrete, functional areas have been identified at Anyang through extensive, ongoing excavations. The two most important elite components discussed here are the primary residential/temple area at Xiaotun (Hsiaot'un) and the royal cemetery at Xibeigang (Hsi-p'ei-kang; Bagley 1999; Chang 1986; Keightley 1999). An earlier, walled settlement called Huanbei was recently discovered in the Anyang area (Tang et al. 2000). By the end of the occupation period the site of Anyang had expanded to 24 km² (Bagley 1999:187). Several other sites dating to the late Shang period have been discovered, such as Tianhu (see Figure 8.1).

Gradually, more information is emerging about earlier phases of the Shang period (c. 1570–1200 B.C.). Details about the chronology of sites such as Zhengzhou, Yuanqu, Taixi, and Yanshi, however, are in dispute (see Bagley 1999; Chang 1986; Chang and Zhang 1998; Tang et al. 2000). This chapter also considers economic and political organization during earlier phases of the Shang state, before Anyang became the capital.

It should be noted that sites yielding bronze objects contemporary with the Erlitou and Shang periods have been found in the eastern province of Shandong. Increasingly, archaeologists refer to these early Bronze Age sites in northern China as part of independent polities rather than parts of state territories centered farther west. The Yueshi period (c. 1800–1450 B.C.) in Shandong is contemporary with the Erlitou period and the Erligang phase of the earlier Shang period in Henan (Fang 1998). Shang period sites in Shandong discussed here are Daxinzhuang (Ta-hsin-chuang), Sufutun (Su-fu-t'un), and Qianzhangda (see Figure 8.1).

THE LATE SHANG STATE AND ITS NEIGHBORS

Textual data from the late Shang period (oracle bone inscriptions, inscriptions on bronze vessels) show that the core of the state territory consisted of areas where the king had control over economic resources, where he could receive harvests and hunt or extract other resources. Beyond that, there were rulers of towns at varying distances from Anyang with which the Shang rulers attempted to establish and maintain friendly relations. Interpreting the extent of the late Shang state territory on the basis of this textual information has been the subject of considerable debate. Both textual and archaeological data are needed to shed light on the situation, as discussed below.

The oracle bone inscriptions mention lands (called *tu*) in four directions that are relatively close to Anyang and within the core state area, inhabited by people regarded as Shang by descent. These appear to be cultivable lands headed by partially autonomous local rulers. Also, the Shang king performed harvest divinations on behalf of these rulers (see Keightley 1999:272, 2000:62; David Keightley, personal communication 2003). This effort by the king could indicate that there was an economic relationship between the Shang king and these local rulers, who occasionally provided grain as tribute. State officials, however, could not always rely on the duration of friendly relations with people living in the relatively close *tu* lands, as the oracle bone inscriptions mention that the army was sometimes sent to attack these areas (Keightley 2000:63).

The oracle bone inscriptions also refer to four general areas, or *fang*, surrounding the capital of Anyang to the east, south, west, and north, considered beyond the borders of Shang territory. The inscriptions indicate frequent interaction between the Shang state and the people regarded as non-Shang in these areas. The quantity, nature, and size of these non-Shang independent polities are not clear. These border areas are commonly referred to as the territories of neighboring small states (*fang guo*). The inscriptions also mention that some of these polities were larger and more powerful than others (Du 1996), so that not all of them should be thought of as states. Estimates of the quantity of the separate *fang guo* polities in contact with the Shang during the Anyang period have varied widely. For more than 30 years, many scholars have interpreted the oracle bone inscriptions to indicate that there were 50 to 100 separate states (Chen 1956; Yue 1998; Zhang 1988). Zhao (1988) believes there were more than 110 states. In contrast, a passage in the *Yi Zhou Shu*, a Western Zhou period document, claims that when the Zhou conquered the Shang, they subjugated 99 states that likely were allied with the Shang. In addition, it comments that there were 652 other recognized states (Kong 1929). The issue is complicated by the fact that individual polities could be allies of the late Shang state for a few years and enemies at a later time.

State officials at Anyang made great efforts to appease people in the *fang* areas because they relied on them for extraction of resources that could not be obtained in the vicinity of the capital. According to the inscriptions, the king often had to send soldiers to fight the rebellious, non-Shang people in these areas (Keightley 1999:269, 284). In addition, some *fang* polities cooperated with the Shang to fight against other *fang* polities at various times (Lin 1982). The lack of success of extracting resources from the *tu* and *fang* areas as often as desired may have led Shang officials to establish alliances with peoples at even greater distances. As discussed below, however, these alliances also were fragile and fluctuating.

The oracle bone inscriptions indicate that the Shang recognized roughly a thousand towns beyond Anyang, primarily in the western Shandong–eastern Henan area, southern Hebei, the western Henan–eastern Shanxi area, northern Anhui, and Jiangsu (Chang 1980, 1983b:25). On this basis Chang infers that there were several early states (*guo*) in northern China during the late Shang period, each composed of a hierarchical network of towns. According to Han period (206 B.C.–A.D. 220) texts, the total number of independent polities that existed during the Shang and Xia periods ranges even in the thousands. Clearly, more regional archaeological fieldwork is needed to clarify the quantity and nature of these polities. Another important issue is how the political landscape changed from the earlier Shang (Erligang phase) to the late Shang (Anyang) period. Chang (1980, 1983b) estimates that during earlier phases of the Shang period there were numerous small states. By the late Anyang phase there were fewer states but the territory of each one was larger.

Scholars in North America and in China are equally divided about the issue of the size of the late Shang state. Chang (1980:220) argues that the core area controlled by the Shang rulers at Anyang was relatively large, consisting of northern and central Henan and southwestern Shandong. Others (Maisels 1990; Trigger 1999) also view the late Shang state as relatively large and powerful. Conversely, Keightley (1983, 1999) views the state as relatively small. These same issues are debated in the scholarly literature in China (Du 1996).

We conclude that the late Shang state should be viewed instead as a confederation of allied polities (*fang guo lian meng*; see Lin 1982) that were patrilineal descent groups. Based on oracle bone inscriptions, there were numerous territories inhabited by different patrilineages spread across the landscape (Chang 1980:216; Keightley 1999:269–270). Rather than a stable territory of fixed size, the late Shang state was a dynamic polity that often fluctuated in size and composition. The Shang kings used both persuasion and force to maintain these alliances. Yue (1998) suggests that some *fang guo* leaders came to Anyang to join in sacrifices to Shang royal ancestors and that Shang kings sometimes even went to the *fang* territories to participate in sacrifices there.

CONTROL OF FARMERS AND UTILITARIAN CRAFT SPECIALISTS

Textual and archaeological data reveal a degree of control over agricultural production to support ruling elites during the late Shang period at capitals such as Anyang. Grain and other foodstuffs flowed into the capitals as tribute on a periodic basis, from short and long distances. The extant writing from the late Shang period has a ritual and divinatory function. Therefore, any economic information provided by the oracle bone inscriptions tends to concern the acquisition of prestigious goods to offer as sacrifices to powerful royal ancestors. The king probably also had to ensure that adequate grain was available for officials such as military officers and for craft specialists who made bronze vessels and other key prestige goods. Presumably, the royal household would have attempted to achieve tight economic control over villages near Anyang to acquire adequate quantities of foodstuffs.

There is no consensus, however, about the degree of control that state authorities had over laborers for farming or craft production in the vicinity of Anyang. The oracle bone inscriptions mention workers (gong) who specialized in specific tasks for the state and belonged to distinct groups (described as zuo gong, or left; zhong gong, or middle; and you gong, or right; Xiao 1981). There are specific terms for officials who managed craft production (Yang 1992). Although the inscriptions are not clear, specific officials may have been in charge of each division of farmers and craftspeople, as in the military system (Keightley 1999:285). Some scholars maintain that all workers were slaves (Xiao 1981), although Yang (1986) argues that these laborers were commoners. Yang (1992) interprets the inscriptions as meaning that there were two classes of craftworkers: common people and slaves. In any case, the oracle bone inscriptions show that labor for farming, craft production, and the military was a resource that was in constant demand (Keightley 1999:280). The term dependent laborer most usefully describes the nature of the social relations that existed (Keightley

1999:285–286). These farmers can be regarded as peasants who periodically did agricultural labor for the state.

The inscriptions note that the king could order common people to harvest crops and that he frequently expressed concern about harvests. It is conceivable that all land was regarded as belonging to the king (Chang 1980:223, 226–227, 236; National Museum of Chinese History 1997:137). What probably was more critical, however, was the control of labor by the state (David Keightley, personal communication 2003). Various ranks of officers managed farm workers, and others were responsible for clearing land and preparing cultivation areas. The king often personally inspected the fields and, therefore, the work of his managers (Keightley 1999: 278–280). In addition, officials with specific titles were in charge of animal husbandry and of animal sacrifices (Keightley 1999:280). The oracle bones describe great quantities of cattle and other animals brought to state authorities for sacrificial offerings to royal ancestors (Chang 1980). It is likely that the sacrificial meat was shared during feasts by elite ritual participants (Keightley 1999:280–281; Underhill 2002).

It is likely that there also was mandatory labor for some public construction projects, such as digging royal tombs (see Keightley 1999:268 on the labor required). Even though cooperative labor also may have played a role in economic organization during the Shang period (R. McIntosh 1999), there would have been some powerful incentives, both physical and ideological, motivating people to comply with the demands of the royal household, particularly the sacred authority of the ruling elites and their ancestors.

There is some archaeological evidence to support the interpretation that state authorities at least partially controlled agricultural production in the vicinity of Anyang. Cheng (1960:197) and Haas (1982:98) note the significance of a pit containing a large quantity of stone tools in the Xiaotun section of Anyang, the same district where the palaces and temples were discovered. Although originally described as knives (Li 1952:590–591;

Shi 1933:723), these tools are called sickles in later publications (Cheng 1960:197; National Museum of Chinese History 1997: 146, providing a photograph). In either case they look feasible for harvesting grain. There is some confusion in the literature about the contents and nature of this important pit, called E181. Cheng (1960:197) mistakenly reports that 3,500 sickles were discovered in it. In the earliest report Shi (1933) states that 444 tools were found (also reported by National History Museum 1997). Li (1952:590) provides the necessary details. The pit contained a total of 3,640 artifacts, 1,122 of which were whole and incompletely manufactured "knives" (based on adding up the list in the report). Only 237 of the tools were finished. The rest were in various stages of production, with 244 nearly complete.

The interpretation that the pit provides evidence for some elite management of agricultural production at Anyang is still plausible. Shi (1933) explains that the deep pit or cellar containing the tools was located in a southern section (Area E) of Xiaotun, at a considerable distance from the palace but perhaps closer to the agricultural fields. Furthermore, the large percentage of unfinished tools in one pit, seemingly representing most stages in the manufacture of these tools, points to a single workshop. Therefore, state officials probably also managed production of stone tools for the workers who provided grain for the royal household and other key personnel.

The unusual nature of the pit in question also has not been adequately reported. According to the description provided by Shi (1933), the feature was not an average trash or storage pit. It was very narrow and deep, such that the excavators were not able to reach the bottom. The pit was rectangular in shape, measuring about 1 m by 2 m in plan view and 8 m deep. It appears that there was a deliberate arrangement of the contents, with objects of the same kind placed in piles. There were 3,155 egg-shaped stone pebbles in an upper level and an assortment of presumably valued objects below, including decorative gold foil, bronze artifacts such as *zu* projectile points, tortoise shells, broken jade

decorative *huan* rings, and other decorative objects (Shi 1933:722–724). We suggest that the function of the pit was to hold sacrificial offerings by elites to ancestors. The fact that agricultural tools, both complete and in the process of manufacture, were included illustrates the importance of agricultural production in the political economy.

Storage of grain at Anyang was in structures built above ground (called *lin*), judging from graphs in oracle bone inscriptions. Certain officials were ordered by the ruling elite to monitor the security of these storage areas (Liu 1993:322). Some of the numerous underground pits from the south-central part of Xiaotun also may have been used for grain storage, according to Guo (1933:605–606).

Textual data from more than one early historic period reveal that Shang elites also controlled some craftspeople who made utilitarian goods. The *Zuo Zhuan*, a text dating to the Spring and Autumn period (771–476 B.C.), describes craft specialists for utilitarian goods such as rope and pottery vessels who were organized by descent group. After acquiring all resources from the conquered Shang king, the new Western Zhou king ordered specialist producers for rope, pottery vessels, fermented beverages, and other goods to labor for the leader of Lu, a vassal of the new Western Zhou state located in what is now western Shandong province (see Guo 1963; Yang 1981). Now there is archaeological evidence that provides some support for the text describing the migration of craftspeople to Shandong: Guo et al. (1990) report the discovery of two early Western Zhou bronze vessels in southwestern Shandong (context unclear) with inscriptions and symbols depicting the name of a descent group (Suo) that made rope.

During the Shang period state authorities probably controlled a number of craftspeople who made utilitarian goods for the royal household and for officials who lived in or near the capital (Chang 1980, 1983b). Xiao (1981) argues that small graves in the large cemetery in the western district of Anyang provide evidence to support the conclusion that there was a high degree of occupational specialization. In more than one section of the cemetery some graves contain distinct sets of bronze, stone, and bone tools that appear to represent specialized production. In Area Eight 24 percent of the small graves contain bronze knives and awls interpreted as tools used in the production of bone objects. The same tools were found in the remains of a bone workshop nearby in the Beixinzhuang section of Anyang.

CONTROL OF SKILLED LABOR TO PRODUCE PRESTIGE GOODS

State officials also needed to control skilled labor to make highly valued prestige goods, particularly bronze vessels. The numerous bronze vessels in elite graves at Anyang attest to the importance of these goods in symbolizing economic power. The oracle bone inscriptions also indicate that bronze food vessels were symbols of political power and authority. The vessels were crucial for sacrificial rites to royal ancestors, who were regarded as a key source of power. Archaeological remains of workshops for bronze production near elite contexts at Anyang are additional grounds for concluding that there was attached specialization for production of bronze vessels, weapons, and other goods (Brumfiel and Earle 1987; Chang 1980, 1983a; Underhill 2002). Judging from the large quantities of bronze vessels recovered from graves at Anyang, state authorities would have required control over a considerable force of skilled specialists. There would have been a number of specialists for each step in production: smelting, alloying, preparing the clay models, preparing the piece molds, assembling the molds and pouring the molten metal, and finishing the vessels (Chase 1991:22–25, 29; Franklin 1983:96–97; Hua 1999). The system of attached specialization began during earlier phases of the Shang state, judging from the bronze workshop remains at Zhengzhou (Chang 1980). As discussed below, mining of ores also would have been supervised by state officials during the Shang period.

It is likely that late Shang state officials also controlled other skilled craft specialists who made prestige goods for elite consumption at Anyang. Jade objects are abundant in elite graves, notably the unlooted tomb of Fu Hao (regarded as a consort of the king), containing 755 items. Skilled workers who made prestige goods such as bronze vessels and jade objects probably had higher status than others. A house interpreted as a workshop for stone and jade objects at Xiaotun had rammed-earth floors and painted murals and contained bronze projectile points and turquoise inlaid hairpins (see Chang 1980:235; Institute of Archaeology 1976:266).

Elite graves at Anyang also contain lacquer objects inlaid with mother-of-pearl designs in the shape of animal masks (Fang 2001). According to Cheng (1960:126–127), the Shang extracted mother-of-pearl from thick freshwater *Lamprotula* shells that were native to the Yangzi River area. Several species in this genus are known to China and are distributed over a wide area, including parts of Hebei, Jiangsu, Anhui, Zhejiang, and Hubei provinces (Liu et al. 1979).

Ruling elites in other states contemporary with the late Shang also may have controlled some skilled craftspeople. There probably were efforts to make some prestige goods to emulate those from Anyang, the capital of the most powerful state in northern China at the time. At the Shang period site of Qianzhangda in southern Shandong, archaeologists recovered elaborate lacquer objects inlaid with shell (Fang 2001; Shandong Team 1992). The consensus is that Qianzhangda represents a separate state identified as Xue in later historical texts (Shandong Team 1992). The rich graves here have other Anyang-style prestige goods, including bronze vessels and jade animals.

Oracle bone inscriptions mention another important material that has remained relatively elusive to archaeologists, silk textiles. Traces of silk textiles have been found on the back of bronze weapons and vessels (Kuhn 1982:383–385). Several other cases have been reported during the last 20 years. For instance, rolled silk was found in a sacrificial pit in the Hougang section of Anyang (about 1 km to the southeast of elite residences at

Xiaotun) with 73 slain human victims and other prestige goods (Institute of Archaeology 1987:268). Oracle bone inscriptions from the late Shang period mention worry (presumably by the king) about the success of silk production (both the silkworms and the cloth), and certain managers were held accountable. Women raised the silkworms (Kuhn 1982:378). The production system of elite textiles may have resembled that of the Inca, in which state officials managed scores of female weavers (Costin 1998b).

REGIONAL ECONOMIC ORGANIZATION DURING THE LATE SHANG PERIOD

The prevailing regional model for late Shang economic organization has been that villages surrounding the capital of Anyang provided labor and basic goods to the state. Some farmers and craft specialists in the core capital areas contributed their labor to support state officials. There also were craftspeople who were independent specialists supplying commoner households with utilitarian goods. The assumption has been that villages were largely self-sufficient (Chang 1975, 1980). The alternative possibility that there was large-scale production of utilitarian goods such as pottery has not been tested, however.

The prevailing model of economic organization assumes that the late Shang state was relatively large. The model also stipulates that lower-ranking elites in secondary centers served the state by monitoring the flow of goods and raw materials into Anyang (Chang 1975, 1980:210; Trigger 1999). On this basis some scholars emphasize differences between urban and rural production systems, assuming a steady state of integration between primary and secondary centers (Maisels 1990; Trigger 1999). These debates cannot be resolved until more regional-scale data for the late Shang period are available, although more information about regional settlement patterns is emerging through the initiation of systematic survey in the Anyang area (Jing et al. 1997; Liu and Chen 2001; Tang et al. 2000). There is a great need for economic information from rural sites as well as urban centers, a problem identified in other areas of

the world where early states developed (Wattenmaker 1998).

As discussed above, textual data reveal that relations between the capital at Anyang and outlying settlements were fragile and fluctuating. Other scholars advocate a city-state model for early China that emphasizes economic integration between each center and its hinterlands (Charlton and Nichols 1997:13; Yates 1997). These two competing models for Shang political and economic organization probably represent a false dichotomy, since little regional-scale data currently are available for northern China during the Shang period. One method of approaching the topic of economic integration between settlements is to consider exchange of goods. As discussed below, evidence has been accumulating for the interregional exchange of goods and raw materials during the Shang period. More than one kind of exchange system existed, including gift exchange among elites and exchange of valuable raw materials. Investigation of interacting polities can reveal the effect that different kinds of intercommunity social networks had on social change in an area (Stein 1999:174–175).

EXCHANGE OF PRESTIGE GOODS AND WEALTH ITEMS AMONG ELITES

Shang-style bronze vessels have been found in a wide area of eastern China, as far south as modern Hunan and Jiangxi provinces (Chang 1980). They are common in Shang-style elite graves in outlying areas of northern China, such as the late Shang site of Tianhu in southeastern Henan (CPAM 1986). At most of these Shang period sites there is no direct evidence for independent bronze production, and therefore it is likely that elites at capitals such as Anyang gave these vessels to elites in peripheral areas for service to the state. These areas could have provided goods, raw materials, or labor, including protection of exchange routes. The system of elite gift exchange with bronze vessels documented from the Western Zhou period (Cook 1997) may have begun sometime during the Shang period (Underhill 2002). Elite spheres of gift exchange would have been important mechanisms for maintaining alliances between Anyang and outlying areas that were essential for extraction of resources.

Elites in these peripheral areas desired foreign prestige goods and emulated Shang elite burial practices. As Helms (1993) observes, local elites seek to adopt elements of foreign elite ideology and ritual practices. For example, elite Shang-style graves became increasingly common in western and central Shandong during the late Shang period (Gao 2000). Gift exchange also must account for the bronze vessels in elite graves at Qianzhangda (Shandong Team 1992, 2000) and Sufutun (Shandong Provincial Museum 1972). As discussed below, state officials at Anyang evidently initiated alliances with outlying polities at even greater distances to extract resources. In more than one of these peripheral areas the process of interaction between local elites and the Shang could have accelerated development of social stratification or political centralization.

There is increasing evidence that late Shang state officials at Anyang interacted with independent complex societies in southern China that also had the means to produce bronze items. The process of interacting with the Shang state probably helped motivate the initial production of bronze items in these areas (Bagley 1999:213). The rich, elite tomb at Xingan in southern Jiangxi contains a few Shang-style bronzes but a number that are totally different from northern ones, such as large masks. Some of the jades also are in styles different from those of objects at Anyang (Bagley 1993; Jiangxi Institute of Archaeology et al. 1997). Contacts with the north were under way by the early phases of occupation at Anyang or somewhat earlier, judging from artifact styles (Bagley 1999: 172). The presence of the few Shang elite styles of bronze vessels probably represents gift exchange from northern capitals or, as suggested by Bagley (1999), local copies of northern styles. Bagley (1999:172–174) proposes that local styles became more abundant during later phases of occupation, when bronze production in the area increased in scale. It is likely that elites in southern

Jiangxi, like their counterparts in Henan, sponsored production of ritually important bronze items and jade items. This process allowed political, economic, and ideological power to increase.

Similarly, at the remarkable Shang period site of Sanxingdui in Sichuan, archaeologists recovered unique life-sized bronze statues along with even fewer Shang-style bronze vessels. The scale of the remains, including a relatively large walled settlement and abundant wealth items, points to a state society contemporary with the Shang. Although contacts between people from the Sanxingdui and Shang state polities in Henan probably began during the middle (Erligang) Shang period, bronze production may not have begun in Sichuan until later (Bagley 1999:217–218; see also Shen 2002; Sichuan Province Institute of Archaeology 1999).

During earlier phases of the Shang period as well, there were efforts by state officials to expand the territory from which resources could be extracted. The consensus is that officials at capitals such as Zhengzhou (Erligang phase) established colonies in outlying areas. The settlement of Panlongcheng in eastern Hubei bears many similarities to Zhengzhou (see Figure 8.1). Panlongcheng also is surrounded by a wall of rammed earth, contains clear evidence (smelting crucibles, slag) for production of bronze vessels and weapons, and has Shang-style elite burials (see Bagley 1977, 1999; Hubei Province Institute of Archaeology 2001). The attempt to expand the economic network of the state ended when Panlongcheng was abandoned at the end of the middle Shang period. The earlier Shang state did not have extensive control over Hubei. Sites with local, distinctively non-Shang traits are common, such as Zhongbaodao in western Hubei (Three Gorges Team 2001). The bronze tools at the settlement may represent independent production. The territory under state control probably was narrow and linear in shape, consisting only of the exchange route that led from the capital at Zhengzhou in Henan directly to Panlongcheng.

Other settlements established in the earlier

(pre-Anyang) Shang period, such as Daxin-zhuang in western Shandong (Shandong University Archaeology Department et al. 1995), may represent territories that were controlled on a more regular basis. Bronze production has been documented at the settlement of Yanshi in Henan (Wang 1999) as well as the capital at Zhengzhou (Chang 1980). Other relatively early Shang settlements with bronze vessels but no evidence for bronze production are Taixi (Hebei Province Institute of Archaeology 1985) and Yuanqu (National Museum of Chinese History et al. 1996). It is likely that some of these areas were important for extraction of resources, including ores, as discussed below.

OTHER PRESTIGE GOODS

It is debated whether certain oracle bone inscriptions refer to the exchange of silk textiles among elites (see Kuhn 1982:379). Given the effectiveness of clothing for marking elite status throughout the world and growing evidence for sponsored production of valued textiles in early states, as discussed above, more evidence for the Shang should emerge.

A long-standing debate in Shang archaeology is the economic function of cowrie shells. Some scholars believe these shells and those of the same shape made in bone or bronze that have been found at Anyang represent a form of currency (Dai 1981). Others argue that the shells were symbols of wealth, used to decorate clothing, horse gear, and other items (Chen 2000; Guo 1963; Kondo 1998). Peng and Zhu (1999) point out that cowrie shells appear in late Neolithic as well as earlier Bronze Age sites in several areas of China, and they become more numerous in sites of the late Shang period.

The same species of cowrie shell (*Monetaria moneta*) has been known as a form of currency in modern cultures in several areas of the world. *Monetaria* has a huge range, including the Indian Ocean to the South China Sea (Lorenz and Hubert 2000:204–205; Ma 1997). Peng and Zhu (1999) assume that the early use of cowrie shells in western China indicates an origin area in western Asia. Given the natural distribution of the species, however, during the late Shang period people most likely acquired the shells through a system of long-distance exchange to the south. One bronze *ding* tripod vessel in the Sackler collections in New York has an inscribed figure interpreted as standing on a boat and holding a string of cowries. Other inscriptions show simply a string of cowries (Bagley 1987:459). Some scholars have proposed that there were specialist traders by lineage (Chang 1975:221).

On the basis of textual and archaeological data from the late Shang period, we suggest that cowrie shells were a wealth item used only by elites for display or for acquisition of other valuables. In Shang oracle bone inscriptions cowries could have been standard units, such that five *bei* (shells) equaled one *peng*, or string of cowries. There is inadequate evidence to conclude that they represent a form of currency used by a wide range of households during the Shang period. Currency would imply a relatively large scale of production for a range of goods and a market economy. The shells are found only in a few elite graves, indicating that they were accessible exclusively to elites. For instance, 6,880 were found in the grave of Fu Hao (Institute of Archaeology 1980:220). There also is inscriptional evidence that the king would give cowries to officials. As Bagley (1987:522) and Kondo (1998) conclude, the king bestowed gifts of cowries on military and other officials to honor them for meritorious service to the state. We further suggest that nobles could have used them to acquire other wealth items. A bronze vessel in a sacrificial pit at Hougang bears an inscription stating that a person received 20 *peng* of shells and then made a *ding* tripod vessel in honor of his father (Institute of Archaeology 1987:272). The cowrie shell became a true form of currency available to a wide range of households only after the Shang period.

TRIBUTE FOR STATE OFFICIALS: RAW MATERIALS AND GOODS

Another debate concerns the nature and extent of resources that flowed into the capital at Anyang as tribute to the late Shang state.

Table 8.1. Tribute Sent to Northern China by Territories Mentioned in the *Yu Gong*
During the Early Historic Period

Territory	Modern Area	Kinds of Tribute
Ji Zhou	Hebei, Liaoning	grain
Yan Zhou	western Shandong, eastern Henan	lacquer, silk
Qing Zhou	northern Shandong	salt, hemp cloth, flax, sea resources, tin, fine stone
Xu Zhou	southern Shandong, northern Anhui, Jiangsu	five colors of soil to make altars; pheasants, tung wood, chime stones, silk, mussels, fish
Yang Zhou	southern Jiangsu, southern Anhui, Zhejiang	copper, jade, animal teeth, rhinoceros leather, feathers, catalpa wood, silk, shell, oranges, tin
Jing Zhou	Hubei, southern Anhui, Hunan	feathers, leather, animal teeth, copper, various woods for making bows, sandstone, cinnabar, bamboo, oranges, silk, jade, large tortoises
Yu Zhou	Henan	lacquer, flax, special sands for abrasion in jade production
Liang Zhou	Shanxi	jade, silver, leather
Yong Zhou	Gansu	jade

Exaction of resources through tribute was a major activity of early states in several areas of the world (Brumfiel 1994). Evaluating this debate requires reassessing textual and archaeological evidence for interregional political and economic relations. The oracle bone inscriptions emphasize receipt of ritual goods from other territories (presumably near and far) for divination and sacrifices to royal ancestors, such as turtle shells, cattle, sheep, and humans, as well as cowrie shells (Chang 1980; Keightley 1999). Although at least some turtle shells originated in South China, some may have been given as tribute by other states in northern China (Chang 1980:156). According to textual data, the tribute system of the late Shang state consisted primarily of ritual goods, many of which came from distant areas (Keightley 1999:281–282). As discussed above, human labor was in demand by the state, and war captives probably also were important tribute items. More archaeological research is needed to discern whether utilitarian goods or raw materials also were given to late Shang leaders as tribute.

One later historical text, the *Yu Gong*, a chapter of the *Shang Shu* (or *Shu Jing*, Book of Documents), describes tributary relations between polities. The consensus is that most sections were written during the late Eastern Zhou period (771–221 B.C.), but some sections could date to as late as the Qin dynasty (221–206 B.C.; Shaughnessy 1993). Archaeological discoveries at Shang period sites in recent years have led scholars to suggest that some information in the *Yu Gong* refers to earlier periods. Shao (1987) proposes that the *Yu Gong* refers to nine state territories as early as the late Longshan to the Shang period.

The *Yu Gong* provides potential economic information (Li 1999) about the late Shang period. This text describes different kinds of tribute that the various territories provided to powerful states in northern China sometime during the early historic period (Table 8.1). Parts of the text therefore may describe goods sent to the Shang ruling elite at Anyang, although some tribute items listed, such as oranges (wild or domesticated), may refer to post-Shang periods. Oranges are mentioned in the *Shi Jing* (Book of Songs), which contains passages interpreted as dating from the early Western Zhou to the Spring and Autumn period (c. 1046–476 B.C.). There is some evidence to suggest that one or more of the territories described in the *Yu Gong* (Figure 8.2) could have provided

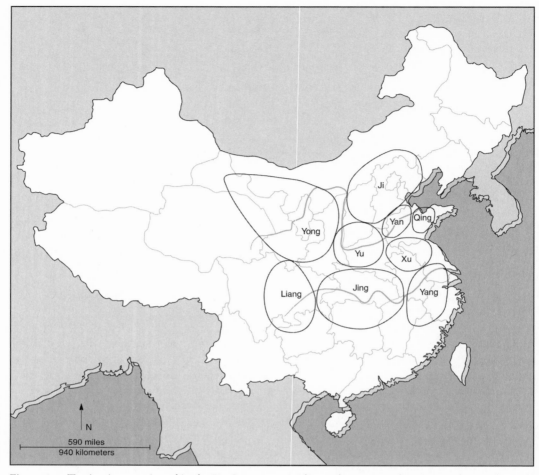

Figure 8.2. Territories mentioned in the *Yu Gong* as providing tribute to northern states during the early historic period. (Adapted from Li and Chen 1982:Figure 1; illustration by Jill Seagard)

goods or raw materials to the capital of Anyang during the late Shang period, such as salt, jade, and ores for bronze production.

Another key question is the nature of sociopolitical organization in these areas during the late Shang period. Most contemporary polities would have had relations of dependency with Anyang, providing raw materials or goods as tribute in exchange for goods or other services from the center. The Shang could have interacted with chiefdoms or weak states in these areas. In either case the territory most likely was smaller than depicted in the Eastern Zhou document. The interaction could have been mutually beneficial, eventually instigating significant social change in the smaller polities. For example,

local leaders in smaller-scale polities could have furthered their own economic and political agendas by managing the flow of goods with the Shang. Junker (1999) provides a relevant example of the impact of trade between chiefdoms in peripheral areas and state societies. Some exchange of goods between the late Shang state and independent polities could have involved equally strong independent states rather than relations of dependency. In this case the relations should be characterized as exchange between peer polities (Renfrew 1986a).

ACQUISITION OF SALT, JADE, AND ORES
The oracle bone inscriptions mention that the late Shang kings tried more than one method

to obtain salt. Yang (1998) argues that the Shang conquered a location somewhere in the northwest to acquire salt. The oracle bones mention a title (Lu Xiu Chen) of an official in charge of salt production, and they also mention that some individuals sent salt to Anyang as tribute (Yang 1992). The king could have attempted to obtain salt from an area closer to the capital, such as sea salt from an area to the east (Fang 2004). Possibly referring to an earlier period, the *Yu Gong* text mentions that sea salt was sent as tribute from the Qing Zhou area in northern Shandong to another state.

Recent compositional analyses show that some jade (nephrite) in Shang sites was acquired from very distant areas. An inscription on one jade *ge* dagger-ax found in the Fu Hao tomb at Anyang mentions that a *fang* territory named Lu sent five dagger-axes as tribute, perhaps for funeral rites, as a token of respect. This tomb also yielded a *qing* chime stone bearing an inscription indicating that the Zhu state sent the item as tribute (Institute of Archaeology 1980:139, 199). In addition, a few jade artifacts in the Fu Hao tomb were made from stone that was quarried in Xinjiang. Similarly, a compositional analysis of jade artifacts in the Xingan tomb in Jiangxi reveals two distant source areas, Shanxi province and Xinjiang province (the majority; Chen 2000). These very distant source areas may not have been used on a frequent basis; it is likely that source areas closer to Anyang were relied on more often.

Jade could have been acquired by more than one form of exchange. Wen and Jing (1992) identify potential nephrite sources in the Yangzi Delta area near Shanghai and in southern Henan. Similarly, the *Yu Gong* mentions that jade was provided by three areas in the Yangzi River valley (Jing Zhou, Yang Zhou, Liang Zhou) and two more northern areas that were closer to Anyang (Yu Zhou, Yong Zhou). Of course, more compositional analyses of jade artifacts and source areas are needed to evaluate this hypothesis.

There is a growing amount of information on source areas for tin and copper used in the production of bronze vessels during the late

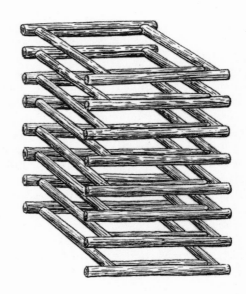

Figure 8.3. Facilities for copper mining at the Shang site of Tongling at Ruichang, Jiangxi. (Illustration by Jill Seagard)

Shang period. Ingots were prepared near the mines and transported to the capital settlements in Henan. At Anyang, for example, archaeologists found ingots in bronze production areas (Institute of Archaeology 1987). Important source areas for copper have been identified in the Yangzi River valley, particularly Tongling (Ruichang), in northern Jiangxi, and Tonglushan, in southern Hubei (see Figure 8.1). Radiocarbon analyses of associated wooden structures and analysis of associated artifacts show that Tongling was first exploited during the middle Shang period, representing the earliest known mining site in China (Hua and Lu 1996; Liu and Lu 1998). Archaeologists found early evidence for strip mining techniques and then tunnel mining (Hua and Lu 1996; Liu and Lu 1998). During the middle Shang period miners entered the shaft by crawling through a tunnel with horizontal wooden supports (Figure 8.3). During the late Shang period miners went through a deep tunnel (Liu and Lu 1998). Golas (1999) notes that given the friable rock, mining in the Yangzi River area would not have been difficult, and the river greatly facilitated transportation.

Abundant radiocarbon dates and artifacts clearly indicate that Tonglushan was used during the Zhou period. A number of scholars conclude from radiocarbon dates on wooden shafts that mining began during the Shang period, although no Shang artifacts have been discovered. Smelting could have taken place near the mining areas, given the abundant local timber (Golas 1999:79–82).

Other mining sites in southern Anhui dating to the Shang period also have been discovered (Hua and Lu 1996). Tongling and Tonglushan fall within the territory described in the *Yu Gong* as Jing Zhou, which was said to have provided copper. Southern Anhui is in the area described as Yang Zhou, which was noted for its copper and tin. Some scholars regard these areas as the most important for providing copper during the Shang period. The copper is higher in quality and easier to extract than in other areas because it is shallower (Hua and Lu 1996).

In addition, the importance of the remote province of Yunnan for providing copper to the Shang state is becoming increasingly acknowledged. Hua and Lu (1996) regard it as secondary only to the Yangzi River area. Compositional analyses show that some bronze vessels from the Fu Hao tomb in Anyang were made from ores originating in Yunnan, which have distinctive low ratios of lead isotopes (Li 1993). More bronzes of this kind date to the Shang period than other periods. However, the degree to which late Shang officials at Anyang relied on such distant sources is not clear, nor is the nature of the exchange system represented.

Peng et al. (1999) propose that during middle (Erligang) Shang there was greater reliance on sources from northern areas such as Hebei and Liaoning provinces, with high ratios of lead isotopes. During the late Shang

period state authorities needed to exploit new areas to the south. One possible explanation is that northern polities that had been allies in the middle Shang period became hostile in late Shang. Or perhaps some northern areas ran out of ore. Regardless, periodic acquisition of ores from South China required a strong state organization. As Bagley (1993: 36) notes, contacts between the Shang and local elites in other distant areas such as southern Jiangxi where Xingan is located could have been initiated when the Shang royal court sought new sources for copper.

Compositional analyses show that bronze vessels from the southern states represented at Xingan and Sanxingdui in Sichuan tend to have high radiogenic lead (Jin et al. 1998), as do bronze vessels from the early and middle Shang sites of Yanshi, Zhengzhou, and Panlongcheng. This pattern also characterizes vessels from phases Yinxu I and II at Anyang. Vessels with high radiogenic lead from phases III and IV are much less common. Therefore, some of the same sources may have been used from the early Shang period to the first half of the Anyang (Yinxu) period (Jin et al. 1998).

Less research has been conducted on source areas for tin, another crucial ore for bronze production. Modern tin (more properly, cassiterite) deposits are concentrated in mountainous areas of southern China, including the modern provinces of Yunnan, Hunan, and Jiangxi (Golas 1999:91). An unresolved issue is the degree to which ore sources in the south were exploited in comparison with sources closer to the Shang capitals.

As Golas (1999:78) notes, it does not seem feasible for the Shang in central Henan (Zhengzhou) and northern Henan (Anyang) to have relied totally on distant sources from the Yangzi River area. There must have been some ore sources closer to Shang capitals to accommodate the great intensity and scale of production, particularly during the late Shang period.

Golas (1999:72–74) estimates that more than 20 copper sources and 10 tin deposits would have been available within a 350-km radius of Anyang. His maps of pre-twentieth-century historically documented source areas show a number of locations for tin and lead in west-central Henan, northern Shanxi, and Shandong. Copper sources are known in northern Shanxi, central Hebei, and several locations in central Shandong (Golas 1999:55, 62, 92). During the early-middle Shang periods political elites would have established contacts with people in northern areas to extract copper, tin, or lead. The site of Taixi in central Hebei could represent an alliance with elites at Zhengzhou. During the late Shang period the rich burials containing a few bronze vessels and other local-style wealth items at Qianzhangda and Sufutun in Shandong (at the periphery of the central Shandong mountains) could represent local elites who managed the flow of copper or other resources to Anyang. Similarly, the *Yu Gong* mentions that the Qing Zhou territory in northern Shandong provided tin as tribute to powerful states. Unfortunately, documenting archaeological evidence for actual exploitation of particular copper sources in China has been difficult because of the highly variable impurities in smelted copper and the likelihood that sources once exploited by the Shang were exhausted (Golas 1999:76).

CONCLUSIONS

In this chapter we have employed textual and archaeological data to provide a sketch of the political economy in the late Shang state centered at Anyang, circa 1200–1046 B.C. The earliest known writing system in China, the inscriptions on oracle bones and bronze vessels, reveals that control over the economy by state officials required constant effort, whether the interaction was with people from settlements close to Anyang or far away. Cooperative relations with people living in areas where important resources were required were fragile and fluctuated over time. Alliances with distant communities in particular would have had to be constantly negotiated.

The most basic requirement was grain and other foodstuffs for the royal household, officials, and craftspeople who made highly valued prestige goods such as bronze vessels and jade items at Anyang. State officials attempted to fill this need by obtaining tribute and people to labor in the fields. It appears that the state also controlled production of stone harvesting tools for its farm workers. There is additional textual evidence to infer that the Shang controlled the labor of a few craft specialists who made utilitarian items for the royal household, such as rope and pottery vessels. A number of villages near Anyang must have been under tight control of the state. Beyond that, allied settlements would have varied over time, as there were few cost-effective methods of enforcing the status quo.

There is abundant archaeological evidence for elite-sponsored production of prestige goods at Anyang and at earlier Shang capitals such as Zhengzhou, particularly bronze vessels. During the late Shang state at least, there also was sponsored production of jade items, lacquered goods inlaid with mother-of-pearl, and silk textiles. We propose that cowrie shells acquired from South China were exchanged among elites as wealth items.

The oracle bone inscriptions state that the military was often called on to subdue people in other settlements, even those inhabited by people regarded as Shang. We infer that another method of enlisting cooperation in providing economic resources and loyalty to the state was to provide local elites with bronze vessels and other prestige goods made at Anyang. The interactions between Shang officials and elites of other areas may have led to an increase in acquisition of economic, political, and ideological power in each social system. Regionally oriented research projects in areas such as southern Shandong (Qianzhangda) and southern Jiangxi (Xingan) are essential for evaluating this hypothesis. Elites at Qianzhangda could have monitored the flow of copper ores into Anyang for bronze production. Elites at Xingan may have sponsored production of ritually important bronze items after initial contacts with the Shang.

Early texts such as the *Yu Gong* provide tantalizing clues about possible exchange relations between the late Shang state and other areas. Recent archaeological discoveries such as copper mines in some of these areas could mean that parts of the *Yu Gong* actually refer to the Shang period. Basic issues that need to be addressed include the degree of reliance on distant copper mines in comparison with those farther north.

These issues regarding intersettlement economic relations have implications for understanding the size and degree of integration of the Shang state. More surveys and excavations of capital sites and their surrounding areas are needed for identifying core areas of the state that provided periodic labor for farming and craft production as well as foodstuffs. Such research also is crucial for identifying possible secondary centers that could have monitored the flow of goods to the capitals. More investigations of intersettlement relations during each phase of the Shang period are needed for determining the boundaries of the state territory. These boundaries should not be viewed as static or fixed, for either the late Shang or earlier periods. We propose instead that state officials at the capitals frequently cast out the "royal net" in different directions and at varying distances to obtain important resources (foodstuffs, craft goods, human labor). The territory of the state had to be constantly negotiated, and it was loosely integrated. Future studies also are needed to evaluate how the size and regional organization of the Shang state changed over time.

Note

We thank Jonathan Haas (Department of Anthropology, The Field Museum) and David Keightley for their valuable comments on a draft of this chapter. Jochen Gerber (Department of Zoology, The Field Museum) generously provided information on various shell species. Jill Seagard (Department of Anthropology, The Field Museum) skillfully prepared the figures.

9

Appropriative Economies
Labor Obligations and Luxury Goods in Ancient Maya Societies

Patricia A. McAnany

At the Classic Maya capital of Copan, Honduras, royal sculptors depicted the passage of the years on the back of Stela D as a bundle transported via a tumpline (Schele and Mathews 1998:168–169). Literally the burden of time, this metonymic convention imparted cosmic significance to the pedestrian task of burden bearing (*kuch* in Yucatec Mayan), at the same time appropriating to Maya royalty a key signifier of manual labor. This example is but one of many in which a locally grounded concept was blended with a hierarchical ideology to produce a notion of natural "order" (à la Baines and Yoffee 1998, 2000:14). Key to the establishment and maintenance of hierarchy, "order" implies an ideology of authority. This chapter explores how such ideologies were established and came to be "the natural order of things." In more specific economic terms, this study examines the manner in which power and materials deemed of great value came to be concentrated in Classic Maya palace courts and, in the process, to alter irrevocably the "logic of practice" (Bourdieu 1990:80–97) among those who lived outside of but linked with court society.

CONSTRUCTS, THEORIES, AND CASE DATA

Studies of economies of ancient states often are reduced to a tug-of-war between polar extremes: market versus redistributive or administered economies, horizontal exchange relationships versus vertical transfers of labor and goods, Marxist versus agency-centered approaches, and historically, substantivist versus formalist approaches. For the Maya region, another dyad of opposing views can be cited: those who embrace the ethnographically based model of self-sufficient Maya households, championed during the previous century by Morley (1956:34) and others, versus those who detect the presence of marketplaces and active regional exchange networks (Andrews 1983; Freidel 1981; Masson 2002; Sabloff and Rathje 1975; Shafer and Hester 1991; Tourtellot and Sabloff 1994 among many others). Twenty-plus years of household archaeology in combination with elemental sourcing and petrographic studies has shifted the weight of evidence in favor of locally active networks of production and distribution and eroded the credibility of the notion of self-sufficient Maya households. Similarly, the traditional idea that Classic Maya seats of power—places as far-flung as Caracol, Tikal, Chunchucmil, and Sayil—were not also economic central places increasingly has been challenged by the discovery of architectural features and artifact patterns suggestive of production and marketplace activities.

As observed by Freidel (1981), the general trend within Maya archaeology has been to recognize that ancient economic arrangements were more, rather than less, complex. At various times and places Maya economies included reciprocal exchange; marketplace trading; tribute in labor and goods; household production beyond that needed for consumption by family members; crafting by artisans attached to palace courts; traders (of variable status) operating on local, regional, and long-distance scales; and—assuredly documented for the Postclassic period—economic transactions based on several media of convertibility (money), of which cacao, or the chocolate bean, played an important role (see Masson 2002 for a comprehensive overview). Thus the types of economic arrangements that existed within Maya society at any one point in time, though not infinite, certainly defy facile generalization. For this reason, I approach the topic by relying on case studies, or vignettes, to put flesh on the rather stark structure of economic form and to focus discussion on a strong characteristic of Maya economies—appropriation—and the attendant labor obligations and luxury goods that underwrote this and many other archaic state economies.

According to Baines and Yoffee (2000:15), compounded wealth is a key social and civilizational phenomenon underpinning "high culture." Largely restricted to the elite sector, compounded wealth permits the long-term stability of an aristocratic and generally ruling component of society. Although Baines and Yoffee have isolated one of the stabilizing factors of hierarchy, they do not discuss the remarkable means by which such stability was achieved—the sweat and toil of countless commoners. As Gose (1994:238, 243) has observed in the Peruvian Andes, "Hierarchy involves not just a distinction between the dominant and the subordinate, but also a logical and substantive connection between them, such that neither could exist without the other.... Power is necessarily based on cooperation and not just transgression." Thus one of the most intriguing questions that pervades the study of the "abnormal process" of civilization making (Mann 1986: 124) is how compounded wealth nested within hierarchical relations came to transpire and to increasingly characterize most

human societies (see also Stanish, this volume). As this chapter shows, Maya high culture would have been nonexistent without the cooperation of commoners who physically built the "seats of power," supplied and maintained the elite residences, and engaged in some form of ongoing dialogue with palace courts. In this respect, study of the emergence of an appropriative economy (defined here as one in which political power initiates the hierarchical transfer of goods and services) is explicitly an examination of the restructuring of sociopolitical relations (in favor of an ideology of authority), of the concentration of wealth, and of the deployment of labor in the service of rulers, the final change representing an acceptance of burden bearing by those in service. These factors likely were embedded within a changing ethos of privilege, responsibility, and value that was ascribed to material things as well as persons of differing rank. In choosing to focus on the intersection of hierarchy and economy, I seek not to compress the significant variation that once existed in Maya economic arrangements but to highlight some of the powerful forces that shaped and transformed Maya economic structure.

This analysis attempts to balance two agency-centered perspectives: the desires and appetites of royal Maya courtiers and the productive capacities of residents of sustaining communities. A longitudinal time frame is achieved by basing the analysis on both primary and secondary data that span the Formative through the Postclassic periods (in this study, specifically 800 B.C. until c. A.D. 1000). Primary data from the site of K'axob, Belize (Figure 9.1), help clarify the conditions surrounding the emergence of appropriative economies during the latter part of the Formative period, generally extending from 400 B.C. to A.D. 250. On the other end of the temporal spectrum, archaeological investigations in the Sibun River valley (Figure 9.1) of central Belize have yielded information relevant to the dynamic restructuring of economic arrangements during the Epiclassic period (A.D. 700/800–1000). Sandwiched

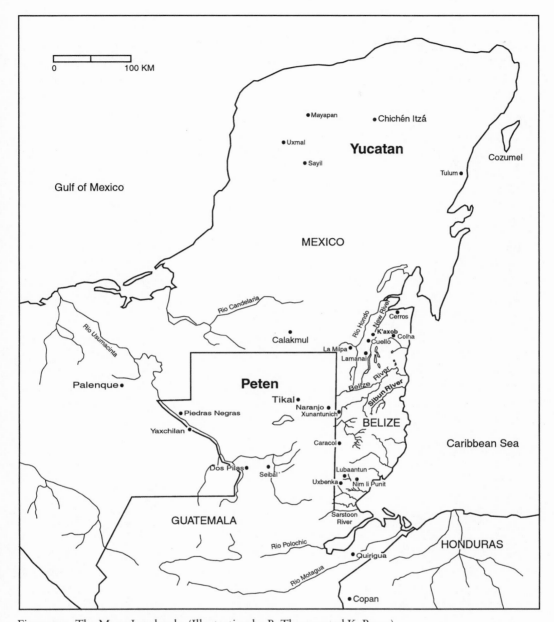

Figure 9.1. The Maya Lowlands. (Illustration by B. Thomas and K. Berry)

temporally between these two studies is a consideration of Classic period (A.D. 250–900) palace economies that is based on published literature.

The well-preserved deposits of K'axob from the Middle to Terminal Formative period (800 B.C.–A.D. 250) display sensitivity to large-scale societal changes that materialized around 200 B.C. (here imputed to have been connected with the emergence of appropriative economies attendant on political centralization). Information from K'axob is directly relevant to understanding how the legitimacy of a new order, with its signature concentration of wealth and need for human labor, affected life in a Formative village. The

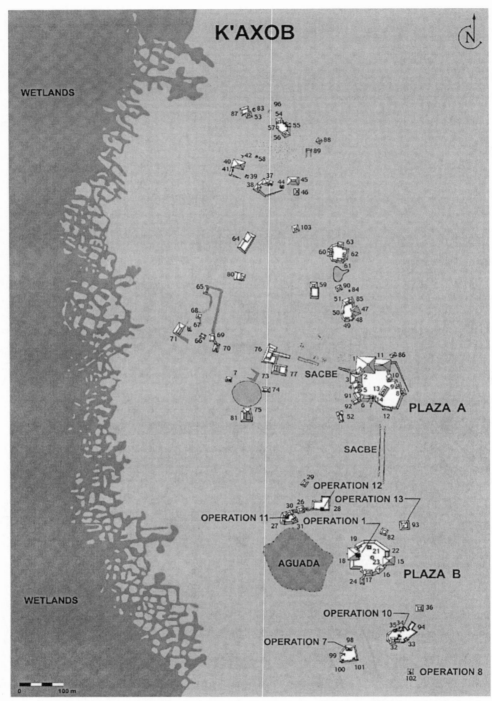

Figure 9.2. K'axob: structures built during the Formative and Classic periods. (Illustration by T. Martz, K. Berry, and E. Hall)

Operation 1: Phase 2d

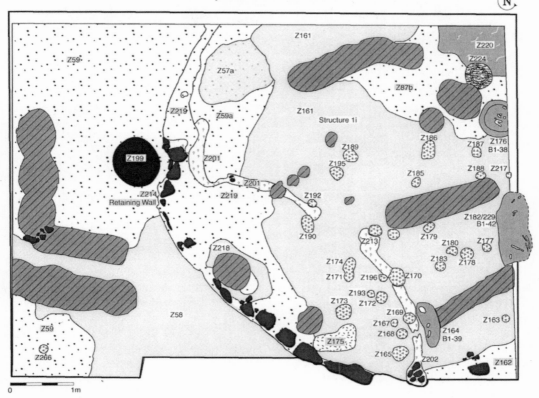

Figure 9.3. Floor plan of Middle Formative apsidal domicile and associated features at K'axob, Operation 1, Phase 2. (Illustration by T. Martz, K. Berry, and E. Hall)

archaeological record of the Sibun Valley, on the other hand, refers to a time when the hereditary dynasties of the central Peten (of Guatemala) were foundering and northern Yucatec sites such as Chichén Itzá were asserting greater dominance. In spite (or perhaps because) of this political turbulence, settlement within the Sibun Valley thrived at this time, most likely because of local cacao (chocolate) production and an uninterrupted appetite for cacao in courtly society. Information from the Sibun Valley informs us of the workings of a prestige economy and the production of a luxury good. Between these two anchor points exist the lowland Maya Classic period and a wealth of hieroglyphic, iconographic, artifactual, and architectural information relevant to understanding the specific historical circumstances around which hierarchy and economy converged.

LIVELIHOOD IN THE FORMATIVE VILLAGE OF K'AXOB

Although settlement before 1000 B.C. is curiously underrepresented in the Maya Lowlands, the latter part of the Middle Formative period (800–400 B.C.) is a time of many village founding events at selected locales across the lowlands. Elsewhere (McAnany and López Varela 1999:157) I have described this phenomenon as analogous to the colonization of Polynesia by hierarchically organized groups transporting a full suite of domesticates, an elaborated material culture, and a sophisticated cosmology. The wetland and riverine environments of northern Belize provided one of the favored environs for settlement, as exemplified by K'axob, which is located on a patch of fertile soil between the New River and a large perennial wetland called Pulltrouser Swamp (Figure 9.2).

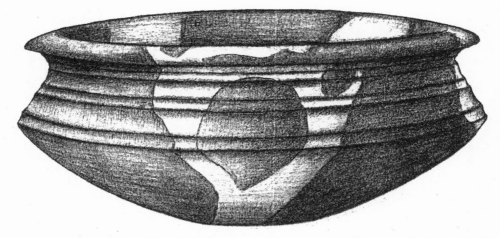

Figure 9.4. Timax Incised bowl from foundation Burial 1-43, K'axob. (Illustration by J. A. Labadie)

Lacking domesticated animals, Formative Maya settlers seem to have focused on colonizing areas in which good farming soil was located near the protein-rich resources of wetlands and rivers.

At K'axob the earliest known domicile (built before 600 B.C.) is a large (64 m²), solidly built apsidal structure with a white, packed-marl floor, wattle-and-daub walls, and an appended kitchen structure (Figure 9.3). Shortly before this domicile was constructed, an adult male and female were buried in the midden-rich soil under the future house location. The male, adorned with more than 2,000 shell beads and two distinctive pottery vessels, may have been one of the village founders. His interment contained two of the three artifact types characterized by Joyce (2000:69) as the earliest recognizable products of high culture in Mesoamerica: well-made pottery and marine shell costume ornaments. This burial contrasted sharply with that of the accompanying female, who was interred with no adornment or pottery.

The basis on which such gender inequality was constituted is not clear; however, these basal interments accent the fact that social life at the Formative village of K'axob was not structured around an ethos of egalitarianism. One of the pottery vessels interred with the putative apical ancestor—a Timax Incised bowl (Figure 9.4)—was decorated with a faux resist technique; both the tech-

nique and the paste are foreign to K'axob. In fact, during this early settlement phase much of the pottery, chipped-stone tools and debitage, and ground stone was procured or traded from distances up to 100 km. The scale of this expansive and integrated network of procurement never again was achieved at K'axob (Bartlett et al. 2000:129–130; López Varela 2004; McAnany and Ebersole 2004; McAnany and Peterson 2004). This pattern stands in great contrast with the post-200 B.C. period, during which procurement zones became tightly circumscribed around K'axob. Even during the earlier time period, however, two prestige-linked valuables from the distant, mountainous southern Maya region—jade and obsidian—were scarce items at K'axob, indicating the spatial and social limits of the procurement net. It was not until the Late Classic period that the site became relatively well supplied with volcanic glass, probably as a consequence of restructured trade pathways that used marine and freshwater routes, including the nearby New River.

Macrobotanical remains from the basal levels of K'axob point toward a fully agricultural village that subsisted on maize and cultivated several orchard species including cacao, avocado, and *mamey zapote* (Miksicek 1983; Turner and Miksicek 1984:Table 1). Additionally, the plenitude of fish and turtle remains in the basal levels (Masson 2004) indicates that the faunal resources of adjacent wetlands provided a valuable source of protein not always present in the Mesoamerican diet. Excavations in the island fields that border the terra firma have yielded evidence of Formative period canal and raised-field construction (Berry 2003), indicating that the island fields were cultivated well before the population maximum of the Late Classic period. With the capacity to produce crops well into the dry season, wetland farming (as one component of a tropical agricultural regimen) may have offered another attraction to Formative settlers.

How should the economy of this Middle Formative village be characterized? Local agrarian production complemented by the harvesting of aquatic resources seems to have fed the village just fine, and osteological analysis indicates a low incidence of nutritionally related paleopathologies (Storey 2004). Mortuary remains are suggestive of the early presence of leadership positions, but architectural remains are those of domiciles rather than palaces, indicating leadership based on kinship and seniority. Active maintenance of networks of procurement that extended well beyond the limits of the village indicates that village leaders enjoyed the authority to initiate and participate in trading relationships without meddling from overlords. This situation would soon change.

ASSERTING VILLAGE IDENTITY IN THE FACE OF POLITICAL CENTRALIZATION

By 200 B.C. the physical and political geometry of the lowland Maya landscape began to change radically. New peaks in the topography of rolling hills, wetlands, and valleys were created by the construction of towering pyramids, conceived and scripted in Classic times as built mountains, places for the storage and display of great spiritual and political power. Although residential construction greatly accelerated at K'axob during this time, no pyramids were built. In contrast, ambitious construction projects at the nearby centers of Nohmul, San Estevan, and Cerros, as well as the raising of a massive, 33-m-tall pyramid (Structure N10-43) only 50 km up-

river at the long-term capital of Lamanai (Pendergast 1981:41), suggest that "contributions" of labor likely were solicited during this time. As noted elsewhere (Freidel and Schele 1988:550), iconographic programs decorating Formative pyramids thematically focus on deities and not rulers. Given this fact and the rarity of interior tombs—particularly among the monumental pyramids of the Mirador Basin of the northern Peten (Hansen 1998:89–95)—Formative pyramids likely were not construed as mortuary shrines for dead dynasts (McAnany 2001:133). Likewise, the paucity of palace structures dating to the end of the Formative (as well as the beginning of the Early Classic period) suggests that the royal court, as it is known for the Late Classic period (Inomata and Houston 2001), was not fully constituted. In other words, the tradition of divine rulers had not yet crystallized during the Late Formative period; rather, elites seem to have competed to centralize a power base that was materialized in massive construction programs dedicated primarily to deities. Such culturally constructed "mountains" dedicated to the gods required the recruitment of a large seasonal labor force, suggesting the institutionalization of an ethos of labor service couched within hierarchical power relations. The imposition of labor obligations on local villages need not be perceived as an occasion of naked domination, however. The organization and deployment of labor is a skill that generally is well developed among village leaders, and dialogue between village headmen and emerging rulers before labor mobilization likely involved some commitment of reciprocity. Building activities are assumed to have taken place during the dry season and thus need not have detracted from agricultural labor. More likely, there was considerable village pride in participating in the construction of a massive shrine to the deities. Dealing with the aftermath of a landscape altered both physically and politically, however, may have been a very different proposition. In Mesoamerica there existed a tight synergism between religious hierarchy and political centralization. A shrine that provided an earthly home for a deity could become a tool of political power and thus increase the influence of those who initiated its construction.

The onset of monumental construction at nearby emergent seats of power is reflected at K'axob in profound changes in mortuary practices, a diminished scale of exchange spheres and of imports, and the assertion of village identity and centrality, expressed stylistically in ritual contexts. After 200 B.C. the mortuary pattern of K'axob shifted from one that emphasized adults and children to one in which young males increasingly were accorded burial in the ancestral heartland of the village (Storey 2003). These burials were often interred as secondary remains, and their age and sex is consonant with that of warriors, suggesting that young men either were actively involved in "homeland defense" in the sense of resistance to emergent overlords or were drawn into the inevitable conflicts between competing seats of power. Either way, this pattern suggests that the ushering in of a new order may not have been a pacific process.

For residents of K'axob, the emergence of a political economy with centralized nodes of power resulted in the elimination of the far-flung procurement networks of earlier times. Procurement zones became highly localized and entrenched. Petrographic and neutron-activation analyses of pottery pastes indicate that most vessels were fabricated from clays available within 7 km of K'axob (Bartlett et al. 2000:127). Gone also were the exotic cherts whose source of origin remains unknown. Instead, chert tools increasingly bore the production mark of Colha, a massive tool-producing site located only 30 km to the south (Shafer and Hester 1991). There is little debitage to indicate anything but the refurbishing and recycling of imported, finished tools (McAnany 1989; McAnany and Peterson 2003; Shafer 1983). In short, procurement efforts within the immediate catchment of K'axob were intensified while acquisition of goods from distances greater than 10 km seems to have become highly controlled.

As political centralization, labor drafts,

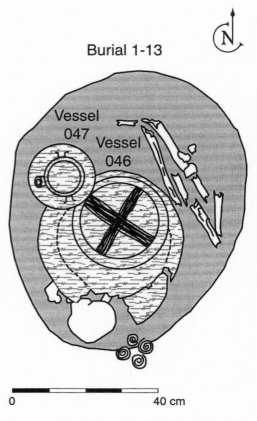

Burial 1-13

Vessel 047 Vessel 046

0   40 cm

Figure 9.5. Late Formative flexed male burial (1-13) covered by a large bowl whose base was painted with a prominent cross motif. (Illustration by B. Thomas, K. Berry, and E. Hall)

and controlled resource acquisition became facts of life, the residents of K'axob responded by manipulating their material culture to express their own identity and centrality within a changing world. Pottery represents a very plastic medium of identity assertion, and although the monochromatic Sierra Red tradition of the Late Formative period often has been characterized as a homogeneous horizon, closer inspection reveals that the artisans of K'axob and surrounding communities crafted distinctive shapes and decorative motifs (Bartlett and McAnany 2000:108–113). At K'axob seven vessels associated with centrally positioned burial features dating from Late to Terminal Formative times (specifically 200 B.C. to c. A.D. 250) were painted with a cross motif and inverted over the head or body of a deceased male (Figure 9.5). The ritual context in which these vessels were used before interment is not clear; it is clear, however, that the quadripartite motif is a Maya symbol of centrality and centering, used to mark an *axis mundi* (Headrick 2004).

The marking of K'axob as a central place was carried one step further with the circa 100 B.C. dedication of a new plaza floor in the center of the ancestral village, which was marked by the placement of four small red bowls arranged in a cross pattern. The bones of a fetal deer and frog were placed inside the bowls, and a scattering of golden chert microdebitage was sprinkled over the entire offering (Harrison 2004; Masson 2004; McAnany and Peterson 2004). These statements of identity and centrality were materialized at a time when larger political forces appear to have marginalized and impoverished the village. Such a response bears ideological similarities to self-referential practices in the highland Guatemalan Tzutujil village of Santiago Atitlán. In particular, Prechtel (1999:5) describes the residents' way of conceiving of their village in terms of "internal bigness." Villagers are well aware of their disadvantageous position in economic and political hierarchies external to their village and of the demands that a modern nation-state places on them. Yet their identity is vested in a very localized existence that is given meaning and graphically illustrated by a cycle of rituals keyed to their "home" landscape and meteorological conditions. In this manner, external political and economic forces harden the outlines of identity consciousness.

The localization of the production economy of K'axob and the assertion of village identity and centrality were related synergistically to the establishment of seats of power as signified by monumental architecture constructed outside K'axob. The hierarchical relations engendered by this political centralization fundamentally changed the organization of labor and production within K'axob. The extent to which this single village presents a pattern typical or atypical of the Formative Maya period remains to be demonstrated by careful analysis of chronological sequences elsewhere, but it is widely anticipated that similar patterns accented by locally nuanced variation will prove to be pervasive. As the ensuing Classic period demonstrates, palace themes of centralization, artisan production, and conspicuous consumption were counterpoised against evidence of more modest subsistence and artisan production and lower levels of consumption in commoner households. Such contrastive identities reverberated and were amplified through time and into the colonial period (Restall 1997:87–97). During the Classic period, hierarchy and appropriation were signified unambiguously in hieroglyphic texts, polychrome painting, and monumental sculpture of the royal court.

"NATURAL" LORDS AND LADIES IN THEIR PALATIAL DOMAIN

During the colonial period members of Yucatec Maya aristocratic families routinely petitioned the Spanish provincial courts for recognition of their *hidalgo* (elite) status. If granted, such recognition conferred on the applicant many privileges, including abstention from tribute obligations and the power to draft local labor for domestic service. Commoners were asked to testify as to the lordly status of the applicant, and in this regard the 1641 testimony provided by Diego Tzut of Yaxakumche, translated and paraphrased by Roys (1941:649), is particularly revealing: "And this witness saw that for don Alonso Xiu, father of the said don Juan Xiu and his sister, while he lived the community cultivated his cornfield and provided service for his house every week. And when a new house was needed, the community constructed it, and they always respected him as a *natural lord* [emphasis added]. And so for these reasons his children, as descendants of natural lords, should enjoy what their fathers, grandfathers and ancestors enjoyed, not paying tribute nor rendering personal services like the other plebeian Indians."

Assuming that Roys's translation has captured the spirit of this testimony, we can discern the ready acceptance of a concept of a natural lord who by virtue of pedigree is accorded the labor of others. Burden bearing in the form of labor service undertaken for the benefit of natural lords and ladies appears to have been the normal and orderly course of events. On social grounds, Diego Tzut sharply demarcated the distinction between lords and commoners, and that distinction carried significant political and economic privilege. Although one must exercise caution in transplanting colonial testimony back to Classic times, it was during the earlier Classic period that the seeds of distinction between elite and commoner matured. This testimony indicates that the benefits derived from this arrangement were reaped well into colonial times.

It is doubtful that Classic period elites (royalty as well as subregnal statuses) constituted a class in the Marxist sense of a self-interested group that controlled the means of production, exploited and appropriated the labor of individuals, and acted as a unified faction according to class interests. On the other hand, ruling kin groups and their cohorts monopolized power and most certainly appropriated labor and services from subordinate kin groups living in their realm. Within a polity these ruling factions were differentiated diacritically from commoners by genealogy, residential locale, material accouterments, hieroglyphic texts, and possibly language (Houston et al. 2000:334–337). During the Classic period there were multiple, competing political centers of varying sizes and areal extent, including about a dozen royal courts and as many as 50 courts of secondary and tertiary kingdoms. Epigraphic information has been interpreted as indicative of hierarchical relations that permeated intercourt diplomacy as well as relations between court and constituency (Martin and Grube 2000:17–21). Hieroglyphic texts also contain documentation of the pervasive practice of intercourt visitation. Such visits were undertaken in order to participate in rituals linked to events in the lives of royalty (heir designation, marriage, accession, or death), to witness the dedication of new constructions, and to observe period-ending calendrical rituals. Ruling families and their cohorts—regardless of their large archaeological visibility—represented only a small fraction of both the total Lowland Maya Classic period population (which numbered in the millions) and the residents of any one kingdom. Their frequent trips of diplomacy may be have been motivated partly by a desire to participate actively in high culture with other royalty; the reality of such interconnectedness is underscored by the standardization in Late Classic hieroglyphic texts. Consequently, the extent to which we can identify material remains distributed across the lowlands that exhibit a homogeneous flavor suggestive of class may be a result of the high intensity of articulation among ruling families of the Maya Lowlands. Frequent visits of nobility plus the ongoing events of the court generated many occasions for banquets and ritual feasting, to which we shall return shortly.

APPROPRIATIVE BUSINESS OF PALACE COURTS

Sometime around A.D. 400, Maya statecraft moved toward a system of governance in which rulers—named and recorded for posterity in hieroglyphic texts—were described as holy lords, or *ch'uhul/k'uhul ajaw* (Houston and Stuart 2001:59). Rulers and their families, competing noble families, lesser elites, and a large support staff constituted a palace court, recently characterized as "a vortex of intersecting power relations" (Houston and Stuart 2001:55). Ranked in power and opulence, a dozen or so royal courts and many smaller palace courts existed during the Late Classic period (A.D. 550–800). Architecturally, a palace court generally included a grouping of courtyards raised several meters above ground level. Buildings (called range structures) were situated in a roughly geometric plan around the perimeter of each courtyard. Range structures are long, rectangular, stone-walled buildings with internal room divisions that often contain a stone bench or throne feature (Harrison 2001). Sometimes, but not always, the roof of a range structure was constructed with a corbelled arch, thereby doubling the amount of stone needed for construction. As Abrams (1994:53) has noted, transport of raw materials is a costly process, and labor estimates can skyrocket if long-distant transport is required. Based on an architectural energetics study of a sample of structures at Copan, Honduras, Abrams (1994:128) concludes that although substantial amounts of labor were needed to build stone structures, the labor demands "were relatively modest and clearly distinct from oppressive conscriptive systems within many historic empires." Nevertheless, an estimate of 24,705 person-days needed to build one stone temple (Structure 10L-22) at Copan is a significant investment of human labor (Abrams 1994:53).

Based on archaeological and ethnohistorical information, Inomata (2001a:28–33) has characterized the business of Maya palace courts as including polity administration, diplomacy, military duties, ceremonies, scribal and artistic work, and management of the royal household. To the final category—which included domestic staff, guards, and entertainers—should be added managers and workers of the agricultural lands controlled by the palace (although colonial records indicate the possibility that some agricultural work may have been undertaken as part of labor service). Inomata (2001a:29) points out that palace courts likely also required an individual in charge of procurement, known as a *caluac* in colonial period Yucatec palace courts (Tozzer 1941:26). Described as securing provisions from local households of the realm, a *caluac* ensured the centripetal flow of goods and services necessary to sustain a court. The gendered nature of many of these goods and services highlights the very visible contribution of female work to the support of palace courts. For instance, royalty appear to have been provided with prepared food (generally female-gendered work) that was

cooked elsewhere. Excavation in royal courts such as the Caana complex of Caracol and the Central Acropolis of Tikal reveal a conspicuous absence of cooking hearths, burned cooking vessels, and midden deposits contemporary with Classic period occupancy (Chase and Chase 2001:131–132; Harrison 1999:195–198). Prepared food may have been gathered from the surrounding populace or, more likely, prepared in royal kitchens located on the periphery of palaces and supervised by members of the royal court although staffed by women completing their labor service. Either way, feeding a royal family required the combined efforts of agricultural production and hunting (traditionally male gendered) combined with female-gendered transformation of raw food into cuisine. The onerous and potentially abusive nature of these obligations is revealed in colonial period documents that include complaints filed by commoners that labor service in *hidalgo* residential compounds could drag on for the better part of a year (Morley 1941: 236–243).

It is not clear whether a *caluac* also assumed responsibility for securing luxury goods, artisan supplies, and valuables that were not locally available. From Spanish accounts of the Aztec courts, we are aware of the conspicuous display and consumption of wealth at royal courts (Díaz 1956:211; Evans 1998:170). The simple presence of a royal court initiated an upward flow of goods and services, as Folan et al. (2001:Figure 8.16) have noted for Calakmul. Artisans of the court required raw materials not locally available, such as jade, marine shell, and obsidian. As noted by Helms (1993:13–27) and Reents-Budet (1994), the crafting of finely made and highly valuable objects of personal adornment and ritual paraphernalia played a significant role in defining the identity of the palace court. The marine shell-working activities documented by Inomata and Stiver (1998) for the inland Aguateca court provide a ready example. Additionally, spindle whorls are frequent finds from palace contexts, and the weaving and fine embroidering of cotton cloth may have been a defining activity of elite females (Hendon 1997:41–43; McAnany and Plank 2001:95–96). Yet not all Maya courts were located in an environment suitable for cotton cultivation, and this fact likely necessitated either trade or appropriation (or both) of raw materials. Hieroglyphic and iconographic evidence discussed below indicates minimally the presence of the latter.

Artisan production aside, ritual feasts and banquets necessitated the acquisition of comestibles in quantities beyond the production capabilities of even a royal household. For instance, many texts painted on polychrome pottery vessels and wall murals or carved in stone make ready reference to cacao (chocolate) beans. During the last 15 years the hieroglyphic compound for cacao (spelled syllabically *ka-ka-w[a]* or *kakaw*) has been deciphered (Stuart 1988, 1989) and found to be common on text bands encircling Classic period cylindrical vessels recovered from tomb contexts. Such texts follow a formulaic structure, identifying the royal person for whom the vessel was crafted as well as the routine contents of the vessel (generally a cacao or maize-based drink). The ritual context in which such vessels were used is suggested by the text and imagery of a well-known palace scene from Piedras Negras (Panel 3) that depicts a formal gathering of nobles (Houston and Stuart 2001:69–73); part of the text describes a nocturnal ritual involving a chili-laced cacao drink. The need for labor and goods to meet the courtly imperatives of feasting and artisan production theoretically was unlimited and capable of absorbing significant resources.

One means by which palace courts acquired their chocolate beans is intimated in the murals of Structure 1, Room 1, at Bonampak. A recent infrared photography project conducted by Miller (1997) and colleagues has clarified the throne scene on the end wall as a royal family surrounded by five large white bundles, one of which is labeled "five *pih kakaw*" (Houston 1997:40). If *pih* stands for a unit of 8,000 (as Miller 2001:210 asserts), then 40,000 chocolate beans were contained within the sacks. Significantly, the individual beans and not the sacks are the subject of this seemingly precise count; the practice of recording cacao beans by counting also is described for the early colonial period (Morley 1941:159; Roys 1943:186) and may be linked to the use of cacao as a medium of currency. In the Bonampak murals, sacks were placed at the base of the throne; an adjacent wall contains a painted procession of "messengers" wearing long white robes—costumes linked with tribute-presentation events at Yaxchilan and Tikal also (Houston 2000:173–174). These scenes suggest two conclusions relevant to Classic period political economy: first, material transfers might accompany statements of political allegiance and/or subservience, and second, the court of a minor kingdom such as Bonampak apparently received sizable "gifts" of desired luxury goods such as cacao.

Within Maya epigraphy a highly pertinent development of the 1990s centered on the recognition that hieroglyphic texts coupled with the pictorial content of polychrome vessels are highly informative about the political economy of Classic period courts. The hieroglyphic compound *i-ka-tsi* is now read as "cargo" and *pa-ta* or *patan* as "tribute" (Stuart 1997:9, 1998:385, 410–414); Stuart has noted a textual association between *ikats* or *ikazts* and the glyph for "step" or "ascend" (Stuart 1998:409–417). Pictorially, most tribute-presentation scenes painted on cylindrical vessels are placed within a palace context and contain a striking hierarchical dimension in which the presenter ascends from a lowly position to present a gift (generally cotton cloth, cacao, or *Spondylus* spp. shells) to a ruler seated on a throne. These three items, in particular, typify the needs of the court and, for cotton cloth, the gendered labor responsible for tribute production. The rare *Spondylus* spp. marine shell was valuable in raw form and even more so when crafted into an item of bodily adornment by a palace artisan. Cacao eased the royal thirst and lubricated ritual festivities; cotton *mantas* represented goods of great value and convertibility and also highlight the contribution of female labor to the political economy.

Encoding unambiguous information regarding hierarchy, such presentation scenes unfortunately do not allow the extrapolation of quantitative data on the amounts or the periodicity with which goods were delivered to the palace court. When titles are used and can be deciphered, the presenter generally holds a lesser rank than the enthroned, but there is little explicit information regarding the situational relation between the two. Stuart (1998:414–416) observes, however, that textual references to *ikats* often co-occur with references to warfare and conquest, and thus some of the presentation scenes have a clearly punitive context. In short, based on current information on the acquisition of prestige goods at Classic Maya courts, tribute played a major role in material transfers, particularly of jadeite, cotton, quetzal feathers, and cacao (Houston 1997; Houston and Stuart 2001:69; Miller 1997; Stuart 1998: 410–414).

In light of this information, a courtly role for an official who tabulated the goods presented to nobles must be considered. Given the mathematical prowess of Classic Maya scribes, there likely was an individual dedicated to a careful accounting of all goods presented to the court. In reference to cacao beans that were enumerated individually rather than weighed, this role gives new meaning to the old expression "bean counter." A Classic Maya tributary list has yet to be uncovered, however, and the hieroglyphic corpus known to date does not contain the economic specificity of cuneiform texts or the colonially produced and Spanish-annotated Codex Mendoza of the Mexican Highlands. Nevertheless, current understanding points to the fact that hieroglyphic texts are not mute on the subject of political economy, as previously thought, and, significantly, that conquest followed by tribute exaction was not foreign to principles of Maya statecraft.

From the perspective of political economy, the provisioning of courts (both royal and secondary), in addition to their physical construction and maintenance, was an expensive and time-consuming endeavor requiring the compliance and toil of innumerable elites and commoners who existed in a web of hierarchical obligations. Truly an institutionalized form of burden bearing, such obligations served to maintain an aristocracy in which godlike rulers dwelled among the living, near commoners and elites alike. Baines and Yoffee (2000) note, however, that civilizational order is fragile and costly to maintain, and this statement rings true for both members of high culture and commoners. In the Maya Lowlands a political economy focused on the creation, maintenance, and expansion of royal courts housing divine rulers survived for about 400 years before rends in the fabric began to appear. The economic restructuring attendant on the demise of governance by divine rulers can be perceived particularly keenly in a region linked to the prestige sector of the political economy. Surviving the collapse of divine rulers and flourishing under more relaxed hierarchical relations, the cacao-production sector—as it is represented in the Sibun Valley of central Belize—holds clues to the nature of a new order that possibly weakened and definitely replaced the old aristocracy.

CACAO PRODUCTION AND THE PRESTIGE ECONOMY

Polychrome vessels name-tagged and reserved for cacao quaffing in addition to tribute-presentation scenes featuring sacks of counted cacao beans highlight the central role of this cultigen in courtly life and ritual. Yet agronomic, ethnohistorical, paleoenvironmental, and demographic information points to the difficulty of growing cacao precisely where royal courts abounded—the Peten and the Yucatan. The northern Yucatan was simply too dry to grow cacao anywhere but within small, collapsed sinkholes, or *rellojadas* (Gómez-Pompa et al. 1990; Pérez Romero 1988). Although there may have been sufficient rainfall to grow this tree crop in the Peten, it thrives primarily in soils of well-drained alluvial river valleys (Muhs et al. 1985:124), a rare landform in the Peten. Extracting information from colonial records, Jones (1989:102) bluntly states that "cacao did not grow well in the central Petén, however, and the Itzas and their neighbors had to depend on importation of the product or control over subject populations who could supply them with it."

Cacao blossoms produce small amounts of large, heavy pollen that are laboriously transported from the stamen to the pistil by species of midge insects that belong to the ceratopoginid family and prefer a high-canopy forest habitat (Young 1994:124–127). Cacao growers today sustain high rates of pollination only when their orchards are small and surrounded by stands of mature forest (Young 1994:167–172), an ecological imperative that can be satisfied only in zones of high rainfall and low population density where large tracts of forest are allowed to stand. Vegetation communities reconstructed from pollen cores taken from lakes of the Peten as well as population estimates based on archaeological survey data indicate that neither high-canopy forest nor low population densities in any way characterized the central lowlands during the peak of the Classic period (Rice 1993:40–43; Turner 1990:Figure 15.1). On ecological as well as paleodemographic grounds, it seems that cacao production was extremely limited in the immediate surroundings of most Classic period royal courts.

Acquiring sacks of beans must have been a high priority of Maya elites from the Classic through the colonial period. Scholes and Roys (1968:316) note that during Late Postclassic times, northern Yucatec Maya were engaged in brisk trade with cacao producers along the Gulf coast of Tabasco, Mexico, and had established trade relations and some measure of political influence in the cacao-producing valleys bordering the Caribbean. Classic period iconography and hieroglyphic texts discussed above reveal that one mechanism by which this valued prestige good was transferred to the palace courts of the Peten entailed postbattle coercion and established hierarchical relationships involving obligations of labor and goods. The exact production locales of Classic period cacao orchards are not known from hieroglyphic texts, al-though poorly understood epithets, often glossed as "tree fresh" or "frothy" cacao, may actually refer to varieties or flavors specific to production regions. Regardless, the river valleys of the Caribbean watershed, located less than 100 km east of the Peten, were proximate to many palace courts. Central and southern Belize would have been particularly strategic locales because this zone is drained by river valleys that contain alluvial soil capable of producing a highly desirable luxury crop such as cacao. Because of the presence of a substantial but not dense population, areas of high canopy could be reserved for cacao production while the local population provided labor for its cultivation. Materializations of power (DeMarrais et al. 1996) such as monumental architecture and hieroglyphic texts, sine qua non of political importance in Classic Maya society, are underrepresented in these river valleys, suggesting peripheral political status.

A relevant construct for understanding the production and distribution of cacao can be built by combining the competitive and acquisitive elements of prestige-goods theory (Friedman and Rowlands 1978) with the explicit power differentials of core-periphery or world-systems theory (Blanton and Feinman 1984; Champion 1989; Peregrine and Feinman 1996; Rowlands et al. 1987; Smith and Berdan 2000; Stein 1999; Wallerstein 1974; Wolf 1982). Following Champion (1989:14), we assume that cores are "the net consumers of the products of the periphery, and to be the dominant partners in the network of political relationships of which the exchange may be the visible manifestation, while the peripheries are the net providers and the dominated partners." New field data from recent archaeological investigations within one valley in the periphery, the Sibun River valley, provide a point of departure for unraveling the complexities of the prestige economy from the perspective of producers.

Into the Deep History of the Sibun Valley
By the end of the sixteenth century, Spanish *entradas* accompanied by missionaries had penetrated the Caribbean drainages, includ-

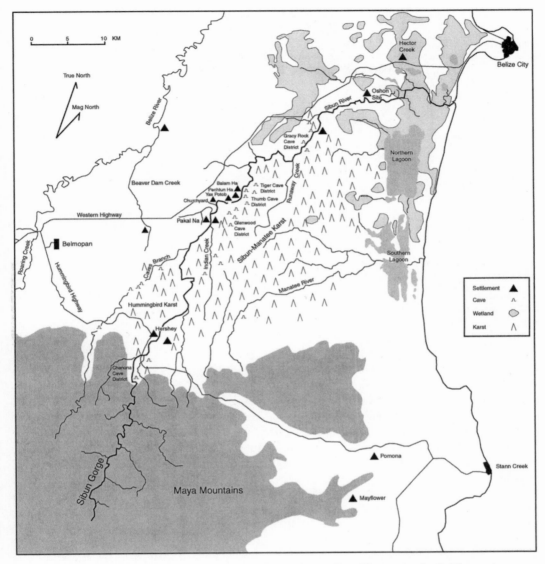

Figure 9.6. Selected settlements and caves in the Sibun River valley. (Illustration by B. Thomas)

ing a river valley called the Xib'um or Xibun (Jones 1998:map 1, pronounced *sheeb' oon*), now identified on Belize national maps as the Sibun. There, as elsewhere, Spaniards sought to establish control over any significant resources, including cacao orchards. Little specific detail regarding these early colonial incursions is known; it is clear, however, that a chapel, complete with a bell, was built in the Sibun Valley. In 1630 a wave of resistance to Spanish domination spread across the southern lowlands, and the colonial settlement was abandoned by indigenous Xib'um Maya residents, who removed the church bell and took it with them (Jones 1989:200). During later centuries cacao production in the Americas suffered major setbacks and eventually was eclipsed by production in Africa and Asia. Even today, however, cacao is grown commercially in the Sibun Valley. Several decades ago Hershey Foods operated a sprawling chocolate orchard that surrounds a large Classic Maya center (locally called the Hershey site) situated at the head of the valley.

Figure 9.7. Idealized view of a "chiefly" residence (Structure 109) at Pechtun Ha, Sibun River valley. (Illustration by K. Acone)

The Sibun River originates in the Maya Mountains and flows across a limestone plain to empty into the Caribbean Sea about 100 km downstream (Figure 9.6). It crosses a karstic landscape of caves and hidden valleys, many of which were visited repeatedly in ancient times for ritual practice. Ongoing survey of the valley floor and caverns is complemented by a program of surface collection in the caves and excavation at surface sites. Results to date indicate that there was little settlement of the valley before the Late Classic period. This fact, which contrasts greatly with the Middle Formative founding of K'axob, located about 100 km to the north, may be attributed to the severe annual flooding regime of the Sibun River (McAnany et al. 2003). Occurring during the growing season, floods frequently cover even the highest river terraces and are debilitating to all but orchard species such as cacao that can tolerate severe, short-term flooding. During the Late Classic period settlements were founded up and down the valley, and the caverns of the Sibun-Manatee karst became sites of repeated ritual offerings. We can only speculate on the motivations behind this late settlement of the Sibun Valley. Independent kin groups may have opted to expand into a sparsely settled valley with significant cacao production potential during a period that is known to have been the population maximum of Classic society. Alternatively, the colonization may have been directed from and supported

by one of the palace courts to the west, undertaken expressly for the purpose of generating a ready source of cacao. Information to date indicates that construction during Late Classic times was primarily residential. With the exception of the upper valley center, called Hershey, seats of power—as materialized in pyramid plazas—were underdeveloped in the Sibun Valley, where large elongated platforms, possibly "chiefly residences," represent the bulk of construction (Figure 9.7).

This pattern crystallized during the time Ringle et al. (1998) refer to as the Epiclassic period (A.D. 700–1000). During this liminal time the power and reach of the Peten core dynasties declined precipitously, and northern Yucatec centers of power, particularly Chichén Itzá, extended their influence in all directions, including south along the Caribbean seaboard. In effect, the Epiclassic period was witness to the ushering in of a new order in which power was vested in rulers who were not described as divine, monumental architecture was somewhat devalued, and great emphasis was placed on maintaining large, water-based procurement networks navigated by means of cargo canoes. The core not only shifted to the north, it transformed.

Materialization of a New Order
Far from resulting in the depopulation of the Sibun Valley, the collapse of the old core seems to have invigorated occupants of the

XARP 2001
SAMUEL OSHON SITE
STRUCTURE 402
RECONSTRUCTION
K. ACONE

Figure 9.8. Idealized view of a circular shrine (Structure 402) from the Samuel Oshon site, Sibun River valley. (Illustration by K. Acone)

valley, particularly in its middle and lower sections, where new construction programs were initiated during the Epiclassic period. One distinctive architectural feature—circular shrine structures—were added to the primary plazas of three sites: Pechtun Ha, Samuel Oshon, and Augustine Obispo (Figure 9.8). Stone monuments, both altars and repositioned stelae, are associated with these distinctive buildings, as are incense burners characteristic of this time period, namely, ladle-handled varieties as well as studded forms (Figure 9.9). Ringle et al. (1998:Figure 29) suggest that this ceramic complex, found throughout the Mesoamerican highlands and lowlands at this time, is indicative of a network of shrine and pilgrimage centers connected to the emergent, militaristic cult of Quetzalcoatl/Kukulkan. Leaving aside the cult interpretation for the moment, we can readily interpret this complex as indicating a restructuring of the political orientation of the Sibun Valley. Links with the Peten, immediately to the west, gave way to a rapport with Yucatec sites, located farther to the

north; this realignment seems to have fostered prosperity within the valley.

The wealth is manifest not only in construction activities but also in high densities of long-distance trade goods such as obsidian that are present at small house platforms as well as large plaza groups. Just as low densities of obsidian at K'axob indicate a small-scale procurement network, the high densities of volcanic glass in the Sibun Valley suggest a larger trading network and the possession of a highly desired commodity, such as cacao, with which to trade. Contrasts between the relative frequency of obsidian at K'axob versus the Sibun Valley must be tempered, however, by the fact that across the lowlands the amount of obsidian in domestic contexts rose dramatically at the end of the Classic period. As Rice (1987:82, 84) has suggested, such greater availability of obsidian may indicate that it had been "devalued" as an luxury good. Certainly the old interior routes of transport—supply lines likely controlled by the large sites of the central Peten—were supplanted by coastal networks. Regardless, the net effect of reorientation to more distant northern sites seems to have been beneficial to the wealth and well-being of ancient Sibun Valley farming households.

The old adage "distance makes the heart grow fonder" may be pertinent to relations between the Sibun Valley and the northern sites. Based on size, the sites of the Sibun Valley could have been dominated easily by powerful centers to the north. The great distance separating the two, however, may have favored a loose hierarchical relationship, closer to the "favored trading partnership" status that the United States extends to distant markets. Although Ringle et al. (1998) interpret the Epiclassic package of artifacts and buildings as indicative of a messianic and militaristic cult, its manifestation in the Sibun Valley resembles more of an economic restructuring, except for one telling deposit discussed below. The opportunity to shift allegiance likely was related to the cacao-production role of the valley and the fact that the Sibun River flows to the Caribbean Sea, thus directly linking the valley to an expanding

Figure 9.9. Sherds from Epiclassic incense burners from the Augustine Obispo site: *(a)* studded variety, *(b)* ladle-handed variety. (Photograph by author)

maritime trading network, a long-noted characteristic of the Postclassic period (Sabloff and Rathje 1975). One particular burial deposit from the midvalley site of Pakal Na, however, pertains to the putative militarism of the "cult of Kukulkan." An adult male, placed at the bottom of a 2-m-deep trench that had been excavated on the central axis of the largest platform at Pakal Na, was interred headless. Associated with his extended, postcranial skeleton were secondary remains of at least three other individuals, including a human skull cap carved with a woven mat de-

sign (symbolic of authority) and a human mandible drilled for suspension and carved with zoomorphic glyphs. The primary interment likely was a warrior who met an unfortunate death. The inclusion of an unusual pyriform pedestal vessel (Figure 9.10), similar in form and finish to those found in the Yucatan during the Epiclassic period, intimates that the shift in allegiance among residents of the Sibun Valley either produced or resulted from a cycle of conflict.

Given the coarse grain of archaeological chronologies, a causal linkage, if any, be-

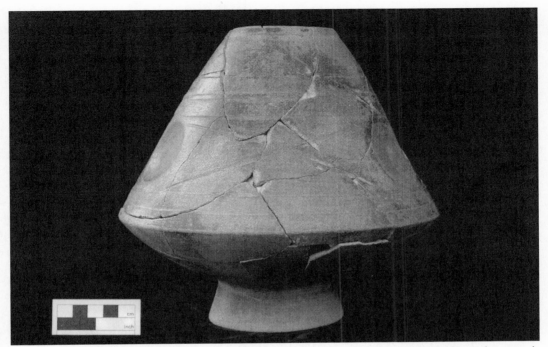

Figure 9.10. Pedestal vessel with highly constricted neck found in axial burial at Pakal Na. (Photograph by author)

tween the fall of the Peten divine rulers and the expansion of northern Yucatec powers is difficult to determine. Did the onset of the locally prosperous, trading "cult of Kukulkan" fill a power vacuum resulting from the weakened influence of Late Classic divine rulers or did this cult actively subvert the power of the old dynasties? If the latter, the appearance of this new order may have hastened or even caused the demise of the older form of governance. From the perspective of the Sibun Valley, the new order entailed a hierarchy that was more diffuse and webs of obligation that were more laterally extended. Under the new order, burden bearing more likely referred to the weight of a tumpline used to transport goods to markets for trading (Feldman 1985) than to onerous labor service.

FINAL THOUGHTS ON
APPROPRIATIVE ECONOMIES

Among the ancient states of Mesoamerica, the Classic Maya style of statecraft was singular in its emphasis on named and imaged rulers, some of whom reigned over polities less than 50 km in diameter. Vested in the materialization of elite identity, Classic Maya royal courts were voracious consumers of food, drink, textiles, and items of personal adornment and ritual attire. This ostentatious display, so apparent in pictorial and textual sources, has profound implications for the structure and relations of production within the multistate system of the Maya Lowlands. This chapter has approached this appropriative economy from three temporally successive angles: (1) the Formative village of K'axob, which bore witness to the emergence of extractive economies; (2) the elaboration of appropriative Classic period palace economies; and (3) the dynamics of core-periphery relations within the prestige economy of the Epiclassic period. Each vignette has yielded a wealth of information relevant to understanding ancient Maya economies and contributes toward illuminating what has been referred to as the "black box" of Maya political economy (Hammond 1991).

During the Formative period the emergence of centralized power seems to have taken place within an environment of "identity politics" as elites attempted to forge alliances and create networks of hierarchical obligations on a regional scale. For the village of K'axob, this process resulted in sharply diminished resource zones and entrenched localized trading networks. The village was well supplied, but its horizons were narrowed; these new boundaries initiated new assertions of village identity and centrality not observed during earlier periods. Given the coincidence between this process, as observed at K'axob, and the initiation of monumental constructions at nearby locales, it appears that a wholesale restructuring of local economies was attendant on the emergence of seats of political power and concomitant appropriative economies. Nevertheless, local and regional exchange networks that supplied households as well as palaces coexisted with the hierarchical appropriation of goods and services. Although hierarchy pervaded ancient Maya society, it did not constitute the sole mechanism by which goods and services were circulated.

The expression of hierarchical relationships of appropriation was elevated to an art form during the Classic period as palace courts inhaled goods and services from near and afar. Palaces were provisioned at least in part with tribute from vanquished foes as well as those enmeshed within well-established relations of obligation. A role for gender-based labor services also is indicated, particularly in the construction and maintenance of palace courts and ritual precincts and in the functioning of royal kitchens. Resources acquired from afar also fueled the prestige and artisan economies of the palaces.

Blanton and colleagues (1996:2, 4) have proposed that the power strategy of Classic Maya rulers emphasized the creation of networks of supply and alliance outside the polity. In general, items that circulate within a prestige-goods system are difficult to acquire, come from a long distance, involve labor-intensive artistry, or display intrinsically desired properties of color, texture, or durability (Blanton et al. 1996:12; Brumfiel and Earle 1987; Helms 1993; Miller 1987: 122; Renfrew 1986b). One of the most desirable prestige items was cacao, or chocolate beans, which could be grown in large quantities only in regions peripheral to the two core areas of power that existed in the central Peten of the Classic period and northern Yucatan of the Epiclassic to colonial period. The Sibun Valley of central Belize is one such cacao-production area where current archaeological research indicates continued, if not increased, vitality attendant on the collapse of the old core of the central Peten and the consolidation of political power at northern Yucatec sites, such as Chichén Itzá. Possibly thriving under the banner of an intrusive "cult of Kukulkan," the Sibun Valley provides a case study in political flexibility and responsiveness to new economic opportunities, a prevalent characteristic of peripheral areas.

Rathje (1971, 1972) introduced the concept of core-periphery interaction to Maya scholarship. Foreshadowing Wallerstein's (1974) codification of a world system, Rathje (1972) modeled the interaction between the core polities of the central Maya Lowlands and the peripheries to the east and south as one of balanced reciprocity; ritually saturated cosmology was exchanged for needed supplies such as salt and metates. The concept of a political or appropriative economy was not a part of Rathje's discourse. Wallerstein (1974) amply addressed power differentials, albeit in a Eurocentric, top-down fashion that focused on the rise of mercantile capitalism. Wolf's (1982) later treatment shifted focus from the centers codified by Wallerstein (1974) to the profound effect of an emergent world economy on the mode and relations of production in the periphery—among the "people without history." In like fashion the final portion of this chapter has shifted focus from the textually rich palaces to the "text-free" Sibun Valley, where production efforts fueled the prestige economies of the core areas. The Sibun case study, especially when contrasted with that of K'axob, demonstrates the temporal dynamism and the situational complexity of ancient Maya economies. Although no single economic arrangement monopolized Maya economies, these case studies show that large-scale trading relationships likely played a more prominent role during both the Middle Formative and Epiclassic periods. From the perspective of K'axob householders, the Late Formative onset of an appropriative political economy resulted in a reduced and somewhat entrenched trading sphere and likely initiated labor obligations. Over time the proximity of K'axob to the resources of the wetlands may have buffered this community from the nutritional deficiencies noted elsewhere at lowland sites, but even the Late Classic deposits of K'axob bespeak a kind of insularity that is distinct from the more international flavor of Sibun Valley sites. Likely participating in the long-distance luxury trade of cacao, Sibun Valley residents led a very different economic life than did the farmers of K'axob and probably enjoyed a fair measure of autonomy from their distant overlords located to the north. Contingencies of history and geography serve to entangle economic relationships in a manner that is profound, at the same time providing us with opportunities to unravel the skein.

10

Unraveling the Prehispanic Highland Mesoamerican Economy

Production, Exchange, and Consumption in the Classic Period Valley of Oaxaca

GARY M. FEINMAN AND LINDA M. NICHOLAS

Several presidential elections ago in the United States, the candidate and his staff swept to victory by sticking in focused fashion to the mantra, "It's the economy, stupid!" Few social scientists or historians today would argue with the basic gist of this statement when it comes to understanding ancient (or for that matter modern) societies. That is, if you do not have some idea of how a society's economy worked, it is hard to truly comprehend the daily workings of that social entity. For example, in a recent encyclopedia synthesis Timothy Earle (1999:608) states: "The economic basis of human society is undeniably important. To understand the operation and evolution of past societies, investigations of production and exchange have become a central concern to archaeologists."

For more than a generation, scholars have had a rudimentary grasp of the nature of the late Prehispanic economy of the Aztecs of central Mexico (Figure 10.1) (e.g., Adams 1966; Vaillant 1941). This understanding has included an awareness of intensive corn farming, tribute, a system of markets, craft specialization, long-distance exchange, and more. Our economic knowledge of the Aztecs and their antecedents is sufficient for some scholars (Smith and Masson 2000:109) to observe that "some of the most notable achievements of the ancient Mesoamerican peoples were in the realm of economics."

Although some basic features of the late Prehispanic Aztec economy have long been known and its complex interweavings have become clearer through recent scholarship (e.g., Berdan et al. 1996; Hodge and Smith 1994), many key questions about the workings of this economic system remain unanswered. Before the last quarter century most of our perspectives on the Aztecs came from documents. Although these ancient texts provided many vivid insights, most came from the heart of the polity and had an elite vantage (e.g., Berdan 1982). In other words, the view was largely top-down and capital-centric.

Recent decades of archaeological research have significantly broadened the focus to some outlying provinces and more rural contexts (e.g., Berdan et al. 1996; Hodge and Smith 1994). Yet even in the case of the Aztecs, for whom we have both documents and archaeological findings, scholars have only recently begun to understand how rural communities articulated economically with one another and in turn with larger centers. At the same time, we have just started to unravel the differences in access and consumption patterns between households. And there is no clear consensus in regard to the scale or context of various production activities. If we think more diachronically to the historical roots and predecessors of the Aztec domain in earlier Mesoamerica, our economic understandings become all the more hazy and speculative.

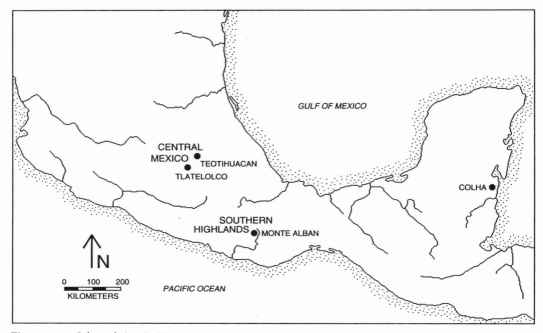

Figure 10.1. Selected sites in Mesoamerica.

In this chapter the goal is to begin to conceptualize and understand in a holistic manner (Berdan 1989:106) a Prehispanic Mesoamerican economy that predated that of the Aztecs by centuries. More specifically, the focus is the Valley of Oaxaca (a large highland valley in certain respects similar to that of the Aztec heartland in the Basin of Mexico) during the Classic period (A.D. 200–800). Our present understanding of Classic period Mesoamerican economies is not particularly complete or detailed for any specific region. The aim of this work is to begin to piece together a framework for the Valley of Oaxaca that not only will strengthen the understanding of this core region (Palerm and Wolf 1957) but may serve as a baseline model or starting point for other Mesoamerican societies. Of course, we firmly suspect, based on the evidence at hand (e.g., Blanton et al. 1993), that Prehispanic Mesoamerican economies were rather diverse, and so no single example (whether Aztec or Oaxacan) can serve as a fully adequate model for any other time or place. Nevertheless, because few efforts have been undertaken to view Classic period Mesoamerican economies holistically,

we first briefly discuss aspects of the central Mexican Aztec economic system (A.D. 1320–1520) as well as late Prehispanic Oaxaca before moving on to the latter region during earlier times.

ENVISIONING ANCIENT ECONOMIES:
PREHISPANIC MESOAMERICA

When thinking broadly (anthropologically) about economic behavior and organization, scholars have stressed three main spheres of activity: production, distribution, and consumption (e.g., Durrenberger 1996:367; Feinman 2001). More specifically, Prehispanic Mesoamerica in the Classic period and later was characterized by urban states, and so economic activities were enacted and interconnected across broad spatial scales (see also Berdan 1989). For that reason, this analysis takes a multiscalar perspective that considers a range of spatial scales from houses to macroregions (Blanton et al. 1993; Smith and Masson 2000).

As noted above, holistic conceptions regarding the economy of ancient Mesoamerica have typically begun with the Aztecs, the late Prehispanic central Mexican peoples who, when the Spanish arrived in 1519, dominated to different degrees a significant segment of ancient Mesoamerica (Berdan et al. 1996). Because the Spanish chronicled many aspects of the Aztec world, we have extensive textual records from which we can infer that marketing and the payment of tribute were key features of the Aztec economy (e.g., Berdan 1982, 1985, 1987a, 1989; Hodge 1998). Descriptions of specialized traders and producers (Sahagún 1950–1982 [1569]) also are well known. Crafted items, including metals, lapidary stone, feathers, and textiles, are detailed (Berdan 1987b; Sahagún 1950–1982 [1569]), although the texts mention comparatively little about the specific contexts or scale (sensu Costin 1991) at which these craft producers worked. The existence of skilled Aztec craft specialists also is manifest through the recovery and in-depth analysis of the elaborate artifacts themselves (e.g., Charlton et al. 1991, 2000; Noguera 1971).

Fortuitously, early Spanish accounts describe key aspects of the Aztec market system in some detail (Berdan 1985; Blanton 1996). The emphasis in the Spanish chronicles may reflect the importance of this economic institution to Aztec society. For example, in one famous account the conquistador Bernal Díaz del Castillo (1956:218–219) writes in regard to the central market at Tlatelolco: "After having examined and considered all that we have seen we turned to look at the great market place and the crowds of people that were in it, some buying and others selling, so that the murmur and hum of their voices and words that they used could be heard more than a league off. Some of the soldiers among us who had been in many parts of the world, in Constantinople, and all over Italy, and in Rome, said that so large a market place and so full of people, and so well regulated and arranged, they had never beheld before." Likewise, López de Gómara (1966:160) recounts: "The market place of Mexico is wide and long, and surrounded on all sides by an arcade; so large is it, indeed, that it will hold seventy thousand or even one hundred thousand people, who go about buying and selling, for it is, so to speak, the capital of the whole country, to which people come, not only from the vicinity, but from farther off. Besides, all the towns about the lake [have their own markets], because of which there are always the vast number of canoes and people that I have mentioned, and even more."

These accounts (and others) provide several important clues regarding the organization of the Aztec economy. (1) The system was hierarchical with large markets and smaller ones (Blanton 1996); the latter met less frequently. (2) Various currencies were used in the market, including cacao beans and reams of cloth (Berdan 1982:43). (3) A wide variety of goods, some exotic and some local, were sold in the markets (Berdan 1982:43). (4) There was some political influence or degree of control over the market (to encourage participation and to arbitrate disputes) (Berdan 1982; Blanton 1996:52; Hicks 1987; Kurtz 1974). Finally, (5) there were elements of a profit motive, as cacao beans, one kind of currency, were apparently counterfeited (Oviedo y Valdés 1851–1855:1: 316; Sahagún 1950–1982 [1569], book 10: 65).

Although the Aztecs provide a reasonable place to begin consideration of Prehispanic Mesoamerican economies, we also know that the Aztecs dominated a large, multiregional, tributary domain and thus were hardly typical for ancient Mesoamerica (even for later Prehispanic Mesoamerica). As a result, we have to use our knowledge about them judiciously when endeavoring to understand other ancient Mesoamerican economies. In addition, whereas Prehispanic Mesoamerica may have been one interconnected economy at the macroscale, particularly in its later history (Blanton and Feinman 1984), the macroregion was composed of various local and regional economic systems that may have operated in rather different ways.

Marketing is just one of three principal modes of exchange that anthropologists have used to describe and characterize the nature of economic exchange (Berdan 1989:83–84; Polanyi 1957; Renfrew 1975). *Reciprocity* describes a mode of exchange or economy based on small-scale, face-to-face exchange generally among equals. *Redistribution* refers to centralized exchange in which goods move through a nodal person or institution and then back out again. *Marketing* is market-based exchange in which the market serves as a key central institution through the mechanisms of supply and demand for the regulation of production and exchange. Of course, as many have discussed (e.g., Earle 1999), these broad modal categories subsume much variation and represent only a starting point for specific analyses. Nevertheless, for ancient Mesoamerica (and many ancient economies), there is no consensus even at this level of generality (e.g., Berdan 1989; Carrasco 1978; Hirth 1998; Sanders et al. 1979:297–298).

Despite its prominent role in sixteenth-century documents, some scholars see the market as a late (possibly Aztec) development in Mesoamerica and suggest that earlier economies were largely or entirely redistributive. They regard the marketing aspect of the Aztec economy as an anomaly that emerged just before Spanish conquest in Mesoamerica, perhaps only related to the process of Aztec empire foundation (the increasing scale of the Aztec political domain). The implication has been that marketing was much less important for other ancient Mesoamerican societies than it was for the Aztecs. What are the practical implications of this view (see Hirth 1998)?

If later Mesoamerican economies were basically redistributive in nature, then we would expect economic networks to have been small and politically bounded. Craft specialization would have been minimal, highly centralized, *and* in large part restricted to the manufacture of elite goods (as opposed to utilitarian items). Most households would have produced the majority of their essential goods themselves. In a large region the movement of heavy bulk items (in significant quantities) to a central place and then out again seems highly cumbersome and thus unlikely.

In contrast, the perspective we propose is that a marketing system and marketplaces

were integral features of many later ancient Mesoamerican economies, long before the Aztec period (Blanton et al. 1993; Feinman et al. 1984; Hirth 1998). We propose that craft specialization for exchange also was significant, with the market and other distributive mechanisms linking specialized producers at several geographic scales. In our view, economic specialization (for elite as well as basic items) was marked between households in the same community, between different sites in a region, and even between different sectors of the same larger area, thereby making exchange, in large part through markets, a key aspect of these economies.

More specifically, the geographic extent and demographic scale of these later Mesoamerican polities was extensive. For example, we estimate, based on full-coverage surveys, that there were more than 100,000 people in the Valley of Oaxaca alone during the Classic period (Kowalewski et al. 1989:249). If we consider the size of the regional population and also account for the seeming volume and nature of specialized production (Kowalewski et al. 1989:213), it would seem unlikely that economic exchanges could have been enacted entirely through either face-to-face transactions between households (reciprocity) or the movement of goods through central political figures (redistribution).

To begin to assess these alternative propositions, we must look beyond the standard ancient Mesoamerican fare of tombs and temples and examine regional settlement patterns and household archaeology. One of the empirical problem areas in the Valley of Oaxaca, which after all is the home of the *Early Mesoamerican Village* (Flannery 1976) and thus household archaeology, is the relative dearth of excavations (and fewer publications) of ancient houses that postdate those unearthed well over 20 years ago for the Formative period (1600 B.C.–A.D. 200). Although some of the most expansive systematic regional archaeological settlement pattern coverage in the world has been conducted in this upland valley and its surrounds in the southern highlands, relatively few

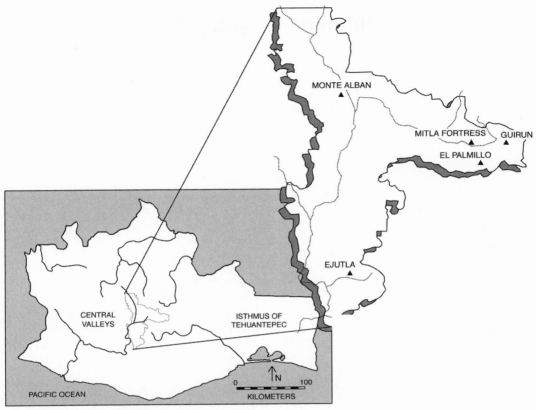

Figure 10.2. Selected sites in the Valley of Oaxaca.

Classic period houses in this area have been excavated and reported (for a notable exception, see Winter 1974).

BACKGROUND TO ANALYSIS: VALLEY OF OAXACA

The Valley of Oaxaca in Mexico's southern highlands—a distant part of the Aztec tributary domain—was home to Zapotec- and Mixtec-speaking peoples. Although the Zapotec and Mixtec are not as popularly known as the Aztecs, the Valley of Oaxaca has long been recognized as one of the core regions of Prehispanic Mesoamerica (Palerm and Wolf 1957). For example, the valley was home to Monte Albán, one of Mesoamerica's first cities (Blanton 1978). The earliest domesticated food plant and some of the first writing in Mesoamerica also have been found in the valley (Marcus 1992; Smith 2000).

For roughly the last 20 years, we have con-

ducted field research in the Valley of Oaxaca (Figure 10.2). We started with the systematic regional settlement pattern project, under the direction of Richard Blanton (Blanton et al. 1982) and Stephen Kowalewski (Kowalewski et al. 1989). Collectively, we have now walked over, mapped, and dated archaeological sites in an area of more than 7,000 km²— one of the largest contiguous areas in the world to be investigated by full-coverage regional survey (Balkansky 1997; Blanton 1978; Blanton et al. 1982; Drennan 1989; Feinman and Nicholas 1990, 1996; Finsten 1996; Kowalewski 1976, 1991; Kowalewski et al. 1989; Spores 1972). We draw from this long-term settlement study in discussing regional-scale findings and patterns.

In addition, our findings are drawn from two other archaeological research efforts. First, at the scale of the site, we have conducted highly intensive surveys and artifact pickups at the valley-floor Ejutla site (Feinman et al. 1991), which sits near the southern end of the central valleys of Oaxaca, and at three hilltop sites—Guirún, the Mitla Fortress, and El Palmillo—located on natural ridges at the eastern or Tlacolula periphery of the valley (Feinman and Nicholas 2000a). Second, we have carried out residential terrace/domestic excavations at two of these sites, Ejutla in the south and El Palmillo in the east (Feinman and Nicholas 1993, 1995, 2000b, 2001; Feinman et al. 2001, 2002; Middleton et al. 2002).

Our focus here is the Classic period (A.D. 200–800), centuries before the Aztecs, whose empire dates to the end of the subsequent Postclassic period (A.D. 1200–1520). We concentrate on the Classic period because we currently have little understanding of the economy of this period, when the valley was at least partly under the hegemony of urban Monte Albán. Although Zapotec writing was first used centuries before the Classic period, written texts from Oaxaca are rare and remain largely undeciphered. These short texts also seem to have little to do with matters economic (Marcus 1992) and so at present are no help for the issue at hand. Instead, we draw on three scales of archaeological data pertaining to the Classic period: domestic contexts (including houses), sites, and regional settlement patterns.

To make this analysis more manageable, we consider the Classic period economy in the Valley of Oaxaca in terms of two main facets—production and distribution—both of which would be expected to differ if the prime mode of exchange was redistribution as opposed to marketing. No one criterion or test implication is determinant or can separate these two alternatives. Yet if a market-based system was central, we would expect to see the following characteristics: (1) production for exchange (specialized production) of both utilitarian and luxury goods; (2) specialized production at the household, site, and even regional scales; (3) no direct or overarching administrative control of production and distribution; (4) widespread (and somewhat even) distribution of goods both geographically and between different houses at a site; (5) absence of large centralized storage features or facilities; and (6) large open and highly accessible plazas that could have served as marketplaces. The existence of a redistributive system would be supported by the alternatives or opposing characteristics.

MARKETING IN PREHISPANIC OAXACA
Today the markets of the Valley of Oaxaca are one of the key economic institutions in this highland, semiarid region (e.g., Cook and Diskin 1976). Interestingly, in the mid-sixteenth century, decades after the Spanish conquest, markets were noted and described by the early Spanish chroniclers who wrote about the Valley of Oaxaca (Appel 1982; Spores 1965). But as with the Aztecs, scholarly opinion often has considered these Oaxaca markets to be late, the postcontact result of Spanish influences. Unfortunately, when it comes to the prior Classic period we lack any such documentary clues.

As we try to understand the economy of ancient Oaxaca, we have little choice but to turn to archaeology. Here we focus first on production. For more than two decades, Mesoamerican archaeologists have looked for evidence of specialized production in the archaeological record. Yet until recently, we faced a bit of a conundrum. Drawing heavily from recent Euro-American experience, archaeologists (including ourselves initially) expected that specialists should generally be associated with nondomestic (that is, non-household) workshops. Alternatively, production that occurred in domestic contexts was expected to be purely for local use. In other words, there was a preconceived conflation between the scale of manufacture (that is, where it occurs—a house or a workshop) with the intensity of production (how much was manufactured and for whom).

For example, although Mesoamerican archaeologists working at Teotihuacan (Spence 1967, 1981) and Colha (Hester and Shafer 1994; Shafer and Hester 1983, 1986, 1991), as well as elsewhere, continually noted dense piles of production-related debris (especially related to stone tools and pottery), such finds usually were made in or near domestic contexts (Roemer 1982; Shafer and Hester 1983; Spence 1987). Meanwhile, few if any definitive nondomestic workshops have ever been found in Mesoamerica. As a result, in spite of the debris residues that clearly appeared to indicate intense manufacture that seemingly had to be carried out in part for exchange, some scholars (such as Clark in his 1986 reinterpretation of Spence's findings for Teotihuacan and Mallory in his 1986 review of Shafer and Hester at Colha) downplayed the evidence for craft specialization based on the apparent domestic settings.

Findings from our excavations at Ejutla and El Palmillo, where we have uncovered *domestic* settings associated with nonsubsistence production that was not for immediate or direct use (Feinman 1999) but rather for exchange, may help unravel this apparent conundrum. Our interpretive problem stems from the discipline's tacit reliance on unilineal models of craft production such as have been proposed by van der Leeuw (1977) and Santley (Santley et al. 1989). These models generally expect that the scale and intensity of production covary in stepwise fashion. The analytical difficulties with these rather unilinear models should not be a surprise. After all, today most craft specialists in rural Mexico—even artisans who send their textiles and pottery as far away as Europe and Asia—still frequently operate out of their houselots. We argue that the broadly expected association (found in the theoretical models proposed by van der Leeuw [1977], Santley et al. [1989], Clark [1986], and others) between domestic production and purely subsistence manufacture for immediate use should not be retained. We suspect that at El Palmillo and Ejutla as well as Colha and Teotihuacan specialized production for exchange was undertaken in household contexts.

Households were a prime unit of production and so a key building block of the ancient Mesoamerican economy. As noted above, most evidence for Prehispanic production activities has been found in residential contexts. At the same time, these units were linked in networks of exchange that circulated surplus manufacture, including non-elite goods. For ancient Oaxaca, this model seems to fit with the little that we know about agricultural production as well. In fact, no massive agricultural works requiring large labor crews, extensive canal systems, or sizable dams are evidenced in Prehispanic times. There is little large-scale water control today in the Valley of Oaxaca, and there was even less in the past (Lees 1973). In addition, the checkerboard nature of valley rainfall very likely fostered exchange connections between different areas of this semiarid valley system. It is important to recognize that if most households were producing basic as well as status-related goods in part for exchange, the economy would not be easy to manage politically through centralized redistribution, especially given the nature of Prehispanic transportation.

ECONOMY OF CLASSIC PERIOD OAXACA:
EMPIRICAL FINDINGS

The perspectives presented above stem from excavations of houses and their immediate surrounds that we have directed at two very different (though largely contemporaneous) sites, Ejutla and El Palmillo (Feinman and Nicholas 1993, 1995, 2000b; Feinman et al. 2001, 2002).

The Ejutla site is located on the floor of the Ejutla Valley, at the southern margin of the larger Valley of Oaxaca. Although mostly destroyed by the modern town—Ejutla de Crespo—parts of the roughly 1-km² site are still visible in numerous houselots and in several fields along the eastern edge of the modern village. Following the discovery of anomalous quantities of marine shell debris on the surface of several fields during regional survey (Feinman and Nicholas 1990), we began a series of excavations in the area of dense surface shell to determine the timing and nature of the shell-working activities at the site (Feinman and Nicholas 1993, 1995; Feinman et al. 1991, 1993).

Over four field seasons (1990–1993) a Classic period house and its immediate surrounds were uncovered (Figure 10.3). The

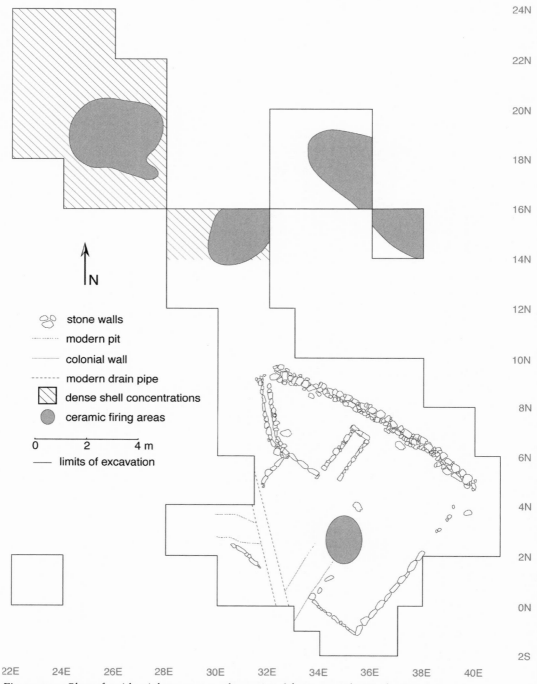

Figure 10.3. Plan of residential structure and associated features at the Ejutla site.

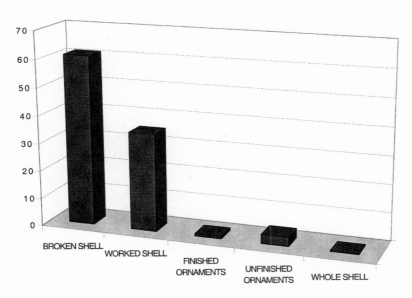

Figure 10.4. Shell assemblage at Ejutla.

excavated structure, roughly 6 × 4 m with a small attached work area to the north, was defined by a stone foundation and a floor of mixed earth and crushed bedrock. Several factors point to the domestic nature of this complex: the discovery of a small subfloor tomb that included at least four individuals, the recovery of a shallow firepit and probable cooking area immediately outside the structure, and the presence of food remains and other residential trash in the middens adjacent to the house. In Classic period Oaxaca (e.g., Winter 1974, 1995), residential complexes often were associated with domestic tombs (on the order of the one found in Ejutla).

The excavations confirmed not only shell working at the Ejutla site but also the presence of several other craft activities. More than 20,000 pieces of marine shell were recovered, much of which was cut, abraded, or in other ways modified. Broken or partially completed ornaments—especially disks, mosaic pieces, and beads—were relatively common whereas finished artifacts were rare (less than 1 percent) (Figure 10.4). Most of the identified shell varieties were native to the

Pacific, including such taxa as *Spondylus*, *Strombus*, and *Pinctada* that were commonly employed to fashion ornaments across Prehispanic Mesoamerica. No known site in the central valleys of Oaxaca equals this sector of the Ejutla site in terms of the concentration of marine shell, especially debris. Comparisons with the shell assemblage at El Palmillo, where we recovered fewer than 100 pieces of shell, mostly ornaments, during three excavation seasons, highlight just how anomalous the amounts of shell at Ejutla are. Given their abundance, the shell ornaments made at Ejutla clearly were not just for immediate local consumption. The excavated domestic tomb in Ejutla included only one small shell bead, and the number of entirely finished shell pieces recovered during the excavations was small.

The Ejutla excavations also yielded ample evidence for ceramic production (Balkansky et al. 1997; Feinman and Balkansky 1997). More than 2,000 figurines were recovered, many of them broken or malformed. Of the more than 75 recovered ceramic molds, 17 were definitely for figurines. Not surprisingly, several molds matched commonly noted

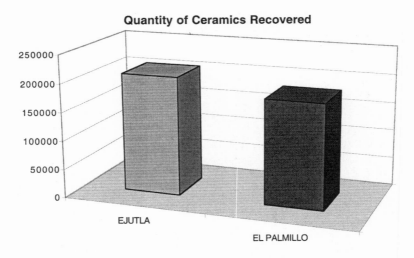

Figure 10.5. Quantity of ceramics and total cubic area excavated at El Palmillo and Ejutla.

figurine varieties. Our collections contain dozens of platelike *moldes* used in forming vessels. Overall, more than 900 pottery wasters (see Feinman 1980; Redmond 1979) were recorded. These defective pieces comprise a range of ceramic forms, including figurines (160 wasters), *comales* (tortilla griddles), and *sahumadores* (incense burners). Preliminary petrographic and elemental (ICP) analyses show that raw clays taken from the current site surface (and from a finer clay bed in a nearby stream cut) are qualitatively (mineralogically and elementally) similar to the pastes of Ejutla figurines and other vessels

(Carpenter and Feinman 1999). Another indicator of ceramic production was the presence of at least four shallow, ash-filled pits in external areas adjacent to the structure. We interpret these features as pit kilns, based on the prevalence of burnt rock, charcoal, and ash lenses in conjunction with kiln wasters, kiln furniture, and heavy densities of fired clay concretions (presumably remnants from temporary earthen roofs that were placed over the firing pits [Balkansky et al. 1997; Stark 1985:176]).

In contrast, at El Palmillo we found fewer ceramic firing features (at present only one),

Evidence for Ceramic Production
Pieces Recovered per Cubic Meter

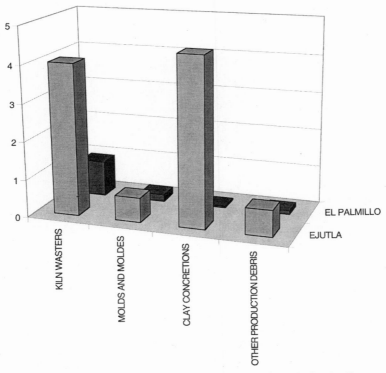

Figure 10.6. Ceramic production assemblage at Ejutla and El Palmillo.

and it is smaller than those at Ejutla. We also recovered a lower volume of ceramics at El Palmillo (Figure 10.5) and fewer artifactual indicators for ceramic production (Figure 10.6).

Based on the quantity of artifactual remains, shell working and ceramic production appear to have been practiced at a fairly high level of intensity at Ejutla. Lapidary crafting also was carried out, but apparently at a lower volume. Rectangular onyx plaques and cylindrical drill plugs, as well as chunks and flakes of greenstone and other nonlocal stones, were recovered in the excavations, principally in the exterior midden. One technique, the use of hollow tubular drills, was employed to work both shell and onyx; the diameter of the majority of the onyx drill plugs matches that of many shell disks, one of the most common shell ornament types re-

covered in the excavations. With chert reduction debris mixed in with the shell debris, it seems likely that the ancient Ejutleños also made the chert microdrills that they used to perforate the shell ornaments.

Several complementary analyses help tie the craft activities to the excavated house. Microartifactual (heavy fraction) analyses of the earthen floor have yielded microscopic flecks of shell, chert flakes, and pieces of greenstone, all too small to be swept away during cleaning (Middleton 1998). The recovery of these microartifacts in the heavy fraction from floor deposits provides support for the argument that these materials were worked inside the excavated house (Feinman et al. 1993). Chemical analysis (ICP) of soil samples taken systematically from the house floor also have left traces of repeated firings (possibly from the adjacent firepits)

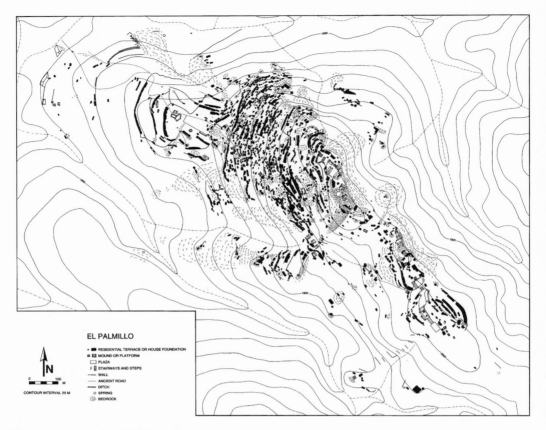

Figure 10.7. The site of El Palmillo.

and signatures from regular shell working (Middleton and Price 1996).

Most of the excavated artifacts (noted above) were recovered from the exterior middens, yet one of the chert microdrills was found on the floor near a flagstone pavement in a work area at the northern edge of the residential complex. Nearby was a small pit filled with sheets of mica, a material often used as an inclusion in the Ejutla ceramics (particularly *comales*). Surprisingly few finished shell ornaments were found inside the house, and only one tiny shell bead was found in the tomb. In the excavated extramural middens, craft debris often was found interspersed with domestic trash, such as food remains and sherds from charred cooking jars. Such remains help tie the craft debris to a domestic context.

As noted above, the high volume of shell debris in the middens, in conjunction with such a small number of finished pieces, indicates that much of the production was for exchange. There is simply no empirical evidence to suggest that this volume of shell ornament production was entirely for immediate household consumption. In addition to the high quantity of ceramic manufacturing debris, the overall volume of pottery was great (more than 1.75 metric tons was excavated). We were not able to excavate the entire area encircling the house (which almost certainly included more midden deposits), nor do we know how much production waste was transported via natural or cultural processes to areas distant from the house. Nevertheless, from the perspective of what was recovered, it seems unlikely that any single household would have used (even over several decades) anything approaching the volumes of figurines (or *comales* and *sahumadores*) that probably were made in this domestic context. In addition, near the base of one excavated firing feature, sherds from at least 9 to 11 different *comales* were found in the same excavation level of one 2-by-2-m unit. As with the thousands of figurines, the output from this particular production context was unlikely to have been for immediate household needs alone. If the Ejutla potters were supplying only their immediate needs, it seems doubtful that they would have concentrated so heavily on figurines, *comales*, and *sahumadores*, as those are not the forms that dominate a household's ceramic inventory.

Our research findings from El Palmillo, although more preliminary, provide an additional vantage on the economy. El Palmillo is a hilltop, terraced site, situated on the top and steep slopes of a rocky ridge at the eastern edge of the dry Tlacolula arm of the Valley of Oaxaca, on the outskirts of the present-day town of Santiago Matatlán (Figure 10.7). The setting is markedly different from alluvial Ejutla. The ancient inhabitants constructed more than 1,400 terraces at the site, the majority of which were residential. As with Ejutla, El Palmillo was most densely occupied during the Classic period.

Because of our interest in houses and the domestic economy, we began the excavations at El Palmillo on several terraces on the lower slopes, far from the public core of the site. We selected three adjacent terraces for excavation in 1999 (1147, 1148, and 1162) and a fourth adjoining terrace in 2000 (1163) (Figure 10.8) (Feinman et al. 2001). In 2001 we selected an additional terrace (925, Figure 10.9) farther up the slope but still far from the summit, with the goal of examining possible spatial and status-related variation in domestic architecture and economic activities, including production and consumption (Feinman et al. 2002).

On the lower terraces we uncovered two multiroom residential complexes, each consisting of a long, narrow, rectangular structure with foundation walls of shaped and flattened stones and well-made plaster floors. These rectangular structures or rooms were situated toward the back (east) edge of the terrace and linked a number of smaller, more

square-shaped rooms to the north and south. Together these sets of rooms form three sides of a central patio that was always open on the front (west) edge of the terrace. The central patios also were plastered, although the plaster was often poorly preserved. This basic layout was retained throughout several rebuilding episodes.

A similar residential complex was constructed on the upper terrace. However, in contrast to the lower terraces, the basic layout of the complex was changed more significantly with each rebuilding episode. During the final occupation of the terrace the domestic architecture was more formal, with an L-shaped grouping of rooms around a small sunken patio with a plastered banquette.

As with Ejutla, domestic refuse, human burials, and fire installations on the terraces—including two large ovens on the lower terraces that appear to have been used to roast maguey—indicate domestic use. The 43 burials uncovered on the terraces were found in the central patios, under house floors, and in the terrace retaining walls. Only one of the burials was a subfloor tomb, with the remains of three individuals, situated under the L-shaped structure on the upper terrace. Mixed in with the domestic debris was evidence of several craft activities.

The inhabitants of the excavated terraces at El Palmillo engaged in a different range of craft activities from their contemporaries at Ejutla. As indicated above, we found only limited evidence of ceramic production at El Palmillo, mostly on the lower terraces and largely of utilitarian wares for local consumption only. Shell working was nonexistent. Rather, the production of chipped-stone tools from local chert sources was a major livelihood at El Palmillo. The lithic assemblage at the site is dominated by chert (over 90 percent of the entire assemblage), specifically chert production waste (74 percent). The chipped-stone tools manufactured at El Palmillo include abraders, bifaces, perforators, points, *raspadores* (large specialized scrapers), generalized scrapers, and unifaces. The quantity of chert tools and production waste most likely represents a high level of

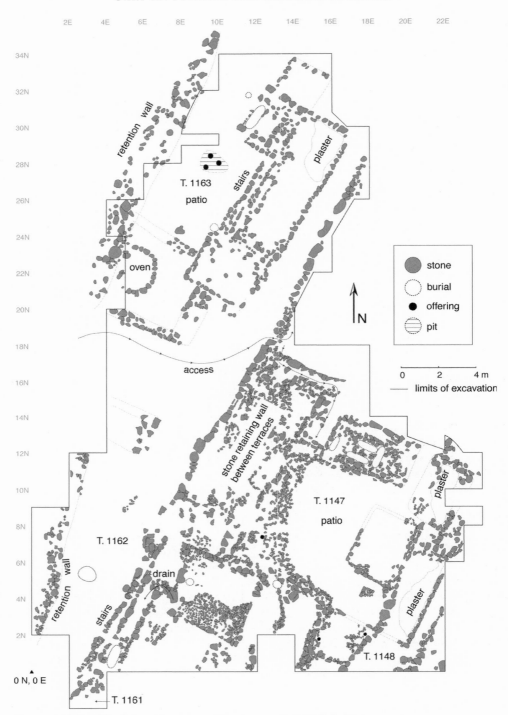

Figure 10.8. Residential architecture on lower terraces at El Palmillo.

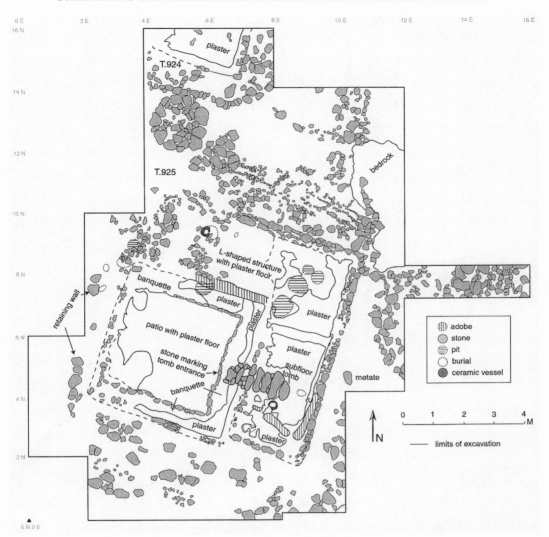

Figure 10.9. Residential architecture on upper terrace at El Palmillo.

lithic production, possibly for exchange to other sites in the region.

A quantitative comparison of the stone materials at El Palmillo and Ejutla shows some, but not striking, differences between the stone assemblages at the two sites. There is more chert (per cubic meter) at El Palmillo and more obsidian at Ejutla (where chert was less readily available) (Figure 10.10, top). There are no local sources of obsidian, and obsidian blades seem to have arrived at both sites as already prepared blades. We found few obsidian cores at either site.

A comparison of the stone assemblages by weight, however, reveals greater differences between the two assemblages (Figure 10.10, bottom). At Ejutla there were considerable quantities of tiny debris created by sharpening and using small tools to work shell and many small microdrills, debris that is all but absent in our El Palmillo excavations. We also recovered small flakes from lapidary work, and the chert assemblage was full of very small flakes. These findings have been confirmed by microscopic debris of greenstone, onyx, rose quartz, and shell that was recovered from flotation samples (Middleton 1998). In contrast, El Palmillo, which sits on

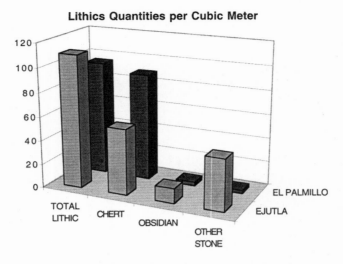

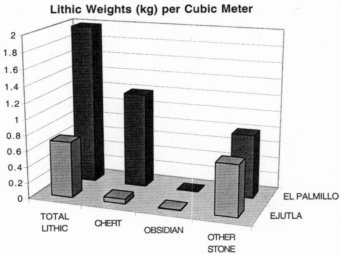

Figure 10.10. Stone materials *(top)* and stone assemblage weights *(bottom)* at El Palmillo and Ejutla.

several local chert sources, was a locus for the preparation of large chert cores, tools, and flakes.

There is a lower percentage of formal chert tools at El Palmillo (2 percent of the chert assemblage compared with 10 percent at Ejutla), which is what would be expected if chipped-stone nodules and chunks were being reduced into cores, usable flakes, and tools at El Palmillo. This mirrors the pattern for the shell debris at Ejutla. More important, the nature of the tool assemblages at the two sites is different. Of the tools we can tie to more specific tasks, there are many more scrapers at El Palmillo and many more micro-drills at Ejutla (Figure 10.11).

At El Palmillo we have found indications of xerophytic plant processing—particularly maguey, which is the economic backbone for the contemporary community where the site is located. We found many tools at El Palmillo that likely were used to process maguey. Scrapers were one of the most abundant chert tools, including the specialized *raspadores* that are thought to have served to extract maguey fiber from the plant's pulpy

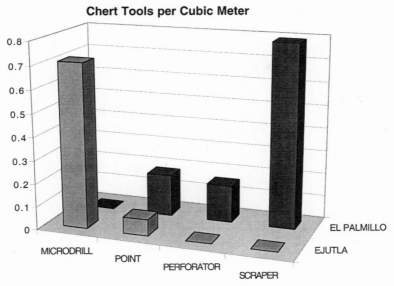

Figure 10.11. Chert tools at El Palmillo and Ejutla.

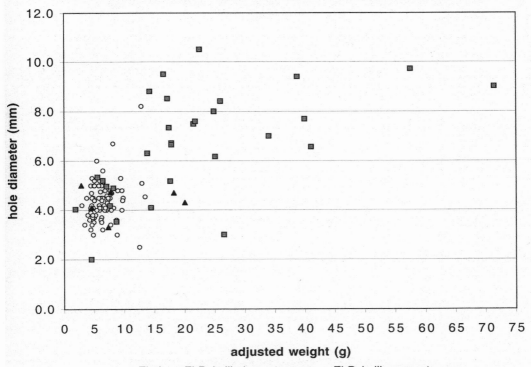

Figure 10.12. Spindle whorl size at El Palmillo and Ejutla.

Table 10.1. Nonlocal Goods and Materials at Ejutla and El Palmillo

	Raw Material	Finished Item
Ejutla	Shell	Obsidian blades
	Greenstone	Chert tools
	Chert nodules	Chalcedony points
		Thin Orange pottery
El Palmillo	Shell	Shell ornaments
	Fine chert	Obsidian blades
		Fine chert tools
		Thin Orange pottery
		Jade beads (?)

leaves (Hester and Heizer 1972; Robles G. 1994). The production of maguey fiber and textiles was a significant activity at El Palmillo, one for which we saw no evidence at Ejutla. Whereas stone working at Ejutla was related to shell ornament manufacture, the majority of stone working at El Palmillo appears to have been related to processing maguey.

We also found a number of spindle whorls at both sites. Although spindle whorls are more variable at El Palmillo, large ceramic spindle whorls, in the size range typically used for maguey fiber (Parsons 1972; Parsons and Parsons 1985, 1990), are more common there and are rare at Ejutla. Most of the whorls at Ejutla, and many fewer at El Palmillo, are of the smaller size likely used to spin cotton (Figure 10.12). Finally, many of the bone tools recovered in the El Palmillo excavations, including battens, needles, perforators, and spindle whorls, are related to textile manufacture. We found more of these bone tools, especially battens and needles, at El Palmillo than Ejutla (Figure 10.13).

To rule out the possibility that the differences we have noted between the two sites were simply the function of the necessarily small sample sizes associated with excavations, we also look beyond the excavated parts of each site. In other words, were the sites similar but we just uncovered the shell workers at Ejutla and the stone workers at El Palmillo? Findings from the intensive site surveys that were enacted at both sites illustrate

that the same patterns found for the excavations are borne out at the scale of the site; there is more chert at El Palmillo and more shell and ceramics at Ejutla (Figure 10.14).

Even at the regional scale, some of these differences remain. There is much more chipped-stone working in the eastern arm of the valley where El Palmillo is located and more shell working in the southern part of the valley near Ejutla (Feinman and Nicholas 1992:Figures 6, 7). Yet given the distribution of these goods, it seems likely that certain finished goods and raw materials were moved considerable distances across the valley. This is not really surprising if we look at distribution (Table 10.1). Shell and obsidian moved into the valley from afar. Certain finer varieties of chert as well as greenstone and onyx were exchanged across the valley system. We also recovered some exotic cherts at Ejutla.

Finished shell items from Ejutla also may have been traded to larger sites such as Monte Albán, which was farther from the coast. We have examined shell collections from this large center and believe that many of the ornaments made in Ejutla were sent to Monte Albán (Feinman and Nicholas 2000b). These movements of goods certainly could have occurred through exchange modes other than the market. Yet widespread exchange patterns with *utilitarian* and elite goods moving over considerable distances is much more indicative of a market than a redistributive system.

Bone Tools per Cubic Meter

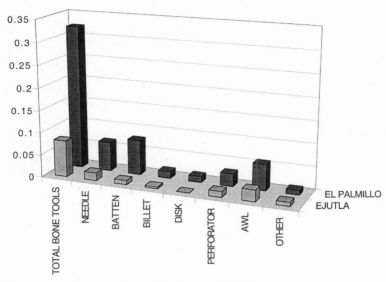

Figure 10.13. Bone tools at El Palmillo and Ejutla.

Quantities Recovered on Intensive Survey

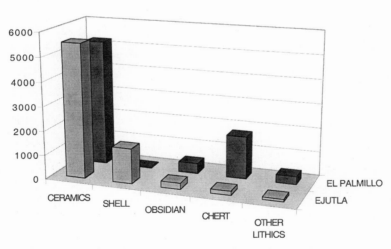

Figure 10.14. Archaeological materials on the surface at El Palmillo and Ejutla.

Finally, it is worth noting that in excavations or surveys we have not found *any* large storage features in Oaxaca of the kind that we might associate with centralized redistribution. In fact, few such features have ever been found in Mesoamerica or were described by the Spanish. Aztec rulers had granaries, but they do not appear to be of a size that could begin to feed even the urban capital of Aztec Tenochtitlan. Suggestively, Pizarro and his crew described, sought out, and even emptied grain storage facilities on their march through Andean Peru. If such features were commonplace, they probably

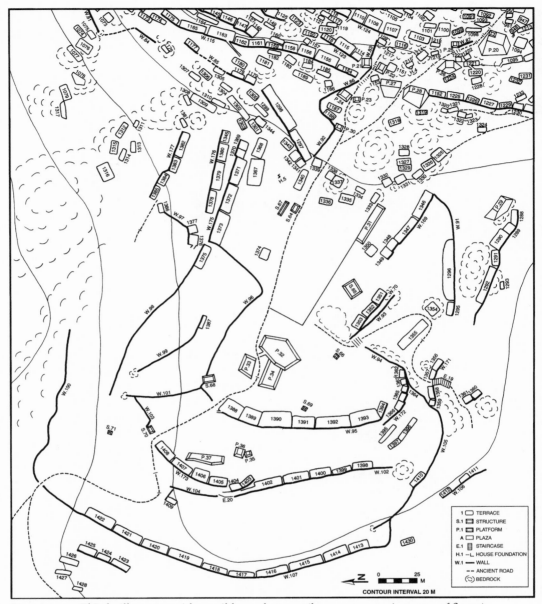

Figure 10.15. El Palmillo sector with possible market area (large open area in center of figure).

would have captured Spanish attention in Mexico. At the same time, recent detailed surface maps completed for El Palmillo reveal an open and accessible plaza area that conceivably could have been a marketplace (Figure 10.15). A series of ancient accessways or paths lead to this open area, which was located on the low hill below most of the defensive walls.

This possible market area may have been a locus for both inter- and intrasite exchange. For example, although stone tool production was a prevalent activity at El Palmillo, there is little evidence that a significant quantity of obsidian tools was fashioned from cores at the site. Few obsidian cores have been found at El Palmillo (Table 10.2). In contrast, clearer indications of obsidian tool produc-

Table 10.2. Obsidian Recovered During Intensive Survey of Three Hilltop Terrace Sites in Eastern Tlacolula

	Mitla Fortress	El Palmillo	Guirún
Total obsidian	389	285	359
% of stone assemblage	33	12	12
Cores	23	4	2
Blades	272	255	304
Flakes	79	20	48
Other	15	6	5

Notes: All materials are from the surface only. All three sites were occupied during the Classic and Postclassic periods, and the obsidian may pertain to either period. Only one additional obsidian core has been found at El Palmillo in three seasons of excavation.

tion have been recovered from elsewhere in eastern Tlacolula, including the Mitla Fortress (which has a sizable occupation from the Classic period as well as from the Postclassic), situated less than 10 km away from El Palmillo.

The inhabitants of El Palmillo may have obtained some of their obsidian tools from these other sites where obsidian cores (and obsidian in general) were more abundant. Of course, all obsidian originated from outside the state of Oaxaca. The greater percentage of obsidian in the total stone assemblage on the upper terrace (9 percent versus 3 percent on the lower terraces) appears to show that its residents had greater access to this nonlocal exotic good, which seemingly was not divided up evenly among households at the site.

Although chert tool production and maguey processing were important economic activities on both sets of terraces at El Palmillo, there were some minor differences in other economic activities. The residents of the lower terrace did make some utilitarian ceramic vessels, as one small pit kiln was noted on those terraces. There was much less evidence of ceramic production on the upper terrace. Spindle whorl comparisons reveal another minor difference. There were relatively fewer whorls on the upper terrace, but the ones we did find there tended to be smaller than the ones on the lower terraces, although not all were as small as the ones at Ejutla. Residents of the lower terraces most

likely were weaving coarser maguey thread whereas on the upper terrace the whorls may have been used to spin wild cotton (which still grows on the site today) or finer maguey thread (see Berdan 1987b). These different household products likely were exchanged through a system that was able to interconnect not only the many hundreds of households at El Palmillo but the tens of thousands more at other settlements in the region where different economic activities were practiced.

SUMMARY AND A LOOK FORWARD

We have outlined a variety of evidential lines (drawn from a range of artifact classes and archaeological scales) that lead us to propose that household production, often for exchange, was a likely building block of the Classic period economy in the Valley of Oaxaca. We also have suggested that the products from this specialized domestic production were more apt to have been circulated through markets than via tribute or redistribution alone. This is not to assert that the latter two methods were not part of a complex economic system involving interwoven means of circulation; rather, we believe that marketing was likely a key mechanism through which a variety of goods produced in different regions and communities were exchanged. We do not suggest that the interpretation we propose for Oaxaca in the Classic period can be extrapolated to all other Mesoamerican regions or periods in a wholesale manner. But as with the Aztec economy, it provides another reasonable foundation on which we can build. Based on our findings, it would appear that there were significant earlier highland Mesoamerican foundations for the later Prehispanic Aztec market network.

If the market was an important institution in Prehispanic Oaxaca and Mesoamerica earlier than Aztec times, then future Mesoamerican archaeologists have their work cut out for them. In Oaxaca we must learn more about the organization of household labor and specifically how households participated in the wider networks of exchange. More broadly for Mesoamerica, we should investigate how the market institution interrelated with the different political institutions that composed ancient Mesoamerica. How did the nature of the market change over time? Critically, when did markets develop, and what factors prompted their emergence? How did such exchanges interrelate with tributary demands and other economic activities? Finally, why was the ancient Mesoamerican economy so different from what was described by the Spanish for the Andean highlands of South America, where market institutions were apparently far less prominent throughout the Prehispanic era (Stanish 1997)? How similar or different were Mesoamerican markets from European markets of the same period? Although certainly not easy to address, questions such as these provide welcome challenges that we hope will guide archaeological investigations—through continued research, analysis, and interpretation—in the decades ahead.

Note

We wish to thank Jeff Grathwohl, Jim Skibo, and the University of Utah Press for sponsoring the conference leading to this volume and making this intellectual exchange possible. Earlier versions of this chapter were presented at The Field Museum, Southern Illinois University, Northern Illinois University, the University of Illinois at Chicago, and Northwestern University. We are indebted to all our colleagues who offered thoughtful comments and suggestions.

We gratefully acknowledge the National Science Foundation support given to the first author for the excavations at El Palmillo (SBR-9805288) and Ejutla (BNS 89-19164, BNS 91-05780, SBR-9304258). We also appreciate the valuable support received from the National Geographic Society, the H. John Heinz III Fund of the Heinz Family Foundation, The Field Museum, the Graduate School of the University of Wisconsin-Madison, and Arvin B. Weinstein. This study would not have been possible without the dedicated assistance of our Oaxacan and North American field and laboratory crews. We also are grateful to Jennifer Ringberg, Jill Seagard, and Helen Haines, who assisted us in the preparation of the graphics. We profoundly thank the Instituto Nacional de Antropología e Historia of Mexico, the Centro Regional de Oaxaca, and the local authorities of Santiago Matatlán and Ejutla de Crespo for the necessary permissions to implement these field studies, as well as for their essential support. Finally, we dedicate this work to the people of Matatlán and Ejutla. Their untiring assistance, interest, and encouragement in various stages of this study has made our effort gratifying in so many ways.

Craft Economies of Ancient Andean States

CATHY LYNNE COSTIN

Craft goods were extraordinarily important in the production and maintenance of ancient chiefdoms and states. In addition to basic domestic functions, they were used in almost all social, political, and ritual activities. Understanding the context and organization of their production is integral to a full understanding of daily life, political economy, and the role of material objects in social and political relations.[1] Archaeologists have made enormous headway in the past several decades in documenting and explaining both technological and organizational aspects of craft production and the concomitant systems of craft distribution and use. At this juncture I suggest it is important to revisit some of our key models and heuristic devices, to consider whether their continued use serves to move the discourse forward or is an impediment to refining our ideas about ancient societies.

In this chapter I attempt to accomplish four objectives related to modeling the organization of production in complex societies, the realization of which will contribute to cross-cultural studies of economies generally and our understanding of craft production specifically. First, the data I present add to a growing recognition that the economies of "complex" societies are enormously complex and not easily reducible to single-type models or generalizations (cf. Sinopoli n.d.). Second, in pulling together what we currently know about ancient Andean artisans, I hope to prod colleagues into paying more attention to artisan identities, which I believe are central to understanding power, control, and the organization of production. As archaeologists embrace agency-based exegesis, it is important to remember that it isn't just consumers/elites who are the active parties in the generation of meaning, action, and social structures. Third, in exploring what we know about the basic contexts of craft production in the Prehispanic Andes, I join the challenge to unilineal models for the development of specialization that suggest production forms evolve such that one "mode" replaces another. In particular, I question the received wisdom that over time household-based production is uniformly replaced by nondomestic "workshop" production (see also Feinman and Nicholas 2000b, this volume; Sinopoli n.d.). Fourth, I hope to advance ongoing discussions about the nature of the social relations of production, reflecting especially on the issue of the distinction between "attached" and "independent" production.

In pursuing these general objectives, I also foster discussions more specific to assessing the nature of Andean economic organization. Like several other contributors to this volume when speaking of the scholarly climate in their areas of study (for example, McAnany, Junker, and Stahl), researchers in "my" area (the Andes) often argue that general socioeconomic models and frameworks do not apply to "our" culture area; rather, distinctively Andean forms of organization and interaction arose and persisted over time. In particular, a model of community self-sufficiency and complementary exploitation of multiple ecological zones derived from early Spanish colonial documents and ethnographic observation is often touted as the uniquely Andean form of socioeconomic organization (Masuda et al. 1985; Murra 1972). In assessing the organization of craft production at various times and places in the Andes, I address three questions of particular interest to Andeanists. First, are these models derived from sixteenth-century colonial documents and twentieth-century peasant strategies applicable in deeper antiquity? Second, did the coast and highlands—with their radically different ecological configurations—have distinctive systems of production and distribution? And third, does this singularly Andean model adequately account for organization across time and space, or were Andean economic activities more variably organized?

WHY FOCUS ON PRODUCTION?

Studies of craft production are a fundamental part of archaeological inquiry in that they are central to the reconstruction of ancient lifeways and the explication of sociocultural evolution. Most recent investigations of craft production are integrated into larger studies of social, economic, and/or political organization and change. There is, for example, a long tradition in archaeology that claims an association between craft *specialization* and complex social organization, in which one is a marker for the other (Arnold 1987; Bayman 1999; Brumfiel and Earle 1987; Cameron 2001:89; Childe 1950; Hayden 1995; McCorriston 1997; Rice 1981; Stanish, this volume; Stein 1998b; Wailes 1996; Wilson 1988) and specialists are seen as integral to the establishment and maintenance of elite power (Clark and Blake 1994; Costin 1996a; D'Altroy and Earle 1985; Earle 1987b, 1997; Helms 1993; Peregrine 1991).

Studies of craft production also are inte-gral to investigations of the role material culture plays in domestic, social, and ritual life. Most objects in preindustrial societies are both utilitarian (in the broadest sense of the word) and a means of social communication (Appadurai 1986; Hodder 1982; Miller 1985; Schiffer 1999). Material culture is fundamental to the expression of identity, power, and social relations (Costin 1998c; Morris 1991, 1995; Wright 1996). The now widely used concept of "materialization" (DeMarrais et al. 1996) refers to the process of transforming intangible ideas and beliefs into visible, concrete symbols and signs. Craft production *is* materialization, as craft producers take ideas about daily maintenance, social identity, and power relations and express them in physical objects that can be experienced by others (see also Pauketat, this volume; cf. Earle 1997:151–155). Studies of the use or meaning of material culture ought to consider how the objects were made and by whom they were made, to gain insight into how meaning was created technologically and stylistically and to consider the perspectives and objectives of those who translated those ideas into their physical form.

CRAFT PRODUCTION SYSTEMS

Recently, I have suggested that the most effective way to study production is to consider it as a system composed of six interrelated components (Costin 2001c, 2004; cf. Bayman 1999).

1. Producers. The social identities of artisans—their gender, class, ethnicity, legal status, and the like—provide important clues useful for reconstructing ancient economies, in terms of both labor organization and the role of craft in broader social processes. Ideally, in addition to a description of social identity, the study of producers includes the investigation of characteristics such as the degree of specialization, labor intensity (the amount of time producers spend in craft production as opposed to other [economic] activities), the nature of compensation (which relates, fundamentally, to producer-consumer relations), producer skill (which is some admixture of proficiency and inherent talent), and principles of labor recruitment (which relate to social relations among producers and between producers and consumers).

2. *Means of production.* The means of production consist of raw materials, tools, and the technical knowledge necessary to transform raw materials into finished goods. Archaeologists study raw materials to reconstruct patterns of resource exploitation and the organization of production and exchange. The performance characteristics of raw materials reflect choices in manufacturing technologies and the intended functions of the finished goods. Studies of technology are used to infer other components of production, especially various aspects of the organization of production such as the degree of specialization and the nature of elite involvement in production activities. Technological differences might be used to identify work groups or even individual artisans, one step in assessing the amount of specialization. In particular, five aspects of technology—complexity, efficiency, output, control, and variability—are seen as linked to the organization of production (see Costin 2001c: 288–292).

3. *Organizing principles.* Production has organizing principles that situate it in time and in physical and social space. Temporal patterns relate to the daily and seasonal scheduling of work and issues of part- as opposed to full-time production. From the spatial and social loci of production, we infer many important aspects of the organization of production, in particular the general organization of work, the relative concentration or dispersal of manufacturing activities, and the sociopolitical context in which production takes place. All are important because they affect how producers interact with consumers and how consumers acquire goods. These aspects of organization also are tied to issues of distribution and control.

4. *Objects.* The principles and practices underlying the use of craft products are closely connected to other aspects of the production systems. The terms of consumption will shape the conditions of production (contra Clark 1995:287). Assumptions about the social and spatial organization of production (and how these manifest themselves archaeologically) are often based on the general "types" of goods under consideration (for example, utilitarian domestic goods as compared with prestige goods or preciosities), the degree of restriction in their use, and/or whether there were relatively few or many of these goods in use. Thus it is important to document the functions and uses of goods when reconstructing the production system.

5. *Principles and mechanisms of distribution.* Distribution entails the means by which goods are transferred from producers to consumers in specialized systems. Implicit in most discussions of specialized production is the belief that there is a correlation between the organization of production and the form of transfer. For example, definitions of independent specialization imply voluntary transfer, whereas attached specialization is seen to entail obligatory or coerced transfer from artisan to sponsor. The distribution of goods is as much a social and political process as an economic one, and it is important to fully describe its contexts and the mechanisms by which it occurs. Unfortunately, archaeologists recently have paid scant attention to documenting the nature of the transfer of goods from producer to consumer (but see, for example, Junker, this volume; Feinman and Nicholas, this volume).

6. *Consumers.* Finally, as already implied above, production is organized to meet the needs of consumers. Models of the organization of production usually posit a relationship between the social identities of consumers and the type of production. In any detailed study of production, then, it is important to ascertain, rather than assert, the intermediate and final consumers of the goods under study.

In this discussion of Prehispanic Andean production systems, I bring to the forefront two of these components: producers and the organizing principles of production. Nevertheless, elucidating the other components is integral to understanding any one aspect of the production system.

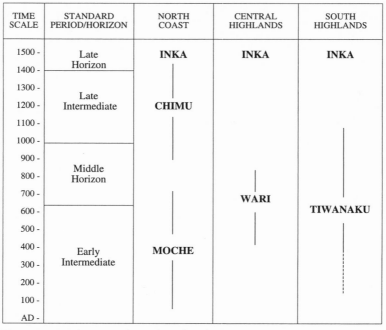

TIME SCALE	STANDARD PERIOD/HORIZON	NORTH COAST	CENTRAL HIGHLANDS	SOUTH HIGHLANDS
1500 - 1400 -	Late Horizon	INKA	INKA	INKA
1300 - 1200 - 1100 - 1000 -	Late Intermediate	CHIMU		
900 - 800 - 700 - 600 -	Middle Horizon		WARI	TIWANAKU
500 - 400 - 300 - 200 - 100 - AD -	Early Intermediate	MOCHE		

Figure 11.1. Schematic chronology for the central Andes.

BACKGROUND

Andean South America has been the locus of complex societies for several millennia. Although the time frame in which indigenous states predominated is often conveniently broken into five chronological epochs, an accurate cultural-historical reconstruction is actually more complex (Figure 11.1). In this chapter I focus on five major state systems: the Moche and Chimu of the north coast, the Wari of the central highlands, the Tiwanaku of the southern highlands, and the Inka empire, which spread throughout the Andes from Ecuador and Colombia in the north to Argentina and Chile in the south (Figure 11.2).[2]

Most Andean "cultures" have been defined traditionally by their distinctive portable art styles, and the extent of their political domains has been inferred from the geographic distribution of those styles. It is only recently that archaeologists and culture historians working in the Andes have sought to systematically investigate and characterize the sociopolitical organization of the groups that created those art works through the analysis of settlement patterns, social stratification, and economic structure. For that reason, our understandings of Andean sociopolitical organization have undergone significant modification in the past few years.

Moche-style artifacts are found on the north coast of Peru in contexts dating from roughly A.D. 100 to 800. Once considered to be a single large state with a population variously estimated at 250,000 to one million people, the Moche world is now seen as divided into two different spheres or polities (Bawden 1996; Castillo and Donnan 1994; Donnan 1990; Pillsbury 2001; Shimada 1994). The multitiered settlement hierarchy, evidence for militarism, and high degree of social stratification all indicate state-level social organization (Shimada 1994:105–115). The intricate, often figurative designs on Moche objects undoubtedly communicated complex ideas about the natural world, social structure, power hierarchies, and supernatural domain. Much of the Moche imagery in both portable and monumental art seems tied to battle and its ceremonial aftermath, emphasizing relations of dominance and sub-

Figure 11.2. The Andes: approximate boundaries of the polities mentioned in the text. (Map created by David Deis)

jugation. These scenes are not just "purely" mythological, as similar events were (re)enacted by human impersonators (Alva and Donnan 1993; Bourget 2001; Donnan and Castillo 1992; Verano 2001).

The highland Wari and Tiwanaku polities of the Middle Horizon (c. A.D. 600–1000) were clearly related to each other—they share complex iconographic images and themes—but the nature of the relationship is poorly understood. Some models postulate that the Tiwanaku polity arose first and exported its "ideology" to the north; others see the two cultures as deriving from a common source close to the Tiwanaku heartland and then diverging through evolutionary processes as yet unidentified. Interestingly, the iconic images of both polities echo themes that first appeared in the Chavin style nearly a thousand years earlier, suggesting there were ideological continuities that survived the oscillations of political consolidation and fragmentation that characterized the highlands from 500 B.C. to A.D. 500/600 (cf. van Buren 2000).

There is little doubt that both corporate art styles are associated with state-level polities, although the exact structure of their individual political organizations is uncertain. Wari and Tiwanaku have been variously characterized as military states or empires based on aggressive religious proselytizing; what both models attempt to explain is the presence of portable objects in the Wari and Tiwanaku corporate styles hundreds of kilometers from their presumed political centers.

The sociopolitical character of the protohistoric Chimu "empire" is much more clear than those of the polities that preceded it, in large measure because Spanish colonial documents complement the available archaeological material. After consolidating power in the traditional Moche heartland of the north coast during the early Chimu period (roughly A.D. 900–1100), the Chimu lords set off on a series of military conquests, first to the south and then to the north. The empire was ruled from the capital of Chan Chan in the Moche Valley. A hierarchy of administrative centers was established in the conquered lands. There is some debate as to whether the Chimu expansion was aimed primarily at controlling agricultural land (e.g., Keatinge and Conrad 1983) or acquiring raw materials, artisan labor, and finished craft goods (Topic 1990). The expansion of the Chimu stopped only when they encountered and were defeated by the Inka army in about A.D. 1470.

The Inka constituted a true empire. The Inka polity began as a small chiefdom centered in the central Andean highlands, but through a series of military and diplomatic maneuvers the Inka spread rapidly throughout both highland and coastal regions, beginning in about A.D. 1400. Before their conquest by the Spanish in the early sixteenth century, the Inka controlled an area of western South America running 3,000 km from modern-day Colombia and Ecuador in the north to Chile and Argentina in the south and encompassing eight to twelve million people associated with 80 different ethnic and/or language groups. The empire was governed by a complex bureaucracy of centralized and provincial administrators. The economy has traditionally been characterized as highly centralized, with the state controlling most production and distribution, although recent research indicates that the state used a number of different strategies to finance its activities (e.g., D'Altroy 1992, 2002).

Although these cases are discussed in chronological order, I do not mean to imply a set of necessary evolutionary relationships or an inevitable developmental sequence among them. Certainly there are historical connections among these polities, but I make no a priori claims to continuity from one chronological phase to the next. Indeed, the antiquity of patterns and the developmental relationships among Andean cultures are desperately in need of documentation; too much of the Andean literature is content to argue through assertion, no more. I have organized the presentation of the data around the analytic components of the production system rather than as holistic, integrated cases because I do not wish to generalize about or reify specific constructs such as "the Moche" or "the Inka" craft production system, given the state of the data and analyses.

ANDEAN CRAFTS

Andean peoples have created awe-inspiring craft goods for thousands of years. Their textiles and metal goods are some of the most technologically sophisticated produced by preindustrial peoples. Pottery served mundane functions as well as carried religious, social, and political messages, often executed with astonishing artistry. Aside from their aesthetic appeal, the Andean cases are instructive for a number of reasons. Both utilitarian and luxury goods provide comparative cases that add significantly to our general understanding of the technology and organization of craft production (see Feinman 1999 on the need for more comparative and cross-cultural studies of craft production). Moreover, craft goods have long been considered among the primary means by which state ideologies—political and religious—were spread from one region to another (e.g., Burger 1995; Lavallée and Lumbreras 1985:400; Morris 1991, 1995; Stone-Miller 1995). Thus it is of prime importance to understand the nature of their production.

Despite the elaborate character of metal, textile, and ceramic crafts in Andean states, the data on Andean craft production remain remarkably scant, creating real challenges for preparing a synthesis such as this one. There are few detailed studies of either craft technology or production loci. Most discussions of production still rely on assertion and speculation to fill in the gaps of missing data. There is little published archaeological work on households, so we lack data on an important context of production and consumption. In several cases we have evidence for production loci but no information on associated public or private contexts, so it is difficult to assess the social relations of production. Often production loci are identified, but there is little evidence for the specific type or types of goods produced or the identities of the consumers who used the finished products. It is still rare to have multiple studies of the same craft in the same culture, needed in order to gauge the amount of variation in the organization of production. Finally, much more has been said about luxury, prestige goods than utilitarian goods. The bias toward the organization of the "political economy" implicit in many of the chapters in this volume holds for research in the Andes generally.

On a more general level, there is surprisingly little documentation of variation in the social and political organization of most Andean societies. Studies of Andean socioeconomic organization have been strongly shaped by two contrasting models. The first, more dominant model is most often applied to highland societies. This model posits that individual communities maintained their self-sufficiency by rotating members among tasks in a variety of production zones in the form of a "vertical archipelago" (so named because the characteristics of ecological niches are largely determined by altitude in the Andes; Murra 1972). Thus production was largely "unspecialized" beyond the intracommunity level. This model primarily addresses agricultural and pastoral activities; it says little about the production and circulation of noncomestible goods other than wool. "Specialization" in this model is implicitly limited to the production of wealth items for use by the elite and governing institutions. Producers of sumptuary goods are assumed to be (full-time) retainers of the paramount leaders, often resident in their houses. In contrast, in the second, subsidiary model each river valley of the coast is portrayed as organized into dozens of interdependent communities, each of which "specialized" in a specific "profession" such as fishing, farming, or potting (Rostworowski 1977a, 1977b, 1989). Both these models, derived from colonial-era documents, are assumed to have great antiquity in the Andes (e.g., Russell and Jackson 2001; Stanish 1992; but see Isbell's [1997] scathing critique of this practice). There is limited debate as to whether the "highland" model (i.e., the idea of ecological complementarity) might also be applicable to the coast (see, for example, Netherly 1977; Ramírez 1996; Shimada 1985, 1987), but there has been implicit agreement that the "coastal" model (i.e., one of village specialization) is not applicable in the highlands notwithstanding evidence to the contrary (e.g., Costin 1986, 2001a; D'Altroy and Hastorf 2001; Julien 1982; LeVine 1987; Russell 1988).[3]

Despite these limitations, a careful review of the literature on Andean craft production reveals patterns that relate to my objectives. First, there is tremendous complexity in Andean craft production, with multiple production systems operating simultaneously. As Hayashida (1998) has demonstrated specifically for the Andes, there is enormous diversity even in the production of a single commodity type (ceramics) for a single consuming entity (the Inka state). This observation that states have heterogeneous economies with multiple sectors supports similar conclusions drawn by many of my colleagues in this volume (e.g., Stein and Storey; see also Sinopoli 1994b). Second, there is tremendous variability in the social identities of Andean artisans. Simplistic unidimensional explanations for the division of labor and task allocation—such as those arguing that artisans are largely distressed peasant agriculturists (e.g., Arnold 1985; Mohr-Chávez 1992; Stark 1991; Tschauner 2001)—are insufficient for elucidating the Andean cases presented below. New models that also consider the control of esoteric knowledge (e.g., Inomata 2001b; cf. comments in Stahl, this volume), the availability of labor (Kramer 1997), and social agency (e.g., Brumfiel 1998; Sinopoli 1998) need to inform our discussions. In part, in the Andean cases artisan identity is linked to the contexts of distribution and the functions of craft goods. Third, in the Andes there is little "industrial-scale" utilitarian production, in contrast to trends predicted by many models for the development of specialization in state societies (e.g., Wilson 1988: 87–88). As Feinman and Nicholas (2000b, this volume) demonstrate, we should not conflate the scale (or setting) of production with its intensity; neither should we assume a necessary correlation between specialization and nondomestic production loci. Fourth, to characterize social relations of production simply as either "attached" or "independent" is inadequate. To begin with, the context—or locus of control—must be characterized along a continuum rather than dichotomized; the degree of elite involvement in production varies (cf. Sinopoli 1988). There also is no simple correlation between types of goods and contexts of production. The Andean cases demonstrate that the production of some ideologically charged goods was not in the hands of attached specialists as they are classically defined. There is less evidence for close elite or institutional supervision of a broad array of iconographically potent goods than might be predicted by traditional models. However, this class of ideologically charged goods is primarily distributed among the commoners. This observation has important implications for our ideas about the

growth of political economies and the nature of political power and control. In general, the Andean data indicate that there are many ways that both independent and attached production can be organized to meet the overall objectives of producers, patrons, and consumers.

ANDEAN ARTISANS

The sociopolitical relations of production cannot be understood fully without understanding producer identity. Gender, age, kinship relations, and place of residence, among other things, are a significant part of economic and social relations. Social identity is often critical in establishing claims to resources; it is central to principles of labor recruitment. Therefore, artisan identity must figure into models of who crafts and why they craft. Through craft production, artisans transform ideas and social meaning into material objects. As archaeologists place greater emphasis on social agency and the role of material culture in mediating social, political, and supernatural relations, an understanding of the multiplicity of perspectives that contribute to the creation of iconic images and goods ought to inform analyses.

Artisan identity is among the most difficult components of the production system to reconstruct in preliterate and nonliterate societies (see Costin 1996b, 2001c:282–285). Until recently, characterizations of Andean artisans derived either from Spanish colonial documents that described life in the Inka empire or from ethnographic analogy. Some archaeological data now complement the ethnohistoric data and additionally provide information on artisans in societies for which there are no textual data. These archaeological data primarily consist of detailed examination of production contexts, although it is important to remember that the production setting is not the same thing as artisan identity. In a few cases burial data and figurative representations of artisans provide evidence for artisan identity.

As Storey (this volume) points out, in "complex" economies we should expect to

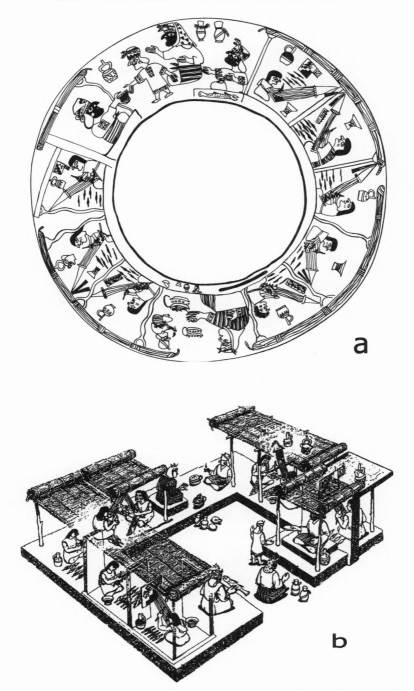

Figure 11.3. Reconstruction of a Moche weaving workshop: *(a)* inner rim of fineline flaring bowl depicting women weaving in a possible workshop setting (drawing courtesy of Christopher Donnan and Donna McClelland); *(b)* reconstruction of a Moche textile workshop based on the ceramic vessel illustrated in *(a)* (redrawn from Campana 1994:Figure 15.9).

Figure 11.4. Moche ceramic vessel representing metalworking. (Photograph courtesy of Christopher Donnan)

find a wide variety of workers. For those Andean cases in which artisan identity is demonstrated rather than asserted a priori, that indeed appears to be the case.

Moche Artisans

Gender. Much of what we infer about the social identities of Moche weavers is based on a painted ceramic vessel that depicts a textile "workshop" (Figure 11.3a). Eight female weavers of diverse ages are depicted on the inner rim of this flaring bowl. All are seated and using backstrap looms attached to posts or the ramada of a building. Each seated weaver is accompanied by various weaving accoutrements such as spindles and a single elaborate fineware ceramic vessel. Several of the women appear to have samples or templates from which they copy their designs. The scene includes six males, five of whom are dressed in elegant garb and are seated in poses usually reserved for individuals of power or authority. Campana (1994) has interpreted this scene literally, reconstructing it as a workshop staffed by women with elite male supervisors or patrons (Figure 11.3b). The association between women and weaving is supported by burial data from the site of Pacatnamu, where women were consistently accompanied by spinning and weaving tools in their graves (Donnan and McClelland 1997:36).

Another Moche ceramic vessel—again,

the only one of its kind published—depicts four metalworkers (Figure 11.4). Three are blowing on tubes into a closed chamber (a kiln or oven). The fourth is holding an oval object. That object and several others depicted on the top of the chamber are likely scrap metal being remelted or blanks or half-finished objects in the process of being annealed. All these metalworkers are male.

Status. Artisan status is inferred primarily from the physical setting in which production occurred. Based on the diversity of settings in which Moche craft production took place, it is possible to conclude that Moche artisans were drawn from many social sectors, urban and rural, commoner and elite. Even within a single craft type, artisan identity is variable. For example, there are four well-documented Moche ceramic workshops, all from relatively urban loci. At Cerro Mayal in the Chicama Valley, inferred kilns and other production-activity areas were found interspersed among and adjacent to habitation areas that were likely occupied by commoner populations (Russell et al. 1998; Russell and Jackson 2001). A variety of medium-quality, decorated serving and consuming vessels, as well as figurines and musical instruments associated with household rituals, were produced at the Cerro Mayal locus. The production area at the Moche V site of Galindo was similarly located on the outskirts of a commoner residential zone. However, evidence indicates that plain utilitarian wares were produced there (Bawden 1982). In both cases the artisans are inferred to be of commoner status. A third ceramic production workshop was located at the base of Huaca de la Luna at the city also called Moche. The excavators believe the excavated production area is part of a larger potters' barrio and suggest the potters themselves were of the elite class (Uceda and Armas 1998:107; cf. Chapdelaine 2001:75). They base this conclusion on the location of the workshop in the central Sol/Luna urban complex, near the locus of the most important elite and ritual activities at the site, and on the presence of large quantities of high-quality grave goods—including elaborate metal items—found in two of the burials under the floor of the potters' compound. According to osteological evidence, the buried individuals were potters (Uceda and Armas 1998:93). These elite potters were making a wide variety of items whose forms and iconography point to elite and ritual use (for example, musical instruments, elaborate painted vessels with depictions of ritual hunting and warfare, and luxury burial goods). The fourth well-documented ceramic production locus was identified at Moche V Pampa Grande. It was located in a nonresidential area not too far from the city center, which is interpreted as an elite context (Shimada 1994:195–197). Shimada does not believe, however, that the transient artisans who worked there were elites.

In addition to these reasonably well-described urban ceramic production loci, other possible utilitarian ceramic production locations have been mentioned (e.g., Russell et al. 1998), but none has been investigated. The implication, however, is that these production areas are located in small village sites inhabited by commoner-peasant populations.

There is limited archaeological evidence for the activities of other artisans at Moche sites. Chapdelaine (2001) has recovered evidence for metal, textile, and cloth production in the residential compounds that housed the lower elites at Moche. Like Uceda and Armas, excavators of the pottery workshop discussed above, Chapdelaine argues that the elite residents of these compounds—not resident or transient commoner retainers—were themselves the artificers and artisans. Shimada (1994, 2001) postulates a different arrangement at Moche V Pampa Grande, where he identified six areas in which *Spondylus* shell, cotton, and copper were worked. None of these workshops is located in a residential sector of the site. Although most of these activities were carried out in elite sectors of the city, Shimada argues that because there is no habitational debris nearby, the (non-elite) workers were housed elsewhere and must have traveled to the workshops

each day. Evidence for metalworking was identified in an elite sector of Galindo (Bawden 1977:202–207). Because this was not a residential zone, it is difficult to ascertain the identities of the artisans with certainty.

Neither of the two figurative ceramic vessels discussed above in the context of artisan gender definitively indicates the artisans' social status. In both scenes the workers are dressed in plain cloth, usually an indicator of commoner status in Andean figural representations. The weaving women's dress and head ornaments are set apart from the more elaborate dress of the seated males (cf. Shimada 1994:209). The presence of these higher-status males might also indicate that the women are being supervised by and/or are in the employ of higher-status individuals.

The evidence for Moche artisan status, then, is complex. Both figural and contextual data suggest that men and women crafted—although perhaps they worked at different crafts—and that artisans held a range of socioeconomic statuses, from commoner to lower elite. Women weavers held generally low status, although some weaving occurred in elite contexts. Potters apparently held a range of statuses, largely but perhaps not entirely linked to the sociopolitical value of the goods they produced. Domestic wares were produced by commoners. Some finer ceramic wares that carried ritually potent symbols also were produced by commoners at the Cerro Mayal workshop(s). These images were created in molds, so most of the workers did not have to command or manipulate esoteric knowledge in order to properly craft their goods. The production of the finest wares for which we have solid evidence appears to be the domain of (lower) elites. Some of the goods from the ceramic workshop at Moche bore painted designs, which would require greater skill and knowledge on the part of the artisan. That members of the elite would take responsibility for manufacturing goods associated with communicating and upholding elite power is consistent with recent thinking about the control of esoteric

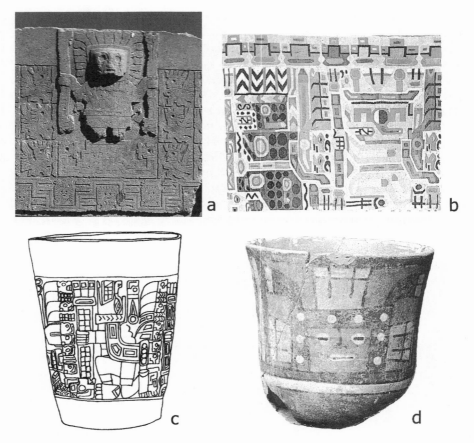

Figure 11.5. Key Middle Horizon iconic image represented in multiple media: *(a)* central portion of carved stone "doorway" at Tiwanaku depicting central Portal God and attendant running figures; *(b)* fragment of a tunic depicting stylized attendant running figures; *(c)* carved wooden beaker with attendant running figure; and *(d)* small cup with Portal God. (All photographs and drawings by author)

knowledge and cultural capital in highly stratified societies (Costin 2001b; Inomata 2001b; Stahl, this volume).

Middle Horizon:
Wari and Tiwanaku Artisans

The importance of craft goods in the spread of Middle Horizon political and religious ideologies in the central and southern Andes goes unchallenged in the Andean literature (e.g., Kolata 1993; Stone-Miller 1995). This is an era of highly standardized iconography reproduced on ceramics and textiles and in stone (Figure 11.5). Yet until recently, little was said of the organization of production of these goods. Given the centrality of material culture in models for the spread of these polities and their ideologies, understanding the organization of their production is of the essence.

There are four well-documented production loci that pertain to the Middle Horizon Wari and Tiwanaku polities. The ceramic workshop at Maymi, in the Pisco Valley, however, lacks information on the larger social context—there is no evidence yet analyzed regarding the habitations or other settlements in the area (Anders et al. 1998), and so we cannot reconstruct the social identities of the artisans who worked there. A second ceramic workshop is reported from the site of Conchopata, a political and religious center in the Ayacucho Valley. When Conchopata was at its height, elaborate decorated ritual ceramic vessels were produced there. The production location is near, but outside, an elite habitation zone. The domestic architecture in which production was situated is much cruder than the elite residences to the north, and the excavators imply that it was commoners who actually made the pottery, although the pottery was of central ritual importance (Pozzi-Escot et al. 1998). Only two craft workshops are reported for the Tiwanaku area. The production of low-quality decorated ceramic service wares took place in a commoner household context at the Tiwanaku "imperial" capital (Janusek 1999; Kolata 1993:170), as did bone panpipe production at the Tiwanaku regional center of Lukurmata (Janusek 1999). These last two cases exemplify the production of nonutilitarian goods by commoners for commoners.

Chimu Artisans

There is fragmentary documentary evidence for craft production in the Chimu empire, and there have been varying, almost contradictory, interpretations of these Spanish colonial documents. There is little doubt that a wide variety of craft *specialists* were producing in the Chimu area (Ramírez-Horton 1981, 1982; Rostworowski 1977a, 1989). Little has been written about the social identities of these artisans, however. Of greater concern has been the nature of their relationship to the ruling elite (cf. Tschauner 2001; see discussion below).

Ramírez-Horton (1982:Table 1) lists 24 types of specialists named in early colonial documents from Lambayeque and Pacasmayo. The specialists are discussed in the context of the labor and resources under the jurisdiction of local leaders; the implication is that the artisans had commoner status. The professions are all named in Spanish, although a few titles—for example, *cumbicos* (weavers) and *chicheros* (*chicha* [maize beer] brewers)—are derived from native Quechua

terms (but note that Quechua was not the indigenous language of the north coast, and so these terms must have been introduced by the Inka when they conquered the Chimu or by the Spaniards, who continued to use some Quechua terms in their administration of the conquered Andean region). All occupational titles are listed in the masculine form; whether this reflects the traditional Chimu or Inka division of labor or the Spanish worldview is uncertain. Thus it would be unwise at this point to assume that these are all masculine professions.

Some information on artisan identity can be derived from the locales in which production occurred. Secure-context archaeological data for craft production in the Chimu empire come primarily from the imperial capital at Chan Chan. Chan Chan is perhaps unique among Andean cities in that the bulk of the population is inferred to have been either state bureaucrats or artisans (Topic 1990). Excavations at Chan Chan yielded evidence for production in both commoner and elite contexts, although different kinds of goods and/or different stages of production were carried out at the different locales (see discussion below). This range of social statuses for Chimu artisans is in keeping with findings in the other Andean cases.

Aside from Chan Chan, there is little information on Chimu craft production locales. Epstein and Shimada (1984) describe a multicomponent smelting site in the Leche Valley. The presence of distinctive Chimu administrative architecture suggests that state functionaries supervised production, but there is no evidence for the social identity of the workforce itself. Detailed evidence for Chimu craft production comes from only one other site, the Pampa de Burros potting community in the Lambayeque Valley to the north. At that site Tschauner (2001) recovered evidence for fairly large-scale pottery production in a dedicated workshop compound. The potting compound was adjacent to a domestic complex, which Tschauner argues housed the potting families. Detailed investigation of the residential unit revealed no evidence for an elite or socially elevated presence, indicating that the potters who worked there were of commoner status.

Inka Artisans

Labor. Analyses of colonial texts suggest that Inka artisans fell within one of four categories of labor in the imperial system.

1. *Mit'a* laborers were those general subjects of the empire who worked to pay their labor taxes. The Spanish documents indicate that commoners fulfilled this obligation by working at their customary occupations.[4]

2. *Mitmaqkuna* laborers consisted of production groups—likely kin units—who were physically relocated by the empire, partially for strategic reasons and partially to fill perceived labor gaps. Some were relocated within their natal provinces, and others were moved fairly long distances from one region of the empire to another. Artisans, especially potters and weavers, are among the documented *mitmaqkuna*. Most *mitmaqkuna* groups were not provisioned directly by the state; rather, the state allocated lands and herds to them in their new homes, and the *mitmaqkuna* were expected to feed, house, and clothe themselves as well as manufacture craft goods for state institutions. Evidence suggests that *mitmaqkuna* groups retained at least some of their "traditional" kin and governance structure despite the co-option of their labor by the state.

3. *Yanakuna* were individuals who were alienated from their natal communities and relocated as retainers to individual estates and nobles.

Crosscutting these three designations was the title *kamayoq*. The term is a suffix appended to a variety of objects and services to denote those responsible for making or providing them (e.g., *qompikamayoq* [fine cloth maker], *qhipukamayoq* [quipu manipulator, or accountant]). The term seems to be applied only to specialists. Moreover, it is applied only to some categories of specialists; in particular, I have argued that the term translates as "skilled man" and was applied to male specialists (Costin 1998b).

4. The fourth category of artisans consisted of the *aqllakuna*. These were women removed from their natal villages and housed in special state facilities, where they wove cloth and brewed beer for use in state functions. Significantly, the *aqllakuna* are never referred to as *kamayoq*, supporting my contention that they were kept conceptually apart from the other artisans (Costin 1998b).

Status. Most artisans in the Inka empire were of generally low, certainly commoner, status. The ethnohistoric data indicate that *mit'a* applied only to commoners and that *mitmaqkuna* were drawn from the commoner class, although their local leaders might be relocated along with them to oversee production and provide community governance. Early colonial censuses in the highlands list artisans such as potters, sandal makers, and woodworkers along with farmers among the residents of the commoner villages in the hinterland of the provincial center of Huánuco Pampa in the north (LeVine 1987; Ortiz de Zuñiga 1967) and Chucuito in the south (Díez de San Miguel 1964; Julien 1982). In the Yanamarca Valley of the central highlands, archaeological evidence for the production of pottery and stone tools was found primarily in commoner households (Costin 2001a; see also Russell 1988).

The one exception to this generalization of low artisan status appears to be the status of female weavers. I found archaeological evidence for weaving differentially concentrated in elite households in the Yanamarca Valley (Costin 1993). Although this finding does not disallow the possibility that commoner women went to elite households to work there periodically, ethnohistoric documents suggest that it was the wives and daughters of the households themselves who were the primary textile producers in elite households (Falcón 1918 [1565]:154; Polo de Ondegardo 1940 [1561]:141). The *aqllakuna* had special ideological status in the empire. I have argued that their high status was both "real" and socially (re)constructed within the state ideology (Costin 1998b; see also Silverblatt 1987). Social rank was an important criterion for selecting girls to become *aqllakuna*, along with age, beauty, and virginity. There is evidence that girls were chosen disproportionately from elite households in conquered provinces. As the metaphorical wives, sisters, and daughters of the emperor and supreme deity, *aqllakuna* were afforded a position at the apex of the Inka status hierarchy.

A unique set of burials recovered at the Inka provincial capital at Túcume on the north coast supports this interpretation of *aqllakuna* status. At Túcume a group of 19 female burials was recovered from under the floor of one room in the most elaborate building at the site used during the Inka period. Mostly young women, these burials contained many items associated with weaving (spindles, spindle whorls, balls of thread, needles, loom boards; small items were stored in the closed, rectangular baskets consistently recovered with women) as well as high-status objects such as fine pottery, jewelry, and fancy cloth. The excavators believe the women were interred simultaneously, perhaps to accompany the elaborate burial of a man recovered in an adjacent room. This man is inferred by the excavators to be the last Inka provincial governor at Túcume (Narvaez 1995:93–96), and the women are presumed to be *aqllakuna* in his retinue.[5]

Gender and Age. The most detailed textual information on the Inka gendered division of labor comes from the work of Guamán Poma de Ayala (1980 [1615]). This document presents a generalized, normative perspective on the division of labor and includes a section in which work responsibilities are systematically described for males and females. Each gender is divided into 10 age categories. Although these groupings have been characterized as age grades by some writers (e.g., Dilke 1978), in fact they represent the census categories of Inka bureaucrats, who were interested in extracting goods and services from the conquered populace.[6] Thus the extensive list of tasks is not a complete discussion of work patterns; the tasks enumerated were those of particular interest to the state: matters of warfare, mining, camelid herding, textile production, and the supply of personal services to elites and bureaucrats. In addition, Guamán discusses other aspects of work in the context of describing the annual agricultural cycle. Other early chroniclers also refer to men's and women's tasks.

Taking these sources together, I develop a general understanding of the division of labor by gender and age in a household context. Adult females were responsible for food preparation; they did much of the agricultural work (planting, hoeing, weeding, harvesting), fetched water, and took primary responsibility for watching young children. They also invested large amounts of their time spinning and weaving to meet familial and political obligations. In contrast, adult males' primary responsibilities were plowing and combat; indeed, these were the archetypal masculine activities (Silverblatt 1987: 14). In addition, men helped in other agricultural work (especially planting and harvesting), collected firewood, built houses, and herded camelids. Subadults in particular collected grass and firewood, cared for camelid herds, and collected wild resources such as medicinal and industrial plants and birds. Although some distinct tasks were enumerated for girls and boys, many labor assignments for subadults were the same for both genders, and task allocation seems to have differentiated young people by gender less than it did adults. Older adults (those past their reproductive prime)—perhaps those freed from heavy agricultural work and (for men) combat duty—were responsible for small animal care and craft production, particularly spinning, weaving, and rope making. They also aided in childcare.

In addition to the information on the household division of labor, there are lists of *specialists* who produced crafts for the state (e.g., Falcón 1977 [1571]; Ortiz de Zuñiga 1967). Spanish documents almost invariably translate the native terms for artisans in the masculine; it is not certain whether this reflects the paradigmatic division of labor among the Inka or colonial Spanish biases. Censuses appear to list the occupations of the (male) heads of households; again, whether this reflects work allocation among the Inka or the Spanish worldview is not clear. Many craft activities—for example, production of stone tools—are seldom if ever mentioned. I suggest we can only cautiously apply ethnographic analogy. Although continuities in technology and certain organizational aspects from precolonial to present times are clear (e.g., Cleland and Shimada 1998; Hagstrum 1989), the economies of the native peoples have nevertheless experienced significant disruption and reorganization, enough to warrant changes in the division of labor as household tasks were reallocated to meet family needs in a monetized and more globalized economy.

PRODUCTION SETTING: SPATIAL ORGANIZATION, CONTEXT OF PRODUCTION, AND ORGANIZATION OF WORK GROUPS

Study of the physical setting of production begins with locating the places where the various production tasks occurred. With this information we can describe the geographic distribution of production activities, the context(s) in which production occurred, and the size of production loci, as well as infer the internal organization of production loci. Identifying production locations is also the foundation for further analyses of specialization and the social relations of production.

In the Andes, production, even when specialized, remained fairly localized in scope. Although many Andean decorative styles had broad geographic distribution, compositional and technological analyses consistently indicate that stylistically similar goods were produced at multiple workshops, even within small regions such as coastal and highland valleys (e.g., Costin 2001a; D'Altroy and Bishop 1990; Hayashida 1998:325; Russell et al. 1998).

Evidence for craft production has been recovered from a variety of settings in the central Andes. Most has been found in nondomestic contexts, but I suspect this is more a function of the focus of Andean archaeology than it is a realistic representation of the social organization of production. When Andean archaeologists have pursued excavation of household contexts in complex societies,

strong evidence for some types of craft production has been consistently recovered (e.g., Bermann 1994; Costin 1986, 2001a; D'Altroy and Hastorf 2001; Goldstein 1989; Janusek 1994; Russell 1988; Topic 1982).

One pattern that recurs across time and space is the differentiation into production spheres for the manufacture of utilitarian domestic wares (those used in cooking and storage) and finer wares such as decorated service vessels and ritual objects. Somewhat less consistent but still evident is the maintenance of separation between production for local populations' domestic consumption and for that of a conquering polity or elite institution. This greater ambiguity might be a function of an overlap between workforces, as discussed below. A third emergent pattern characterizes what Shimada (1998, 2001) calls modular or segmented production. This pattern reflects a relatively high degree of task specialization within certain crafts and/or media, a phenomenon that has not been adequately addressed in studies of craft production generally.

Moche Production Settings

Moche crafts were made in a variety of contexts. There is evidence for household-based ceramic production at Moche (Chapdelaine 2001; Uceda and Armas 1998) and non-household-based ceramic production at Cerro Mayal (Russell et al. 1998), Galindo (Bawden 1977, 1982), and Pampa Grande (Shimada 1994, 2001). Neither the Cerro Mayal nor the Galindo workshop shows evidence for controlled access to the premises. The Galindo example is notable because it is one of the few cases we have from the Andes in which utilitarian pottery was produced in a nondomestic context. The Galindo ceramic workshop also manufactured the small figurines frequently found in commoner residences, as did the Cerro Mayal potters. The contexts of Moche ceramic production, then, are variable, and there does not seem to be an immediate correlation between the setting (residential or nondomestic) and class of goods (luxury or utilitarian). Indeed, the conclusion based on available data, limited as they are, runs counter to some models of the organization of production in that more highly specialized sumptuary production was household based; at least some of the more mundane goods were produced in larger-scale, nondomestic settings.

Moche metal workshops are located in nonresidential zones of major administrative centers at the Moche V sites of Pampa Grande and Galindo. In both cases there are metalworking loci adjacent to administrative architecture in areas where access could be carefully controlled; additionally, at Pampa Grande there is evidence for small-scale metal production in less elite locations (Bawden 1996:97; Shimada 1994:200–206). At Galindo the nature of the items produced—copper bells, copper disks used to decorate clothing, and small ritual axes—suggests production for elite consumption, and the location makes sense in light of models for the organization of production. The situation for metal production at Pampa Grande parallels that proposed for ceramic production: more highly valued items (e.g., copper *tumis*) were produced in elite areas, whereas mundane utilitarian items such as needles and fishhooks were produced in more peripheral, commoner locales (Shimada 1994:225). A third small metalworking locus has been reported from the elite residential zone at Moche, but the published information on the context and its contents is scant (Chapdelaine 2001).

Middle Horizon Production Settings and Internal Organization

As with Moche, production took place in both domestic and nondomestic settings during the Middle Horizon. Many different types of goods were manufactured in household settings. At the site of Omo in the Moquegua Valley, camelid thread, spindle whorls, and needles were ubiquitous in household contexts, indicating domestic production of cloth (Kolata 1993:258). The data from Conchopata situate production of high-status pottery in a residential compound (Pozzi-Escot et al. 1998). This area is close to but distinct from another area with remains

of high-status residences and ritual activities. The excavators posit a relatively large workforce using the production locus overall, based on the number of tools recovered. However, it is unclear how large the individual work groups might have been.

In the Ch'iji Jawira sector of the Tiwanaku capital, huge quantities of ceramic production debris were found in a residential zone near the outskirts of the city. The pottery produced at Ch'iji Jawira incorporated important Tiwanaku forms and iconography but was not the highest quality or most politically charged pottery used at the site. To date, this is the only area of the city that has yielded evidence for ceramic production. Janusek (1999) has argued that the Ch'iji Jawira potters represent a distinct social/corporate group in Tiwanaku society, possibly an *ayllu* associated with the populations of Cochabamba. At Lukurmata, a secondary Tiwanaku administrative center, Janusek (1999) identified the production of panpipes—used in social gatherings and ritual activities—in a household context. Significantly, in both cases production was of socially visible, nonutilitarian goods, but not goods used by the ruling elite. In neither case is there evidence for direct elite supervision of production.

The only well-documented nondomestic Middle Horizon production locus is at the coastal site of Maymi. Ceramics related stylistically to early Wari wares were produced at this location. The site consists of a integrated complex of at least three pit kilns and a work area identified by the presence of well-preserved tools, raw clay, and manufacturing debris. The work area is significantly larger than potting households in the Andes today and lacks domestic refuse. The differential distribution of production-associated remains suggests to the excavators a highly structured organization of production in which different steps in the production process were carried out at different areas within the workshop. The excavators posit suprahousehold organization, speculating that four potters likely worked together in this production area (Anders et al. 1998).

Chimu Production
Settings and Organization

As with the other Andean states, there is evidence for the production of craft goods in both domestic and nondomestic contexts in the Chimu polity. The evidence from the capital of Chan Chan is particularly clear-cut, as the city was stripped of its artisans abruptly at the time of Inka conquest, when the Inka forcibly removed Chimu artisans to the Inka capital at Cuzco and other strategic locations throughout the empire (Rowe 1948). The abandonment was so sudden that large quantities of tools and raw materials were left in place by the artisans who had used them (Topic 1990:150).

Topic (1990) suggests that craft production at Chan Chan took place in several different settings. The barrios are large, commoner residential zones on the outskirts of the city where workshops are interspersed among the houses. Production debris was found in the houses and in dedicated crafting areas. Evidence for metal and textile production was found together at most houses, indicating to Topic that both men and women worked at craft production. The nondomestic workshops seem to be largely given over to metalworking, although one workshop might have concentrated on woodworking in preparation for metal inlay. Most evidence for craftwork in the barrios points to the preliminary stages of production, especially the fabrication of sheet metal and fiber spinning. The second setting for production at Chan Chan is what Topic (1990:158) calls the retainer areas. These are manufacturing loci found on platforms immediately adjacent to the *ciudadelas*, huge architectural complexes that were the palaces of the Chimu rulers. The architecture in which these activities occurred speaks to a higher status for the artisans there, and the artifactual remains indicate less emphasis on the preliminary steps of craft manufacture, such as beating out sheet metal and spinning, and more emphasis on the formation and finishing of objects. The third setting for craft production at Chan Chan is in the lower-class domestic architectural context of the SIAR (small, irregularly

agglutinated rooms; Topic 1982). Large quantities of production debris pertaining to the manufacture of utilitarian metal items such as needles were recovered in the SIAR. These buildings were scattered throughout the site, and access to them was relatively unrestricted.

One interesting point about the archaeological evidence for craft production at Chan Chan is that it contradicts somewhat the descriptions of the organization of north coast craft production found in early colonial documents. Those documents describe a situation in which each occupational specialty was associated with its own *parcialidad*, or social unit (usually a separate village). In contrast, the archaeological data from Chan Chan indicate greater integration of what are traditionally considered different crafts (e.g., wood- and metalworking; cf. Shimada 1998). Topic (1990:165) suggests that this might have been a state-imposed structure at the capital to facilitate the production of elaborate compound sumptuary objects (such as inlay or textiles decorated with metal bangles) or to integrate the artisans who made tools used by other artisans, such as the woodworkers who made weaving and spinning tools.

The evidence for Chimu craft production outside the capital is minimal. Some evidence for metal and textile production has been found at Chimu provincial centers, but the overall scale (output) is considerably lower than that assumed for the capital at Chan Chan (Mackey and Klymyshyn 1990; Moore 1981). A large-scale smelting facility at Cerro Huaringa, which had supplied the Sicán lords who ruled Lambayeque before the Chimu conquest, was co-opted for state-controlled processing of copper ores (Epstein and Shimada 1984; Shimada 1985). This production took place in a nondomestic setting associated with distinctive state-style administrative architectural features.

Outside Cerro de los Cementerios there is limited evidence for other craft production at Chimu administrative centers. At Túcume the excavators uncovered a large *Spondylus* shell bead workshop. Despite the significance of *Spondylus* as a rare, imported commodity used in public rituals, this workshop was located in a compound relatively far removed from the administrative core of the site (Sandweiss 1995). Traces of possible pottery and metal production were recovered from surface collections several hundred meters away from the shell bead workshop, but the area has not been excavated or extensively published.

Conklin (1990:Figure 13) illustrates a rare Late Intermediate period unprovenienced textile that depicts a weaving scene in what he identifies as Chimu style. In this textile two weavers work in front of, perhaps even on the "porch" of, an elite building that he refers to as a "temple." This structure is very much like the elite structures with ramadas depicted in Moche and Chimu ceramics and reconstructed for the *ciudadelas* at Chan Chan. The weavers work on an elaborate, multicolored textile. Given the centrality of elaborate textiles to Chimu statecraft, this representation of weavers working in the direct shadows of an elite institutional building conforms to our archetypal model of attached production.

As with other Andean cultures, pottery is the most ubiquitous portable craft type recovered at Chimu sites. However, of the major Chimu crafts, we know the least about pottery production. No pottery production areas have been located at Chan Chan or at any other Chimu administrative site. Mold-made Chimu-style pottery was produced at at least one nondomestic workshop, identified at the site of Pampa de Burros in the Lambayeque Valley (Tschauner 2001; Tschauner et al. 1994). Several forms of small, usually decorated serving and consumption vessels were produced at this workshop. Vessels tied to the production site by chemical analyses were recovered both at local habitation sites and at several Chimu administrative centers in the Lambayeque Valley.

The pottery workshop at Pampa de Burros consists of a large, multiroom compound. Each room has yielded evidence of one or more stages of ceramic production, from forming to firing. The primary technologies

employed were mold forming and paddle-stamp decorating. Evidence indicates that the molds and paddle stamps were produced within the workshop. Although molds, mold matrices, and paddle stamps are generally *made* by accomplished artisans, they can be *used* by relatively unskilled workers. The combination of these shaping and decorating technologies and the presence of multiple, contemporaneous kilns, each in a separate room or courtyard within the potting compound, suggests the simultaneous use of the compound by several different work groups, each internally differentiated and headed by a master potter overseeing less-skilled workers (Tschauner 2001:210–220). The Pampa de Burros pottery production area lacked domestic debris. The potters likely lived in an adjacent residential compound southeast of the production facility.

There is no evidence for the manufacture of large storage or cooking vessels at Pampa de Burros. These forms—found in much greater quantities than the serving and consuming vessel types produced at Pampa de Burros—were manufactured using a different technology (paddle and anvil) altogether. Tschauner (2001) argues that the lack of concentrated evidence for their production indicates highly dispersed, household-based production (cf. Cleland and Shimada 1998). The implication is that there were at least two separate ceramic production systems operating simultaneously in the Lambayeque Valley. They made different types of goods and were organized differently, but neither one was supervised or sponsored by the elites or government institutions. An important aside for model building and cross-cultural analyses is that the more ubiquitous types were produced in dispersed, low-output settings and the less common forms in nucleated, high-output workshops, an observation that runs counter to some assumptions about the relationship between aggregate levels of consumption and the scale of production.

Inka Period Production Settings
Given the multiplicity of types of craft goods and their various uses during the rule of the

Inka empire, it is not surprising that there was a tremendous amount of variation in craft production settings and their organization. As in the other cases for state societies already discussed, some goods were produced for use only within the domestic economy while others were produced for circulation and use within the extradomestic political economy. A key imperial strategy was to co-opt artisan labor to produce both utilitarian and luxury goods. Utilitarian wares were used to provision other state functionaries.[7] Higher-quality goods in the state style were used in a wide range of state activities. Some ethnohistoric documents distinguish between artisans who made fine goods for the Inka and those who made lesser-quality items (e.g., Murúa 1946 [1590]: 334). Yet other evidence indicates that there was a high degree of interdigitation between the two sectors and their personnel. It has long been my contention (e.g., Costin and Hagstrum 1995) that the same artisans often produced for both state and utilitarian use (see also Hyslop 1976:144; Spurling 1992), particularly when the "state" goods were of low quality, low technological or design complexity, or low value.[8] Hayashida's research on potters on the north coast suggests that local and state-style vessels were made in the same production facilities (1995, 1998). In contrast, my work in the central highlands indicates that although the same potters might have made both local ceramic utilitarian wares and vessels in the state style, they did so in different locations (Costin 2001a; Costin and Hagstrum 1995).

All the published direct evidence for the production of Inka-style pottery comes from nondomestic contexts at Inka administrative centers. Hayashida (1995, 1998) has excavated two workshop complexes at small Inka administrative centers on the north coast adjacent to the Inka trunk road. There is no domestic refuse directly associated with the work areas, although she believes the potters lived nearby. Similarly, evidence for pottery production was found in nondomestic contexts at the Inka administrative center of

Potrero-Chiquiago in Argentina (D'Altroy et al. 1998).[9] At Milliraya, in the Titicaca Basin, there are no architectural remains on the surface of the site, where evidence for Inka ceramic production has been recovered. However, the excavator, Spurling (1992:292), concludes that this was a specialized work area because the production site is too small to have housed the 100 potting families reported in the colonial documents to have been living there.

Textile production took place in a variety of settings. Much of this work was household based, reflecting the organization of labor to meet the textile tribute demands imposed on conquered populations. Apparently, women continued to labor within their homes, as they had before conquest, to meet state demands for spun thread and woven cloth. According to the ethnohistoric documents, some weaving specialists went to state facilities to weave (e.g., LeVine 1987:24). Although they are listed in colonial documents, none of the places where the *mitmaqkuna qompikamayoq* (relocated fine-cloth weavers) worked have been identified archaeologically. Spurling (1992) surveyed intensively one of the communities that purportedly housed 1,000 state weavers but found no evidence for textile production. This is somewhat surprising, since spindle whorls are often found in surface collections of even small domestic sites (e.g., Costin 1993:Figure 10). On the other hand, structures identified as *aqllawasi* (the compounds where the *aqllakuna* lived and worked) have been located at several Inka provincial administrative centers (LeVine 1985; Morris 1974; Morris and Thompson 1985). All the buildings that presumably housed the *aqllakuna* were constructed in the finest imperial architectural style. Their design and layout served to effectively restrict movement in and out of the compounds, keeping the residents well isolated from the other goings-on at the sites.

In addition to the production of goods for use within the political economy, craft items were produced for daily household use, although less is known about their production than about production of goods for state use. Available archaeological evidence suggests that there were low levels of localized specialization in pottery and lithic production in the highlands, mirroring a pattern still found in traditionally organized regions today (Costin 1986, 2001a; Hagstrum 1989; Russell 1988). Colonial documents from several different parts of the highlands convey a similar picture, reporting settlements where "all" the occupants produced the same commodities (Julien 1982; LeVine 1987). Carpenters, potters, weavers, rope makers, sandal makers, and salt miners are among those listed. This pattern is one of village specialization, in which many households in one community within a small region specialize in the production of a particular good or suite of goods for distribution to other local villages. In contrast, evidence for textile production is ubiquitous, supporting the observation made in the colonial documents that all women spun and wove to meet the needs of their own households (Costin 1993; Murra 1962). This pattern is little different from the one observed in immediately pre-Inka communities.

For the coastal provinces, there is some evidence for a greater degree of specialization for commoner consumption, perhaps reflecting more intensive specialized production prior to Inka conquest. On the north coast, relocated potters continued to make traditional vessels, manufacturing them at the same workshops where they made ceramics for state use (Donnan 1997; Hayashida 1998).

It appears that there was great organizational continuity from immediately pre-Inka to Inka times in the production of utilitarian goods for domestic use as well as the production of goods destined for circulation in the political economy. Even when potters were relocated, they continued to serve their traditional consumers (so long as they were relocated locally). This generalization appears to hold whether artisan groups were moved as *mitmaqkuna* (Hayashida 1995, 1998) or whole villages were strategically relocated (Costin 2001a; D'Altroy and Hastorf 2001).

SOCIAL RELATIONS OF PRODUCTION

The social relations of production locate artisans in social space. This component of the production system encompasses the relationships among artisans and between artisans and consumers. The relationships among artisans consist largely of work-group composition and the nature of social ties and connections among them. The characterization of the relationship between producers and consumers is twofold. First, herein lies the crux of specialization, a form of economic organization in which not all consumers of a particular good are its producers. But as Storey (this volume) points out, economies are just one facet of social life more generally. Specialization is as much a social relation as it is an economic one, as it diminishes autonomy and creates new kinds of interdependencies that underwrite complex forms of social integration (Costin 1998b, 1998c, 2001a; Durkheim 1984 [1933]). The second aspect of producer-consumer relations is the context of production, which entails the nature of elite power and control in the production system and beyond (see Costin 1991:11–13, 2001c:297–301; Earle 1987b).

Archaeologists study the social relations of production because these relations are at the heart of studies that situate craft production in other sociopolitical structures and processes. Many elements of the organization of production—including but not limited to the development of specialization generally and nondomestic workshop production specifically—are considered central to the development of sociopolitical complexity (i.e., the rise of chiefdoms and states). Because specialization *requires* exchange, production organization also is close to the core of social relations and social networks, both kin based and non-kin based. Differential participation in production and exchange networks can result in different levels of social participation and integration and can affect autonomy, power, prestige, and status within the community as well.

Studies of the social organization of production include investigation of work-group composition, which describes the size of the production unit and the type(s) of relationships among work-group members. Its assessment is important not only because it manifests the general workings of the production unit but also because models of increasing sociopolitical complexity posit a shift from kin-based to non-kin-based (for example, contractual, territorial, or forced) labor relations and an overall increase in the size of nonfood-producing work units. A second aspect of the social organization of production that is central to discussions of chiefdoms and states is specialization. Defining and identifying specialization have both proven challenging to archaeologists in many regards (see Clark 1995; Costin 2001c; Rice 1991).

The third element of the social organization of production of concern to archaeologists, and the one I focus on here, is the sociopolitical context in which production takes place. These contexts, which in part denote relations between producers and consumers, are often described as either attached or independent, a distinction first proposed by Earle (1981; see also Brumfiel and Earle 1987). Although the concepts are entrenched in the archaeological inquiry on craft production, the exact nature of these categories and their usefulness has been debated extensively (for just a few examples, see Ames 1995; Clark 1995; Clark and Parry 1990; Costin 1991, 2001a; Inomata 2001b; Stein 1996). Attempts to provide short and simple formulas for distinguishing attached and independent production have failed, largely for three reasons. First, the terms best refer to relations of production, and only secondarily to types of artisans, and particularly not to specific individuals or work groups, as the same artisans can produce in both attached and independent contexts, albeit not at the same time. Second, the types of objects produced in systems of attached and independent production cannot necessarily be used to distinguish between them. Third, the distinction between attached and independent production is best seen not as a dichotomy but as a continuum that reflects the nature and degree of control.

At the heart of the distinction between attached and independent production is control. In systems of attached production, elites or political/religious institutions have the authority to control directly some or all components of the production system, including access to raw materials, technical choices, the location of production activities, labor deployment and organization, object appearance and information content, and the distribution of finished goods. This control attests to the function of attached production: these forms of craft organization (and they are plural) serve to enhance or uphold one social group's privileged access to resources, labor, power, and/or wealth. Systems of attached production facilitate control of the distribution and consumption of objects used to secure privilege and inequality through the exercise of economic, political, military, or ideological power. The items produced in systems of attached production can be military gear, ritual objects, prestige goods, clothing, service ware, or trinkets. It is not the proximate use of the objects that conditions the social context of production; rather, it is their underlying use in the political economy and power structure.

In contrast, in systems of independent production, elites and institutions do not maintain direct authority to exercise control over raw materials, artisans, the organization of production, or distribution. The objects produced under independent specialization tend to be utilitarian, but they might be elements in social communication or potent sources of supernatural power. What distinguishes them from objects made by attached specialists is that, ideally, access to the products of independent specialists is open, and possession of these objects does not confer institutionalized advantage. In other words, *by definition, the products of attached specialists serve to directly uphold institutionalized sociopolitical differentiation, but the products of independent specialists do not.*

The reason the concepts of attached and independent production remain potent is that they encapsulate many notions about sociopolitical process. When using them, however, it is imperative to remember that labels are not explanations (see Pauketat, this volume; also Feinman 2000b). Although somewhat ambiguous, they are useful as heuristic devices because they describe different social relations of production. These relations of production are in turn connected to larger issues of social organization and integration. In noncapitalist socioeconomic systems, attached forms of production promote and reinforce many kinds of social, political, and economic inequality because they facilitate the efforts of some privileged members of society to gain unequal access to labor, appropriate production, and control information and ideology. In contrast, independent types of production likely contribute to social solidarity by creating more balanced reliance among producers and consumers through the circulation of specialized goods and services through a community or region.[10]

Although the concepts of attached and independent production are useful in analyses of stratified societies, they are problematic in cases that lack the economic and political differentiation theorized to underwrite attached specialization (i.e., to control production by others for elite and institutional purposes). In response to this dilemma, Ames (1995) introduced the concept of *embedded production*, which he describes as production by high-status individuals for their own use or for the use of other high-status individuals, usually within their household (see also the discussion of *intensified elite household production* in Costin 1996a:211).[11] Although Ames initially applied the concept to middle-range societies, this type of production can occur in many sociopolitical contexts, from relatively simple chiefdoms (Costin 1993; Trubitt 1996) to states (Feinman and Nicholas 2000b; Inomata 2001b). Embedded production has been inferred archaeologically when evidence for craft manufacture is recovered from high-status domestic contexts. Thus the issue of embedded production, as defined by Ames, is closely tied to artisan identity. The methodological key to differentiating attached specialization from embedded production lies in resolving whether artisans were (elite) household members or (commoner) non-kin who came to the elite residence specifically to participate in craftwork. This distinction may be impossible to demonstrate with purely archaeological data.

Here I discuss the social relations of production in the cases presented above, relying primarily on the direct evidence we have for the organization of production. Where Andean archaeologists have discussed the context of craft production, primary concern has been with attached forms of production—that is, with production of luxury goods—and little attention has been directed toward investigating independent specialization.[12] Careful examination of the data reveals that in many cases much of what is written about the context of production is based on assertion or speculation rather than demonstration with analysis of hard data. Nevertheless, where there are solid data, the Andean cases allow for a much more nuanced view of the distinction between attached and independent production than has previously appeared in the craft production literature.

Moche Social Relations of Production
Moche elite goods seem a prime example of those that "should" have been produced by attached specialists. Elaborate metal, ceramic, textile, shell, and semiprecious stone goods were central to Moche statecraft and expressions of ideology (Donnan and McClelland 1999). They are labor intensive, demonstrate tremendous technical skill and sophistication, are often made of rare materials, and incorporate a complex iconographic content. All these indirect indicators point to some form of attached production (cf. Costin and Hagstrum 1995). Unfortunately, we don't have *direct* evidence for the production of the most valuable Moche goods, such as the items found in elite burials at Sipán (Alva 1994, 2001; Alva and Donnan 1993), San José de Moro (Donnan and Castillo 1992), and Moche (Chapdelaine 2001) and the unprovenienced masterworks that grace museum displays and private collections (Donnan 1978; Donnan and McClelland 1999).

The imperative for control over at least

some Moche prestige-goods production is taken as a given among Andeanists. Because there is no direct evidence for the production of the finest Moche ceramics and metal objects, little can be said of the specific mechanisms by which Moche elites controlled the most valuable materials and expressions of esoteric knowledge. Evidence for the production of goods from a slightly lower echelon indicates that control over production was achieved in several ways, suggesting different forms or degrees of artisan attachment. The painters of Moche fineline vessels were among the most skilled and knowledgeable of all Andean artisans, controlling a complex repertoire of images and lore necessary to re-create mythological "texts" and iconic scenes (see Donnan and McClelland 1999). The use of elite artisans in the pottery workshop at the capital of Moche discussed above (Uceda and Armas 1998) represents one way to maintain control over the spread of esoteric knowledge and iconographically potent images. Metal items and textiles also were produced in the elite residential zone at Moche. Chapdelaine (2001) argues that over time, access to at least one of the elite compounds that housed artisans became more restricted through the reduction of entryways and a re-orientation of the entrance away from the main street and toward a narrow, secondary street. Thus Moche elites sought to increase control over some types of production. It is hoped that further research will identify the specific sociopolitical circumstances that facilitated or required this increase in control.

Moche artisans also produced ideologically potent goods of lesser quality and elaboration. Cerro Mayal is an example of a locus of production for this type of goods. There is little tangible evidence for direct control of production at Cerro Mayal other than the use of mold technology.[13] The use of molds at Cerro Mayal facilitated the accurate replication of important iconographic elements. Not only did this practice allow the images and associated concepts to be recognized easily by the consuming populations (Russell et al. 1998; see also Cummins 1998), it also permitted the use of relatively un-trained labor and contributed to the control of esoteric knowledge, since only the master potters needed to understand the concepts in order to design the molds.

A third form of control over production is evidenced at Pampa Grande. The architectural contexts of metal and textile workshops at Pampa Grande suggest restricted access to the craft production zones in the elite areas of the city (Shimada 1994). Unlike the situation at Moche, however, craft production at Pampa Grande did not take place in a household setting. The proximity of the Pampa Grande workshops to the central walled compound that presumably housed the most important elites in the city further bolsters the idea that the artisans were associated with—that is, sponsored by—the elites. In a careful analysis of traffic flow, Shimada postulates that commoner artisans living in other parts of the city traveled to these manufacturing areas each day and worked under the direction of elite supervisors, a more classic form of attached production. Campana's (1994) reconstruction of a weavers' workshop (Figure 11.3b) follows from Shimada's reconstruction of the weavers' workshop at Pampa Grande.

The Moche period also yields some evidence for large-scale craft production with no overt mechanism of control, Galindo ceramic production being the primary example.

Middle Horizon Social Relations of Production

The data on Middle Horizon production contexts are sparse. As with Moche, the indirect indicators suggest that the finest Wari and Tiwanaku wares "should" have been produced in carefully controlled contexts. There is insufficient evidence from the ceramic production area at Conchopata to determine how much and what type of control was exerted over the production of finewares there. Proximity to elite residences and key ritual locales certainly would facilitate supervision, however.

There is no evidence for elite control over the production of serving wares at Ch'iji

Jawira at the Tiwanaku capital or of pan-pipes at the Tiwanaku provincial center of Lukurmata. Thus it appears that many forms of socially important goods used by commoners were manufactured outside the direct control of political elites.

Chimu Social Relations of Production
Craft production in the Chimu empire has been largely modeled as attached production. As a conclusion derived primarily from archaeological data, this is not surprising, since few non-elite contexts have been excavated in great detail, especially outside the capital city of Chan Chan. Drawing this conclusion from the ethnohistoric documents, however, is somewhat more tortured and depends on how the general Chimu economy is modeled. Those who see it as a highly centralized, redistributive economy argue that even artisans working outside Chan Chan were patronized by and/or offered up (all) their goods as tribute to the elites (e.g., Netherly 1977; Ramírez-Horton 1982). In contrast, other interpretations of the documentary evidence model the system on the coast as one with large numbers of independent specialists exchanging among themselves without elite or administrative involvement (e.g., Rostworowski 1989).

Aside from the capital at Chan Chan (discussed below), the presence of an *audiencia* —a hallmark of Chimu administrative architecture—at the metal workshop at Cerro de los Cementerios supports the supposition that the state directly controlled at least some forms of craft production (Epstein and Shimada 1984). The textile depicting weavers working physically under a temple or administrative building (Conklin 1990:Figure 13) also reinforces the idea that artisans worked directly for state institutions. However, consistent with findings from other Andean groups, there is limited evidence for the production of corporate, state-style goods at Late Intermediate period workshops and no clear evidence for elite or institutional supervision. For example, the Pampa de Burros potters produced what are usually termed Imperial Chimu-style ceramics (Tschauner

2001; Tschauner et al. 1994). There is no evidence for direct state or elite supervision of production on-site, and the site is located at a considerable distance from the nearest Chimu administrative center (of which there were several in the region). The ubiquity of diagnostic Chimu-style pottery throughout the north coast coupled with the absence of pottery production facilities at Chimu administrative centers suggests that the inferred lack of elite control over pottery production was the rule rather than the exception. Tschauner (2001) argues that there was no difference in the quality of workmanship or degree of labor investment in Chimu-style pottery found at administrative centers when compared with pottery recovered at local villages in the Lambayeque Valley. This indicates to him that elites and commoners used the same source(s) for their ceramic vessels, a sign of independent specialization. Thus the limited evidence for craft production outside Chan Chan indicates both attached and independent forms of production. Although it is necessary to be cautious when drawing conclusions from a limited number of cases, the difference between controlled metal production on the one hand and unencumbered pottery production on the other is telling, as pottery was not nearly as important as metal in political relations and ideology in the Chimu world.

The notion that the Chimu economy was highly centralized, physically and administratively, comes in part from the uncritical application of Murra's (1972) model to coastal economies and in part from the plethora of evidence for high-output production and large-scale storage at the capital of Chan Chan. In contrast, much smaller quantities of production debris and storage rooms have been identified at Chimu secondary and tertiary administrative centers (Mackey and Klymyshyn 1990). There is, however, a lack of large-scale excavation at secondary centers and habitation sites, so the reconstruction of the Chimu economy might be an artifact of research rather than a complete representation of Chimu economic structures and processes.

Nevertheless, there is no doubt that the scale of craft production at Chan Chan was enormous. The common interpretation is that as much as three-fourths of the population was engaged in craftwork (Moseley 1992:256; Topic 1990:149). Topic's (1990) data from Chan Chan provide nuanced information for the production of socially valuable, politically charged goods such as metal and cloth. The evidence suggests varying degrees of official control at different stages of the production process, with an emphasis on control over valuable raw materials and the esoteric knowledge embodied in finished goods. The presence of "administrative" architecture interspersed among some of the commoner production areas at Chan Chan indicates a level of elite supervision of some crafts, particularly metalworking and textile production. These administrative rooms, called *arcones*, contained storage bins filled with raw materials such as cotton fiber, tools, and partially finished goods, suggesting that supervisors provided raw materials and tools and collected finished goods (Topic 1990:156). Significantly, supervision is over metal and textile production, goods valued both for their raw inputs and for the importance of their final products in the status hierarchy. At Chan Chan the final stages of metal and textile production were even more carefully supervised in workshops directly adjacent to the rulers' palaces. The relatively higher status of the workers responsible for the end products, as opposed to the low status of the workers charged with preparing the raw materials (sheet metal and thread, for example), along with evidence for closer direct interaction with elite personnel, again points to the mechanisms by which elites could effectively control esoteric knowledge and valuable goods.

Inka Period Social Relations of Production
The availability of textual material to complement the archaeological data allows for a more detailed reconstruction of the social relations of production in the Inka empire. Goods were produced for use by the state in a number of contexts. The ethnohistoric documents indicate that artisans making goods to be used and/or distributed by the state were supervised by a complex hierarchy of bureaucrats, from provincial Inka functionaries down to traditional *ayllu* (kin) leaders (LeVine 1987). To simply identify this production as "attached" is to obscure the range of variability in organizational forms (see Hayashida 1998). The amount and nexus of control the state exerted over artisans was highly variable. That the Inka were able to relocate thousands of skilled artisans and demand goods from hundreds of thousands more speaks to the coercive potential of the state. But in fact, in many ways they exercised control sparingly to meet particular objectives. In large measure the degree and mode of control and the organization of production is explainable in relation to the function of the goods.

The largest-scale craft production for the state was the cloth tax imposed on "all" women. With a total imperial population of eight to twelve million, it is not extravagant to visualize more than a million women working part-time for the state! The provision of rough cloth, called *awasqa*, was one of two primary tribute obligations owed by conquered populations to the state.[14] Although this tribute was phrased in terms of labor as part of a woman's *mit'a* obligations, women were required to provide a set amount of cloth to the state each year (Costin 1993:5; LeVine 1987). That the state's nominal exaction was labor is evidenced by the consistent report in the colonial documents that the state provided the women with fiber to spin and/or thread to weave (e.g., Murra 1962:715).[15]

There is little evidence that the state exerted much control over the form or quality of this requisitioned rough cloth beyond providing the raw materials and setting quotas. For example, in the archaeological record for the Mantaro Valley, I observed a dramatic increase in the number of spindle whorls after the Inka conquest, coinciding with Inka demands for tribute cloth (Costin 1993). However, there was no perceptible change in the types, sizes, or shapes of spindle whorls used

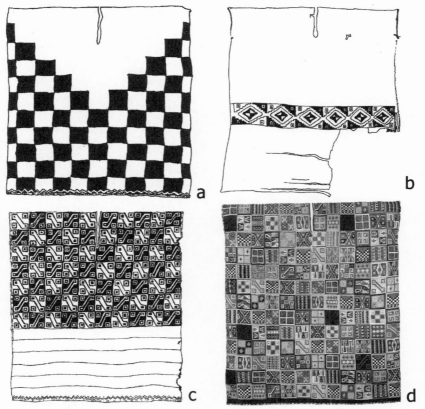

Figure 11.6. Inka-style tunics of varying degrees of elaborateness: *(a)* military checkerboard; *(b)* diamond waistband; *(c)* repeated Inka key motif; *(d)* "royal" tunic (motifs include miniature military tunics and the Inka key, among many others). *(a–c,* drawn by Harris Wells; *d,* drawn by author)

by local women, nor does there appear to be any change in weaving technology. Since whorl form, size, and weight are all related to the type of yarn spun (Brumfiel 1996; Fauman-Fichman 1999), I infer that local women spun the same kind(s) of thread and wove the same kind(s) of cloth before and after the Inka conquest.

This organization of production for rough cloth was particularly well suited to state needs and logistics. The recipients of the cloth were common soldiers and some *mit'a* workers, and there was no need for elaborate decoration or even standardization. What was important was that the state acquire large quantities of cloth at low cost to itself. As Storey (this volume) points out, all states consider costs and benefits in deciding which strategies to use to meet their objectives.

Many discussions of attached production assume that "cost" is not a factor in attached specialization, but in fact, it is. The ideological importance was that the cloth (like all other items associated with state largesse) came from the state, a point reinforced by universal female participation in tribute cloth production. This example underscores the point that attached production takes on many forms and that state-sponsored manufacture involved more than just the highly controlled production of luxury goods (although even this rough cloth was in many ways a *prestige* good, albeit not a "prestige good" as often defined in the literature).

In contrast with rough cloth production is the production of fine cloth. Even within this category, called *qompi* by the Inka, there was a range of qualities and elaborateness (Figure

Figure 11.7. Inka ceramic vessels illustrating variation in formal and stylistic elements. (Collections of the Field Museum: *a*, FM 2645; *b*, FM 2859; *c*, FM 2752; photographs by author)

11.6). The simplest of these textiles were the checkerboard tunics issued to warriors who distinguished themselves in battle and their leaders (Figure 11.6a). Slightly more elaborate were a class of tunics with repetitive designs worn by low-level Inka bureaucrats (Figure 11.6b; for a full discussion, see Costin 1998b). Although the corpus of extant tunics is small, those that have survived are highly standardized in their format, metric attributes, manufacturing techniques, and formal design layout (A. Rowe 1978; J. Rowe 1979), suggesting to me that their manufacture was carefully supervised, likely because they were distributed by the state to signal important information about the social identity and political prerogatives of those who wore them. In contrast with these relatively simple, fine garments are those that combine many design elements on one garment (Figure 11.6c). These tunics are not standardized. I have suggested that each of the design elements on these shirts communicates some aspect of the social identity of the wearer and that these elaborate garments were woven for specific individuals who had a distinctive combination of rank and office. Although weavers of the more standardized, less elaborate examples of *qompi* might have worked from templates (see the one illustrated in Mackey 1984:Figure 3), I have argued that the weavers of the finest, most elaborate cloth were likely high-status women with access to a full understanding of the meaning of the Inka design system and knowledge of how to apply it (Costin 1998b).

The state also used large quantities of ceramic cooking and service ware in its various activities, including the provisioning of soldiers, *aqllakuna*, and other state retainers, and in the large-scale feasting that marked the end of *mit'a* rotations and other instances of state hospitality. A range of ceramic types was used at these events, and it appears that a range of procurement strategies was used as well. At some Inka provincial centers nearly 100 percent of the pottery recovered is in the official state style; at others the percentage of state-style pottery recovered is far lower. It has been argued that the state used local-style pottery for some official activities (e.g., D'Altroy et al. 1998).

Because all documented Inka ceramic production loci are at state installations, it is tempting to regard pottery production as fairly tightly supervised. Yet other evidence suggests uneven application of state "control" during the production process. Although Inka pottery is usually characterized as highly standardized[16] and politically charged, there is in fact a tremendous amount of variation in the quality, degree of stylistic elaboration, and even adherence to imperial stylistic canons when one considers the recognizable variants of Inka pottery, often referred to as "provincial," "local," "imitation," or "hybrid" wares (Figure 11.7). The archaeological work at the production facilities of Tambo Real and La Viña on the north coast (Hayashida 1995) and at Milliraya in the southern highlands (Spurling 1992) suggests that state, imitation, and hybrid goods were all made at the same workshops. Thus the state did not maintain uniform control over all aspects of the goods produced.[17]

The evidence strongly suggests that the state recruited local potters and provided them with only minimal training (see also Costin and Hagstrum 1995). There is a high degree of technological variation among Inka-style wares recovered in different parts of the empire, indicating that the Inka were more concerned with the ends of production than the means or methods. The use of different forming, finishing, and decorating techniques in different parts of the Andes reflects continuity with diverse pre-Inka technological traditions. This technological variation can even be identified at the regional level. At two state pottery production facilities in the Leche Valley located approximately 10 km apart, potters used different techniques to form vessels (both molds and paddle-and-anvil; Hayashida 1995, 1998). Both technologies have a long history on the north coast; Tschauner (2001) has documented the contemporaneity of both technological styles

in the Lambayeque Valley, located just south of the Leche. Hayashida believes different workshops represent different *mitmaqkuna* groups recruited from among local potting *parcialidades* (communities) with their own distinct technological traditions. There is some evidence that the work groups were organized differently at the two Inka facilities.

I have recently begun a study of formal design symmetry patterns in Inka-style pottery. My initial hypothesis was that local potters, though ostensibly "copying" Inka vessels or implementing the Inka design repertoire, would adhere to their culturally specific traditional symmetry patterns in the specifics of the design layout and organization. Although the sample analyzed to date is small and the results are preliminary and not quantified, it appears that imperial design symmetries were actually quite simple and therefore easy to conform to with minimal training or supervision. On the north coast, where painted pottery declined in importance after the disintegration of the Moche polity(ies) 700 years before the Inka conquest, Inka forms and designs are often rendered through traditional plastic techniques.

In contrast with the pattern suggested by the data on ceramic vessel forming and decorating, and perhaps somewhat counterintuitively, the state apparently intervened more directly in the supply of raw materials and in the firing process. The pastes used to make Inka pottery consistently differ from those used to make local types (Costin 1986, 2001a; D'Altroy and Bishop 1990). I have argued that this differentiation among raw material inputs relates to state strategies aimed at minimizing the impact of tribute obligations on the local economies (Costin 1998a; compare D'Altroy et al. 1998) as well as state policies of providing raw materials and requiring only labor from subject populations. Inka-style pottery also is often fired differently from local pottery (Costin and Hagstrum 1995; Hayashida 1995). It is unclear whether this difference relates to the introduction of new firing strategies to improve the quality of the final product (Inka-style goods are consistently better—i.e., harder—fired than local types) or whether it relates to the need to adjust firing processes for the different raw materials and only inadvertently resulted in more highly fired wares.

As with the other cases discussed in this chapter, the workshops where the finest Inka goods were made have not been identified archaeologically. Even without them, however, it is apparent that there was a range of ways in which production could be organized and controlled. Production under the Inka was highly variable in structure and process, and the Inka state appears to have been quite strategic in its craft procurement tactics. Despite arguments that attached production cannot be analyzed as "economic" (i.e., economizing) behavior (e.g., Tschauner 2001), it is quite clear that elite and institutional sponsors can choose from among many methods of acquiring craft goods, and what we observe in the ethnohistoric and archaeological records are the results of the decisions that were made.

CONCLUSIONS

The cases presented here provide important insights into craft production in state societies and the nature of Andean economies. In regard to the Andean economy specifically, we observe that playing off the archaeological data with models drawn from the ethnohistoric record underscores the superficiality of the textual evidence. Even archaeological investigation of just a part of Inka production indicates that production was organized in a much more variable fashion than the normalized model inferred from descriptions in the colonial documents. This does not mean we should disregard the textual material; it provides irreplaceable complementary evidence. However, we cannot settle with reconstructions drawn from sixteenth-century reports as the exclusive basis of our archetypes for ancient Andean economies. Particular care must be taken in extending very late Prehispanic patterns further into the past. Although it is reasonable to use these texts to develop models to test explicitly with archaeological

data, care must be taken to demonstrate, not merely assert, the workings of more ancient Andean economies.

Similarly, we cannot simply dichotomize the coastal and highland economies. For example, there was likely far more commodity specialization at independent villages in the highlands than allowed for in the strict archipelago model. Larger, more urban communities on the coast might require a third model, although even with limited excavations evidence points to variation among contemporaneous communities (e.g., Moche and Cerro Mayal; Galindo and Pampa Grande).

The Andean cases also provide insights useful in cross-cultural and comparative research. The first of these, not surprisingly, is the observation of a high degree of complexity generally and a multiplicity of organizational forms operating in any one polity, even for a single craft type. Related to this is a more refined understanding about the developmental sequence of production systems. It does not appear that elementary economic forms were simply replaced by more intensive, specialized, differentiated, and/or elaborate ones as more complex sociopolitical structures developed. Rather, traditional forms continued to exist side by side with newer forms that developed to meet the expanding demands of consumers, elites, and institutions in state-level societies. Often the new forms were modifications or elaborations of existing forms rather than created de novo. In the Andean cases we see clearly the importance of considering the specific historical circumstances in which craft production systems develop. In any developmental trajectory the technology, organization, and social relations of production are bound to change, but the new or changed forms are contingent on the preexisting forms, as both Stahl and Pauketat (this volume) also observe.

A concomitant observation is that household-based production remains viable and central in complex societies, even for the production of some ideologically important goods. Illustrations can be drawn from the

Moche and Tiwanaku cases, among others. "Meaning" can be embodied in many ways, derived from any (or all) of the components of the production system. For example, artisan identity and/or principles of distribution can imbue goods with sufficient and appropriate signification, even in the absence of overt decoration or particular technological characteristics. This is the case for plain cloth in the Inka empire, where the mere fact that the state first commanded and then redistributed it took this cloth out of the realm of the domestic and the mundane.

These cases permit refinement and redirection of models that explain the division of labor, and they underscore the importance of documenting the division of labor in reconstructing economic organization. In several of the cases—for example, Moche and Inka—the social identities of those who craft are generally linked to the sociopolitical value of goods and means of control over the production process. Nevertheless, there is not always a straightforward correlation between the social identity of artisans and the function of goods, as there is more than one way to control production, particularly access to esoteric knowledge and technical skill. Where techniques (e.g., Moche ceramic molds) or processes (Inka textile design boards) allow goods to be produced by rote or imitation, it is possible to recruit semiskilled, commoner laborers and even have them work under minimal official supervision. However, for the most powerful, politically and ideologically loaded goods, whose successful crafting requires an understanding of the full spectrum of iconic meanings and how to deploy them, it is likely that production will be limited to the elite or to artisans who can be fully controlled by them (for example, the Inka *aqllakuna*).

Finally, there exists a large body of socially and symbolically charged goods produced outside direct elite control. Examples discussed herein include Moche, Tiwanaku, and Chimu decorated serving wares and other ritual objects. Here attached specialization does not operate in the extreme form that tradi-tional models posit, in that there are few if any tangible indicators of the direct elite or institutional control over the production of these goods. The study of these middle-range goods also tells us something important about state procurement and distribution strategies. It looks as though in most of these cases neither elites nor state institutions intervened directly in the production of *all* goods made in the corporate style or carrying ideological load. There is often a strong element of conformity to state stylistic and iconographic canons, but it appears not to be always and uniformly enforced directly by the state. Rather, these states often seemed to tolerate the production of goods that carried important social and political messages outside their direct control. This was a remarkably cost-effective measure through which to disseminate state ideologies. Both producers and consumers internalized some measure of corporate identity. Even the hybrid goods are an effective means by which state symbols and ideas come to permeate culture and daily life. These imitations and local derivatives of "official" art do not afford individuals any particular or important prerogatives; rather, they demonstrate the degree to which the dominating group has penetrated local society. Possession of these goods allows individuals to feel affiliated (cf. Janusek 1999), but the inferior quality or hybridization of style and form surely reminds the "locals" that they are not truly at one with the dominating, conquering group.

As I said at the outset of this chapter, it is difficult to fully reconstruct any one aspect of the production system without a fairly complete understanding of the other components. Thus a fundamental shortcoming in this discussion of the social relations of production is the lack of concrete evidence for the mechanisms used to distribute most of these wares. Strikingly, we often posit different models of production and distribution for the Inka and for those who came before them. In the Inka case the presence of state-style goods is frequently linked to state hospitality and largesse. In contrast, for the pre-Inka cases more independent, laissez-faire modes of distribution are often asserted (cf. Janusek 1999). In the former case the ethnohistoric texts inform about state practices; interpretations of the Inka archaeological record are colored by these narratives as buildings are interpreted as places of state hospitality and certain artifacts as the remnants of those activities. As I have noted elsewhere, without the documentary evidence for the Inka case, we would be hard pressed to identify some production as state sponsored, especially household-based spinning and weaving (Costin 2001c:299; see Charlton et al. 1993, which makes a similar point for Aztec period Otumba).

We have made enormous progress in understanding both the role and production of craft products in the creation and maintenance of complex societies. A reassessment and refinement of some of our cherished models and terms at this point can serve us well as we continue to redefine the processes and institutions that differentiate the economies of diverse chiefdoms and states.

Notes

I am grateful to Gary Feinman and the University of Utah Press for inviting me to participate in this project. Chris Donnan, Frances Hayashida, Izumi Shimada, and Hartmut Tschauner all provided thoughtful comments, unpublished papers, and stimulating ideas that helped me enormously, and I thank them profusely. In the end, all interpretations of the data remain my own, and I apologize to all who feel I've trampled their data in my attempt to find some broader patterns among them.

1. Until recently, archaeological discussions of "craft" have focused on tangible objects, primarily portable goods such as ceramics, lithics, textiles, and beads, largely because of the nature of the materials we recover and the unacknowledged influence of Western art historical traditions. However, ethnographic and ethnohistoric studies indicate that there is no universal line drawn between the skilled elaboration of noncomestible material goods (plastic and visual arts) and the skilled elaboration of movement (dance), sound (music), language (poetry, narrative, drama), and food (cuisine). In all instances the end products exhibit the same key features and functions in that they are the result of transformational processes involving skill (knowledge, talent and proficiency, effort), conform to culturally defined systems of aesthetics, and encode cultural meaning.

2. This list does not include all the presumed state-level societies of the Prehispanic Andes, nor all those that produced stylistically distinct crafts. However, it does include all those for which there is a substantial literature on the direct evidence for craft production. In a few instances there is excellent work on craft production but it is limited to one or two studies (e.g., Sicán [Cleland and Shimada 1998; Shimada 1998; Shimada and Wagner 2001; Tschauner 2001]); in many cases systematic work on the technology or organization of production of craft goods has yet to be done.

3. Associated with these models for the organization of production are, of course, conflicting reconstructions of distribution mechanisms. The archipelago model allows for tribute payments and subsequent redistribution of some special items manufactured by sponsored or patronized specialists while precluding regular exchange of utilitarian goods among commoner communities. In contrast, the coastal model requires extensive exchange (barter) of utilitarian goods and services among specialists residing in different productive communities, perhaps with some form of fixed exchange values among commodities.

4. The existence of customary occupations suggests, of course, that there were occupational specialists among the conquered populations before Inka domination.

5. The burial of an elite male with several "attendant" females has precedence on the north coast at the Chimu capital of Chan Chan. The identification of these "weaving women" at Túcume as aqllakuna rests largely on the identification of the principal burial as that of an Inka (as opposed to a local) lord. This identification is based on the nature of the architecture of the building, the goods accompanying the primary burial, and unfortunately, the identification of the women as aqllakuna (a case, perhaps, of circular reasoning). Even if they aren't aqllakuna, however, they are clearly high-status women who are associated with weaving.

6. After describing the work of adolescent boys, Guamán Poma (1980 [1615]:181) comments, "*Toda estas diligencias se hacía por amor de la república y aumento de la grandesa de la magestad del Ynga*" (All this work is done for love of country and the increase of the majesty of the Inka ruler; my translation).

7. Large quantities of goods were needed to service laborers during their *mit'a* rotations. Potters in the Chillon Valley were required to make ceramics for the *aqllakuna* stationed nearby (Hayashida 1998:323). Similarly, the relocated *mitmaqkuna* recorded for Milliraya in the southern Andes and Cajamarca in the northern Andes were likely moved to those locations to both serve the provincial administrators and provision the large contingents of warriors in those areas.

8. Exceptions would be the *aqllakuna* and perhaps some artisans who produced the most highly valued objects, although even some metalworkers producing for the state were allowed to make small items to distribute as they chose (Rostworowski 1989:235).

9. The room in which the evidence was recovered was part of a larger residential sector of the site, however.

10. This conceptualization also answers charges that independent production is conceived of as economic behavior—governed by principles of efficiency and increasing output—whereas attached production is characterized as social and political behavior (Clark 1995; Hayashida 1995; Tschauner 2001:3).

11. Janusek (1999) uses the term to refer more generally to specialized production that takes place in a domestic context, as in these cases he sees the relations of production *embedded* in kin relations. Storey (this volume) sees all economies as embedded, as they are just one aspect of social life more generally.

12. Tschauner (2001) argues that this emphasis is a result of the insistence of most Andean archaeologists that Murra's (1972) vertical-archipelago model is valid for highlands and coast and extends into fairly deep antiquity. In this model, members of the same community exploited different ecozones in order to provide the full range of necessary goods to other community members. Differential task allocation within the community is not considered specialization, and ethnohistoric documents that discuss craft specialists are variously explained away. Few archaeological projects have dealt explicitly with the issue of the organization of production for commoner consumption (but see Costin 1986; D'Altroy and Hastorf 2001).

13. The excavators have posited an elaborate form of patronized (i.e., attached) production at Cerro Mayal, in which the Cerro Mayal artisans "owed" some portion of their output to the rulers of the nearby center of Mocollope (Russell and Jackson 2001). This reconstruction is based on an analogy drawn from documents that describe craft production in the late Prehispanic and early historic periods, nearly a thousand years after production ceased at Cerro Mayal. No published data demonstrate the plausibility of this analogy.

14. The other was work in the state-owned agricultural fields.

15. Note, however, that among the tribute obligations of farmers and herders was the production of cotton and wool.

16. Most people take their lead from the following comment made by John Rowe, the "dean" of Inka studies: "Cuzco-Polychrome (i.e., Inka) and related types bear the mark of mass-production. The design consists of a few elements, always executed in the same manner, and repeated in the same positions on the jars. They are types noted for economy of effort and usefulness rather than for imagination or originality. They are the only Peruvian pottery types so consistent that a whole jar can confidently be reconstructed from a single sherd" (Rowe 1944:48). In fact, no detailed studies of Inka-style pottery either from the capital region or from the provinces have truly tested this notion.

17. The situation is not unique to the Inká. There are a plethora of imitation and hybrid styles throughout time and space in the Andes; the only difference is that we have the manufacturing locales for the Inka period but generally not for the earlier ones (although see Shimada's [e.g., Shimada and Wagner 2001] work at Huaca Sialupe).

12

Political Economy in the Historic Period Chiefdoms and States of Southeast Asia

LAURA LEE JUNKER

At the time of European contact the Southeast Asian mainland and the major island archipelagoes to the south had a politically fragmented landscape, controlled by numerous maritime trading kingdoms of varying scale and complexity lying at the intersection of sea routes linking China, mainland Southeast Asia, India, East Africa, and the Middle East in a vast network of spice and luxury-goods trade (Figure 12.1). These maritime trading polities centered on coastal or river-based capitals such as Palembang, Melaka, Ayudhya, Thang-long, Pegu, Johor, Brunei, Manila, Ternate, Majapahit, Makassar, Kedah, Jolo, and Cotabato, large-scale cities that controlled the flow of tropical forest products and raw materials from the hinterlands (such as spices, aromatics, hardwoods, wax, resins, ivory, animal pelts, and gold ore) for export to China and other foreign lands in exchange for luxury-goods wealth (including porcelains, silks, gold jewelry, lacquerware, and other "prestige goods"). Many Southeast Asian indigenous states and chiefdoms, such as Srivijaya (Sumatra), Funan (Cambodia), Champa (southern Vietnam), Brunei (Borneo), and P'u-tuan (Philippines), had official trade relations with the Chinese that date to at least the first millennium A.D., and many of the others enumerated above entered the official trade records by the early second millennium A.D. These Southeast Asian "tributary" polities not only received Chinese merchants and diplomats at their ports but also made "tributary trade missions" to the Chinese court, creating a substantial body of Chinese writings on political relations, economic affairs, and other matters pertaining to specific polities. In addition, many Southeast Asian maritime trading kingdoms adopted Sanskrit-based writing systems (but in Malay script), along with Hindu religious elements, from their Indic trade partners. Therefore, we have a substantial number of both contact period European records and early non-European texts going back more than a millennium with information on polity location and scale, political structures, foreign trade and military relations, and local political economy in these island Southeast Asian complex societies.

An archaeological emphasis on widespread architectural styles and historical reliance on epigraphically prominent polities have in the past given the impression that Southeast Asian political history was the progression from one enduring civilization to another—Funan, Champa, Srivijaya, Angkor, Pagan, Majapahit (e.g., Coedes 1972; Hall 1968). However, the advent of regional-scale archaeological investigations and new approaches to historical analysis have begun to emphasize the multicenter nature of premodern Southeast Asia and the generally fragmented structure of power relations that resulted only rarely in coalescing local power centers into a tenuously cohering centralized state (B. Andaya 1992; Andaya and Andaya

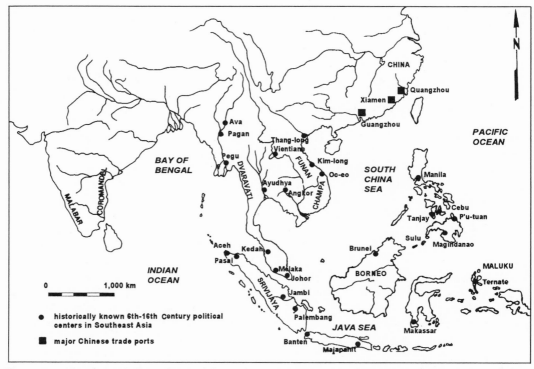

Figure 12.1. Southeast Asian polities of the sixth–sixteenth centuries known through texts and archaeological evidence.

1982:20; Hall 1985, 1992; Reid 1993a; Wheatley 1975, 1983; Winzeler 1976, 1981). As summarized by historian Barbara Andaya (1992:409): "The typical Southeast Asian 'kingdom' was a coalescence of localized power centers, ideally bound together not by force but through a complex interweaving of links engendered by blood connections and obligation. Leadership, conceived in personal and ritual terms, required constant reaffirmation. On the death of each ruler, therefore, his successor's authority had to be reconstituted with a renewal of marriage bonds and a vow of loyalty."

Southeast Asian polities were characterized by political structures that were weakly centralized and lacked long-term political stability. A number of factors combined to create highly decentralized polities, built on shifting alliance networks, that were structurally quite distinct from complex societies elsewhere in the world. Comparatively low population densities relative to productive

agricultural land led to an emphasis on control of labor rather than fixed geographic spheres of political authority. In Southeast Asian kingdoms and chiefdoms, particularly those of island Southeast Asia, extreme environmental diversity between closely spaced ecological niches, the geographic fragmentation of island archipelagoes and narrow mountain-ringed valleys, and the absence of unilineal descent principles for inheriting leadership undermined long-term political stability.

Alliance networks surrounding chiefs and kings were created and maintained through the charismatic attraction of individuals (e.g., Tambiah 1976), through the theatrical ceremonialism of the polity center (Geertz 1980b), and most importantly through voluminous gift exchanges between allied leaders and between elite patrons and their cadre of supporters (e.g., Wheatley 1983; Winzeler 1976; Wolters 1999). Political relationships and hierarchies of authority had to be constantly reinforced through the strategic disbursement of wealth to cronies and clients, unlike in strongly centralized polities. An elaborate series of bridewealth exchanges for polygamous marriages, the circulation of status-symboling goods as part of competitive feasting events, elite gift exchange associated with royal investitures, and other institutionalized forms of exchange were core to Southeast Asian political economies and were the very foundations of political power. In the absence of strong genealogical claims to leadership and with the difficulties of militaristic control, only those leaders who had the means to amass large quantities of prestige goods could be ultimately successful in consolidating their power base.

In attempting to define what are seen as relatively unique characteristics of Southeast Asian political structure, historians and anthropologists have developed a variety of models and conceptual frameworks. The "segmentary polity" model of Southall (1988, 1991) and Fox (1977), applied to Southeast Asian states by Kiefer (1972b) and Winzeler (1976, 1981), emphasizes the weakly integrated leader-focused factions at the core of Southeast Asian political structures. Geertz's (1967, 1980b) concept of Bali and the Hinduized polities of Java as "theater states" and Tambiah's (1976) description of Thai states as galactic polities instead emphasize the ideology of divine rule, which stabilizes the cosmological image of a centralized state even though ruling personnel and political configurations undergo frequent transformations through revolt and usurpation. The traditional Sanskrit term *mandala* also has been applied by historians, most notably Wolters (1999), to simultaneously describe these political and ideological aspects of the Southeast Asian state. Underlying these models is the implicit view that Southeast Asian political structures are unique, even aberrant, and difficult to analyze within broader frameworks of cultural evolutionary theory, actor-based models, or other approaches. Not surprisingly, Southeast Asian complex societies are rarely mentioned and almost never figure prominently in cross-culturally comparative

studies of political structure and political economy (but see Blanton et al. 1996; Earle 1997; Flannery 1995). Yet based on recent work on comparative political structures, such as Blanton's (Blanton et al. 1996) and Feinman's (1995) distinction between "corporate-based" and "network-based" power strategies, these ubiquitous features of Southeast Asian polities are not extraordinary in state-level and chiefly societies; instead, they represent an extreme emphasis on network strategies of political power relations that have profound implications for political economy.

In this chapter I attempt to elucidate some of the specific material and ideological means whereby Southeast Asian rulers built and maintained alliance-structured political coalitions, including control of foreign prestige-goods trade and foreign religious ideologies, the circulation of women and bridewealth to create affinal networks, the exchange of wealth in the context of ritual feasting, and the circulation of labor through institutionalized slave raiding. In addition, I look at some of the ecological, geographic, demographic, and cultural factors that may have contributed to the pervasiveness of network political strategies and portable wealth-based forms of political economy in Southeast Asian complex societies. Because there is an exceptionally rich historic and ethnographic record we can bring to bear on the discussion of political structure and political economy in early Southeast Asian complex societies of the first millennium and early second millennium A.D., much of what is presented here is documentary or ethnohistoric in nature. Archaeology, however, has recently contributed to our understanding of the long-term development of maritime trading polities in specific regions of Southeast Asia, using excavations at coastal centers, regional settlement surveys, and particularly investigations of how political expansion within certain polities might have been effected through control of foreign prestige-goods trade, militarism, the strategic disbursement of wealth in marriage exchanges, and ritual feasting prestations. In terms of archaeological investigations, I focus primarily on work that has been carried out by myself and others in the Philippine archipelago and nearby regions of island Southeast Asia for the period spanning the early first millennium A.D. to European contact.

Considerably less is known about the origins and longer-term dynamics of these alliance-focused political structures and foreign prestige trade-oriented political economies in Southeast Asia, as the archaeological evidence is much more limited for the prehistoric Metal Age societies that preceded the historically known kingdoms and chiefdoms of Southeast Asia. A significant issue is whether historically documented political structures and aspects of political economy can be extrapolated back in time to these earlier, pre-state complex societies, spanning the first millennium B.C. to mid-first millennium A.D., or if the scale and nature of the recent South China Sea–Indian Ocean trade radically transformed the nature of Southeast Asian political formations. I do not attempt to treat this earlier period in depth here but instead offer some limited comparisons with the historic period and discuss some of the problems with the archaeological evidence that have limited our understanding of these longer-term political dynamics.

POLITICAL STRUCTURES IN SOUTHEAST ASIA: NETWORKS OF POWER

Southeast Asian complex societies are generally characterized by a "decentralized" political structure in which political hierarchies are weakly integrated even in the most developed "states." Political authority relies less on hereditary ascription and territorial control than on cultivating ties of personal loyalty through gift giving and ceremonialism. Anthropologists and historians have developed a diverse and often confusing range of conceptual frameworks aimed at differentiating these uniquely Southeast Asian political forms from those of "ordinary" centralized polities. For example, Leach (1965:56–59), emphasizing the relatively weak and ephemeral authority of the Shan rulers over their subjects, the lack of a permanent territorial power base, and the highly personal nature of

power relations, describes the historic states of Burma as "charismatic kingships." Geertz (1973:331–338, 1980b:11–25), who saw cosmological ideals of political order and court ceremonialism as the ultimate creator and maintainer of political structure in historic Bali and Java rather than strong corporate political units, refers to these polities as "theater states." According to Geertz, participation in court pageantry and displays of prestige by local elites bound them to the Balinese and Javanese rulers at the polity center, but this grandiose ceremonialism masked the institutional reality of a fragile pyramid of political dominance and subordination. Emphasizing both ecological factors that create centrifugal tendencies toward political fragmentation and indigenous cosmological notions that promote political and cultural integration, Tambiah (1976:69) proposed the term *galactic polity* to describe the perpetual cycles of coalescence and disintegration that characterize the traditional Thai state as well as other Southeast Asian polities. Both Geertz's (1967, 1980b) and Tambiah's (1976) descriptions of Thai states as galactic polities emphasize the overarching importance of ideology, ritual, and state pageantry at the polity center in reinforcing and maintaining political power in these societies that lack the politically cohering institutions of centralized states. An ideology of divine rule stabilizes the cosmological "image" of a centralized state even though ruling personnel and political configurations undergo frequent transformations through revolt and usurpation.

Borrowing from Southall's (1956, 1988, 1991) African-based concept of "segmentary polities" and Fox's (1977) later elaboration of this concept as a comparative form of political organization, anthropologists Kiefer (1972b) and Winzeler (1981:462) have suggested the utility of a segmentary-state model in describing the historic Sulu sultanate of the southern Philippines (Kiefer) and island Southeast Asian polities in general (Winzeler). As in many Iron Age and historic sub-Saharan African kingdoms, the general availability of land and relative underpopulation of much of the region meant that the acquisition of loyal subjects and their labor through personalized reciprocity or seizure in warfare was a major preoccupation of rulers who lacked the permanent power base of land and immovable wealth. The consequence in parts of Africa and much of Southeast Asia was the formation of political pyramids that were highly unstable, particularly as one moved from core centers to more distant local centers of power. Geertz (1980b:16) uses the analogy of an intricately constructed house of cards that becomes more weakly integrated and inevitably collapsible as it spreads "horizontally" over the landscape and "vertically" across generations. In the Philippines these features of political structure can be found in societies running the gamut from simple chiefdoms to Islamic sultanates of significantly greater complexity. This suggests that the alliance-structured nature of political relations was not a function of polity scale in Southeast Asia but instead was a fundamental organizational principle of complex societies in the region. In contact period Philippine chiefdoms, political allegiance was given only to the leader immediately above an individual, with whom he had personal ties of reciprocity and loyalty (Junker 1999:68–78; Kiefer 1972a, 1972b). Alliance units were formed out of perpetually shifting, leader-focused factions whose members were recruited through material exchanges of prestige goods and maintained through chiefly sponsored ceremonialism.

Historians of premodern Southeast Asian states, most notably Wolters (1999) and Wheatley (1983), have tended to favor the term *mandala* (a traditional Southeast Asian Sanskrit term borrowed from Indian states of the period) to describe this type of nonterritorial, fluctuating political structure characteristic of early historic Southeast Asian kingdoms. Again, the focus in *mandala*-type states was on a style of political authority in which all political relations were personal and immediate rather than remote and hereditarily imbued. Individuals competed for ideological and material supremacy through the controlled circulation of foreign prestige goods and through adopting exotic arts, religions (Hinduism, Buddhism, Islam), and literary traditions (particularly Sanskrit writing). In recognizing that *mandala*-like features of political structure could be found in the Philippines and other areas of island Southeast Asia lacking full-blown states, Wolters (1999) joined the contemporaneous struggles of anthropologists such as Geertz, Tambiah, and Winzeler to define panregional patterns of social and political organization. Historians, however, have typically been more cautious about broadly painted pan-Southeast Asian generalities in political structure, instead emphasizing the importance of "local" culture histories that examine the varying local meanings and functions attached to foreign materials and ideas circulated in foreign trade (Andaya and Ishii 1992; Taylor 1992; Wheatley 1983; Wolters 1999).

Thus a number of models, which vary primarily in nomenclature on their relative emphasis on materialist versus ideological elements of rulership, and on the relative significance of "localized" versus panregional processes, have been developed to describe ubiquitous features of political structure in Southeast Asian kingdoms and chiefdoms (Brown 1976; Geertz 1973, 1980b; Gullick 1958; Tambiah 1976; Wheatley 1975, 1983; Winzeler 1976, 1981; Wolters 1999). These features include highly decentralized power bases and weak regional integration, with relations of political subjugation maintained primarily through personal alliance and clientage ties involving continual gifting, ceremonialism, and prestige display. However, recent work on comparative political structures by Blanton (Blanton et al. 1996) and Feinman (1995) has suggested that these ubiquitous features of Southeast Asian polities are not extraordinary in state-level and chiefly societies but instead represent an extreme emphasis on network strategies of political power relations and political economy, a strategy for maintaining rulership that is practiced to a lesser or greater degree in many complex societies. Blanton and Feinman have contrasted corporate-based and network-based, or exclusionary, power strategies as differing but not mutually exclusive ways of achieving political dominance in complex societies. They suggest that these strategies are part of the political dynamics in all complex societies, but political actors in a particular society and historical context may emphasize one mode of control more than the other.

In the *exclusionary or network power strategy* political actors try to create personal networks of political dominance through the strategic distribution of portable wealth items and symbolic capital (such as ritual potency and religious knowledge). Alliances are typically created and maintained outside local groups through "prestational events" (Blanton et al. 1996:4), involving exchanges of marriage partners, prestige goods, esoteric knowledge, and labor. Individuals who can most successfully translate these exchanges into patronage over a large network of allies and followers gain political preeminence in the community. However, as noted by Blanton and Feinman, in societies in which a network strategy is the predominant mode in the political economy, leadership is generally highly conflictive, unstable, and prone to relatively short cycles of expansion and collapse. In contrast, attempts at monopolistic control of resources and power-imbuing symbols are inhibited by a *corporate political strategy*, which instead disperses power across different groups and sectors of society through bureaucratic institutions promoting consensus, solidarity, and collective action and often large-scale public architecture emphasizing these values. In societies characterized by corporate politics and political economies, a strong "cognitive code" defines social relations between elite rulers and their subjects, among kinsmen (e.g., unilineal descent groups), and in various subgroups in the society.

The emphasis on unstable, personalized alliances cemented through exchanges of prestige goods, spouses, labor, and esoteric knowledge as the core elements of political structure in Southeast Asian societies exemplifies a strongly network-oriented strategy of political control. This is not to say that Southeast Asian complex societies did not

also have elements of corporate political strategy, in which certain highly structured institutions provided an opposing force to monopolistic power relations and promoted corporate values of group solidarity, collective empowerment, and diffuse participation in political action. In traditional Southeast Asian kingdoms these corporate-oriented institutions tend to be religious in nature, often associated with the adoption of Hinduism and Buddhism (Andaya and Ishii 1992). These religion-based corporate structures also appear to operate more strongly in Southeast Asian societies with comparatively higher population densities, with a heavier focus on control of productive agricultural land (versus labor), and with more state investment in large-scale land modification and water control systems.

An example is the contact period Balinese state, in which the entire realm was divided into Hindu temple-centered irrigation units, with religious functionaries not only performing life-sustaining agricultural rites but also organizing the labor to construct the irrigated rice terraces, coordinating cultivation schedules to maximize production, and allocating water to farmers (Geertz 1980b; Lansing 1991). Although there is some disagreement among ethnohistorians who have analyzed the Balinese political system about the relative power of secular authorities (i.e., the king and "men of prowess" at the center of clientage networks) versus religious authorities, the Balinese system has much stronger corporate elements than many other Southeast Asian political systems because of the focus on temple groups as centers of collective action and social solidarity that crosscut the clientage networks of power-accruing chiefs and diffuse royal authority. Elaborate Hindu temple complexes and the religious ritual held there are the symbolic locus of a corporate identity that ultimately limits the ability of kings and charismatic leaders to monopolize wealth and political power. The simultaneous complementarity of and tension between corporate and exclusionary political strategies is emphasized by Blanton et al. (1996). This polarity is nicely summarized for the Balinese case by Valeri (1991:137), who views the contrast as between "the most fundamental, most unquestionable grounds for social existence (relative to which all are ultimately equal) and the noble values (wealth, military force, ability to attract, generative potency, etc.), which are unequally distributed and which allow those who have them most to weave and reweave around their persons hierarchical networks defined by relationships of clientage, alliance, descent, debt, or even servitude."

In contrast, in the Philippines, where population densities are relatively low, land-based corporate units are absent, native religious systems focus on individualized rather than collective forms of worship, and there is no independently powerful priesthood, it is not surprising that there are no monumental material symbols of corporate identity such as large-scale tombs, temples, or statuary (Junker 1999). Even in the Philippine chiefdoms that converted to Islam in the few centuries before European contact and built the requisite mosques (e.g., Sulu, Magindanao, Manila), the secular political authority of sultans was fully merged with religious potency in the Islamic tradition. That is, there were no separate religious hierarchies to disperse the power of traditional chiefs, who continued to build patronage networks through the strategic control and disbursement of prestige goods, religious knowledge, exotic symbols gained through foreign contacts, labor, and marriage partners. In contrast to Bali, corporate political strategies did not appear to have played a strong role in shaping power relations in the Philippines.

ECOLOGICAL, DEMOGRAPHIC, AND CULTURAL FACTORS IN THE POLITICAL ORGANIZATION OF SOUTHEAST ASIAN POLITIES

A number of historians and archaeologists have pointed to the fragmented geography and diverse environments of Southeast Asia as promoting diffuse centers of political power and frustrating attempts at large-scale political integration (B. Andaya 1992:405; Hall 1985; Reid 1993a:3). Although main-land Southeast Asia and some of the larger islands of insular Southeast Asia had extensive river basins and lowland alluvial plains, these river plains were often separated by rugged mountain chains or stretches of nearly impenetrable tropical forest. Whereas many coastal peoples were favored by sheltered harbors that promoted maritime interactions, other lowland populations were isolated by coastal swamp forests that prevented sea-going vessels from penetrating the coast. The inhabitants of insular Southeast Asia, comprising dozens of island archipelagoes and thousands of additional isolated islands, depended on wind, currents, and weather patterns to determine the direction and intensity of cultural interaction.

As noted by Barbara Andaya (1992:405), the result of these isolating factors was an astonishing cultural and linguistic diversity, in which numerous distinct dress styles, customs, and languages developed within close proximity. This is particularly true of the Philippines, where it is estimated that more than 200 languages were spoken at the time of European contact (with 80 languages remaining today). Linguistic and cultural differences among Philippine societies were displayed in a wide range of regional variation in textiles, basketry, ornamentation, and other distinct material markers (Casal et al. 1982; Lebar 1977). This linguistic and material diversity is not surprising, given the complex cultural amalgam recorded in the sixteenth century, composed of Islamic sultanates, hundreds of chiefdoms of varying scale and complexity, and small-scale upland tribal societies and hunter-gatherer populations spread over eleven major islands and thousands of smaller ones together only slightly larger than the landmass of the British Isles.

Related to the unique ecology and geography of Southeast Asia were factors of demography, which had their own effects on the structure of political relations. Until almost the European colonial period most of Southeast Asia (with the possible exception of Bali, Java, and parts of Vietnam) had exceedingly low population densities relative to land and

Table 12.1. Estimated Population Numbers and Densities for Southeast Asia and Comparative Regions in Approximately A.D. 1600

	Estimated Population	Density Persons/km^2
Southeast Asia[a]	23,000,000	5.7
Burma	3,100,000	4.6
Laos (including northeast Thailand)	1,200,000	2.9
Siam (minus northeast)	1,800,000	5.3
Cambodia-Champa	1,230,000	4.5
Vietnam (north and central)	4,700,000	18.0
Malaya (including Patani)	500,000	3.4
Sumatra	2,400,000	5.7
Java	4,000,000	30.3
Borneo	670,000	0.9
Sulawesi	1,200,000	6.3
Bali	600,000	79.7
Lesser Sunda Islands	600,000	9.1
Maluku	275,000	3.7
Northern Philippines (Luzon and Visayas)	800,000	4.0
Southern Philippines (Mindanao and Sulu)	150,000	1.5
China[b]	150,000,000	37.5
India[b]	135,000,000	32.0
Japan[b]	22,000,000	59.5
Polynesia[c]	453,700	17.8
Europe[b]	100,000,000	10.4

[a]Reid 1988:14. See Reid for details of original historical sources and calculation of estimates.

[b]McEvedy and Jones 1978. China includes China proper but not inner Mongolia, Manchuria, or Chinese Turkestan. India includes Pakistan and Bangladesh. If population densities for Japan are corrected for habitable arable land only, the figure is 366.7 people/km^2. Europe includes continental Europe, Scandinavia, and the British Isles.

[c]Kirch 1984:19. West Polynesia, East Polynesia, and the Polynesian outliers were combined to obtain an overall density for the region. New Zealand was removed from the estimate because of its unique environmental and demographic characteristics.

resources (Reid 1988:11–18, 1992:460–463). Density (persons/km^2) estimates from A.D. 1600 for most areas of Southeast Asia, as well as the overall average of 5.5 persons/km^2 for the region, are less than a fifth of that of India and China and roughly half that of Europe (Table 12.1). The highest proportion of the population in Southeast Asia was concentrated in the large coastal trading cities of the western archipelago and in limited areas of intensive wet-rice farming, such as the Red River delta of Vietnam, central and eastern Java, Bali, and South Sulawesi. The eastern archipelagoes of island Southeast Asia, including the Maluku (the Moluccas), the Philippines, and Borneo, were the least densely populated parts of Southeast Asia, with Mindanao and Sulu supporting lower population densities than Luzon and the Visayas (see Table 12.1).

Given the relative bounty of land and marine resources, studies of health and nutrition showing adequate diets at the period of contact, and the apparent lack of any cultural prescriptions for delayed marriage or child bearing, the low population densities in Southeast Asia before the nineteenth century have been somewhat puzzling to historians and demographers (Owen 1987). Reid (1992: 461), however, suggests a number of factors that might have contributed to these relatively low population levels, including extended breast-feeding of children, heavy agricultural workloads of mothers and consequent depression of fertility, the widespread practice of abortion, the ubiquity of fertility-reducing diseases such as malaria, and the high rate of warfare. Although warfare in Southeast Asia did not usually take a large death toll, it was costly for already low-density areas that were decimated by enforced migration or enslavement of the productive workforce (Reid 1992:461–462).

Because of relatively low population levels, combined with an economic emphasis on swidden cropping rather than intensive permanent agriculture, an abundance of unoccupied fertile land, and a seemingly inexhaustible supply of wood and bamboo for the easy rebuilding of even large settlements, many island Southeast Asian populations were inherently mobile and not particularly concerned with control of land as a political and economic commodity (Hall 1992:187; Reid 1983a:157; Winzeler 1981:462). An obvious conclusion is that shortages of labor relative to land engendered a political system in which a ruler's power base was measured in terms of the size of the labor force bound to him through extensive alliance networks rather than fixed geographic territories. Thus competition between political leaders (and between rulers and would-be rulers) focused on commanding labor rather than commandeering land, which may explain the enormously strong emphasis in Southeast Asian complex societies on alliance-building activities such as the gifting of prestige goods, the creation of extensive marriage ties, ritualized feasting, and religious pageantry aimed at so-

cial cohesion (see discussion below). Even political expansion through militarism appears to have been primarily oriented toward the capture of slave labor to augment local productive capacities rather than the seizure of land and territory (Andaya and Andaya 1982:61; Reid 1983b:27–33, 1992:461; see below).

Certain cultural features that were related to environments, demography, and traditional economic modes also tended to constrain intergenerational continuity in political leadership and to promote political fissioning in Southeast Asian complex societies. One of these was the widespread emphasis on bilateral descent rules in inheritance and cognatic descent (Brown 1976; Eggan 1967). Fox (1971, 1977) has emphasized the significance of corporate unilineal descent groups and particularly stratified lineages or "conical clans" in the development and maintenance of strongly centralized state structures in India, as well as China, Mesopotamia, and Prehispanic Mexico and Peru. Societies adhering to strong unilineal principles of descent can control the smooth transfer of political authority from one generation to another with minimal disruption, and corporate descent groups can form the basis for state bureaucratic units, ensuring the steady flow of resources from periphery to center. In most ethnographically or historically known complex societies of Southeast Asia, kinship is generally reckoned bilaterally, corporate descent groups are lacking, postmarital residence is bilocal or neolocal, and rank and wealth are inherited along both the maternal and paternal lines (Hall 1985:110–111; Kirsch 1976; Reid 1988:147; Winzeler 1976:628). Even though imported Indian or Muslim law codes in some polities identified the eldest son as the legitimate heir, succession disputes were almost inevitable between the eldest son and younger sons, as well as both maternal and paternal uncles (B. Andaya 1992:419). In addition, in many Southeast Asian complex societies, polygamy was the cultural norm, at least among the rulers and other nobility (e.g., B. Andaya 1992:409, 419; L. Andaya 1993:37; Geertz

1980b:5; Reid 1988:152), who produced multiple heirs and further exacerbated the conflict over succession.

Adding to the chaos of kingly and chiefly succession in some regions of Southeast Asia was a pronounced mythology of folk heroism in which ordinary individuals rise up and rebel against a tyrannical leader and usurp political power (B. Andaya 1992:421; Taylor 1992:178). Kingship in Southeast Asia depended strongly on the association with the inherited spiritual power of royal ancestors, which automatically set kings above their followers, "reinforced by ideas and vocabulary of imported religions" (Andaya and Ishii 1992:546). As noted by Earle (1987a:299), this emphasis on foreign origins serves to segregate the local elite from the remainder of society as being "connected to a universal (rather than a local) order." In Southeast Asian complex societies, where charismatic leadership is more important than hereditary succession, court ceremonialism incorporating exotic religions would be a particularly important strategy for expanding political power bases. The seemingly arbitrary adoption and often rapid discard of foreign religious ideologies such as Hinduism, Buddhism, and Islam by Southeast Asian maritime trading polities was initially viewed by historians as part of a politically shaping "indianization" process (see Casparis 1961; Coedes 1968, 1972; Majumdar 1963; Van Leur 1967). More recently, scholars have begun to recognize that Southeast Asian sovereigns often expediently used religious conversion as one of a number of mechanisms to establish their "cosmopolitanism" and to expand the universe of symbols validating their political hegemony (B. Andaya 1975; Christie 1979; Hall 1977, 1985:6, 9, 47, 51–53; Wheatley 1979; Wolters 1979).

The perception of ritual potency in a ruler, however, was vulnerable to any decline in general prosperity within his political sphere (B. Andaya 1992:420). Southeast Asian ideologies often left the door open for ordinary individuals, through revelation or the acquisition of sacred objects, to acquire spiritual power that could lead to a kind of popular messianic rebellion (Andaya and Ishii 1992: 551). Whereas the construction of a strong military was critical to protecting a ruler's economic activities (particularly for controlling trade and launching plunder-aimed raiding expeditions), warrior-elite often were able to garner significant wealth and establish independent power bases through their close association with elite patrons (Hall 1992:260), ultimately threatening the latter's hegemony (Reid 1988:167).

The fragility of political alliance and clientage networks created by these ecological, cultural, and social factors likely magnified the type of competitive interactions for labor and resources among elites, both within and between polities, that ultimately resulted in frequent reconfiguration of the political landscape. Political cycling, or the oscillatory expansion and contraction of polities within an unstable political landscape (Anderson 1994a; Champion and Champion 1986; Renfrew and Cherry 1986; Wright 1984), would be expected to occur with greatest frequency in societies with this type of weakly integrated, network-based political structures. Not surprisingly, detailed historical work and regional-scale archaeological investigations in parts of Southeast Asia have demonstrated that what were once thought of as large-scale, highly centralized, and enduring polities, such as the Vietnamese coastal kingdom of Champa (Hall 1992; Taylor 1992), were actually a series of competing polities almost continuously in a state of political flux, whose political fragmentation was archaeologically masked by shared aspects of elite material culture (Higham 1989). This also has been historically and archaeologically demonstrated for the smaller-scale maritime trading polities of the Philippines, where chiefdoms such as Manila, Sulu, Magindanao, Cebu, Butuan, and Tanjay rose and fell with astounding rapidity as chiefs and would-be chiefs competed to establish ultimately brittle patronage networks through various ideological and material means (Junker 1999).

Network-type political formations involve the expansion of political influence through both material exchanges and ideological means. In Southeast Asia competition for wealth, social prestige, and political power was enacted through varying strategies for controlling people and resources, most overtly through strategic marriage alliances and ritualized "feasts of merit" in which elites' capacity for attracting followers, mobilizing resources, and theatrical ceremonialism was on public display. Extreme local diversity in resources, combined with geographic factors favoring the development of gateway ports and dendritic networks of interaction (Bronson 1977; Hall 1985; Reid 1983a), engendered a political economy focused on foreign prestige-goods trade as the primary source of political currency.

FOREIGN PRESTIGE-GOODS TRADE AND THE GIFT-SEALED ALLIANCE

As early as the Chinese Tang period (A.D. 618–906) and probably before, Chinese trade records, indigenous Southeast Asian texts, and archaeological finds of foreign goods at Southeast Asian sites document the beginnings of long-distance trade in prestige goods within a vast maritime network connecting China, emerging Southeast Asian polities, India, and Arab traders from the west (Hall 1985; Reid 1988; Wheatley 1983; Wolters 1967, 1971) (Figure 12.1). Chinese porcelains, silks, and lacquerware, Indian glass beads and textiles, and other foreign luxury goods procured through maritime trade became increasingly key symbols of social prestige and political power for Southeast Asian elite in kingdoms such as Funan (southern Vietnam), Champa (Vietnam and Cambodia), Srivijaya (Sumatra), Java, Majapahit, Melaka (Malay Peninsula), Brunei (Borneo), and Maluku (Moluccas Islands), as well as in the smaller-scale chiefdoms of the Philippine and Indonesian archipelagoes. Most significant for discussions of political structure, foreign prestige goods became the most important source of politically manipulable wealth for maintaining network-based political units in historic period Southeast Asian chiefdoms and kingdoms. Although historic sources suggest that most Southeast Asian complex societies supported full-time luxury-good artisans (particularly gold and bronze metallurgists, fine textile weavers, and fine ceramic specialists) (Reid 1988:101–103), it was primarily foreign wealth that provided the strategic material prestations to cronies and clients that structured political relations (Junker 1999:14–15). These foreign goods, along with labor in the form of captured slaves, were circulated as bridewealth payments for politically strategic marriages, as elite gifts in the context of ritual feasting, as part of royal ceremonies of investiture, and in other contexts in which political relations were materially negotiated. Underhill and Fang (this volume) show that in the early Chinese states of the Shang period, the material embodiment of political relations was strongly focused on internally produced bronzes rather than exotic forms of political currency, but Shang bronze vessels functioned in political networking in the same way as porcelains in Southeast Asia. Underhill and Fang suggest that elites at Shang centers such as Anyang presented gifts of bronze vessels to obtain political and military allies and to exact economic resources from obligated subordinates; these gifting events included politically charged contexts similar to those in Southeast Asia such as ritual feasts and mortuary rites.

That control of foreign prestige-goods trade became critical to the political economy of Southeast Asian polities by the first millennium A.D. is evidenced in the complex competitive strategies developed by rival kingdoms and chiefdoms in various periods to monopolize the South China Sea luxury trade. Many island Southeast Asian states of the late first millennium and early second millennium A.D., such as Srivijaya, Samudra-Pasai, Melaka, Majapahit, Johor, and Kedah, developed entrepôts, or "ports of trade," with well-organized harbor facilities, port administrators, and in some cases a monetized economy to attract Chinese, Arab, Indian, and Southeast Asian traders (Geertz 1980a; Van Leur 1967; Wheatley 1961). The eminence of polity rulers in administering and controlling foreign luxury-good trade in traditional Southeast Asian kingdoms is particularly well documented by Wolters (1967, 1971), Hall (1976, 1985:78–102), and others for the seventh-eleventh-century Malay state of Srivijaya. The bulk of foreign trade revenues flowing into the Srivijaya coastal center were channeled by the Srivijayan rulers into central coffers through a well-established system of obligatory customs duties and "tribute" payments collected not only at the state's major entrepôt but also at numerous subordinate ports. Nonroyal "elite" associated with the ruler's court were placed in positions of control over port and market areas to facilitate and enforce fee collections; alliances reinforced by redistributing luxury imports to local chiefs ensured the continuing flow of commodities through various segments of the internal trade network.

As outlined by Hall (1985:99–100), trade in the capital's market area was carried out under strict royal control. This oversight was effected through a well-developed bureaucracy of state officials known as "supervisors of trade and crafts," state-established rates of value for various commodities in gold and silver equivalents, and strict regulation of the movement and activities of foreign merchants. Hall (1985:100) suggests that in its earliest phases of development the Srivijaya political economy may have amassed external wealth primarily through skimming profits (using port fees, tribute, and the like) from what was essentially a "free trade" system in which access to foreign luxury goods was not wholly exclusive to the royal elites. The Srivijayan monarch and associated elite, however, gradually tightened their control over access to luxury goods by establishing monopolies over local commodities that were the major export items in this foreign trade. Srivijaya's ultimate success in attracting foreign traders was in large part due to its ability to guarantee safe passage for trading vessels through its economic patronage of Malay sea nomads who protected its sea-lanes (Hall 1992:201–202).

Similarly, the principality of Melaka gained international trade prominence in the fifteenth and sixteenth centuries because of the strategic location of its primary coastal entrepôt along the Melaka Straits, which separate the Indian Ocean from the South China Sea. An early European visitor to Melaka, the Portuguese explorer and trader Tome Pires, described a bureaucratically complex port management system designed to ensure maximum profit and economic control for the Malaysian rulers (Andaya and Andaya 1982: 31–51; Gullick 1981:11–18; Miksic 1984; Thomaz 1993). Melaka's strategies for monopolizing trade in the region continued the successful traditions of Srivijaya by providing the administrative infrastructure and resources necessary to meet the needs of foreign traders, by ensuring the safety of passing ships through winning the allegiance of traditional pirate groups inhabiting the straits area, and by controlling an efficient system for funneling resources from hinterland areas to the port. Like the Srivijayan polity, the Melakan rulers dealt with the problem of piracy by steering some trade profits to the *orang laut*, the mercenary Malay raiders inhabiting the straits area, who in turn protected vessels traveling to Melakan ports and attacked ships of trade rivals (Andaya and Andaya 1982:42; Thomaz 1993:77; Wheatley 1961:307–320).

Because most of Melaka's foreign traders coming from the west were Muslims (including Indians, Persians, and already Islamicized Malays such as those of the Pasai kingdom), it is not surprising that the Melakan rulers quickly embraced Islam at the beginning of the fifteenth century, establishing cultural as well as economic ties with their most lucrative trade partners (Andaya and Andaya 1982:52; Andaya and Ishii 1992:516–517; Thomaz 1993:79–81). The success of Melaka's trade infrastructure is evidenced in its growth to become the largest urban center in Southeast Asia in the early sixteenth century (with an estimated population of 100,000–200,000) (Thomaz 1993:71), trade volumes that nearly rivaled those of the wealthiest European ports such as Seville (Andaya and Andaya 1982:44), and its role as the intersection of maritime trading networks that stretched from the Red Sea and Persian Gulf to Japan and the Philippines.

The elite rulers of many Southeast Asian polities were not content to remain passive beneficiaries of foreign trading expeditions into their ports but instead took an active role in soliciting foreign traders and expanding the trade volumes so critical to political alliance building. "Tributary missions" by gift-bearing Southeast Asian chieftains and kings to the Chinese court have been analyzed by historians as a competitive strategy for gaining favored trade status with the Chinese state (e.g., L. Andaya 1992:346; Andaya and Andaya 1982:23–24; Hall 1976; Wolters 1971:39–48), with such missions growing in frequency during periods of increased political fragmentation and interpolity trade conflict (Hall 1985:78–79; Smith 1979:445–451). These tributary missions involved sea and overland voyages to the imperial court by Southeast Asian leaders, accompanied by large entourages of nobility, bodyguards, and servants, and armed with formal petitions requesting a "tributary" relationship. The bestowal of tributary status was not commensurate with actual political hegemony or economic sovereignty by the Chinese but a well-tuned Chinese strategy for controlling the flow of wealth in and out of its borders, for carefully selecting advantageous trade partners, and for perpetuating the emperors' view of China as the center of the universe, to which all other polities were naturally subservient. In exchange for recognizing imperial China as nominal overlord, a tributary polity would be accorded privileged trade relations and a constant source of foreign wealth, as well as court titles and imperial regalia that enhanced the polity ruler's prestige and political legitimacy at home. The massive cargoes of tributary offerings accompanying the contingent were viewed by the Chinese as proper material recognition of their superior role in the political and economic relationship. From the perspective of the tributary polity, however, the large volume and diversity of its gifts were proof of its ability to pro-

vide trade goods of the type and scale desired by the Chinese and its superiority to rival maritime trading polities.

The frequency and elaborateness of tributary missions by Southeast Asian polities between the seventh and sixteenth centuries exhibits a periodicity that simultaneously reflects Chinese foreign trade policies and the degree of political fragmentation and interpolity competition in Southeast Asia. For example, a flurry of tributary missions by the early Hinduized kingdom of Funan (encompassing the lower Mekong region) in the mid-third century A.D. were likely aimed at establishing Funan ports such as Oc-eo as the primary Southeast Asian commercial entrepôts in the burgeoning Indian-Chinese maritime trade (Hall 1985:70). At the peak of Funan's political and economic power in the fourth century—when historical records suggest that Funan centers were unsurpassed in Southeast Asia in their architectural splendor, Hindu ceremonialism, commercial wealth, and cosmopolitan mix of Chinese, Indian, Persian, and Southeast Asian traders (Hall 1992:192–196)—tributary missions were few, as there were few threats to Funan trade supremacy (Hall 1985:43). With the establishment of an all-sea route from India to China through the Melaka and Sunda Straits in the fifth century, Funan commercial dominance was directly challenged by Malay trading kingdoms to the south. The fifth century saw a large upsurge in tributary missions by Funan, by former Funan satellites, and by rising polities along the Sumatran and Javanese coasts (Hall 1985:43).

Srivijaya's political and economic fortunes are similarly chronicled in peaks of tributary embassies in the seventh century, as Srivijaya attempted to consolidate its ascendancy over other straits-area polities such as the Jambi-Malayu, and in the late tenth century and early eleventh century, when Srivijaya's trade hegemony was challenged by the rise of multiple competing trade centers in Java and regions to the east (Andaya and Andaya 1982: 23–24; Hall 1992:207–215). The late tenth century and early eleventh century was a peak of tributary trade for Southeast Asia in general (as measured in terms of both the frequency of missions by individual polities and the number of Southeast Asian polities launching trade missions). The coalescence of several new major regional powers in the thirteenth and early fourteenth centuries (e.g., Sukothai, Ayutthaya, Majapahit) resulted in a lull in tributary embassies (Wolters 1971:4). However, the massive upsurge in the demand for Southeast Asian products in China, India, the Near East, and Europe at the beginning of the fifteenth century, and the consequent proliferation of Southeast Asian trade centers, encouraged a renewed competition among polities to launch lavish tributary missions as a means of ensuring a share of the lucrative trade "pie" (Reid 1993a:15).

Even in the smaller-scale and less-developed maritime trading polities of the Philippine archipelago, there is some evidence for large-scale investment in port facilities and administrators, residential areas for foreign traders, and competitive tributary missions to the Chinese court. At the Sulu capital of Jolo the Sulu sultan and influential *datus* (chiefs) held exclusive rights to foreign luxury commodities through a number of institutionalized trade practices (Majul 1966, 1973; Warren 1982, 1985). These included a formal system of port fees administered directly by the royal court, obligations on foreign merchants to extend "credit" to the sultan and other elite (frequently forcing the foreign traders to exchange below the "going" rate or forgo payment altogether), and enforcement of the ruler's monopoly over trade of particularly valuable local export items (such as pearls, forest hardwoods, tortoise shell, and bird nests). Sixteenth-century descriptions of Manila record the presence of a well-fortified, heavily populated trade port, with special quarters for resident Chinese and Japanese merchants, craft specialists associated with elite residences, and a well-organized port area, administered by a single paramount chieftain and a number of lesser chiefs (Anon. 1570, in Blair and Robertson 1903–1909:3:92–104, 141–158). The tradi-

tional seafaring group known as the Ilanun served the Sulu rulers as maritime raiders and as the primary naval force for protecting Sulu sea-lanes (Tarling 1963; Warren 1985); the *maharlika,* or warrior-elite, performed the same function for the Tagalog chiefs at Manila (Loarca 1903–1909 [1582]:149–151). At least eight Philippine polities (including Sulu, several chiefdoms at or near Manila, and various chiefdoms on the islands of Mindoro and Mindanao) launched tributary missions to the Chinese court between the eleventh and fifteenth centuries (Junker 1998:296–297, 1999:212–218).

Archaeologists carrying out settlement surveys in regions associated with these early maritime trading kingdoms and chiefdoms in Southeast Asia document socially restricted patterns of distribution consistent with the circulation of prestige goods as political currency. In a recent archaeological study of the Musi River basin of Palembang, the probable locale of the seventh–twelfth-century kingdom of Srivijaya, McKinnon (1985, 1993) demonstrates that foreign prestige goods and elite architectural styles were the material cement of political alliance between coastal nobility and hinterland leaders who controlled interior export resources critical to foreign trade. McKinnon notes that large riverbank sites up to 80 km inland have megalithic architecture, in the form of limestone menhirs and dolmens that mirror the style of stone monuments (but have no Sanskrit inscriptions) found at one of the probable locations of the Srivijaya capital at the mouth of the Musi River near modern Palembang. Burials in association with the limestone monuments at these interior sites, as well as scattered surface debris, include bronze jewelry and blades, glass beads, and imported Chinese stoneware and porcelains dating from the ninth to the thirteenth century; these goods are stylistically and materially similar to luxury goods found along the coast and correspond chronologically to the period of Srivijaya dominance (also see Manguin 1992:69–72). Because the logistics of fieldwork in Sumatra precluded large-scale excavations, systematic surface collections, and even the preparation of accurate site maps, McKinnon is cautious in interpreting these interior sites as clear evidence for Srivijaya-connected hinterland elites. I would argue, however, that the significant investment in construction of stone ritual structures and tombs coupled with the sizable quantities of foreign prestige goods at these riverine sites suggest the long-term presence of high-status individuals who may have controlled the flow of riverine trade supporting the coastal port. McKinnon (1993:236) in fact proposes that iron, salt, and textiles might be added to these archaeologically visible coastal imports. These large inland centers may have been the concentration points for alluvial gold, ivory, rhinoceros horns, resins, honey, bird nests, and possibly pepper collected by upland groups for export to the coastal populations directly under Srivijaya hegemony. The local chiefs were likely part of the alliance network of the coastal royalty, facilitating the river movement of these exportable resources in exchange for ceremonially bestowed titles and status-enhancing exotics such as Chinese porcelain (Miksic 1984).

Similarly, Allen (1991) has compiled archaeological data from the hinterlands of the seventeenth–eighteenth-century Kedah maritime trading polity of western coast of the Malay Peninsula. Her regionally focused work has demonstrated the presence of numerous large riverbank interior centers that probably functioned as intermediaries in the Kedah-centered regional trade, as evidenced in concentrations of Kedah-derived ceramics and Indian-style ritual structures. Historic sources suggest that leaders at these upriver centers were allied to the rulers at the polity center through the flow of prestige goods and that sometimes elite kinsmen of the ruler were sent to the hinterland as trade and tribute administrators (Hall 1985:92). These upriver secondary centers, particularly those inhabited by second-tier chiefs and located near the polity center, were significantly larger than the typical interior village and were often fortified (although they were still

considerably dwarfed by the primate coastal port) (Gullick 1965:28). In addition, the presence of second-tier chiefs or local leaders whose close ties to the coastal rulers are cemented through the presentation of prestige goods (frequently of foreign derivation) would be manifested in similar status and wealth differences in the polity center but on a smaller scale—that is, spatially discrete commoner and elite occupation areas, with trade wealth concentrated in the households of the latter. Unfortunately, extensive excavations have not been carried out at any of these riverbank trade centers, and these assumptions about site patterns and inferred functions have yet to be tested. However, through careful geological reconstruction of the Merbok and Muda Rivers, Allen (1991) was able to demonstrate that the economic and political significance of various upriver settlements shifted according to rapidly changing alluvial configurations, that is, inland centers that were well situated for efficiency of transport at one point in time were displaced when river shifts reduced their advantageous position as trade bulking centers. Again, poorly developed methodologies for locating and surveying the multitude of less visible village sites have precluded the kinds of quantitative studies of site size differentials, rank-size patterns, and the differential distribution of prestige goods that would provide a wider understanding of political dynamics in the region.

The Bais-Tanjay region of Negros Island in the central Philippines is another such locale where systematic regional survey, combined with extensive excavations at the coastal trade port and related sites, has produced sufficient regional-scale settlement pattern data to document the long-term growth of a Southeast Asian maritime trading polity over nearly a millennium and its prestige goods-focused political economy (Hutterer and Macdonald 1982; Junker 1990, 1994, 1996, 1998, 1999). Tanjay was known through mid-sixteenth-century documents to have been one of a number of coastal complex societies in the Philippines engaged in maritime trade for Chinese porcelain and other prestige goods. The chiefdom of Tanjay was centered on the alluvial plain of the Tanjay River, adjacent to upland tropical forest zones occupied by swiddening tribal groups and mobile hunter-gatherers who traded valuable forest products to the coastal elites for foreign export. Between 1979 and 1995 a program of systematic archaeological survey, combined with systematic auger coring, test excavations, and more extensive excavations of selected survey zones and sites within the 315-km² region, allowed the identification, mapping, and dating of more than 500 Prehispanic settlements spanning the second millennium B.C. to European contact.

A two-tiered settlement hierarchy was present in the Bais-Tanjay region as early as the A.D. 500–1000 Aguilar phase, dominated by the coastal center of Tanjay, strategically located at the intersection of riverine and maritime trade routes. Even in this phase, prior to any archaeologically visible evidence for prestige goods from outside the archipelago, the regional settlement organization was riverine oriented and "dendritic" in form, with distinct upriver secondary centers that controlled significant volumes of prestige goods (primarily decorated earthenware, bronze objects, and paste beads). By the eleventh century Tanjay emerged as a coastal port of significant size, with elite and nonelite habitation zones and burial areas, ceramic and iron production areas, ritual paraphernalia not found at other sites, and large concentrations of foreign trade goods (porcelain, bronze, ivory objects, and glass beads from China, India, and other Southeast Asian polities). Not only were foreign prestige goods differentially distributed in houses and burials at the chiefly center, but they also were flowing inland, presumably through elite exchange networks, to interior riverbank centers where allied chiefs and nobility may have resided.

By the fifteenth and sixteenth centuries Tanjay had grown in size to an estimated 30–50 ha, emerging as a hyper-large "primate" center that controlled a large river network of connected secondary centers in the Tanjay River drainage. Excavations within the fifteenth–sixteenth-century occupation levels at Tanjay revealed a coastal trade port that was not only larger than before but had more extensive areas for the production of iron and earthenware pottery (Junker 1993, 1999:274–291) and more striking differences in wealth between both households and burials (Junker 1999:152–158, 171–179; Junker et al. 1996; Junker et al. 1994). The growth of Tanjay as a polity center in the two centuries before Spanish contact corresponded with a significant expansion in foreign trade, marked by two- to fivefold increases in densities of porcelain (Chinese, Annamese, and Siamese), bronze (of unknown derivation), glass beads (Indian and Malay), and exotic earthenware (Siamese and from other Philippine islands) found in burials, household middens, and contexts of ritual feasting (Junker 1999:152–158; 2001). Several upriver secondary centers connected to Tanjay reached 7–10 ha in size in this period, and excavations have revealed the presence of significant quantities of foreign porcelain, beads, metal products, and other symbols of prestige and power. Statistical analyses of the spatial relationships between sites (using linear nearest-neighbor analysis and various statistical measures of site clustering) show that these upriver secondary centers that formed the middle tier in the settlement hierarchy became more regularly spaced in the fifteenth–sixteenth-century Osmena phase (Junker 1999:227–231). This increased "centrality" of river trade centers is significant because historic sources suggest that like the riverbank centers of the Musi and Merbok Rivers of Srivijaya and Kedah, they served as the primary points of interaction between lowland coastal chiefs and interior populations who were the ultimate collectors of the raw materials that were essential to foreign trade.

Thus far, all the archaeological examples of prestige-goods exchange and alliance network building in Southeast Asian kingdoms and chiefdoms have focused on the late first millennium to mid-second millennium A.D., the period of historically known complex societies and after the advent of the South China Sea maritime porcelain trade. Less well documented in archaeological terms are the political structures and political economies of prehistoric complex societies that appear to have preceded developed maritime trading polities such as Srivijaya, Kedah, Melaka, Sulu, Brunei, and Tanjay. The tremendous wealth-manipulating opportunities during the period of expanding South China Sea–Indian Ocean trade may have fueled Southeast Asian political economies, already heavily based on personal alliance networks shaped by material and labor exchanges. In simple terms the issue is whether the political forms and contexts of exchange documented in historic period Southeast Asian complex societies (i.e., after about A.D. 500) can be projected into the more distant past, or if we need to think differently about political structure and political economy in early Southeast Asian complex societies.

The period from about 1000 B.C. to A.D. 500 has been designated by Southeast Asian archaeologists as the sequentially named Bronze Age–Iron Age, or more generally the Metal Age. In regions of mainland Southeast Asia, particularly southern China, northern Vietnam, Cambodia, and central Thailand, this period saw the emergence of rich burials (in wood- or stone-lined pits) containing bronze implements (such as socketed axes, decorated blades), bronze vessels, bronze drums, bronze bells, iron implements (after about 500 B.C.), beads of precious and exotic materials (including agate, carnelian, rock crystal), shell ornaments, clay animal and human figurines, and elaborately decorated ceramics (see summaries in Higham 1989, 1996). By the mid-first millennium B.C. there is evidence for larger-scale settlements along major rivers, some moated with elaborate earthworks, in areas such as central Thailand (e.g., Ho 1992; Welch and McNeill 1991) and in the lower Mekong Valley (Stark et al. 1999), many of which contain evidence for sophisticated copper and iron metallurgy and

the concentration of metal, stone, and ceramic luxury goods. Although systematic, regional-scale settlement surveys are still relatively rare compared with excavations of single sites, several such surveys in central Thailand have revealed the emergence of settlement hierarchies by the early first millennium B.C. (McNeill and Welch 1991). An example is Mudar's (1993) analysis of archaeological survey data from the Lam Maleng Valley, where a landscape of relatively similarly sized, probably autonomous, small-scale villages transformed by around 1000 B.C. to one in which there were substantial centers with significant evidence for exotic status goods and copper and iron working. Many archaeologists investigating these Bronze Age and Iron Age sites have interpreted the wide-ranging variability in mortuary treatment, the construction of at least moderate-scale earthworks around large settlements, the beginnings of specialized metal production, and the appearance of regional settlement hierarchies as strong evidence for emerging sociopolitical complexity. Given the widespread circulation over considerable distances of certain types of status goods within Southeast Asia, such as Dongson bronze drums, decorated bronze implements, carnelian beads, and decorated ceramics, alliance-building exchanges of prestige goods may have been a significant element of the political economies of these early complex societies.

In the island archipelagoes of insular Southeast Asia there is similar archaeological evidence for developing sociopolitical complexity among coastal and river valley people in the first millennium B.C. to the early first millennium A.D. Most striking is the widespread appearance of elaborate burials with prestige goods, indicative of some degree of social ranking and possibly hereditary social stratification. For example, stone slab-lined burial chambers discovered in southern Sumatra contain a rich array of bronze ornaments, exotic glass and carnelian beads, and carved boulders with scenes of men carrying bronze Dongson-style ritual drums and arrayed in elaborate clothing and ornaments (Bellwood 1992:132–133). In the Philippines during the same period, developing social status differences are apparent in stone and pottery jar burials, often with spectacularly carved anthropomorphic lids and containing large quantities of shell and bronze bracelets, glass and carnelian beads, and decorated earthenware pottery (Bellwood 1992:135; Hutterer 1977; Junker 1999:168–171). The wide distribution throughout the island archipelagoes of bronze and gold ornaments, iron objects, glass and carnelian beads, Dongson-like bronze drums, and certain distinctive styles of paddle-impressed, stamped, painted, and burnished earthenware pottery, often originating in a limited locale, suggests the operation of prestige-goods exchange systems similar to those of the later historic period kingdoms but of more limited volume and geographic scale.

Unfortunately, regional settlement data and even substantial excavations of isolated habitation sites are almost nonexistent for this period, making it difficult to surmise the relative significance of prestige-goods exchanges in local political economies, the origins of many so-called exotic goods, and the social and political contexts (other than possibly mortuary feasts) in which these goods might have been circulated. However, the regional settlement pattern evidence from the Tanjay region of the Philippines, as discussed above, reveals the presence of a two-tiered settlement hierarchy and substantial regional-scale movement of prestige goods (bronze, beads, and decorated pottery) well before the advent of Chinese trade in the late first millennium A.D., suggesting that this type of alliance-oriented political structure fueled by the circulation of portable wealth has some time depth in Southeast Asia prior to the emergence of the historic maritime trading kingdoms.

At the same time, a few areas of island Southeast Asia (specifically, parts of Sumatra, Java, and Bali) have yielded megalithic stone monuments, including terraced platforms, large stone-lined tombs, and large boulders carved into animal or human figures, that ap-

pear to be associated with mortuary ritual at Metal Age burial sites (Bellwood 1985:292–302; Christie 1979). Such constructions indicate the importance of more permanent, corporate symbols of political authority in some early complex societies of the region but their striking absence in others (specifically, the Philippines, Borneo, Maluku, and areas with early complex societies). Although we should avoid simplistic explanations of this variability, it is interesting to note that megalithic constructions appear to be concentrated in those regions of island Southeast Asia with the highest precolonial population densities (Junker 1999:82), where the impact of labor diversion on agricultural workforces would be less than in areas of low population density. Archaeologists working outside Southeast Asia have suggested that in addition to conveying a symbolic message of chiefly political power and association with the sacred, such monumental works often symbolize "proprietary control over the economic landscape" (Earle 1997:101; also see Kirch 1990; Trigger 1990). In southern Sumatra, Java, and Bali higher prehistoric population densities may have emphasized territorial control of fixed resources, corporate political strategies, and monumental architecture as symbols of more enduring collective forms of sovereignty, more than in other parts of island Southeast Asia. As noted earlier, this pattern of greater emphasis on monumental landscapes and corporate forms of political authority (later embedded in Buddhist religious organization) persisted as a defining feature of historic period kingdoms in Bali.

In sum, the little archaeological evidence we have for the period of early complex society development in Southeast Asia suggests that although portable prestige-goods wealth appears to have a significant role in many early Metal Age political economies, intersocietal contacts were more localized, and there is evidence that ideological coordination of groups through monumental construction may have been more common than in the historic period in some areas of Southeast Asia. Although the tremendous increase in geographic scope and scale of the South China

Sea–Indian Ocean trade beginning in the mid-first millennium A.D. is assumed by historians and archaeologists alike to have had profound effects on Southeast Asian complex societies (e.g., Hall 1985, 1992; Higham 1989, 1996; Wheatley 1983; Wolters 1999), we simply cannot yet adequately assess the specifics of these transformations without the types of regional-scale archaeological investigations of long-term sequences of complex society development that we have for regions such as the Yellow River valley of China, Mesopotamia, and pre-Roman Europe.

In his chapter comparing the political economies of Neolithic and Metal Age complex societies in Europe, Sherratt (this volume) emphasizes that Bronze Age and Iron Age societies represented a sharp break from the earlier monument-building Neolithic societies because their emerging political structures, social relations, economies, and ideological systems were shaped by prestige-goods trade and cultural contacts with expanding urban states to the south. Innovations and exotic materials were transferred to new cultural contexts, were incorporated and reinterpreted, and in the process transformed these societies in unpredictable ways. Sherratt argues that because these later complex societies were part of world systems that their predecessors were not, it is important to recognize that these two periods of complex society florescence are in a sense "disassociated" and do not form an evolutionary cultural sequence with strong continuities in power structures. In the Southeast Asian case we cannot assume that the prehistoric Metal Age complex societies were similar to historically known maritime trading kingdoms in political organization and political economy. We need to be more critical of attempts to project the rich historical evidence on the significance of political networking and prestige-goods exchanges in recent Southeast Asian polities into the prehistoric past. Thus most of the following discussion of alliance-building material exchanges and their specific sociopolitical contexts, known primarily through ethnohistoric analysis, focuses exclusively on more recent Southeast Asian

kingdoms and chiefdoms of the historic period.

POLITICALLY STRATEGIC MARRIAGES, RITUAL FEASTS, AND THE CIRCULATION OF PRESTIGE GOODS

Based on history and archaeology, political ties in Southeast Asian kingdoms, at least for the last millennium before European contact, were highly volatile and predicated on maintaining networks of personal allegiance. Strategic disbursements of prestige goods by political patrons were essential to attracting and retaining a large cadre of tribute-producing supporters. Marriage exchanges and ritualized feasting events allying elites almost invariably involved gift offerings of porcelain, gold, bronze, or other valuables as symbols of political connectedness and a shared "culture" that segregated elites from the lower social tiers (Andaya and Ishii 1992; Friedman 1979; Reid 1988). Southeast Asian rulers, however, also attracted followers and maintained the highly volatile factions at the core of their political structure by formal gift presentations, often involving foreign porcelains and other exotic status goods, to loyal subordinates. Here I consider prestige-goods gifting as the material cement of political relations in the context of marriage alliances and ritual feasting.

Marriage negotiations and bridewealth payments were one of the most important social contexts in which prestige goods were strategically disbursed to expand political networks in Southeast Asian complex societies. For chiefs and kings in particular, the creation of a widespread network of affinal ties that ramified horizontally and vertically through the sociopolitical hierarchy was of supreme importance in political coalition building. Subordinates presented their daughters and sisters to rulers as acts of fealty, and elites exchanged wives to consolidate their alliance, with elite polygamy "both an indication of status and a diplomatic weapon" (Reid 1988:151). Because bridewealth payments traditionally passed from prospective grooms to the families of selected brides throughout Southeast Asia (Reid 1988:146), it was incumbent on Southeast Asian maharajahs, sultans, and chiefs to accrue the enormous surpluses of prestige-goods wealth that would allow them to acquire numerous high-status and politically strategic wives for their sons and heirs.

In Southeast Asian societies, where overlord-vassal relationships involved continued reciprocity and were modeled after the kinship bonds of families, "it was the exchange of women which made these bonds tangible, for the children that resulted from subsequent unions became the living symbol of irrevocable kinship" (B. Andaya 1992:408). In the sixteenth–seventeenth-century Maluku (Moluccan) polities of Ternate and Tidore, which expanded under the Portuguese spice trade, the king's court contained hundreds of royal wives supplied by high-ranking chiefs of the outlying districts under his dominion: "it was not uncommon for a sultan to have a wife in every major settlement in the kingdom" (L. Andaya 1993:37). Some elite women from smaller polities and outlying districts were designated royal spouses before leaving their mother's wombs (B. Andaya 1992:408). The giving of women in polygamous marriages to the ruler and other high-ranking elites at the polity center was an act of fealty and subordination that was rewarded with a return flow of elevated status and bridewealth valuables.

Geertz (1980b) also has written extensively about the significance of marriage alliances in defining, and sometimes redefining, political clients and social asymmetries in nineteenth-century Balinese kingdoms. Polygynous, hypergamous marriages in the royal court and within the noble class were one of the most important mechanisms for political integration, establishing a wide network of ties that bound high-ranking Balinese *dadias* (agnatic descent groups) to similarly constructed but lower-ranking descent groups in clientage relationships. Geertz describes the political ramifications of the Balinese marriage system:

> Though marriage was preferentially *dadia* [agnatic descent group]-endogamous, title-group hypergamy—that is to say,

marriage of a woman of lower title to a man of higher—was permitted. As a result, the higher it was in the title-group ladder, at least among the ruling gentry, the more endogamous a marriage could be, from the point of view of the women of the *dadia*; while, from the point of view of the men, and especially the lord, the larger the man's complement of endogamous and hypergamous wives could be. The degree to which a *dadia* could keep its own women and still bring in others from outside was an almost quantitative measure of its status. The lower, or less powerful, *dadias* were obliged to send some of their women to the higher, or more powerful, in order to secure their place in the polity. The relationship thus established was called *wargi*. That is, the lower *dadia* was *wargi* to the higher, by virtue of having given a woman to it in marriage and acknowledging thereby both its own inferiority and its loyalty to the higher. Wives were given as a form of tribute, an act of homage, and an oath of fealty. (1980b:35)

In addition to these asymmetrical marriage alliances aimed at cementing vertical ties and extending ties to subordinates, Geertz (1980b:39) notes the importance of "crosswise" (i.e., horizontal or symmetrical) exchanges between locally dominant *dadias* of different regions. Ongoing prestations of heirlooms, trade goods, and theatrical or artistic performances were tied to these elite marriage alliances and were a formalized aspect of ceremonial occasions.

Ethnohistoric sources suggest that intermarriage between elites also was a significant political integrating mechanism in the smaller-scale chiefdoms of the Prehispanic Philippines. Both Spanish sources and early ethnographic accounts of extant chiefdoms such as the Magindanao, Bagobo, and Kulaman indicate that *datus*, or chiefs, were frequently polygamous, selecting wives from a large number of villages where strategic alliances were necessary to consolidate political power (e.g., Anon. 1572, in Zaide 1990:2:111; Cole 1913:103, 157; Ileto 1971:34; Legaspi 1990 [1569]:42; Saleeby 1905:60; Vicencio 1990 [1534]:359). The marriage arrangements made by chiefs were almost invariably predicated on political considerations and were a significant element of interpolity alliance-building strategies. This is exemplified in a case described by Spanish chronicler Pedro Chirino (1903–1909 [1604]:294–295), in which a Visayan chief's daughter was married to the son of a chief of a small neighboring island with attendant exchange of substantial bridewealth and gifts. As a "wife taker," the chief on the neighboring island became politically superior to the wife-giving Visayan chief and was able to draw him and the bulk of his supporters into his sphere of political influence. Subsequent hostilities, however, resulted in "the marriage last[ing] no longer than did peace between them," and the political coalition dissolved. Chirino (1903–1909 [1604]:294) notes that such alliance-building marriage contracts frequently involved multigenerational wife exchanges between allied individuals, with betrothal negotiations sometimes initiated well before the potential spouses were even born.

The Magindanao *tarsilas* (genealogical records of the sultans and pre-Islamic chiefs, known through oral tradition and encoded in writing during the historic period) indicate a long history of inter-elite marriage aimed at cementing political relationships in these Mindanao polities (Saleeby 1905). Ileto (1971:2) suggests that an analysis of the directional flow of women (i.e., which *datus* were most often wife givers and which *datus* were most often wife takers) can reveal which of the Magindanao polities enjoyed relative political dominance in particular periods. Like the case of nineteenth-century Bali (Geertz 1980b), but unlike the Burmese Shan and Kachin studied by Leach (1965), the wife-receiver position appears to have conferred greater prestige. The genealogies of the mid to late sixteenth century indicate an almost unidirectional flow of women from the coastal Magindanao polity centered at Cotabato into the interior Buayan-centered chiefdom, which is claimed in Antonio Morga's account (1903–1909 [1609]) to have been a

significantly larger and more powerful political center than that of the coast.

By the seventeenth and eighteenth centuries the Buayan polity was eclipsed by the Cotabato sultans, whose ties with Maluku polities such as Ternate and Tidore and the rising Portuguese spice trade catapulted Cotabato to primacy as an international trading port with a powerful naval force (Majul 1966). At this time the flow of elite women reversed and most of the interpolity elite marriages involved the betrothal of the daughters and sisters of the Buayan *datus* to Cotabato rulers and the rulers of even more distant polities. The Cotabato Magindanao chiefs are reported to have taken wives not only from the Buayan Magindanao but also from powerful *datus* elsewhere in Mindanao and from the sultan and other elites of Sulu (Saleeby 1905:57), creating a widening web of affinal alliances that strengthened the regional predominance of this polity. By the end of the eighteenth century the Cotabato sultans' political preeminence was eroding because of the Spanish presence at Zamboanga, whereas the Buayan rulers, buffered by their interior location, expanded their power through intensive surplus agricultural production and control of interior resources (Ileto 1971:11). Accordingly, the Buayan rajahs in the nineteenth century received wives from the Cotabato rulers and from numerous neighboring smaller polities (Ileto 1971:34).

Elite intermarriages and the flow of women through hypergamous marriages to men, and especially *datus*, of higher rank are tied to the prestige-goods economy through bridewealth payments, which redistributed foreign porcelains and other accumulated status goods between wife takers and wife givers. According to Spanish writers of the contact period (e.g., Bobadilla 1990 [1640]: 337; Dasmarinas 1958 [1590]:410–411; Santa Ines 1990 [1676]:89–90; San Antonio 1990 [1738]:336–339), social mobility of the entire kin group was achieved not only through marrying its women to higher-ranking men but also by accumulating the resources (e.g., slaves, porcelain, gold, fine textiles, water buffalo, pigs, and other prestige goods) to meet the high bride-prices necessary to acquire high-status women for the group's male members. Therefore, success in accumulating high bride-prices for previous marriage matches, in obtaining prestige goods and slaves through maritime raiding and trading activities, in controlling the labor of luxury-good artisans, and in accruing goods and status in the competitive feasting arena all contributed to a pool of wealth that could be used for making politically and socially enhancing marriages for the kin group. Heirlooms and other status goods flowed to the woman's kin group whereas primarily prestige flowed to the man's kin group. This prestige derived both from the relative status of the woman and from public opinion about the relative extravagance of the bridewealth payment that the man's family was able to offer (see ethnographic accounts of Biernatzki 1985; Claver 1985; Cole 1913, 1956; Manuel 1971; as well as Junker 1999:294–300).

Of significance in the construction of political alliance networks is the reported practice among the Manuvu and Bukidnon of chiefs or other elites "sponsoring" young men, assisting with bridewealth payments when the prospective groom and his kinsmen cannot meet the expense of a desired high-status match (Biernatzki 1985:33; Manuel 1971:230, 332). Manuel (1971:333) summarizes the practice for the Manuvu: "Sons of ordinary citizens, unless assisted by kinsmen, may not be able to meet the bride wealth requirements, and it is usually the *datu* who comes with a helping hand to tide over a tight situation. [In addition], the concept of 'extending our waters and expanding our lands' [i.e., 'influence'] is used for practical purposes by *datus* when their sons or daughters marry.... Thus, political influence may spread fanwise in all directions." These surrogate bridewealth payments created subordinate relationships for chiefs that could be called on whenever labor, resources, or military support were required. Thus chiefs aimed to acquire politically manipulable wealth not only to finance their own status-enhancing marriages and those of their sons

but also as a "fund of power" that could be used strategically to sponsor marriages for young men from lower-ranking families who recognized their debt through future loyalty and service to the *datu*. The result was a wide-ranging network of clients who were bound to the chief through bridewealth debts that extended his political sway over time as well as space.

Many components of status rivalry, circulation of portable wealth, and political competition for followers also converge within the "feasts of merit," or competitive feasting complexes that are an almost ubiquitous feature of Southeast Asian complex societies (Beatty 1991; Biernatzki 1985; Kirsch 1973; Reid 1988; Schnitger 1964; Volkman 1985). In Philippine chiefdoms of the contact period, both community cohesion and social-rank differentiation were expressed through elite gift exchange, chiefs' oral narratives, animal sacrifice, food prestations, and ancestor-invoking ritual (Junker 1999:313–335, 2001; Junker et al. 1994). Ritual feasts were generally associated with elite life-crisis events and events critical to the political economy (e.g., chiefly succession, trading, warfare, the agricultural cycle), for which the ability to draw on the resources of a chief's constituency to finance them demonstrated a status-enhancing power to mobilize productivity. Furthermore, chiefly generosity in lavish presentations of valuables as gifts to elite guests served both to maintain politically significant reciprocal exchange relationships (the material glue of alliance building) and to symbolize overtly a chief's rank in the social and political hierarchy (as measured through his control of people and wealth).

The control of foreign prestige-goods wealth, particularly Chinese porcelain, was essential to successful participation in the feasting system. Food distributions were displayed on the elite sponsor's array of fine porcelain plates and bowls (e.g., Alcina 1960b [1668]:133–136; Cole 1913:88, 92; Pigafetta 1521: 59), and porcelains, silks, metal gongs, and other imported valuables were exchanged between elites attending the feast

(Claver 1985:74–75; Cole 1913:111–112; Kiefer 1972a:26, 97). Elite prestations occurring at any single feast represented links in intertwined chains of ongoing reciprocal exchange partnerships between allied nobility, reflecting the unique state of political and social ties at any one time. As in marriage arrangements and bridewealth payments, the prestige gained from sponsorship of feasts came from the creation of social debt among the people attending the feast (see Voss 1987: 131). By expending huge amounts of his wealth in feeding the attendees at the feast, many of whom did not have the resources to reciprocate in kind, a feast's host expanded the number of people in an asymmetrical relationship to him, as well as reinforced the debt of existing ties of patronage.

A number of anthropologists have suggested that competitive feasts aimed at the establishment of permanent economic inequalities and political power are primarily a structural feature of "transegalitarian," "aggrandizing," or "big-man" societies characterized by unstable criteria of social ranking and political succession (e.g., Clark and Blake 1994; Friedman and Rowlands 1978; Hayden 1995; Rossman and Rubel 1978). According to this view, the need for competitive feasts is largely obviated in more complex societies, since the competition for political succession and economic surplus has been resolved in the emergence of inheritable rulership and enforceable tribute, maintaining permanent labor pools and stored wealth. In other words, political authority is no longer a matter to be negotiated in contexts of social interaction like competitive feasting but rather an inalienable fact of ascribed rulership. However, where cognatic descent ruled, where polygamy was widely practiced, and where demographic factors created an emphasis on coalition building rather than territorially based political power, inheritance was problematic. Thus political authority and the status of elites and pretenders to elitehood appear to have been renegotiated continually in Southeast Asian polities through the institution of competitive feasting.

Ethnographic and historical work on the Kachin and Shan of Burma (Friedman 1979; Lehman 1989) has shown that the availability of external sources of wealth can set off an inflationary cycle in the feasting system, expanding alliance networks sealed with prestige goods and contributing to the evolution of larger-scale political units. Once foreign serving vessels and exchangeable goods enter the feasting system as prestige symbols of exceptionally high value, other feast givers must obtain similar exotic goods and/or inflate their distributions of now-devalued locally manufactured goods to maintain their relative ranking in the feasting system and their political alliance networks. In addition, the feasting system often expands in terms of the diversity of social groups participating in status display, as the availability of exotic prestige goods creates a two-tiered system of value in which local luxury goods are more widely available for lower-ranking groups to use in elite-emulating ceremonial feasts.

Archaeological work in the Philippines has shown that ritual feasting was probably a component of chiefly political economies at least by the eleventh century A.D. In addition, there appears to be a strong link between the coalescence of larger-scale chiefly polities at Cebu and Tanjay and a widening scale and social participation in ritual feasting by the height of foreign prestige-goods trade in the fifteenth century (Junker 1998, 2001; Nishimura 1992). The Philippine chiefdoms present an almost ideal case for studying the development and expansion of competitive feasting as a form of ritual alliance building and wealth circulation; ethnohistoric analysis has shown that feasts generally took place within archaeologically identifiable locales (the sponsoring elite's houseyard), they involved the use of specific kinds of highly visible serving pieces (primarily imported porcelain dishes and cups), and they included specific kinds of high-status "feasting foods" (including water buffalo, pig, certain marine delicacies, and rice rather than the daily staple of starchy tubers). Excavations of elite and non-elite habitation zones at Cebu (dated from the fourteenth to sixteenth centuries) and Tanjay (dated from the eleventh to sixteenth centuries) revealed the concentration of foreign porcelain serving wares and probable feasting foods (pig bones, water buffalo bones, and charred rice) in the elite sectors of the settlements. However, in comparisons of pre-fifteenth-century and fifteenth–sixteenth-century residential areas at both Tanjay and Cebu, significantly greater densities of water buffalo, pig, and porcelain serving vessels were recovered from trash deposits in the two centuries before European contact, possibly marking a generally increased scale and frequency of ritual feasts at these fifteenth–sixteenth-century chiefly centers as the polities expanded (Junker 1999:325–333, 2001; Junker et al. 1994; Nishimura 1992). Even more significant, however, is the appearance of emulative "feasting wares" and proportionally larger densities of feasting foods such as pig and water buffalo in the non-elite sector of these sites by the fifteenth century. The "emulative" feasting wares consist of inferior-quality porcelain serving pieces, mass-produced at Siamese and Vietnamese kilns, that mimicked popular Chinese styles, as well as locally produced earthenware pedestaled plates and serving bowls with burnished surfaces and/or incised and stamped decoration. The politically integrating and wealth-circulating exchanges at the core of ritual feasting events were becoming increasingly important at multiple levels in the political hierarchy.

MARITIME RAIDING AND THE EXPANSION OF POLITICAL NETWORKS

Even the ubiquitous maritime raiding between rival Southeast Asian trading polities was geared toward expanding the alliance networks that were the basis for political power relations. Rather than contribute to political growth primarily through a process of territorial conquest (Carneiro 1981, 1990; Redmond 1994:123–124; Vayda 1961; Webster 1975:467), warfare in Southeast Asian kingdoms and chiefdoms focused on the capture of labor and portable resources that could enhance the economic base and political sway of rulers (Junker 1999:336–369; Reid 1988:121–129, 1992:461; Scott 1994: 153). As summarized by Reid (1988:122): "The perception of forest land as infinitely available and manpower as scarce ensured that competition was fundamentally over control of people. It was often status questions which gave rise to conflict, but the physical objective of the combatants was to seize people rather than territory. Both the constant small-scale raiding of the Philippines, eastern Indonesia, and upland regions everywhere, and the cumbrous encounters of great armies in the mainland states and Java, were essentially aimed at increasing the human resources at the disposal of a chief or king." The emphasis on labor capture in warfare resulted in battle strategies aimed at taking captives and seizing other portable resources rather than large-scale slaughter of enemies (Reid 1983a, 1983b, 1988:123). The dominant military leader in Southeast Asia was one who could mobilize large warrior forces, cause his enemy to retreat through intimidation and supernatural intervention rather than engage in a pitched battle, and leave the battleground with more warriors (including both uninjured warriors and captives) than he started with (1988:121–129). In the Philippines the Spaniards were often puzzled by the fierce initial display by chiefly military forces that was followed by a reluctance to press their advantage over less well-equipped and well-manned forces. Instead of inflicting greater casualties and seizing control of the attacked coastal town, they generally retreated as soon as they pushed their enemies back sufficiently to take desired captives and booty (Alcina 1960b [1688]:161; Artieda 1903 [1569]:197). Expansion of polities through warfare appears to have involved not direct seizure of geographic territories but simply a realignment of political loyalties as lower-ranking chiefs previously allied with the defeated ruler expediently forged ties with the more powerful patron, who now controlled additional slaves and other seized resources for distribution.

Interpolity warfare had a direct impact on a Southeast Asian ruler's ability to engage in material largesse for political coalition building. Raids against rival groups enhanced a leader's status and political sway by providing women for polygamous marriages, increasing agricultural and craft productivity through enslaved labor, providing sacrificial victims for status-enhancing ritual feasts, and damaging maritime trade opportunities for political rivals. Historical studies of precolonial slavery in Southeast Asia (Reid 1983a; Scott 1983; Watson 1980) have shown that although debt-bondage was practiced, warfare captivity was the major avenue whereby a slave labor force was accrued to support the expanding political economies of growing kingdoms and chiefdoms. Slaves were rapidly incorporated into the social and economic fabric of their captor society, serving as agricultural laborers, artisans, warriors, and traders and generally augmenting the surplus-producing labor force under a ruler's control. Most significant, it was generally polities arising in regions of particularly low population density in Southeast Asia that were the fiercest slave-raiding predators and who relied most heavily on captured labor to expand their economic base (Schwalbenberg 1993).

An example of the spiraling economic and political effects of expanding maritime raiding is the sixteenth–eighteenth-century Sulu sultanate of the southern Philippines, situated in one of the least-populated regions of island Southeast Asia and largely independent of colonial rule until the early twentieth century. The Sulu, Magindanao, Maranao, and other groups in the southwestern corner of the archipelago were notorious for their large-scale raiding activities focused on slave acquisition not only in the Philippines but over much of island Southeast Asia. A number of ethnohistorians claim that the Sulu economy was economically dependent on this form of negative trade (Majul 1973; Kiefer 1972a, 1972b; Warren 1982, 1985). Warren estimates that in the eighteenth century, on average, two to three thousand slaves were imported annually and more than 50 percent of the productive labor within the polity was derived from captured slaves. For-

eign slaves were incorporated into the local workforce as rice farmers, fishermen, craftsmen, and even traders and warriors (Reid 1983b:22; Warren 1985:222–228). Warren suggests that the use of slave labor in agricultural production and other basic economic tasks expanded chiefly surplus and freed up a larger portion of the nonslave population to serve the chief in the types of trading and raiding activities that contributed to his wealth and political power (Warren 1985: 221–222). In Sulu, as in many Southeast Asian chiefdoms and states, captured slaves also could be directly invested in bridewealth to expand a chief's alliance network. Women captured in raids, if of sufficiently high status, were sometimes added to a ruler's polygamous harem of wives to enhance his regional notoriety.

Southeast Asian concepts of slavery were puzzlingly mild in European eyes because slave captives were easily manumitted after a period of service, entering into the tribute-paying patronage network of the successful king or chief (Reid 1983a). Paradoxically, this high degree of social mobility and depletion of the slave ranks fueled intensified slave raiding to replenish laborers at the bottom level of the social hierarchy (Schwalbenberg 1993; Warren 1985). A strong ideology of warrior prestige, encoded in epic tales of slave-capturing prowess, material status insignia, and identification with a formalized warrior class, perpetuated this emphasis on war captives as politically manipulable wealth (Junker 1999:347–349). For example, in the Philippines, orally recounted epic tales are peopled by warrior-elites whose elaborate tattoos, filed and gold-pegged teeth, and blood-red clothing marked them as individuals capable of acquiring hundreds of valued captives in a single battle and amassing a huge political following through the distribution of plundered wealth (e.g., Alcina 1960a [1688]:20–23, 77–78, 1960b [1688]: 165–169; Morga 1903–1909 [1609]:175; also see Cole 1913:96; Junker 1999:347–349; Scott 1994:166–169). Fourteenth–sixteenth-century burials in the Philippines containing males with filed and gold-pegged teeth, boar's-teeth pendants, and other standardized warrior-associated emblems (Junker et al. 1996) are consistent with the historic evidence for a specialized warrior class (known as *maharlika* among the Tagalogs), which formed the core of a chief's supporters.

Given the great economic value of war captives, it is somewhat surprising that head taking, human sacrifice, and the use of enemy body parts as war trophies were tied to status displays in postwar feasts, harvest ceremonies, and elite mortuary ritual in the Prehispanic Philippines (e.g., Morga 1903–1909 [1609]:175). In his 1913 ethnography of the Bagabo chiefdoms, Cole (1913:105–107) describes a human sacrifice associated with the Gin Em harvest ceremony, and he notes that special raids were often launched to provide sacrificial victims on the death of an important chief. I would argue that it is precisely the great value of humans, as sources of labor and political support, that makes them the ultimate prestige-enhancing sacrificial victims for competitive feasts. Among the Bagabo a lower-ranking person could gain some measure of status by "purchasing a piece" of the victim or victims sacrificed annually at the Gin Em ceremony, while others had to be content with animal or plant offerings (Cole 1913:115; also see Keesing 1962:164–165, 189–190). This practice of head taking and human sacrifice, with subsequent interment of the enemy body parts in the graves of prominent individuals, is evidenced in the archaeological recovery of high-status burials with human grave accompaniments at sites such as Tanjay (Junker 1993, 1999:347–349).

In Southeast Asian kingdoms and chiefdoms, maritime piracy of trade vessels and raids against the coastal settlements of trade rivals also were deliberate strategies in interpolity competition for foreign prestige-goods trade. Island Southeast Asian kingdoms such as Srivijaya and Melaka had professional seafaring warriors who protected the kingdoms' sea-lanes, attacked ships attempting to enter rival trade ports, and continuously raided the coastal settlements of trade competitors in an attempt to disrupt their foreign commerce

(Wheatley 1961:307–320). Foreign ships studiously avoided ports known to be attacked frequently and trading partners who could not ensure export goods or subsistence support for traders in transit. Chinese records going back to the thirteenth century (Craig 1914:4; Laufer 1907:253–255), early Spanish writings (e.g., Artieda 1903 [1569]:197–198; Lavezaris 1903–1909 [1569]:287; Legaspi 1903–1909 [1567]:55), and ethnographic accounts of Maranao and Ilanun sea marauders serving the Sulu and Magindanao sultans (Warren 1985) suggest that a similar tactic of maritime raiding was practiced as a form of chiefly trade competition in the Philippines.

Slaves and other portable resources seized in maritime raiding were invested by Southeast Asian rulers in alliance-building exchanges, competitive feasting, attracting more foreign prestige-goods trade, and other activities critical to expanding their political power base. Thus it is not surprising that archaeological evidence for the Philippines demonstrates a significant increase in the intensity of interpolity warfare and slave raiding in the fifteenth and sixteenth centuries, a period when we also see evidence for expanded foreign prestige-goods trade and a larger scale of competitive feasting in many coastal Philippine maritime trading chiefdoms (Junker 1999:356–368). In the Bais-Tanjay region and in polities centered at Cebu, Manila, and Jolo (the Sulu polity), there is a substantial increase in the volumes of iron and bronze implements (probably weapons) being produced at coastal centers in this period (a tenfold increase from the fourteenth to fifteenth century at Tanjay), as well as an influx of foreign military technology obtained through foreign trade (including Chinese swivel guns, cannons, and swords and Japanese peaked helmets and armor). There also is an archaeologically visible shift by the fifteenth century from a defensive strategy favoring inland "refuge" hilltop fortifications to "homeland" defense systems (coral block fortifications or ditch-and-stockade complexes) surrounding most of the major trade ports (Dizon and Santiago 1994;

Junker 1999:354–356). Large-scale special-ized warrior groups or maritime mercenaries known by European and Chinese writers in the sixteenth century (e.g., the *maharlika* of the northern Philippines and the Malay *orang laut* of coastal Sumatra) may have emerged around this period with an ex-panded scale and intensity of warfare, along with emblems of warrior prestige (e.g., tooth filing and gold pegging, trophy skulls) that show up in increasing frequency in fifteenth–sixteenth-century cemeteries in the Philip-pines (Junker 1999:362–365). Analyses of burials in the Philippines also have demon-strated a startling increase in the numbers of violent deaths, mass graves, and decapita-tions, probably associated with ritual head taking, found in cemeteries dated to the last two centuries before European contact (Junker 1999:363).

Warfare and slave raiding were clearly one of the many competitive strategies of political alliance building and wealth accumulation by Southeast Asian elites. Expanding investment in militarism was an important means of pro-tecting foreign trade interests and jeopardiz-ing the flow of politically manipulable trade wealth to competing leaders. Since most cap-tured slaves were put to work in agricultural labor or exportable craft production, which freed up existing labor for wealth-enhancing foreign trade activities, or were used as ex-changeable wealth in politically significant bridewealth payments, slave raiding became a significant means of expanding a leader's political currency and extending his political sway. Ritual sacrifice of some captives during life-crisis or calendrical ceremonies and feasts perpetuated the image of rulers and other coalition builders as extraordinarily wealthy and powerful, further adding to their mag-netism for followers. The archaeological evidence from the Tanjay region of the Philip-pines emphasizes the significance of mili-tarism as a component of political economy: intensifying warfare and slave raiding ap-pears to have accompanied the increased em-phasis on foreign prestige-goods trade, the expanding circulation of wealth in ritual feasting contexts, and the emergence of polit-ical networks of expanding scale and com-plexity in fifteenth–sixteenth-century Philip-pine chiefdoms.

CONCLUSIONS: ALLIANCE NETWORKS IN SOUTHEAST ASIAN POLITICAL STRUCTURE AND POLITICAL ECONOMY

Perhaps as a consequence of certain demo-graphic, geographic, ecological, and cultural factors discussed in this chapter, precolonial Southeast Asian kingdoms and chiefdoms tended to be organized around personal al-liance and clientage networks rather than strongly corporate political entities. These highly volatile alliance networks were main-tained through the charismatic attraction of individuals, through theatrical ceremonial-ism highlighting the sacred power of rulers, and most important, through the circulation of wealth among allied leaders and between elite patrons and their fluctuating cadre of supporters. Power monopolies in early-second-millennium Southeast Asian states such as Melaka, Brunei, Makassar, Sulu, Pegu, Majapahit, and Ayudhya, as well as in the chiefdoms of the western archipelagoes, were created through tightly controlled prestational events that expanded political networks. These included exchanges of bridewealth for polygamous marriages, cir-culation of prestige goods as part of competi-tive feasting events, and even the capture of valuables and labor in maritime raiding.

Much of the politically manipulable wealth that circulated in these prestational contexts was obtained through long-distance prestige-goods trade, linking the island archi-pelagoes of insular Southeast Asia with the coastal ports of river valley states on the Southeast Asian mainland, the various Chi-nese empires (beginning at least as early as the third-century A.D. Han), the Hindu king-doms of southern India (by at least the sec-ond century A.D.), Arab trade ports along the Persian Gulf and Red Sea (sometime in the early first millennium A.D.), and later even East African maritime trading groups such as the Swahili. Indirectly, these vast South

China Sea–Indian Ocean trade networks even affected populations on the European and Australian continents at a surprisingly early date. Second-century A.D. Roman coins have been excavated in the tombs of nobility at the coastal Vietnam port of Oc-eo (the presumed capital of the second-fifth-century early Khmer kingdom), and Chinese silks and Southeast Asian metal goods have been reported at Roman sites. At the other end of the trade spectrum are foragers along the northern Australian coast who, for several archaeologically documented millennia, collected *trepang* (sea slug) and other products for exchange with Southeast Asian middleman traders such as the Macassans (of Sulawesi) for eventual export to China, obtaining metal axes and foreign art styles in return. The considerable significance of foreign trade as a source of political currency in the alliance-structured polities of Southeast Asia is probably best seen in the detailed Chinese records of competitive tributary missions to the Chinese court launched by Southeast Asian polities of varying scale and complexity (in the tenth century both the vastly powerful Srivijaya state on Sumatra and the tiny P'u-tuan chiefdom of the southern Philippines sponsored these expensive trade-focused royal junkets). Archaeological evidence, in the form of great volumes of foreign porcelains in elite habitation and burials, as well as the adoption of exotic writing systems (primarily Sanskrit based) and foreign religious ideologies in monumental inscriptions, supports the documentary evidence for an enduring emphasis in Southeast Asian kingdoms on exotic wealth and foreign cosmologies in political coalition building.

More significant than documenting the foreign trade itself, however, are the effects on local political economies and the expansion-contraction of political alliance networks. Because of their strong focus on network or alliance strategies of political power building, and perhaps also because of their heavy reliance on the vagaries of foreign trade, historically known Southeast Asian kingdoms and chiefdoms of the first millennium and early second millennium A.D. were generally characterized by highly conflictive political leadership, political configurations with little long-term stability, and a political history of repeated and short-term cycles of expansion and collapse. Most of what we know about the political history of specific polities, however, is due to the work of historians using Chinese documents and indigenous inscriptions, records that tell us little about how foreign trade was articulated with other aspects of local political economies and how fluctuating access to foreign wealth may have influenced relations of power in these polities. Archaeological work on Southeast Asian maritime trading polities has been extremely limited, particularly on the crucial regional scale, and I necessarily relied here on only a few examples of how archaeological research at both the site and regional levels has begun to deal with these issues of political structure and political economy. However, archaeological investigations on the Tanjay chiefdom of the early to mid-second millennium in the central Philippines, and on state-level polities such as Srivijaya and Kedah in present-day Malaysia and Indonesia, demonstrate that we can trace the dynamics of these alliance-structured political systems over long periods of time through the movement and deposition contexts of prestige goods and symbols of power. The archaeological evidence from Tanjay in particular shows that expansion of the polity scale in the fifteenth and sixteenth centuries was connected to, if not predicated on, competitive success in attracting foreign trade and in using that foreign trade wealth to support politically significant exchanges in ritual feasts, to finance greater wealth-generating maritime raiding, and to generally expand the regional reach of the chiefs' power through other forms of exchange (perhaps including the political opportunities created through polygamy and large bridewealth payments).

The Tanjay investigations, as well as archaeological research on historically known maritime trading kingdoms such as Srivijaya and Kedah, illustrate the necessity of regional-scale archaeological work rather than limited excavations at individual burial and settlement sites if we are to gain a better understanding of how the foreign connections emphasized in historical records actually shaped and transformed local political structures and political economies. In addition, long-term regional-scale archaeological investigations of specific polities or areas of complex society development in Southeast Asia will allow us to move away from the pitfalls of assuming panregional forms of political and economic organization and largely parallel cultural evolutionary trajectories (see Wolters 1999 for a historian's significant views on this issue). As emphasized in the chapters by Pauketat, Sherratt, and Stein (this volume), the tendency for archaeologists to talk about "Mississippian chiefdoms," "European Bronze Age chiefdoms," and "early Mesopotamian states" as if they were unitary sociopolitical phenomena obscures the significant ecological, historical, and cultural forces that shaped specific polities at particular points in time.

What is even more problematic in the Southeast Asian case is the comparative lack of archaeological evidence for the period of complex society development before the advent of the South China Sea–Indian Ocean trade in the early to mid-first millennium, the birth of an interaction network that not only linked the farthest reaches of Southeast Asia into an expansive "world system" of foreign states and empires but also spread the writing systems that recorded some of the impacts of these expanding foreign contacts. If, as argued here, long-standing geographic and ecological features endemic to the region and consequent demographic patterns were significant in creating decentralized, alliance-structured political units maintained through continuous material gifting, then we would expect that early Metal Age complex societies of the region would to some degree share this emphasis on network power strategies with later maritime trading states. Although archaeological evidence from Metal Age sites suggests that long-distance prestige-goods exchanges were significant elements of local political economies, this period also saw a significant amount of monumental construction, elaborate tombs, and other manifestations of strongly corporate power bases that are not as evident in many complex societies of the later historic period. Thus archaeologists working on Southeast Asian complex societies would be wise to heed Sherratt's warning that early and later complex societies in the region may not have any smooth "evolutionary" connection. They may be radically different from one another because of the latter's rapid insertion into a very complex world system that created new cultural values, social and political forms, and types of economic interactions within already varying local cultural systems.

Note

Many of the theoretical aspects of this work were developed while I was teaching in the Department of Anthropology at Western Michigan University. I would like to acknowledge the contributions of my colleagues there, particularly Allen Zagarell and Michael Nassaney, in influencing my thoughts on social and political structures in complex societies. Lauretta Eisenbach, also at Western Michigan, provided essential assistance in getting the revised chapter to the volume editors with the untimely breakdown of my computer system and graphics program. The archaeological fieldwork in the Tanjay region of the Philippines reported on here was carried out in 1992, 1993, 1994, and 1995 with funding from the National Geographic Society, the Mellon Foundation, and the University Research Council. My sincere appreciation goes to all the participants in the University of Utah Press roundtable at Snowbird; their comments and critiques contributed greatly to my revisions of this chapter. I would like to acknowledge particularly the assistance of Gary Feinman, whose insightful and detailed comments helped me rethink many of my arguments.

13

Comparative Insights into the Ancient Political Economies of West Africa

ANN BROWER STAHL

The tendency to parse studies of ancient economies into two categories—comparative, evolutionary, and generalizing approaches on one hand, and specific, historical, and contextual approaches on the other—glosses the complexities of studies that work to move beyond reductionist neoevolutionary logic and attend to the context and complexity of regional cultural sequences (Yoffee 1993; Yoffee and Sherratt 1993). Empirically grounded case studies have tempered the excesses of earlier evolutionary approaches, particularly with respect to the growing recognition that the formative stages of complex social forms cannot adequately be modeled on the basis of ethnographic cases perceived as "survivals" of earlier forms (Shennan 1993b; Sherratt, this volume; Yoffee 1993). The histories of "simple" societies were linked to the emergence of "complex" societies with which they interacted, and these cannot be taken as separable units for analysis (for an insightful ethnographic commentary, see Sharpe 1986; also Sherratt, this volume; Stahl 1999c; Stein, this volume).

Although I am convinced, along with Yoffee and Sherratt (1993; also Sherratt, this volume), that the question of what preceded complex societies is primarily an archaeological one, the models that inform our imaginings of ancient political economies continue to be grounded in historic and ethnographic exemplars (e.g., prestige-goods models; see

Sherratt, this volume). Given the centrality of political economies, an important component of our investigations into ancient ones needs to be a comparative historical analysis of more recent ones that inform our models of understanding. Thus a central argument of this chapter is that understanding the linkages and trajectories of more recent political economies provides an important comparative platform for engaging in analysis of ancient ones. Comparative analyses allow us to explore commonalities and divergences between ancient and recent patterns and can help us expand on the partialities of ethnographic models of political order, production, and consumption. But a related argument that I develop here is that the limits of our understanding do not lie in a paucity of data alone. Rather, the preoccupations we bring to the study of past political economies shape the contours of our knowledge in often unacknowledged ways. My focus in this chapter is on how the intellectual and political economic contexts that have informed African archaeology have influenced the directions of research and modes of investigation into ancient political economies. I argue that African archaeology, and therefore our knowledge of Africa's ancient political economies, has been shaped by three special burdens: (1) the widespread negative imagery of Africa, (2) a rich ethnographic heritage, and (3) a complex and turbulent history of interaction with Europe

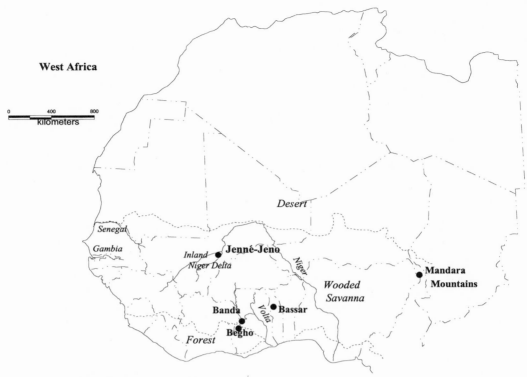

Figure 13.1. Selected sites in West Africa

and the Americas. Though these burdens are overlapping and related, I discuss each in turn, exploring their implications for our research priorities, investigative strategies, and the evidential sources we deem relevant (see also Stahl 1999c, 2001). I pay particular attention to how our understanding of production, consumption, and exchange has been shaped by these factors and conclude by highlighting some new perspectives of recent research and their implications for our images of Africa.

IMAGES OF AFRICA

Our understanding of Africa's past has been fundamentally shaped by deeply rooted, negative Western imagery of the continent. The portrayal of Africa as a "dark continent" (Achebe 1978; Hammond and Jablow 1970; Keim 1999; Mudimbe 1988; Rigby 1996) served as a foil for postindependence African history and archaeology as scholars embarked on a program of recuperating positive images of Africa. This emphasis directed his-

torical and archaeological investigations toward (1) demonstrating the complexity of African societies, (2) countering the image of Africans as uninventive and reliant on outside stimuli for technological or sociopolitical innovation (Sinclair et al. 1993:9–12), and (3) documenting the dynamism of African societies (Connah 1998). Whereas colonial scholars assumed that complex African societies (such as the Sudanic states of Ghana, Mali, and Songhai) were a product of external contact (e.g., with Islamic North Africa through the trans-Saharan caravan trade; Levtzion 1976:114–118), the 1970s witnessed a concerted effort to investigate the pre-Islamic roots of the Sudanic states (e.g., at Jenné-Jeno, Figure 13.1; McIntosh and McIntosh 1993; also Connah 1987). In similar fashion, archaeologists worked to demonstrate the antiquity and independent origins of other hallmarks of progress (agriculture, metallurgy, and state-level organization; Stahl 1999c:43). In the 1960s and 1970s, then, historians and archaeologists sought to show that Africa had a past worthy of respect and independent of outside influence.

Scholars working to decolonize African history framed Africa's claim to respect in terms of universal criteria of progress and civilization—that Africa, like other world areas, had cities, kings, sophisticated art, and other markers of civility (Fuglestad 1992; Neale 1985, 1986). At one extreme, Afrocentric scholars insisted that these hallmarks of civilization developed first in Africa and diffused from there (e.g., Asante and Asante 1990; Diop 1974; for critiques, see Blakey 1995; Holl 1995:194–208). Afrocentrism thus reversed the direction of influence but left the theoretical and methodological foundations of colonial historiography intact (Holl 1995:204). Other reformulations similarly failed to question universal criteria of progress (Fuglestad 1992; Neale 1985, 1986). The typological separation of states, chieftaincies, and tribes into discrete evolutionary units went unquestioned and thus diverted attention from the intermeshing political economies that connected societies of different scales (Sharpe 1986; see also Shennan 1993b; Sherratt, this volume; Yoffee 1993). Our understanding of ancient West African political economies was thus skewed toward centers and long-distance trade rather than so-called peripheries and broader patterns of production and consumption (McIntosh 1995; McIntosh and McIntosh 1993; Posnansky 1973, 1987).

The effort to demonstrate that Africa's past was "just as good as Europe's, because it was the same" (Neale 1985:10) gave way in the 1980s and 1990s to greater attention to the *distinctive* features of African societies. Multiculturalism in the West was accompanied by a sense that respect for African patterns of cultural development did not hinge on their universality; now distinctiveness and divergence were valued (R. McIntosh 1998; S. McIntosh 1999; Schmidt and Patterson 1995). Scholars argued that heterarchical configurations of power characterized many African societies and that Africa provided examples of "alternative pathways to complexity" (S. McIntosh 1999:20):

While it is certainly possible to identify African societies that look and function in many ways like classic Polynesian chiefdoms—with conical clans, elite control of craft production, and differential access of elites to land and, especially, cattle—the real story of interest...lies in the many complex African societies that are not so configured. In many African kingdoms, the chief's domestic unit (including wives and slaves) is directly involved in subsistence pursuits; attached craft specialists are rare or non-existent; and it is the king's job to ensure adequate access to land for all his subjects. (S. McIntosh 1999:22)

These distinctive forms of social political organization were arguably underwritten by alternative forms and conceptualizations of power that flowed less from material wealth than from less tangible but nonetheless potent resources—what Schoenbrun (1999: 139) terms "creative power" (as distinct from "instrumental" power). Whereas instrumental power flows from control of people's actions, creative power "manipulates and invents forms of meaning...[in the] semantic universe of moral agency" (Schoenbrun 1999:139; cf. Guyer and Belinga 1995). This distinction has led to growing concern with the phenomenology of power, with its semantic conceptualizations and manifestations in African sociopolitical life, particularly in the multiethnic societies of West Africa (e.g., David 1992; MacEachern 1994; McIntosh 1998; McNaughton 1988; Schoenbrun 1998, 1999; Sterner 1992). Again, the emphasis in recent literature is on *distinctive* aspects of African sociopolitical life, though broader relevance is developed in terms of how African examples might illuminate variability in other world areas (S. McIntosh 1999) or act as "deep-time sources of successful social plurality" (McIntosh 1998:xvi–xvii) that can serve as models for sociopolitical organization today.

The attention to social plurality is associated with a growing concern for the complex intermeshing of societies of different scales. In Africa this interest has played out most visibly in debates over the identity of the Kalahari San as isolated foragers or as peasants participating in a complex political economy shaped by the demands of long-distance exchange and capitalist production (Gordon and Douglas 2000; Lee 1990, 1992; Solway and Lee 1990; Wilmsen 1989, 1995; Wilmsen and Denbow 1990). Though this debate had considerable visibility, archaeologists and historians working elsewhere in Africa also have paid increasing attention to the interactions of societies formerly viewed as occupying different evolutionary stages (i.e., tribes, chiefdoms, states; e.g., Azarya 1996; Brooks 1993; Denbow 1999; MacEachern 1993, 2001; McIntosh 1998; Robertshaw 1999).

In sum, negative images of Africa have directed the attention of historians and archaeologists to particular aspects of ancient political economies, those deemed relevant to demonstrating the civility and complexity of African peoples. More recent concerns with plurality and the distinctive features of African polities have broadened the scope of investigations, focusing on the relations between societies of different scales and the cultural specificity of power relations. A concern with the distinctive aspects of African forms of organization and conceptualizations of power have led historians and archaeologists alike to renewed study of the ethnographic literature on Africa as sources of comparative models. For example, Susan McIntosh's (ed. 1999) recent edited volume includes a number of studies that explore alternate forms of political organization drawn from the "ethnographic record"—a term that roughly means the twentieth century. This leads us to the second burden that frames our understanding of ancient West African political economies—a rich ethnographic heritage.

AFRICA'S ETHNOGRAPHIC HERITAGE
Though African societies have been marginalized in theoretical discussions of cultural complexity (S. McIntosh 1999:22), they have been central to the development of theory and methodology in social anthropology (Moore 1993:3). Africa's special place in anthropology was shaped by its colonial history. Colonization occurred relatively late over much of the continent and took the form of administrative rather than settler colonization in most areas. Although ethnographic study of African societies was shaped by the colonial context in which it was conducted (Asad 1973; cf. Lewis 1998), this context differed dramatically from that of North American ethnographic research: "Many African rural economies continued long-established agricultural and pastoral practices. Indigenous languages, and social and cultural frameworks, though profoundly affected by the colonial transformations, remained strikingly different from those of the Europeans. There was an African Africa that was a going concern" (Moore 1993:6).

Yet Africa's rich ethnographic heritage has been a mixed blessing for those interested in historical studies (Koponen 1986; Stahl 2001:3–15; Vansina 1987). Just as archaeologists highlighted certain kinds of sites for investigation, anthropologists focused ethnographic inquiry on certain kinds of societies; they were drawn to the study of "coherent," bounded societies and eschewed more heterogeneous societies typical of interstitial areas between homogenous tribes (what Kopytoff [1987] terms the "internal African frontier;" see also Amselle 1993, 1998). These ethnographic accounts provided rich sources of comparative insight into the social, political, and economic organization of African societies. Yet they portrayed African societies in a timeless ethnographic present (or what Chance [1996] terms an "ethnographic past") in accounts shaped by anthropology's preoccupation with the social statics of rural "tribal" societies (Ekeh 1990; Goody 1990; Thornton 1983). The belief that formal colonial relations had a limited and recent impact on rural African societies contributed to the sense that Africans were among the "people without history" (Wolf 1982). This is not to say that anthropologists were unaware of the changes wrought by colonial expansion (Goody 1998); rather, pioneering ethnographers tended to produce two types of accounts: "One was the closed description of the way of life of particular African peoples, a kind of timeless abstraction of 'the way it probably was' before the colonial period, as if native life could be conceived as a self-contained system uncontaminated by outside contacts. The second mode of description was…concerned with the historical moment at which the fieldwork was done. This genre provided data on everything from labor migration to the impact of colonial institutions" (Moore 1994:39). The first set of accounts was central to the theoretical development of social anthropology and focused on social and cultural practices in the "before time," before the disruptions associated with the imposition of colonial authority. Methodologically, these accounts derived from a combination of remembrances and sorting among extant practices that were deemed more or less "traditional," as if "the original pre-colonial tribal society still existed inside a carapace of colonial and postcolonial bureaucracy and western technology. Chip the colonial shell away and you will be back to the traditional core" (Leach 1989:43). Change was assumed to be recent and superficial (Adas 1995; Koponen 1986; Thornton 1983), an assumption that underwrote the practice of extrapolating contemporary "traditional" practices into the past, contributing to what Owusu (1978:321) describes as the "essential anachronism of the ethnographic enterprise." Practices and arrangements perceived as traditional were taken out of time, severed from the material political economic contexts that shaped them, and used to reconstruct past practices and arrangements associated with other times and contexts.

The growing recognition of historical global connections (e.g., Wolf 1982) made this approach untenable. In recent decades the historical dynamics of African societies have become central to anthropological inquiry (e.g., Berry 1993; Jean Comaroff and John Comaroff 1991; John Comaroff and Jean Comaroff 1997; Guyer 1995; H. Moore and Vaughan 1994; S. Moore 1986; Stoller 1995). Recent studies explore the impact of colonization on African systems of produc-

tion and consumption, forms of political organization, identity, and so on. Today it is well recognized that many of the ethnic groups that formed the core of colonial ethnography were a product of colonial processes (Lentz 1994, 1995; Peel 1983, 1989; Sharpe 1986). Yet even now there persists a lingering sense of a definable *precolonial* period during which African societies were relatively stable or perhaps varied only within certain limits that can be adequately modeled from ethnographic sources (cf. Chanock 1985; David and Sterner 1999; Ekeh 1990; Guyer and Belinga 1995). These "autonomous preconditions" (Thomas 1991:37, 88) provide a baseline against which to assess change in the colonial period, implying that before their incorporation into a capitalist world system, African political economies were relatively unchanging. But this approach in turn raises questions about how scholars reconstruct autonomous preconditions. The degree of change and dynamism is a question to be asked rather than an assumption to be made, one best addressed through archaeological sources (given the paucity of written sources before formal colonization).

I take up the question of evidence and methodology below but for the moment observe that archaeologists, historians, and historical anthropologists rightly treat recent African societies as informative sources for modeling past African societies. Yet we often use ethnographic models to create a past in the image of the present (Stahl 1993, 2001: 19–40), particularly when modeling aspects of life that are assumed to have endured relatively unchanged through global historical processes (e.g., subsistence and local craft production, and village life more generally). Ethnoarchaeological studies, for example, seldom include a historical or archaeological component to assess how contemporary patterns of production and consumption may have altered through time. Further, many historical anthropologists and historians have felt comfortable using ethnographic accounts to establish a precolonial baseline against which to judge change in the colonial period. In the process, we have largely ignored the possibility that the practices and structures captured in ethnographic accounts emerged through a long history of interaction with Europe, Asia, and the Americas, a history with much deeper roots than the rather shallow time frame of formal colonization (see Sherratt, this volume). Before returning to questions of sources and methods, I turn now to the third burden of African archaeology: Africa's long and turbulent history of interaction with Europe and the Americas.

"TURBULENCE AND LOSS": THE LEGACY OF AFRICA'S GLOBAL CONNECTIONS

In a thought-provoking work Guyer (1999) argues that Africa's history has been shaped by the thematics of turbulence and loss. West Africa's involvement in European-dominated commercial networks extends back some five centuries; its involvement in the Saharan trade extends back at least a millennium. These complex and variable commercial and political networks have been associated with periods of turbulence and uncertainty that in some cases opened the way to innovation. At the same time, turbulence has been associated with loss—the disappearance of certain pathways and possibilities for action that previously gave shape to African societies but that are lost to historical memory (Guyer 1999; see also David and Sterner 1999). For example, Guyer and Belinga (1995) suggest that past processes of social differentiation in central Africa are inadequately captured by the vocabulary of markets, accumulation, and divisions of labor because wealth rested as much on the possession of knowledge as on the possession of things. Here leadership was rooted in *composition*—the bringing together of people with different knowledges (of crafts, the supernatural, diverse ecologies, and so on)—rather than in *accumulation* (see also Kopytoff 1999:93). Social theory has neglected compositional practices because of their "relative decline as an organizational principle in the colonial period. Kinship and kingship survived the disorder and demographic collapse of colonial rule that may have eliminated enough of the wealth that was 'people' to profoundly impoverish the compositional process" (Guyer and Belinga 1995:118). In a related vein, Ekeh (1990) suggests that forms of lineage organization that are taken as an enduring and quintessential feature of African social organization may be a legacy of the disruption associated with the slave trade. Relatively weak African states offered insufficient protection from the threat of enslavement, and thus lineage organizations may have been strengthened to offer some measure of protection to their members. The implication is that Africa's rich ethnographic heritage must be viewed *in temporal context and in relation to the contingent global relations* that shaped it. We know little of how the daily lives of African peoples were shaped and reshaped through periods of demographic collapse associated with the slave trade, with the introduction of New World crops, and with new forms of production and consumption.[1] Although processes of change—including turbulence and loss—may have intensified in the period immediately preceding and during formal colonization, they were ongoing processes with a long, complex history that we are only beginning to unravel. As a starting point we should assume that the ancient political economies of West Africa are inadequately captured by historical and ethnographic sources and that we must work to develop research strategies that will help us move beyond the limits of ethnography.

These "special burdens"—Western imagery of Africa, Africa's rich ethnographic heritage, and its history of turbulence and loss—have shaped the contours of inquiry and knowledge of ancient political economies. In an effort to recuperate more positive images, scholars have trained attention on particular aspects and qualities of Africa's past—first, signs of complexity; more recently, signs of distinctiveness. As we have become aware of the complex, intermeshing relations between societies of different scales, we have drawn unevenly on Africa's rich ethnographic heritage, using insights of ethnography to provide information on aspects of daily life or smaller-scale societies that have been overlooked in an archaeology of complexity. Finally, we have been insufficiently attentive to the effects of turbulence and loss (Guyer 1999)—particularly in the centuries leading up to formal colonization—on twentieth-century African societies as described in ethnographies. Below I discuss evidential sources and their potential for illuminating Africa's ancient political economies before turning to an exploration of case studies that anticipate new strategies and research directions.

EVIDENTIAL SOURCES OF INSIGHT INTO AFRICA'S ANCIENT POLITICAL ECONOMIES

A variety of evidential sources—documents, oral histories, comparative ethnographic and linguistic data, and material remains—provide information on ancient West African political economies. These sources have different temporal and spatial relations to the past practices and arrangements we want to learn about (Stahl 1999b). Archaeological materials were generated by the people whose lives we are attempting to reconstruct whereas documents were often produced in distant areas by foreigners (Arab chroniclers, European traders, colonial officials, etc.). Oral sources, which play a prominent role in African history, are generated by descendant peoples but in contemporary contexts. Comparative ethnographic and linguistic data are generated in the present through a study of descendant communities (loosely construed) under the assumption that a "direct historical" connection links the community to its antecedents. Such connections have long been assumed to strengthen the veracity of ethnographic models (Stahl 2001:21–23).

We must attend to the obvious strengths and weaknesses of each evidential source (the material evidence of archaeology sheds light on rather different aspects of daily life than, say, texts); but we have been less careful to attend to what we might think of as the "formation processes" that shape these disparate archives (see Trouillot 1995:1–30). In other words, each archive (of documents, oral histories, ethnographies, archaeological data sets) has a distinct formation history that

shapes its strengths and weaknesses as a source of insight into past political economies. Archives are differentially shaped by the disciplinary preoccupations of archaeologists (with states, cities, and long-distance trade), anthropologists (with tribal societies perceived as outside history), and historians (with chieftaincy histories and matters of state; Stahl 2001:1–18). As such, they present challenges for how we use them to frame our understanding of ancient political economies. My concern here is with how we triangulate among these diverse sources to arrive at insights into ancient economies, and particularly with our use of historic and ethnographic analogues (for an extended discussion, see Stahl 2001:19–40).

Early reconstructions of ancient economic practices and sociopolitical arrangements took an "illustrative" approach to analogy (Stahl 1993:236). Ethnography was assumed to provide a reasonable guide to "traditional" society and culture in the "before time" and could therefore be used to flesh out the bare bones of archaeological evidence. Ethnographic sources were thought to be particularly relevant to the reconstruction of local economic phenomena—that is, production for local consumption—as it was assumed that the structure of traditional subsistence or craft production was only superficially affected by broader geopolitical economic changes. Historical linguistic reconstructions were linked to the archaeological sources based on glottochronological/lexicostatistical insights and were similarly used to fill out the details of cultural inventories—for example, the presence of crops and technologies that might not survive archaeologically (e.g., Ehret 1982, 1984). Because the evidence culled from these diverse archives (textual, oral historical, linguistic, archaeological) was shaped by the concerns of the scholars who generated them, these sources tended to shed light on different aspects of societies and on societies of different scales (texts and oral histories, on complex societies and political struggles; archaeology, on centers, long-distance trade, and other aspects of cultural complexity; ethnography, on social arrangements and political organization among less complex societies). This contributed to the sense that these sources could be used *additively*, one line of evidence filling in the gaps of others (cf. Trouillot 1995).

Yet an illustrative, additive approach obscures the different temporal and spatial relations among sources, as for example when an early-twentieth-century account on the social organization of craft production is used to animate archaeological evidence for specialized craft production in ancient sites (Stahl 1999b; cf. Costin, this volume). The organization of cloth production provides a useful illustration. In the early twentieth century, strip-woven cloth was produced in many areas across West Africa; though arrangements varied, women often grew and spun cotton, men dyed and wove it. Production was often household based and intended for household use. Etienne (1977) and Roberts (1984) stressed the role of cloth production in creating reciprocal obligations between husbands and wives; both argued that these obligations were transformed in the colonial period as local cloth production was first commercialized and later collapsed in the face of competition with imported cloth. They presented a compelling case based on historical and ethnographic sources of how cloth production was reshaped by the colonial political economy, but they assumed that early colonial accounts adequately captured the nature of precolonial cloth production. In other words, they assumed that the form of household production and gendered division of labor described by early colonial officials had deep temporal roots. Yet this is a question that must be posed and addressed through comparative evaluation with temporally appropriate archaeological sources, not an assumption to be made. We need to be attuned to the possibility that the dynamics of cloth production changed in relation to contingent political economic circumstances in the so-called precolonial period as well (see below; Stahl and Cruz 1998).

In some senses the problems associated with an illustrative, additive use of ethnographic models have been exacerbated by

the desire to expand our understanding of ancient political economies across societal scales, to capture how the lives of city dwellers were intertwined with those of villagers in smaller-scale societies. Because archaeologists have paid little attention to small-scale societies, local production, or consumption, we draw heavily on ethnography in modeling village life, local and regional exchange, patterns of craft production, and so on. This tendency has been encouraged by the florescence of ethnoarchaeological studies in Africa.[2] Because many crafts persisted into the twentieth century, we have comparatively robust documentation of potting and to a lesser extent weaving and iron production. Unfortunately, many ethnoarchaeological accounts reproduce the limitations of early ethnographic accounts in being insufficiently attentive to the broader context and contingencies that shape practices in the present. In other words, "traditional practices" continue to be viewed as outside historical process. Nonetheless, contemporary studies can provide invaluable comparative data for exploring craft production in the past. Their comparative value is lost, however, when it is assumed that contemporary arrangements adequately model past arrangements.

We should anticipate that ancient economic practices and arrangements varied from historically and ethnographically documented ones (see Storey, this volume)—that even though potting, weaving, and smithing continue to be vital crafts in many rural areas, the organization of these pursuits was likely altered as villagers were incorporated into a colonial, capitalist political economy (Cruz 2003). Pressures of monetization in the twentieth century (Guyer 1995) have restructured production. New materials and/or techniques may have reshaped production practices (i.e., use of imported threads in weaving; see Sherratt, this volume). Subsistence production was reshaped by the introduction of new crops and pressures to produce cash crops. In this sense we need to embrace a *comparative* approach, one that explores the points of similarity and divergence in our diverse lines of evidence—ethnographic, historical, and archaeological. As Wylie (1985) argues, divergences are especially important because they show how past and present may have differed. But particularly important for our understanding of *ancient* economies is a historically contingent study of more *recent* economies. Historians and historically oriented anthropologists are producing valuable accounts of how production and consumption were transformed over the last century or two by changing involvement in a global political economy (e.g., Frank 1993; Guyer 1995; Isaacman and Roberts 1995; Roberts 1992; Steiner 1985, among others). But we are only now beginning to realize archaeology's potential to investigate how African political economies were reshaped through a long history of global interaction (see also Yoffee 1993; Yoffee and Sherratt 1993). A focus on *origins* and *antiquity* associated with the effort to recuperate positive images of Africa has directed attention to early-period sites (the earliest cities, the earliest metallurgy, etc.) that promised to demonstrate Africa's active role in world prehistory (Stahl 1999c). Investigations of more recent sites have focused primarily on coastal "historic" sites directly associated with European colonial occupations (e.g., Bredwa-Mensah and Crossland 1997; DeCorse 1992, 1993, 1998a, 1998b, 2001; K. Kelly 1997a, 1997b, 2001). Findings on the consumption of European goods, spatial relations between African and Europeans, and other aspects of daily life valuably augment the (comparatively) robust historical documentation on coastal societies. But we know little of how these relations reshaped production, consumption, and exchange in inland areas, where we face a "parched documentary landscape" (Cohen and Odhiambo 1989:16) and a virtually unexplored archaeological landscape.

I turn now to several recent case studies that focus on precisely these issues in interior West Africa, arguing that these sorts of studies are crucial if we are to develop historically sensitive comparative models for the exploration of more ancient political economies.

PRODUCTION, CONSUMPTION, AND EXCHANGE IN RECENT CENTURIES: CASE STUDIES

De Barros's (1985, 1987, 2001) research on Bassar ironworking combines archaeological, oral historical, and documentary sources to explore the changing nature of production in West Africa over the last millennium. His work, focused in northern Togo, represents one of the few areal studies in West Africa to explore temporal changes in the organization and output of iron production. The varied topography of the Bassar area is associated with iron-rich hills that both supplied high-grade ore and served as a refuge during periods of political unrest and slave raiding. Drawing on small-scale survey and excavation, de Barros argues that the scale of iron production intensified through time, particularly in the western reaches of his study area, where higher-grade ores were found. Increased demand for finished iron products (weapons, horse paraphernalia, and perhaps protective devices such as helmets) was associated with the emergence of cavalry-based states to the west in the sixteenth and seventeenth centuries (Dagomba, Mamprusi, Gonja). Iron production in Bassar increased in response by an estimated 400–600 percent in the period circa A.D. 1550–1800.[3] At the same time, specialization increased: some settlements focused on smelting, others on smithing, some on charcoal making, others on potting. This period was characterized by higher population densities, which de Barros (2001) suggests may have been due to the importation of slaves (who served as laborers) and the in-migration of ironworkers, as well as natural population increase.

Historical sources suggest that Bassar settlement strategies were altered by periodic but intensive slave raiding in the late eighteenth and nineteenth centuries (de Barros 2001). Though the area had been subject to occasional raiding from the fifteenth century, more intensive raiding was prompted by Asante's tribute demands against Dagomba. After imposing its hegemony over its northern neighbors, the forest state of Asante demanded annual tribute in cattle, sheep, cloth, and slaves. Dagomba's annual levy is estimated to have been on the order of 2,000 slaves, 800 cattle, and 1,600 sheep. "Bassar, with its flourishing iron industry, growing population, and abundant cattle, was a natural place for the Dagomba to turn to meet their annual quota" (de Barros 2001:69). In response, Bassar's population abandoned open areas and established settlements close to the hills, where they could flee in times of attack. The Bassar peneplain was virtually abandoned as population concentrated in four historical centers. The Bassar chieftaincy appears to have been founded in the late eighteenth or early nineteenth century, and de Barros (2001) suggests that it may have developed as a defense against intensive slave raiding. Yet ironworking did not suffer any major decreases in Bassar until the final decades of the nineteenth century, following a Dagomba siege on the town of Bassar in the 1870s. Production increased again in the early years of the German protectorate (after 1894) but finally succumbed under combined pressure from competing imports and a 1951 ban on smelting instituted by French colonial authorities to control deforestation.

Potting too was affected by the changing political economic fortunes of the Bassar area. The pressure of Dagomba slave raiding led to decreased supplies of pottery, originating in the northern and eastern reaches of Bassar. Local production around the town of Bassar became increasingly important, and de Barros (2001:75) suggests that the cluster of specialized potting villages around Mount Bassar may have been founded in this period.

De Barros's study presents a dynamic picture of craft production and consumption, one that was fundamentally shaped and reshaped by contingent regional and interregional political economic circumstances. Levels of production variably intensified or declined across the region through time; intensification was achieved in multiple ways— through use of enslaved labor or increased specialization. Neither ethnographic nor historical sources adequately capture the complex changes, and de Barros's contribution is substantially strengthened by the com-

parative use of archaeological sources that reveal changing patterns of craft production through time.

Research associated with the Mandara Archaeological Project (MAP), centered on the Mandara Mountains of northern Cameroon, also provides historically sensitive comparative models that may prove useful in investigating ancient political economies. The Mandara Mountains are home to a diverse array of lineage-based ethnic groups collectively referred to as Montagnards, whereas the surrounding plains are home to a variety of Muslim groups characterized by centralized polities. MAP used ethnoarchaeological and historical sources to focus on issues of identity, style, symbols, and ideology (David 1992; David et al. 1988; Lyons 1998; MacEachern 1998; Sterner 1989, 1992). But the project also generated insights into the changing nature of technology and the relations between societies of different scales. Here I focus on MAP's findings about how settlement systems and economic relations were restructured by the region's growing involvement in the North African trade.

MacEachern's work focused on the northern Mandara Mountains, where a diverse array of Montagnard groups came under pressure from the predatory Wandala state that dominated the surrounding lowlands (MacEachern 1993, 2001, 2003). Historically, these groups lived in uneasy tension. The Islamic Wandala were organized into a centralized polity with a cavalry and access to firearms. In recent centuries the Wandala depended on Montagnard populations for supplies of iron, which the Wandala in turn traded to larger states west and north in what is today Nigeria and Chad (Bornu, Kanem) in return for horses, guns, chain mail, cloth, and salt (MacEachern 1993:256). Yet the Montagnard populations provided an equally important resource for the Wandala: slaves, who were incorporated into Wandala society or traded on to Kanem or Bornu for consumption by North African markets. Though their mountain home provided some measure of protection from mounted Wandala raiders, kidnapping and raiding were ongoing threats to Montagnards into the twentieth century. As one Montagnard man observed: "The Wandala are clever. They bought our iron, then used it to make the shackles that they held us with" (MacEachern 1993:257–258).

The Montagnard/Wandala relationship was thus fraught with ambivalence—Montagnard populations relied on their Wandala trade connections to obtain salt and protein (in the form of dried fish), which were in short supply in their densely inhabited mountainous home (MacEachern 1993:257); yet at the same time, the Wandala threatened the integrity of Montagnard society through repeated slave raids. The Wandala depended on the Montagnards for access to vital trade commodities (iron, slaves) but also for access to mountain refuge in times when the Wandala were subject to attacks from their more powerful neighbors. "Such occupations could not have taken place without the cooperation of Montagnard lineages; stored goods could disappear, wells could be poisoned or rendered unusable, and resistance could make the Wandala's position untenable" (MacEachern 1993:258).

According to archaeological evidence, Montagnard occupation of the Mandara highlands began comparatively recently (David 1998). Survey has revealed no evidence of occupation before about 500 years ago; this is consistent with oral sources that stress the immigrant origins of the Montagnards (MacEachern 1993:259). Occupation of the highlands coincides with an abandonment of the plains by the so-called Sao (an ambiguous term used historically to refer to the indigenous inhabitants of the plains south of Lake Chad; MacEachern 2001:136, 144). The plains, by contrast, were occupied from circa A.D. 300. Site densities here indicate relatively high population densities, though there is no evidence for site hierarchies. In the period before the hills were colonized, iron smelting occurred at a variety of locations throughout the plains and near the base of the mountains where iron ore was available (MacEachern 2001:135).

Drawing on oral historical, documentary, and archaeological sources, MacEachern posits that the northern Mandara highlands were colonized as indigenous plains-dwelling peoples came under increasing pressure from mounted slave raiders, first from larger states (Kanem) and later (by the seventeenth century) from the Wandala, who operated as "subcontractors" for Bornu (MacEachern 2001:141–143). Colonization of the mountains probably began in the sixteenth century. Although many colonists may have arrived as families or kin groups, MacEachern (2001: 145) suggests that the terrace systems that sustained Montagnard agriculture required relatively high population densities for construction and maintenance. The Wandala embrace of slave raiding thus drove other plains-dwelling people into the mountains in substantial numbers, with effects on regional craft production. Whereas iron had previously been smelted at plains sites, smelting became confined to the mountain edges near the source of iron ore. Collecting the ore that occurs in the form of alluvial deposits at the base of the Mandara Mountains is labor intensive. Wandala access to these ores became more difficult with Montagnard occupation of the mountains as Wandala became subject to surprise attacks from nearby Montagnards. The Wandala thus depended on Montagnard smelters to gain access to the ores or smelted blooms, which were subsequently modified into tools by Wandala smiths (MacEachern 1993:257).

A strength of the Mandara project is its attention to variability in this area of astonishing cultural diversity. The organization of recent iron production in the northern highlands, for example, differed considerably from that among other Montagnard groups, where ironworking is the province of "casted" endogamous technological specialists ("blacksmiths"; David and Robertson 1996; MacEachern 2003; Sterner and David 1991).[4] In the central Mandara highlands, iron production is the province of castes (among the Kapsiki and Mafa) whose members are also responsible for divination, curing, and burial. Women of these castes practice potting and midwifery (David and Robertson 1996:129–130; Sterner and David

1991). By contrast, there were no restrictions on who could smelt or pot in the northern Mandara Mountains, and here many families produced iron and pottery for both household use and sale (MacEachern 2003). Among casted groups in the central mountains there is no standard repertoire of specializations (Sterner and David 1991:361), though as elsewhere in West Africa these groups are regarded with a combination of fear and respect for their power (e.g., McNaughton 1988). The concentration of technological specialists among a casted minority has important archaeological ramifications since a socially distinct group produces the vast majority of durable material culture (ceramics and metal; MacEachern 1998:127; 2003). We might expect considerable homogeneity in style and technology, though homogeneity in raw material would depend on the mobility of these specialists (i.e., whether they were itinerant).

In some cases Montagnard groups with and without castes speak closely related languages. These close relationships have led MacEachern (2003) to suggest that the dichotomy probably was due not to different group origins but instead to processes that took place after the mountains were initially settled. In other words, casted technological and ritual specialists may be a recent innovation among some groups, or conversely a casted form of organization may have disappeared among some Montagnards. MacEachern (2003) suspects that the unrestricted form of specialization in the northern mountains was well suited to meet export demands since production could be expanded in caste-based production systems by recruiting additional personnel in numbers that could probably be met only over generational time spans. The specific trajectory remains to be worked out through a comparative assessment of diverse sources. But an important implication is that although casted groups may be an ancient feature of the West African social landscape, castes are dynamic and subject to transformation. In her historical study of West African castes Tamari (1991:247) observes that "the most frequent transforma-

tions included: increase in importance of a secondary occupation, until it became the primary occupation; a complete change in occupation; change in rank and in the nature of relations with the majority population." Moreover, in some cases formal castes have disappeared; in others immigrant castes have been assimilated into host societies (Tamari 1991:248). Further, we lack a clear understanding of how slaving might have shaped caste organization. Historically, casted people formed a minority of the population in West African societies (from less than 5 to at most 20 percent of the population); "in contrast, slaves formed up to fifty per cent of the population in certain areas in the estimates of some eighteenth- and nineteenth-century explorers" (Tamari 1991:224). Caste membership in some cases offered a measure of protection against enslavement, but again it remains a question of how the dynamics of caste may have been shaped and reshaped by changing forms and modes of slavery. This example underscores the ways in which labor organization was reshaped by intensified production (Costin, this volume) and cautions us against assuming that ethnographic models of caste adequately capture ancient forms.

The Mandara Archaeological Project also has generated useful data on changes in iron production after World War II, when local craftsmen gained access to large supplies of imported scrap metal. This new source reversed the flow of metal; Wandala towns that were formerly recipients of blooms smelted in the highlands now supplied scrap metal to Montagnard peoples (David and Robertson 1996:133). Wandala smiths, who had long stressed forging over smelting, took advantage of expanded supplies to broaden their repertoire and produce tool forms targeted at specific ethnic groups. Their organization into guilds minimized competition among Wandala smiths and fostered specialization (by age, technical skill, and so on). They embraced marketing innovations and relied on middlemen to ply their goods, which allowed them more time at the forge (David and Robertson 1996:134). By contrast, Montagnard smiths now obtained raw material from Wandala markets and continued to operate as "generalists"—individual smiths producing an array of tool forms that they marketed themselves. This study offers general insights into how technological change affects the organization of labor and marketing strategies, but as David and Robertson (1996:140) emphasize, context and contingencies shaped the direction of change.

Though the Mandara case study offers interesting preliminary insight into the changing character of production in relation to changing political economic conditions, published materials provide limited insight into the organization of production as revealed by archaeological sources. Nonetheless, the Mandara project has produced a number of robust hypotheses regarding settlement, production, consumption, and exchange that can be assessed through expanded archaeological testing. As in de Barros's study, the project provides a framework for assessing how "turbulence and loss" (Guyer 1999) reshaped economic practices over the last five centuries, promising a temporally sensitive comparative model that can be used to assess the character of political economic arrangements in more ancient contexts. Such projects are crucial if we want to know to what extent and how practices of craft production, consumption, and exchange were reshaped by (minimally) several centuries of transformation and upheaval associated with the slave trade (in its various forms; see Lovejoy 1983; Manning 1996; Watson 1980), among other geopolitical processes.

A third case study demonstrates archaeology's potential to inform how production and consumption on the local level were shaped by larger geopolitical contingencies. Banda Research Project investigations have focused on how life in the rural Banda area of west-central Ghana was affected by geopolitical economic changes over the last eight to ten centuries. Banda is today a small multiethnic chieftaincy that encompasses about 25 villages (for an early ethnographic description, see Goody 1963; also Stahl 1991). Four of the five ethnic groups that make up the contemporary Banda chieftaincy trace their origins to elsewhere; only the minority Kuulo (Dumpo) people claim to be autochthons (Stahl 2001:51–60). According to oral and documentary sources, the Banda chieftaincy was founded in the uncertain conditions that ensued as trade shifted southward from a Saharan to an Atlantic focus. Before the eighteenth century the savanna woodland/forest boundary was home to entrepôts that prospered from trade with the Niger River area and ultimately the trans-Saharan trade. Begho was a prominent center where forest products (gold, ivory, kola) were exchanged for those brought south by the caravan trade (salt, copper alloys; Arhin 1987; Posnansky 1973, 1987). Begho and its environs came under increasing pressure from the emergent Asante state, centered in the forest to the south (Wilks 1975). Asante mounted attacks against Begho and its neighboring polities in the first two decades of the eighteenth century, and disruption of its mercantile economy left a political economic vacuum in the western Volta Basin. It was in these conditions of uncertainty that the Banda chieftaincy was founded (Stahl 2001:149–155). Within decades (1773–1774; Yarak 1979) Banda was forcibly incorporated into the expansionist Asante state, which dominated the Atlantic trade along the so-called Gold Coast. Asante control over Banda waxed and waned through the nineteenth century, a period characterized by a changing landscape of international trade. Britain's abolition of the slave trade (1807) and transition to the "legitimate" trade in raw materials (palm oil, rubber, and later cacao; Grier 1981; McSheffrey 1983) reshaped labor demands. Internal slavery intensified as slaves formerly bound for external markets were used to produce cash crops. Unstable political economic conditions prevailed at the end of the nineteenth century as Volta Basin societies came under threat from the mounted troops of Imam Samori, who, in waging *jihad*, pursued a scorched-earth policy north of Banda, burning crops and villages and enslaving survivors (Haight 1981). New military elites emerged who were associated with new forms of wealth (i.e., intensified consumption of salt and cloth; McDougall 1990:255–256; Roberts 1992). The relatively brief formal colonial period (60 years) commenced when Britain officially annexed Asante's hinterland in 1897, though British administrators did not make their presence felt in Banda until the second decade of the twentieth century. Banda history is thus associated with a complex pattern of migration, changing trade connections, and shifting political hegemonies.

The Banda Research Project has since 1986 been directed toward understanding how daily life in the area was reshaped by these changing political economic circumstances. The project combines oral historical, documentary, and archaeological sources to investigate change and continuity in patterns of settlement, exchange, craft production, and subsistence through time (Stahl 1991, 1994, 1999a, 2001; Stahl and Cruz 1998). We employ a modified direct historical approach (Stahl 2001:27–40). Initial excavations focused on Makala Kataa, a late-nineteenth–early-twentieth-century village abandoned under British village relocation schemes. An earlier component of Makala Kataa was occupied from the late eighteenth to early nineteenth century, when it was abruptly abandoned. The nearby site of Kuulo Kataa is claimed by the autochthonous Kuulo as the site where their female ancestor descended to earth. Archaeological deposits here range from the period of the Niger trade (contemporary with Begho) through at least the early nineteenth century. Our excavations have focused on the earliest occupation of Kuulo Kataa (Stahl 1999a). I briefly summarize what we have learned of the changing mosaic of production and exchange in relation to this broader political economic canvas, focusing particularly on weaving and potting.

During the Kuulo phase (c. A.D. 1300–1650) Kuulo Kataa was a village-sized settlement that operated in the orbit of Begho and other large towns of the period (Old Bima; Bravmann and Mathewson 1970). Though the character of political organization in the Begho period is unclear (Posnansky 1987), our data suggest a long-lived occupation (signaled by the rebuilding and/or refurbishing of houses). Residents participated in regional trade in craft and subsistence goods and in interregional exchange in prestige goods (including ivory, copper alloys, and gold, as suggested by several figurative gold weights recovered from secure archaeological proveniences; see Stahl 1999a:38). Trade was northward looking, but a glimmer of Atlantic connections is evidenced by New World crops with which Kuulo villagers experimented (maize, suggested by phytoliths, and tobacco, suggested by smoking pipes). Clay sources in the region have distinctive chemical signatures, and neutron activation analysis (NAA) has discriminated among clays east and west of the Banda hills (Cruz 1996, 2003). Diverse ceramic forms at Kuulo Kataa were homogeneous in their chemical composition, and the chemical signature of the source is consistent with a local origin east of the Banda hills (Stahl 1999a, 2001). The volume of discarded pottery on this village site hints at on-site production for a regional market. The volume of slag and two furnace features suggest on-site production of iron as well. But in contrast to Begho, where spindle whorls were common (Crossland 1975), we have no evidence for thread production at Kuulo Kataa, suggesting that cloth may have been an "object of distinction" (Bourdieu 1984) that was not produced (and perhaps not consumed) by Kuulo villagers. The wide range of wild fauna attests the importance of wild resources in the diet and hints at diverse strategies for acquiring wild animal products (including "garden hunting" and trade in animal products). Dog bones were ubiquitous and dominated the identifiable domestic fauna; evidence of dog butchery and special treatment of dog mandibles presented a marked departure from both later occupations and contemporary practice. Similar disjunctures in settlement and craft production suggest dislocation in the wake of Begho's decline (after A.D. 1722) and raise questions about the applicability of ethnographic models to the period before about A.D. 1750.

According to historical sources, uncertainty ensued after circa A.D. 1722 as a result of the southward shift in trade and a political economic reconfiguration of forest societies (Wilks 1982a, 1982b). Though there is no trace of abrupt abandonment at Kuulo Kataa, it appears that the relatively large villages characteristic of the Begho period broke apart. Although we as yet have no sites that can be confidently assigned to the period between 1700 and 1780, the roots of the contemporary Banda chieftaincy may extend to as early as the 1730s (Stahl 2001:150). Banda was forcibly incorporated into Asante not long after its founding, but a period of relative stability followed. Early Makala villagers consumed objects derived from both sub- and intercontinental trade, now mediated by Asante, but imports had less impact on household reproduction than did a reorganized regional trade. Unlike residents of Kuulo Kataa, those at early Makala appear not to have produced the basic tools required for household reproduction (metal implements, pottery). Based on NAA data, early Makala villagers consumed pottery made on the other side of the Banda hills; jars and bowls came from different sources (Cruz 1996, 2003; Stahl and Cruz 1998). Smoking pipes were common and heterogeneous and derived from a variety of sources. Given the modest numbers of spindle whorls, textiles were domestically produced and the production of textiles shifted "downward," perhaps to the household level (as documented through early-twentieth-century sources; Stahl and Cruz 1998). Thus the ethnographic pattern of household production of textiles that some scholars have taken as typical of precolonial arrangements is a relatively recent development in this area. The shift from specialist to household craft would have altered the role of cotton cloth as an object of distinction. According to historical sources, prestige cloths now derived from the south, with taste shaped by fashions in Kumase, the Asante capital (Stahl 1999b, 2002; see also Steiner 1985). Wild and domestic fauna contributed to the diet, but consumption of dog was uncommon, hinting at discontinuities in

belief systems between Kuulo Kataa and early Makala. Specialized hunting or trade in large dangerous animals appears to have declined, with greater emphasis on opportunistic "garden hunting." The Atlantic world impinged on daily life more fully now; some Banda captives faced the middle passage in the wake of Asante's conquest (Yarak 1979), and firearms were a factor in the balance of power. Gun flints at early Makala suggest access to this new technology of destruction (Goody 1971), which was likely turned against neighboring groups in times of conflict. We can only speculate how firearms shaped dislocation in the Volta Basin in the early nineteenth century; however, we have good evidence that early Makala was abruptly abandoned. Quantities of usable material culture were left behind, an abandonment pattern (Cameron and Tomka 1993) that hints at a traumatic disjuncture in daily life. Ironically, because maize is more portable and storable than indigenous staples, New World crops may have helped displaced people cope. Thus trauma may have hastened adoption of crops first introduced through the slave trade (Chrétien 1988; Ohadike 1981).

Settlers at late Makala (established c. 1896) had lived through a traumatic period. Volta Basin peoples were under pressure from the mounted troops of the Imam Samori (Muhammed 1977). Household routines would have been repeatedly disrupted. There is an air of impermanence about the village established after 1896—houses were minimal residential units constructed with less durable techniques than their counterparts at Kuulo or early Makala. Household reproduction drew on more localized resources (pottery made of local clays, locally available wild animals, domestically produced textiles); at the same time, late Makala villagers were drawn into more substantial involvement in the colonial market economy. Monetization introduced new pressures on production as villagers reallocated labor to produce marketable goods (e.g., tobacco; Stahl and Cruz 1998). Villagers now had access to a wider array of goods, some of which were unit packaged to encourage increased consumption. None of the European goods (primarily bottle glass, ornaments, and smoking pipes) at late Makala were required for household reproduction, though all reshaped bodily practice and the practices of taste (Stahl 2002; see John Comaroff and Jean Comaroff 1997). New labor demands imposed by the colonial administration reshaped household labor allocation with implications for household reproduction (Cruz 2003; Stahl and Cruz 1998). Some craft production may have intensified as male labor shortages forced women to find alternative means to feed and clothe household members. Cruz (2003) has tracked twentieth-century changes in potting, which is today confined to villages west of the hills. She has documented changing marketing strategies that allowed women west of the hills to concentrate more fully on their craft while women east of the hills abandoned potting.

We have just completed a phase of regional site testing that will shed light on whether the patterns at these "core" sites are characteristic of the Banda area as a whole. Analyses of these data will provide a robust understanding of how local subsistence and craft production (of cloth, pottery, and iron) were reshaped through these long series of "global encounters." The relevance of such studies to the investigation of more ancient economies is that they provide us with temporally sensitive comparative models that can be used to assess patterns of *both* continuity *and* change in political economic strategies and arrangements that emerged through West Africa's long and turbulent involvement in broader geopolitical economic processes. The strength of these studies lies in their exploration of the specific histories of culturally embedded economies (Pauketat, this volume) that nonetheless give rise to comparative understandings of global processes.

CONCLUSIONS

Our understanding of Africa's ancient political economies is partial, more partial perhaps than in other world areas for a variety of his-

torical and political reasons (Schmidt and Patterson 1995). I have suggested that those partialities are shaped by special burdens that confront African archaeology: widespread negative imagery, rich ethnography, and a long and turbulent history of interaction. My goal was to take stock of how those burdens have shaped our knowledge and to suggest that the limits to our understanding do not lie in a paucity of data alone. More robust understandings require attention to the factors that shape those partialities (i.e., the preoccupation of different disciplines with societies of different scales) and the research efforts to expand our "archives" to account for them. I have suggested that we need to be better attuned to the temporality of sources and their contingencies and to embrace a more explicitly comparative approach that is attentive to disjunctures and disparities among diverse sources from different periods (Stahl 2001). If we are to develop historically sensitive analogical models, we must explore the effects of recent geopolitical economic processes on the contemporary societies that inform our imaginings of ancient ones. We need to take account of the "turbulence and loss" (Guyer 1999) that has been a fact of life in West Africa for centuries. Africa is not alone here, although the slave trade surely placed a distinctive cast on these processes in Africa compared with the Western Hemisphere. In each case study highlighted here the complexities of the slave trade (both internal and external) shaped sociopolitical organization, settlement strategies, subsistence and craft production, and consumption practices (see also Gronenborn 2001; McIntosh 2001). In short, they reshaped the political economies of societies of varying scales whose daily lives were intimately entwined. Archaeology has much to contribute to understanding the varying trajectories and consequences of these involvements, particularly if archaeological sources are viewed comparatively in relation with ethnographic and historical sources. But our work is just beginning.

As we attempt to expand our knowledge of West Africa's past, we need to be keenly aware of the first of our special burdens—the negative imagery that animates Western imaginings of Africa. The popular imagination continues to be fed by media portrayals of Africa as a land of underdevelopment, brutality, and radical "otherness." Africa continues to have "tribal wars" while other world areas have "ethnic conflicts," for example (Jean Comaroff and John Comaroff 1993; John Comaroff and Jean Comaroff 1992:4). The most troubling recycling of long-standing negative images is found in Kaplan's (2000) *The Coming Anarchy: Shattering the Dreams of the Post Cold War*. In an account first published as a cover essay in the *Atlantic Monthly* (Kaplan 1994), Kaplan extrapolates a grim future for "our civilization" from a portrayal of West Africa that "is becoming *the* symbol of worldwide demographic, environmental, and societal stress" (1994:46). Kaplan's vision has gained prominence in the corridors of power—he lectures to the U.S. military, was a consultant to the U.S. Army's Special Forces Regiment, and is a fellow at the New America Foundation. West Africa in Kaplan's view is likely to become isolated by a "wall of disease"; its cities are "a nightmarish Dickensian spectacle to which Dickens himself would never have given credence. The corrugated metal shacks and scabrous walls were coated with black slime. Stores were built out of rusted shipping containers, junked cars, and jumbles of wire mesh" (Kaplan 1994:52, 54).[5] Kaplan cites polygamy and extended family structures (which he terms "communalism") along with animism as providing a "weak shield against the corrosive social effects of life in cities" (1994:46). West Africa's environment is denuded through logging conducted at a "madcap speed" (Kaplan 1994:54), signaling an irrational overexploitation of the region's natural resources. Kaplan's rhetorical strategy is a variant of the familiar "barbarians at the gates" (di Leonardo 1998:40–43)—albeit one with a perverse twist: whereas Africa has long been deployed to imagine a dark and savage past, it is now the source for imaginings of a dark and savage future. There is, of

course, some truth in Kaplan's account—West Africa's forests are being stripped at an alarming rate, diseases such as drug-resistant malaria and AIDS are pressing problems, and West Africa's cities are home to many impoverished people. Yet Kaplan ignores the extent to which these "truths" are a product of Africa's long history of global entanglements. Africa's hardwoods are harvested to meet consumer demand in Europe, America, and Asia. Malaria, like many other diseases, has become more virulent because of drug therapies developed and introduced by Western medicine. And the inability of poor Africans to sustain themselves in urban settings is related to a long history of systematic underdevelopment (Grier 1981).

Kaplan closed his 1994 essay with the observation that as he was returning to the United States, businessmen were boarding planes for Asia while "the only non-Africans off to West Africa had been relief workers in T-shirts and khakis. Although the borders within West Africa are increasingly unreal, those separating West Africa from the outside world are in various ways becoming more impenetrable" (1994:76). By recycling entrenched stereotypes and refusing thoughtful historical analysis, Kaplan reinforces those barriers and contributes to Africa's marginalization. Scholars of Africa, archaeologists among them, are rightly concerned to counter his message. McIntosh, for example, counterposes Kaplan's image of African despotism with the ancient societies of the Middle Niger, which provide a model of an "original civil society" based in a resilient pluralism and heterarchy that has relevance today (McIntosh 1998:6–10, 294–303). McIntosh works to trace the "deep time" roots of an alternative pluralism in the origins of complex societies in this part of West Africa, observing that "those who would marginalize Africa's later history must now contend with the Middle Niger people's original solution to the global (and very modern) conundrum of counterpoised power" (McIntosh 1998:xviii). Yet we must avoid falling prey to the old dilemma of countering offensive images with their obverse (Fuglestad 1992; Neale 1985, 1986). This strategy leads to romanticized accounts that do not confront the "isms" (racism, ethnocentrism) that underwrite these images. Different players may be privileged, but the rules of the game remain the same. In this sense we succumb to one of anthropology's two fatal moves:

> The first is conspiring with the morality play, taking the stage to advocate the "cultural richness" of one stigmatized population after another. After all, if culture can be rich, it then also can be poor, or lacking altogether. The second is delimiting anthropology's purview to a truncated "culture" in the first place, as if human beings' apprehensions of reality can be studied apart from the reality they are apprehending. Despite their lofty intentions, anthropologists' idealized concept of culture, torn from history and political economy, has come to serve as a fetish, a systematic falsification in public political discourse. (di Leonardo 1998: 132)

Redressing our myopia requires paying attention to the interconnections between societies of varying scales (within and between continents) and to the structures and processes that underwrite those interconnections (di Leonardo 1998:121). Through comparative use of historically sensitive analogical models developed with their contingencies fully in view, archaeologists can bring to public discussions a more nuanced understanding of the historical political economic processes that shape our world. This requires keeping a broad temporal and geographical scope in view, one that recognizes the relational quality of sociopolitical economic processes; but at the same time, it requires that we pursue empirically robust case studies that track these processes and contingencies in specific localities through time (e.g., Junker, Pauketat, Stein, Storey, all this volume). The hard work of developing such understandings of West Africa's ancient and recent political economies is just beginning, with consequences for our perceptions of the region's past as well as its future.

Notes

1. The impact of the slave trade has been a particularly thorny issue; it was long treated as a "family affair" (Neale 1985:15), and scholars have been reluctant to address the complex and diverse roles of Africans in it (cf. Inikori 1982; Manning 1996; Watson 1980).

2. The florescence of ethnoarchaeological research in Africa is shaped in part by the political economy of research funding. In the face of shrinking resources, ethnoarchaeological research became an attractive alternative to more expensive archaeological research. This shift is reflected in the large number of B.A. long essays and M.A. theses devoted to ethnoarchaeological research filed in West African departments of archaeology.

3. The volume of iron produced was estimated on the basis of the volume of slag from sites of different periods. De Barros corrected for varying lengths of occupations as well the variable yield of different qualities of ores throughout the area. The potential for error remains, though de Barros (1987:158) argues that the resulting estimates are "probably of the right order of magnitude."

4. The term *caste* is viewed with ambiguity in African studies because of its connotations with the distinctive caste system of India. Debate focuses particularly on the hierarchical aspects of caste systems since ranking does not seem to be necessarily implied in West African examples (for a discussion, see McNaughton 1988:156–161; but cf. Tamari 1991:230).

5. Kaplan's portrayal of West Africa is highly selective, partial, and irresponsible. He writes as a journalist, bases his account on a brief visit to a handful of countries, and emphasizes the worst of what he has perceived through the lens of Western ethnocentrism in a form of "drive-by journalism" (to borrow a phrase from a letter to the editor in response to one of Kaplan's later pieces in the *Atlantic Monthly*). Could we not as easily describe the use of junked shipping containers and cars as recycling? It is more environmentally responsible and no more offensive to the eye than the junkyards that scar America's landscape.

References

Abrams, Elliot M.
1994   *How the Maya Built Their World.* University of Texas Press, Austin.

Abrams, Philip
1988   Notes on the Difficulty of Studying the State (1977). *Journal of Historical Sociology* 1:58–89.

Achebe, Chinua
1978   An Image of Africa. *Research in African Literatures* 9(1):2–15.

Adams, Robert McC.
1966   *The Evolution of Urban Society.* Aldine, Chicago.
1974   Anthropological Perspectives on Ancient Trade. *Current Anthropology* 15:239–258.
1978   Strategies of Maximization, Stability, and Resilience in Mesopotamian Society, Settlement, and Agriculture. *Proceedings of the American Philosophical Society* 122(5):329–335.
1981   *Heartland of Cities: Surveys of Ancient Settlement and Land Use on the Central Floodplain of the Euphrates.* University of Chicago Press, Chicago.
2002   Steps Toward Regional Understanding of the Mesopotamian Plain. In *Material Culture and Mental Spheres: Rezeption archäologischer Denkrichtungen in der vorderasiatischen Altertumskunde. International Symposium for Hans J. Nissen, Berlin, 23–24 June 2000,* edited by Susanne Kerner and Bernd Müller-Neuhof. Alter und Altes Testament (AOAT) 293. Münster.

Adams, Robert McC., and Hans J. Nissen
1972   *The Uruk Countryside: The Natural Setting of Urban Societies.* University of Chicago Press, Chicago.

Adas, Michael
1995   The Reconstruction of "Tradition" and the Defense of the Colonial Order: British West Africa in the Early Twentieth Century. In *Articulating Hidden Histories: Exploring the Influence of Eric R. Wolf,* edited by Jane Schneider and Rayna Rapp, pp. 291–307. University of California Press, Berkeley.

Albarracin-Jordan, Juan
1996   *Tiwanaku: Arqueología regional y dinámica segmentaria.* Editores Plural, La Paz.

Alcina, Francisco I.
1960a   Historia de las islas e indios de las
[1688]   Bisayas, Book 3, Part 3. In *The Muñoz Text of Alcina's History of the Bisayan Islands,* edited by Paul Lietz. Philippine Studies Program, University of Chicago, Chicago.
1960b   Historia de las islas e indios de las
[1688]   Bisayas, Book 3, Part 4. In *The Muñoz Text of Alcina's History of the Bisayan Islands,* edited by Paul Lietz. Philippine Studies Program, University of Chicago, Chicago.

Alcock, Susan A.
1993   *Graecia Capta: The Landscapes of Roman Greece.* Cambridge University Press, New York.

Algaze, Guillermo
1993   *The Uruk World System: The*

Dynamics of Expansion of Early Mesopotamian Civilization. University of Chicago Press, Chicago.

1999   Trends in the Archaeological Development of the Upper Euphrates Basin of Southeastern Anatolia During the Late Chalcolithic and Early Bronze Ages. In *Archaeology of the Upper Syrian Euphrates: The Tishreen Dam Area,* edited by Gregorio del Olmo Lete and Juan-Luis Montero Fenollós, pp. 535–570. Editorial AUSA, Barcelona, Spain.

2001a   *The Prehistory of Imperialism: The Case of Uruk Period Mesopotamia.* In *Uruk Mesopotamia and Its Neighbors: Cross-cultural Interactions in the Era of State Formation,* edited by Mitchell S. Rothman, pp. 27–83. School of American Research Press, Santa Fe, New Mexico.

2001b   Initial Social Complexity in Southwestern Asia: The Mesopotamian Advantage. *Current Anthropology* 42:199–233.

Algaze, Guillermo, Gulay Dinckan, Britt Hartenberger, Timothy Matney, Jennifer Pournelle, Lynn Rainville, Steven Rosen, Eric Rupley, Duncan Schlee, and Regis Valley

2001   Research at Titris Höyük in Southeastern Turkey: The 1999 Season. *Anatolica* 27:23–106.

Algaze, Guillermo, Paul Goldberg, Dierdre Honca, Timothy Matney, Adnan Misir, Arlene Rosen, Duncan Schlee, and Lewis Somers

1995   Titris Höyük: A Small Early Bronze Age Urban Center in Southeast Anatolia: The 1994 Season. *Anatolica* 21:13–64.

Allen, Jane

1991   Trade and Site Distribution in Early Historic-Period Kedah: Geoarchaeological, Historical, and Locational Evidence. In *Indo-Pacific Prehistory 1990, Volume 1,* edited by Peter S. Bellwood, pp. 307–319. Bulletin of the Indo-Pacific Prehistory Association No. 10. Indo-Pacific Prehistory Association, Canberra.

Alt, Susan

1999   Spindle Whorls and Fiber Production at Early Cahokian Settlements. *Southeastern Archaeology* 18:124–134.

2001a   Cahokian Change and the Authority of Tradition. In *The Archaeology of Traditions: Agency and History Before and After Columbus,* edited by Timothy R. Pauketat, pp. 141–156. University Press of Florida, Gainesville.

2001b   Keeping Order in the Uplands: A Look at a Cahokian Administrative Center. Paper presented at the 58th Southeastern Archaeological Conference, Chattanooga.

2002   *The Knoebel Site: Tradition and Change in the Cahokian Suburbs.* Unpublished Master's thesis, Department of Anthropology, University of Illinois, Urbana.

Alva, Walter

1994   *Sipán.* Colección Cultura y Artes del Perú, Lima.

2001   The Royal Tombs of Sipán: Art and Power in Moche Society. In *Moche Art and Archaeology in Ancient Peru,* edited by Joanne Pillsbury, pp. 223–246. National Gallery of Art, Washington, D.C.

Alva, Walter, and Christopher B. Donnan

1993   *Royal Tombs of Sipán.* Exhibition catalogue, Fowler Museum of Cultural History, University of California, Los Angeles.

Ambrose, Stanley H., Jane Buikstra, and Harold W. Kruger

2001   Gender and Status Differences in Diet at Mound 72, Cahokia, Revealed by Isotopic Analysis of Bone. Paper presented at the 66th Annual Meeting of the Society for American Archaeology, New Orleans.

Ames, Kenneth M.

1995   Chiefly Power and Household Production on the Northwest Coast. In *Foundations of Social Inequality,* edited by T. Douglas Price and Gary M. Feinman, pp. 155–187. Plenum Press, New York.

Amselle, Jean-Loup

1993   Anthropology and Historicity. In *History Making in Africa,* edited by V. Y. Mudimbe and Bogumil Jewsiewicki, pp. 12–31. Beiheft 32.

History and Theory Studies in the Philosophy of History. Wesleyan University, Middletown, Connecticut.

1998 *Mestizo Logics: Anthropology of Identity in Africa and Elsewhere.* Translated by C. Royal. Stanford University Press, Palo Alto.

Andaya, Barbara W.

1975 The Nature of the State in Eighteenth-Century Perak. In *Pre-colonial State Systems in Southeast Asia: The Malay Peninsula, Sumatra, Bali-Lombok, South Celebes,* edited by Anthony Reid and Lance Castles, pp. 22–35. Monographs of the Malaysian Branch of the Royal Asiatic Society No. 6. Royal Asiatic Society, Hong Kong.

1992 Political Development Between the Sixteenth and Eighteenth Centuries. In *The Cambridge History of Southeast Asia, Volume 1: From Early Times to c. 1800,* edited by Nicholas Tarling, pp. 402–459. Cambridge University Press, Cambridge.

Andaya, Barbara W., and Leonard Andaya

1982 *A History of Malaysia.* Macmillan, London.

Andaya, Barbara W., and Yoneo Ishii

1992 Religious Developments in Southeast Asia, c. 1500–1800. In *The Cambridge History of Southeast Asia, Volume 1: From Early Times to c. 1800,* edited by Nicholas Tarling, pp. 508–571. Cambridge University Press, Cambridge.

Andaya, Leonard

1992 Interactions with the Outside World and Adaptation in Southeast Asian Society, 1500–1800. In *The Cambridge History of Southeast Asia, Volume 1: From Early Times to c. 1800,* edited by Nicholas Tarling, pp. 345–401. Cambridge University Press, Cambridge.

1993 Cultural State Formation in Eastern Indonesia. In *Southeast Asia in the Early Modern Era: Trade, Power, and Belief,* edited by Anthony Reid, pp. 23–41. Cornell University Press, Ithaca.

Anders, Martha, Susana Arce, Izumi Shimada, Victor Chang, Luis Tokuda, and Sonia Quiroz

1998 Early Middle Horizon Pottery Production at Maymi, Pisco Valley, Peru. In *Andean Ceramics: Technology, Organization, and Approaches,* edited by Izumi Shimada, pp. 233–251. MASCA Research Papers in Science and Archaeology Vol. 15 supplement. University of Pennsylvania Museum, Philadelphia.

Anderson, David G.

1994a *The Savannah River Chiefdoms: Political Change in the Late Prehistoric Southeast.* University of Alabama Press, Tuscaloosa.

1994b Factional Competition and the Political Evolution of Mississippian Chiefdoms in the Southeastern United States. In *Factional Competition in the New World,* edited by Elizabeth M. Brumfiel and John W. Fox, pp. 61–76. Cambridge University Press, Cambridge.

1997 The Role of Cahokia in the Evolution of Southeastern Mississippian Society. In *Cahokia: Domination and Ideology in the Mississippian World,* edited by Timothy R. Pauketat and Thomas E. Emerson, pp. 248–268. University of Nebraska Press, Lincoln.

Andreau, Jean

1999 *Banking and Business in the Roman World.* Cambridge University Press, New York.

2002 Markets, Fairs, and Monetary Loans: Cultural History and Economic History in Roman Italy and Hellenistic Greece. In *Money, Labour, and Land: Approaches to the Economies of Ancient Greece,* edited by Paul Cartledge, Edward E. Cohen, and Lin Foxhall, pp. 113–129. Routledge, New York.

Andreoni, James, and John H. Miller

1993 Rational Cooperation in the Finitely Repeated Prisoner's Dilemma: Experimental Evidence. *Economic Journal* 103:570–585.

Andrews, Anthony P.

1983 *Maya Salt Production and Trade.* University of Arizona Press, Tucson.

Appadurai, Arjun (editor)
1986   *The Social Life of Things: Com-
        modities in Cultural Perspective.*
        Cambridge University Press, Cam-
        bridge.

Appel, Jill
1982   Addendum to Chapter 8: The Post-
        classic: A Summary of the Ethnohis-
        toric Information Relevant to the In-
        terpretation of Late Postclassic
        Settlement. In *Monte Albán's Hin-
        terland, Part I: The Prehispanic Set-
        tlement Patterns of the Central and
        Southern Parts of the Valley of Oax-
        aca, Mexico,* by Richard E. Blanton,
        Stephen A. Kowalewski, Gary M.
        Feinman, and Jill Appel, pp.
        139–148. Memoirs No. 15. Museum
        of Anthropology, University of
        Michigan, Ann Arbor.

Archi, Alfonso
1985   The Royal Archives of Ebla. In *Ebla
        to Damascus,* edited by Harvey
        Weiss, pp. 140–148. Smithsonian
        Institution Press, Washington, D.C.

1990   The City of Ebla and the Organiza-
        tion of the Rural Territory. In *The
        Town as Regional Economic Center
        in the Ancient Near East,* edited by
        Erik Aertz and Horst Klengel, pp.
        15–19. Leuven University Press,
        Leuven.

Archibald, Zofia H.
2001   Setting the Scene. In *Hellenistic
        Economies,* edited by Zofia H.
        Archibald, John Davies, Vincent
        Gabrielson, and G. J. Oliver, pp.
        1–9. Routledge, New York.

Archibald, Zofia H., John Davies, Vincent
Gabrielson, and G. J. Oliver (editors)
2001   *Hellenistic Economies.* Routledge,
        New York.

Arhin, Kwame
1987   Savanna Contributions to the
        Asante Political Economy. In *The
        Golden Stool: Studies of the Asante
        Center and Periphery,* edited by
        Enid Schildkrout, pp. 51–59. An-
        thropological Papers Vol. 65, Part 1.
        American Museum of Natural His-
        tory, New York.

Arnold, Dean
1985   *Ceramic Theory and Cultural
        Process.* Cambridge University
        Press, Cambridge.

Arnold, Jeanne
1987   *Craft Specialization in the Prehis-
        toric Channel Islands, California.*
        University of California Publications
        in Anthropology Vol. 18. University
        of California Press, Berkeley.

Artieda, Diego de
1903   Relation of the Western Islands. In
[1569] *The Philippines, 1493–1898,* vol. 3,
        edited by Emma H. Blair and James
        A. Robertson, pp. 190–208. Arthur
        H. Clark, Cleveland.

Asad, Talal (editor)
1973   *Anthropology and the Colonial En-
        counter.* Humanities Press, Atlantic
        Heights, New Jersey.

Asante, Molefi Kete, and Kariamu Welsh
Asante (editors)
1990   *African Culture: The Rhythms of
        Unity.* Africa World Press, Trenton,
        New Jersey.

Azarya, Victor
1996   *Nomads and the State in Africa:
        The Political Roots of Marginality.*
        African Studies Centre, Leiden.

Bagley, Robert W.
1977   P'an-lung-ch'eng: A Shang City in
        Hupei. *Artibus Asiae* 39:165–219.

1987   *Shang Ritual Bronzes in the Arthur
        M. Sackler Collections.* Arthur M.
        Sackler Foundation, Washington,
        D.C., and Arthur M. Sackler Mu-
        seum, Harvard University, Cam-
        bridge.

1993   An Early Bronze Age Tomb in
        Jiangxi Province. *Orientations*
        24(7):20–36.

1999   Shang Archaeology. In *The Cam-
        bridge History of Ancient China,* ed-
        ited by Michael Loewe and Edward
        Shaughnessy, pp. 124–231. Cam-
        bridge University Press, New York.

Baines, John, and Norman Yoffee
1998   Order, Legitimacy, and Wealth in
        Ancient Egypt and Mesopotamia. In
        Archaic States, edited by Gary M.
        Feinman and Joyce Marcus, pp.
        199–260. School of American Re-
        search Press, Santa Fe, New Mexico.

2000   Order, Legitimacy, and Wealth: Set-
        ting the Terms. In *Order, Legiti-*

macy, and Wealth in Ancient States, edited by Janet Richards and Mary van Buren, pp. 13–17. Cambridge University Press, Cambridge.

Balkansky, Andrew K.

1997   Archaeological Settlement Patterns of the Sola Valley, Oaxaca, Mexico. *Mexicon* 19:12–18.

Balkansky, Andrew K., Gary M. Feinman, and Linda M. Nicholas

1997   Pottery Kilns of Ancient Ejutla, Oaxaca, Mexico. *Journal of Field Archaeology* 24:139–160.

Barnes, Gina

1993   *China, Korea, and Japan: The Rise of Civilization in East Asia*. Thames and Hudson, New York.

Bartlett, Mary L., and Patricia A. McAnany

2000   "Crafting" Communities: The Materialization of Formative Maya Identities. In *The Archaeology of Communities: A New World Perspective*, edited by Marcello A. Canuto and Jason Yaeger, pp. 102–122. Routledge, London.

Bartlett, Mary L., Hector Neff, and Patricia A. McAnany

2000   Differentiation of Clay Resources on a Limestone Plain: The Analysis of Clay Utilization During the Maya Formative at K'axob, Belize. *Geoarchaeology* 15:95–133.

Bass, George F.

1991   Evidence of Trade from Bronze Age Shipwrecks. In *Bronze Age Trade in the Mediterranean: Papers Presented at the Conference Held at Rewley House, Oxford, in December 1989*, edited by Noël Gale, pp. 69–82. Studies in Mediterranean Archaeology Vol. 90. P. Åströms Förlag, Jonsered, Sweden.

Bauer, Brian, and Charles Stanish

2001   *Ritual and Pilgrimage in the Ancient Andes*. University of Texas Press, Austin.

Bawden, Garth

1977   *Galindo and the Nature of the Middle Horizon on the North Coast of Peru*. Unpublished Ph.D. dissertation, Department of Anthropology, Harvard University, Cambridge.

1982   Galindo: A Study in Cultural Transi-tion During the Middle Horizon. In *Chan Chan: Andean Desert City*, edited by Michael E. Moseley and Kent C. Day, pp. 285–320. University of New Mexico Press, Albuquerque.

1996   *The Moche*. Blackwell, Cambridge.

1999   *The Moche*. 2nd ed. Blackwell, Malden, Massachusetts.

Bayman, James

1999   Craft Economies in the North American Southwest. *Journal of Archaeological Research* 7:249–299.

Beatty, Andrew

1991   Ovasa: Feasts of Merit in Nias. *Bijdragen: Tot de Taal-, Land-en Volkenkunde* 147:216–235.

Belisario, M. V., M. Follieri, and L. Sadori

1994   Nuovi dati archaeobotanici sulla coltivazione di *Vitis vinifera* L. ad Arslantepe (Malatya, Turchia). In *Drinking in Ancient Societies: History and Culture of Drinks in the Ancient Near East*, edited by Lucio Milano, pp. 77–90. Sargon, Padua.

Bellwood, Peter

1985   *Prehistory of the Indo-Malaysian Archipelago*. Academic Press, Sydney.

1992   Southeast Asia Before History. In *The Cambridge History of Southeast Asia, Volume 1: From Early Times to c. 1800*, edited by Nicholas Tarling, pp. 55–136. Cambridge University Press, Cambridge.

Benn, David W.

1997   Who Met the Mississippians at the Mouth of the Apple River? Investigations at 11Ca44. *Illinois Archaeology* 9:1–35.

Bennett, Wendell C.

1936   Excavations in Bolivia. *Anthropological Papers of the American Museum of Natural History* 35(4): 329–507.

Berdan, Frances F.

1982   *The Aztecs of Central Mexico: An Imperial Society*. Holt, Rinehart and Winston, New York.

1983   The Reconstruction of Ancient Economies: Perspectives from Archaeology and Ethnohistory. In *Economic Anthropology: Topics and Theories*, edited by Sutti Ortiz, pp.

83–95. Monographs in Economic Anthropology No. 1. University Press of America, Lanham, Maryland.

1985   Markets in the Economy of Aztec Mexico. In *Markets and Marketing*, edited by Stuart Plattner, pp. 339–367. University Press of America, Lanham, Maryland.

1987a   The Economics of Aztec Luxury Trade and Tribute. In *The Aztec Templo Mayor*, edited by Elizabeth Hill Boone, pp. 161–184. Dumbarton Oaks, Washington, D.C.

1987b   Cotton in Aztec Mexico: Production, Distribution, and Uses. *Mexican Studies/Estudios Mexicanos* 3(2):235–262.

1989   Trade and Markets in Precapitalist States. In *Economic Anthropology*, edited by Stuart M. Plattner, pp. 78–107. Stanford University Press, Palo Alto.

Berdan, Frances F., Richard E. Blanton, Elizabeth H. Boone, Mary G. Hodge, Michael E. Smith, and Emily Umberger

1996   *Aztec Imperial Strategies*. Dumbarton Oaks, Washington, D.C.

Bermann, Mark P.

1994   *Lukurmata: Household Archaeology in Prehispanic Bolivia*. Princeton University Press, Princeton.

Bernbeck, Reinhard

1993   *Steppe als Kulturlandchaft*. Dietrich Reimer, Berlin.

Berry, Kimberly A.

2003   *Farming the Scales of the Crocodile: Cultural and Geoarchaeological Evidence for Ancient Maya Wetland Reclamation at K'axob, Belize*. Unpublished Ph.D. dissertation, Department of Archaeology, Boston University, Boston.

Berry, Sara S.

1993   *No Condition Is Permanent: The Social Dynamics of Agrarian Change in Sub-Saharan Africa*. University of Wisconsin Press, Madison.

Biernatzki, William E.

1985   Bukidnon Datuship in the Upper Pulangi River Valley. In *Bukidnon Politics and Religion*, edited by Alfonso de Guzman II and Esther M. Pacheco, pp. 15–49. Papers No. 11.

Institute for Philippine Culture, Ateneo de Manila Press, Quezon City, Philippines.

Blair, Emma H., and James A. Robertson (editors and translators)

1903   *The Philippines, 1493–1898*. 55 –1909   vols. Arthur H. Clark, Cleveland.

Blakey, Michael L.

1995   Race, Nationalism, and the Afrocentric Past. In *Making Alternative Histories: The Practice of Archaeology in History in Non-Western Settings*, edited by Peter R. Schmidt and Thomas C. Patterson, pp. 213–228. School of American Research Press, Santa Fe, New Mexico.

Blanton, Richard E.

1978   *Monte Albán: Settlement Patterns at the Ancient Zapotec Capital*. Academic Press, New York.

1983   Factors Underlying the Origin and Evolution of Market Systems. In *Economic Anthropology: Topics and Theories*, edited by Sutti Ortiz, pp. 51–66. Monographs in Economic Anthropology No. 1. University Press of America, Lanham, Maryland.

1996   The Basin of Mexico Market System and the Growth of Empire. In *Aztec Imperial Strategies*, by Frances F. Berdan, Richard E. Blanton, Elizabeth H. Boone, Mary G. Hodge, Michael E. Smith, and Emily Umberger, pp. 47–84. Dumbarton Oaks, Washington, D.C.

Blanton, Richard E., and Gary M. Feinman

1984   The Mesoamerican World System. *American Anthropologist* 86:673–682.

Blanton, Richard E., Gary M. Feinman, Stephen A. Kowalewski, and Peter N. Peregrine

1996   A Dual-Processual Theory for the Evolution of Mesoamerican Civilization. *Current Anthropology* 37:1–14.

Blanton, Richard E., Stephen A. Kowalewski, and Gary M. Feinman

1992   The Mesoamerican World-System. *Review* 15:419–426.

Blanton, Richard E., Stephen A. Kowalewski, Gary M. Feinman, and Jill Appel

1982   *Monte Albán's Hinterland, Part I: The Prehispanic Settlement Patterns* of the Central and Southern Parts of the Valley of Oaxaca, Mexico. Memoirs No. 15. Museum of Anthropology, University of Michigan, Ann Arbor.

Blanton, Richard E., Stephen A. Kowalewski, Gary M. Feinman, and Laura Finsten

1993   Ancient Mesoamerica: A Comparison of Change in Three Regions. 2nd ed. Cambridge University Press, Cambridge.

Blanton, Richard E., Peter N. Peregrine, Deborah Winslow, and Thomas D. Hall (editors)

1997   Economic Analysis Beyond the Local System. University Press of America, Lanham, Maryland.

Blitz, John H.

1993   Ancient Chiefdoms of the Tombigbee. University of Alabama Press, Tuscaloosa.

Boas, Franz

1932   The Aims of Anthropological Research. Science 76:605–613.

1964   The Central Eskimo. University of Nebraska Press, Lincoln. Originally published 1884–85.

Bobadilla, Diego de

1990   Relation of the Philippine Islands.
[1640] In Documentary Sources of Philippine History, vol. 4, edited and translated by Gregorio F. Zaide, pp. 329–343. National Bookstore Publications, Manila.

Bogucki, Peter (editor)

1993   Case Studies in European Prehistory. CRC Press, Boca Raton, Florida.

Booth, Don, Timothy R. Pauketat, and Andrew Fortier

2001   Competitors or Colleagues: The Archaeology of the East St. Louis Mound Group. Paper presented at the 47th Annual Midwest Archaeological Conference, La Crosse, Wisconsin.

Bornstein, Gary, and Ilan Yaniv

1998   Individual and Group Behavior in the Ultimatum Game: Are Groups More "Rational" Players? Experimental Economics 1:101–108.

Bourdieu, Pierre

1977   Outline of a Theory of Practice. Translated by Richard Nice. Cambridge University Press, Cambridge.

1984   Distinction: A Social Critique of the Judgement of Taste. Translated by Richard Nice. Harvard University Press, Cambridge.

1990   The Logic of Practice. Stanford University Press, Palo Alto.

Bourget, Steve

2001   Rituals of Sacrifice: Its Practice at Huaca de la Luna and Its Representation in Moche Iconography. In Moche Art and Archaeology in Ancient Peru, edited by Joanne Pillsbury, pp. 89–110. National Gallery of Art, Washington, D.C.

Bowles, Samuel, Robert Boyd, Ernst Fehr, and Herbert Gintis

1997   Homo reciprocans: A Research Initiative on the Origins, Dimensions, and Policy Implications of Reciprocal Fairness. Ms. available at http://www.unix.oit.umass.edu/~gintis/homo_abst.html.

Bozell, John R.

1993   Vertebrate Faunal Remains. In Temples for Cahokia Lords: Preston Holder's 1955–1956 Excavations of Kunnemann Mound, by Timothy R. Pauketat, pp. 107–123. Memoirs No. 26. Museum of Anthropology, University of Michigan, Ann Arbor.

Bradley, Richard

1982   The Destruction of Wealth in Later Prehistory. Man 17:108–122.

Bravmann, René A., and R. Duncan Mathewson

1970   A Note on the History and Archaeology of "Old Bima." African Historical Studies 3:133–150.

Bredwa-Mensah, Y., and L. B. Crossland

1997   A Preliminary Report on Archaeological Investigations at the Danish Plantation Settlements along the South Akuapem Ridge, Ghana. Papers from the Institute of Archaeology (UCL) 8:59–72.

Bronson, Bennet

1977   Exchange at the Upstream and Downstream Ends: Notes Towards a Functional Model of the Coastal State in Southeast Asia. In Economic Exchange and Social Interaction in Southeast Asia, edited by Karl Hutterer, pp. 39–52. Michigan Papers on South and Southeast Asia No. 13.

Center for South and Southeast Asian Studies, University of Michigan, Ann Arbor.

Brooks, George E.
1993   *Landlords and Strangers: Ecology, Society, and Trade in Western Africa, 1000–1630.* Westview Press, Boulder, Colorado.

Brown, Douglas E.
1976   *Principles of Social Structure: Southeast Asia.* Duckworth, London.

Brown, James A.
1996   *The Spiro Ceremonial Center: The Archaeology of Arkansas Valley Caddoan Culture in Eastern Oklahoma.* Memoirs No. 29. Museum of Anthropology, University of Michigan, Ann Arbor.

Brumfiel, Elizabeth M.
1994   The Economic Anthropology of the State: An Introduction. In *The Economic Anthropology of the State*, edited by Elizabeth M. Brumfiel, pp. 1–16. Monographs in Economic Anthropology No. 11. University Press of America, Lanham, Maryland.

1996   The Quality of Tribute Cloth: The Place of Evidence in Archaeological Argument. *American Antiquity* 61:453–462.

1998   The Multiple Identities of Aztec Craft Specialists. In *Craft and Social Identity*, edited by Cathy Lynne Costin and Rita P. Wright, pp. 145–152. Archeological Papers No. 8. American Anthropological Association, Washington, D.C.

Brumfiel, Elizabeth M., and Timothy K. Earle
1987   Specialization, Exchange, and Complex Societies: An Introduction. In *Specialization, Exchange, and Complex Societies*, edited by Elizabeth M. Brumfiel and Timothy K. Earle, pp. 1–9. Cambridge University Press, New York.

Burger, Richard
1995   *Chavín and the Origins of Andean Civilization.* Thames and Hudson, London.

Cameron, Catherine M.
2001   Pink Chert, Projectile Points, and the Chacoan Regional System. *American Antiquity* 66:79–102.

Cameron, Catherine M., and Steve A. Tomka (editors)
1993   *Abandonment of Settlements and Regions: Ethnoarchaeological and Archaeological Approaches.* Cambridge University Press, Cambridge.

Campana D., Cristóbal
1994   El entorno cultural de un dibujo mochica. In *Moche: Propuestas y perspectivas*, edited by Santiago Uceda and Elías Mujica, pp. 449–477. Travaux de l'Institut Français d'Etudes Andines 79. Universidad Nacional de la Libertad, Trujillo and Lima, Peru.

Cancian, Frank
1965   *Economics and Prestige in a Maya Community.* Stanford University Press, Palo Alto.

1989   Economic Behavior in Peasant Communities. In *Economic Anthropology*, edited by Stuart M. Plattner, pp. 127–170. Stanford University Press, Palo Alto.

Carandini, Andrea
1983   Columella's Vineyard and the Rationality of the Roman Economy. *Opus* 2:177–203.

Carneiro, Robert L.
1981   The Chiefdom: Precursor of the State. In *The Transition to Statehood in the New World*, edited by Grant D. Jones and Robert R. Kautz, pp. 37–79. Cambridge University Press, Cambridge.

1990   Chiefdom Level Warfare as Exemplified in Fiji and the Cauca Valley. In *The Anthropology of War*, edited by Jonathan Haas, pp. 190–211. Cambridge University Press, Cambridge.

1998   What Happened at the Flashpoint? Conjectures on Chiefdom Formation at the Very Moment of Conception. In *Chiefdoms and Chieftaincy in the Americas*, edited by Elsa Redmond, pp. 19–42. University Press of Florida, Gainesville.

Carpenter, Andrea, and Gary M. Feinman
1999   The Effects of Behaviour on Ceramic Composition: Implications for the Definition of Production Locations.

Journal of Archaeological Sciences 26:783–796.

Carrasco, Pedro
1978   La economía del México prehispánico. In *Economía política e ideología en el México prehispánico*, edited by Pedro Carrasco and Johanna Broda, pp. 15–76. Editorial Nueva Imagen, Mexico City.
1983   Some Theoretical Considerations about the Role of the Market in Ancient Mexico. In *Economic Anthropology: Topics and Theories*, edited by Sutti Ortiz, pp. 67–81. Monographs in Economic Anthropology No. 1. University Press of America, Lanham, Maryland.

Carter, Elizabeth, and Andrea Parker
1995   Pots, People, and the Archaeology of Death in Northern Syria and Southern Anatolia in the Latter Half of the Third Millennium B.C. In *The Archaeology of Death in the Ancient Near East*, edited by Stuart Campbell and Anthony Green, pp. 96–115. Oxbow Monograph No. 51. David Brown Book Company, Oakville, Connecticut.

Cartledge, Paul, Edward E. Cohen, and Lin Foxhall (editors)
2002   *Money, Labour, and Land: Approaches to the Economies of Ancient Greece*. Routledge, London.

Casal, Gabriel, R. Jose, Eric Casino, G. Ellis, and Wilhelm Solheim (editors)
1982   *The People and Art of the Philippines*. Museum of Cultural History, University of California, Los Angeles.

Casparis, J. G. de
1961   Historical Writing on Indonesia (Early Period). In *Historians of Southeast Asia*, edited by D. G. E. Hall, pp. 121–163. Oxford University Press, London.

Castillo, Luis Jaime, and Christopher Donnan
1994   La ocupación Moche de San José de Moro, Jequetepeque. In *Moche: Propuestas y perspectivas*, edited by Santiago Uceda and Elías Mujica, pp. 93–146. Travaux de l'Institut Français d'Etudes Andines 79. Universidad Nacional de la Libertad, Trujillo and Lima, Peru.

Champion, Timothy C.
1989   Introduction. In *Centre and Periphery: Comparative Studies in Archaeology*, edited by Timothy C. Champion, pp. 1–21. Unwin Hyman, London.

Champion, Timothy, and Sara Champion
1986   Peer Polity Interaction in the European Iron Age. In *Peer Polity Interaction and Socio-Political Change*, edited by Colin Renfrew and John Cherry, pp. 59–68. Cambridge University Press, Cambridge.

Chance, John K.
1996   Mesoamerica's Ethnographic Past. *Ethnohistory* 43:379–403.

Chang, Kwang-chih
1975   Ancient Trade as Economics or as Ecology. In *Ancient Civilization and Trade*, edited by Jeremy Sabloff and C. C. Lamberg-Karlovsky, pp. 211–224. University of New Mexico Press, Albuquerque.
1980   *Shang Civilization*. Yale University Press, New Haven.
1983a   Sandai Archaeology and the Formation of States in Ancient China: Processual Aspects of the Origins of Chinese Civilization. In *Origins of Chinese Civilization*, edited by David Keightley, pp. 495–521. University of California Press, Berkeley.
1983b   *Art, Myth, and Ritual*. Harvard University Press, Cambridge.
1986   *The Archaeology of Ancient China*. 4th ed. Yale University Press, New Haven.

Chang, Kwang-Chih, and Changshou Zhang
1998   Looking for City Shang of the Shang Dynasty in Shangqiu. *Symbols* 1:5–10.

Chanock, Martin
1985   *Law, Custom, and Social Order: The Colonial Experience in Malawi and Zambia*. Cambridge University Press, Cambridge.

Chapdelaine, Claude
2001   The Growing Power of a Moche Urban Class. In *Moche Art and Archaeology in Ancient Peru*, edited by Joanne Pillsbury, pp. 69–88.

National Gallery of Art, Washington, D.C.

Charlton, Cynthia O., Thomas H. Charlton, and Deborah L. Nichols

1993   Aztec Household-Based Craft Production: Archaeological Evidence for the City-State of Otumba, Mexico. In *Prehispanic Domestic Units in Western Mesoamerica: Studies of the Household, Compound, and Residence*, edited by Robert Santley and Kenneth Hirth, pp. 147–171. CRC Press, Boca Raton, Florida.

Charlton, Thomas H., and Deborah L. Nichols

1997   The City-State Concept: Development and Applications. In *The Archaeology of City-States*, edited by Deborah Nichols and Thomas Charlton, pp. 1–14, Smithsonian Institution Press, Washington, D.C.

Charlton, Thomas H., Deborah L. Nichols, and Cynthia L. O. Charlton

1991   Aztec Craft Production and Specialization: Archaeological Evidence from the City-State of Otumba, Mexico. *World Archaeology* 23:98–114.

2000   Otumba and Its Neighbors: Ex Oriente Lux. *Ancient Mesoamerica* 11:247–265.

Chase, Arlen F., and Diane Z. Chase

2001   The Royal Court at Caracol, Belize: Its Palaces and People. In *Royal Courts of the Ancient Maya, Volume 2: Data and Case Studies*, edited by Takeshi Inomata and Stephen D. Houston, pp. 102–137. Westview Press, Boulder, Colorado.

Chase, W. Thomas

1991   *Ancient Chinese Bronze Art: Casting the Precious Sacral Vessel*. China Institute in America, New York.

Chase-Dunn, Christopher

1992   The Comparative Study of World-Systems. *Review* 15:313–333.

Chase-Dunn, Christopher, and Thomas D. Hall

1997   *Rise and Demise: Comparing World-Systems*. Westview Press, Boulder, Colorado.

Chase-Dunn, Christopher, and Thomas D. Hall (editors)

1991   *Core/Periphery Relations in Precapitalist Worlds*. Westview Press, Boulder, Colorado.

Chávez, Karen

1988   The Significance of Chiripa in Lake Titicaca Basin Developments. *Expedition* 30(3):17–26.

Chayanov, Aleksandr V.

1966   *The Theory of Peasant Economy*. Edited by Daniel Thorner, Basile Kerblay, and R. E. F. Smith. American Economic Association, Homewood, Illinois.

Chen, Mengjia

1956   *Yinxu buci zongshu* (Summary of oracle bones from Yinxu). Science Press, Beijing.

Chen, Xu

2000   *Xia Shang wenhua lunji* (Collection of essays on Xia and Shang culture). Science Press, Beijing.

Cheng, Te-K'un

1960   *Archaeology in China, Volume 2: Shang China*. W. Heffer and Sons, Cambridge.

Chernykh, Evgenii N.

1992   *Ancient Metallurgy in the USSR: The Early Metal Age*. Cambridge University Press, Cambridge.

Childe, V. Gordon

1950   The Urban Revolution. *Town Planning Review* 21:3–17.

1957   *The Dawn of European Civilization*. 6th ed. Routledge and Kegan Paul, London.

1958   *The Prehistory of European Society*. Harmondsworth, Middlesex, U.K.

Chirino, Pedro

1903   Relación de las Islas Filipinas. In
–1909   *The Philippines, 1493–1898*, vol.
[1604]   12, edited and translated by Emma H. Blair and James A. Robertson. Arthur H. Clark, Cleveland.

Chrétien, Jean-Pierre

1988   The Historical Dimension of Alimentary Practices in Africa. *Diogenes* 144:92–115.

Christie, A. H.

1979   Lin-i, Funan, Java. In *Early Southeast Asia: Essays in Archaeology, History, and Historical Geography*, edited by Robert B. Smith and W. Watson, pp. 281–287. Oxford University Press, New York.

Civil, Miguel

1980   Les limites de l'information textuelle. In *L'archéologie de l'Iraq du début de l'époque néolithique à avant notre ère*, edited by Marie-Therese Barrelet, pp. 225–232. CNRS, Paris.

1987   Ur III Bureaucracy: Quantitative Aspects. In *The Organization of Power: Aspects of Bureaucracy in the Ancient Near East*, edited by McGuire Gibson and Robert D. Biggs, pp. 43–53. Studies in Ancient Oriental Civilization No. 46. Oriental Institute, University of Chicago, Chicago.

1994   *The Farmer's Instructions: A Sumerian Agricultural Manual*. Editorial Ausa, Barcelona.

Clark, John E.

1986   From Mountains to Molehills: A Critical Review of Teotihuacan's Obsidian Industry. In *Research in Economic Anthropology, Supplement 2: Economic Aspects of Prehispanic Highland Mexico*, edited by Barry L. Isaac, pp. 23–74. JAI Press, Greenwich, Connecticut.

1995   Craft Specialization as an Archaeological Category. *Research in Economic Anthropology* 14:267–294.

Clark, John E., and Michael Blake

1994   The Power of Prestige: Competitive Generosity and the Emergence of Rank Societies in Lowland Mesoamerica. In *Factional Competition and Political Development in the New World*, edited by Elizabeth M. Brumfiel and John W. Fox, pp. 17–30. Cambridge University Press, Cambridge.

Clark, John E., and William Parry

1990   Craft Specialization and Cultural Complexity. *Research in Economic Anthropology* 12:289–346.

Claver, Francisco

1985   Dinawit Ogil: High Datu of Namnam. In *Bukidnon Politics and Religion*, edited by Alfonso de Guzman II and Esther Pacheco, pp. 51–114. Institute for Philippine Culture, Papers No. 11. Ateneo de Manila Press, Quezon City, Philippines.

Cleland, Kate M., and Izumi Shimada

1998   Paleteada Potters: Technology, Production Sphere, and Sub-Culture in Ancient Peru. In *Andean Ceramics: Technology, Organization, and Approaches*, edited by Izumi Shimada, pp. 111–152. MASCA Research Papers in Science and Archaeology Vol. 15 supplement. University of Pennsylvania Museum, Philadelphia.

Coedes, Georges

1968   *The Indianized States of Southeast Asia*. East-West Center Press, Honolulu.

1972   *The Making of South East Asia*. 2nd ed. University of California Press, Berkeley.

Cohen, David W., and E. S. Atieno Odhiambo

1989   *Siaya: The Historical Anthropology of an African Landscape*. James Currey, London.

Cohen, Edward E.

1992   *Athenian Economy and Society: A Banking Perspective*. Princeton University Press, Princeton.

2002   Introduction. In *Money, Labour, and Land: Approaches to the Economies of Ancient Greece*, edited by Paul Cartledge, Edward E. Cohen, and Lin Foxhall, pp. 1–7. Routledge, London.

Cole, Fay Cooper

1913   *Wild Tribes of the Davao District*. Publication No. 162. Anthropology Series 13, No. 1. Field Museum of Natural History, Chicago.

1956   *The Bukidnon of Mindanao*. Chicago Natural History Museum, Chicago.

Collins, James M.

1997   Cahokia Settlement and Social Structures as Viewed from the ICT-II. In *Cahokia: Domination and Ideology in the Mississippian World*, edited by Timothy R. Pauketat and Thomas E. Emerson, pp. 124–140. University of Nebraska Press, Lincoln.

Collins, Randall

1992   The Geopolitical and Economic World-Systems of Kinship-Based and Agrarian-Coercive Societies. *Review* 15:373–388.

Colloredo-Mansfeld, Rudi

1999   *The Native Leisure Class: Consumption and Cultural Creativity in the Andes*. University of Chicago Press, Chicago.

2002   An Ethnography of Neoliberalism: Understanding Competition in Artisan Economies. *Current Anthropology* 43:113–137.

Columella

1941   *On Agriculture*. 3 vols. Loeb Classical Library. Harvard University Press, Cambridge.

Comaroff, Jean, and John L. Comaroff

1991   *Of Revelation and Revolution, Volume 1: Christianity, Colonialism, and Consciousness in South Africa*. University of Chicago Press, Chicago.

1993   Introduction. In *Modernity and Its Malcontents: Ritual and Power in Postcolonial Africa*, edited by Jean Comaroff and John L. Comaroff, pp. xi–xxxvii. University of Chicago Press, Chicago.

Comaroff, John L., and Jean Comaroff

1992   *Ethnography and the Historical Imagination*. Westview Press, Boulder, Colorado.

1997   *Of Revelation and Revolution, Volume 2: The Dialectics of Modernity on a South African Frontier*. University of Chicago Press, Chicago.

Conklin, William J.

1990   Architecture of the Chimu: Memory, Function, and Image. In *The Northern Dynasties: Kingship and Statecraft in Chimor*, edited by Michael E. Moseley and Alana Cordy-Collins, pp. 43–74. Dumbarton Oaks, Washington, D.C.

Connah, Graham

1987   *African Civilizations: Precolonial Cities and States in Tropical Africa: An Archaeological Perspective*. Cambridge University Press, Cambridge.

1998   Static Image: Dynamic Reality. In *Transformations in Africa: Essays on Africa's Later Past*, edited by Graham Connah, pp. 1–13. Leicester University Press, London.

Connerton, Paul

1989   *How Societies Remember*. Cambridge University Press, Cambridge.

Cook, Constance

1997   Wealth and the Western Zhou. *Bulletin of the School of Oriental and African Studies* 60(2):253–294.

Cook, Scott, and Martin Diskin (editors)

1976   *Markets in Oaxaca*. University of Texas Press, Austin.

Costin, Cathy Lynne

1986   *From Chiefdom to Empire State: Ceramic Economy Among the Prehispanic Wanka of Highland Peru*. Ph.D. dissertation, University of California, Los Angeles. University Microfilms, Ann Arbor.

1991   Craft Specialization: Issues in Defining, Documenting, and Explaining the Organization of Production. In *Archaeological Method and Theory*, vol. 3, edited by Michael B. Schiffer, pp. 1–56. University of Arizona Press, Tucson.

1993   Textiles, Women, and Political Economy in Late Prehispanic Peru. *Research in Economic Anthropology* 14:3–28.

1996a   Craft Production and Mobilization Strategies in the Inka Empire. In *Craft Specialization and Social Evolution: In Memory of V. Gordon Childe*, edited by Bernard Wailes, pp. 211–225. University of Pennsylvania Museum Publications, Philadelphia.

1996b   Exploring the Relationship Between Gender and Craft in Complex Societies: Methodological and Theoretical Issues of Gender Attribution. In *Gender and Archaeology: Essays in Research and Practice*, edited by Rita P. Wright, pp. 111–142. University of Pennsylvania Press, Philadelphia.

1998a   Concepts of Property and Access to Nonagricultural Resources in the Inka Empire. In *Property in Economic Context*, edited by Robert C. Hunt and Antonio Gilman, pp. 119–137. Monographs in Economic Anthropology No. 14. University Press of America, Lanham, Maryland.

1998b   Housewives, Chosen Women, and Skilled Men: Cloth Production and Social Identity in the Late Prehispanic Andes. In *Craft and Social Identity*, edited by Cathy Lynne Costin and Rita P. Wright. Archeological Papers No. 8. American Anthropological Association, Washington, D.C.

1998c   Introduction. In *Craft and Social Identity*, edited by Cathy Lynne Costin and Rita P. Wright. Archeological Papers No. 8. American Anthropological Association, Washington, D.C.

2001a   Ceramic Production and Distribution. In *Empire and Domestic Economy*, by Terence D'Altroy and Christine Hastorf, pp. 203–242. Kluwer Academic/Plenum, New York.

2001b   Comment on "The Power and Ideology of Artistic Creation: Elite Craft Specialists in Classic Maya Society," by Takeshi Inomata. *Current Anthropology* 42:334–335.

2001c   Craft Production Systems. In *Archaeology at the Millennium: A Sourcebook*, edited by T. Douglas Price and Gary M. Feinman, pp. 273–327. Kluwer Academic/Plenum, New York.

2004   The Study of Craft Production. In *Handbook of Methods in Archaeology*, edited by Christopher Chippindale and Herbert Maschner. Alta-Mira Press, Walnut Creek, California, in press.

Costin, Cathy Lynne, and Melissa Hagstrum
1995   Standardization, Labor Investment, Skill, and the Organization of Ceramic Production in Late Prehispanic Peru. *American Antiquity* 60:619–639.

Cowgill, George L.
1988   Onward and Upward with Collapse. In *The Collapse of Ancient States and Civilizations*, edited by Norman Yoffee and George L. Cowgill, pp. 244–276. University of New Mexico Press, Albuquerque.

CPAM, Henan Province, Xinyang District, and Luoshan County
1986   Luoshan Tianhu Shang Zhou mudi (The Shang and Zhou cemetery at Tianhu, Luoshan County). *Kaogu Xuebao* 2:153–197.

Craig, Austin
1914   *A Thousand Years of Philippine History Before the Coming of the Spaniards*. Philippine Education Company, Manila.

Crawford, Michael H.
1985   *Coinage and Money Under the Roman Republic*. Routledge, New York.

Creekmore, Andrew
2002   In the Throes of Death: A General Comparison of Burial Practices in Northern and Southern Mesopotamia During the Third Millennium B.C. Seminar paper, Anthropology Department, Northwestern University, Evanston.

Crossland, L. B.
1975   Traditional Textile Industry in North-West Brong Ahafo, Ghana—The Archaeological and Contemporary Evidence. *Sankofa* 1:69–73. *Legon Journal of Archaeological and Historical Studies*, University of Ghana.

Cruz, Maria das Dores
1996   Ceramic Production in the Banda Area (West-Central Ghana): An Ethnoarchaeological Approach. *Nyame Akuma* 45:30–37.

2003   *Shaping Quotidian Worlds: Ceramic Production in the Banda Area (West-Central Ghana): An Ethnoarchaeological Approach*. Unpublished Ph.D. dissertation, Department of Anthropology, State University of New York, Binghamton.

Cummins, Tom
1998   The Figurine Tradition of Coastal Ecuador: Technological Style and the Use of Molds. In *Andean Ceramics: Technology, Organization, and Approaches*, edited by Izumi Shimada, pp. 199–212. MASCA Research Papers in Science and Archaeology Vol. 15 supplement. University of Pennsylvania Museum, Philadelphia.

Dai, Zhiqiang
1981   Anyang Yinxu chutu bei hua chutan (Preliminary discussion of cowrie shells excavated at Anyang). *Kaogu* 3:72–77.

D'Altroy, Terence N.
1992   *Provincial Power in the Inka Empire*. Smithsonian Institution Press, Washington, D.C.

1994   Public and Private Economy in the Inka Empire. In *The Economic Anthropology of the State*, edited by Elizabeth M. Brumfiel, pp. 169–209. Monographs in Economic Anthropology No. 11. University Press of America, Lanham, Maryland.

2002   *The Incas*. Blackwell, Cambridge.

D'Altroy, Terence N., and Ronald Bishop

1990   The Provincial Organization of Inka Ceramic Production. *American Antiquity* 55:120–138.

D'Altroy, Terence N., and Timothy K. Earle

1985   Staple Finance, Wealth Finance, and Storage in the Inka Political Economy. *Current Anthropology* 26:187–206.

D'Altroy, Terence N., and Christine Hastorf

2001   *Empire and Domestic Economy*. Kluwer Academic/Plenum, New York.

D'Altroy, Terence N., Anna Lorandi, and Vanessa Williams

1998   Ceramic Production and Use in the Inka Political Economy. In *Andean Ceramics: Technology, Organization, and Approaches*, edited by Izumi Shimada, pp. 283–312. MASCA Research Papers in Science and Archaeology Vol. 15 supplement. University of Pennsylvania Museum, Philadelphia.

D'Andrade, Roy

2000   The Sad Story of Anthropology, 1950–1999. *Cross-Cultural Research* 34:219–232.

D'Arms, John H.

1980   Senators' Involvement in Commerce in the Late Republic: Some Ciceronian Evidence. In *The Seaborne Commerce of Ancient Rome: Studies in Archaeology and History*, edited by John H. D'Arms and E. C. Kopff, pp. 77–89. Memoirs No. 36. American Academy in Rome, Rome.

1981   *Commerce and Social Standing in Ancient Rome*. Harvard University Press, Cambridge.

Dasmarinas, Gomez Perez

1958   The Manners, Customs, and Beliefs
[1590] of the Philippine Inhabitants of Long Ago. Translated by Carlos Quirino and M. García. *Philippine Journal of Science* 87:389–445.

David, Nicholas

1992   The Archaeology of Ideology: Mortuary Practices in the Central Mandara Highlands, Northern Cameroon. In *An African Commitment: Papers in Honour of Peter Lewis Shinnie*, edited by Judy Sterner and Nicholas David, pp. 181–210. University of Calgary Press, Calgary.

1998   The Ethnoarchaeology and Field Archaeology of Grinding at Sukur, Adamawa State, Nigeria. *African Archaeological Review* 15:13–63.

David, Nicholas, and Ian Robertson

1996   Competition and Change in Two Traditional African Iron Industries. In *The Culture and Technology of African Iron Production*, edited by Peter R. Schmidt, pp. 128–144. University of Florida Press, Gainesville.

David, Nicholas, and Judy Sterner

1999   Wonderful Society: The Burgess Shale Creatures, Mandara Polities, and the Nature of Prehistory. In *Beyond Chiefdoms: Pathways to Complexity in Africa*, edited by Susan K. McIntosh, pp. 97–109. Cambridge University Press, Cambridge.

David, Nicholas, Judy Sterner, and Kodzo Gavua

1988   Why Pots Are Decorated. *Current Anthropology* 29:365–389.

David, Nicholas, Robert Heimann, David Killick, and Michael Wayman

1989   Between Bloomery and Blast Furnace: Mafa Iron-Smelting Technology in North Cameroon. *African Archaeological Review* 7:183–208.

Davies, John K.

1998   Ancient Economies: Models and Muddles. In *Trade, Traders, and the Ancient City*, edited by Helen Parkins and Christopher Smith, pp. 225–256. Routledge, New York.

2001   Hellenistic Economies in the Post-Finley Era. In *Hellenistic Economies*, edited by Zofia H. Archibald, John Davies, Vincent Gabrielson, and G. J. Oliver, pp. 11–62. Routledge, New York.

de Barros, Philip

1985   *The Bassar: Large-Scale Iron Producers of the West African Savanna*.

Unpublished Ph.D. dissertation, Department of Anthropology, University of California, Los Angeles.

1987   Bassar: A Quantified, Chronologically Controlled, Regional Approach to a Traditional Iron Production Centre in West Africa. *Africa* 57(2):148–173.

2001   The Effects of the Slave Trade on the Bassar Ironworking Society of Togo. In *West Africa During the Atlantic Slave Trade: Archaeological Perspectives*, edited by Christopher R. DeCorse, pp. 59–80. Leicester University Press, London.

DeBoer, Warren R., and Alice B. Kehoe

1999   Cahokia and the Archaeology of Ambiguity. *Cambridge Archaeological Review* 9:261–267.

De Cecco, Marcello

1985   Monetary Theory and Roman History. *Journal of Economic History* 45:809–822.

2000   Conclusioni. In *Mercati permanente e mercati periodici nel mondo romano*, edited by Elio Lo Cascio, pp. 269–273. Edipuglia, Bari.

DeCorse, Christopher R.

1992   Culture Contact, Continuity, and Change on the Gold Coast, A.D. 1400–1900. *African Archaeological Review* 10:163–196.

1993   The Danes on the Gold Coast: Culture Change and the European Presence. *African Archaeological Review* 11:149–173.

1998a   Culture Contact and Change in West Africa. In *Studies in Culture Contact: Interaction, Culture Change, and Archaeology*, edited by James G. Cusick, pp. 358–377. Occasional Paper No. 25. Center for Archaeological Investigations, Southern Illinois University, Carbondale.

1998b   The Europeans in West Africa: Culture Contact, Continuity, and Change. In *Transformations in Africa: Essays on Africa's Later Past*, edited by Graham Connah, pp. 219–244. Leicester University Press, London.

2001   *An Archaeology of Elmina: Africans and Europeans on the Gold Coast,* 1400–1900. Smithsonian Institution Press, Washington, D.C.

De Ligt, Luuk

1993   *Fairs and Markets in the Roman Empire.* J. C. Gieben, Amsterdam.

2000   Governmental Attitudes Towards Markets and *Collegia.* In *Mercati permanente e mercati periodici nel mondo romano*, edited by Elio Lo Cascio, pp. 237–252. Edipuglia, Bari.

Delougaz, Pinhas

1940   *The Temple Oval at Khafajah.* Oriental Institute Publication No. 53. University of Chicago, Chicago.

DeMarrais, Elizabeth, Luis J. Castillo, and Timothy Earle

1996   Ideology, Materialization, and Power Strategies. *Current Anthropology* 37:15–31.

Dematte, Paula

1999   Longshan-Era Urbanism: The Role of Cities in Predynastic China. *Asian Perspectives* 38(2):91–153.

Denbow, James

1999   Material Culture and the Dialectics of Identity in the Kalahari: A.D. 700–1700. In *Beyond Chiefdoms: Pathways to Complexity in Africa*, edited by Susan K. McIntosh, pp. 110–123. Cambridge University Press, Cambridge.

Denmark, Robert A., Jonathan Friedman, Barry K. Gills, and George Modelski (editors)

2000   *World System History: The Social Science of Long-Term Change.* Routledge, London.

de Vries, Jan

1993   Between Purchasing Power and the World of Goods: Understanding the Household Economy in Early Modern Europe. In *Consumption and the World of Goods*, edited by John Brewer and Roy Porter, pp. 85–132. Routledge, London.

Diakonoff, Igor M.

1982   The Structure of Near Eastern Society Before the Middle of the Second Millennium B.C. *Oikumene* 8:7–100.

Díaz del Castillo, Bernal

1956   *The Discovery and Conquest of Mexico,* 1517–1521. Edited by Genaro García, translated by Alfred

P. Maudslay. Farrar, Straus, and Cudahy, New York.

Diehl, Michael (editor)
2000   *Hierarchies in Action: Cui Bono?* Occasional Paper No. 27. Center for Archaeological Investigations, Southern Illinois University, Carbondale.

Dietler, Michael
1990   Driven by Drink: The Role of Drinking in the Political Economy and the Case of Early Iron Age France. *Journal of Anthropological Archaeology* 9:352–406.
1996   Feasts and Commensal Politics in the Political Economy: Food, Power, and Status in Prehistoric Europe. In *Food and the Status Quest*, edited by Polly Wiessner and Wulf Schiefenhövel, pp. 87–125. Berghahn Books, Providence.
1998   Consumption, Agency, and Cultural Entanglement: Theoretical Implications of a Mediterranean Colonial Encounter. In *Studies in Culture Contact: Interaction, Culture Change, and Archaeology*, edited by James G. Cusick, pp. 288–315. Occasional Paper No. 25. Center for Archaeological Investigations, Southern Illinois University, Carbondale.

Dietler, Michael, and Brian Hayden (editors)
2001   *Feasts: Archaeological and Ethnographic Perspectives on Food, Politics, and Power.* Smithsonian Institution Press, Washington, D.C.

Dietler, Michael, and Ingrid Herbich
1998   Habitus, Techniques, Style: An Integrated Approach to the Social Understanding of Material Culture and Boundaries. In *The Archaeology of Social Boundaries*, edited by Miriam T. Stark, pp. 232–263. Smithsonian Institution Press, Washington, D.C.

Díez de San Miguel, Garci
1964   *Visita hecha a la Provincia de Chucuito por Garci Díez de San Miguel en el año 1567.* Casa de la Cultura del Perú, Lima.
[1547]

di Leonardo, Micaela
1998   *Exotics at Home: Anthropologies, Others, American Modernity.* University of Chicago Press, Chicago.

Dilke, Christopher (editor)
1978   *Letter to a King: A Peruvian Chief's Account of Life Under the Incas and Under Spanish Rule*, by Don Felipe Guamán Poma de Ayala. E. P. Dutton, New York.

Diop, Cheikh Anta
1974   *The African Origin of Civilization: Myth or Reality.* L. Hill, New York.

Dizon, Eusebio, and Rey Santiago
1994   Preliminary Report on the Archaeological Explorations in Batan, Sabtang and Ivuhos Islands, Batanes Province, Northern Philippines. Unpublished report submitted to the Archaeology Division, National Museum of the Philippines, Manila.

Dobres, Marcia-Anne
2000   *Technology and Social Agency.* Blackwell, Oxford.

Donnan, Christopher
1978   *Moche Art of Peru: Precolumbian Symbolic Communication.* Exhibition catalogue, Fowler Museum of Cultural History. University of California, Los Angeles.
1990   An Assessment of the Validity of the Naymlap Dynasty. In *The Northern Dynasties: Kingship and Statecraft in Chimor*, edited by Michael E. Moseley and Alana Cordy-Collins, pp. 243–274. Dumbarton Oaks, Washington, D.C.
1997   A Chimu-Inka Ceramic Manufacturing Center from the North Coast of Peru. *Latin American Antiquity* 8:30–54.

Donnan, Christopher, and Luis Jaime Castillo
1992   Finding the Tomb of a Moche Priestess. *Archaeology* 45(6):38–42.

Donnan, Christopher, and Donna McClelland
1997   Moche Burials at Pacatnamu. In *The Pacatnamu Papers, Volume 2: The Moche Occupation*, edited by Christopher B. Donnan and Guillermo A. Cock, pp. 17–189. Fowler Museum of Cultural History, University of California, Los Angeles.
1999   *Moche Fineline Painting: Its Evolution and Its Artists.* Fowler Museum of Culture History, University of California, Los Angeles.

Douglas, Mary, and Baron Isherwood
1979   *The World of Goods: Towards an*

Anthropology of Consumption.
Basic Books, New York.

Drechsel, Emanuel J.
1994 Mobilean Jargon in the "Prehistory" of Southeastern North America. In *Perspectives on the Southeast: Linguistics, Archaeology, and Ethnohistory*, edited by Patricia B. Kwachka, pp. 25–43. University of Georgia Press, Athens.

Drennan, Robert D.
1989 The Mountains North of the Valley. In *Monte Albán's Hinterland, Part II: The Prehispanic Settlement Patterns in Tlacolula, Etla, and Ocotlán, the Valley of Oaxaca, Mexico,* by Stephen A. Kowalewski, Gary M. Feinman, Richard E. Blanton, Laura Finsten, and Linda M. Nicholas, pp. 367–384. Memoirs No. 23. Museum of Anthropology, University of Michigan, Ann Arbor.

Du, Zhengsheng
1996 Buci suo jian de chengbang xingtai (The structure of city-states from the oracle bones). In *Jin xin ji: Zhang Zhenlang xiansheng bashi qingshou lunwenji* (Collection of essays to show respect for the eightieth birthday of Mr. Zhang Zhenlang), edited by Rongzeng Wu, pp. 12–31. Institute of Archaeology, CASS, Beijing.

Duncan-Jones, Richard P.
1982 *The Economy of the Roman Empire: Quantitative Studies.* 2nd ed. Cambridge University Press, New York.
1990 *Structure and Scale of the Roman Economy.* Cambridge University Press, New York.
1994 *Money and Government in the Roman Empire.* Cambridge University Press, New York.

Durkheim, Emile
1984 *The Division of Labor in Society.*
[1933] Translated by W. D. Halls. Free Press, New York.

Durrenburger, E. Paul
1996 Economic Anthropology. In *Encyclopedia of Cultural Anthropology*, edited by David Levinson and Melvin Ember, pp. 365–371. Henry Holt, New York.

Dyson, Stephen
1985 The Villas of Bucino and the Consumer Model of Roman Rural Development. In *Papers in Italian Archaeology IV*, edited by Carol Malone and Simon Stoddart, pp. 67–84. BAR International Series No. 246. British Archaeological Reports, Oxford.

Earle, Timothy K.
1981 Comment on P. Rice, "Evolution of Specialized Pottery Production: A Trial Model." *Current Anthropology* 22:230–231.
1987a Chiefdoms in Archaeological and Ethnohistorical Perspective. *Annual Review of Anthropology* 16:279–308.
1987b Specialization and the Production of Wealth: Hawaiian Chiefdoms and the Inka Empire. In *Specialization, Exchange, and Complex Societies*, edited by Elizabeth Brumfiel and Timothy Earle, pp. 64–75. Cambridge University Press, Cambridge.
1991 The Evolution of Chiefdoms. In *Chiefdoms: Power, Economy, and Ideology*, edited by Timothy Earle, pp. 1–15. Cambridge University Press, Cambridge.
1997 *How Chiefs Come to Power: The Political Economy in Prehistory.* Stanford University Press, Palo Alto.
1999 Production and Exchange in Prehistory. In *Companion Encyclopedia of Archaeology*, edited by Graeme Barker, pp. 608–636. Routledge, London.

Eggan, Fred
1967 Some Aspects of Bilateral Social Systems in the Northern Philippines. In *Studies in Philippine Anthropology*, edited by Mario D. Zamora, pp. 186–201. Alemar-Phoenix, Quezon City, Philippines.

Ehret, Christopher
1982 The First Spread of Food Production to Southern Africa. In *The Archaeological and Linguistic Reconstruction of African History*, edited by Christopher Ehret and Merrick Posnansky, pp. 158–181. University of California Press, Berkeley.

1984 Historical/Linguistic Evidence for Early African Food Production. In *From Hunters to Farmers: The Causes and Consequences of Food Production in Africa*, edited by J. D. Clark and Steven A. Brandt, pp. 26–35. University of California Press, Berkeley.

Ekeh, Peter P.
1990 Social Anthropology and Two Contrasting Uses of Tribalism in Africa. *Comparative Studies in Society and History* 32:660–700.

Ekholm, Kajsa, and Jonathan Friedman
1982 Capital Imperialism and Exploitation in Ancient World-Systems. *Review* 6:87–110.

Emerson, Thomas E.
1991 Some Perspectives on Cahokia and the Northern Mississippian Expansion. In *Cahokia and the Hinterlands: Middle Mississippian Cultures of the Midwest*, edited by Thomas E. Emerson and R. Barry Lewis, pp. 221–236. University of Illinois Press, Urbana.
1997 *Cahokia and the Archaeology of Power*. University of Alabama Press, Tuscaloosa.

Emerson, Thomas E., and Eve Hargrave
2000 Strangers in Paradise? Recognizing Ethnic Mortuary Diversity on the Fringes of Cahokia. *Southeastern Archaeology* 19:1–23.

Emerson, Thomas E., and Randall E. Hughes
2000 Figurines, Flint Clay Sourcing, the Ozark Highlands, and Cahokian Acquisition. *American Antiquity* 65:79–101.

Emerson, Thomas E., and Timothy R. Pauketat
2002 Embodying Power and Resistance at Cahokia. In *The Dynamics of Power*, edited by Maria O'Donovan, pp. 105–125. Occasional Paper No. 30. Center for Archaeological Investigations, Southern Illinois University, Carbondale.

Englund, Robert K.
1991 Hard Work—Where Will It Get You? Labor Management in Ur III Mesopotamia. *Journal of Near Eastern Studies* 50:255–280.
1995 Late Uruk Period Cattle and Dairy Products: Evidence from Proto-Cuneiform Sources. *Bulletin on Sumerian Agriculture* 8:33–48.
1998 Texts from the Late Uruk Period. In *Mesopotamien: Späturuk-Zeit und Frühdynastische Zeit*, edited by Pascal Attinger and Marcus Wäfler, pp. 15–233. Orbis Biblicus et Orientalis 160/1. Universitätsverlag, Freiburg, and Vandenhoeck and Ruprecht, Gottingen.

Ensminger, Jean
2002 Introduction: Theory in Economic Anthropology at the Turn of the Century. In *Theory in Economic Anthropology*, edited by Jean Ensminger, pp. ix–xix. Altamira Press, Walnut Creek, California.

Epstein, Steven M., and Izumi Shimada
1984 Metalurgia de Sicán: Una reconstrucción de la producción de la aleación de cobre en el Cerro de los Cementerios, Perú. *Beiträge zur Allgeinen und Vergleichenden Archäologie* 5:379–430.

Etienne, Mona
1977 Women and Men, Cloth and Colonization: The Transformation of Production-Distribution Relations Among the Baule (Ivory Coast). *Cahiers d'Etudes Africaines* (65)17:41–64.

Evans, Susan T.
1998 Sexual Politics in the Aztec Palace: Public, Private, and Profane. *RES* 33:167–183.

Falcón, Francisco
1918 Representación hecha en Concilio
[1565] Provincia.... In *Collección de libros y documentos referentes a la historia de Perú*, Serie I, Vol. 11. Lima.
1977 Oficios y cosas en que seruian al
[1571] Ynga. In *Etnía y sociedad: Costa peruana prehispánica*, by María Rostworowski de Diez Canseco, pp. 248–250. Instituto de Estudios Peruanos, Lima.

Falkenstein, Adam
1953 Le cité-temple Sumérien. *Cahiers
–1954 d'Histoire Mondiale* 1:784–814. Revised and translated by Maria de J. Ellis as *The Sumerian Temple-City*. Undena, Los Angeles, 1974.

Fang, Hui
1998   Yueshi wenhua de fenqi yu niandai (Periodization and dating of the Yueshi culture). *Kaogu* 4:55–71.
2001   Shang dai bang xi qi qi qianshuo (Preliminary discussion of mother-of-pearl inlaid objects). *Huaxia Kaogu* 2:48–61.
2004   Shang Zhou shiqi Haidai diqu de haiyan shengchan (Production of sea salt in the Haidai area during the Shang and Zhou periods). *Kaogu*, in press.

Farb, Peter
1969   *Man's Rise to Civilization as Shown by the Indians of North America from Primeval Times to the Coming of the Industrial State*. Secker and Warburg, London.

Farber, H.
1978   A Price and Wage Study for Northern Babylonia During the Old Babylonian Period. *Journal of the Economic and Social History of the Orient* 21:1–51.

Farnsworth, Rodney
1996   Contextualizing the Pliny/Trajan Letters: A Case for Critiquing the (American) Myth of Deliberative Discourse in (Roman) Society. *Rhetoric Society Quarterly* 26(1):29–46.

Fauman-Fichman, Ruth
1999   *Postclassic Craft Production in Morelos, Mexico: The Cotton Thread Industry in the Provinces*. Ph.D. dissertation, University of Pittsburgh. University Microfilms, Ann Arbor.

Feinman, Gary M.
1980   *The Relationship Between Administrative Organization and Ceramic Production in the Valley of Oaxaca, Mexico*. Unpublished Ph.D. dissertation, Department of Anthropology, Graduate Center, City University of New York, New York.
1995   The Emergence of Inequality: Focus on Strategies and Processes. In *Foundations of Social Inequality*, edited by T. Douglas Price and Gary M. Feinman, pp. 255–279. Plenum Press, New York.
1998   Scale and Organization: Perspectives on the Archaic State. In *Archaic States*, edited by Gary M. Feinman and Joyce Marcus, pp. 95–133. School of American Research Press, Santa Fe, New Mexico.
1999   Rethinking Our Assumptions: Economic Specialization at the Household Scale in Ancient Ejutla, Oaxaca, Mexico. In *Pottery and People: A Dynamic Interaction*, edited by James M. Skibo and Gary M. Feinman, pp. 81–98. University of Utah Press, Salt Lake City.
2000a   Cultural Evolutionary Approaches and Archaeology. In *Cultural Evolution, Contemporary Viewpoints*, edited by Gary M. Feinman and Linda Manzanilla, pp. 3–12. Kluwer Academic/Plenum, New York.
2000b   Dual-Processual Theory and Social Formations in the Southwest. In *Alternative Leadership Strategies in the Prehispanic Southwest*, edited by Barbara J. Mills, pp. 207–224. University of Arizona Press, Tucson.
2001   Economic Organization. In *Archaeology of Ancient Mexico and Central America: An Encyclopedia*, edited by Susan T. Evans and David L. Webster, pp. 229–234. Garland, New York.

Feinman, Gary M., and Andrew K. Balkansky
1997   Ceramic Firing in Ancient and Modern Oaxaca. In *Prehistory and History of Ceramic Kilns*, edited by Prudence Rice, pp. 129–147. American Ceramic Society, Westerville, Ohio.

Feinman, Gary M., Richard E. Blanton, and Stephen A. Kowalewski
1984   Market System Development in the Prehispanic Valley of Oaxaca, Mexico. In *Trade and Exchange in Early Mesoamerica*, edited by Kenneth G. Hirth, pp. 157–178. University of New Mexico Press, Albuquerque.

Feinman, Gary M., and Joyce Marcus (editors)
1998   *Archaic States*. School of American Research Press, Santa Fe, New Mexico.

Feinman, Gary M., and Linda M. Nicholas
1990   At the Margins of the Monte Albán State: Settlement Patterns in the Ejutla Valley, Oaxaca, Mexico.

Latin American Antiquity 1:216–246.

1992 Prehispanic Interregional Interaction in Southern Mexico: The Valley of Oaxaca and the Ejutla Valley. In *Resources, Power, and Interregional Interaction*, edited by Edward M. Schortman and Patricia A. Urban, pp. 75–116. Plenum Press, New York.

1993 Shell Ornament Production in Ejutla: Implications for Highland-Coastal Interaction in Ancient Oaxaca. *Ancient Mesoamerica* 4:103–119.

1995 Household Craft Specialization and Shell Ornament Manufacture in Ejutla, Mexico. *Expedition* 37(2):14–25.

1996 Defining the Eastern Limits of the Monte Albán State: Systematic Settlement Pattern Survey in the Guirún Area, Oaxaca, Mexico. *Mexicon* 18:91–97.

2000a Intensive Survey of Hilltop Terrace Sites in Oaxaca, Mexico. *Antiquity* 74(2000):21–22.

2000b High-Intensity Household-Scale Production in Ancient Mesoamerica: A Perspective from Ejutla, Oaxaca. In *Cultural Evolution, Contemporary Viewpoints*, edited by Gary M. Feinman and Linda Manzanilla, pp. 119–142. Kluwer Academic/Plenum, New York.

2001 Excavations at El Palmillo: A Hilltop Terrace Site in Oaxaca, Mexico. *In The Field* 72(2):2–5. Field Museum, Chicago.

Feinman, Gary M., Linda M. Nicholas, and Scott Fedick

1991 Shell Working in Prehispanic Ejutla, Oaxaca (Mexico): Findings from an Exploratory Field Season. *Mexicon* 13:69–77.

Feinman, Gary M., Linda M. Nicholas, and Helen R. Haines

2002 Houses on a Hill: Classic Period Domestic Life at El Palmillo, Oaxaca, Mexico. *Latin American Antiquity* 13:251–277.

Feinman, Gary M., Linda M. Nicholas, and William D. Middleton

1993 Craft Activities at the Prehispanic

Ejutla Site, Oaxaca, Mexico. *Mexicon* 15:33–41.

2001 Domestic Life at Classic Period Hilltop Terrace Sites: Perspectives from El Palmillo, Oaxaca. *Mexicon* 23:42–48.

Feldman, Lawrence H.

1985 *A Tumpline Economy*. Labyrinthos, Culver City, California.

Finley, Moses I.

1973 *The Ancient Economy*. Chatto and Windus, London.

Finsten, Laura

1996 Periphery and Frontier in Southern Mexico: The Mixtec Sierra in Highland Oaxaca. In *Pre-Columbian World Systems,* edited by Peter N. Peregrine and Gary M. Feinman, pp. 77–95. Prehistory Press, Madison, Wisconsin.

Firth, Raymond

1959 *Economics of the New Zealand Maori*. 2nd ed. Government Printer, Wellington, New Zealand. Originally published 1929.

1967 *The Work of the Gods in Tikopia*. Athlone Press, London.

Flannery, Kent V.

1993 Will the Real Model Please Stand Up: Comments on Saidel's "Round House or Square?" *Journal of Mediterranean Archaeology* 6:109–117.

1995 Prehistoric Social Evolution. In *Research Frontiers in Anthropology,* edited by Carol R. Ember and Melvin Ember, pp. 3–25. Prentice-Hall, Englewood Cliffs, New Jersey.

1998 The Ground Plans of Archaic States. In *Archaic States*, edited by Gary M. Feinman and Joyce Marcus, pp. 15–57. School of American Research Press, Santa Fe, New Mexico.

Flannery, Kent V. (editor)

1976 *The Early Mesoamerican Village*. Academic Press, New York.

Folan, William J., Joel D. Gunn, and Maria del Rosario Domínguez C.

2001 Triadic Temples, Central Plazas, and Dynastic Palaces: A Diachronic Analysis of the Royal Court Complex, Calakmul, Campeche, Mexico. In *Royal Courts of the Ancient Maya, Volume 2: Data and Case*

Studies, edited by Takeshi Inomata and Stephen D. Houston, pp. 223–265. Westview Press, Boulder, Colorado.

Foraboschi, Daniele
2000   The Hellenistic Economy: Indirect Intervention by the State. In *Production and Public Powers in Classical Antiquity*, edited by Elio Lo Cascio and Dominic W. Rathbone, pp. 37–43. Supplementary Vol. No. 26. Cambridge Philological Society, Cambridge.

Foster, Benjamin R.
1981   A New Look at the Sumerian Temple-State. *Journal of the Economic and Social History of the Orient* 24:225–241.

1993   Management and Administration in the Sargonic Period. In *Akkad: The First World Empire,* edited by Mario Liverani, pp. 25–39. Herder Editrice, Rome.

1999   A Century of Mesopotamian Agriculture. In *Landwirtschaft im Alten Orient,* edited by Horst Klengel and Johannes Renger, pp. 1–19. Dietrich Reimer, Berlin.

Fowler, Melvin L., Jerome Rose, Barbara Vander Leest, and Steven R. Ahler
2000   *The Mound 72 Area: Dedicated and Sacred Space in Early Cahokia*. Reports of Investigations No. 54. Illinois State Museum, Springfield.

Fox, Richard
1971   *Kin, Clan, Raja, and Rule: State-Hinterland Relations in Pre-industrial India*. University of California Press, Berkeley.

1977   *Urban Anthropology: Cities in Their Cultural Settings*. Prentice-Hall, Englewood Cliffs, New Jersey.

Frangipane, Marcella
1997   A Fourth-Millennium Temple/Palace Complex at Arslantepe-Malatya: North-South Relations and the Formation of Early State Societies in the Northern Regions of Greater Mesopotamia. *Paléorient* 23(1): 45–73.

Frank, Andre G.
1978   *World Accumulation, 1492–1789*. Macmillan, London.

1998   *ReOrient: Global Economy in the Asian Age*. University of California Press, Berkeley.

Frank, Andre G., and Barry K. Gills (editors)
1993   *The World System: Five Hundred Years or Five Thousand?* Routledge, London.

Frank, Barbara E.
1993   Reconstructing the History of an African Ceramic Tradition: Technology, Slavery, and Agency in the Region of Kadiolo (Mali). *Cahiers d'Etudes Africaines* (131)33:381–401.

Frank, Robert H., and Philip J. Cook
1995   *The Winner-Take-All Society: Why the Few at the Top Get So Much More Than the Rest of Us*. Penguin Books, New York.

Frankenstein, Susan, and Michael J. Rowlands
1978   The Internal Structure and Regional Context of Early Iron-Age Society in South-Western Germany. *Bulletin of the [London University] Institute of Archaeology* 15:73–112.

Franklin, Ursula
1983   The Beginnings of Metallurgy in China: A Comparative Approach. In *The Great Bronze Age of China: A Symposium*, edited by George Kuwayama, pp. 94–99. Los Angeles County Museum of Art, Los Angeles.

Frayn, Joan M.
1993   *Markets and Fairs in Roman Italy: Their Social and Economic Importance from the Second Century B.C. to the Third Century A.D.* Clarendon Press, Oxford.

Freidel, David A.
1981   The Political Economics of Residential Dispersion Among the Lowland Maya. In *Lowland Maya Settlement Patterns*, edited by Wendy Ashmore, pp. 371–382. University of New Mexico Press, Albuquerque.

Freidel, David A., and Linda Schele
1988   Kingship in the Late Preclassic Maya Lowlands. *American Anthropologist* 90:547–567.

Fried, Morton H.
1967   *The Evolution of Political Society: An Essay in Political Anthropology*. Random House, New York.

Friedman, Jonathan
1979   *System, Structure, and Contradiction in the Evolution of "Asiatic" Social Formations*. National Museum Press, Copenhagen.

Friedman, Jonathan, and Michael J. Rowlands
1978   Notes Towards an Epigenetic Model of the Evolution of "Civilization." In *The Evolution of Social Systems*, edited by Jonathon Friedman and Michael J. Rowlands, pp. 201–276. University of Pittsburgh Press, Pittsburgh.

Frier, Bruce W.
1980   *Landlords and Tenants in Imperial Rome*. Princeton University Press, Princeton.

Fuglestad, Finn
1992   The Trevor-Roper Trap or the Imperialism of History: An Essay. *History in Africa* 19:309–326.

Fülle, Gunnar
1997   The Internal Organization of the Arretine *Terra Sigillata* Industry: Problems of Evidence and Interpretation. *Journal of Roman Studies* 87:111–155.

Gailey, Christine W., and Thomas C. Patterson
1987   Power Relations and State Formation. In *Power Relations and State Formation*, edited by Thomas C. Patterson and Christine W. Gailey, pp. 1–26. American Anthropological Association, Washington, D.C.

Gallant, Thomas W.
1991   *Risk and Survival in Ancient Greece*. Stanford University Press, Palo Alto.

Gao, Guangren
2000   Haidai qu de Shangdai wenhua yicun (Shang period cultural remains in the Haidai region). *Kaogu Xuebao* 2:183–198.

Geertz, Clifford
1967   *Religion of Java*. Free Press, Glencoe, Illinois.
1973   *The Interpretation of Cultures*. Basic Books, New York.
1980a   Ports of Trade in Nineteenth-Century Bali. *Research in Economic Anthropology* 3:109–122.
1980b   *Negara: The Theatre State in Nineteeth-Century Bali*. Princeton University Press, Princeton.

Gelb, Ignace J.
1969   On the Alleged Temple and State Economies in Ancient Mesopotamia. In *Studi in onore di Edoardo Volterra*, 6:137–154. Giuffr'e, Milan.
1986   Ebla and Lagash: Environmental Contrast. In *The Origins of Cities in Dry Farming Syria and Mesopotamia in the Third Millennium B.C.*, edited by Harvey Weiss, pp. 157–167. Four Quarters, Guilford, Connecticut.

Gelb, Ignace J., Piotr Steinkeller, and Robert M. Whiting
1991   *Earliest Land Tenure Systems in the Near East: The Ancient Kudurrus*. Publication Vol. 104. Oriental Institute, University of Chicago, Chicago.

Gintis, Herbert
2000   Strong Reciprocity and Human Sociality. *Journal of Theoretical Biology* 206:169–179.

Gladwin, Christina H.
1989   On the Division of Labor Between Economics and Economic Anthropology. In *Economic Anthropology*, edited by Stuart Plattner, pp. 397–425. Stanford University Press, Palo Alto.

Golas, Peter
1999   *Chemistry and Chemical Technology, Part XIII: Mining*. Science and Civilisation in China, Vol. 5, general editor Joseph Needham. Cambridge University Press, Cambridge.

Goldstein, Lynne G., and John D. Richards
1991   Ancient Aztalan: The Cultural and Ecological Context of a Late Prehistoric Site in the Midwest. In *Cahokia and the Hinterlands: Middle Mississippian Cultures of the Midwest*, edited by Thomas E. Emerson and R. Barry Lewis, pp. 193–206. University of Illinois Press, Urbana.

Goldstein, Paul
1989   *Omo, a Tiwanaku Provincial Center in Moquegua, Peru*. Unpublished Ph.D. dissertation, Department of Anthropology, University of Chicago, Chicago.

Gómez-Pompa, Arturo, José Salvador Flores, and Mario Aliphat Fernández
1990 The Sacred Cacao Groves of the Maya. *Latin American Antiquity* 1:247–257.

Goody, Jack R.
1963 Ethnological Notes on the Distribution of the Guang Languages. *Journal of African Languages* 2:173–189.
1971 *Technology, Tradition, and State in Africa*. Oxford University Press, London.
1986 *The Logic of Writing and the Organization of Society*. Cambridge University Press, Cambridge.
1990 The Political Systems of the Tallensi and Their Neighbors, 1888–1915. *Cambridge Anthropology* 14(2):1–25.
1998 Establishing Control: Violence along the Black Volta at the Beginning of Colonial Rule. *Cahiers d'Etudes Africaines* (150–152)38:227–244.

Gordon, Robert T., and Stuart Sholto Douglas
2000 *The Bushman Myth: The Making of a Namibian Underclass*. 2nd ed. Westview Press, Boulder, Colorado.

Gose, Peter
1994 *Deathly Waters and Hungry Mountains: Agrarian Ritual and Class Formation in an Andean Town*. University of Toronto Press, Toronto.

Granovetter, Mark
1985 Economic Action and Social Structure: The Problem of Embeddedness. *American Journal of Sociology* 91:481–510.
1992 The Nature of Economic Relations. In *Understanding Economic Process*, edited by Sutti Ortiz and Susan Lees, pp. 21–37. University Press of America, Lanham, Maryland.

Green, William, and Roland L. Rodell
1994 The Mississippian Presence and Cahokia Interaction at Trempealeau, Wisconsin. *American Antiquity* 59:334–359.

Greene, Kevin
1986 *The Archaeology of the Roman Economy*. University of California Press, Berkeley.

Grier, Beverly
1981 Underdevelopment, Modes of Production, and the State in Colonial Ghana. *African Studies Review* 24(1):21–47.

Griffin, James B.
1952 Culture Periods in Eastern United States Archeology. In *Archeology of Eastern United States*, edited by James B. Griffin, pp. 352–364. University of Chicago Press, Chicago.

Gronenborn, Detlef
2001 Kanem-Borno: A Brief Summary of the History and Archaeology of an Empire of the Central *bilad al-sudan*. In *West Africa During the Atlantic Slave Trade: Archaeological Perspectives*, edited by Christopher R. DeCorse, pp. 101–130. Leicester University Press, London.

Guamán Poma de Ayala, Felipe
1980[1615] *El primer nueva corónica y buen gobierno*. Edición crítica de John Murra y Rolena Adorno; traducciones y análisis textual del Quechua por Jorge Urioste. Siglo Veintiuno Editores, Madrid.

Gudeman, Stephen
1986 *Economics as Culture: Models and Metaphors of Livelihood*. Routledge and Kegan Paul, London.

Gullick, John M.
1958 *Indigenous Political Systems of Western Malaya*. Athlone Press, London.
1965 *Indigenous Political Systems of Western Malaya*. 2nd ed. Athlone Press, London.
1981 *Malaysia: Economic Expansion and National Unity*. Ernest Benn, London.

Guo, Baojun
1933 B qu fajue ji zhi yi (Excavations in Area B). In *Excavations at Anyang, Part IV*, edited by Li Chi, pp. 579–608. Bulletin of the Institute of History and Philology, Shanghai.
1963 *Zhongguo qingtongqi shidai* (The Bronze Age of China). New China Press, Beijing.

Guo Keyu, Huaduo Sun, Fangjian Liang, and Chaoming Yang
1990 Suo shi qi de faxian ji qi zhongyao yiyi (The significance of the discovery

of the Rope Clan vessel). *Wenwu* 7:36–38.

Guyer, Jane I.
1999   Turbulence and Loss in African History and Anthropology. Paper presented at the 98th Annual Meeting of the American Anthropology Association, Chicago.

Guyer, Jane I. (editor)
1995   *Money Matters: Instability, Values, and Social Payments in the Modern History of West African Communities*. Heinemann, Portsmouth, New Hampshire.

Guyer, Jane I., and Samuel M. E. Belinga
1995   Wealth in People as Wealth in Knowledge: Accumulation and Composition in Equatorial Africa. *Journal of African History* 36:91–120.

Haas, Jonathan
1982   *The Evolution of the Prehistoric State*. Columbia University Press, New York.

Hagstrum, Melissa
1989   *Technological Continuity and Change: Ceramic Ethnoarchaeology in the Peruvian Andes*. Ph.D. dissertation, University of California, Los Angeles. University Microfilms, Ann Arbor.

Haight, Bruce M.
1981   *Bole and Gonja: Contributions to the History of Northern Ghana*. Unpublished Ph.D. dissertation, Department of History, Northwestern University, Evanston.

Hall, Daniel G. E.
1968   *A History of South-East Asia*. 3rd ed. St. Martin's Press, New York.

Hall, Kenneth R.
1976   State and Statecraft in Early Srivijaya. In *Explorations in Early Southeast Asian History: The Origins of Southeast Asian Statecraft*, edited by Kenneth R. Hall and John K. Whitmore, pp. 61–105. Michigan Papers on South and Southeast Asia No. 11. Center for South and Southeast Asian Studies, University of Michigan, Ann Arbor.
1977   The Coming of Islam to the Archipelago: A Reassessment. In *Economic Exchange and Social Interaction in Southeast Asia: Perspectives from Prehistory*, edited by Karl Hutterer, pp. 177–196. Michigan Papers on South and Southeast Asia No. 13. Center for South and Southeast Asian Studies, University of Michigan, Ann Arbor.
1985   *Maritime Trade and State Development in Early Southeast Asia*. University of Hawaii Press, Honolulu.
1992   Economic History of Early Southeast Asia. In *The Cambridge History of Southeast Asia, Volume 1: From Early Times to c. 1800*, edited by Nicholas Tarling, pp. 183–275. Cambridge University Press, Cambridge.

Hall, Thomas D., and Christopher Chase-Dunn
1993   The World-Systems Perspective and Archaeology: Forward into the Past. *Journal of Archaeological Research* 1:121–143.

Hally, David J. (editor)
1994   *Ocmulgee Archaeology: 1936–1986*. University of Georgia Press, Athens.

Halperin, Rhoda H.
1988   *Economies Across Cultures: Toward a Science of the Economy*. St. Martin's Press, New York.
1994   *Cultural Economies: Past and Present*. University of Texas Press, Austin.

Halstead, Paul
1993   Banking on Livestock: Indirect Storage in Greek Agriculture. *Bulletin on Sumerian Agriculture* 7:63–75.
1995   Plough and Power: The Economic and Social Significance of Cultivation with the Ox-Drawn Ard in the Mediterranean. *Bulletin on Sumerian Agriculture* 8:11–22.

Hammond, Dorothy, and Alta Jablow
1970   *The Africa That Never Was: Four Centuries of British Writing about Africa*. Waveland Press, Prospect Heights, Illinois.

Hammond, Norman
1991   Inside the Black Box: Defining Maya Polity. In *Classic Maya Political History: Hieroglyphic and Archaeological Evidence*, edited by T. Patrick Culbert, pp. 253–284. Cambridge University Press, Cambridge.

Hansen, Richard D.
1998   Continuity and Disjunction: The Pre-Classic Antecedents of Classic Architecture. In *Form and Meaning in Classic Maya Architecture*, edited by Stephen D. Houston, pp. 49–122. Dumbarton Oaks, Washington, D.C.

Harding, A. F.
1983   The Bronze Age in Central and Eastern Europe: Advances and Prospects. *Advances in World Archaeology* 2:1–50.

Harris, Rivkah
1964   The Naditu Woman. In *Studies Presented to A. Leo Oppenheim*, edited by Robert D. Biggs and J. A. Brinkman, pp. 106–135. Oriental Institute, University of Chicago, Chicago.

1975   *Ancient Sippar: A Demographic Study of an Old Babylonian City (1894–1595 B.C.)*. Historisch-Archaeologisch Instituut te Istanbul, Leiden.

Harris, William V.
1993   Between Archaic and Modern: Some Current Problems in the History of the Roman Economy. In *The Inscribed Economy: Production and Distribution in the Roman Empire in the Light of Instrumentum domesticum*, edited by William V. Harris, pp. 11–29. Supplement No. 6. Journal of Roman Archaeology, Ann Arbor, Michigan.

Harrison, Eleanor
2004   Nourishing the Animus of Lived Space Through Ritual Caching. In *K'axob: Ritual, Work, and Family in an Ancient Maya Village,* edited by Patricia A. McAnany. Cotsen Institute of Archaeology, University of California, Los Angeles, in press.

Harrison, Peter D.
1999   *The Lords of Tikal: Rulers of an Ancient Maya City*. Thames and Hudson, London.

2001   Thrones and Throne Structures in the Central Acropolis of Tikal as an Expression of the Royal Court. In *Royal Courts of the Ancient Maya, Volume 2: Data and Case Studies,* edited by Takeshi Inomata and Stephen D. Houston, pp. 74–101. Westview Press, Boulder, Colorado.

Hart, Keith
1982   On Commoditization. In *From Craft to Industry: The Ethnography of Proto-Industrial Cloth Production,* edited by Esther N. Goody, pp. 38–49. Cambridge University Press, Cambridge.

Hastorf, Christine
2004   The Upper Formative in the Titicaca Region. In *Advances in the Archaeology of the Titicaca Basin*, edited by Charles Stanish, Amanda B. Cohen, and Mark S. Aldenderfer. Cotsen Institute of Archaeology, University of California, Los Angeles, in press.

Hastorf, Christine (editor)
1999   *Early Settlement at Chiripa, Bolivia.* Contributions of the University of California Archaeological Research Facility, Berkeley.

Hayashida, Frances
1995   *State Pottery Production in the Inka Provinces.* Unpublished Ph.D. dissertation, Department of Anthropology, University of Michigan, Ann Arbor.

1998   New Insights into Inka Pottery Production. In *Andean Ceramics: Technology, Organization, and Approaches*, edited by Izumi Shimada, pp. 313–338. MASCA Research Papers in Science and Archaeology, Vol. 15 supplement. University of Pennsylvania Museum, Philadelphia.

Hayden, Brian
1995   Pathways to Power: Principles for Creating Socioeconomic Inequalities. In *Foundations of Social Inequality*, edited by T. Douglas Price and Gary M. Feinman, pp. 15–86. Plenum Press, New York.

1996   Feasting in Prehistoric and Traditional Societies. In *Food and the Status Quest*, edited by Polly Wiessner and Wulf Schiefenhövel, pp. 127–147. Berghahn Books, Providence.

Hayden, Brian, and Rob Gargett
1990   Big Man, Big Heart? A Meso-american View of the Emergence of

Complex Society. *Ancient Meso-america* 1:3–20.

Headrick, Annabeth
2004   The Quadripartite Motif and the Centralization of Power. In *K'axob: Ritual, Work, and Family in an Ancient Maya Village*, edited by Patricia A. McAnany. Cotsen Institute of Archaeology, University of California, Los Angeles, in press.

Hebei Province Institute of Archaeology
1985   *Gaocheng Taixi Shang dai yizhi* (The Shang site of Taixi at Gaocheng). Wenwu Press, Beijing.

Helms, Mary W.
1993   *Craft and the Kingly Ideal: Art, Trade, and Power*. University of Texas Press, Austin.

Hendon, Julia A.
1997   Women's Work, Women's Space, and Women's Status Among the Classic-Period Maya Elite of the Copan Valley, Honduras. In *Women in Prehistory: North America and Mesoamerica*, edited by Cheryl Claassen and Rosemary Joyce, pp. 33–46. University of Pennsylvania Press, Philadelphia.

Henrickson, Elizabeth
1981   Non-religious Residential Settlement Patterning in the Late Early Dynastic of the Diyala Region. *Mesopotamia* 16:43–141.

Hester, Thomas R., and Robert F. Heizer
1972   Problems in the Functional Interpretation of Artifacts: Scraper Planes from Mitla and Yagul, Oaxaca. *University of California Archaeological Research Facility* 14:107–123.

Hester, Thomas R., and Harry J. Shafer
1994   The Ancient Maya Craft Community at Colha, Belize, and Its External Relationships. In *Archaeological Views of the Countryside: Village Communities in Early Complex Societies*, edited by Glenn M. Schwartz and Steven E. Falconer, pp. 48–63. Smithsonian Institution Press, Washington, D.C.

Hicks, Frederic
1987   First Steps Toward a Market-Integrated Economy in Aztec Mexico. In *Early State Dynamics*, edited by Henri J. M. Claessen and Pieter van de Velde, pp. 91–107. Studies in Human Society No. 2. E. J. Brill, Leiden.

Higham, Charles
1989   *The Archaeology of Mainland Southeast Asia*. Cambridge University Press, Cambridge.
1996   *The Bronze Age of Southeast Asia*. Cambridge University Press, Cambridge.

Hirth, Kenneth G.
1998   The Distributional Approach: A New Way to Identify Marketplace Exchange in the Archaeological Record. *Current Anthropology* 39:451–476.

Ho, C.-M.
1992   An Analysis of Settlement Patterns in the Lopburi Area. In *Early Metallurgy, Trade, and Urban Centres in Thailand and Southeast Asia*, edited by Ian Glover, Pornchai Suchitta, and John Villiers, pp. 39–46. White Lotus Press, Bangkok.

Hodder, Ian
1982   *Symbols in Action: Ethnoarchaeological Studies of Material Culture*. Cambridge University Press, Cambridge.

Hodge, Mary G.
1998   Archaeological Views of Aztec Culture. *Journal of Archaeological Research* 6:197–238.

Hodge, Mary G., and Michael E. Smith (editors)
1994   *Economies and Polities in the Aztec Realm*. Institute for Mesoamerican Studies, State University of New York, Albany.

Hodges, Richard
1988   *Primitive and Peasant Markets*. Blackwell, Cambridge.

Holl, Augustin F. C.
1995   African History: Past, Present, and Future: The Unending Quest for Alternatives. In *Making Alternative Histories: The Practice of Archaeology in History in Non-Western Settings*, edited by Peter R. Schmidt and Thomas C. Patterson, pp. 183–211. School of American Research Press, Santa Fe, New Mexico.

Hopkins, Keith
1980   Taxes and Trade in the Roman Empire. *Journal of Roman Studies* 70:101–125.

2000 Rents, Taxes, Trade, and the City of Rome. In *Mercati permanente e mercati periodici nel mondo romano*, edited by Elio Lo Cascio, pp. 253–267. Edipuglia, Bari.

Houston, Stephen D.
1997 A King Worth a Hill of Beans. *Archaeology* 50(3):40.
2000 Into the Minds of Ancients: Advances in Maya Glyph Studies. *Journal of World Prehistory* 14: 121–201.

Houston, Stephen D., John Robertson, and David Stuart
2000 The Language of Classic Maya Inscriptions. *Current Anthropology* 41:321–356.

Houston, Stephen D., and David Stuart
2001 Peopling the Classic Maya Court. In *Royal Courts of the Ancient Maya, Volume 1: Theory, Comparison, and Synthesis*, edited by Takeshi Inomata and Stephen D. Houston, pp. 54–83. Westview Press, Boulder, Colorado.

Howgego, Christopher
1992 The Supply and Use of Money in the Roman World. *Journal of Roman Studies* 82:1–31.
1994 Coin Circulation and the Integration of the Roman Economy. *Journal of Roman Archaeology* 7:5–21.

Hua, Jueming
1999 *Zhongguo gudai jinshu jishu* (Metallurgical technology in ancient China). Daxing Press, Zhengzhou, Henan.

Hua, Jueming, and Benshan Lu
1996 Changjiang zhong xia liu tong kuang dai de zaoqi kai fa he Zhongguo qingtong wenming (Bronze civilization of China and early period mining in the middle and lower reaches of the Yangzi River area). *Ziran Kexue Li Yanjiu* 15(1):1–16.

Hubei Province Institute of Archaeology
2001 *Panlongcheng: 1963–1994 nian kaogu fajue baogao* (Report on the 1963–1994 archaeological excavations at Panlongcheng). Wenwu Press, Beijing.

Hudson, Michael, and Baruch A. Levine (editors)
1996 *Privatization in the Ancient Near East and Classical World*, Vol. 1. Bulletin 5. Peabody Museum of Archaeology and Ethnology, Harvard University, Cambridge.
1999 *Urbanization and Land Ownership in the Ancient Near East*, Vol. 2. Bulletin 7. Peabody Museum of Archaeology and Ethnology, Harvard University, Cambridge.

Humphreys, Sarah C.
1978 *Anthropology and the Greeks*. Routledge and Kegan Paul, Boston.

Hunt, Edwin S.
1987 Multinational Corporations: Their Origin, Development, and Present Forms. *Research in Economic Anthropology* 8:317–375.

Hutterer, Karl L.
1977 Prehistoric Trade and the Evolution of Philippine Societies: A Reconsideration. In *Economic Exchange and Social Interaction in Southeast Asia: Perspectives from Prehistory*, edited by K. Hutterer, pp. 177–196. Michigan Papers on South and Southeast Asia No. 13. University of Michigan Center for South and Southeast Asian Studies, Ann Arbor.

Hutterer, Karl L., and William K. Macdonald (editors)
1982 *Houses Built on Scattered Poles: Prehistory and Ecology in Negros Oriental, Philippines*. University of San Carlos Press, Cebu City, Philippines.

Hyslop, John
1976 *An Archaeological Investigation of the Lupaka Kingdom and Its Origin*. Unpublished Ph.D. dissertation, Department of Anthropology, Cornell University, Ithaca.

Ileto, Reynaldo
1971 *Maguindanao, 1860–1888: The Career of Datu Uto of Buayan*. Southeast Asian Paper No. 32. Cornell University, Ithaca.

Inikori, J. E. (editor)
1982 *Forced Migration: The Impact of the Export Slave Trade on African Societies*. Hutchinson, London.

Inomata, Takeshi
2001a King's People: Classic Maya Courtiers in a Comparative Perspective. In *Royal Courts of the Ancient*

Maya, Volume 1: Theory, Comparison, and Synthesis, edited by Takeshi Inomata and Stephen D. Houston, pp. 27–53. Westview Press, Boulder, Colorado.

2001b The Power and Ideology of Artistic Creation: Elite Craft Specialists in Classic Maya Society. *Current Anthropology* 42:321–350.

Inomata, Takeshi, and Stephen D. Houston (editors)

2001 *Royal Courts of the Ancient Maya*, vols. 1 and 2. Westview Press, Boulder, Colorado.

Inomata, Takeshi, and Laura Stiver

1998 Floor Assemblages from Burned Structures at Aguateca, Guatemala: A Study of Classic Maya Households. *Journal of Field Archaeology* 25:431–452.

Institute of Archaeology, CASS

1976 1975 Nian Anyang Yinxu de xin faxian (New discoveries at the site of Yinxu at Anyang in 1975). *Kaogu* 4:264–272, 263.

1980 *Yinxu Fu Hao mu* (Tomb of Fu Hao at Yinxu). Wenwu Press, Beijing.

1987 *Yinxu fajue baogao, 1958–1961* (Excavations at Yinxu, 1958–1961). Wenwu Press, Beijing.

1999 *Yanshi Erlitou, 1959–1978: Nian kaogu fajue baogao* (The Erlitou site in Yanshi: Excavations, 1959–1978). Encyclopedia of China Press, Beijing.

Isaac, Barry L.

1993 Retrospective on the Formalist-Substantivist Debate. *Research in Economic Anthropology* 14:213–233.

1996 Approaches to Classic Maya Economies. *Research in Economic Anthropology* 17:297–334.

Isaacman, Allen, and Richard Roberts (editors)

1995 *Cotton, Colonialism, and Social History in Sub-Saharan Africa*. Heinemann, Portsmouth, New Hampshire.

Isbell, William H.

1997 *Mummies and Mortuary Monuments: A Postprocessual Prehistory of Central Andean Social Organization*. University of Texas Press, Austin.

Iseminger, William R., Timothy R. Pauketat, Brad Koldehoff, Lucretia S. Kelly, and Leonard Blake

1990 East Palisade Excavations. In *The Archaeology of the Cahokia Palisade, Part I*. Illinois Cultural Resource Study No. 14. Illinois Historic Preservation Agency, Springfield.

Jacobs, Jane

1970 *The Economy of Cities*. Jonathan Cape, London.

Jacobsen, Thorkild

1943 Primitive Democracy in Ancient Mesopotamia. *Journal of Near Eastern Studies* 2:159–172.

1953 On the Textile Industry at Ur Under Ibbi-Sin. In *Studia Orientalia Ioanni Pedersen*, pp. 172–187. Copenhagen. Reprinted in *Toward the Image of Tammuz*, edited by William L. Moran, pp. 216–230. Harvard University Press, Cambridge.

1976 *The Treasures of Darkness: A History of Mesopotamian Religion*. Yale University Press, New Haven.

Janusek, John

1994 *State and Local Power in a Prehispanic Andean Polity: Changing Patterns of Urban Residence in Tiwanaku and Lukurmata, Bolivia*. Ph.D. dissertation, University of Chicago, Chicago. University Microfilms, Ann Arbor.

1999 Craft and Local Power: Embedded Specialization in Tiwanaku Cities. *Latin American Antiquity* 10:107–131.

Jiangxi Institute of Archaeology, Jiangxi Museum, Xingan County Museum

1997 *Xingan Shang dai da mu* (The large Shang dynasty tomb at Xingan). Wenwu Press, Beijing.

Jin, Zhengyao, Weiliangguang Ping, Xizhang Yang, W. Thomas Chase, Yuanjiufu Ma, and Lunjialiu San

1998 Zhongguo lianghe liuyu qingtong wenming zhijian de lianxi: Yi chutu Shang qingtongqi de qian tong wei su bi zhi yanjiu jieguo wei kaocha zhongxin (Relationship between the Bronze Age of Mesopotamia and that of China: Results of a lead isotope analysis of excavated Shang bronzes). In *Zhongguo Shang Wenhua Guoji Xueshu Taolunhui Lunwenji* (Papers of the International Symposium of Shang Culture in China), edited by Institute of Archaeology, pp. 425–433. Encyclopedia Press of China, Beijing.

Jing, Zhichun, George Rapp, and Tianlin Gao
1997 Geoarchaeological Aids in the Investigation of Early Shang Civilization on the Floodplain of the Lower Yellow River, China. *World Archaeology* 29:36–50.

Joffe, Alexander H.
1998 Alcohol and Social Complexity in Ancient Western Asia. *Current Anthropology* 39:297–322.

Johnson, Allen W., and Timothy K. Earle
1987 *The Evolution of Human Societies: From Foraging Group to Agrarian State*. Stanford University Press, Palo Alto.

2000 *The Evolution of Human Societies: From Foraging Group to Agrarian State*. 2nd ed. Stanford University Press, Palo Alto.

Johnson, Jay K.
1987 Cahokia Core Technology in Mississippi: The View from the South. In *The Organization of Core Technology*, edited by Jay K. Johnson and Carol A. Morrow, pp. 187–205. Westview Press, Boulder, Colorado.

Jones, Grant D.
1989 *Maya Resistance to Spanish Rule: Time and Resistance on a Colonial Frontier*. University of New Mexico Press, Albuquerque.

1998 *The Conquest of the Last Maya Kingdom*. Stanford University Press, Palo Alto.

Jongman, Willem
2000 Wool and the Textile Industry of Roman Italy: A Working Hypothesis. In *Mercati permanente e mercati periodici nel mondo romano*, edited by Elio Lo Cascio, pp. 187–197. Edipuglia, Bari.

Joyce, Rosemary A.
2000 High Culture, Mesoamerican Civilization, and the Classic Maya Tradition. In *Order, Legitimacy, and Wealth in Ancient States*, edited by Janet Richards and Mary van Buren,

pp. 64–76. Cambridge University Press, Cambridge.

Joyce, Rosemary A., and Julia A. Hendon
2000 Heterarchy, History, and Material Reality: "Communities" in Late Classic Honduras. In *The Archaeology of Communities: A New World Perspective*, edited by Marcello A. Canuto and Jason Yaeger, pp. 143–160. Routledge, London.

Julien, Catherine
1982 Inca Decimal Administration in the Lake Titicaca Region. In *The Inca and Aztec States, 1400–1800: Anthropology and History*, edited by George A. Collier, Renato I. Rosaldo, and John D. Wirth, pp. 119–152. Academic Press, New York.

Junker, Laura L.
1990 The Organization of Intra-regional and Long-Distance Trade in Prehispanic Philippine Complex Societies. *Asian Perspectives* 29:167–209.

1993 Archaeological Excavations at the Twelfth–Sixteenth-Century Settlement of Tanjay, Negros Oriental: The Burial Evidence for Social Status Symboling, Head-taking, and Interpolity Raiding. *Philippine Quarterly of Culture and Society* 21(1):39–82.

1994 Trade Competition, Conflict, and Political Transformations in Sixth-to Sixteenth-Century Philippine Chiefdoms. *Asian Perspectives* 33:229–260.

1996 Hunter-Gatherer Landscapes and Lowland Trade in the Prehispanic Philippines. *World Archaeology* 27:389–410.

1998 Integrating History and Archaeology in the Study of Philippine Chiefdoms. *International Journal of Historical Archaeology* 2:291–320.

1999 *Raiding, Trading, and Feasting: The Political Economy of Philippine Chiefdoms*. University of Hawaii Press, Honolulu.

2001 The Evolution of Ritual Feasting Systems in Prehispanic Philippine Chiefdoms. In *Feasts: Archaeological and Ethnographic Perspectives on Food, Politics, and Power*, edited by Michael Dietler and Brian

Hayden, pp. 267–310. Smithsonian Institution Press, Washington, D.C.

Junker, Laura L., Mary Gunn, and Mary J. Santos
1996   The Tanjay Archaeological Project: A Preliminary Report on the 1994 and 1995 Field Seasons. *Convergence* 2(2):30–68.

Junker, Laura L., Karen Mudar, and Marla Schwaller
1994   Social Stratification, Household Wealth, and Competitive Feasting in Fifteenth–Sixteenth-Century Philippine Chiefdoms. *Research in Economic Anthropology* 15:307–358.

Kaplan, Robert D.
1994   The Coming Anarchy. *Atlantic Monthly* 273(February):44–76.
2000   *The Coming Anarchy: Shattering the Dreams of the Post Cold War.* Random House, New York.

Kardulias, P. Nick (editor)
1999   *World-Systems Theory in Practice: Leadership, Production, and Exchange.* Rowman and Littlefield, Lanham, Maryland.

Kauffman, Stuart
1995   *At Home in the Universe: The Search for Laws of Self-Organization and Complexity.* Oxford University Press, New York.

Keatinge, Richard, and Geoffrey W. Conrad
1983   Imperialist Expansion in Peruvian Prehistory: Chimu Administration of a Conquered Territory. *Journal of Field Archaeology* 10:255–283.

Keesing, Frederick
1962   *The Ethnohistory of Northern Luzon.* Stanford University Press, Palo Alto.

Kehoe, Alice B.
1998   *The Land of Prehistory: A Critical History of American Archaeology.* Routledge Press, London.

Kehoe, Dennis P.
1988   Allocation of Risk and Investment on the Estates of Pliny the Younger. *Chiron* 18:15–42.
1989   Approaches to Economic Problems in the "Letters" of Pliny the Younger: The Question of Risk in Agriculture. In *Aufsteig und Niedergang de Römischen Welt (ANRW), Teil II: Principat, Band 33, Sprache und Literatur (Allgemeines zur Literatur des 2. Jahrhunderts und Einzelne Autoren der Trajanischen und Frühhadrianischen Zeit)*, edited by Wolfgang Haase, pp. 555–590. Walter de Gruyter, New York.
1990   Pastoralism and Agriculture. *Journal of Roman Archaeology* 3:386–398.
1993   Economic Rationalism in Roman Agriculture. *Journal of Roman Archaeology* 6:476–484.
1997   *Investment, Profit, and Tenancy: The Jurists and the Roman Agrarian Economy.* University of Michigan Press, Ann Arbor.

Keightley, David
1983   The Late Shang State: When, Where, What? In *The Origins of Chinese Civilization*, edited by David Keightley, pp. 523–564. University of California Press, Berkeley.
1984   Late Shang Divination: The Magico-Religious Legacy. In *Explorations in Early Chinese Cosmology*, edited by Henry Rosemont, pp. 11–34. Scholars Press, Chico, California.
1999   The Shang: China's First Historical Dynasty. In *The Cambridge History of Ancient China*, edited by Michael Loewe and Edward Shaughnessy, pp. 232–291. Cambridge University Press, New York.
2000   *The Ancestral Landscape.* Institute of East Asian Studies, University of California, Berkeley.

Keim, Curtis A.
1999   *Mistaking Africa: Curiosities and Inventions of the American Mind.* Westview Press, Boulder, Colorado.

Kelly, John E.
1980   *Formative Developments at Cahokia and the Adjacent American Bottom: A Merrell Tract Perspective.* Unpublished Ph.D. dissertation, Department of Anthropology, University of Wisconsin, Madison.
1991   The Evidence for Prehistoric Exchange and Its Implications for the Development of Cahokia. In *New Perspectives on Cahokia: Views from the Periphery*, edited by James B. Stoltman, pp. 65–92. Prehistory Press, Madison, Wisconsin.

1997   Stirling-Phase Sociopolitical Activity at East St. Louis and Cahokia. In *Cahokia: Domination and Ideology in the Mississippian World*, edited by Timothy R. Pauketat and Thomas E. Emerson, pp. 141–166. University of Nebraska Press, Lincoln.

Kelly, Kenneth

1997a   The Archaeology of African-European Interaction: Investigating the Social Roles of Trade, Traders, and the Use of Space in the Seventeenth- and Eighteenth-Century Hueda Kingdom, Republic of Benin. *World Archaeology* 28: 350–369.

1997b   Using Historically Informed Archaeology: Seventeenth and Eighteenth Century Hueda-Europe Interaction on the Coast of Benin. *Journal of Archaeological Method and Theory* 4:353–366.

2001   Change and Continuity in Coastal Benin. In *West Africa During the Atlantic Slave Trade: Archaeological Perspectives*, edited by Christopher R. DeCorse, pp. 81–100. Leicester University Press, London.

Kelly, Lucretia S.

1997   Patterns of Faunal Exploitation at Cahokia. In *Cahokia: Domination and Ideology in the Mississippian World*, edited by Timothy R. Pauketat and Thomas E. Emerson, pp. 69–88. University of Nebraska Press, Lincoln.

2000   *Social Implications of Faunal Provisioning for the Cahokia Site: Initial Mississippian, Lohmann Phase.* Unpublished Ph.D. dissertation, Department of Anthropology, Washington University, St. Louis, Missouri.

2001   A Case of Ritual Feasting at the Cahokia Site. In *Feasts: Archaeological and Ethnographic Perspectives on Food, Politics, and Power*, edited by Michael Dietler and Brian Hayden, pp. 334–367. Smithsonian Institution Press, Washington, D.C.

Kemp, Barry

1997   Why Empires Rise. *Cambridge Archaeological Journal* 7:125–131.

Kepinski, C.

1990   Tell Khoshi. In *Archaeology in Iraq*, edited by Khaled Nashef, pp. 275–277. *American Journal of Archaeology* 94.

Kiefer, Thomas

1972a   *The Tausug: Violence and Law in a Philippine Moslem Society.* Holt, Rinehart and Winston, New York.

1972b   The Tausug Polity and the Sultanate of Sulu: A Segmentary State in the Southern Philippines. *Sulu Studies* (1):19–64.

Kim, H. S.

2002   Small Change and the Moneyed Economy. In *Money, Labour, and Land: Approaches to the Economies of Ancient Greece*, edited by Paul Cartledge, Edward E. Cohen, and Lin Foxhall, pp. 44–51. Routledge, London.

King, Adam

2001   Long-Term Histories of Mississippian Centers: The Develomental Sequence of Etowah and Its Comparison to Moundville and Cahokia. *Southeastern Archaeology* 20:1–17.

Kirch, Patrick

1984   *The Evolution of Polynesian Chiefdoms.* Cambridge University Press, Cambridge.

1990   Monumental Architecture and Power in Polynesian Chiefdoms: A Comparison of Tonga and Hawaii. *World Archaeology* 22:206–221.

Kirsch, A. Thomas

1973   *Feasting and Social Oscillation: A Working Paper on Religion and Society in Upland Southeast Asia.* Southeast Asian Data Paper No. 92. Department of Asian Studies, Cornell University, Ithaca.

1976   Kinship, Genealogical Claims, and Social Integration in Ancient Khmer Society: An Interpretation. In *Southeast Asian History and Historiography*, edited by C. D. Cowan and O. W. Wolters, pp. 190–202. Cornell University Press, Ithaca.

Klengel, Horst

1987   Non-slave Labour in the Old Babylonian Period: The Basic Outline. In *Labor in the Ancient Near East*, edited by Marvin A. Powell, pp.

159–66. American Oriental Series 68. American Oriental Society, New Haven.

1992   *Syria, 3000 to 300 B.C.: A Handbook of Political History.* Akademie, Berlin.

Knight, Vernon James, Jr.

1986   The Institutional Organization of Mississippian Religion. *American Antiquity* 51:675–687.

1997   Some Developmental Parallels Between Cahokia and Moundville. In *Cahokia: Domination and Ideology in the Mississippian World*, edited by Timothy R. Pauketat and Thomas E. Emerson, pp. 227–249. University of Nebraska Press, Lincoln.

Knight, Vernon James, Jr., and Vincas P. Steponaitis

1998   *Archaeology of the Moundville Chiefdom.* Smithsonian Institution Press, Washington, D.C.

Kohl, Philip

1978   The Balance of Trade in Southwestern Asia in the Mid-Third Millennium B.C. *Current Anthropology* 19:463–492.

1987a   The Ancient Economy, Transferable Technologies, and the Bronze Age World-System: A View from the Northeastern Frontier of the Ancient Near East. In *Centre and Periphery in the Ancient World*, edited by Michael Rowlands, Mogens Larsen, and Kristian Kristiansen, pp. 13–24. Cambridge University Press, Cambridge.

1987b   The Use and Abuse of World-Systems Theory: The Case of the Pristine West Asian State. In *Advances in Archaeological Method and Theory*, vol. 11, edited by Michael B. Schiffer, pp. 1–36. Academic Press, New York.

Kolata, Alan

1993   *The Tiwanaku: Portrait of an Andean Civilization.* Blackwell, Cambridge, Massachusetts.

Kondo, Tengchaoyi

1998   Shang dai hai bei de yanjiu (Research on cowrie shells from the Shang period). In *Zhongguo Shang Wenhua Guoji Xueshu Taolunhui Lunwenji* (Papers of the International Symposium of Shang Culture in China), edited by the Institute of Archaeology, CASS, pp. 389–412. Encyclopedia of China Press, Beijing.

Kong, Chao (editor)

1929   *Yi Zhou Shu* (Lost records of the Zhou), vol. 4. Shanghai Shangwu Press, Shanghai.

Koponen, J.

1986   Written Ethnographic Sources and Some Problems Connected with Their Use in African Historiography. *Scandinavian Journal of History* 11:55–69.

Kopytoff, Igor

1987   The Internal African Frontier: The Making of African Political Culture. In *The African Frontier: The Reproduction of Traditional African Societies*, edited by Igor Kopytoff, pp. 3–84. Indiana University Press, Bloomington.

1999   Permutations in Patrimonialism and Populism: The Aghem Chiefdoms of Western Cameroon. In *Beyond Chiefdoms: Pathways to Complexity in Africa*, edited by Susan K. McIntosh, pp. 88–96. Cambridge University Press, Cambridge.

Kouchoukos, Nicholas

1998   *Landscape and Social Change in Late Prehistoric Mesopotamia.* Unpublished Ph.D. dissertation, Department of Anthropology, Yale University, New Haven.

Kowalewski, Stephen A.

1976   *Prehispanic Settlement Patterns of the Central Part of the Valley of Oaxaca, Mexico.* Unpublished Ph.D. dissertation, Department of Anthropology, University of Arizona, Tucson.

1991   Peñoles: Archaeological Survey in the Mixtec Sierra, Mexico. Report to the National Science Foundation and the National Geographic Society.

Kowalewski, Stephen A., Gary M. Feinman, Laura Finsten, Richard E. Blanton, and Linda M. Nicholas

1989   *Monte Albán's Hinterland, Part II: The Prehispanic Settlement Patterns*

*in Tlacolula, Etla, and Ocotlán, the
Valley of Oaxaca, Mexico.* Memoirs
No. 23. Museum of Anthropology,
University of Michigan, Ann Arbor.

Kramer, Carol
1997 *Pottery in Rajasthan: Ethnoarchaeology in Two Indian Cities.* Smithsonian Institution Press, Washington, D.C.

Kuhn, Dieter
1982 The Silk Workshops of the Shang
Dynasty (Sixteenth–Eleventh Century B.C.). In *Explorations in the
History of Science and Technology
in China,* edited by Guohao Li,
Mengwen Zhang, and Tianqin Cao,
pp. 367–408. Chinese Classics Press,
Shanghai.

Kuhrt, Amelie
1995 *The Ancient Near East, c. 3000–330
B.C.* 2 vols. Routledge, London.

Kupper, Jean Robert
1957 *Les nomades en Mésopotamie au
temps des rois de Mari.* Société
d'Édition "Les Belles Lettres," Paris.

Kurtz, Donald V.
1974 Peripheral and Transitional Markets: The Aztec Case. *American Eth-
nologist* 1:685–705.

Lansing, J. Stephen
1991 *Priests and Programmers: Technologies of Power in the Engineered
Landscape of Bali.* Princeton University Press, Princeton.

Larsen, Mogens T.
1989 Introduction: Literacy and Social
Complexity. In *State and Society:
The Emergence and Development of
Social Hierarchy and Political Cen-
tralization,* edited by John Gledhill,
Barbara Bender, and Mogens T.
Larsen, pp. 173–191. Unwin
Hyman, London.

Laufer, Berthold
1907 *The Relations of the Chinese to the
Philippine Islands.* Bureau of Printing, Washington, D.C.

Lavallée, Danielle, and Luis G. Lumbreras
1985 *Les Andes, de la préhistoire aux
incas.* Gallimard, Paris.

Lavezaris, Guido de
1903 Letter to Felipe II. In *The Philippine
–1909 Islands, 1493–1803,* vol. 3, edited
[1569] and translated by Emma H. Blair

and James A. Robertson, pp. 29–32.
Arthur H. Clark, Cleveland.

Leach, Edmund R.
1965 *Political Systems of Highland
Burma.* Beacon Press, Boston.
1989 Tribal Ethnography: Past, Present,
and Future. In *History and
Ethnicity,* edited by Elizabeth
Tonkin, Maryon McDonald, and
Malcolm Chapman, pp. 34–47. ASA
Monographs No. 27. Routledge,
London.

Leach, Jerry W.
1983 Introduction. In *The Kula: New Perspectives on Massim Exchange,* edited by Jerry W. Leach and Edmund
Leach, pp. 1–26. Cambridge University Press, Cambridge.

Lebar, Frank M. (editor)
1977 *Insular Southeast Asia: Ethno-
graphic Studies. Section 4: The
Philippines.* Human Relations Area
Files (HRAF) Publications, New
Haven.

Lebeau, Marc
2000 Stratified Archaeological Evidence
and Compared Periodizations in the
Syrian Jezirah During the Third Millennium B.C. In *Chronologies des
pays du Caucase et de l'Euphrate
aux IVe–IIIe millenaires,* edited by
Catherine Marro and Harald
Hauptmann, pp. 167–192. Varia
Anatolica XI. Institut Français
d'Etudes Anatoliennes, Istanbul.

Lee, Richard B.
1990 Primitive Communism and the Origins of Social Inequality. In *The Evolution of Political Systems: Sociopol-
itics in Small-Scale Sedentary
Societies,* edited by Steadman Up-
ham, pp. 225–246. Cambridge University Press, Cambridge.
1992 Art, Science, or Politics? The Crisis
in Hunter-Gatherer Studies. *American Anthropologist* 94:31–54.

Lees, Susan H.
1973 *Sociopolitical Aspects of Canal Irrigation in the Valley of Oaxaca.*
Memoirs No. 6. Museum of Anthropology, University of Michigan, Ann
Arbor.

Legaspi, Miguel de
1903 Letters to Felipe II of Spain. In *The*

−1909   *Philippine Islands, 1493–1803*, vol.
[1567]   2, edited and translated by Emma H. Blair and James A. Robertson, pp. 232–243. Arthur H. Clark, Cleveland.

1990   Relation of the Filipinas Islands and
[1569]   of the Character and Conditions of the Inhabitants. In *Documentary Sources of Philippine History*, vol. 2, edited and translated by Gregorio F. Zaide, pp. 37–42. National Bookstore Publications, Manila.

Lehman, Frederick K.
1989   Internal Inflationary Pressures in the Prestige Economy of the Feast of Merit Complex: The Chin and Kachin Cases from Upper Burma. In *Ritual, Power, and Economy: Upland-Lowland Contrasts in Mainland Southeast Asia*, edited by Susan D. Russell, pp. 89–101. Occasional Paper No. 14. Center for Southeast Asian Studies, Northern Illinois University, DeKalb.

Lentz, Carola
1994   "They Must Be Dagaba First and Any Other Thing Second . . . ": The Colonial and Post-colonial Creation of Ethnic Identities in North-Western Ghana. *African Studies* 53(2):57–91.
1995   "Tribalism" and Ethnicity in Africa: A Review of Four Decades of Anglophone Research. *Cahiers de Sciences Humaines* 31(2):303–328.

Levine, David K., and Wolfgang Pesendorfer
2001   The Evolution of Cooperation Through Imitation. Ms. available at http://ideas.uqam.ca/ideas/data/clalevarc.html.

LeVine, Terry Y.
1985   *Inka Administration in the Central Highlands: A Comparative Study*. Unpublished Ph.D. dissertation, Archaeology Interdepartmental Program, University of California, Los Angeles.
1987   Inka Labor Service at the Regional Level: The Functional Reality. *Ethnohistory* 34:14–46.

Levtzion, Nehemia
1976   The Early States of the Western Sudan to 1500. In *History of West Africa*, vol. 1. 2nd ed. Edited by J. F. Ade Ajayi and Michael Crowder, pp. 114–151. Longman Group, London.

Lewis, Herbert S.
1998   The Misrepresentation of Anthropology and Its Consequences. *American Anthropologist* 100:716–731.

Li, Ji (Chi)
1952   Yinxu you ren shiqi tu shuo (An illustrated catalog of edged stone tools from Yinxu). *Bulletin of the Institute of History and Philology* 23:523–619.

Li, Xiaochen
1993   Shang Zhou zhongyuan qingtongqi kuang liao laiyuan de zai yanjiu (Further study of sources of ores for bronze vessels from the Shang and Zhou periods in the Central Plain). *Ziran Kexue Shi Yanjiu* 12(3):264–267.

Li, Xueqin
1999   *Shang Shu zheng yi* (Explanation of the Shang Shu). Beijing University Press, Beijing.

Li, Chenfu (posthumously), and Chen, Daiguang (editor)
1982   *Yu Gong shi di* (An explanation of places mentioned in the *Yu Gong*). Zhong Zhou Shu Huashe Press, Zhengzhou, Henan.

Lin, Yun
1982   Jiaguwen zhong de Shang dai fang-guo lianmeng (Alliances of *fang* states during the Shang period from the oracle bone inscriptions). *Guwenzi Yanjiu* 6:67–92.

Lipinski, Edward (editor)
1979   *State and Temple Economy in the Ancient Near East*. Orientalia Lovaniensia Analecta 5. Departement Oriëntalistiek, Leuven.

Little, Keith J.
1999   The Role of Late Woodland Interactions in the Emergence of Etowah. *Southeastern Archaeology* 18:45–56.

Liu, Li, and Xingcan Chen
2000   Xia Shang shiqi dui ziran ziyuan de kongzhi wenti (Questions concerning the control of natural resources in the Xia and Shang periods). *Dongnan Wenhua* 3:45–60.
2001   Settlement Archaeology and the Study of Social Complexity in

China. *Review of Archaeology* 22(2):4–22.

Liu, Shizhong, and Benshan Lu
1998   Jiangxi Tongling tong kuang yizhi de fajue yu yanjiu (Research and excavation at the copper mining site of Tongling in Jiangxi). *Kaogu Xuebao* 4:465–498.

Liu, Xing
1993   *Xin bian jiaguwen zidian* (A new dictionary of the oracle bones). Guoji Wenhua Chuban Gongsi, Beijing.

Liu, Yueying, Wenzhen Zhang, Yaoxian Wang, and Enyi Wang
1979   *Zhongguo jingji dongwu zhi* (The economic fauna of China). Science Press, Beijing.

Liverani, Mario
1996   Reconstructing the Rural Landscape of the Ancient Near East. *Journal of the Economic and Social History of the Orient* 39:1–41.

Loarca, Miguel de
1903   Relación de las Islas Filipinas. In
–1909   *The Philippines, 1493–1898*, vol. 5,
[1582] edited and translated by Emma H. Blair and James A. Robertson, pp. 32–187. Arthur H. Clark, Cleveland.

Lo Cascio, Elio
1981   State and Coinage in the Late Republic and Early Empire. *Journal of Roman Studies* 71:76–86.

Lo Cascio, Elio (editor)
2000   *Mercati permanenti e mercati periodici nel mondo romano: Atti degli Incontri capresi di storia dell'economia antica, Capri, 13–15 ottobre 1997*. Edipuglia, Bari.

Lo Cascio, Elio, and Dominic W. Rathbone
2000   Introduction. In *Production and Public Powers in Classical Antiquity*, edited by Elio Lo Cascio and Dominic W. Rathbone. Supplementary Vol. No. 26. Cambridge Philological Society, Cambridge.

Lo Cascio, Elio, and Dominic W. Rathbone (editors)
2000   *Production and Public Powers in Classical Antiquity*. Supplementary Vol. No. 26. Cambridge Philological Society, Cambridge.

López de Gómara, Francisco
1966   *Cortés: The Life of the Conqueror by His Secretary*. Translated by Lesley B. Simpson. University of California Press, Berkeley.

López Varela, Sandra L.
2004   Ceramic History of K'axob: The Early Years. In *K'axob: Ritual, Work, and Family in an Ancient Maya Village*, edited by Patricia A. McAnany. Cotsen Institute of Archaeology, University of California, Los Angeles, in press.

Lorenz, Franz, and Alex Hubert
2000   *A Guide to Worldwide Cowries*. 2nd ed. Conch Books, Hackenheim, Germany.

Love, John R.
1991   *Antiquity and Capitalism: Max Weber and the Sociological Foundations of Roman Civilization*. Routledge, New York.

Lovejoy, Paul E.
1983   *Transformations in Slavery: A History of Slavery in Africa*. Cambridge University Press, Cambridge.

Lyons, Diane
1998   Witchcraft, Gender, Power, and Intimate Relations in Mura Compounds in Déla, Northern Cameroon. *World Archaeology* 29:344–362.

Ma, Xiutong (editor)
1997   *Zhongguo dongwu zhi* (Fauna in China: Mollusca). Science Press, Beijing.

MacEachern, Scott
1993   Selling the Iron for Their Shackles: Wandala-Montagnard Interactions in Northern Cameroon. *Journal of African History* 34:247–270.
1994   "Symbolic Reservoirs" and Cultural Relations Between Ethnic Groups: West African Examples. *African Archaeological Review* 12:203–222.
1998   Scale, Style, and Cultural Variation: Technological Traditions in the Northern Mandara Mountains. In *The Archaeology of Social Boundaries*, edited by Miriam Stark, pp. 107–131. Smithsonian Institution Press, Washington, D.C.
2001   State Formation and Enslavement in the Southern Lake Chad Basin. In *West Africa During the Atlantic*

Slave Trade: Archaeological Perspectives, edited by Christopher R. DeCorse, pp. 131–151. Leicester University Press, London.

2003   Blacksmiths, Iron-Working, and State Societies in the Northern Mandara Mountains. In *Iron, Master of Them All*, edited by William Dewey. Iowa Studies in African Art 5. School of Art and Art History, University of Iowa, Iowa City, in press.

Mackey, Carol J.

1984   Chimu and Chimu-Inca Textiles from Manchan. *National Geographic Society Research Reports* 21:273–278.

Mackey, Carol J., and A. M. Ulana Klymyshyn

1990   The Southern Frontier of the Chimu Empire. In *The Northern Dynasties: Kingship and Statecraft in Chimor*, edited by Michael E. Moseley and Alana Cordy-Collins, pp. 195–226. Dumbarton Oaks, Washington, D.C.

MacMullen, Ramsay

1970   Market-Days in the Roman Empire. *Phoenix* 24:333–341.

1984   The Roman Emperor's Army Costs. *Latomus* 3–4:571–580.

Macve, Richard H.

1985   Some Glosses on "Greek and Roman Accounting." In *Crux: Essays in Greek History Presented to G. E. M. de Ste. Croix on His 75th Birthday*, edited by Paul A. Cartledge and F. D. Harvey, pp. 233–264. Duckworth and Imprint Academic, London.

Maekawa, Kazuya

1973   The Development of the e-mi in
–1974   Lagash During Early Dynastic III. *Mesopotamia* 8–9:77–144.

1980   Female Weavers and Their Children in Lagash: Presargonic and Ur III Periods. *Acta Sumerologica* 2:81–125.

1987   Collective Labor Service in Girsu-Lagash: The Pre-Sargonic and Ur III Periods. In *Labor in the Ancient Near East*, edited by Marvin A. Powell, pp. 49–71. American Oriental Series 68. American Oriental Society, New Haven.

Maisels, Charles

1990   *The Emergence of Civilization.* Routledge, New York.

Maital, Shlomo

1998   Foreword. In *Rationality Gone Awry? Decision Making Inconsistent with Economic and Financial Theory*, by Hugh H. Schwartz, pp. ix–xiii. Praeger, Westport, Connecticut.

Majul, Cesare

1966   Chinese Relationships with the Sultanate of Sulu. In *The Chinese in the Philippines, 1550–1770*, edited by Alfonso Felix, Jr., pp. 142–159. Solidaridad Press, Manila.

1973   *Muslims in the Philippines.* University of the Philippines Press, Quezon City.

Majumdar, Ramesh Chandra

1963   *Ancient Indian Colonisation in South-East Asia.* Bhatt, Baroda, India.

Malinowski, Bronislaw

1961   *Argonauts of the Western Pacific.* E. P. Dutton, New York. Originally published 1922.

Mallory, Jack K.

1986   "Workshops" and "Specialized Production" in the Production of Maya Chert Tools: A Response to Shafer and Hester. *American Antiquity* 51:152–158.

Mallowan, Max E. L.

1947   Excavations at Brak and Chagar Bazar. *Iraq* 9:1–266.

Manguin, Pierre-Yves

1992   Excavations in South Sumatra, 1988–1990: New Evidence for Sriwijayan Sites. In *Southeast Asian Archaeology 1990*, edited by Ian C. Gover, pp. 62–73. Centre for South-East Asian Studies, University of Hull, Hull, U.K.

Mann, Michael

1986   *The Sources of Social Power: A History of Power from the Beginning to A.D. 1760*, vol. 1. Cambridge University Press, Cambridge.

Manning, Patrick (editor)

1996   *Slave Trades, 1500–1800: Globalization of Forced Labour.* Variorum, Aldershot, Hampshire, United Kingdom.

Manuel, E. Arsenio
1971   *Manuvu Social Organization.*
        University of the Philippines Press,
        Quezon City.
Marcus, Joyce
1992   *Mesoamerican Writing Systems:
        Propaganda, Myth, and History in
        Four Ancient Civilizations.* Prince-
        ton University Press, Princeton.
Marcus, Joyce, and Gary M. Feinman
1998   Introduction. In *Archaic States*, ed-
        ited by Gary M. Feinman and Joyce
        Marcus, pp. 3–13. School of Ameri-
        can Research Press, Santa Fe, New
        Mexico.
Marfoe, Leon
1987   Cedar Forest to Silver Mountain: So-
        cial Change and the Development of
        Long-Distance Trade in Early Near
        Eastern Societies. In *Centre and Pe-
        riphery in the Ancient World*, edited
        by Michael Rowlands, Mogens
        Larsen, and Kristian Kristiansen, pp.
        25–35. Cambridge University Press,
        Cambridge.
Margueron, Jean-Claude
1987   Etat présent des recherches sur
        l'urbanisme de Mari I. *MARI*
        5:483–498.
1988   Espace agricole et aménagement
        régional a Mari au début du IIIe
        millennaire. *Bulletin on Sumerian
        Agriculture* 4:49–60.
1996   Mari, reflet du monde mésopotami-
        enne au IIIe millennaire. *Akkadica*
        98:11–30.
Martin, Mary
1982   Conservation at the Local Level:
        Individual Perceptions and Group
        Mechanisms. In *Desertification and
        Development: Dryland Ecology in
        Social Perspective*, edited by Brian
        Spooner and H. S. Mann, pp.
        145–169. Academic Press, London.
Martin, Simon, and Nikolai Grube
2000   *Chronicle of the Maya Kings and
        Queens: Deciphering the Dynasties
        of the Ancient Maya.* Thames and
        Hudson, London.
Masson, Marilyn
2002   Introduction. In *Ancient Maya Polit-
        ical Economies*, edited by Marilyn
        A. Masson and David A. Freidel, pp.

        1–30. Altamira Press, Rowman and
        Littlefield, Lanham, Maryland.
2004   Contribution of Fishing and Hunt-
        ing to Subsistence and Symbolic Ex-
        pression. In *K'axob: Ritual, Work,
        and Family in an Ancient Maya Vil-
        lage,* edited by Patricia A. McAnany.
        Cotsen Institute of Archaeology,
        University of California, Los Ange-
        les, in press.
Masuda, Shozo, Izumi Shimada, and
Craig Morris (editors)
1985   *Andean Ecology and Civilization.*
        University of Tokyo Press, Tokyo.
Mathews, James Edward
1992   *Prehispanic Settlement and Agricul-
        ture in the Middle Tiwanaku Valley,
        Bolivia.* Unpublished Ph.D. disserta-
        tion, Department of Anthropology,
        University of Chicago, Chicago.
Matthiae, Paolo
1980   *Ebla: An Empire Rediscovered.*
        Doubleday, New York.
Mattingly, D. J.
1988   Oil for Export? A Comparison of
        Libyan, Spanish, and Tunisian Olive
        Oil Production in the Roman Em-
        pire. *Journal of Roman Archaeology*
        1:33–56.
1997   Africa: A Landscape of Opportu-
        nity? In *Dialogues in Roman Imperi-
        alism: Power, Discourse, and Dis-
        crepant Experience in the Roman
        Empire*, edited by D. J. Mattingly,
        pp. 117–139. Supplementary Series
        No. 23. Journal of Roman Archaeol-
        ogy, Portsmouth, Rhode Island.
Mattingly, D. J., and J. Salmon (editors)
2001   *Economies Beyond Agriculture in
        the Classical World.* Routledge,
        New York.
Mauss, Marcel
1990   *The Gift: The Form and Reason for
        Exchange in Archaic Societies.*
        Translated by W. D. Hall. Norton,
        New York. Originally published
        1925.
Mazzoni, Stefania
1988   Economic Features of the Palace
        Equipment of Palace G. In
        *Wirtschaft und Gesellschaft von
        Ebla*, edited by Hartmut Waetzoldt
        and Harald Hauptmann, pp.

81–105. Heidelberger Orientverlag, Heidelberg.

McAnany, Patricia A.

1989 Stone Tool Production and Exchange in the Eastern Maya Lowlands: The Consumer Perspective from Pulltrouser Swamp, Belize. *American Antiquity* 54:332–346.

2001 Cosmology and the Institutionalization of Hierarchy in the Maya Region. In *Leaders to Rulers*, edited by Jonathan Haas, pp. 125–148. Kluwer Academic/Plenum, New York.

McAnany, Patricia A., Kimberly A. Berry, and Ben Thomas

2003 Wetlands, Rivers, and Caves: Agricultural and Ritual Practice in Two Lowland Maya Landscapes. In *Perspectives on Ancient Maya Rural Complexity*, edited by Gyles Iannone and Samuel V. Connell, pp. 71–81. Cotsen Institute of Archaeology, University of California, Los Angeles.

McAnany, Patricia A., and Justin P. Ebersole

2004 Ground and Polished Stone Tools. In *K'axob: Materiality, Ritual, Work, and Family in an Ancient Maya Village,* edited by Patricia A. McAnany. Cotsen Institute of Archaeology, University of California, Los Angeles, in press.

McAnany, Patricia A., and Sandra L. López Varela

1999 Re-creating the Formative Maya Village of K'axob: Chronology, Ceramic Complexes, and Ancestors in Architectural Context. *Ancient Mesoamerica* 10:147–168.

McAnany, Patricia A., and Polly A. Peterson

2004 Tools of the Trade: Acquisition, Use, and Recycling of Chipped Stone. In *K'axob: Ritual, Work, and Family in an Ancient Maya Village,* edited by Patricia A. McAnany. Cotsen Institute of Archaeology, University of California, Los Angeles, in press.

McAnany, Patricia A., and Shannon Plank

2001 Perspectives on Actors, Gender Roles, and Architecture at Classic Maya Courts and Households. In *Royal Courts of the Ancient Maya, Volume 1: Theory, Comparison, and Synthesis*, edited by Takeshi Ino-

mata and Stephen D. Houston, pp. 84–129. Westview Press, Boulder, Colorado.

McClellan, Thomas

1999 Urbanism on the Upper Syrian Euphrates. In *Archaeology of the Upper Syrian Euphrates: The Tishreen Dam Area*, edited by Gregorio del Olmo Lete and Juan-Luis Montero Fenollós, pp. 413–425. Editorial AUSA, Barcelona.

McClellan, Thomas, and Anne Porter

1999 Survey of Excavations at Tell Banat: Funerary Practices. In *Archaeology of the Upper Syrian Euphrates: The Tishreen Dam Area*, edited by Gregorio del Olmo Lete and Juan-Luis Montero Fenollós, pp. 107–116. Editorial AUSA, Barcelona.

McCloskey, Deidre N.

1997 Other Things Equal: Polanyi Was Right, and Wrong. *Eastern Economic Journal* 23:483–487.

McCorriston, Joy

1997 The Fiber Revolution: Textile Extensification, Alienation, and Social Stratification in Ancient Mesopotamia. *Current Anthropology* 38:517–549.

McDougall, E. Ann

1990 Salts of the Western Sahara: Myths, Mysteries, and Historical Significance. *International Journal of African Historical Studies* 23:231–257.

McEvedy, Colin, and Richard Jones

1978 *Atlas of World Population History*. Facts on File, New York.

McIntosh, Robert

1999 Clustered Cities and Alternative Courses to Authority in Prehistory. *Journal of East Asian Archaeology* 1(1–4):63–86.

McIntosh, Roderick J.

1998 *The Peoples of the Middle Niger: The Island of Gold*. Blackwell, Oxford.

McIntosh, Susan Keech

1999 Pathways to Complexity: An African Perspective. In *Beyond Chiefdoms: Pathways to Complexity in Africa*, edited by Susan K. McIntosh, pp. 1–30. Cambridge University Press, Cambridge.

2001   Tools for Understanding Transformation and Continuity in Senegambian Society, 1500–1900. In *West Africa During the Atlantic Slave Trade: Archaeological Perspectives*, edited by Christopher R. DeCorse, pp. 14–37. Leicester University Press, London.

McIntosh, Susan Keech (editor)

1995   *Excavations at Jenné-Jeno, Hambarketolo, and Kaniana (Inland Niger Delta, Mali), the 1981 Season*. University of California Publications in Anthropology, Vol. 20. University of California Press, Berkeley.

1999   *Beyond Chiefdoms: Pathways to Complexity in Africa*, edited by Susan K. McIntosh. Cambridge University Press, Cambridge.

McIntosh, Susan K., and Roderick J. McIntosh

1993   Cities Without Citadels: Understanding Urban Origins along the Middle Niger. In *The Archaeology of Africa: Food, Metals, and Towns*, edited by Thurstan Shaw, Paul Sinclair, Bassey Andah, and Alex Okpoko, pp. 622–641. Routledge, London.

McKinnon, Edward

1985   Early Polities in Southern Sumatra: Some Preliminary Observations Based on Archaeological Evidence. *Indonesia* 40:1–36.

1993   A Note on Finds of Early Chinese Ceramics Associated with Megalithic Remains in Northwest Lampung. *Journal of Southeast Asian Studies* 24:227–238.

McNaughton, Patrick R.

1988   *The Mande Blacksmiths: Knowledge, Power, and Art in West Africa*. Indiana University Press, Bloomington.

McNeill, Judith, and David Welch

1991   Regional and Interregional Interaction on the Khorat Plateau. *Bulletin of the Indo-Pacific Prehistory Association* 10:327–340.

McSheffrey, Gerald M.

1983   Slavery, Indentured Servitude, Legitimate Trade, and the Impact of Abolition in the Gold Coast, 1874–1901: A Reappraisal. *Journal of African History* 24:349–368.

Mehrer, Mark, and James Collins

1995   Household Archaeology at Cahokia and in Its Hinterlands. In *Mississippian Communities and Households*, edited by J. Daniel Rogers and Bruce D. Smith, pp. 32–57. University of Alabama Press, Tuscaloosa.

Meijer, Diedrik

1986   *A Survey in Northeastern Syria*. Netherlands Historical-Archaeological Institute, Istanbul.

Meskell, Lynn

1999   *Archaeologies of Social Life: Age, Sex, Class et cetera in Ancient Egypt*. Blackwell, Oxford.

Michalowski, Piotr

1987   Charisma and Control: On Continuity and Change in Early Mesopotamian Bureaucratic Systems. In *The Organization of Power: Aspects of Bureaucracy in the Ancient Near East*, edited by McGuire Gibson and Robert D. Biggs, pp. 55–68. Studies in Ancient Oriental Civilization No. 46. Oriental Institute, University of Chicago, Chicago.

Mickwitz, G.

1937   Economic Rationalism in Greco-Roman Agriculture. *English Historical Review* 108:577–589.

Middleton, Paul S.

1980   La Graufesenque: A Question of Marketing. *Athenaeum* 58:186–191.

1983   The Roman Army and Long Distance Trade. In *Trade and Famine in Classical Antiquity*, edited by Peter Garnsey, Keith Hopkins, and C. R. Whittaker, pp. 75–83. Cambridge University Press, New York.

Middleton, William D.

1998   *Craft Specialization at Ejutla, Oaxaca, Mexico: An Archaeometric Study of the Organization of Household Craft Production*. Unpublished Ph.D. dissertation, Department of Anthropology, University of Wisconsin, Madison.

Middleton, William D., Gary M. Feinman, and Linda M. Nicholas

2002   Domestic Faunal Assemblages from the Classic Period Valley of Oaxaca, Mexico: A Perspective on the Subsistence and Craft Economies. *Journal*

of Archaeological Science
29:233–249.

Middleton, William D., and T. Douglas Price
1996   Identification of Activity Areas by Multi-element Characterization of Sediments from Modern and Archaeological House Floors Using Inductively Coupled Plasma-Atomic Emission Spectroscopy. *Journal of Archaeological Science* 23:673–687.

Miksic, John
1984   A Comparison Between Some Long-Distance Trading Institutions of the Malacca Straits Area and of the Western Pacific. In *Southeast Asian Archaeology at the 15th Pacific Science Congress*, edited by Donn T. Bayard, pp. 235–253. Studies in Prehistoric Archaeology Vol. 1b. University of Otago, Otago, New Zealand.

Miksicek, Charles H.
1983   Paleoecology and Subsistence at Pulltrouser Swamp: The View from the Float Tank. Ms. on file, Department of Archaeology, Boston University, Boston.

Millar, Fergus
1981   The World of the *Golden Ass. Journal of Roman Studies* 71:63–75.

2000   Trajan: Government by Correspondence. In *Trajano emperador de Roma*, edited by Julián González, pp. 363–388. L'Erma di Bretschneider, Rome.

Millard, Alan
1988   The Bevelled-Rim Bowls: Their Purpose and Significance. *Iraq* 50:49–57.

Miller, Daniel
1985   *Artefacts as Categories: A Study of Ceramic Variability in Central India.* Cambridge University Press, Cambridge.

1987   *Material Culture and Mass Consumption.* Blackwell, Oxford.

Miller, Mary
1997   Imaging Maya Art. *Archaeology* 50(3):34–40.

2001   Life at Court: The View from Bonampak. In *Royal Courts of the Ancient Maya, Volume 2: Data and Case Studies*, edited by Takeshi Inomata and Stephen D. Houston, pp. 201–222. Westview Press, Boulder, Colorado.

Milner, George R.
1998   *The Cahokia Chiefdom: The Archaeology of a Mississippian Society.* Smithsonian Institution Press, Washington, D.C.

Mohr-Chávez, Karen
1992   The Organization of Production and Distribution of Traditional Pottery in South Highland Peru. In *Ceramic Production and Distribution: An Integrated Approach*, edited by George J. Bey and Christopher Pool, pp. 49–92. Westview Press, Boulder, Colorado.

Monfort, César C.
1994   *A Macroeconomic and Spatial Analysis of Long-Distance Exchange: The Amphora Evidence from Roman Britain.* Unpublished Ph.D. dissertation, Southampton University. British Thesis Service, British Library.

Moore, Henrietta, and Megan Vaughan
1994   *Cutting Down Trees: Gender, Nutrition, and Agricultural Change in the Northern Province of Zambia, 1890–1990.* Heinemann, Portsmouth, New Hampshire.

Moore, Jerry D.
1981   Chimu Socio-Economic Organization: Preliminary Data from Manchan, Casma Valley, Peru. *Nawpa Pacha* 19:115–128.

Moore, Sally Falk
1986   *Social Facts and Fabrications: "Customary" Law on Kilimanjaro, 1880–1980.* Cambridge University Press, Cambridge.

1993   Changing Perspective on a Changing Africa: The Work of Anthropology. In *Africa and the Disciplines: The Contributions of Research in Africa to the Social Sciences and Humanities*, edited by Robert H. Bates, V. Y. Mudimbe, and Jean O'Barr, pp. 3–57. University of Chicago Press, Chicago.

1994   *Anthropology and Africa: Changing Perspectives on a Changing Scene.*

University of Virginia Press, Charlottesville.

Moorey, Peter R. S.
1994   *Ancient Mesopotamian Materials and Industries: The Archaeological Evidence.* Clarendon Press, Oxford.

Morga, Antonio
1903   Sucesos de las Islas Filipinas. In *The*
–1909   *Philippine Islands, 1493–1803*, vol.
[1609] 16, edited by Emma H. Blair and James A. Robertson, pp. 75–133. Arthur H. Clark, Cleveland.

Morley, Neville
2000   Markets, Marketing, and the Roman Elite. In *Mercati permanente e mercati periodici nel mondo romano*, edited by Elio Lo Cascio, pp. 211–221. Edipuglia, Bari.

Morley, Sylvanus G.
1941   The Xiu Chronicle, Part I: The History of the Xiu. Unpublished manuscript, Tozzer Library, Harvard University, Cambridge.
1956   *The Ancient Maya.* Revised by George W. Brainerd, 3rd ed. Stanford University Press, Palo Alto.

Morris, Craig
1974   Reconstructing Patterns of Non-agricultural Production in the Inca Economy: Archaeology and Documents in Institutional Analysis. In *Reconstructing Complex Societies: An Archaeological Colloquium*, edited by Charlotte B. Moore, pp. 46–68. Supplement to the Bulletin of the American Schools of Oriental Research 20. Cambridge, Massachusetts.
1991   Signs of Division, Symbols of Unity: Art in the Inka Empire. In *Circa 1492: Art in the Age of Exploration*, edited by Jay A. Levenson, pp. 521–528. National Gallery of Art, Washington, D.C.
1995   Symbols to Power: Styles and Media in the Inka State. In *Style, Society, and Person*, edited by Christopher Carr and Jill E. Neitzel, pp. 419–433. Plenum Press, New York.

Morris, Craig, and Donald E. Thompson
1985   *Huánuco Pampa: An Inca City and Its Hinterland.* Thames and Hudson, London.

Morris, Ian
1994   The Athenian Economy Twenty Years after the Ancient Economy. *Classical Philology* 89:351–366.

Moseley, Michael
1992   *The Incas and Their Ancestors.* Thames and Hudson, London.

Mudar, Karen
1993   *Prehistoric and Early Historic Settlements in the Central Plain: Analysis of Archaeological Survey in Lopburi Province, Thailand.* Unpublished Ph.D. dissertation, Department of Anthropology, University of Michigan, Ann Arbor.

Mudimbe, V. Y.
1988   *The Invention of Africa: Gnosis, Philosophy, and the Order of Knowledge.* Indiana University Press, Bloomington.

Muhammed, Akbar
1977   The Samorian Occupation of Bondoukou: An Indigenous View. *International Journal of African Historical Studies* 10:242–258.

Muhs, Daniel R., Robert R. Kautz, and J. Jefferson MacKinnon
1985   Soils and the Location of Cacao Orchards at a Maya Site in Western Belize. *Journal of Archaeological Science* 12:121–137.

Muller, Jon
1984   Mississippian Specialization and Salt. *American Antiquity* 49:489–507.
1987   Salt, Chert, and Shell: Mississippian Exchange and Economy. In *Specialization, Exchange, and Complex Societies*, edited by Elizabeth Brumfiel and Timothy Earle, pp. 10–21. Cambridge University Press, Cambridge.
1995   Regional Interaction in the Later Southeast. In *Native American Interactions: Multiscalar Analyses and Interpretations in the Eastern Woodlands*, edited by Michael S. Nassaney and Kenneth E. Sassaman, pp. 317–340. University of Tennessee Press, Knoxville.
1997   *Mississippian Political Economy.* Plenum Press, New York.

Murra, John V.

1962   Cloth and Its Functions in the Inca
        State. *American Anthropologist*
        64:710–728.

1972   El "control vertical" de un máximo
        de pisos ecológicos en la economía
        de las sociedades andinas. In *Visita
        de la Provincia de León de Huánuco
        en 1562, Iñigo Ortiz de Zuñiga, visi-
        tador*, vol. 2, edited by John V.
        Murra, pp. 429–476. Universidad
        Nacional Hermilio Valdizán, Facul-
        tad de Letras y Educación,
        Huánuco, Peru.

Murúa, Martín de

1946   *Los orígenes de los inkas, crónica
[1590] sobre el antiguo Perú, escrita en el
        año de 1590.* Lima.

Narváez, Alfredo

1995   The Pyramids of Túcume. In *Pyra-
        mids of Túcume: The Quest for
        Peru's Forgotten City*, by Thor
        Heyerdahl, Daniel H. Sandweiss,
        and Alfredo Narváez, pp. 79–130.
        Thames and Hudson, New York.

National Museum of Chinese History

1997   *A Journey into China's Antiquity,
        Volume 1: Palaeolithic Age, Spring
        and Autumn Period.* Morning Glory
        Publishers, Beijing.

National Museum of Chinese History, Shanxi
Province Institute of Archaeology, Museum of
Yuanqu County

1996   *Yuanqu Shang cheng* (The Shang
        city at Yuanqu). Science Press,
        Beijing.

Neale, Caroline

1985   *Writing "Independent" History:
        African Historiography,
        1960–1980.* Greenwood, Westport,
        Connecticut.

1986   The Idea of Progress in the Revision
        of African History, 1960–1970. In
        *African Historiographies: What His-
        tory for Which Africa?* edited by
        Bogumil Jewsiewicki and David
        Newbury, pp. 112–122. Sage, Bev-
        erly Hills, California.

Neeve, Pieter W. de

1990   A Roman Landowner and His Es-
        tate: Pliny the Younger. *Athenaeum*
        78:363–402.

Netherly, Patricia

1977   *Local Level Lords on the North

Coast of Peru.* Ph.D. dissertation,
        Cornell University, Ithaca. Univer-
        sity Microfilms, Ann Arbor.

Neumann, Hans

1987   *Handwerk in Mesopotamien.*
        Schriften zur Geschichte und Kultur
        des alten Orients 19. Akademie,
        Berlin.

1992   Zur privaten Geschäftstätigkeit in
        der Ur III Zeit. In *Nippur at the Cen-
        tennial*, edited by Maria de J. Ellis,
        pp. 161–176. University of Pennsyl-
        vania Museum, Philadelphia.

Nishimura, Masao

1992   *Long Distance Trade and the Devel-
        opment of Complex Societies in the
        Prehistory of the Central Philip-
        pines: The Cebu Central Settlement
        Case.* Unpublished Ph.D. disserta-
        tion, Department of Anthropology,
        University of Michigan, Ann Arbor.

Nissen, Hans J.

1976   Geographie. In *Sumerological Stud-
        ies in Honour of Thorkild Jacobsen*,
        edited by Stephen J. Lieberman, pp.
        9–40. Assyriological Studies 20.
        Oriental Institute, University of
        Chicago, Chicago.

1982   Die Tempelstadt: Regierungsform
        der frühdynasischen Zeit in Baby-
        lonien? In *Gesellschaft und Kultur
        im alten Vorderasien*, edited by
        Horst Klengel, pp. 195–200.
        Akademie der Wissenchaften,
        Berlin.

1999   *Geschichte Alt-Vorderasiens.* Olden-
        bourg, Munich.

2001   Cultural and Political Networks in
        the Ancient Near East During the
        Fourth and Third Millennia B.C. In
        *Uruk Mesopotamia and Its Neigh-
        bors: Cross-cultural Interactions in
        the Era of State Formation*, edited
        by Mitchell S. Rothman, pp.
        149–179. School of American Re-
        search Press, Santa Fe, New Mexico.

Nissen, Hans J., Peter Damerow, and
Robert K. Englund

1993   *Archaic Bookkeeping: Early Writing
        and Techniques of Economic Ad-
        ministration in the Ancient Near
        East.* Translated by Paul Larsen.
        University of Chicago Press,
        Chicago.

Noguera, Eduardo
1971   Minor Arts in the Central Valleys. In *Handbook of Middle American Indians, Volume 10: Archaeology of Northern Mesoamerica*, edited by Gordon F. Ekholm and Ignacio Bernal, pp. 258–269. University of Texas Press, Austin.

North, Douglass C.
1994   Economic Performance Through Time. *American Economic Review* 84:359–368.

Nowak, Martin A., Karen M. Page, and Karl Sigmund
2000   Fairness versus Reason in the Ultimatum Game. *Science* 289:1773–1775.

Oates, David, and Joan Oates
1994   Tell Brak: A Stratigraphic Summary, 1976–1993. *Iraq* 56:167–176.

Oates, Joan
1969   Choga Mami, 1967–8: A Preliminary Report. *Iraq* 31:115–152.
1977   Seafaring Merchants of Ur? *Antiquity* 51:221–234.

O'Brien, Patricia J.
1991   Early State Economics: Cahokia, Capital of the Ramey State. In *Early State Economics*, edited by Henri J. M. Claessen and Pieter van de Velde, pp. 143–175. Transaction, London.

Ohadike, D. C.
1981   The Influenza Pandemic of 1918–19 and the Spread of Cassava Cultivation in the Lower Niger: A Study in Historical Linkages. *Journal of African History* 22:379–391.

Oliver, Douglas
1955   *A Solomon Island Society*. Harvard University Press, Cambridge.

Oppenheim, A. Leo
1965   Comment. In *Third International Conference of Economic History*, pp. 33–40. Mouton, London.
1977   *Ancient Mesopotamia*. University of Chicago Press, Chicago.

Orthmann, Winfried
1990   *Tell Chuera*. Rudolf Habelt, Bonn.

Ortiz de Zuñiga, Iñigo
1967   *Visita de la Provincia de León de*
[1562]   *Huánuco en 1562. Tomo I: Visita de los cuatro waranqa de los chupachu.* Edición a cargo de John V. Murra. Documentos para la Historia y Etnología de Huánuco y la Selva Central, Vol. 1. Universidad Nacional Hermilio Valdizán, Facultad de Letras y Educación, Huánuco, Peru.

Ortner, Sherry B.
2001   Commentary. *Journal of Social Archaeology* 1:271–278.

Oviedo y Valdés, Gonzalo F. de
1851   *Historia general y natural de las*
–1855   *indias, islas y tierra firme del mar océano.* 4 vols. Edited by José Amador de los Ríos. Real Academia de la Historia, Madrid.

Owen, Norman (editor)
1987   *Death and Disease in Southeast Asia.* Oxford University Press, Singapore.

Owusu, Maxwell
1978   Ethnography of Africa: The Usefulness of the Useless. *American Anthropologist* 80:310–334.

Özbal, Rana
2002   Household Organization and City Layout in North and South Mesopotamia in the Third Millennium B.C. Seminar paper, Anthropology Department, Northwestern University, Evanston.

Palerm, Angel, and Eric R. Wolf
1957   Ecological Potential and Cultural Development in Mesoamerica. *Pan American Union Social Science Monograph* 3:1–37.

Parkins, Helen, and Christopher Smith (editors)
1998   *Trade, Traders, and the Ancient City.* Routledge, New York.

Parsons, Mary H.
1972   Spindle Whorls from the Teotihuacan Valley, Mexico. In *Miscellaneous Studies in Mexican Prehistory*, by Michael W. Spence, Jeffrey R. Parsons, and Mary H. Parsons, pp. 45–79. Anthropological Papers No. 45. Museum of Anthropology, University of Michigan, Ann Arbor.

Parsons, Jeffrey R., and Mary H. Parsons
1985   Otomí Maguey Utilization: An Ethnoarchaeological Perspective. Preliminary report submitted to the National Geographic Society.

1990 *Maguey Utilization in Highland Central Mexico: An Archaeological Ethnography.* Anthropological Papers No. 82. Museum of Anthropology, University of Michigan, Ann Arbor.

Paterson, Jeremy

1998 Trade and Traders in the Roman World. In *Trade, Traders, and the Ancient City*, edited by Helen Parkins and Christopher Smith, pp. 149–167. Routledge, New York.

2001 Hellenistic Economies: The Case of Rome. In *Hellenistic Economies*, edited by Zofia H. Archibald, John Davies, Vincent Gabrielson, and G. J. Oliver, pp. 367–378. Routledge, New York.

Pauketat, Timothy R.

1992 The Reign and Ruin of the Lords of Cahokia: A Dialectic of Dominance. In *Lords of the Southeast: Social Inequality and the Native Elites of Southeastern North America*, edited by Alex W. Barker and Timothy R. Pauketat, pp. 31–52. Archeological Papers No. 3. American Anthropological Association, Washington, D.C.

1993 *Temples for Cahokia Lords: Preston Holder's 1955–1956 Excavation of Kunnemann Mound.* Memoir No. 26. Museum of Anthropology, University of Michigan, Ann Arbor.

1994 *The Ascent of Chiefs: Cahokia and Mississippian Politics in Native North America.* University of Alabama Press, Tuscaloosa.

1996 The Place of Post-Circle Monuments in Cahokian Political History. *Wisconsin Archeologist* 77:73–83.

1997a Cahokian Political Economy. In *Cahokia: Domination and Ideology in the Mississippian World*, edited by Timothy R. Pauketat and Thomas E. Emerson, pp. 30–51. University of Nebraska Press, Lincoln.

1997b Specialization, Political Symbols, and the Crafty Elite of Cahokia. *Southeastern Archaeology* 16:1–15.

1998a *The Archaeology of Downtown Cahokia: The Tract 15A and Dunham Tract Excavations.* Studies in Archaeology No. 1. Illinois Transportation Archaeological Research Program, University of Illinois, Urbana.

1998b Refiguring the Archaeology of Greater Cahokia. *Journal of Archaeological Research* 6:45–89.

2000a Politicization and Community in the Pre-Columbian Mississippian Valley. In *The Archaeology of Communities: A New World Perspective*, edited by Marcello A. Canuto and Jason Yaeger, pp. 16–43. Routledge, London.

2000b The Tragedy of the Commoners. In *Agency in Archaeology*, edited by Marcia-Anne Dobres and John Robb, pp. 113–129. Routledge, London.

2001a A New Tradition in Archaeology. In *The Archaeology of Traditions: Agency and History Before and After Columbus*, edited by Timothy Pauketat, pp. 1–16. University Press of Florida, Gainesville.

2001b Practice and History in Archaeology: An Emerging Paradigm. *Anthropological Theory* 1:73–98.

2002 Materiality and the Immaterial in Historical-Processual Archaeology. Ms. on file, Department of Anthropology, University of Illinois, Urbana.

2003 Resettled Farmers and the Making of a Mississippian Polity. *American Antiquity* 68:39–66.

Pauketat, Timothy R., and Susan M. Alt

2003 Mounds, Memory, and Contested Mississippian History. In *Archaeologies of Memory*, edited by Ruth M. Van Dyke and Susan E. Alcock, pp. 151–179. Blackwell, Oxford.

Pauketat, Timothy R., and Thomas E. Emerson

1991 The Ideology of Authority and the Power of the Pot. *American Anthropologist* 93:919–941.

Pauketat, Timothy R., and Thomas E. Emerson (editors)

1997 *Cahokia: Domination and Ideology in the Mississippian World.* University of Nebraska Press, Lincoln.

Pauketat, Timothy R., Lucretia S. Kelly, Gayle J. Fritz, Neal H. Lopinot, Scott Elias, and Eve Hargrave

2002 The Residues of Feasting and Public

Ritual at Early Cahokia. *American Antiquity* 67:257–279.

Pauketat, Timothy R., and Neal H. Lopinot
1997   Cahokian Population Dynamics. In *Cahokia: Domination and Ideology in the Mississippian World*, edited by Timothy R. Pauketat and Thomas E. Emerson, pp. 103–123. University of Nebraska Press, Lincoln.

Paz Soria, José Luis
1999   Excavations in the Llusco Area. In *Early Settlement at Chiripa, Bolivia*, edited by Christine Hastorf, pp. 31–35. Contributions of the Archaeological Research Facility, University of California, Berkeley.

Pearson, Harry W.
1957   The Secular Debate on Economic Primitivism. In *Trade and Market in the Early Empires: Economies in History and Theory*, edited by Karl Polanyi, Conrad M. Arensberg, and Harry W. Pearson, pp. 3–11. Free Press and Falcon's Wing Press, Glencoe, Illinois.

Peel, J. D. Y.
1983   *Ijeshas and Nigerians: The Incorporation of a Yoruba Kingdom, 1890s–1970s*. Cambridge University Press, Cambridge.
1989   The Cultural Work of Yoruba Ethnogenesis. In *History and Ethnicity*, edited by Elizabeth Tonkin, Maryon McDonald, and Malcolm Chapman, pp. 198–215. ASA Monographs No. 27. Routledge, London.

Peltenburg, Edgar
1999   The Living and the Ancestors: Early Bronze Age Mortuary Practices at Jerablus Tahtani. In *Archaeology of the Upper Syrian Euphrates: The Tishreen Dam Area*, edited by Gregorio del Olmo Lete and Juan-Luis Montero Fenollós, pp. 427–442. Editorial AUSA, Barcelona.

Pendergast, David M.
1981   Lamanai, Belize: Summary of Excavation Results, 1974–1980. *Journal of Field Archaeology* 8:29–53.

Peng, Ke, and Yanshi Zhu
1999   Zhongguo gudai yong hai bei laiyuan xi tan (New ideas on origins and uses of cowrie shells in ancient China). *Kaoguxue Jikan* 12:119–147.

Peng, Zicheng, Yonggang Liu, Shizhong Liu, and Jueming Hua
1999   Gan E Yu diqu Shang dai qingtongqi he bufen tong qian kuang liao laiyuan de chutan (Discussion of source areas for copper and lead for bronze production during the Shang period in Jiangxi, Hubei, and Henan provinces). *Ziran Kexue Li Yanjiu* 18(3):241–249.

Peregrine, Peter
1991   Some Political Aspects of Craft Specialization. *World Archaeology* 23:1–11.
1992   *Mississippian Evolution: A World-System Perspective*. Prehistory Press, Madison, Wisconsin.

Peregrine, Peter N., and Gary M. Feinman (editors)
1996   *Pre-Columbian World Systems*. Prehistory Press, Madison, Wisconsin.

Pérez Romero, José A.
1988   *Algunas consideraciones sobre cacao en el norte de la península de Yucatán*. Tesis de licenciatura en ciencias antropológicas, Universidad Autónoma de Yucatán, Mérida, Mexico.

Pfälzner, Peter
1996   Activity and Social Organisation of Third Millennium B.C. Households. In *Houses and Households in Ancient Mesopotamia*, edited by Klaas R. Veenhof, pp. 117–127. Nederlands Historisch-Archaeologisch Instituut te Istanbul, Istanbul.

Pigafetta, Antonio
1521   First Voyage Around the World. In *The Philippines at the Spanish Contact*, edited and translated by F. Landa Jocano, pp. 44–80. Garcia Publications, Quezon City, Philippines.

Pillsbury, Joanne
2001   Introduction. In *Moche Art and Archaeology in Ancient Peru*, edited by Joanne Pillsbury, pp. 9–20. National Gallery of Art, Washington, D.C.

Pinnock, Frances
1984   Trade at Ebla. *Bulletin of the Society for Mesopotamian Studies* 7:19–36.

1988   Observations on the Trade of Lapis Lazuli in the IIIrd Millennium B.C. In *Wirtschaft und Gesellschaft von Ebla*, edited by Hartmut Waetzoldt and Harald Hauptmann, pp. 107–110. Heidelberger Orientverlag, Heidelberg.

Pittman, Holly

2001   Mesopotamian Intraregional Relations Reflected Through Glyptic Evidence in the Late Chalcolithic 1–5 Periods. In *Uruk Mesopotamia and Its Neighbors: Cross-cultural Interactions in the Era of State Formation*, edited by Mitchell S. Rothman, pp. 403–443. School of American Research Press, Santa Fe, New Mexico.

Plattner, Stuart

1989   Introduction. In *Economic Anthropology*, edited by Stuart Plattner, pp. 1–20. Stanford University Press, Palo Alto.

Polanyi, Karl

1944   *Origins of Our Time: The Great Transformation*. Farrar and Rinehart, New York.

1957   The Economy as Instituted Process. In *Trade and Market in the Early Empires*, edited by Karl Polanyi, Conrad M. Arensbert, and Harry W. Pearson, pp. 243–270. Regnery, Chicago.

1968   Societies and Economic Systems. In *Primitive, Archaic, and Modern Economies: Essays of Karl Polanyi*, edited by George Dalton, pp. 3–25. Beacon Press, Boston. Reprinted from *The Great Transformation*.

Polanyi, Karl, Conrad M. Arensberg, and Harry W. Pearson (editors)

1957   *Trade and Market in the Early Empires: Economies in History and Theory*. Free Press and Falcon's Wing Press, Glencoe, Illinois.

Pollock, Susan

1991   Of Priestesses, Princes, and Poor Relations: The Dead in the Royal Cemetery of Ur. *Cambridge Archaeological Journal* 1:171–189.

2001   The Uruk Period in Southern Mesopotamia. In *Uruk Mesopotamia and Its Neighbors: Cross-cultural Interactions in the Era of State Formation*, edited by Mitchell S. Rothman, pp. 181–231. School of American Research Press, Santa Fe, New Mexico.

Polo de Ondegardo, Juan

1940   Informe al Licenciado Briviesca de
[1561]   Muñatones. *Revista Histórica* 13:128–196.

Porter, Anne

1995   Tell Banat—Tomb 1. *Damaszener Mitteilungen* 8:1–50.

2000   *Mortality, Monuments, and Mobility*. Unpublished Ph.D. dissertation, Department of Near Eastern Languages and Civilizations, University of Chicago, Chicago.

Porter, James W.

1977   The Mitchell Site and Prehistoric Exchange Systems at Cahokia: A.D. 1000 ± 300. In *Explorations into Cahokia Archaeology*, edited by Melvin L. Fowler, pp. 137–164. Bulletin No. 7. Illinois Archaeological Survey, Urbana. Reprint.

Portugal Ortiz, Max

1988   Excavaciones arqueológicos en Titimani (II). In *Arqueología boliviana*, pp. 51–81. Instituto Nacional de Arqueología, La Paz, Bolivia.

Porubcan, Paula J.

2000   Human and Nonhuman Surplus Display at Mound 72, Cahokia. In *Mounds, Modoc, and Mesoamerica: Papers in Honor of Melvin L. Fowler*, edited by Steven R. Ahler, pp. 207–225. Scientific Papers, Vol. 28. Illinois State Museum, Springfield.

Posnansky, Merrick

1973   Aspects of Early West African Trade. *World Archaeology* 5:149–162.

1987   Prelude to Akan Civilization. In *The Golden Stool: Studies of the Asante Center and Periphery*, edited by Enid Schildkrout, pp. 14–22. Anthropological Papers Vol. 65, Part 1. American Museum of Natural History, New York.

Postgate, J. N.

1988   A View from Down the Euphrates. In *Wirtschaft und Gesellschaft von Ebla*, edited by Hartmut Waetzoldt and Harald Hauptmann, pp. 111–117. Heidelberger Orientverlag, Heidelberg.

1992   *Early Mesopotamia: Society and Economy at the Dawn of History.* Routledge, London.

1994   How Many Sumerians per Hectare? Probing the Anatomy of an Early City. *Cambridge Archaeological Journal* 4:47–65.

Potter, Stephen R.

1993   *Commoners, Tribute, and Chiefs: The Development of Algonquian Culture in the Potomac Valley.* University of Virginia Press, Charlottesville.

Powell, Marvin

1990   Urban-Rural Interface: Movement of Goods and Services in a Third Millennium City-State. In *The Town as Regional Economic Centre in the Ancient Near East*, edited by Erik Aerts and Horst Klengel, pp. 7–14. Leuven University Press, Leuven.

Powell, Mary Lucas

1992   *Status and Health in Prehistory.* Smithsonian Institution Press, Washington, D.C.

Pozzi-Escot, Denise, Marleni M. Alarcón, and Cirilo Vivanco

1998   Wari Ceramics and Production Technology: The View of Ayacucho. In *Andean Ceramics: Technology, Organization, and Approaches*, edited by Izumi Shimada, pp. 63–90. MASCA Research Papers in Science and Archaeology Vol. 15 supplement. University of Pennsylvania Museum, Philadelphia.

Prechtel, Martín

1999   *Long Life, Honey in the Heart: A Story of Initiation and Eloquence from the Shores of a Mayan Lake.* Penguin Putnam, New York.

Price, T. Douglas (editor)

2000   *Europe's First Farmers.* Cambridge University Press, Cambridge.

Price, T. Douglas, and Gary M. Feinman (editors)

1995   *Foundations of Social Inequality.* Plenum Press, New York.

Purcell, Nicholas

1985   Wine and Wealth in Ancient Italy. *Journal of Roman Studies* 75:1–19.

Qiu, Shihua, and Lianzhen Cai

2001   Xia Shang Zhou duandai gongcheng zhong de tanshisi niandai kuangjia (A chronological framework for the Xia-Shang-Zhou Chronology Project). *Kaogu* 1:90–100.

Ramírez, Susan E.

1996   *The World Upside Down: Cross-cultural Contact and Conflict in Sixteenth-Century Peru.* Stanford University Press, Palo Alto.

Ramírez-Horton, Susan

1981   La organización económica de las costa norte: Un análisis preliminar del período prehispánico tardío. In *Etnohistoria y antropología andina*, edited by Amalia Castelli, Marcia Koth de Paredes, and Mariana Mould de Pease, pp. 281–297. Centro de Proyección Cristiana, Lima, Peru.

1982   Retainers of the Lords or Merchants: A Case of Mistaken Identity? In *El hombre y su ambiente en los Andes centrales: Ponencias presentadas en el cuarto simposio internacional*, edited by Luis Milliones and Hiroyasu Tomoeda, pp. 123–136. Senri Ethnological Studies No. 10. National Museum of Ethnology, Osaka.

Rathbone, Dominic

1991   *Economic Rationalism and Rural Society in Third Century A.D. Egypt: The Heroninos Archive and the Appianos Estate.* Cambridge University Press, New York.

Rathje, William L.

1971   The Origin and Development of Lowland Classic Maya Civilization. *American Antiquity* 36:275–285.

1972   Praise the Gods and Pass the Metates: A Hypothesis of the Development of Lowland Rainforest Civilizations in Mesoamerica. In *Contemporary Archaeology: A Guide to Theory and Contributions*, edited by Mark P. Leone, pp. 365–392. Southern Illinois University Press, Carbondale.

Reade, Julian

1973   Tell Taya (1972–73): Summary Report. *Iraq* 35:155–187.

Redmond, Elsa M.

1979   A Terminal Formative Ceramic Workshop in the Tehuacan Valley. In *Prehistoric Social, Political, and*

Economic Development in the Area of the Tehuacan Valley: Some Results of the Palo Blanco Project, edited by Robert D. Drennan, pp. 111–125. Technical Reports No. 11. Museum of Anthropology, University of Michigan, Ann Arbor.

1994   *Tribal and Chiefly Warfare in South America.* Memoirs No. 28. Museum of Anthropology, University of Michigan, Ann Arbor.

1998   Introduction: The Dynamics of Chieftaincy and the Development of Chiefdoms. In *Chiefdoms and Chieftaincy in the Americas*, edited by Elsa M. Redmond, pp. 1–17. University Press of Florida, Gainesville.

Reents-Budet, Dorie
1994   *Painting the Maya Universe: Royal Ceramics of the Classic Period.* Duke University Press, Durham.

Rees, Mark A.
2001   Historical Science or Silence? Toward a Historical Anthropology of Mississippian Political Culture. In *The Archaeology of Traditions: Agency and History Before and After Columbus*, edited by Timothy R. Pauketat, pp. 121–140. University Press of Florida, Gainesville.

Reid, Anthony
1983a   "Closed" and "Open" Slave Systems in Pre-colonial Southeast Asia. In *Slavery, Bondage, and Dependency in Southeast Asia*, edited by Anthony Reid, pp. 156–181. St. Martin's Press, New York.

1983b   Introduction: Slavery and Bondage in Southeast Asian History. In *Slavery, Bondage, and Dependency in Southeast Asia*, edited by Anthony Reid, pp. 1–43. St. Martin's Press, New York.

1988   *Southeast Asia in the Age of Commerce, 1450–1680, Volume 1: The Lands Below the Winds.* Yale University Press, New Haven.

1992   Economic and Social Change, c. 1400–1800. In *The Cambridge History of Southeast Asia, Volume 1: From Early Times to c. 1800*, edited by Nicholas Tarling, pp. 460–507.

Cambridge University Press, Cambridge.

1993a   Introduction: A Time and a Place. In *Southeast Asia in the Early Modern Era*, edited by Anthony Reid, pp. 1–22. Cornell University Press, Ithaca.

1993b   *Southeast Asia in the Age of Commerce, 1450–1680, Volume 2: Expansion and Crisis.* Yale University Press, New Haven.

Renfrew, Colin
1972   *The Emergence of Civilisation: The Cyclades and the Aegean in the Third Millennium B.C..* Methuen, London.

1973   *Before Civilisation: The Radiocarbon Revolution and European Prehistory.* Jonathan Cape, London.

1974   Beyond a Subsistence Economy: The Evolution of Social Organization in Prehistoric Europe. In *Reconstructing Complex Societies*, edited by Charlotte B. Moore, pp. 69–96. Supplement to the Bulletin of the American School of Oriental Research No. 20. Cambridge, Massachusetts.

1975   Trade as Action at a Distance: Questions of Integration and Communication. In *Ancient Civilization and Trade*, edited by Jeremy A. Sabloff and C. C. Lamberg-Karlovsky, pp. 3–59. School of American Research, Santa Fe, and University of New Mexico Press, Albuquerque.

1986a   Introduction: Peer Polity Interaction and Socio-Political Change. In *Peer Polity Interaction and Socio-Political Change*, edited by Colin Renfrew and John F. Cherry, pp. 1–18. Cambridge University Press, Cambridge.

1986b   Varna and the Emergence of Wealth in Prehistoric Europe. In *The Social Life of Things: Commodities in Cultural Perspective*, edited by Arjun Appadurai, pp. 141–168. Cambridge University Press, Cambridge.

Renfrew, Colin, and John Cherry (editors)
1986   *Peer Polity Interaction and Socio-*

Political Evolution. Cambridge University Press, Cambridge.

Renger, Johannes M.

1994   On Economic Structures in Ancient Mesopotamia. *Orientalia* 63:157–208.

1995   Institutional, Communal, and Individual Ownership or Possession of Arable Land in Ancient Mesopotamia from the End of the Fourth to the End of the First Millennium B.C. *Kent Law Review* 71:269–319.

Restall, Matthew

1997   *The Maya World: Yucatec Culture and Society, 1550–1850.* Stanford University Press, Palo Alto.

Rice, Don S.

1993   Eighth-Century Physical Geography, Environment, and Natural Resources in the Maya Lowlands. In *Lowland Maya Society in the Eighth Century A.D.*, edited by Jeremy A. Sabloff and John S. Henderson, pp. 11–63. Dumbarton Oaks, Washington, D.C.

Rice, Prudence M.

1981   Evolution of Specialized Pottery Production: A Trial Model. *Current Anthropology* 22:219–240.

1987   Economic Change in the Lowland Maya Late Classic Period. In *Specialization, Exchange, and Complex Societies*, edited by Elizabeth M. Brumfiel and Timothy K. Earle, pp. 76–85. Cambridge University Press, Cambridge.

1991   Specialization, Standardization, and Diversity: A Retrospective. In *The Ceramic Legacy of Anna O. Shepard*, edited by Ronald L. Bishop and Frederick W. Lange, pp. 257–279. University Press of Colorado, Niwot.

Rigby, Peter

1996   *African Images: Racism and the End of Anthropology.* Berg, Oxford.

Ringle, William M., Tomás Gallareta N., and George J. Bey III

1998   The Return of Quetzalcoatl: Evidence for the Spread of a World Religion During the Epiclassic Period. *Ancient Mesoamerica* 9:183–232.

Roberts, Richard

1984   Women's Work and Women's Property: Household Social Relations in the Maraka Textile Industry of the Nineteenth Century. *Comparative Studies in Society and History* 26:229–250.

1992   Guinée Cloth: Linked Transformations within France's Empire in the Nineteenth Century. *Cahiers d'Etudes Africaines* (128)32: 597–627.

Robertshaw, Peter

1999   Seeking and Keeping Power in Bunyoro-Kitara, Uganda. In *Beyond Chiefdoms: Pathways to Complexity in Africa*, edited by Susan K. McIntosh, pp. 124–135. Cambridge University Press, Cambridge.

Robles G., Nelly M.

1994   *Las canteras de Mitla, Oaxaca: Tecnología para la arquitectura monumental.* Publications in Anthropology No. 47. Vanderbilt University, Nashville.

Rocha, Jorge M.

1996   Rationality, Culture, and Decision Making. *Research in Economic Anthropology* 17:13–41.

Roemer, Erwin

1982   Investigation at Four Lithic Workshops at Colha, Belize: 1981 Season. In *Archaeology at Colha, Belize: The 1981 Interim Report*, edited by Thomas R. Hester, Harry J. Shafer, and Jack D. Eaton, pp. 75–84. Center for Archaeological Research, University of Texas at San Antonio, San Antonio.

Roobaert, Arlette, and Guy Bunnens

1999   Excavations at Tell Ahmar-Til Barsip. In *Archaeology of the Upper Syrian Euphrates: The Tishreen Dam Area*, edited by Gregorio del Olmo Lete and Juan-Luis Montero Fenollós, pp. 163–178. Editorial Ausa, Barcelona.

Rossman, Abraham, and Paula Rubel

1978   Exchange as Structure, or Why Doesn't Everyone Eat His Own Pigs. *Research in Economic Anthropology* 1:105–130.

Rostovtzeff, Mikhail

1941   *Social and Economic History of the Hellenistic World*. Clarendon Press, Oxford.

1957   *Social and Economic History of the Roman Empire*. Clarendon Press, Oxford.

Rostworowski de Diez Canseco, María

1977a   Coastal Fishermen, Merchants, and Artisans in Pre-Hispanic Peru. In *The Sea in the Pre-Columbian World*, edited by Elizabeth P. Benson, pp. 167–186. Dumbarton Oaks, Washington, D.C.

1977b   *Etnia y sociedad: Costa peruana prehispánica*. Instituto de Estudios Peruanos, Lima.

1989   *Costa peruana prehispánica*. 2nd ed. Historia Andina No. 15. Instituto de Estudios Peruanos, Lima.

Rothman, Mitchell S.

1996   Palace and Private Agricultural Decision-Making in the Early 2nd Millennium B.C. City-State of Larsa, Iraq. In *The Economic Anthropology of the State*, edited by Elizabeth Brumfiel, pp. 149–166. Monographs in Economic Anthropology No. 11. University Press of America, Lanham, Maryland.

2001   The Local and the Regional: An Introduction. In *Uruk Mesopotamia and Its Neighbors: Cross-cultural Interactions in the Era of State Formation*, edited by Mitchell S. Rothman, pp. 3–26. School of American Research Press, Santa Fe, New Mexico.

Rothman, Mitchell S. (editor)

2001   *Uruk Mesopotamia and Its Neighbors: Cross-cultural Interactions in the Era of State Formation*. School of American Research Press, Santa Fe, New Mexico.

Rountree, Helen C.

1989   *The Powhatan Indians of Virginia: Their Traditional Culture*. University of Oklahoma Press, Norman.

Rowe, Ann P.

1978   Technical Features of Inca Tapestry Tunics. *Textile Museum Journal* 17:5–28.

Rowe, John H.

1944   *An Introduction to the Archaeology of Cuzco*. Papers of the Peabody Museum of Anthropology and Ethnology Vol. 27, No. 2. Harvard University, Cambridge.

1948   The Kingdom of Chimor. *Acta Americana* 6(1–2):26–59. Mexico City.

1979   Standardization in Inca Tapestry Tunics. In *The Junius Bird Pre-Columbian Textile Conference*, edited by Ann P. Rowe, Elizabeth P. Boone, and Anne-Louise Schaffer, pp. 239–264. Textile Museum and Dumbarton Oaks, Washington, D.C.

Rowlands, Michael J., Mogens Larsen, and Kristian Kristiansen (editors)

1987   *Centre and Periphery in the Ancient World*. Cambridge University Press, Cambridge.

Roys, Ralph L.

1941   The Xiu Chronicle, Part II: The Xiu Chronicle. Unpublished manuscript, Tozzer Library, Harvard University.

1943   *The Indian Background of Colonial Yucatan*. Publication No. 548. Carnegie Institution of Washington, Washington, D.C.

Russell, Glenn

1988   *The Impact of Inka Policy on the Domestic Economy of the Wanka, Peru: Stone Tool Production and Use*. Ph.D. dissertation, University of California, Los Angeles. University Microfilms, Ann Arbor.

Russell, Glenn, and Margaret A. Jackson

2001   Political Economy and Patronage at Cerro Mayal, Peru. In *Moche Art and Archaeology in Ancient Peru*, edited by Joanne Pillsbury, pp. 159–176. National Gallery of Art, Washington, D.C.

Russell, Glenn, Banks Leonard, and Jesus Briceno

1998   The Cerro Maya Workshop: Addressing Issues of Craft Specialization in Moche Society. In *Andean Ceramics: Technology, Organization, and Approaches*, edited by Izumi Shimada, pp. 63–90. MASCA Research Papers in Science and Archaeology Vol. 15 supplement. University of Pennsylvania Museum, Philadelphia.

Sabloff, Jeremy A., and William L. Rathje
1975   The Rise of a Maya Merchant Class. *Scientific American* 233:72–82.

Sahagún, Bernadino de
1950   *General History of the Things of*
–1982   *New Spain* (Florentine Codex). 12
[1569] vols. Translated by Arthur J. O. Anderson and Charles Dibble. School of American Research, Santa Fe, and University of Utah, Salt Lake City.

Sahlins, Marshall
1972   *Stone Age Economics*. Aldine, New York.

Saitta, Dean J.
1994   Agency, Class, and Archaeological Interpretation. *Journal of Anthropological Archaeology* 13:201–227.

Saleeby, Najeeb M.
1905   *Studies in Moro History, Law, and Religion*. Ethnological Survey Publications, Vol. 4, Part 1. Bureau of Printing, U.S. Department of the Interior, Manila.

San Antonio, Francisco
1990   Crónicas de la apostólica provincia
[1738] de San Gregorio de religiosos descalzados de N.S.P.S. Francisco de las Philipinas, China, Japón, etc. In *Documentary Sources of Philippine History*, vol. 5, edited and translated by Gregorio F. Zaide, pp. 299–341. National Bookstore Publications, Manila.

Sanders, William T., Jeffrey R. Parsons, and Robert S. Santley
1979   *The Basin of Mexico: Ecological Processes in the Evolution of a Civilization*. Academic Press, New York.

Sandford, Stephen
1982   Pastoral Strategies and Desertification: Opportunism and Conservatism in Arid Lands. In *Desertification and Development: Dryland Ecology in Social Perspective*, edited by Brian Spooner and H. S. Mann, pp. 61–80. Academic Press, London.

Sandweiss, Daniel
1995   Life in Ancient Túcume. In *Pyramids of Túcume: The Quest for Peru's Forgotten City*, by Thor Heyerdahl, Daniel H. Sandweiss, and Alfredo Narváez, pp. 142–168. Thames and Hudson, New York.

Santa Ines, Francisco de
1990   Crónica de la provincia de San
[1676] Gregorio Magno de China, Japón, etc. In *Documentary Sources of Philippine History*, vol. 5, edited and translated by Gregorio F. Zaide, pp. 67–92. National Bookstore Publications, Manila.

Santley, Robert S., Philip J. Arnold, and Christopher A. Pool
1989   The Ceramics Production System at Matacapan, Veracruz, Mexico. *Journal of Field Archaeology* 16:107–132.

Schele, Linda, and Peter Mathews
1998   *The Code of Kings: The Language of Seven Sacred Maya Temples and Tombs*. Scribner, New York.

Schiffer, Michael B.
1999   *The Material Life of Human Beings: Artifacts, Behavior, and Communication*. Routledge, London.

Schmidt, Peter R., and Thomas C. Patterson
1995   Introduction: From Constructing to Making Alternative Histories. In *Making Alternative Histories: The Practice of Archaeology in History in Non-Western Settings*, edited by Peter R. Schmidt and Thomas C. Patterson, pp. 1–24. School of American Research Press, Santa Fe, New Mexico.

Schneider, Jane
1977   Was There a Pre-capitalist World System? *Peasant Studies* 6:20–29.

Schnitger, F. M.
1964   *Forgotten Kingdoms in Sumatra*. Brill, Leiden.

Schoenbrun, David L.
1998   *A Green Place, a Good Place: Agrarian Change, Gender, and Social Identity in the Great Lakes Region to the Fifteenth Century*. Heinemann, Portsmouth, New Hampshire.
1999   The (In)visible Roots of Bunyoro-Kitara and Buganda in the Lakes Region, A.D. 800–1300. In *Beyond Chiefdoms: Pathways to*

Complexity in Africa, edited by Susan K. McIntosh, pp. 136–150. Cambridge University Press, Cambridge.

Scholes, France V., and Ralph L. Roys
1968   *The Maya Chontal Indians of Acalan-Tixchel*. 2nd ed. University of Oklahoma Press, Norman. Originally published 1948.

Schwalbenberg, Henry
1993   The Economics of Slavery in the Prehispanic Philippines. *Philippine Quarterly of Culture and Society* (21)1:370–390.

Schwartz, Glenn
1987   The Ninevite V Period and the Development of Complex Society in Northern Mesopotamia. *Paléorient* 13(2):93–100.

1994   Before Ebla: Models of Pre-state Political Organization in Syria and Northern Mesopotamia. In *Chiefdoms and Early States in the Near East: The Organizational Dynamics of Complexity*, edited by Gil Stein and Mitchell Rothman, pp. 153–174. Prehistory Press, Madison, Wisconsin.

Schwartz, Glenn, Hans H. Curvers, and Barbara Stuart
2000   A Third-Millennium Elite Tomb from Tell Umm el-Marra, Syria. *Antiquity* 74:771–772.

Schwartz, Hugh H.
1998   *Rationality Gone Awry? Decision Making Inconsistent with Economic and Financial Theory*. Praeger, Westport, Connecticut.

Scott, James
1976   *The Moral Economy of the Peasant: Subsistence and Rebellion in South East Asia*. Yale University Press, New Haven.

Scott, William Henry
1983   *Oripun* and *Alipin* in the Sixteenth-Century Philippines. In *Slavery, Bondage, and Dependency in Southeast Asia*, edited by Anthony Reid, pp. 138–155. St. Martin's Press, New York.

1994   *Barangay: Sixteenth-Century Philippine Culture and Society*. Ateneo de Manila Press, Quezon City, Philippines.

Service, Elman R.
1962   *Primitive Social Organization: An Evolutionary Perspective*. Random House, New York.

1972   *Origins of the State and Civilization*. Norton, New York.

Shafer, Harry J.
1983   Lithic Artifacts of the Pulltrouser Area: Settlement and Fields. In *Pulltrouser Swamp: Ancient Maya Habitat, Agriculture, and Settlement in Northern Belize*, edited by B. L. Turner and Peter D. Harrison, pp. 212–245. University of Texas Press, Austin.

Shafer, Harry J., and Thomas R. Hester
1983   Ancient Maya Chert Workshops in Northern Belize, Central America. *American Antiquity* 48:519–543.

1986   Maya Stone-Tool Craft Specialization and Production at Colha, Belize: Reply to Mallory. *American Antiquity* 51:158–166.

1991   Lithic Craft Specialization and Product Distribution at the Maya Site of Colha, Belize. *World Archaeology* 23:79–97.

Shalizi, Cosma Rohilla
1999   *Homo reciprocans*: Political Economy and Cultural Evolution. *Bulletin of the Santa Fe Institute* 14(2):1–5.

Shandong Provincial Museum
1972   Shandong Yidu Sufutun diyihao nuli xunzang mu (Slave sacrifice tomb 1 of the Sufutun site at Yidu in Shandong). *Kaogu* 9:17–30.

Shandong Team, IA, CASS
1992   Tengzhou Qianzhangda Shang dai muxang (Shang dynasty burials at Qianzhangda in Tengzhou). *Kaogu Xuebao* 3:365–392.

2000   Shandong Tengzhou shi Qianzhangda Shang Zhou mudi 1998 nian fajue jianbao (Archaeological report of excavations in 1998 at the Shang and Zhou cemeteries in Qianzhangda village, Tengzhou, Shandong). *Kaogu* 2000(7):13–28.

Shandong University Archaeology Department, Shandong Province Institute of Archaeology, Jinan City Museum
1995   1984 Nian qiu Jinan Daxinzhuang

yizhi shijue shuyao (Important results from test excavations at the
Daxinzhuang site in Jinan in fall
1984). *Wenwu* 6:12–27.

Shao, Wangping
1987   *Yu Gong* jiu zhou de kaoguxue yan-
        jiu (Archaeological research on the
        nine territories of the *Yu Gong*).
        Jiu Zhou Xuekan 5:9–18.

Sharpe, Barrie
1986   Ethnography and a Regional Sys-
        tem: Mental Maps and the Myth of
        States and Tribes in North-Central
        Nigeria. *Critique of Anthropology*
        6(3):33–65.

Shaughnessy, Edward
1993   Shang Shu (Shu Ching). In *Early
        Chinese Texts: A Bibliographical
        Guide*, edited by Michael Loewe,
        pp. 376–389. Institute of East Asian
        Studies, University of California,
        Berkeley.

Shaw, Brent D.
1979   Rural Periodic Markets in Roman
        North Africa as Mechanisms of So-
        cial Integration and Control. *Re-
        search in Economic Anthropology*
        2:91–117.
2001   Challenging Braudel: A New Vision
        of the Mediterranean. *Journal of
        Roman Archaeology* 14:419–453.

Shen, Chen
2002   *Anyang and Sanxingdui: Unveiling
        the Mysteries of Ancient Chinese
        Civilizations*. Royal Ontario Mu-
        seum, Toronto.

Shennan, Stephen
1986   Central Europe in the Third Millen-
        nium B.C.: An Evolutionary Trajec-
        tory for the Beginning of the Euro-
        pean Bronze Age. *Journal of
        Anthropological Archaeology*
        5:115–146.
1993a   Settlement and Social Change in
        Central Europe, 3500–1500 B.C.
        Journal of World Prehistory
        7:121–161.
1993b   After Social Evolution: A New Ar-
        chaeological Agenda? In *Archaeo-
        logical Theory: Who Sets the
        Agenda?* edited by Norman Yoffee
        and Andrew Sherratt, pp. 53–59.
        Cambridge University Press, Cam-
        bridge.

1999   Cost, Benefit, and Value in the Or-
        ganisation of Early European Cop-
        per Production. *Antiquity*
        73:352–363.

Sherratt, Andrew
1981   Plough and Pastoralism: Aspects of
        the Secondary Products Revolution.
        In *Pattern of the Past: Studies in Ho-
        nour of David Clarke*, edited by Ian
        Hodder, Glynn Isaac, and Norman
        Hammond, pp. 261–305. Cam-
        bridge University Press, Cambridge.
        Reprinted, with additions, in Sher-
        ratt 1997.
1993   What Would a Bronze Age World
        System Look Like? Relations Be-
        tween Temperate Europe and the
        Mediterranean in Later Prehistory.
        Journal of European Archaeology
        1:1–57.
1994a   The Transformation of Early Agrar-
        ian Europe: The Later Neolithic and
        Copper Ages, 4500–2500 B.C. In
        *The Oxford Illustrated Prehistory of
        Europe*, edited by Barry Cunliffe,
        pp. 167–201. Oxford University
        Press, Oxford.
1994b   The Emergence of Elites: Earlier
        Bronze Age Europe, 2500–1300 B.C.
        In *The Oxford Illustrated Prehistory
        of Europe*, edited by Barry Cunliffe,
        pp. 244–276. Oxford University
        Press, Oxford.
1995a   Reviving the Grand Narrative: Ar-
        chaeology and Long-Term Change.
        David Clarke Memorial Lecture,
        University of Cambridge, 1995.
        Journal of European Archaeology
        3:1–32.
1995b   Alcohol and Its Alternatives: Symbol
        and Substance in Pre-industrial Cul-
        tures. In *Consuming Habits: Drugs
        in History and Anthropology*, edited
        by Jordan Goodman, Paul E. Love-
        joy, and Andrew Sherratt, pp.
        11–46. Routledge, London.
1997   *Economy and Society in Prehistoric
        Europe: Changing Perspectives*.
        Princeton University Press,
        Princeton.
1998   The Human Geography of Europe:
        A Prehistoric Perspective. In *An His-
        torical Geography of Europe*, edited
        by Robert A. Dodgshon and Robin

A. Butlin, pp. 1–25. Clarendon Press, Oxford.

2002a   The Horse and the Wheel: The Dialectics of Change in the Circum-Pontic Region and Adjacent Areas, 4500–1500 B.C. In *Prehistoric Steppe Adaptation and the Horse*, edited by Colin Renfrew and Marsha Levine, pp. 233–352. McDonald Institute, Cambridge.

2002b   Diet and Cuisine: Farming and Its Transformations as Reflected in Pottery. *Documenta Praehistorica* 29:61–71.

Sherratt, Andrew, and Susan Sherratt

1991   From Luxuries to Commodities: The Nature of Mediterranean Bronze Age Trading Systems. In *Bronze Age Trade in the Mediterranean: Papers Presented at the Conference Held at Rewley House, Oxford, in December 1989*, edited by Noël Gale, pp. 351–386. Studies in Mediterranean Archaeology Vol. 90. P. Åströms Förlag, Jonsered, Sweden.

1998   Small Worlds: Interaction and Identity in the Ancient Mediterranean. In *The Aegean and the Orient in the Second Millennium: Proceedings of the 50th Anniversary Symposium*, edited by Eric H. Cline and Diane Harris-Cline, pp. 329–342. Aegaeum 18. University of Texas, Austin.

2001   Technological Change in the East Mediterranean Bronze Age: Capital, Resources, and Marketing. In *The Social Context of Technological Change: Egypt and the Near East, 1650–1150 B.C.*, edited by Andrew Shortland, pp. 15–38. Oxbow, Oxford.

Sherratt, Susan, and Andrew Sherratt

1993   The Growth of the Mediterranean Economy in the Early First Millennium B.C. *World Archaeology* 24:361–378.

Shi, Zhangru

1933   Di qi ci Yinxu fajue: E qu gongzuo baogao (Report on work in Area E during the seventh season of excavation at Yinxu). In *Excavations at Anyang, Part IV*, edited by Li Chi, pp. 709–728. Bulletin of the Institute of History and Philology, Shanghai.

Shimada, Izumi

1985   Perception, Procurement, and Management of Resources: Archaeological Perspectives. In *Andean Ecology and Civilization*, edited by Shozo Masuda, Izumi Shimada, and Craig Morris, pp. 357–399. University of Tokyo Press, Tokyo.

1987   Horizontal and Vertical Dimensions of Prehistoric States in North Peru. In *The Origins and Development of the Andean State*, edited by Jonathan Haas, Shelia Pozorski, and Thomas Pozorski, pp. 130–144. Cambridge University Press, Cambridge.

1994   *Pampa Grande and the Mochica Culture*. University of Texas Press, Austin.

1998   Sican Metallurgy and Its Cross-craft Relationships. *Boletín Museo del Oro* 41:27–62.

2001   Late Moche Urban Craft Production: A First Approximation. In *Moche Art and Archaeology in Ancient Peru*, edited by Joanne Pillsbury, pp. 177–206. National Gallery of Art, Washington, D.C.

Shimada, Izumi, and Ursel Wagner

2001   Peruvian Black Pottery Production and Metalworking: A Middle Sicán Craft Workshop at Huaca Sialupe. *MRS Bulletin* 26(1):25–30.

Shipley, Graham

1993   Distance, Development, Decline? World-Systems Analysis and the "Hellenistic" World. In *Centre and Periphery in the Hellenistic World*, edited by Per Bilde, Troels Engberg-Pedersen, Lise Hannestad, Jan Zahle, and Klavs Randsborg, pp. 271–284. Aarhus University Press, Aarhus, Denmark.

Sichuan Province Institute of Archaeology

1999   *Sanxingdui jisi keng* (The sacrificial pits at Sanxingdui). Wenwu Press, Beijing.

Silliman, Stephen

2001   Agency, Practical Politics, and the Archaeology of Culture Contact. *Journal of Social Archaeology* 1:190–209.

Silverblatt, Irene

1987   *Moon, Sun, and Witches: Gender*

Ideologies and Class in Inca and Colonial Peru. Princeton University Press, Princeton.

Sinclair, Paul J. J., Thurstan Shaw, and Bassey Andah

1993   Introduction. In *The Archaeology of Africa: Food, Metals, and Towns*, edited by Thurstan Shaw, Paul Sinclair, Bassey Andah, and Alex Okpoko, pp. 1–31. Routledge, London.

Sinopoli, Carla M.

1988   The Organization of Craft Production at Vijayanagara, South India. *American Anthropologist* 90:580–597.

1994a   The Archaeology of Empire. *Annual Review of Anthropology* 23:159–180.

1994b   Political Choices and Economic Strategies in the Vijayanagara Empire. In *The Economic Anthropology of the State*, edited by Elizabeth M. Brumfiel, pp. 223–242. Monographs in Economic Anthropology No. 11. University Press of America, Lanham, Maryland.

1998   Identity and Social Action Among South Indian Craft Producers of the Vijayanagara Period. In *Craft and Social Identity*, edited by Cathy Lynne Costin and Rita P. Wright, pp. 161–172. Archeological Papers No. 8, American Anthropological Association, Washington, D.C.

n.d.   Crafting Empire: Craft Production and Political Economy in Fourteenth through Seventeenth Century South India. Ms. on file, Department of Anthropology, California State University, Northridge.

Small, David B.

2001   Discussant. "Colonial Praxis," symposium at the 66th Annual Meeting of the Society for American Archaeology, New Orleans.

Smith, Adam

1976   *The Wealth of Nations*. Edited by
[1776] Edward Cannan. University of Chicago Press, Chicago.

Smith, Adam T.

2001   The Limitations of Doxa. *Journal of Social Archaeology* 1:155–171.

Smith, Bruce D.

1978   Variation in Mississippian Settlement Patterns. In *Mississippian Settlement Patterns*, edited by Bruce D. Smith, pp. 479–503. Academic Press, New York.

2000   Guilá Naquitz Revisited: Agricultural Origins in Oaxaca, Mexico. In *Cultural Evolution: Contemporary Viewpoints*, edited by Gary M. Feinman and Linda Manzanilla, pp. 15–60. Kluwer Academic/Plenum, New York.

Smith, M. Estellie

1989   The Informal Economy. In *Economic Anthropology*, edited by Stuart M. Plattner, pp. 292–317. Stanford University Press, Palo Alto.

Smith, Michael E., and Frances F. Berdan

2000   The Postclassic Mesoamerican World System. *Current Anthropology* 41:283–286.

Smith, Michael E., and Marilyn A. Masson (editors)

2000   *The Ancient Civilizations of Mesoamerica: A Reader*. Blackwell, Malden, Massachusetts.

Smith, Robert B.

1979   Mainland South East Asia in the Seventh and Eighth Centuries. In *Early South East Asia*, edited by Robert B. Smith and W. Watson, pp. 443–456. Oxford University Press, New York.

Smith, Stuart Tyson

1997   Ancient Egyptian Imperialism: Ideological Vision or Economic Exploitation? Reply to Critics of *Askut in Nubia*. *Cambridge Archaeological Journal* 7:301–307.

Snell, Daniel C.

1997   *Life in the Ancient Near East, 3100–332 B.C.E.* Yale University Press, New Haven.

Snodgrass, Anthony

1986   *An Archaeology of Greece: The Present State and Future Scope of a Discipline*. University of California Press, Berkeley.

Solway, Jacqueline S., and Richard B. Lee

1990   Foragers, Genuine or Spurious: Situating the Kalahari San in History. *Current Anthropology* 31:109–146.

Southall, Aidan

1956   *Alur Society*. W. Heffer, Cambridge.

1988   The Segmentary State in Africa and
        Asia. *Comparative Studies in Society
        and History* 30:52–82.
1991   The Segmentary State: From the
        Imaginary to the Material Means of
        Production. In *Early State Econom-
        ics*, edited by Henri Claessen and
        Pieter van de Velde. Transaction,
        New Brunswick.

Spence, Michael W.
1967   The Obsidian Industry of Teotihua-
        can. *American Antiquity*
        32:507–514.
1981   Obsidian Production and the State
        in Teotihuacan. *American Antiquity*
        46:769–788.
1987   The Scale and Structure of Obsidian
        Production in Teotihuacan. In *Teoti-
        huacan: Nuevos datos, nuevas sínte-
        sis, nuevos problemas*, edited by
        Emily McClung de Tapia and Ellen
        C. Rattray, pp. 429–450. Universi-
        dad Nacional Autónoma de México,
        Mexico City.

Spencer, Charles S.
1993   Human Agency, Biased Transmis-
        sion, and the Cultural Evolution of
        Chiefly Authority. *Journal of An-
        thropological Archaeology*
        12:41–74.
1997   Evolutionary Approaches in Archae-
        ology. *Journal of Archaeological Re-
        search* 5:209–264.

Spores, Ronald
1965   The Zapotec and Mixtec at Spanish
        Contact. In *Handbook of Middle
        American Indians*, vol. 3, edited by
        Robert Wauchope and Gordon R.
        Willey, pp. 962–986. University of
        Texas Press, Austin.
1972   *An Archaeological Settlement Sur-
        vey of the Nochixtlán Valley, Oax-
        aca*. Publications in Anthropology
        No. 1. Vanderbilt University,
        Nashville.

Spurling, Geoffrey
1992   *The Organization of Craft Produc-
        tion in the Inka State: The Potters
        and Weavers of Milliraya*. Ph.D.
        dissertation, Cornell University,
        Ithaca. University Microfilms, Ann
        Arbor.

Spurr, M. S.
1986   *Arable Cultivation in Roman Italy,
        c. 200 B.C.–c. A.D. 100*. Society for
        the Promotion of Roman Studies,
        London.

Sraffa, Piero
1960   *The Production of Commodities by
        Means of Commodities*. Cambridge
        University Press, Cambridge.

Stahl, Ann B.
1991   Ethnic Style and Ethnic Boundaries:
        A Diachronic Case Study from West
        Central Ghana. *Ethnohistory*
        38:250–275.
1993   Concepts of Time and Approaches
        to Analogical Reasoning in Histori-
        cal Perspective. *American Antiquity*
        58:235–260.
1994   Change and Continuity in the Banda
        Area, Ghana: The Direct Historical
        Approach. *Journal of Field Archae-
        ology* 21:181–203.
1999a   The Archaeology of Global Encoun-
        ters Viewed from Banda, Ghana.
        African Archaeological Review
        16(1):5–81.
1999b   The History of Practice and the
        Practice of History: Materiality and
        Temporal Scales in the Historical
        Conjuncture. Paper presented at the
        98th Annual Meeting of the Ameri-
        can Anthropological Association,
        Chicago.
1999c   Perceiving Variability in Time and
        Space: The Evolutionary Mapping
        of African Societies. In *Beyond
        Chiefdoms: Pathways to Complex-
        ity in Africa*, edited by Susan K.
        McIntosh, pp. 39–55. Cambridge
        University Press, Cambridge.
2001   *Making History in Banda: Anthro-
        pological Visions of Africa's Past*.
        Cambridge University Press, Cam-
        bridge.
2002   Colonial Entanglements and the
        Practices of Taste: An Alternative to
        Logocentric Approaches. *American
        Anthropologist* 104:827–845.

Stahl, Ann B., and Maria das Dores Cruz
1998   Men and Women in a Market Econ-
        omy: Gender and Craft Production
        in West Central Ghana, c.
        1775–1995. In *Gender in African
        Prehistory*, edited by Susan Kent,
        pp. 205–226. Altamira Press, Wal-
        nut Creek, California.

Stanish, Charles
1992　*Ancient Andean Political Economy.* University of Texas Press, Austin.
1997　Nonmarket Imperialism in the Prehispanic Americas: The Inka Occupation of the Titicaca Basin. *Latin American Antiquity* 8:195–216.
1999　Settlement Pattern Shifts and Political Ranking. In *Fifty Years after Virí*, edited by Brian R. Billman and Gary M. Feinman, pp. 116–128. Smithsonian Institution Press, Washington, D.C.
2003　*Ancient Titicaca: The Evolution of Social Power in the Titicaca Basin of Peru and Bolivia.* University of California Press, Berkeley.

Stanish, Charles, Edmundo de la Vega, Lee Steadman, Cecília Chávez J., Kirk Lawrence Frye, Luperio Onofre, Matthew Seddon, and Percy Calisaya Chuquimia
1997　*Archaeological Survey in the Juli-Desaguadero Area, Lake Titicaca Basin, Peru.* Fieldiana Anthropology, new series 29. The Field Museum, Chicago.

Stark, Barbara L.
1985　Archaeological Identification of Pottery Production Locations: Ethnoarchaeological and Archaeological Data in Mesoamerica. In *Decoding Prehistoric Ceramics*, edited by Ben A. Nelson, pp. 158–194. Southern Illinois University Press, Carbondale.

Stark, Miriam T.
1991　Ceramic Production and Community Specialization: A Kalinga Ethnoarchaeological Study. *World Archaeology* 23:64–78.

Stark, Miriam, P. Bion Griffin, Judy Ledgerwood, Michael Dega, C. Mortland, N. Dowling, J. M. Bayman, Bong Savath, Tea Vin, Chhan Chamroven, and Kyle Latinis
1999　Results of the 1995–6 Archaeological Field Investigations at Angkor Borei, Cambodia. *Asian Perspectives* 38:7–36.

Ste. Croix, G. E. M. de
1956　Greek and Roman Accounting. In *Studies in the History of Accounting*, edited by Ananias C. Littleton and B. S. Yamey, pp. 14–74. Richard D. Irwin, Homewood, Illinois.
1981　*The Class Struggle in the Ancient Greek World: From the Archaic Age to the Arab Conquest.* Cornell University Press, Ithaca.

Stein, Gil
1987　Regional Economic Integration in Early State Societies: Third Millennium B.C. Pastoral Production at Gritille, Southeast Turkey. *Paléorient* 13(2):101–111.
1988　*Pastoral Production in Complex Societies: Mid–Late Third Millennium B.C. and Medieval Faunal Remains from Gritille Höyük in the Karababa Basin, Southeast Turkey.* Unpublished Ph.D. dissertation, Department of Anthropology, University of Pennsylvania, Philadelphia.
1993　Segmentary States and Organizational Variation in Early Complex Societies: A Rural Perspective. In *Archaeological Views from the Countryside: Village Communities in Early Complex Societies*, edited by Glenn Schwartz and Steven Falconer, pp. 10–18. Smithsonian Institution Press, Washington, D.C.
1996　Producers, Patrons, and Prestige: Craft Specialists and Emergent Elites in Mesopotamia from 5500–3100 B.C. In *Craft Specialization and Social Evolution: In Memory of V. Gordon Childe*, edited by Bernard Wailes, pp. 25–38. University of Pennsylvania Museum, Philadelphia.
1998a　World Systems Theory and Alternative Modes of Interaction in the Archaeology of Culture Contact. In *Studies in Culture Contact: Interaction, Culture Change, and Archaeology*, edited by James G. Cusick, pp. 220–255. Occasional Paper No. 25. Center for Archaeological Investigations, Southern Illinois University, Carbondale.
1998b　Heterogeneity, Power, and Political Economy: Some Current Research Issues in the Archaeology of Old World Complex Societies. *Journal of Archaeological Research* 6:1–44.
1999　*Rethinking World-Systems: Diasporas, Colonies, and Interaction in Uruk Mesopotamia.* University of Arizona Press, Tucson.

2001a   Who Was King and Who Was Not King? Social Group Composition in Early Mesopotamian State Societies. In *From Leaders to Rulers*, edited by Jonathan Haas, pp. 205–231. Kluwer Academic/Plenum, New York.

2001b   Understanding Ancient State Societies in the Old World. In *Archaeology at the Millennium: A Sourcebook*, edited by Gary M. Feinman and T. Douglas Price, pp. 353–379. Kluwer Academic/Plenum, New York.

Stein, Gil, and M. James Blackman
1993   The Organizational Context of Specialized Craft Production in Early Mesopotamian States. *Research in Economic Anthropology* 14:29–59.

Stein, Gil, and Patricia Wattenmaker
1990   The 1987 Tell Leilan Regional Survey: Preliminary Report. In *Economy and Settlement in the Near East: Analyses of Ancient Sites and Materials*, edited by Naomi F. Miller, pp. 8–18. MASCA Research Papers in Science and Archaeology Vol. 7 supplement. University of Pennsylvania Museum of Archaeology and Anthropology, Philadelphia.

Steiner, Christopher B.
1985   Another Image of Africa: Toward an Ethnohistory of European Cloth Marketed in West Africa, 1873–1960. *Ethnohistory* 32:91–110.

Steinkeller, Piotr
1987   The Administrative and Economic Organization of the Ur III State: The Core and the Periphery. In *The Organization of Power: Aspects of Bureaucracy in the Ancient Near East*, edited by McGuire Gibson and Robert D. Biggs, pp. 19–41. Studies in Ancient Oriental Civilization No. 46. Oriental Institute, University of Chicago, Chicago.

1996   The Organization of Crafts in Third Millennium Babylonia: The Case of Potters. *Altorientalische Forschungen* 23:232–253.

1999   Land-Tenure Conditions in Third Millennium Babylonia: The Problem of Regional Variation. In *Privatization in the Ancient Near East and Classical World*, 1, edited by Michael Hudson and Baruch A. Levine, pp. 289–329. Bulletin No. 5. Peabody Museum of Archaeology and Ethnology, Harvard University, Cambridge.

2001   New Light on the Hydrology and Topography of Southern Babylonia in the Third Millennium. *Zeitschrift für Assyriopogie* 91:22–84.

Steponaitis, Vincas P.
1991   Contrasting Patterns of Mississippian Development. In *Chiefdoms: Power, Economy, and Ideology*, edited by Timothy Earle, pp. 193–228. Cambridge University Press, Cambridge.

Sterner, Judy
1989   Who Is Signaling Whom? Ceramic Style, Ethnicity, and Taphonomy among the Sirak Bulahay. *Antiquity* 63:451–459.

1992   Sacred Pots and "Symbolic Reservoirs" in the Mandara Highlands of Northern Cameroon. In *An African Commitment: Papers in Honour of Peter Lewis Shinnie*, edited by Judy Sterner and Nicholas David, pp. 171–179. University of Calgary Press, Calgary.

Sterner, Judy, and Nicholas David
1991   Gender and Caste in the Mandara Highlands: Northeastern Nigeria and Northern Cameroon. *Ethnology* 30:355–369.

Stoller, Paul
1995   *Embodying Colonial Memories: Spirit Possession, Power, and the Hauka in West Africa*. Routledge, London.

Stoltman, James B.
1991   Cahokia as Seen from the Peripheries. In *New Perspectives on Cahokia: Views from the Periphery*, edited by James B. Stoltman, pp. 349–354. Prehistory Press, Madison, Wisconsin.

Stone, Elizabeth C.
1982   The Social Role of the Naditu Women in Old Babylonian Nippur. *Journal of the Economic and Social History of the Orient* 25:50–70.

Stone-Miller, Rebecca
1995   *Art of the Andes: From Chavin to Inca.* Thames and Hudson, London.

Storey, Glenn R.
1999a   Archaeology and Roman Society: Integrating Textual and Archaeological Data. *Journal of Archaeological Research* 7:203–248.

1999b   The Origin of Social Inequality and the Rise of Urbanism: The Case of the Roman State. Paper presented at the 64th Annual Meeting of the Society for American Archaeology, Chicago.

2000   *Cui Bono?* An Economic Cost/Benefit Analysis of Statuses in the Roman Empire. In *Hierarchies in Action: Cui Bono?* edited by Michael Diehl, pp. 340–374. Occasional Paper No. 27. Center for Archaeological Investigations, Southern Illinois University, Carbondale.

Storey, Rebecca
2004   Ancestors: Bioarchaeology of the Human Remains. In *K'axob: Materiality, Ritual, Work, and Family in an Ancient Maya Village,* edited by Patricia A. McAnany. Cotsen Institute of Archaeology, University of California, Los Angeles, in press.

Stuart, David
1988   The Río Azul Cacao Pot: Epigraphic Observations on the Function of a Maya Ceramic Vessel. *Antiquity* 62:153–157.

1989   Hieroglyphs on Maya Vessels. In *The Maya Vase Book, Volume 1,* edited by Justin Kerr, pp. 149–160. Kerr Associates, New York.

1997   Kinship Terms in Maya Inscriptions. In *The Language of Maya Hieroglyphs,* edited by Martha J. Macri and Annabel Ford, pp. 1–11. Pre-Columbian Art Research Institute, San Francisco.

1998   "The Fire Enters His House": Architecture and Ritual in Classic Maya Texts. In *Function and Meaning in Classic Maya Architecture,* edited by Stephen D. Houston, pp. 373–425. Dumbarton Oaks, Washington, D.C.

Su, Bingqi
1994   *Hua ren. Long de chuan ren. Zhong-guo ren* (Searching for the origins of the Chinese people). Liaoning University Press, Shenyang.

Tamari, T.
1991   The Development of Caste Systems in West Africa. *Journal of African History* 32:221–250.

Tambiah, Stanley
1976   *World Conqueror and World Renouncer: A Study in Religion and Polity in Thailand Against an Historical Background.* Cambridge University Press, Cambridge.

Tang, Jigen, Zhichun Jing, and George Rapp
2000   The Largest Walled Shang City Located in Anyang, China. *Antiquity* 74:479–480.

Tarling, Nicholas
1963   *Piracy and Politics in the Malay World.* F. W. Chesire, Melbourne.

Taylor, Keith
1992   The Early Kingdoms. In *The Cambridge History of Southeast Asia, Volume 1: From Early Times to c. 1800,* edited by Nicholas Tarling, pp. 137–182. Cambridge University Press, Cambridge.

Tchernia, André
2001   La vente du vin. In *Mercati permanente e mercati periodici nel mondo romano,* edited by Elio Lo Cascio, pp. 199–209. Edipuglia, Bari.

Teuber, Michael
1995   How Can Modern Food Technology Help to Identify Dairy Products Mentioned in Sumerian Texts? *Bulletin on Sumerian Agriculture* 8:23–31.

Thomas, Julien
1996   *Time, Culture, and Identity: An Interpretive Archaeology.* Routledge, London.

Thomas, Nicholas
1991   *Entangled Objects: Exchange, Material Culture, and Colonialism in the Pacific.* Harvard University Press, Cambridge.

Thomaz, Luis Felipe
1993   The Malay Sultanate of Melaka. In *Southeast Asia in the Early Modern Era,* edited by Anthony Reid, pp. 69–90. Cornell University Press, Ithaca.

Thompson, Wesley E.
1979   A View of Athenian Banking.
        Museum Helveticum 36:224–241.

Thornton, R.
1983   Narrative Ethnography in Africa,
        1850–1920: The Creation and Cap-
        ture of an Appropriate Domain for
        Anthropology. *Man* 18:503–520.

Thorp, Robert
1991   Erlitou and the Search for the Xia.
        Early China 16:1–38.

Three Gorges Team
2001   *Chaotianzui yu Zhongbaodao* (The
        sites of Chaotianzui and Zhongbao-
        dao). Wenwu Press, Beijing.

Topic, John R.
1982   Lower-Class Social and Economic
        Organization at Chan Chan. In
        Chan Chan: Andean Desert City, ed-
        ited by Michael Moseley and Kent
        Day, pp. 145–175. University of
        New Mexico Press, Albuquerque.

1990   Craft Production in the Kingdom of
        Chimor. In *The Northern Dynasties:
        Kingship and Statecraft in Chimor*,
        edited by Michael E. Moseley and
        Alana Cordy-Collins, pp. 145–176.
        Dumbarton Oaks, Washington,
        D.C.

Tourtellot, Gair, and Jeremy A. Sabloff
1994   Community Structure at Sayil: A
        Case Study of Puuc Settlement. In
        *Hidden Among the Hills: Maya Ar-
        chaeology of the Northwest Yucatán
        Peninsula: First Maler Symposium,
        1989*, edited by Hanns J. Prem, pp.
        71–92. Acta Mesoaméricana 7.
        Verlag von Fleming, Möckmuhl.

Tozzer, Alfred M. (translator)
1941   *Landa's relación de las cosas de Yu-
        catán*. Papers of the Peabody Mu-
        seum of American Archaeology and
        Ethnology Vol. 18. Harvard Univer-
        sity, Cambridge.

Trigger, Bruce G.
1990   Monumental Architecture: A Ther-
        modynamic Explanation of Sym-
        bolic Behaviour. *World Archaeology*
        22:119–132.

1999   Shang Political Organization: A
        Comparative Approach. *Journal of
        East Asian Archaeology* 1:43–62.

Trouillot, Michel-Rolph
1995   *Silencing the Past: Power and the
        Production of History*. Beacon
        Press, Boston.

Trubitt, Mary Beth
1996   *Household Status, Marine Shell
        Bead Production, and the Develop-
        ment of Cahokia in the Mississip-
        pian Period*. Unpublished Ph.D.
        dissertation, Department of Anthro-
        pology, Northwestern University,
        Evanston.

2000   Mound Building and Prestige Goods
        Exchange: Changing Strategies in
        the Cahokia Chiefdom. *American
        Antiquity* 65:669–690.

Tschauner, Harmut
2001   *Socioeconomic and Political Orga-
        nization in the Late Prehispanic
        Lambayeque Sphere, Northern
        North Coast of Peru*. Unpublished
        Ph.D. dissertation, Department of
        Anthropology, Harvard University,
        Cambridge.

Tschauner, Harmut, Marianne Vetters-
Tschauner, Jalh Dulanto, Marcelo Saco, and
Carlos Wester La Torre
1994   Un taller alfarero chimú en el Valle
        de Lambayeque. In *Tecnología y or-
        ganización de la producción
        cerámica prehispánica en los Andes*,
        edited by Izumi Shimada, pp. 349–
        393. Pontificia Universidad Católica
        del Perú, Fondo Editorial, Lima.

Turner, B. L., II
1990   Population Reconstruction for the
        Central Maya Lowlands: 1000 B.C.
        to A.D. 1500. In *Precolumbian Popu-
        lation History in the Maya Low-
        lands*, edited by T. Patrick Culbert
        and Don S. Rice, pp. 301–324. Uni-
        versity of New Mexico Press, Albu-
        querque.

Turner, B. L., II, and Charles H. Miksicek
1984   Economic Plant Species Associated
        with Prehistoric Agriculture in the
        Maya Lowlands. *Economic Botany*
        38:179–193.

Tyers, Paul A.
1996   *Roman Pottery in Britain*. Batsford,
        London.

Uceda, Santiago, and José Armas
1998   An Urban Pottery Workshop at the
        Site of Moche, North Coast of Peru.
        In *Andean Ceramics: Technology,
        Organization, and Approaches*, ed-

ited by Izumi Shimada, pp. 91–110. MASCA Research Papers in Science and Archaeology Vol. 15 supplement. University of Pennsylvania Museum, Philadelphia.

Underhill, Anne
2002   Craft Production and Social Change in Northern China. Kluwer Academic/Plenum, New York.

Ur, Jason
2002   Settlement and Landscape in Northern Mesopotamia: The Tell Hamoukar Survey, 2000–2001. Akkadica 123:57–88.

Vaillant, George C.
1941   Aztecs of Mexico: Origin, Rise, and Fall of the Aztec Nation. Doubleday, Doran and Company, Garden City, New York.

Valeri, Valerio
1991   Afterword. In Priests and Programmers, by John Stephen Lansing, pp. 134–143. Princeton University Press, Princeton.

Van Buren, Mary
2000   Political Fragmentation and Ideological Continuity in the Andean Highlands. In Order, Legitimacy, and Wealth in Ancient States, edited by Janet Richards and Mary Van Buren, pp. 77–87. Cambridge University Press, Cambridge.

Van de Mieroop, Marc
1992   Society and Enterprise in Old Babylonian Ur. Dietrich Raimer, Berlin.
1997   The Ancient Mesopotamian City. Clarendon, Oxford.
1999a   Cuneiform Texts and the Writing of History. Routledge, London.
1999b   Thoughts on Urban Real Estate in Ancient Mesopotamia. In Privatization in the Ancient Near East and Classical World, vol. 1, edited by Michael Hudson and Baruch A. Levine, pp. 253–275. Bulletin No. 5. Peabody Museum of Archaeology and Ethnology, Harvard University, Cambridge.
2000   Review of Privatization in the Ancient Near East and Classical World, vol. 1, edited by Michael Hudson and Baruch A. Levine. Journal of Near Eastern Studies 59:40–43.

van der Leeuw, Sander E.
1977   Towards a Study of the Economics of Pottery Making. In Ex Horreo, edited by B. L. Beek, R. W. Brant, and W. Gruenman van Watteringe, pp. 68–76. Cingvla 4. Albert Egges van Giffen Instituut voor Prae- en Protohistoire, University of Amsterdam, Amsterdam.

Van Dyke, Ruth, and Susan Alcock (editors)
2003   Archaeologies of Memory. Blackwell, Oxford.

Van Leur, Jacob C.
1967   Indonesian Trade and Society. Van Hoeve, The Hague.

Vance, James E.
1970   The Merchant's World: The Geography of Wholesaling. Prentice-Hall, Englewood Cliffs, New Jersey.

Vansina, Jan
1987   The Ethnographic Account as a Genre in Central Africa. Paideuma 33:433–444.

Vayda, Andrew
1961   Expansion and Warfare Amongst Swidden Agriculturalists. American Anthropologist 63:346–358.

Verano, John
2001   War and Death in the Moche World: Osteological Evidence and Visual Discourse. In Moche Art and Archaeology in Ancient Peru, edited by Joanne Pillsbury, pp. 111–126. National Gallery of Art, Washington, D.C.

Veyne, Paul
1991   La société romaine. Seuil, Paris.

Vicencio of Naples
1990   Narrative of the Voyage of Alvaro
[1534] de Saavedra from Mexico to the Philippines and Moluccas (1527–1529). In Documentary Sources of Philippine History, vol. 1, edited and translated by Gregorio F. Zaide, pp. 359–375. National Bookstore Publications, Manila.

Vickers, Michael J., and David Gill
1994   Artful Crafts: Ancient Greek Silverware and Pottery. Clarendon Press, Oxford.

Volkman, Toby
1985   Feasts of Honor: Ritual and Change in the Toralja Highlands. Illinois

Studies in Anthropology No. 16. University of Illinois Press, Urbana.

Voss, Jeremy

1987   The Politics of Pork and the Rituals of Rice: Redistributive Feasting and Commodity Circulation in Northern Luzon, the Philippines. In *Beyond the New Economic Anthropology*, edited by John Clammer, pp. 121–141. St. Martin's Press, New York.

Waetzoldt, Hartmut

1972   *Untersuchungen zur neusumerischen Textilindustrie.* Studi Economici e Tecnologici 1. Rome.

Waetzoldt, Hartmut, and Harald Hauptmann (editors)

1988   *Wirtschaft und Gesellschaft von Ebla.* Heidelberger Orientverlag, Heidelberg.

Wailes, Bernard (editor)

1996   *Craft Specialization and Social Evolution: In Memory of V. Gordon Childe.* University of Pennsylvania Museum, Philadelphia.

Waines, David (editor and translator)

1992   *The History of al-Tabarî,* vol. 36. State University of New York Press, Albany.

Wallerstein, Immanuel

1974   *The Modern World-System: Capitalist Agriculture and the Origins of the World-Economy in the Sixteenth Century.* Academic Press, New York.

Walters, Kenneth R.

1996   Time and Paradigm in the Roman Republic. *Syllecta Classica* 7:69–97.

Wang, Xuerong

1999   Yanshi Shang chengshi ju de tansuo he sikao (Discussion and thoughts about the Shang city site at Yanshi). *Kaogu* 2:24–34.

Warren, James F.

1982   Slavery and the Impact of External Trade: The Sulu Sultanate in the Nineteenth Century. In *Philippine Social History*, edited by Alfred W. McCoy and Ed. C. de Jesus, pp. 415–444. Ateneo de Manila Press, Quezon City, Philippines.

1985   *The Sulu Zone, 1768–1898: The Dynamics of External Trade, Slavery, and Ethnicity in the Transfor-* *mation of a Southeast Asian Maritime State.* New Day Publications, Quezon City, Philippines.

Watson, James L. (editor)

1980   *Asian and African Systems of Slavery.* University of California Press, Berkeley.

Wattenmaker, Patricia

1987   Town and Village Economies in an Early State Society. *Paléorient* 13(2):113–122.

1997   Kazane Höyük, 1995: Excavations at an Early City. In *XVIII Kazi Sonuçlari Toplantisi*, pp. 81–91. Republic of Turkey, Ministry of Culture, General Directorate of Monuments and Museums, Ankara.

1998   *Household and State in Upper Mesopotamia.* Smithsonian Institution Press, Washington, D.C.

Weber, Jill

1997   Faunal Remains from Tell es-Sweyhat and Tell Hajji Ibrahim. In *Subsistence and Settlement in a Marginal Environment: Tell es-Sweyhat, 1989–1995 Preliminary Report*, edited by Richard L. Zettler, pp. 133–168. MASCA Research Papers in Science and Archaeology Vol. 14. University of Pennsylvania Museum of Archaeology and Anthropology, Philadelphia.

Webster, David

1975   Warfare and the Evolution of the State: A Reconsideration. *American Antiquity* 40:464–470.

Weiss, Harvey

1983   Excavations at Tell Leilan and the Origins of North Mesopotamian Cities in the Third Millennium B.C. *Paléorient* 9(2):39–52.

1986   The Origins of Tell Leilan and the Conquest of Space in Third Millennium Mesopotamia. In *The Origins of Cities in Dry Farming Syria and Mesopotamia in the Third Millennium B.C.*, edited by Harvey Weiss, pp. 71–108. Four Quarters, Guilford, Connecticut.

Weiss, Harvey, and Marie-Agnès Courty

1993   The Genesis and Collapse of the Akkadian Empire: The Accidental Refraction of Historical Law. In *Akkad: The First World Empire*, edited by Mario Liverani, pp. 131–155. Sargon, Padua.

Weiss, Harvey, Marie-Agnes Courty, Wilma Wetterstrom, F. Guichard, Louise Senior, Richard Meadow, and Anna Curnow

1993 The Genesis and Collapse of Third Millennium North Mesopotamian Civilization. *Science* 261:995–1004.

Welch, David, and Judith McNeill

1991 Settlement, Agriculture, and Population Changes in the Phimai Region, Thailand. *Bulletin of the Indo-Pacific Prehistory Association* 11:210–228.

Welch, Paul D.

1990 Mississippian Emergence in West-Central Alabama. In *The Mississippian Emergence*, edited by Bruce D. Smith, pp. 197–225. Smithsonian Institution Press, Washington, D.C.

1991 *Moundville's Economy.* University of Alabama Press, Tuscaloosa.

Wen, Guang, and Zhichun Jing

1992 Chinese Neolithic Jade: A Preliminary Geoarchaeological Study. *Geoarchaeology* 7:251–275.

Wesson, Cameron

2001 Creek and Pre-Creek Revisited. In *The Archaeology of Traditions: Agency and History Before and After Columbus*, edited by Timothy R. Pauketat, pp. 94–106. University Press of Florida, Gainesville.

Wheatley, Paul

1961 *The Golden Khersonese: Studies in the Historical Geography of the Malay Peninsula Before A.D. 1500.* University of Malaya Press, Kuala Lumpur.

1975 Satyanrta in Suvarnadvipa: From Reciprocity to Redistribution in Ancient Southeast Asia. In *Ancient Civilizations and Trade*, edited by Jeremy A. Sabloff and C. C. Lamberg-Karlovsky, pp. 227–283. University of New Mexico Press, Albuquerque.

1979 Urban Genesis in Mainland South East Asia. In *Early Southeast Asia: Essays in Archaeology, History, and Historical Geography*, edited by Robert B. Smith and W. Watson, pp. 288–314. Oxford University Press, New York.

1983 *Nagara and Commandery: Origins of Southeast Asian Urban Traditions.* Research Paper No. 207–208. Department of Geography, University of Chicago, Chicago.

White, Leslie A.

1959 *The Evolution of Culture: The Development of Civilization to the Fall of Rome.* McGraw-Hill, New York.

Whittaker, C. R.

1985 Trade and Aristocracy in the Roman Empire. *Opus* 4:49–75.

1988 *Pastoral Economies in Classical Antiquity.* Supplementary Vol. 14. Cambridge Philological Society, Cambridge.

Wiesheu, Walburga

1997 China's First Cities: The Walled Site of Wangchenggang in the Central Plain Region of North China. In *Emergence and Change in Early Urban Societies*, edited by Linda Manzanilla, pp. 87–105. Plenum Press, New York.

Wigg, David G.

1999 The Development of the Monetary Economy in N. Gaul in the Late La Tène and Early Roman Periods. In *Roman Germany: Studies in Cultural Interaction*, edited by J. D. Creighton and Roger J. A. Wilson, pp. 99–123. Supplementary Series No. 23. Journal of Roman Archaeology, Portsmouth, Rhode Island.

Wilkinson, T. J.

1982 The Definition of Ancient Manured Zones by Means of Extensive Sherd Sampling Techniques. *Journal of Field Archaeology* 9:323–333.

1993 Linear Hollows in the Jazira, Upper Mesopotamia. *Antiquity* 67(256):548–562.

1994 The Structure and Dynamics of Dry Farming States in Upper Mesopotamia. *Current Anthropology* 35:483–520.

2000a Regional Approaches to Mesopotamian Archaeology: The Contribution of Archaeological Surveys. *Journal of Archaeological Research* 8:219–267.

2000b Settlement and Land Use in the Zone of Uncertainty in Upper Mesopotamia. In *Rainfall and Agriculture in Northern Mesopotamia*, edited by Remko M. Jas, pp. 3–35. Nederlands Historisch-Archaeologisch Instituut, Leiden.

n.d.   An Introduction to the Archaeology of the Near Eastern Landscape. Ms. on file, Oriental Institute, University of Chicago, Chicago.

Wilkinson, T. J., and D. J. Tucker

1995   *Settlement Development in the North Jazira, Iraq: A Study of the Archaeological Landscape.* Iraq Archaeological Reports No. 3, British School of Archaeology in Iraq. Aris and Phillips, Warminster, U.K.

Wilks, Ivor

1975   *Asante in the Nineteenth Century: The Structure and Evolution of a Political Order.* Cambridge University Press, Cambridge.

1982a   Wangara, Akan, and Portuguese in the Fifteenth and Sixteenth Centuries. I: The Matter of Bitu. *Journal of African History* 23:333–349.

1982b   Wangara, Akan, and Portuguese in the Fifteenth and Sixteenth Centuries. II: The Struggle for Trade. *Journal of African History* 23:463–472.

Williams, Stephen, and Jeffrey P. Brain

1983   *Excavations at the Lake George Site, Yazoo County, Mississippi, 1958–1960.* Papers of the Peabody Museum of Archaeology and Ethnology Vol. 74. Harvard University, Cambridge.

Wills, W. H.

2000   Political Leadership and the Construction of Chacoan Great Houses, A.D. 1020–1140. In *Alternative Leadership Strategies in the Prehispanic Southwest*, edited by Barbara J. Mills, pp. 19–44. University of Arizona Press, Tucson.

Wilmsen, Edwin N.

1989   *Land Filled with Flies: A Political Economy of the Kalahari.* University of Chicago Press, Chicago.

1995   Who Were the Bushmen? Historical Process in the Creation of an Ethnic Construct. In *Articulating Hidden Histories: Exploring the Influence of Eric R. Wolf*, edited by Jane Schneider and Rayna Rapp, pp. 308–321. University of California Press, Berkeley.

Wilmsen, Edwin N., and James R. Denbow

1990   Paradigmatic History of San-Speaking Peoples and Current Attempts at Revision. *Current Anthropology* 31:489–524.

Wilson, David

1988   *Prehispanic Settlement Patterns in the Lower Santa Valley, Peru: A Regional Perspective on the Origins of Complex North Coast Society.* Smithsonian Institution Press, Washington, D.C.

Wilson, Gregory D.

2001   Crafting Control and the Control of Crafts: Rethinking the Moundville Greenstone Industry. *Southeastern Archaeology* 20:118–128.

Winter, Irene

1985   After the Battle Is Over: The Stele of the Vultures and the Beginning of Historical Narrative in the Art of the Ancient Near East. In *Pictorial Narrative in Antiquity and the Middle Ages*, edited by Herbert Kessler and Marianna Simpson, pp. 11–32. Studies in the History of Art, Vol. 16. National Gallery of Art, Washington, D.C.

Winter, Marcus C.

1974   Residential Patterns at Monte Albán, Oaxaca, Mexico. *Science* 186:981–987.

Winter, Marcus C. (editor)

1995   *Entierros humanos de Monte Albán: Dos estudios.* Contribución No. 7 del Proyecto Especial Monte Albán, 1992–1994. Centro INAH Oaxaca, Oaxaca, Mexico.

Winzeler, Robert

1976   Ecology, Culture, Social Organization, and State Formation in Southeast Asia. *Current Anthropology* 17:623–640.

1981   The Study of the Southeast Asian State. In *The Study of the State*, edited by Henri Classen and Peter Skalník, pp. 455–467. Mouton, The Hague.

Wolf, Eric R.

1982   *Europe and the People Without His-*

tory. University of California Press, Berkeley.

Wolters, O. W.

1967   *Early Indonesian Commerce.* Cornell University Press, Ithaca.

1971   *The Fall of Srivijaya in Malay History*. Cornell University Press, Ithaca.

1979   Khmer "Hinduism" in the Seventh Century. In *Early South East Asia: Essays in Archaeology, History, and Historical Geography*, edited by Robert B. Smith and W. Watson, pp. 427–442. Oxford University Press, New York.

1999   *History, Culture, and Region in Southeast Asian Perspectives.* Southeast Asian Program Publications No. 26. Cornell University, Ithaca.

Wood, James W.

1998   A Theory of Preindustrial Population Dynamics: Demography, Economy, and Well-Being in Malthusian Systems. *Current Anthropology* 39:99–135.

Woolf, Greg

1990   World-Systems Analysis and the Roman Empire. *Journal of Roman Archaeology* 3:44–58.

Woolley, Leonard

1934   *Ur Excavations, Volume 2: The Royal Cemetery.* British Museum, London, and University of Pennsylvania Musem, Philadelphia.

Wright, Henry T.

1984   Prestate Political Formations. *On the Evolution of Complex Societies*, edited by Timothy K. Earle, pp. 41–77. Undena, Malibu, California.

2000   Modeling Tributary Economies and Hierarchical Polities. In *Cultural Evolution: Contemporary Viewpoints*, edited by Gary M. Feinman and Linda Manzanilla, pp. 197–213. Kluwer Academic/Plenum, New York.

Wright, Henry T., and Eric S. A. Rupley

2001   Calibrated Radiocarbon Age Determinations of Uruk-Related Assemblages. In *Uruk Mesopotamia and Its Neighbors: Cross-cultural Interactions in the Era of State Formation*, edited by Mitchell S. Rothman, pp. 85–122. School of American Research Press, Santa Fe, New Mexico.

Wright, Rita P.

1996   Contexts of Specialization: V. Gordon Childe and Social Evolution. In *Craft Specialization and Social Evolution: In Memory of V. Gordon Childe*, edited by Bernard Wailes, pp. 123–132. University of Pennsylvania Museum, Philadelphia.

Wylie, Alison

1985   The Reaction Against Analogy. In *Advances in Archaeological Method and Theory*, vol. 8, edited by Michael B. Schiffer, pp. 63–111. Academic Press, New York.

Xenophon

1923   *Memorabilia, Oeconomicus.* Translated by E. C. Marchant. Loeb Classical Library. Harvard University Press, Cambridge.

Xiao, Nan

1981   Shilun buci zhong de "gong" yu "bai gong" (Preliminary discussion of the workers and hundred craft workers in the oracle bones). *Kaogu* 3:266–270.

Yang, Bojun (editor)

1981   *Chun Qiu Zuo Zhuan zhu* (The Zuo Zhuan from the Spring and Autumn period). Zhonghua Shu Ju Press, Jinan, Shandong.

Yang, Shengnan

1992   *Shangdai jingji shi* (A history of the economy during the Shang period). Guizhou Peoples Press, Guiyang.

1998   Cong lu xiao chen shuo Wu Ding dui xi bei zhengfa de jingzhi mudi (Economic goals from military expeditions in the northwest from salt officials under King Wu Ding). In *Jiaguwen Faxian 100 Zhounian Xueshu Yantaohui Lunwenji* (Papers of the conference on the 100th anniversary of the discovery of oracle bones), edited by Taiwan Shifan University Editing Group, pp. 221–230. Taiwan Shifan University, Taipei.

Yang, Xizang

1986   The Shang Dynasty Cemetery

System. In *Studies of Shang Archaeology*, edited by Kwang-chih Chang, pp. 49–79. Yale University Press, New Haven.

Yarak, Larry W.
1979   Dating Asantehene Osei Kwadwo's Campaign against the Banna. *AsantesEm* 10:58.

Yates, Robin
1997   The City-State in Ancient China. In *The Archaeology of City-States*, edited by Deborah Nichols and Thomas Charlton, pp. 71–90. Smithsonian Institution Press, Washington, D.C.

Yoffee, Norman
1988a   Orienting Collapse. In *The Collapse of Complex Societies*, edited by Norman Yoffee and George Cowgill, pp. 1–20. University of Arizona Press, Tucson.

1988b   The Collapse of Ancient Mesopotamian States and Civilization. In *The Collapse of Ancient States and Civilizations*, edited by Norman Yoffee and George Cowgill, pp. 44–68. University of Arizona Press, Tucson.

1993   Too Many Chiefs? (or, Safe Texts for the '90s). In *Archaeological Theory: Who Sets the Agenda?* edited by Norman Yoffee and Andrew Sherratt, pp. 60–78. Cambridge University Press, Cambridge.

1995   Political Economy in Early Mesopotamian States. *Annual Review of Anthropology* 24:281–311.

Yoffee, Norman, Suzanne K. Fish, and George R. Milner
1999   Comunidades, Ritualities, Chiefdoms: Social Evolution in the American Southwest and Southeast. In *Great Towns and Regional Polities in the Prehistoric American Southwest and Southeast*, edited by Jill E. Neitzel, pp. 261–271. University of New Mexico Press, Albuquerque.

Yoffee, Norman, and Andrew Sherratt
1993   Introduction: The Sources of Archaeological Theory. In *Archaeological Theory: Who Sets the Agenda?* edited by Norman Yoffee and Andrew Sherratt, pp. 1–9. Cambridge University Press, Cambridge.

Yoffee, Norman, and Andrew Sherratt (editors)
1993   *Archaeological Theory: Who Sets the Agenda?* Cambridge University Press, Cambridge.

Young, Allen M.
1994   *The Chocolate Tree: A Natural History of Cacao*. Smithsonian Institution Press, Washington, D.C.

Young, Arthur
1770   *A Course of Experimental Agriculture: Containing an Exact Register of All the Business Transacted During Five Years on Near Three Hundred Acres of Various Soils . . . the Whole Stated in Near Two Thousand Original Experiments*. 2 vols. J. Dodsley, London.

Yue, Hongqin
1998   Shang wang chao dui fangguo de jisi yingxiang (The influence of sacrificial rites on the relation between the Shang king and the *fang* states). *Yin Du Xuekan* 3:9–12.

Zaide, Gregorio F. (editor and translator)
1990   *Documentary Sources of Philippine History*. 12 vols. National Bookstore Publications, Manila.

Zeder, Melinda
1994   Of Kings and Shepherds: Specialized Animal Economy in Ur III Mesopotamia. In *Chiefdoms and Early States in the Near East: The Organizational Dynamics of Complexity*, edited by Gil Stein and Mitchell Rothman, pp. 175–191. Prehistory Press, Madison, Wisconsin.

1995   The Archaeobiology of the Khabur Basin. *Bulletin of the Canadian Society for Mesopotamian Studies* 29:21–32.

Zelener, Yan
2000   Market Dynamics in Roman North Africa. In *Mercati permanente e mercati periodici nel mondo romano*, edited by Elio Lo Cascio, pp. 223–235. Edipuglia, Bari.

Zettler, Richard L.
1996   Written Documents as Excavated Artifacts and the Holistic Interpretation of the Mesopotamian Archaeological Record. In *The Study of the Ancient Near East in the Twenty-*

first Century, edited by Jerrold S. Cooper and Glenn M. Schwartz, pp. 81–101. Eisenbrauns, Winona Lake, Indiana.

Zettler, Richard, and Lee Horne (editors)
1998   *Treasures from the Royal Tombs of Ur*. University of Pennsylvania Museum of Archaeology and Anthropology, Philadelphia.

Zhang, Bingquan
1988   *Jiaguwen yu jiaguxue* (Studies on oracle bones and oracle bone inscriptions). National Press, Taipei, Taiwan.

Zhang, Xuehai
1997   Dong tu gu guo tansuo (Discussion of ancient states in the East). *Huaxia Kaogu* 1:60–72.

Zhao, Cheng
1988   *Jiaguwen jianming cidian* (A brief dictionary of the oracle bones). Zhonghua Shuju Press, Beijing.

Contributors

Robert McC. Adams, Department of Anthropology, University of California–San Diego, La Jolla, California 92093–0532

Cathy Lynne Costin, Department of Anthropology, California State University–Northridge, Northridge, California 91330

Hui Fang, Department of Archaeology, Shandong University, Jinan, China

Gary M. Feinman, Department of Anthropology, The Field Museum, Chicago, Illinois 60605

Laura Lee Junker, Department of Anthropology, University of Illinois at Chicago, Chicago, Illinois 60607

Patricia A. McAnany, Department of Archaeology, Boston University, Boston, Massachusetts 02215

Linda M. Nicholas, Department of Anthropology, The Field Museum, Chicago, Illinois 60605

Timothy R. Pauketat, Department of Anthropology, University of Illinois, Urbana, Illinois 61801

Andrew Sherratt, Ashmolean Museum, University of Oxford, Oxford OX1 2PH, U.K.

Ann Brower Stahl, Department of Anthropology, State University of New York at Binghamton, Binghamton, New York 13902-6000

Charles Stanish, Department of Anthropology, Cotsen Institute of Archaeology, University of California–Los Angeles, Los Angeles, California 90095

Gil Stein, Oriental Institute, University of Chicago, Chicago, Illinois 60637

Glenn R. Storey, Departments of Classics and Anthropology, University of Iowa, Iowa City, Iowa 52242-1322

Anne P. Underhill, Department of Anthropology, The Field Museum, Chicago, Illinois 60605

Index